OXFORD MONOGRAPHS IN
PRIVATE INTERNATIONAL LAW

GENERAL EDITOR: P.B. CARTER QC.
Emeritus Fellow of
Wadham College, Oxford

DECLINING JURISDICTION IN PRIVATE INTERNATIONAL LAW

OXFORD MONOGRAPHS IN
PRIVATE INTERNATIONAL LAW

The series aims to publish work of high quality and originality in a number of important areas of private international
law. The series is intended for both scholarly and practitioner
readers.

FORTHCOMING TITLES INCLUDE

Foreign Law in English Courts
RICHARD FENTIMAN

Insolvency in Private International Law
IAN FLETCHER

Intangible Property in Private International Law
PHILLIPA ROGERSON

DECLINING JURISDICTION IN PRIVATE INTERNATIONAL LAW

Reports to the XIVth Congress
of the International Academy
of Comparative Law
Athens, August 1994

J. J. FAWCETT
*Professor of Law
and Dean of the Faculty of Law,
University of Leicester, England*

CLARENDON PRESS · OXFORD
1995

Oxford University Press, Walton Street, Oxford OX2 6DP

Oxford New York
Athens Auckland Bangkok Bombay
Calcutta Cape Town Dar es Salaam Delhi
Florence Hong Kong Istanbul Karachi
Kuala Lumpur Madras Madrid Melbourne
Mexico City Nairobi Paris Singapore
Taipei Tokyo Toronto
and associated companies in
Berlin Ibadan

Oxford is a trade mark of Oxford University Press

Published in the United States
by Oxford University Press Inc., New York

British library Cataloguing in Publication Data
Data available

Library of Congress Cataloging in Publication Data
Declining jurisdiction in private international law: reports to the
XIV Congress of the International Academy of Comparative Law,
Athens/Delphi, August 1994 / [edited by] J. J. Fawcett.
p. cm.
1. Conflict of laws—Jurisdiction—Congresses. I. Fawcett, J. J.
II. International Congress of Comparative Law (14th: 1994: Athens,
Greece)
K7625.D43 1995
340.9—dc20 95-4189
ISBN 0-19-825959-X

1 3 5 7 9 10 8 6 4 2

Typeset by Best-set Typesetter Ltd., Hong Kong
Printed in Great Britain
on acid-free paper by
Biddles Ltd., Guildford and King's Lynn

General Editor's Preface

This book is the first contribution to a new series, *Oxford Monographs in Private International Law*. The aim of the series is to publish works of originality and quality on a number of important and developing areas of private international law. Contemporary private international law is a subject characterised by a marked interaction between scholarly and practitioner interests. The series is designed to accommodate this.

Declining to exercise jurisdiction is a topic which is both intellectually challenging and of great practical importance. Progressive relaxation of rigid legal limitations upon the very existence of jurisdiction has, not surprisingly, given rise to a need for restraint in its exercise. It is important that this need be met in a sophisticated, but well-ordered, way. The present book draws upon the experiences of, and developments in, a wide range of countries. The comparisons and contrasts which emerge are illuminating and could prove to be influential.

Wadham College, Oxford.   P. B. CARTER
5 April, 1995

Preface

This book contains the General Report and the National Reports on the topic of 'Rules for Declining to Exercise Jurisdiction in Civil and Commercial Matters: *Forum Non Conveniens, Lis Pendens,* and Other Rules'. These Reports were written for the XIVth Congress of the International Academy of Comparative Law, held in Athens, Greece, in August 1994.

National Reports were submitted prior to the Congress in relation to the following eighteen law districts: Argentina, Australia, Belgium, Canada (common law jurisdictions), Finland, France, Germany, Great Britain, Greece, Israel, Italy, Japan, The Netherlands, New Zealand, the province of Quebec, Sweden, Switzerland, the USA. The National Reporters had previously been sent a questionnaire (see the Appendix) which sets out the issues that they might be expected to address in relation to declining jurisdiction. The General Report is based on the National Reports, and draws together themes that emerge from these Reports. A few of the Reports have been published elsewhere. However, putting together the General Report and all the National Reports in one thematic book is designed to provide a unique insight into the topic of 'Declining Jurisdiction'. Moreover, this book contains the latest version of the Reports, taking into account discussion at the Athens Congress and developments in the law up to 1 September 1994.

By and large, National Reports have not been amended for the purposes of inclusion in this book. A uniform system of headings and sub-headings has been introduced and, in a few places, I have corrected the English. The Belgian and French Reports were originally submitted in French. However, the Reporters and the International Academy of Comparative Law have kindly agreed to an English translation appearing in this book.

Finally, I would like to express my gratitude to the International Academy of Comparative Law, without whose work this book would not have been possible.

Leicester, October 1994   J. J. FAWCETT

Contents

Table of Cases

Page numbers in bold type refer to where the case is mentioned in the text, page numbers in normal type refer to where the case is mentioned in the footnotes.

European Court of Justice

France

Gibraltar

Great Britain

Greece

Hong Kong

Israel

Italy

Japan

Table of Cases

Table of Legislation

Page numbers in bold type refer to where a law is mentioned in the text, page numbers in normal type refer to where a law is mentioned in the footnotes.

Canada

Germany

Great Britain

Greece

New Zealand

United States of America

Table of Conventions and Treaties

Page numbers in bold type refer to where the Convention/Treaty is mentioned in the text, page numbers in normal type refer to where the Convention/Treaty is mentioned in the footnotes.

1

General Report

J. J. FAWCETT

Professor of Law and Dean of the Faculty of Law, University of Leicester, England*

CONTENTS

---

* An earlier version of the General Report was presented at the Athens Congress in August 1994.

I
INTRODUCTION

The topic of declining jurisdiction in private international law is one of enormous practical importance and academic interest. It is also a topic where a comparative approach is particularly revealing, not only as to differences between the common law and civil law worlds but also as between one common law jurisdiction and another, and as between one civil law jurisdiction and another. Before making these comparisons, a few words need to be said about what is meant by 'declining jurisdiction' and about the scope of the present inquiry.

The phrase 'declining jurisdiction' refers to the situation where a court which has jurisdiction refuses to exercise it. This is a situation with which lawyers from both common law and civil law jurisdictions are familiar.[1] It is to be distinguished from the situation where the rules on jurisdiction are not satisfied and a court therefore dismisses the action on the basis that it has no jurisdiction. Of course, in both situations, the result is the same: the court refuses to try the action.

It is well known that in many States a court may decline to exercise jurisdiction/or assert that it has no jurisdiction on the basis of *forum non conveniens* (i.e. the appropriate forum for trial is abroad or the local forum is inappropriate) or *lis pendens* (i.e. parallel proceedings involving the same parties and cause of action are continuing in two different States at the same time). The rules in relation to both these doctrines will be examined in sections III and IV of this chapter. However, a court may also decline jurisdiction/assert that it has no jurisdiction because of a foreign choice of jurisdiction agreement or arbitration agreement. The rules in relation to such agreements also merit attention and are examined in sections V and VI. Finally, the closely related problem of forum shopping abroad, and how this can be discouraged, will be examined in

---

[1] There is a difference between the terminology used by English judges, who stay proceedings, and US judges, who either suspend or dismiss proceedings on conditions. The effect is the same, in that the plaintiff is forced to go to a foreign forum for trial. In civil law jurisdictions, and in conventions based on civil law concepts, a stay of proceedings may refer, not to declining jurisdiction, but to suspending proceedings pending a decision of a foreign court.

section VII. One limitation on the scope of the present enquiry, though, is that it is confined to 'civil and commercial matters'. This term is a familiar one to lawyers in Western Europe, for it defines the scope of the European Community Convention on Jurisdiction and the Enforcement of Judgments in Civil and Commercial Matters (the Brussels Convention)[2] and the parallel EC/EFTA Convention (the Lugano Convention).[3] It means, for example, that family law matters are, for the most part, excluded.

II
THE JURISDICTIONAL BACKGROUND

Jurisdiction, used in its widest sense, refers to the question whether a court will hear and determine an issue upon which its decision is sought. Before turning to look at the question of declining jurisdiction, something needs to be said more generally in relation to the rules determining when the courts of different States have jurisdiction.

1. Sources of the Rules

There is a wide variety of sources of rules on international jurisdiction. These may be contained in a code, as in the case of Greece and Quebec (which has recently introduced the new Civil Code of Quebec). They may be contained in a statute, as in the Swiss Private International Law Statute of 1987, or in a multilateral convention. The Brussels and Lugano Conventions are well known examples of such multilateral conventions. Alternatively, and less commonly now in Europe, the source may be a bilateral convention, such as the Swiss/Liechtenstein Treaty of 1968. With all these sources case law will have an important role in interpreting the statutory, code, or treaty provisions. However, it is not unknown for the sole direct source of a State's rules on international jurisdiction to be case law. This is the position in Japan, where there are no explicit statutory provisions on international jurisdiction.

In many States there is more than one source. In the United States, Australia, and New Zealand, there are some bases of jurisdiction derived from case law, whereas other bases are derived from statute. In England,

---

[2] See Art. 1 of the Brussels Convention. The original Convention has been amended by three Accession Conventions, see [1978] OJ L304/1 (and at 77 for an amended version of the original Convention); [1982] OJ L388/1; [1989] OJ L285/1. All references to the Brussels Convention refer to it as amended by these three Accession Conventions.

[3] See Art. 1 of the Lugano Convention, [1988] OJ L391/9. Of the EFTA States, Finland, Norway, Sweden, and Switzerland have ratified it. Austria and Iceland have still to do so.

there are three different sources for bases of jurisdiction: case law, procedural rules (the Rules of the Supreme Court), and statutes (implementing the Brussels and Lugano Conventions). Under Belgian law, general rules on international jurisdiction are set out in the *Code judiciaire*, the *Code civil*, and in special acts and treaties ratified in Belgium. French law on jurisdiction is also derived from a number of sources: provisions in the *Code civil* and *Nouveau Code de procédure*, a large body of case law, and International Conventions.

Rules as to jurisdiction may be directly derived from these sources, but they can also be indirectly derived from internal venue provisions. Thus under Swedish law there are special statutory rules (derived from the Lugano Convention) plus general rules derived from the local competence of Swedish district courts. The position is similar in Germany and in The Netherlands where there are statutory and convention rules, plus rules on international jurisdiction derived from rules on internal venue. Japanese cases have based jurisdiction on the venue provisions set out in the Code of Civil Procedure, although there is a debate over whether all these internal provisions reflect the principles on international jurisdiction.

2. DIVERSITY

There is a tremendous variety in the bases of jurisdiction adopted in different States. Starting with common law jurisdictions, there are clear similarities between Britain and other States which historically have come under British influence. England, Australia, New Zealand, Canada (common law jurisdictions), and Israel all base jurisdiction on the service of a writ on the defendant. This can be done where a defendant is transiently present within the jurisdiction. In certain specified circumstances a writ can be served out of the jurisdiction. For instance, is allowed under English law where, in a contractual dispute, the contract is governed by English law.[4] United States law, though, is distinctively different. Nearly all States have long-arm statutes which set out when process may be served on non-resident defendants. However, this jurisdiction is subject to constitutional limits set out in the due process clause of the United States Constitution. As a response to this, some long-arm statutes provide that jurisdiction may be exercised on any basis not inconsistent with the State or United States Constitution.[5] Many long-arm statutes, though, detail the circumstances in which jurisdiction can be asserted over a non-resident defendant. Typically, jurisdiction is allowed where there has been 'the transaction of any business' or 'the commission

---

[4] Ord. 11, r. 1(1)(d)(iii) of the Rules of the Supreme Court.
[5] See e.g. California Code of Civil Procedure, § 410.10 (1991).

of a tortious act' within the State.[6] The United States Supreme Court allows general jurisdiction over any claim against the defendant whenever there are continuous and systematic activities by the defendant within the forum or the defendant is physically present in the forum and served with process. It also allows specific jurisdiction in relation to claims that arise out of the defendant's activities within the forum; in such cases a minimum contacts test is applied.

Moving on to civil law jurisdictions, the same pattern of different rules in different States emerges. Under Belgian law a plaintiff is allowed to proceed in Belgium if the defendant is domiciled or resides in Belgium.[7] A second provision allows a plaintiff to proceed if there is a specified territorial connection with Belgium, such as this being the place of performance of an obligation.[8] Under a third provision a plaintiff may sue in Belgium if he has a domicile or a residence in that State.[9] However, the defendant is allowed to decline this jurisdiction. Under the well-known Article 14 of the French Civil Code a French national is able to bring an action in France against a foreign defendant. In contrast, under German law there is the notorious basis of jurisdiction that the defendant has property in the forum.[10] Swiss law has a general rule on jurisdiction whereby jurisdiction lies with the Swiss judicial or administrative authorities at the defendant's domicile.[11] There are then special rules for particular types of case. For example, for contracts the action may be brought before the Swiss court for the place of performance of the contract.[12] Under Article 3 of the Greek Code of Civil Procedure of 1968 the Greek courts have international jurisdiction when they have territorial jurisdiction.

The position is different in Scandinavian States. There is jurisdiction in Sweden if the defendant is habitually resident or has its seat there. There are also particular rules for special types of dispute. Thus, in disputes concerning debt obligations, a non-domiciliary may be sued at the place where property belonging to him is located. An action for damages in tort may be brought in Sweden if this is the place in which a tortious act occurred or had its impact. Finland takes a very wide jurisdiction based on 'catch where you can' and on the presence of property in the forum.

3. FORUM CONVENIENS

Although there is considerable diversity in the rules on international jurisdiction in different States, one theme that keeps on occurring is that of

[6] See the Illinois long-arm statute, Ill Rev. Stat. Ch. 100, § 2.209 (1983).
[7] Art. 635, 2° of the *Code judiciaire*.   [8] Art. 635, 3° of the *Code judiciaire*.
[9] Art. 638 of the *Code judiciaire*.   [10] S. 23 ZPO (Code of Civil Procedure).
[11] Art. 2 of the Swiss Private International Law Statute of 1987.
[12] Art. 113 of the Swiss Private International Law Statute of 1987.

forum conveniens. *Forum conveniens* can be defined as a court taking jurisdiction on the ground that the local forum is the appropriate forum (or an
appropriate forum) for trial or that the forum abroad is inappropriate. It is
a positive doctrine, unlike the doctrine of *forum non conveniens*, which is a
negative doctrine concerned with declining jurisdiction.

This raises the question: what are the relevant factors when identifying
the appropriate forum? Under English law the concept of appropriateness
involves looking at connecting factors 'and these will include not only
factors affecting convenience or expense (such as availability of witnesses), but also other factors such as the law governing the relevant
transaction . . . and the place where the parties respectively reside or carry
on business'.[13] Ultimately, the object is 'to identify the forum in which the
case can be suitably tried for the interests of all the parties and for the ends
of justice'.[14]

A concern with *forum conveniens* manifests itself in a variety of
different ways, depending on which State one is looking at. These are set
out below:

(a) A DISCRETIONARY RULE

This is a feature to be found in many, but not all, common law jurisdictions. Thus an English court is empowered under its non-convention rules
on jurisdiction to permit service of a writ out of the jurisdiction on a
foreign defendant under Order 11, rule 1(1), of the Rules of the Supreme
Court. The court has to be satisfied that there is a serious issue to be tried,
that one of the heads of rule 1(1) applies, and that the discretion should be
exercised to allow service out of the jurisdiction.[15] The criterion for the
exercise of this discretion is that of *forum conveniens*. The plaintiff has to
show that England is the clearly appropriate forum for the trial.[16]

A number of other Commonwealth common law jurisdictions, for
example Singapore, proceed in the same way as England. However, in
New Zealand, Australia, and Canada there has been a movement towards
allowing service of a writ out of the jurisdiction without permission. Thus
in New Zealand, Rule 219 of the High Court Rules allows service without
leave where the parties or the cause of action have a specified connection
with New Zealand or New Zealand law. Rule 220 allows service with
leave where the court considers New Zealand *forum conveniens*. In most
jurisdictions in Australia no leave is required prior to service of the writ,

---

[13] *Spiliada Maritime Corp* v. *Cansulex Ltd* [1987] AC 460 at 478.   [14] *Ibid.* 480.

[15] *Seaconsar Far East Ltd* v. *Bank Markazi Jomhouri Islami Iran* [1994] 1 AC 438.

[16] *Spiliada Maritime Corp* v. *Cansulex*, n. 13 above. In Australian cases of service out of the
jurisdiction, irrespective of whether leave is required for this or not, the onus is on the
plaintiff to show that the chosen forum is not a clearly inappropriate one.

although leave must be obtained at the hearing if the defendant fails to appear.[17] In Canada five out of nine common law provinces and two territories now allow service out of the jurisdiction without leave if the case comes within one of the relevant heads, and a further two provinces have abolished the list of heads altogether and allow service out of the jurisdiction without leave in any type of case if the person to be served is resident in Canada or the United States.[18] The upshot is that in New Zealand, Australia, and Canada the *forum conveniens* discretion has decreased in importance. Nonetheless, appropriateness can still be considered at the stage after the writ has been served using the doctrine of *forum non conveniens*.

In contrast to the position in Commonwealth States, in the United States there is no *forum conveniens* discretion.

(b) A RULE OF CONSTRUCTION

A German court in a well known decision[19] has, by means of a rule of statutory construction, introduced a requirement of a 'sufficient connection' between the litigation and the forum State in cases where jurisdiction is founded on the presence of the defendant's property in the forum. This requirement introduces one of the main considerations to be taken into account under *forum conveniens*.

(c) AN EXPRESS REFERENCE

Some States have adopted jurisdictional bases which expressly refer to considerations of appropriateness. A good example is Article 3136 of the Civil Code of Quebec which provides jurisdiction 'if the dispute has a sufficient connection with Quebec, where proceedings cannot possibly be instituted outside Quebec or where the institution of such proceedings outside Quebec cannot reasonably be required'.

Many civil jurisdictions in Europe have also adopted *forum conveniens*-type jurisdiction rules. Thus, under French law, a judge is able in two situations to rule on a case, not because of a precise rule giving him competence but because he thinks it is appropriate to do so.[20] The two situations in question are, first, where there would otherwise be a miscarriage of justice and, secondly, where the dispute deals with measures of

---

[17] See Nygh, *Conflict of Laws in Australia* (5th edn. 1991), 39.

[18] There is now a constitutional limit on the jurisdiction of Canadian courts. This is narrower than the doctrine of *forum non conveniens* and is based on minimum standards of order and fairness in intra-Canadian jurisdiction: see *Hunt* v. *T. & N. Plc* (1993) 109 DLR (4th) 16.

[19] BGH, 2 July 1991 (XIth Civil Senate), 115 BGHZ 90.   [20] See below, p. 176.

execution to be performed in France and the judge decides that it is right to determine some underlying question (such as the existence of the debt which justifies the measure of execution). German law has, like Quebec, adopted the concept of *forum conveniens* in the rare case of a negative conflict of competence.[21] The court asserts jurisdiction by necessity if there is an urgent interest in granting domestic legal protection. But the domestic forum has to be positively convenient. Belgian case law also operates a doctrine of jurisdiction by necessity, which has been used in favour of Belgian claimants in family law cases. Dutch courts have from time to time filled in gaps in their rules as to jurisdiction by adopting a concept of *forum necessitatis*. Thus in one case jurisdiction was taken where the deceased had no domicile in The Netherlands but had a major connection with The Netherlands (this was where the estate was located and the heirs were domiciled).[22] Of greater impact in the future, under a Dutch draft bill amending the Code of Civil Procedure, in petition cases (e.g. a dispute over the management of a corporation) a Dutch court will have jurisdiction if the petitioner is domiciled in The Netherlands or the case is otherwise sufficiently connected with the legal sphere of The Netherlands. Moreover, *forum necessitatis* is now explicitly mentioned as constituting jurisdiction. Swiss law has shown some concern that the forum abroad should not be inappropriate. Thus it provides for a subsidiary jurisdiction in cases where a Swiss citizen lives abroad and the action cannot be brought at the regular forum abroad, for example because the foreign courts are not impartial.[23]

This type of provision can also be found in Scandinavia. Under the law of Finland, a court may hear the case in Finland, if litigation abroad would involve extreme injustice and costs for the Finnish party.

Such explicit provisions are exceptional; what is much more common is that in many States appropriateness is seen as the underlying basis of their rules on jurisdiction.

(d) THE UNDERLYING BASIS OF JURISDICTION

Under French law jurisdiction is said to be based on proper adminis-tration of justice and the interests of litigants.[24] The Belgian rules on international jurisdiction are largely based on the common principle of the jurisdictional protection of the foreign defendant.[25] Similarly, the Greek law of jurisdiction is said to take account of all the public and private interests involved and to allocate jurisdiction to the appropriate forum in

---

[21] See below, p. 193.   [22] HR, 26 Oct. 1984, [1985] NJ 696.
[23] See e.g. Arts. 43(2), 47, 60, 67, 76, 80, 87 of the Swiss Private International Law Statute of 1987.
[24] See below, pp. 177–8.   [25] See below, p. 103.

each case.[26] Swiss law bases jurisdiction on a strong connection with the forum. There is no jurisdiction on the basis of the simple presence of the person or mere location of property. Argentinian law has strict rules of jurisdiction related to the territory, parties, and the subject of the claim. German law is based on standardized jurisdictional interests.[27] Under Japanese law it is accepted that international jurisdiction has to be decided in accordance with those principles of justice which would require that fairness be maintained between parties, and a proper and prompt trial be secured. It is also believed that the internal venue provisions, or at least some of these provisions, contained in the Code of Civil Procedure reflect these principles, and can therefore operate as a basis of jurisdiction. Under the Brussels and Lugano Conventions jurisdiction is always allocated to an appropriate forum.[28] The bases of jurisdiction set out in these two conventions all require a close connection with the forum. Normally, the plaintiff is expected to bring the action in the State of the defendant's domicile.[29] Special jurisdiction under Article 5, which provides for trial in a State other than that of the defendant's domicile, has frequently been justified by the European Court of Justice on the basis that it allocates jurisdiction to a Contracting State with which the dispute has a particularly close relationship.[30]

It is worth pointing out, though, that there are different perceptions in different States as to when the local forum is an appropriate one for trial. Thus under Article 5(3)[31] of the Brussels and Lugano Conventions a Contracting State has jurisdiction on the basis of a person being injured in that State. In common law jurisdictions this connection, on its own, is not sufficient to found jurisdiction. There can be differences, too, in relation to how appropriate a local forum must be before it has jurisdiction. The bases of jurisdiction, mentioned above, in the Brussels and Lugano Conventions are, in effect, concerned with allocating jurisdiction to *an appropriate forum*. English courts, when assuming jurisdiction under Order 11 of the Rules of the Supreme Court, are concerned that England is *the clearly appropriate forum*.

4. HARMONIZATION

There have been notable successes in harmonizing rules as to jurisdiction in the European Community and EFTA bloc under the Brussels Convention and the parallel Lugano Convention. However, these conventions do

---

[26] See below, pp. 239–40.   [27] See below, p. 194.
[28] See Fawcett, (1991) 44 *Current Legal Problems* 39.   [29] Under Art. 2.
[30] See e.g. Case 34/82 *Peters* v. *Zuid Nederlandse Aannemers Vereniging* [1983] ECR 987.
[31] As interpreted by the ECJ in Case 21/76 *Handelskwekerij GJ Bier BV* v. *Mines de Potasse d'Alsace SA* [1976] ECR 1735.

not contain all the law on jurisdiction for Western European countries. They only apply to civil and commercial matters and, in broad terms, require the defendant to be domiciled in a European Community or EFTA State. In other cases each Western European State will apply its traditional national rules on jurisdiction. It is interesting to note, though, that in some of these States, for example Spain and, to a lesser extent, Scotland, traditional rules have been amended to bring them into line with the Brussels Convention.

III
FORUM NON CONVENIENS

1. THE OVERALL PICTURE

As has been seen, *forum non conveniens* can be defined as a general discretionary power for a court to decline jurisdiction on the basis that the appropriate forum for trial is abroad or that the local forum is inappropriate.

The common law jurisdictions of Britain, New Zealand, Canada, Israel, and the United States have all adopted a doctrine of *forum non conveniens*, as has the hybrid jurisdiction of Quebec. Japan, although a civil law jurisdiction, has a 'special circumstances' doctrine which bears a resemblance to a doctrine of *forum non conveniens*. Sweden has some general discretion in relation to jurisdiction. In contrast, the civil law jurisdictions of Belgium, France, Germany, Switzerland, Italy, Greece, and The Netherlands have no such general discretionary power to decline jurisdiction. If one turns to the position in Scandinavia, Finland also has not adopted this doctrine: moving to Latin America, nor has Argentina.

The rest of this section will be subdivided to look, first, at the position in States which have adopted a doctrine of *forum non conveniens* and, secondly, at that in States which have not adopted such a doctrine.

2. *FORUM NON CONVENIENS* STATES

The position in States which have adopted a general discretion to decline jurisdiction is complicated by the fact that there is no single doctrine of *forum non conveniens*. Instead, States tend to have their own version of it. The position can best be understood by dividing up the law districts which have adopted a general discretionary power to decline jurisdiction into five groups, and examining the position in relation to each group. The five groups are as follows: Britain and other States whose law has been influenced by British law; the USA; Quebec; Japan; and Sweden.

(a) BRITAIN AND OTHER STATES INFLUENCED BY BRITISH LAW

There are very close similarities between the doctrine of *forum non conveniens* applied in Britain and the doctrine of *forum non conveniens* applied in certain other States whose law is influenced by English and Scots law. Britain has led the way in introducing the doctrine of *forum non conveniens*. The leading case is *Spiliada Maritime Corp.* v. *Cansulex Ltd*,[32] which has had a major influence on the development of the doctrine in other Commonwealth States and in Israel.

(i) The British Lead

The House of Lords in the *Spiliada* case, following Scottish cases,[33] adopted the basic principle that

a stay will only be granted on the ground of *forum non conveniens* where the court is satisfied that there is some other available forum, having jurisdiction, which is the appropriate forum for trial of the action, i.e. in which the case may be tried more suitably for the interests of all the parties and the ends of justice.[34]

Lord Goff then laid down a number of subordinate principles which set out a two-stage process. Under the first stage the burden is on the defendant who seeks a stay to show that there is another available forum which is clearly or distinctly more appropriate than the English forum. Where this cannot be shown, the courts will ordinarily refuse a stay of proceedings. Under the second stage, once it has been shown that there is a clearly more appropriate forum for trial abroad, the burden of proof shifts to the plaintiff to show 'circumstances by reason of which justice requires that a stay should nevertheless not be granted'.[35] The first stage is concerned with the appropriate forum; the second with considerations of justice (including the advantage to the plaintiff of trial in his chosen forum), which have become much less important over the years. The meaning of appropriateness is the same in the present context as that used in the context of *forum conveniens*, examined earlier.

Within a few months of the *Spiliada* decision an important restriction on the use of *forum non conveniens* by United Kingdom courts came into effect. This restriction arises in Brussels Convention cases.[36] This convention contains no general discretionary power to stay actions on the basis of *forum non conveniens*. It is accepted in the United Kingdom that, in cases

---

[32] N. 13 above. The HL accepted the existence of the doctrine in the earlier case of *The Abidin Daver* [1984] AC 398. In Scotland the leading HL case was *Société du Gaz de Paris* v. *SA de Navigation Les Armateurs Français*, 1929 SC (HL) 13.

[33] e.g. *Sim* v. *Robinow* (1892) 19 R (Ct. of Sess.) 665; *Société du Gaz de Paris* case, n 32 above. The development of *forum non conveniens* in the US has also been influenced by Scottish cases.

[34] N. 13 above, at 476.   [35] *Ibid.* 478.

[36] This restriction equally applies in relation to the more recent Lugano Convention.

where jurisdiction is founded on the Brussels Convention, it is not possible to use the doctrine of *forum non conveniens* to decline jurisdiction, at least in intra-EC cases (i.e. ones where the alternative forum to England is another EC State). However, in cases where the alternative forum is a non-EC State, the English Court of Appeal has held that it is still possible to use *forum non conveniens* to decline jurisdiction.[37] This decision, although it has its supporters in England, has been criticized for leading to a lack of harmonization of the law in Europe.[38] Of course, this restriction does not affect any of the other common law jurisdictions covered in the present survey.

(ii) Commonwealth Reaction

The *Spiliada* case has been followed in New Zealand[39] without any obvious difference; this has also happened in Brunei,[40] Hong Kong,[41] and Singapore.[42] It has also been followed in Gibraltar.[43]

The Canadian (common law jurisdictions) doctrine of *forum non conveniens*[44] is very similar to the British model. However, the two doctrines are not entirely the same. First, in Canada the two-stage analysis set out in *Spiliada* has not been followed. Instead, the consideration of the advantage to the plaintiff is part of the overall weighing of factors considered in identifying the natural forum. It is doubtful whether this would affect the outcome in any particular case. Secondly, there is some uncertainty in Canada over the burden of proof in cases where jurisdiction is founded on service of a writ out of the jurisdiction without the leave of the court. Third, in Canada the weight to be given to all the factors considered when ascertaining the appropriate forum may depend to some extent on whether the case is inter-provincial or international, although it is difficult to draw firm conclusions on this.

The High Court of Australia declined to follow the *Spiliada* case, and required there to be vexation or oppression for the grant of a

---

[37] *Re Harrods (Buenos Aires) Ltd* [1992] Ch. 72. The decision was originally referred to the ECJ (Case C–314/92 *Ladenimor SA* v. *Intercomfinanz SA*) but this has been removed from the register because the action has been settled. In a more recent case, the CA has refused to refer the same issue that arose in *Re Harrods* to the ECJ: *The Nile Rhapsody* [1994] 1 Lloyd's Rep. 382. This was because of the expense and delay that such a reference would occasion.

[38] See Cheshire and North, *Private International Law* (12th edn., 1992), 331–4. See also the French report, below, pp. 178–9; Duintjer Tebbens, in Sumampouw *et al.* (eds), *Law & Reality—Voskuil Essays* (1992), 47.

[39] *McConnell Dowell Constructors Ltd* v. *Lloyd's Syndicate 396* [1988] 2 NZLR 257; *Club Meditérranée NZ* v. *Wendell* [1989] 1 NZLR 216 (CA).

[40] *Syarikat Bumiputra Kimanis* v. *Tan Kok Voon* [1988] 3 MLJ 315.

[41] *The Adhiguna Meranti* [1988] 1 Lloyd's Rep. 384 (Hong Kong CA).

[42] *Brinkerhoff Maritime Drilling Corp* v. *PT Airfast Services Indonesia* [1992] 2 SLR 776.

[43] *Aldington Shipping Ltd* v. *Bradstock Shipping Corp and Marbanaft GmbH (The Waylink and Brady Maria)* [1988] 1 Lloyd's Rep. 475 (Gibraltar CA).

[44] See *Amchem Products Inc* v. *British Columbia (Workers' Compensation Board)* (1993) 102 DLR (4th) 96.

stay.[45] However, in a subsequent case the High Court has established that this can be shown by the fact that the forum is a clearly inappropriate one for trial.[46] This formula is loaded in favour of trial continuing in the forum since, in practice, it is going to be harder to show that the local forum is a clearly inappropriate one than it is to show, under the *Spiliada* formula, that the alternative forum abroad is clearly more appropriate. Indeed, if you take the situation where the local forum is *an* appropriate one for trial, there can be no stay under the Australian formula, whereas a stay can still be granted under the *Spiliada* formula as long as the forum abroad is clearly more appropriate.

(iii) Israel

Israeli law on international jurisdiction is based on English law. Since 1980 Israeli case law has adopted the doctrine of *forum non conveniens*. The principles are set out in the very recent decision of the Supreme Court in *Abu-Ghichla* v. *The East Jerusalem Electric Co. Ltd* (not yet reported), decided in December 1993. This case adopts the two stage process set out in the *Spiliada* case. When it comes to the question whether dismissal of the action would cause injustice to the plaintiff, the Israeli Supreme Court followed the position common to both England and the United States that differences, for example, in the amount of damages awarded in the alternative fora do not constitute such injustice. There is, though, one very noticeable difference between the Israeli and the English doctrines. This relates to what are known under United States law as public interest factors. More will be said about these factors when United States law is examined below. Suffice it to say now that, under English law, public interest factors are considered only to a limited extent. Under Israeli law, though, the position remains open on whether the full range of public interest factors can also be considered. There are conflicting judicial statements on this. However, the most recent statement is from Shamgar P in the *East Jerusalem Electric Co* case (not yet reported) where the judge said: 'prima facie, I see no reason why, in Israel, it is not appropriate to consider public interests and even to give them weight, when the party interests are in equilibrium.' One more minor difference between the Israeli and English doctrines of *forum non conveniens* is that an Israeli court will not go into the question of the applicable law if this raises a difficult choice of law issue, whereas an English court is prepared to decide difficult choice of law points at this jurisdictional stage of the litigation.[47]

---

[45] *Oceanic Sun-Line Special Shipping Co Inc* v. *Fay* (1988) 165 CLR 197.
[46] *Voth* v. *Manildra Flour Mills Pty Ltd* (1990) 171 CLR 538.
[47] Compare the Israeli case of *Atiyah* v. *Arbatisi*, 39(1) PD 365 (1985), with the English case of *Metall und Rohstoff AG* v. *Donaldson Lufkin & Jenrette Inc* [1990] 1 QB 391.

(b) THE UNITED STATES

(i) Development of the Doctrine of *Forum Non Conveniens*

The common law doctrine of *forum non conveniens* has been developed by the Supreme Court of the United States. The trend has been for State courts to comply with the federal standard, with the result that the majority of States now recognize the doctrine. There are, though, some notable exceptions. Texas has abolished the doctrine in wrongful death and personal injury actions arising out of an incident in a foreign State or country.[48] The Louisiana courts rejected *forum non conveniens* but a subsequent statute allows for dismissal in limited situations which conform to the federal standard.[49]

Under the United States doctrine of *forum non conveniens* 'a court may decline to exercise its jurisdiction if the court finds that it is a "seriously inconvenient" forum and that the interests of the parties and of the public will be best served by remitting the plaintiff to another, more convenient, forum that is available to him'.[50]

The Supreme Court of the United States in *Gulf Oil Corp.* v. *Gilbert*[51] set out the private and public interest factors to weigh in determining whether a motion to dismiss on the ground of *forum non conveniens* is appropriate. The private interest factors include 'relative ease of access to sources of proof; availability of compulsory process for attendance of unwilling, and the cost of obtaining attendance of willing, witnesses; possibility of view of premises if view would be appropriate to the action; and all other practical problems that make trial of a case easy, expeditious and inexpensive'.[52] Public interest factors include administrative difficulties from court congestion; local interest in having localized controversies decided at home; interest in applying familiar law; avoidance of unnecessary problems in conflict of laws or in the application of foreign law; unfairness of burdening citizens in an unrelated forum with jury duty.

(ii) Similarities and Differences

The similarities between, on the one hand, British, and other Commonwealth States' *forum non conveniens* and, on the other hand, United States *forum non conveniens*, are as follows:

> (i) It is an essential requirement for declining jurisdiction on the basis of *forum non conveniens* in Britain, other Commonwealth

---

[48] See *Dow Chemical Co* v. *Alfaro*, 786 SW 2d 674 (Tex. 1990), *cert. denied*, 498 US 1024 (1991). See also S. 71.031 of the Civil Practice and Remedies Code.

[49] LA Code Civ. Proc. Ann. Art. 123 (West Supp. 1989).

[50] Weintraub, *Commentary on the Conflict of Laws* (3rd edn., 1986), 213.

[51] 330 US 501 (1947).   [52] *Ibid.* 508.

States, and the United States that there is an alternative forum abroad.

(ii) The considerations looked at in the United States as private interest factors would also be considered in Britain and other Commonwealth States when ascertaining the appropriate forum for trial.

(iii) The treatment of the advantage to the plaintiff in trial in the local forum appears to be the same. In *Piper Aircraft Co* v. *Reyno*[53] the Supreme Court of the United States held that the fact that Scots law was less favourable to the plaintiff was not a sufficient basis to defeat the dismissal on *forum non conveniens* grounds of an action brought in the United States. In the *Spiliada* case the House of Lords was concerned to reduce the weight that had previously been given to the advantage to the plaintiff of trial in England. Lord Goff held that this factor cannot be decisive and, by way of example, that an English court would not, in ordinary circumstances, hesitate to stay English proceedings merely because the plaintiff would be deprived of a higher award of damages in England.[54] Both England and the United States also have the same attitude towards time-bars in the foreign forum.[55]

(iv) The relationship with bases of jurisdiction is the same in the sense that, when an action is dismissed or stayed, what the court is saying is that, although it has jurisdiction, it refuses to accept jurisdiction. In the United States this means dismissing a case when what is constitutional is not desirable.

The differences are as follows:

(i) The framework within which the *forum non conveniens* considerations are examined in the United States is more flexible than that which operates in England, with its two-stage process and its rules on the burden of proof.

(ii) In the United States the courts expressly consider public interest factors. This does not happen in England, apart from when the applicable law is considered.[56] In so far as public interest considerations operate under the surface in English law they point towards a public interest in allowing trial in England, even where the dispute is essentially foreign.[57] This public interest is

---

[53] 454 US 235 (1981).   [54] N. 13 above, at 482.   [55] *Ibid.* 483–4.

[56] See Fawcett, (1989) 9 *OJLS* 205 at 220–1. The applicable law is a factor of both public and private interest under English law. The Australian position (in international as opposed to inter-State cases) is the same as the English in relation to public interest factors: see *Oceanic Sun Line Special Shipping Co Inc* v. *Fay* (1988) 79 ALR 9 at 50.

[57] Fawcett, n. 56 above, at 217–8.

founded on the economic benefits of England being a centre for international litigation. This is in direct contrast to the emphasis placed in the United States on the clogging of local courts by foreign litigants.

(iii) Following on from this, a United States court can of its own motion dismiss a case on the basis of *forum non conveniens*, whereas an English court cannot.

(iv) This can affect the weight to be attached in the United States to a forum selection clause which confers jurisdiction on the local court. Normally, this will operate as a strong factor against staying the local proceedings. However, if the court is acting on its own motion this private interest factor, whilst still relevant, is not given as much weight.

(v) A distinction is drawn in the United States between local plaintiffs and foreign plaintiffs. There is a presumption in favour of a local plaintiff's choice of forum, which will normally outweigh any inconvenience to the defendant.[58] There is no such presumption in the case of foreign plaintiffs.[59]

(vi) There is a clear distinction in the United States between international and inter-State cases. Moreover, a change of venue between federal district courts, which involves transfer rather than dismissal, is provided for under section 1404(a) of the United States Code. In Canada there are no such rules. However, in Australia there are cross-vesting provisions,[60] and the philosophy since 1987 is that Australia's States and Territories should be regarded as part of a common nation, and not as foreign law districts.

(c) QUEBEC

(i) Article 3135

Article 3135 of the new Civil Code of Quebec, in force since 1 January 1994, sets out a codified provision on *forum non conveniens*. This states that: 'Even though a Quebec authority has jurisdiction to hear a dispute, it may exceptionally and on application by a party, decline jurisdiction if it considers that the authorities of another country are in a better position to decide.' Previous case law on the existence of a doctrine of *forum non conveniens* in Quebec was contradictory. Now there clearly is such a doctrine, although there is, as yet, no case law on the interpretation of

[58] *Koster* v. *Lumbermans Mut Cass Co*, 330 US 518 (1947).

[59] *Piper Aircraft Co* v. *Reyno*, n. 53 above.

[60] S. 5(2), Jurisdiction of Courts (Cross-vesting) Act 1987 (Cth); see Nygh, n. 17 above, 72–7.

Article 3135. Previous case law[61] suggests that the considerations taken into account when exercising this discretionary power to decline jurisdiction include the following: residence or domicile of the parties; presence of witnesses or evidence in Quebec; enforceability of the Quebecois judgment abroad; assets in Quebec in order to indemnify a victim; abuses of procedure; availability of an alternative forum; interests of the parties or of the child; forum familiar with the substantive law involved.

(ii) Similarities and Differences

On the one hand, Article 3135 employs a very flexible approach which is more reminiscent of the United States doctrine of *forum non conveniens* than the *Spiliada* case's formalized set of sub-principles and two-stage process. On the other hand, the considerations that it is suggested should be taken into account when exercising the Quebec discretion are essentially the same as those employed in Britain and other Commonwealth countries. In particular, most of the public interest factors, which are so important in the United States, do not come into play in Quebec [62] At the same time, the Quebec doctrine has in common with both the United States and British/Commonwealth/Israeli doctrines the notion that, although the court has jurisdiction, it is refusing to exercise it.

(d) JAPAN

(i) The 'Special Circumstances' Doctrine

The Supreme Court, in the *Malaysian Airlines System* case on 16 October 1981,[63] laid down three general rules on international jurisdiction. First, there are no explicit statutory provisions on international jurisdiction in Japan. Secondly, international jurisdiction has to be decided in accordance with those principles of justice which would require that fairness be maintained between parties, and a proper and prompt trial be secured. Thirdly, although the provisions on distribution of venue among local courts are not concerned with international jurisdiction itself, they are believed to reflect the above principles.

The 'special circumstances' doctrine has been developed by the lower courts so as to add a fourth rule to these three general rules on international jurisdiction. It is concerned to ensure that the principles of justice, in accordance with which international jurisdiction has to be decided, are not violated; in other words, that 'fairness be maintained between parties, and a proper and prompt trial be secured'. The factors considered in Japan

---

[61] See below, pp. 154–5.   [62] Quebec is concerned, though, with the applicable law.
[63] *Michiko Goto et al.* v. *Malaysian Airlines System Berhad*, 26 Japanese Annual of International Law 122 (1983).

when applying this doctrine are ones 'such as relative ease of access to source of proof, availability of compulsory process for attendance of un-willing witnesses, the cost of obtaining evidence thereof, the enforce-ability of a judgment, and other relative advantages and obstacles to a fair, proper, and prompt trial'.[64]

(ii) Similarities and Differences

The Japanese 'special circumstances' doctrine bears an obvious resem-blance to the United States doctrine of *forum non conveniens*. It adopts a flexible approach, and the considerations taken into account when applying the Japanese doctrine are very closely modelled on, indeed often identical with, the United States private interest factors. None the less, the Japanese doctrine does not take into account factors of public interest. Because of this, the Japanese doctrine can be said to be closer to the Quebecois than to the United States doctrine of *forum non conveniens*.[65]

However, it is important to note that the Japanese 'special circum-stances' doctrine is distinctly different from all the doctrines of *forum non conveniens* outlined above in three important respects. First, there is no indispensable requirement that there be another more appropriate forum available abroad. Secondly, Japanese courts can only dismiss a case and have no power to stay[66] or dismiss an action subject to conditions. This hinders their ability to deal with cases flexibly. Thirdly, where an action is dismissed on special circumstances grounds, a Japanese court is saying that it has no jurisdiction, as opposed to saying that it has jurisdiction but is refusing to exercise it.

The upshot is that the Japanese 'special circumstances' doctrine is, strictly speaking, not a doctrine of *forum non conveniens*. However, it does bear an obvious resemblance to that doctrine and is accordingly con-sidered in this part of the General Report rather than along with other civil law jurisdictions.

(e) SWEDEN

Swedish courts have a substantial margin of discretion in relation to jurisdiction which allows them to depart from the rules of local compe-tence (on which jurisdiction is based) and dismiss a local action when the connection with Sweden is very weak. This probably requires that the defendant objects to Swedish jurisdiction as being unreasonably burden-

---

[64] See below, p. 310.

[65] For a comparision of *forum non conveniens* in England, Australia, and Japan see Hayes, [1992] *UBC L Rev.* 41.

[66] Except in situations where there are natural disasters or the unavailability of a party due to illness and the like.

some for him. While it is unclear whether the Swedish courts recognize the doctrine of *forum non conveniens*, their general discretion can be used for the same purpose.

(f) AN EXPLANATION

Some explanation is needed why certain States have adopted a doctrine of *forum non conveniens*, and why it is not always the same doctrine. This involves looking at the role of *forum non conveniens* in the different States in which the doctrine has been adopted. It can be regarded as fulfilling the following roles:

(i) The Antidote to Excessively Wide Bases of Jurisdiction

Forum non conveniens performs this role in Britain, Canada (common law jurisdictions), Israel, Quebec, and Japan. In England jurisdiction can be taken in cases of *in personam* jurisdiction on the basis of the transient presence of the defendant in England. In Scotland, owning immovable property in the forum is sufficient to found general jurisdiction against the owner in civil and commercial matters where the Brussels and Lugano Conventions do not apply. Jurisdiction is not being taken on the basis that the forum is *forum conveniens*. There is an obvious risk of injustice if jurisdiction is taken on such wide grounds. At its worst, one party may start an action, including a defensive action for a negative declaration, in a State which has been deliberately chosen because of its inconvenience to the other party.

The Canadian (common law jurisdictions) Reporter states that there are 'few occasions when a Canadian court is absolutely precluded from taking jurisdiction over an action. The discretion to decline jurisdiction has therefore become the means by which disputes as to jurisdiction are most often resolved in the common law jurisdictions of Canada'.[67] Similarly, in the Quebec legal system, although the presence of assets has recently disappeared as a basis of jurisdiction, there are, nevertheless, a number of wide bases of jurisdiction. There is jurisdiction if 'a fault was committed in Quebec, damage was suffered in Quebec, an injurious act occurred in Quebec or one of the obligations arising from a contract was to be performed in Quebec';[68] with such wide, although not necessarily exorbitant, bases of jurisdiction there is a role for *forum non conveniens* in Quebec as an antidote.

In Japan the adoption of the internal venue provisions contained in the Code of Civil Procedure as the criteria for international jurisdiction has had to be countered by the special circumstances doctrine which is concerned to obtain equity in individual cases in a flexible way.

---

[67] See below, p. 144.   [68] Art. 3148–3°, Civil Code of Quebec.

(ii) Providing Flexibility

Bases of jurisdiction employed in common law jurisdictions are not only wide; they can also be crude, sometimes being based on a single, perhaps fortuitous, connection with the forum. Thus, jurisdiction can be invoked without leave of the court under the New Zealand long-arm provision (Rule 219 of the High Court Rules) on the basis that a contract was made in New Zealand or the proceedings concern a claim for damages for an act done in New Zealand. *Forum non conveniens* provides flexibility and allows the court to consider the wide, indeed unlimited, range of considerations which come within the themes of appropriateness and justice.

(iii) Without Excessive Uncertainty

In common law jurisdictions there are many reported cases on private international law. This is a feature of federal systems such as the United States, Canada, and Australia, and of major legal and commercial centres such as England. This has meant that there are numerous precedents explaining the doctrine of *forum non conveniens*, thereby providing a measure of certainty in its operation.

(iv) Preventing Forum-Shopping

The link between forum shopping and *forum non conveniens* is apparent in Canada (common law jurisdictions), where the advantage that the plaintiff obtains from trial in a Canadian forum is condemned if there is no real and substantial connection with that forum, but is regarded as a legitimate advantage where there is such a connection.[69] In the United States *forum non conveniens* has been used with some frequency to deny trial to foreign plaintiffs who forum-shop in the United States. The problem of forum-shopping is particularly acute in the United States, since there are obvious advantages to be obtained from trial in the United States (class actions, contingent fees, juries, higher damages including in many cases punitive damages, extensive pre-trial discovery), and very wide jurisdiction rules which allow trial.[70] It is against this background of forum-shopping that the concern, unique to the United States, with public interest factors, such as the unfairness of burdening citizens in an unrelated forum with jury duty, becomes understandable, as does the distinction drawn between local and foreign plaintiffs.

By way of contrast, there is no such problem of forum-shopping in Quebec, which only has about twenty private international law cases each year, and is very largely concerned under its doctrine of *forum non*

---

[69] See *Amchem Products Inc* v. *British Columbia (Workers' Compensation Board)*, n. 44 above, at 110.   [70] See generally Juenger, (1988/89) 63 *Tul. L Rev.* 553.

conveniens with private interest factors. In New Zealand forum-shopping is also no problem because of the geographical isolation of that State and because there are no obvious substantial advantages in suing in New Zealand over any other common law jurisdiction. Of course, the doctrine of *forum non conveniens* could be used to combat unacceptable forum-shopping in New Zealand, although it was not introduced for this purpose. Sweden is also said to be not popular with forum-shoppers.

(v) Avoiding Contradictory Judgments

In Quebec the doctrine of *forum non conveniens* is seen, like the doctrine of *lis alibi pendens*, which will be examined later, as preventing contradictory judgments from being delivered.

3. States Which have not Adopted a Doctrine of *Forum Non Conveniens*

When looking at the position in those States which have not adopted a doctrine of *forum non conveniens* two important issues need to be addressed. The first is the question why those States have not adopted a doctrine of *forum non conveniens*. The second is the extent to which those States have adopted substitutes for such a doctrine.

(a) why no doctrine of *forum non conveniens*?

There are a number of reasons why States have not adopted a doctrine of *forum non conveniens*. Often it may be for more than one of these reasons.

(i) Open and Closed Systems

The Dutch reporters draw attention to the fact that, in broad terms, there are two alternative systems of control of jurisdiction. First, there is the closed system, under which the law of procedure strictly defines the cases in which the courts have jurisdiction, in principle leaving no room for judicial discretion. This is the system to be found in civil law jurisdictions. Secondly, there is the open system, under which there are broad and general rules of jurisdiction leaving the courts with a discretion whether to accept or decline jurisdiction. This is the system to be found in common law jurisdictions.

(ii) Appropriate Bases of Jurisdiction

More specifically, when discussing the jurisdictional background[71] it has been seen that, in many States, the rules of jurisdiction are such that they take into account the sorts of factors that are considered under a doctrine

---

[71] See above, pp. 7–9.

of *forum non conveniens*; if jurisdiction is taken on the basis of *forum conveniens*, there is no need for a doctrine of *forum non conveniens*.

(iii) No Problem of Forum-Shopping

In many States forum-shopping is not seen as being a problem; accordingly, there is no need for a doctrine of *forum non conveniens* to deal with this. Argentina, Finland, Germany, and Greece all come within this category. However, the precise reason forum-shopping is not seen as being a problem does differ, depending on the State in question. In Argentina the basis of jurisdiction normally coincides with the domicile of the defendant, which prevents persons from bringing actions in Argentina which have no connection with that State. In Germany, forum-shopping is said generally to be perfectly legitimate.[72] There is said to be no advantage in forum-shopping in Greece, and the rules on international jurisdiction deny an opportunity for this. In Finland, it is accepted that a person will have good reasons if that person sues in Finland.

In so far as forum-shopping is perceived to be a problem, many States believe it is better to deal with this by means other than a doctrine of *forum non conveniens*. The French rules on international jurisdiction guarantee, in principle, that a French court is not competent unless it has a strong link with the case. Under Japanese law, forum-shopping is dealt with at the stage of the rules on international jurisdiction and it is suggested that, in developing the law, the courts should be careful not to make rules which unduly favour certain categories of party.

A different way of tackling the problem of forum-shopping is by harmonizing choice of law rules. The German reporter sees harmonization of choice of law rules as being the most suitable answer to forum-shopping, rather than narrowing jurisdiction rules. There is support also from the Italian reporter for using choice-of-law rules to discourage forum-shopping. Moreover, there is a clear precedent for this within the European Community. One of the purposes of the Rome Convention on the law applicable to contractual obligations of 1980, which harmonizes contract choice-of-law rules in the European Community, is to inhibit the forum-shopping that the Brussels Convention allows.[73] However, it should be pointed out that the harmonization of choice of law rules will only stop forum-shopping for substantive law advantages, not for procedural advantages.

(iv) The Position of Judges

The position of judges is different in civil law jurisdictions from that in common law jurisdictions. In France, historically, the power of judges has

---

[72] For a similar English view see Slater, (1988) 104 *LQR* 554. See also Juenger, (1994) 16 *Sydney L Rev*. 5, the reply by Opeskin at 14 and the rejoinder by Juenger at 28.
[73] See the Giuliano and Lagarde Report, [1980] OJ C282/4–5.

been limited so that they are not used to exercising a flexible discretion. The Swiss legal system is not dominated by case law, or by law-making tribunals. There is a fear in Germany of capricious decisions by judges who, if given a wide discretion, may be tempted to get rid of troublesome foreign cases in the name of justice. Greek judges would rather try the case themselves than be accused of such behaviour.

(v) Absence of Cases

Many States lack the case law decisions on private international law which are so necessary to add flesh to the bare bones of a doctrine of *forum non conveniens*, and reduce the uncertainty when exercising the discretion. Sweden and Finland have few cases on private international law. The same is true in Switzerland and in Argentina. More generally, in common law jurisdictions, where much of the law on international jurisdiction is based on case law, it is probably easier to introduce a doctrine of *forum non conveniens* than in civil law States where jurisdiction is laid down by code, statute, or treaty.[74]

(vi) Constitutional Problems

In Germany, there are constitutional difficulties in introducing a doctrine of *forum non conveniens*. There is a constitutional commitment to guaranteeing the legally competent judge; this requires a predictable jurisdiction which must not be manipulated under any circumstances. Similarly, Greek courts are, seemingly, forbidden to take such an initiative under the Constitution. Under Italian law there is the right to adjudication before a court and judge predetermined by a general rule of law. This stems from a provision in the Italian Constitution stating that 'no one shall be denied the right to be tried by his natural judge pre-established by statute'.[75]

(vii) Certainty and Predictability

Civil law States are more concerned with ensuring certainty and predictability than the flexibility that a doctrine of *forum non conveniens* provides. There is no doubt that the uncertainty inherent in exercising a discretionary power leads to litigation, which involves delay and expense to the parties.[76]

(viii) A Negative Conflict of Jurisdiction

Declining jurisdiction can give rise to fears of a negative conflict of jurisdiction, i.e. that no court will try the case.[77] The Dutch reporters comment

---

[74] There is, though, the obvious exception of Quebec with its codified provision on *forum non conveniens*: see above, pp. 16–17.
[75] Art. 25(1).   [76] See generally Robertson, (1987) 103 *LQR* 398.
[77] For German fears see below, p. 195.

that the decision on *forum non conveniens* may decide the case itself because of limitation periods.[78] Common law jurisdictions can get round this danger by refusing a stay of local proceedings in the situation where the plaintiff is time-barred abroad.[79] Alternatively, the staying of local proceedings may be made subject to undertakings by the defendant, which may include an undertaking to consent to the jurisdiction of the foreign court and to continue to waive defences based on statutes of limitations.[80]

(ix) Choice of Law

The Swiss reporter has suggested that another reason for the absence of a doctrine of *forum non conveniens* may be that in these States it is less likely than in common law jurisdictions that the local forum applies the *lex fori*. It follows that the rules on jurisdiction need not be corrected so much in order to avoid the application of the *lex fori*.

(b) FORUM NON CONVENIENS SUBSTITUTES

A *forum non conveniens* substitute is a limited power to decline jurisdiction, or deny that there is jurisdiction, in specific and limited circumstances, on the basis of *forum non conveniens*-type considerations. Nearly all of those States surveyed which have not adopted a general doctrine of *forum non conveniens* have adopted substitutes. The precise details of these substitutes vary from one State to another, and so will be examined on a State-by-State basis.

(i) The Provisions

(i) The Netherlands

There is a statutory *forum non conveniens* rule in proceedings instituted by way of a petition to the court, such as family cases, disputes concerning the management of companies, disputes over the fixing of rent for dwelling-houses, and reduction of liability in transport cases. This rule is set out in section 11 of Article 429c of the Code of Civil Procedure (WBRv) and states that: 'A court has no jurisdiction if the petition is insufficiently connected with the legal sphere of The Netherlands.' This corrects the broad rule which confers jurisdiction by the sole introduction of a petition. There are numerous such cases where *forum non conveniens* has been used. Interestingly, its role in petition cases is the same as that in common law jurisdictions, in that it prevents the forum-shopping which liberal rules on international jurisdiction allow. There is also a *forum non conveniens*-type

---

[78] See below, p. 323.　　　[79] *Spiliada Maritime Corp* v. *Cansulex Ltd*, n. 13 above, at 483–4.
[80] See *In re Union Carbide Corp. Gas Plant Disaster at Bhopal, India in Dec. 1984*, 809 F. 2d 195 (2nd Cir. 1987), *cert. denied sub nom Executive Comm. Members* v. *Union of India*, 484 US 871 (1987).

rule in summons cases which is of case law origin. According to the *Piscator* case[81] the parties are free to confer jurisdiction on a Dutch court by means of a choice of jurisdiction agreement 'unless a reasonable interest is lacking'. Finally, in recent cases involving interim injunction proceedings, district court presidents use *forum non conveniens* considerations more and more to deny jurisdiction.

(ii) Germany

A guardianship court can refrain from placing the ward under its protection if the ward's interests are better served by a foreign court's jurisdiction.[82] Moreover, the principle of *perpetuatio fori*[83] is relaxed in non-contentious proceedings in the interest of the child, especially in adoption cases when the adopting person or child changes his habitual residence to a foreign State. There is also a doctrine of incompatible competence under which, if the applicable foreign law requires from the German court an impossible or unacceptable activity, there is no German international jurisdiction. Finally, there is a doctrine of 'legitimate interest to take legal action', which may be invoked if the plaintiff abuses the judicial procedure.

(iii) Belgium

Belgian law uses a mechanism in uncontested matters which closely resembles the doctrine of *forum non conveniens*. This technique is concerned with the control of *fraude à la loi*. Thus in one case involving an application for divorce by mutual consent involving two foreigners, the Belgian judge verified that the parties had not intended to escape the law that was normally applicable by a foreign court.[84]

(iv) France

In France there is particular criticism of the concept of *forum non conveniens*. However, as in Germany, there is a doctrine of 'legitimate interest to take legal action' which is able to prevent abuse of procedure.

(v) Greece

It is possible to argue that a discretionary power exists by virtue of the prohibition under the Constitution on the 'abusive exercise of [any] rights'.[85] There are also requirements under the Civil Code[86] and the Code of Civil Procedure[87] that the parties act in good faith. The action is to be dismissed as 'abusive' when the litigation does not show any connection

---

[81] HR, 1 Feb. 1985, [1985] NJ 698 JCS, [1989] *NILR* 59.
[82] S. 47 FGG (Code on Non-contentious proceedings).   [83] S. 261 III, No. 2, ZPO.
[84] Brussels, 23 Mar. 1977, [1978] JT 647.
[85] Art. 25.   [86] Art. 281.   [87] Art. 116.

with the Greek court whose jurisdiction has been invoked and the plaintiff seeks to achieve 'improper' aims or other aims than those allowed by the jurisdictional rules.

(vi) Switzerland

The best example of a *forum non conveniens* substitute in Switzerland is to be found in relation to children. Swiss courts regularly refuse to act on behalf of a Swiss child because the authorities at the child's foreign place of residence are better informed, and therefore the foreign State is a more convenient forum.[88]

Swiss law also contains a number of provisions where a *forum conveniens* discretion operates, whereby jurisdiction is taken on the basis that the foreign forum is inappropriate, rather than on the more usual basis of the local forum being appropriate. Thus Swiss law provides for a subsidiary jurisdiction in cases where a Swiss citizen lives abroad and the action cannot be brought in the regular forum abroad, for example because the foreign courts are not impartial.[89] In some respects, this is close to a doctrine of *forum non conveniens*. After all, if the foreign forum is not inappropriate the Swiss court will not try the case and, under *forum non conveniens*, if the foreign forum is more appropriate the same result will follow: the local forum will not try the case. Indeed, the Swiss reporter refers to such subsidiary jurisdiction as a *forum non conveniens* substitute. None the less, the Swiss rule is essentially a positive one, concerned with the assertion of jurisdiction, rather than a negative rule, which denies jurisdiction or leads to a declining of jurisdiction. The emphasis is very different under the Swiss rule from that under a doctrine of *forum non conveniens*. The Swiss rule is biased against jurisdiction being taken; there will only be jurisdiction if it can be shown that the foreign forum is inappropriate. Under *forum non conveniens* the rule is biased in favour of trying the case, for trial continues unless it can be shown that the forum abroad is more appropriate.

(vii) Finland

A discretion is exercised to decide whether there should be a prosecution in Finland in criminal cases concerning an offence committed abroad. The exercise of this discretion involves taking into account typical *forum non conveniens* considerations: nationality, domicile, and residence of the

---

[88] See Art. 85 of the Swiss Private International Law Statute of 1987, which refers to the Hague Convention on Jurisdiction and the Law Applicable to the Protection of Minors of 1961. See Art. 4(1) of that Convention.

[89] See e.g. Arts. 43(2), 47, 60, 67, 76, 80, 87 of the Swiss Private International Law Statute of 1987.

defendant and victim, the availability of evidence, and the probability of a fair trial abroad.

(viii) Argentina

There are a number of procedural mechanisms (for example, involving a motion to dismiss or decline jurisdiction), which come into play in cases of doubt concerning the impartiality of local judges or with a view to ensuring that justice is really done.

(ii) A Comparison with *Forum Non Conveniens*

A comparison with the common law doctrine of *forum non conveniens* shows the following similarities. First, with *forum non conveniens* substitutes, a negative doctrine is being applied so that jurisdiction is declined or denied. Secondly, *forum non conveniens*-type considerations are being employed to justify this declining/denial of jurisdiction.

There are, though, the following important differences. First, with the *forum non conveniens* substitutes, the power to decline/deny jurisdiction operates only in very limited circumstances, such as certain family law matters. It does not involve a general discretionary power. Secondly, normally jurisdiction is denied (i.e. there is no jurisdiction), rather than declined (i.e. there is jurisdiction but this is not exercised). Thirdly, the basis on which jurisdiction is declined/denied is that the local forum is inappropriate. This contrasts with the position in most common law jurisdictions (but not Australia), where the basis is that the alternative forum abroad is more appropriate. As has been seen, this difference in emphasis is a significant one, since it is harder to show that a local forum is inappropriate than that a foreign forum is more appropriate.

IV
LIS PENDENS

1. THE NATURE OF THE PROBLEM

It is widely accepted that it is undesirable to have a situation in which parallel proceedings, involving the same parties and the same cause of action, are continuing in two different States at the same time (*lis pendens*). There is an obvious risk that, if the proceedings continue, this may result in two irreconcilable judgments.[90] In order to avoid this, there may be an ugly rush by the parties to get one action decided ahead of the

---

[90] See Case 144/86 *Gubisch Maschinenfabrik KG* v. *Palumbo* [1987] ECR 4861 at 4874; Case C–351/89 *Overseas Union Insurance Ltd* v. *New Hampshire Insurance Co* [1992] 2 WLR 586.

other,[91] which will lead to problems of *res judicata*. *Lis pendens* is seen by many States as being essentially a problem relating to the recognition and enforcement of foreign judgments. It is certainly true that, the wider the rules on recognition and enforcement of foreign judgments, the more of a problem *lis pendens* becomes. Thus the semi-automatic recognition and enforcement of judgments within Western Europe under the Brussels and Lugano Conventions create a very real risk of being required to recognize a foreign judgment which conflicts with one granted in the recognizing State (or one granted in some other State whose judgments also have to be recognized). In contrast, if a State refuses to recognize and enforce foreign judgments—and this is the position in Sweden and Finland (unless there is a treaty obligation)—*lis pendens* is not seen as being a problem.

There is, though, an additional and less commonly voiced objection to allowing parallel proceedings to continue, in that it creates additional inconvenience and expense to the parties. It is not surprising to find English judges voicing this concern;[92] they also take such considerations into account under the doctrine of *forum non conveniens*. What is perhaps more surprising is to find this concern being voiced by reporters from Greece and Italy, which have no such doctrine.[93]

2. WAYS OF DEALING WITH THE PROBLEM

There are, in theory, four possible ways of dealing with the problem of *lis pendens*.

First, the forum could decline jurisdiction or suspend proceedings.

Secondly, the forum could seek to restrain the foreign proceedings.

Thirdly, both sets of proceedings could be allowed to continue. However, rules of *res judicata* could be used to prevent two judgments; if there are two judgments, rules on recognition and enforcement could be used to decide which one is to have priority.

Fourthly, mechanisms could be adopted to encourage the parties to opt for trial in just one forum (the appropriate forum).

In most States the first method is the one that has found favour. This statement of the overall position should, though, be qualified by the observation that, in a substantial number of States, there is neither explicit statutory/code provision nor established case law on *lis pendens*, so that it is not possible to state with confidence what the position is in these States. This is the situation in Japan, where there are conflicting authorities; in Greece (in non-convention cases), where, because of the lack of authority, the analogy is drawn with *lis pendens* under internal law; in Finland,

---

[91] *The Abidin Daver*, n. 32 above, at 412; *Du Pont (EI) de Nemours & Co* v. *Agnew and Kerr* [1987] 2 Lloyd's Rep. 585 (CA).

[92] See *The Abidin Daver*, n. 32 above.   [93] See below, pp. 249, 282.

where (in non-convention cases) there are no precedents and the basis of the doctrine is vague; and in Sweden, where, apart from convention cases, there is no statutory rule on this topic. Nonetheless, there are suggestions from the national reporters in these States as to how the problem of *lis pendens* could be dealt with.

The four different ways of dealing with the problem of *lis pendens* will now be examined.

(a) DECLINING JURISDICTION/SUSPENDING PROCEEDINGS

Although very many States have adopted rules on declining jurisdiction and/or suspending proceedings in cases of *lis pendens*, there is no uniformity as to the basis for this. It may be on the basis of *forum non conveniens* or a mechanical rule which gives priority to the State which is first seised of the proceedings or a recognition prognosis.

(i) *Forum Non Conveniens*
(i) Lis Pendens as a Factor when Operating the Discretion
In Britain, the Commonwealth States of Australia, Canada, and New Zealand, and Israel, *lis pendens* is not a doctrine in its own right but is regarded as being overall a facet, albeit an important one, of the doctrine of *forum non conveniens*. In exercising the discretion to stay the action in the forum considerable weight may be given to the *lis pendens* factor because of the well recognized undesirability of allowing the two sets of proceedings to continue.

In Canada (common law jurisdictions), *lis pendens* has been given most weight when the same party is the plaintiff in both the local and the foreign proceedings. Although, even in this situation, it may be possible to justify the continuance of the proceedings in the forum. In reversed party cases the *lis pendens* argument is harder to make because it is not one person who has commenced parallel proceedings. It is irrelevant under English law which action is started first, the one in the forum or the one abroad, and under New Zealand law this is said not to be decisive. However, under both English and New Zealand law, what is very relevant is the question how far each set of proceedings has progressed. If no substantial progress has been made in the foreign proceedings, for example there has been no discovery of documents, the *lis pendens* consideration will be given little weight.[94] In the New Zealand case of *McConnell Dowell Constructors Ltd* v. *Lloyd's Syndicate 396*[95] Cooke P said that with

---

[94] *Arkwright Mutual Insurance Co* v. *Bryanston Insurance Co Ltd* [1990] 2 Lloyd's Rep. 70 at 80. See also *De Dampierre* v. *De Dampierre* [1988] AC 92 at 108. Compare *The 'Varna' (No. 2)* [1994] 2 Lloyd's Rep. 41.
[95] [1988] 2 NZLR 257.

actions started more or less contemporaneously (ten days apart in the instant case) the court should move straight to the *forum non conveniens* rule set out in the *Spiliada* case, ignoring the *lis pendens* factor.

In Australia, as an alternative to granting a permanent stay or dismissal of an action, the courts have sometimes granted a temporary stay or lengthy adjournment of a case. In this situation, the Australian rules on *forum non conveniens* have no application.

Under Japanese law, although there is no explicit statutory provision nor well established case law in relation to *lis pendens*, in one case[96] it was taken into consideration under the 'special circumstances' doctrine.[97] The court noted that assuming jurisdiction would run a risk of delivering a judgment conflicting with those of the Californian courts, and that the parallel proceedings would lead to a heavy burden upon the defendant. The result in the case was that the Japanese court denied that it had jurisdiction.

In Quebec *forum non conveniens* has been used to avoid the possibility of contradictory judgments. However, Article 3137 of the recent Civil Code deals with *lis pendens* by the recognition prognosis method.[98]

In the United States there is a rather different approach towards *lis pendens*. Although the *forum non conveniens* doctrine may operate in cases of *lis pendens*, there appears to be no evidence that the *lis pendens* factor is given the weight in favour of declining jurisdiction that it has been given in other common law jurisdictions. Instead, in the United States in *lis pendens* cases the question that normally arises is whether the foreign proceedings should be restrained, i.e. the second way of dealing with the problem of *lis pendens* is employed.[99]

(ii) A Critique

The great virtue of the *forum non conveniens* approach is its flexibility. It can deal with any case involving parallel proceedings, even one where the parties or the cause of action are not the same. This is not a situation of *lis pendens*, as defined above,[100] none the less it is still undesirable that the parallel proceedings should continue in both States, for the risk of additional expense and inconvenience to the parties, and of irreconcilable judgments, is there in such circumstances. Thus, in English law, the concern has been to avoid a multiplicity of proceedings in England and abroad rather than about *lis pendens*, as strictly defined.[101]

---

[96] *Greenlines Shipping Co Ltd* v. *California First Bank*, 28 Japanese Annual of International Law 243 (1985).

[97] As has already been seen, above, pp. 17–18, the special circumstances doctrine is technically not a doctrine of *forum non conveniens*.

[98] See below, p. 37.   [99] See below, pp. 40–1.   [100] Above, p. 27.

[101] See e.g. *Hawke Bay Shipping Co Ltd* v. *The First National Bank of Chicago (The Efthimis)* [1986] 1 Lloyd's Rep. 244 (CA).

The great vice of the *forum non conveniens* approach is that, once proceedings have been commenced in State A, a party may go to State B (a more appropriate forum) and commence proceedings for a negative declaration that State A is not an appropriate forum for trial. This disadvantage stems from the fact that it is not in itself relevant under the *forum non conveniens* doctrine which court was first seised of the proceedings.

For a State such as Japan which, under its domestic procedural law treats jurisdiction and *lis pendens* as being separate, the *forum non conveniens* approach has an obvious lack of attraction. Thus, although there is the one authority adopting the *forum non conveniens* approach, other cases have adopted different solutions.[102]

(ii) The Mechanical First-Seised Approach

This approach requires the courts of the forum to defer to the courts of a foreign State if the latter are first seised of the proceedings.

(i) *The Provisions*

A well known example of a rule adopting this approach is Article 21 of the Brussels and Lugano Conventions which provides that:

Where proceedings involving the same cause of action and between the same parties are brought in the courts of different Contracting States, any court other than the court first seised shall of its own motion stay its proceedings until such time as the jurisdiction of the court first seised is established.

Where the jurisdiction of the court first seised is established, any court other than the court first seised shall decline jurisdiction in favour of that court.

Essentially the same rule has been suggested in a number of Western European States in non-Convention cases. Sweden has entered into a number of other recognition and enforcement treaties besides the Lugano Convention. Even though these do not contain an Article 21-type provision, it is suggested by the Swedish reporter that the *lis pendens* doctrine will be applied to foreign proceedings in these cases too.

Greek law contains no provisions which explicitly deal with *lis pendens*. Nonetheless, most Greek scholars are of the opinion that foreign litispendence must be recognized under certain circumstances. The view is taken that foreign and domestic proceedings are equivalent; resort can therefore be had, by way of analogy, to Article 222 of the Code of Civil Procedure, which is the domestic *lis pendens* rule. This states that 'after the commencement of the litispendence and during the time it lasts no new proceedings are permitted before any other court . . .'. The conditions necessary for domestic *lis pendens* must be fulfilled; there must be the same dispute between the same parties having the same status. Dutch law

---

[102] See below, pp. 310–16.

in non-Convention cases is unusual in that it combines an element of discretion with the first-seised principle. Thus the courts are not obliged to stay proceedings if another court has been first seised. Nonetheless, as a rule in the case of actions between the same parties on the same subject-matter Dutch courts always defer to the court first seised.

Moving outside Western Europe, Argentinian law has a doctrine of *litispendencia*. *Litispendencia* by identity requires that the parties, object, and cause be the same for both sets of proceedings. In this situation the Argentinian judge will decline jurisdiction in respect of the second proceedings.

Even common law jurisdictions sometimes resort to mechanical rules to deal with *lis pendens* in certain narrowly defined circumstances. Under the Canadian federal Divorce Act jurisdiction is given to a province if one spouse has been ordinarily resident there for one year. Resulting problems of *lis pendens* are solved by a rule that gives exclusive jurisdiction to the court of the province or territory in which a petition is first presented.[103] New Zealand also has a specific statutory provision, which is narrow in its scope, being limited to the area of admiralty jurisdiction. Section 6 of the Admiralty Act 1973 provides that the New Zealand courts cannot exercise admiralty jurisdiction *in personam* while proceedings between the same parties are pending in any foreign court, unless the defendant submits or has agreed to submit to their jurisdiction.

(ii) When is a Court Seised of Proceedings?

It is left to the internal law of each State to determine, by reference to its own procedural rules, when its courts are seised of proceedings; normally, the choice is between the moment when the document instituting the proceedings is filed with a local court and the later moment when this document is served on the defendant. Unfortunately, in a number of States the procedural rules do not give a clear answer. Moreover, in those States where a clear answer is given, it is readily apparent that there is no uniformity as to the moment when proceedings become pending.

Uncertainty—In Scotland there is uncertainty simply because there is no authority on when Scots courts are seised of proceedings.[104] The position is also not clear in Greece where one view, favoured by the Greek reporter,[105] is that an action is pending when there is service with a copy of the complaint: the other view is that this occurs when the action is earlier filed before the court.

The position in Switzerland, at first sight, looks to be clear. A Swiss court is seised of proceedings 'when the first act necessary to commence a

---

[103] Divorce Act, RSC 1985, c.3 (2nd Supp.), s. 3(2).
[104] The Schlosser Report ([1979] OJ C59/125) took the view that in Scotland 'proceedings become pending only when service of the summons has been effected on the defender'.
[105] See below, p. 253.

lawsuit is performed'.[106] To commence the lawsuit it is sufficient to initiate conciliation proceedings. However, the Court of Appeal of the Zürich Canton,[107] applying the principle adopted by the European Court of Justice[108] that a court is first seised when the requirements for proceedings to become *definitively* pending are first fulfilled, held that an application for conciliation does not commence proceedings *definitively*. After conciliation proceedings, a Justice of the Peace has to issue a document which entitles the plaintiff to commence court proceedings. This document may be filed with a court. If this is not done within a certain time (in Zürich, within three months), the effect of the document and the proceedings expires. If the plaintiff wants to start new proceedings after the lapse of this time, he has to start proceedings again with the Justice of the Peace.

The English courts have in recent years changed their minds over the precise moment when they are seised of jurisdiction. Initially, this was said to be when proceedings were merely issued. Subsequently, it was decided that, in general, it was to be when the proceedings were served on the defendant.[109] It was suggested, though, that there was an exception to this general rule, whereby if prior to service a provisional measure, such as a Mareva injunction, were granted by the court, it would be seised from the moment that this pre-service jurisdiction was exercised.[110] However, it has recently been decided by the Court of Appeal[111] that there are no exceptions to the simple and practical rule that an English court is seised on the date of service of the writ. When it comes to the grant of provisional measures, a court is not seised of jurisdiction on the merits of the dispute. Neither is a court seised merely by virtue of granting an order for service of process out of the jurisdiction. Leave to appeal to the House of Lords against this decision has, however, been granted.

National courts have enough difficulty in deciding when, under their own procedural rules, their courts are seised of jurisdiction. They will have even more difficulty in working out when a foreign court, under its procedural rules, is so seised, and there is always the risk of getting this wrong.[112] One way of solving this difficulty is to adjourn local proceedings until the foreign court has determined when its own proceedings have become pending.[113]

---

[106] Art. 9(2) of the Swiss Private International Law Statute of 1987.
[107] Obergericht, Zürich, 25 July 1991, 90 *Blätter für Zürcherische Rechtsprechung* 193 (1991).
[108] Case 129/83 *Zelger* v. *Salinitri* [1984] ECR 2398 at 2409.
[109] *Dresser UK Ltd* v. *Falcongate Freight Management Ltd* [1992] 2 QB 502.
[110] *Ibid.* 523 (*per* Bingham LJ).
[111] *Neste Chemicals SA* v. *DK Line SA (The Sargasso)* [1994] 3 All ER 180.
[112] Compare the German view (below, pp. 198–9) that German courts are seised of jurisdiction at the moment of service, with an Italian decision which states that German courts are seised when the action was filed (*Delta GmbH* v. *Mondial Express s.p.a. and Atex sri* (Corte di Cassazione, 12 October 1990, n. 10014) [1992] 4 *Riv. Dir. Int. Priv. Proc.* 956).
[113] *Polly Peck International Ltd* v. *Citibank NA* [1994] ILPr. 71.

Lack of Uniformity—Many States agree that their courts are seised of jurisdiction when the proceedings are served on the defendant (e.g. Italy,[114] Germany, The Netherlands, and England), and so the race by the parties to commence proceedings starts from the same point.[115] However, there is not complete uniformity on this. In Sweden the procedural rule is different; a court is considered seised when the summons application is filed with the court or, if a summons is not necessary, when the claim is presented to the court.[116] This early rule encourages plaintiffs to forum-shop in Sweden. To take an example, a person who knows that an action has been started against him in England, but has not yet been served, can go to Sweden, file an application, and thereby give priority to the Swedish action under the first-seised rule.[117]

As the German reporter points out,[118] the way to produce certainty and uniformity in relation to the first-seised rule, at least within the European Community, is for the European Court of Justice to give an autonomous meaning to the concept of when a court is seised of jurisdiction, rather than leaving it to national procedural law.

(iii) A Critique

The virtue of the first-seised approach is its simplicity. Against this, this approach has the following numerous vices.

First, any mechanical *lis pendens* rule, particularly when enshrined in a code, a convention, or a statute, is going to have to define the meaning of *lis pendens*. Thus Article 21 of the Brussels and Lugano Conventions contains a definition of *lis pendens* in terms of 'the same parties' and 'the same cause of action'. This has led to a considerable body of case law interpreting these terms. The European Court of Justice has clarified the meaning of 'the same cause of action'.[119] This refers to the proceedings being based on the same contractual relationship. This liberal interpretation contrasts with the restrictive view previously taken under Italian law.[120] It has also made clear that there is a separate, albeit closely related, requirement that the subject-matter of the proceedings must be the same. A decision of the European Court of Justice is eagerly awaited on the interpretation of the requirement that the parties must be the same.[121] In England there have

---

[114] See Art. 39(3), Code of Civil Procedure; *Delta GmbH* v. *Mondial Express s.p.a. and Atex srl*, n. 112 above.

[115] See e.g. *AGF* v. *Chiyoda* [1992] 1 Lloyd's Rep. 325—actions pending in England and Italy; *Neste Chemicals SA* v. *DK Line SA (The Sargasso)*, n. 111 above—actions pending in England and The Netherlands.

[116] Ch. 13, s. 4 of the Swedish Code of Judicial Procedure.

[117] See below, p. 376.   [118] See below, p. 199.

[119] Case 144/86 *Gubisch Maschinenfabrik KG* v. *Giulio Palumbo* [1987] ECR 4861. For French criticism see below, pp. 182–3.   [120] See below, p. 292.

[121] This has been referred to the ECJ in Case C–406/92 *The Maciej Rataj*. Tesauro AG gave his opinion on 13 July 1994 that *lis pendens* arises whenever there is total or partial identity

been considerable difficulties over whether this requirement is satisfied in the situation where the two actions are an admiralty action *in rem* and an action *in personam*.[122] There have also been difficulties in the situation in which there is complex litigation involving many parties, some, but not all, of whom may be parties to both actions.[123]

Secondly, if you have a definition in terms of the same parties and cause of action there is an obvious temptation for a party to evade the *lis pendens* provision by adding another party or another cause of action.

Thirdly, it is necessary to make separate provision for certain cases falling outside the definition of *lis pendens*. Thus Article 22 of the Brussels and Lugano Conventions deals with 'related actions'.

Fourthly, which court is first seised may be an accident of timing. Moreover, actions may be started contemporaneously.

Fifthly, the first-seised rule, far from acting as a disincentive to parallel proceedings, acts as a positive incentive to this. It leads to an unseemly race by the parties to be the first to commence proceedings.

Sixthly, a party may start proceedings first in order to block proceedings in another State, and then engage in delaying tactics. This consideration has led to exceptions to the priority principle being created in Italy and Germany, in cases under the Italo–German bilateral Convention.[124]

Seventhly, the lack of uniformity over the question when a court is seised of proceedings means that the race to institute proceedings may commence from different starting points. Moreover, it may not be clear when the race starts because of the uncertainty in some States over when a court is seised of proceedings.

Eighthly, what happens if the court second seised has exclusive jurisdiction; does it still have to give way to the court first seised? The European Court of Justice has left this question open.[125] However, the English Court of Appeal has held that, if the court second seised has jurisdiction conferred on it by the agreement of the parties under Article 17 of the Brussels Convention, this takes precedence over Article 21.[126]

of subject-matter, cause of action, and parties as between two or more actions. In particular, the fact that the forms of the actions differ under the procedural laws of the two States concerned is unimportant. However, the obligation of the court second seised to decline jurisdiction under Art. 21 applies only to that part of the proceedings which has the same subject-matter and parties as the proceedings commenced previously.

[122] See *The Nordglimt* [1988] QB 183; *The Kherson* [1992] 2 Lloyd's Rep. 261.

[123] *The Maciej Rataj* [1992] 2 Lloyd's Rep. 552 (CA); referred to the ECJ. See also *Kinnear* v. *Falconfilms NV* [1994] 3 All ER 42 at 50–51.

[124] See below, p. 39; for the Italian case law see below, p. 290.

[125] Case C–351/89 *Overseas Union Insurance Ltd* v. *New Hampshire Insurance Co* [1992] 1 QB 434.

[126] *Continental Bank NA* v. *Aeakos Compania Naviera SA* [1994] 1 WLR 588.

(iii) Recognition Prognosis

Under this approach a court will decline jurisdiction if the action abroad is likely to lead to a judgment which is recognizable in its State. A recognition prognosis involves the application of a mechanical rule rather than a discretionary rule as understood by common lawyers, who are used to the *forum non conveniens* discretion. At the same time, one should not underestimate the important role and the power that is given to judges when calculating whether a foreign judgment is recognizable.

(i) The Provisions

This method of dealing with *lis pendens* has been commonly adopted in Western European States in non-Convention cases. Thus Article 9 of the Swiss Private International Law Statute of 1987 states that 'If a lawsuit on the same matter between the same parties is already pending abroad, the Swiss courts must stay the proceedings if it is to be expected that the foreign court will, within a reasonable time, render a judgment recognizable in Switzerland.'[127] If there is a foreign judgment abroad the Swiss courts must dismiss the proceedings if that judgment is recognizable in Switzerland. The French and German positions are the same as that in Switzerland. The foreign tribunal must have been *earlier* seised of the proceedings. This rule combines both the mechanical first-seised approach and the recognition prognosis approach.

Italian law operates a similar, albeit not identical, rule under certain bilateral conventions on recognition and enforcement of judgments entered into with France, Germany, Switzerland, and Austria, and which are largely replaced by the multilateral Brussels/Lugano Conventions. These bilateral conventions require dismissal of a local action where: (i) the foreign court was first seised of the proceedings, and (ii) there is identity of or connexity between the concurrent actions, and (iii) the foreign court had jurisdiction under the convention or (in the case of the Italo–Austrian Convention) it is expected that the foreign judgment will be recognized in the forum.

A provision involving dismissal or a stay of the proceedings in the forum, on the basis of a recognition prognosis, is to be found in Article 20 of the Hague Convention on the Recognition and Enforcement of Foreign Judgments in Civil and Commercial Matters of 1971,[128] which has been

---

[127] See also Art. 9(1) of the Swiss–Liechtenstein Treaty of 1968 on the recognition and enforcement of judicial decisions and arbitral awards in civil matters; the decision of the Cour de Cassation in *Miniera di Fragne*, Civ. 1ère, 26 Nov. 1974, [1975] RC 491, note D. Holleaux; [1975] JDI 108, note Ponsard; Grands arrêts . . . 2ème éd., n°. 55.

[128] Art. 20 only applies if two States have concluded a Supplementary Agreement pursuant to Art. 21.

ratified by Cyprus, The Netherlands, and Portugal. However, this does not appear to require that the foreign tribunal was first seised of the proceedings.

The Greek co-reporter suggests that a recognition prognosis should be adopted in cases where the Greek courts are second-seised.

In the Scandinavian States of Finland and Sweden there is no authority dealing with *lis pendens*, so the position is necessarily rather speculative. Nonetheless, it is suggested in Finland that 'the Finnish court seised second should as a rule decline jurisdiction in favour of the court seised first, if the judgment of the first court ought to be recognized and/or enforced in Finland'.[129] This adopts the Swiss, French, and German approach. The suggested rule in Sweden goes even further, in that it is concerned with foreign judgments that have merely evidentiary value in Sweden. It is suggested that the Swedish courts are free to stay proceedings in order to wait for such a judgment, unless the postponement would lead to excessive delay.[130] This limited suggestion arises because under Swedish law, while foreign judgments are not recognized and enforced (outside treaty obligations), they are given certain evidentiary value. It is envisaged that the decision whether to stay would be a matter of discretion for the Swedish court.

Moving outside Western Europe, Quebec has a provision which looks to be similar, although not identical, to the Swiss law. Article 3137 of the Civil Code states that:

On the application of a party, a Quebec authority may stay its ruling on an action brought before it if another action, between the same parties, based on the same facts and having the same object is pending before a foreign authority, provided that the latter action can result in a decision which may be recognised in Quebec, or if such a decision has already been rendered by a foreign authority.

There is, though, one vital difference between this recognition prognosis rule and those so far considered. The fact that a Quebecois authority *may* stay its ruling means that it is arguable that, even if all the conditions of Article 3137 have been met, a Quebecois authority could still refuse to stay its ruling. It is possible that some of the considerations that come into play when applying the Quebecois *forum non conveniens* discretion would operate in this context as well. However, the discretion under Article 3137 is said to operate merely as an antidote to the vagueness of the requirements, particularly for an identity of the objects of each action, under this Article. Moreover, under Article 3137 the Quebecois court stays (i.e. suspends) its ruling, whereas with *forum non conveniens* it declines jurisdiction.

---

[129] See below, p. 171.   [130] See below, p. 375.

There is one Japanese case which has adopted a recognition prognosis.[131] This required a 'reasonable certainty that the first action in the foreign country will result in an irrevocable judgment which can be recognized in Japan'.[132] What is particularly interesting about this case is the attention that was paid by the court to the question how far the proceedings abroad had progressed, a matter which, as has already been seen,[133] is of considerable importance in common law jurisdictions when using the doctrine of *forum non conveniens* to deal with *lis pendens*. In the instant case it was uncertain whether an Ohio case would come to judgment because of a dispute over jurisdiction. It was also too early to predict the possibility of recognition in Japan when the foreign proceedings were still at their starting point.

(ii) A Critique

There is an obvious logic in the recognition prognosis rule in that a foreign action can be regarded as being a premature foreign judgment. At the same time, the problem of irreconcilable judgments will only arise if the foreign judgment is one that is recognized.

Against this, this approach has the following vices:

First, if the foreign judgment is not recognizable, the parallel proceedings will be allowed to continue. But this will create additional expense and inconvenience to the parties. The recognition prognosis method is only suitable for dealing with *lis pendens* if the evils of parallel proceedings are seen solely in terms of the risk of irreconcilable judgments. Moreover, in States like Sweden and Finland, which, in the absence of a treaty obligation, fail to recognize foreign judgments, the court is left with no means of stopping parallel proceedings.

Secondly, the recognition prognosis rule suffers from the same flaw as the mechanical first-seised rule, in that *lis pendens* has to be defined. Article 3137 of the Civil Code of Quebec does this by reference to the actions being 'between the same parties, based on the same facts and having the same object'. These concepts have given rise to definitional problems and to a considerable body of case law.[134] It is interesting to note that, unlike the Brussels and Lugano Conventions, the reference in Quebec is not to the same cause of action, but to the broader and vaguer requirement of the same facts.

Thirdly, there is the same problem of the risk of evasion of the *lis pendens* provision as is encountered with the mechanical first-seised rule.

Fourthly, it is necessary to make separate provision for cases falling

---

[131] The Tokyo District Court judgment of 30 May 1989.   [132] See below, p. 313.
[133] Above, pp. 29–30.   [134] See below, pp. 158–161.

outside the definition of *lis pendens*. Thus the Civil Code of Quebec has, after its provision on *lis pendens*, a provision on linked actions.[135]

Fifthly, in so far as a recognition prognosis, in some States, also refers to the court first seised of the proceedings, the same objections can be made here as were made as the fourth, fifth, sixth, seventh, and eighth objections to the mechanical first-seised rule.

Sixthly, as the Italian reporter points out,[136] it is not easy to predict whether a foreign judgment will be recognized in the forum. There is a particular difficulty with certain defences, such as public policy, which can only properly be considered after the foreign judgment has been granted.

Seventhly, what happens if subsequently it turns out that the foreign judgment cannot be recognized? German law has sought to deal with this problem by adopting a procedure of initially suspending, rather than dismissing, local proceedings. Dismissal will only take place once it is apparent that the plaintiff no longer has a need for domestic legal protection. Swiss courts also adopt a procedure of only suspending proceedings and do not decline jurisdiction. In contrast to this, Japanese law has no power to suspend local proceedings; it can only dismiss them. It therefore requires under its recognition prognosis rule *reasonable certainty* that the first action will be recognized. Nonetheless, it is still possible to envisage a situation arising in Japan whereby the local action is dismissed but the foreign judgment is subsequently not enforced. In the meantime, the claim may have expired in Japan because of the Japanese rules on prescription.[137]

Eighthly, what happens if there is an inordinate delay in the foreign court producing its judgment? Swiss law has attempted to solve this problem by providing that the recognition prognosis only operates if it is expected that the foreign court will, *within a reasonable time*, deliver a judgment. German law meets the problem by providing that the pendency ceases to be recognized when effective legal protection at the foreign forum is no longer guaranteed because of unduly long proceedings. Italian law does not go quite as far as this. However, for the defence of *lis pendens* to apply under the Italo–German Convention, the fact that an action has been instituted abroad is not sufficient. Attention has to be given to the handling and development of the case abroad.

(iv) Problems in Relation to Declining Jurisdiction/Suspending Proceedings

The first problem is how to deal with the situation where there is a challenge to the jurisdiction of the foreign court. What is essential is that

---

[135] Art. 3139, Civil Code of Quebec, discussed below, p. 46.
[136] See below, p. 286.   [137] See below, pp. 315–6.

the local proceedings are not dismissed. Under Article 21 of the Brussels and Lugano Conventions there is a two-stage process whereby any court other than the court first seised stays (i.e. suspends) its proceedings until such time as the jurisdiction of the court first seised is established. Once it has been established, jurisdiction is declined.

Secondly, how long does litispendence continue for? Under Greek law many scholars take the view that litispendence is terminated at the moment that the decision of the first court becomes final. However, according to Greek jurisprudence litispendence is terminated at the moment the first-instance judgment is issued, and revives by the lodging of an appeal.

Thirdly, there can be a problem with provisional measures. Under Japanese law the result of the application of the recognition prognosis rule is the dismissal of the Japanese action. However, in order to obtain provisional measures there has to be an action brought on the merits. Since the local action is barred, the only possible solution is to regard the foreign action as one being brought on the merits. But the judge concerned with the provisional measures may not agree with the judge dealing with the local action on the merits over the recognition prognosis in relation to this foreign action.

(b) RESTRAINING THE FOREIGN PROCEEDINGS

The United States reporters refer to this as a method of dealing with the problem of parallel proceedings,[138] and there are cases in the United States where the inconvenience of parallel proceedings and the ensuing risk of irreconcilable judgments have been used in favour of restraining the foreign proceedings.[139] This is a technique that obviously is only available in those States in which judges have the power to restrain foreign proceedings. As will be seen, this power is confined to common law jurisdictions. This raises the question of the extent to which other common law jurisdictions are prepared to deal with the problem of parallel proceedings by restraining the foreign proceedings.

In England there are cases on restraining foreign proceedings which have taken into account the fact that failure to restrain will result in inconsistent judgments in England and abroad.[140] However, it is also true that, when faced with the situation where England was the natural forum for trial but Illinois also considered itself an appropriate forum for trial, the English Court of Appeal refused to restrain the foreign proceedings, since it was not prepared to resolve a dispute between England and

---

[138] See below, p. 418.

[139] See *Cargill, Inc v. Hartford Accident & Indemnity Co*, 531 F. Supp. 710 (D. Minn. 1982).

[140] See e.g. *Tracomin SA v. Sudan Oil Seed Co Ltd (Nos 1 and 2)* [1983] 1 WLR 1026 at 1035; *Sohio Co v. Gatoil (USA) Inc.* [1989] 1 Lloyd's Rep. 588.

Illinois as to which was the appropriate forum.[141] Of course, under English law the parallel proceedings factor operates strongly in favour of the English courts staying their own proceedings, in a way that does not appear to be the case in the United States, and accordingly there is much less occasion for considering a restraint of foreign proceedings.

(c) ALLOWING BOTH SETS OF PROCEEDINGS TO CONTINUE

In the United States, rather than dismissing local proceedings or restraining the foreign proceedings, the court may allow the parallel proceedings to continue. In one of the leading cases on restraining foreign proceedings, *Laker Airways* v. *Sabena, Belgian World Airlines*,[142] there is a well known quotation that 'the fundamental corollary to concurrent jurisdiction must ordinarily be respected: parallel proceedings on the same *in personam* claim should ordinarily be allowed to proceed simultaneously, at least until a judgment is reached in one which can be pled as *res judicata* in the other'.[143] The United States reporters indicate that, if the parties or cause of action are not the same, then the parallel proceedings will be allowed to continue.

Moving outside the United States, there are a number of Japanese cases where the presence of parallel proceedings was simply ignored.[144] The traditional approach under Italian law has also been to allow parallel proceedings to continue. Indeed, Italian law is unusual in non-Convention cases in positively rejecting a doctrine of *lis pendens*. Article 3 of the Code of Civil Procedure provides that 'Italian jurisdiction is not excluded by the pendency of the same case or another connected with it, before a foreign court'. Belgian law also rejects the use of a *lis pendens* exception in international cases, although the desirability of having such an exception is acknowledged by the Belgian reporter.[145] A *lis pendens* rule is only accepted in Belgium where it is contained in an international convention.

If both sets of proceedings are allowed to continue, the risk of irreconcilable judgments can be dealt with by the use of the doctrine of *res judicata*, provided that the conditions for the operation of this doctrine are met. However, this does nothing to stop the expense and inconvenience to the parties of parallel proceedings in the period leading up to the grant of the judgment necessary for *res judicata*.

If there are eventually two irreconcilable judgments, many States have special recognition and enforcement rules to deal with this. Thus the

---

[141] *Du Pont (EI) de Nemours & Co* v. *Agnew (No. 2)* [1988] 2 Lloyd's Rep. 240.
[142] 731 F.2d 909 (DC Cir. 1984).   [143] *Ibid.*
[144] See e.g. the Tokyo High Court judgment on 18 July 1957, *Kakyusaibansho Minji—Hanreishu*, vol. 8, No. 7, 1282; below, p. 311.
[145] Below, pp. 109–10.

Brussels and Lugano Conventions have provisions dealing with the situation where the judgment (given in a Contracting State) is irreconcilable with a judgment given in the State in which recognition is sought,[146] and that where the judgment (given in a Contracting State) is irreconcilable with an earlier one given in a non-Contracting State.[147] Similarly, the English rules on enforcement of foreign judgments at common law provide a defence where the foreign judgment is on a matter previously determined by an English court.[148] Greek law contains a similar provision in Article 3(1) of the bilateral Treaty between Greece and Germany of 1961, something that is necessary, given the lack of an express provision on *lis pendens* under Greek law. English law has also had to come to grips with the situation where there are two competing foreign judgments. The Privy Council has recently laid down a general rule that the earlier of them is to be recognized and given effect to to the exclusion of the later.[149]

Under Dutch law, the fact that a Dutch court has already decided the matter means that recognition would be against public order. Finally, the Argentinian National Procedural Code lays down a rule whereby a foreign judgment shall not be recognized if it conflicts not only with a previous decision of an Argentinian court on the same matter but also with a simultaneous one.

Italian law operates a very different rule in relation to recognition and enforcement of foreign judgments from those so far mentioned. The Code of Civil Procedure states that[150] 'If an action is instituted in Italy before the foreign judgment becomes final, no proceedings may be brought to validate the foreign judgment.' This means that the mere institution of proceedings in Italy, rather than an Italian judgment, prevents the recognition of the foreign judgment in Italy. This is all part of the traditional nationalistic approach towards jurisdiction that has been adopted in Italy.

(d) ENCOURAGING THE PARTIES TO OPT FOR TRIAL
    IN JUST ONE FORUM

The Conflict of Jurisdiction Model Act,[151] prepared in 1989 by a subcommittee of the American Bar Association and adopted by the State of Connecticut, seeks to solve the problems of parallel proceedings by encouraging the parties early on to opt for trial in the appropriate forum, and discontinue proceedings in other fora. The Model Act sets out criteria for the identification of the appropriate forum, and a discretion is given to

---

[146] Art. 27(3).   [147] Art. 27(5).   [148] *Vervaeke* v. *Smith* [1983] 1 AC 145.
[149] *Showlag* v. *Mansour* [1994] 2 All ER 129.   [150] Art. 797, para. 1, n°. 6.
[151] See Teitz, (1992) 26 *International Lawyer* 21. The Model Act is set out in App. 1.

refuse to enforce judgments granted in any State other than the appropriate forum.

When it comes to child custody cases in the United States all States have enacted the Uniform Child Custody Jurisdiction Act. This is concerned to determine a single 'court of custody'. Where such court is in a particular State, a court seised of the matter in another State must dismiss the action. This Act is also applied by the courts to foreign custody decrees. The Hague Convention on the civil aspects of international child abduction of 1980 forces custody issues to be litigated in the habitual residence of the child prior to the wrongful removal/retention of the child.

3. RELATED ACTIONS

We are concerned here with the situation in which there are two actions, which are closely connected, proceeding in two different States at the same time. This situation may fall outside the definition of *lis pendens* because the parties or the cause of action are not the same in each action. Nonetheless, such related actions may give rise to irreconcilable judgments and to additional expense and inconvenience to the parties. In order to avoid this, the forum can either decline jurisdiction/suspend its proceedings or take jurisdiction over both actions. These two approaches towards the problem of related actions will now be examined.

(a) DECLINING JURISDICTION/SUSPENDING PROCEEDINGS

(i) The Use of *Forum Non Conveniens*

In States which use the doctrine of *forum non conveniens* to deal with the problem of *lis pendens*, there is no need for a separate doctrine to deal with cases which fall outside the definition of *lis pendens*, as strictly understood. As has been seen, one of the great virtues of the *forum non conveniens* approach is that it is flexible enough to deal with the situation where there are parallel proceedings but the parties or cause of action are not the same. Under English law there are examples of the doctrine of *forum non conveniens* being used to stay (in effect, dismiss) the local proceedings when there are such related actions. In the United States, while, in theory, it is possible to use the doctrine of *forum non conveniens* where there are related actions, it seems that, in practice, the courts allow both actions to proceed if not satisfied that the issues in both proceedings are the same or that the parties, either at present or potentially, are not the same.

(ii) A Separate Rule

The real difficulty arises for those States which use the mechanical first-seised approach or the recognition prognosis approach to deal with *lis pendens*, and, having adopted a strict definition of *lis pendens*, are then faced with parallel proceedings which fall outside this definition. The obvious solution for such States is to have a separate rule dealing with related actions. There is a related action provision in the Brussels and Lugano Conventions, which immediately follows the *lis pendens* provision contained in Article 21. Paragraph 1 of Article 22 states that: 'Where related actions are brought in the courts of different Contracting States, any court other than the court first seised may, while the actions are pending at first instance, stay its proceedings'. Related actions are defined under paragraph 3 as ones which 'are so closely connected that it is expedient to hear and determine them together to avoid the risk of irreconcilable judgments resulting from separate proceedings'.[152] Article 22 is similar to the *lis pendens* provision in Article 21, in that it gives priority to the courts of the State which is first seised of the action. However, it is different in that the power to stay local proceedings is a discretionary one. The local court *may* rather than *must* stay its proceedings; it could decide to allow the local action to continue. This raises the question of what the criterion is for the exercise of this discretion. English courts have accepted that it is not a *forum non conveniens* discretion.[153] Normally, the local proceedings should be stayed.[154] The court second seised can take into account the nature of the proceedings in the court first seised.[155] The court must look at the various arguments, both on the merits and in relation to jurisdiction.[156] If the English courts have exclusive jurisdiction under Article 17 of the Brussels Convention (an agreement conferring jurisdiction), this is an important factor against staying the English action.[157] There is an obvious risk with any discretion that courts in different EC States will apply different criteria for the exercise of the discretion. The recent opinion of Advocate General Lenz of the European Court of Justice as to the factors relevant to the exercise of the Article 22 discretion is therefore very welcome. He mentioned three factors in particular (although there may be other important considerations): 'the extent of the relatedness and the risk of mutually irreconcilable decisions; the stage reached in each set of proceedings; and the proximity of the courts to the subject matter of the case'.[158] The effect of the stay under Article 22(1) is to suspend proceedings in the court second seised pending the judgment (or declining of jurisdiction) in the court first seised. That judgment

---

[152] The question whether this provides an exclusive definition has been referred to the ECJ by the English CA in *The Maciej Rataj*, n. 121.

[153] See *The Linda* [1988] 1 Lloyd's Rep. 175 at 179; *Virgin Aviation* v. *CAD Aviation The Times*, 2 Feb. 1990.

[154] *The Linda*, n. 153 above.   [155] *The Maciej Rataj*, n. 121 above (Sheen J).

[156] *IP Metal Ltd* v. *Ruote OZ SpA* [1993] 2 Lloyd's Rep. 60.

[157] *Ibid*. English law was also applied.

[158] Case C–129/92 *Owens Bank Ltd* v. *Bracco and others (No 2)* [1994] 1 All ER 336 at 370.

subsequently may have to be recognized under the Brussels or Lugano Convention.

Dutch law (in non-Convention cases) applies a rule similar to Article 22. Generally, the Dutch courts refer related actions to the court first seised. They use their discretion to refuse to do so only if 'they consider the relationship between the actions too weak or if the proceedings in that other court are already in a too advanced stage'.[159]

There is little authority in France on this topic. There is said to be a psychological resistance to giving way to a foreign tribunal, and there is no significant example of this happening. Nonetheless, the Cour de Cassation has not shown itself hostile to the reception of the doctrine of related actions (*connexité*).

The Italo–French Convention extends its *lis pendens* rule to related actions. There are also proposals in Italy for a more general provision dealing with related claims.[160]

(iii) No Separate Rule

The common law jurisdictions, with their flexible doctrine of *forum non conveniens*, have no need for a separate related-actions rule, and there is nothing more to be said about these States. But there are other States in which there is a need for such a rule, but this is lacking. One such State is Japan and the Japanese reporter acknowledges the difficulty in using its recognition prognosis in cases where the cause of action is not the same in the parallel proceedings.[161] Finland also has no separate rules on related actions.

Switzerland also lacks a rule on related actions in non-Lugano Convention cases. However, the parties may solve the problem by agreeing to stay proceedings until a related cause of action has been decided by a foreign court seised of the cause of action.

German law does not allow for suspension of the domestic proceedings because of their connection with a foreign pending action. But if the decision of the lawsuit *depends* on the outcome of another pending proceeding (which may be foreign) section 148 of the Code of Civil Procedure (ZPO) permits the suspension of the domestic proceedings.

(b) CONSOLIDATION OF ACTIONS

An entirely different approach towards related actions is for the forum to accept jurisdiction over both actions. Many States have provisions which allow this.

---

[159] See below, p. 337.   [160] Art. 7 of the proposed Italian Conflict of Laws Statute.
[161] See below, p. 314.

Article 3139 of the Civil Code of Quebec provides that: 'Where a Quebec authority has jurisdiction to rule on the principal demand, it also has jurisdiction to rule on an incidental demand or a cross demand.'[162] This provision can be invoked where two actions, which may involve different objects or parties, are none the less linked, so that it is difficult to decide one action separately from the other. It can be used to attribute jurisdiction not only to a local court but also to a foreign court if there is a connection between the action and that court. Quebec also has provisions in its Code of Civil Procedure which might be used to allow joinder of actions in cases of connexity (actions having such a close connection that the decision in the first will have a consequence on the second).

The concept of joinder of actions is to be found in Article 6 of the Brussels and Lugano Conventions. Article 6(1) deals with multi-defendant cases and provides that a person domiciled in a Contracting State may also be sued, where he is one of a number of defendants, in the courts for the place in which any one of them is domiciled. The European Court of Justice has held that the actions against the different defendants must be related to the extent that it must be expedient to hear and determine them together in order to avoid the risk of irreconcilable judgments resulting from separate proceedings.[163]

Italian law (in non-Convention cases) also allows for the consolidation of related claims. Thus the litigation of one dispute before an Italian court may form the basis for jurisdiction over another related dispute.[164]

Argentinian law has a doctrine of *litispendencia* by connexity. This applies where one of the three elements (same parties, object, cause) for *lis pendens* (*litispendencia* by identity) is missing. Under this rule the Argentinian court will order the 'accumulation of the proceedings'.

Greek law provides for the exclusive jurisdiction of connexity. Article 31 of the Code of Civil Procedure provides that auxiliary claims are tried before the courts having jurisdiction over the main claim: 'main claims related between them are submitted to the exclusive competence of the first-seised court.'

Article 22(2), of the Brussels and Lugano Conventions deals with declining jurisdiction where the court first seised has jurisdiction over both actions by stating that: 'A court other than the court first seised may also, on the application of one of the parties, decline jurisdiction if the law of that court permits the consolidation of related actions and the court first seised has jurisdiction over both actions.'

---

[162] Scotland has a similar rule under its non-Brussels/Lugano Convention rules: see s. 22(4), Civil Jurisdiction and Judgments Act 1982.

[163] Case 189/87 *Kalfelis* v. *Bankhaus Schröder* [1988] ECR 5565.

[164] Art. 4, n°. 2, Code of Civil Procedure.

V
FOREIGN CHOICE OF JURISDICTION AGREEMENTS

1. EFFECT OF THE AGREEMENT

There is a very clear difference between common law jurisdictions and other States when it comes to the effect given to an agreement conferring jurisdiction on the courts of a foreign State. In common law jurisdictions there is a power to decline jurisdiction but this is discretionary, and a court can, nonetheless, allow the local proceedings to continue, despite the parties' agreement on trial abroad. In other States the declining of jurisdiction is compulsory or, even more fundamentally, the State may have no jurisdiction. The common law discretionary rule and the compulsory declining/no jurisdiction rule of other States will now be examined.

(a) A DISCRETION TO STAY

Under English law the rule set out in the leading case of *The Eleftheria*[165] is that, where a plaintiff sues in England in breach of an agreement to refer disputes to a foreign court, the English court has a discretion whether to stay the English proceedings or not. However, the discretion should be exercised by granting a stay unless strong cause for not doing so is shown. The burden of showing this is on the plaintiff. In exercising this discretion the court will take into account a number of considerations, which are essentially the same as those taken into account under the English doctrine of *forum non conveniens*.[166]

New Zealand case law[167] on foreign jurisdiction clauses is based on *The Eleftheria*. Likewise, this case provides the guidelines for Australian courts. Canadian courts in the common law jurisdictions have also followed the English rule and require strong reasons, from the point of view of convenience or the interests of justice, for allowing the action to proceed in the face of a foreign jurisdiction clause. Examples[168] of where the action was allowed to proceed include the situation where litigation in the foreign court would have led to a multiplicity of proceedings, where the plaintiff could not have compelled its key witnesses to testify in the

---

[165] [1970] P 94. See also *The El Amria* [1981] 2 Lloyd's Rep. 119 (CA); *The Pioneer Container* [1994] 2 All ER 250 (PC).

[166] See below, pp. 223–4.

[167] See e.g. *Apple Computer Inc* v. *Apple Corp SA* [1990] 2 NZLR 598. *The Eleftheria* is also followed in Singapore: *The Vishva Apurva* [1992] 2 SLR 175 (CA).

[168] See below, pp. 137–8.

agreed forum, and where the plaintiff, being relatively impecunious, would have difficulty in suing in the agreed forum.

Israeli law is essentially the same as that in England, so that an Israeli court will dismiss the action where there is a foreign jurisdiction agreement unless there are special circumstances. A good example of such special circumstances is the situation where the plaintiff is unable to bring his action abroad or would be faced with clearly demonstrable discrimination. This was shown in a case where the other State involved was Iraq.[169]

In the United States choice of forum clauses are generally upheld. In *Bremen* v. *Zapata Off-Shore Co* the Supreme Court of the United States held that a foreign forum-selection clause is binding on the parties unless the plaintiff can show that its enforcement would be unreasonable and unjust.[170] The attitude in the United States, as in other common law jurisdictions, is that the parties should normally abide by their agreement. Indeed, the Supreme Court described its approach as being 'substantially that followed in other common law countries including England'.

(b) MANDATORY DECLINING OF JURISDICTION/NO JURISDICTION

In non-common law jurisdictions, there is no discretionary power to allow the proceedings to continue in cases where there is a foreign choice-of-jurisdiction agreement. A local court cannot try the case. The effect is that the court has no jurisdiction or that it must decline jurisdiction.

Thus under German law the effect of a foreign choice of jurisdiction agreement is the *ex officio* dismissal of the local claim as inadmissible. Similarly, under Dutch, Swiss, Greek, Finnish, and Japanese law the effect is that a local court must decline jurisdiction/dismiss the action. Under Article 17 of the Brussels and Lugano Conventions, if the parties have agreed that a court or the courts of a Contracting State are to have jurisdiction, that court or those courts have exclusive jurisdiction. This means that courts in other Contracting States are deprived of jurisdiction. French law (in non-Convention cases) likewise gives exclusive jurisdiction to the designated court, provided a number of conditions are met.[171] This means that, if the parties have agreed on trial abroad and these conditions are met, a French court has no jurisdiction. However, if these conditions are not met, the jurisdiction agreement has no effect. Argentinian law is the same.[172] Under Italian law (in non-Convention

---

[169] *Oneon Insurance Co Ltd* v. *Moshe*, 17 PD 646 (1963).   [170] 407 US 1 at 1 (1972).

[171] Cass. Fr., 1ère ch. civ., 17 Dec. 1985, *CSEE* v. *Soc Sorelec* [1986] Dalloz inf. rap. 265, observ. B. Audit; [1986] *Rev. crit. de dr. internat. pr.* 537, note H. Gaudemet-Tallon; B. Ancel et Y. Lequette, *Grands arrêts de la jurisprudence française de droit international privé* (2nd edn., 1992), 68. The conditions are considered below, pp. 183–4.

[172] *Quilmes Combustibles* v. *Vigon SA*, 15 Mar. 1993.

cases) a court lacks jurisdiction when there is a valid foreign choice of jurisdiction agreement.

Article 17 goes on to deal with the situation where neither party is domiciled in a Contracting State. Here, the agreement does not give exclusive jurisdiction. Its effect is more limited than this, so that 'the courts of other Contracting States shall have no jurisdiction over their disputes unless the court or courts chosen have declined jurisdiction.'

The position under Quebecois law is more complicated. Under Article 3148 of the Civil Code a Quebecois authority has no jurisdiction where the parties have agreed to submit a dispute between them to a foreign authority. Nonetheless, it is suggested[173] that Quebecois courts still retain discretionary powers, given by certain other provisions in the Civil Code, for example to take measures to protect a person or his property in Quebec in case of emergency.

(c) RECOGNITION AND ENFORCEMENT

A choice of jurisdiction clause can have an effect at the stage of recognition and enforcement of foreign judgments. If an action is brought in State A in breach of a choice of jurisdiction agreement, conferring jurisdiction on the courts of State B, the result is that some States will not recognize and enforce the judgment given in State A. There are statutory provisions to this effect under English,[174] United States,[175] and Quebecois law.[176] Under French law the position is the same, even though there are no statutory provisions on this. It is noticeable, however, that the Brussels and Lugano Conventions contain no such provision.

2. THE AGREEMENT

Not every foreign choice of jurisdiction agreement produces the effect outlined above. In order to do so, it has to satisfy certain requirements. Of course, what these are differs from one State to another, but some of the more commonly found requirements are listed below.

(a) AN AGREEMENT CONFERRING JURISDICTION
ON THE COURTS OF A STATE

The English Court of Appeal[177] has held that the *agreement* must be an express one; it cannot be implied. There was no implied choice of jurisdic-

---

[173] See below, pp. 164–5.   [174] S. 32, Civil Jurisdiction and Judgments Act 1982.
[175] See the Uniform Foreign Money-Judgments Recognition Act, adopted by 23 States.
[176] Art. 3165, Civil Code.
[177] *New Hampshire Insurance Co v. Strabag Bau AG* [1992] 1 Lloyd's Rep. 361 at 371.

tion by virtue of the fact that a company was resident in England or by reason of the presence of brokers. However, an express agreement may take an indirect form. According to the European Court of Justice, for the purposes of Article 17 of the Brussels Convention, it can include a jurisdiction clause in the articles of association of a company.[178]

The agreement must confer jurisdiction on the *courts* of a State. According to Greek law, the agreement does not have to determine in advance and by name the concrete court of the foreign State selected; it is enough that the clause permits the foreign court to be determined subsequently under the relevant procedural rules of the chosen State.[179]

Under Article 17 of the Brussels and Lugano Conventions the *State* in question must be a Contracting State, i.e. an EC or EFTA State.

(b) EXCLUSIVE AND NON-EXCLUSIVE JURISDICTION CLAUSES

When it comes to determining whether an agreement is an exclusive or non-exclusive one, the English courts have held that this is a matter for the law governing the agreement. If the parties' contract also contains a choice of law clause, then under English law the jurisdiction clause is regarded as being an exclusive one.[180] This rather wide interpretation of the parties' intentions contrasts with the position in Germany. There, the majority view is that in cases of doubt the assumption is that the parties intended only a simple, non-exclusive agreement. Likewise, in Israel, a clause will only be interpreted as an exclusive one if it expressly so states or that is clearly the necessary intention of the parties; the Israeli Supreme Court has been known to strain in order to interpret a clause as not conferring exclusive jurisdiction.[181]

The distinction between exclusive and a non-exclusive jurisdiction is not a vital one under English law. While it should, in principle, be easier for the plaintiff to convince the court to allow an action in England to proceed when the clause conferring jurisdiction on the foreign court is an exclusive one, recent English decisions have said that, even with a non-exclusive jurisdiction clause, it will take strong reasons not to hold the parties to their agreement.[182]

The position in New Zealand is different. A non-exclusive jurisdiction clause will not prevent a New Zealand court from exercising jurisdiction.

---

[178] Case C–214/89 *Powell Duffryn Plc* v. *Petereit* [1992] ILPr. 300.

[179] See the Areopagus judgment, No. 4/1992, No. B 40 (1992), 707.

[180] *British Aerospace Plc* v. *Dee Howard Co* [1993] 1 Lloyd's Rep. 368.

[181] *Korpol* v. *Horowitz*, 34 (1) PD 260 (1979).

[182] *Berisford (S & W) plc* v. *New Hampshire Insurance Co* [1990] 2 QB 631; *Standard Steamship Owners Protection & Indemnity Association (Bermuda Ltd)* v. *Gann* [1992] 2 Lloyd's Rep. 528. In Australia the burden of adducing evidence justifying trial when there is a foreign choice of jurisdiction agreement is even heavier when it is an exclusive jurisdiction agreement.

It merely indicates that there is an alternative forum abroad when it comes to applying the doctrine of *forum non conveniens*. Similarly, under Canadian law (common law jurisdictions), non-exclusive jurisdiction clauses simply come within the doctrine of *forum non conveniens*, rather than being the basis of some special rule for choice of jurisdiction clauses.[183] Under Scots law less weight is given to a non-exclusive jurisdiction clause than it is in England.[184] Israeli law appears to go even further than this for, when it comes to dismissal, it seems to be only concerned with the effect of exclusive jurisdiction agreements.

In States which have no doctrine of *forum non conveniens* the distinction between an exclusive and a non-exclusive jurisdiction clause can assume even greater importance. Thus, under German law, derogation only takes effect if the parties have agreed that the courts of a State shall have exclusive jurisdiction. The same position is taken under Japanese law, Dutch law,[185] and under the Hague Convention on the Choice of Court, concluded in 1965. According to Article 6, 'Every court other than the chosen court or courts shall decline jurisdiction except—(1) where the choice of court made by the parties is not exclusive.' However, this Convention has only been adopted by Israel and has never come into force.

By way of contrast, it should be noted that under French law no distinction is drawn between exclusive and non-exclusive jurisdiction clauses; all valid clauses confer an exclusive jurisdiction.

The position under the Brussels Convention is less clear. We know that, for agreements conferring jurisdiction coming within Article 17, the effect is to give exclusive jurisdiction. However, Article 17 does not make it clear whether it is referring to exclusive or non-exclusive jurisdiction agreements. It is true that an English court has held that a non-exclusive English jurisdiction clause gives jurisdiction to the English courts.[186] But it is not clear whether it gives exclusive jurisdiction i.e. are courts in other Contracting States prohibited from trying the case? It would be very odd to give exclusive effect to a non-exclusive agreement. The German reporter is of the view[187] that Article 17 allows the parties to agree on a non-exclusive jurisdiction agreement. This does not give exclusive jurisdiction, but only provides an additional forum so that other Contracting States may hear the case on some other basis provided for by the Convention.

---

[183] *PWA Corp* v. *Gemini Group Automated Distribution Systems Inc* (1992) 98 DLR (4th) 227. This may very well also happen in Quebec, where there is no authority on the point.

[184] *Scotmotors (Plant Hire) Ltd* v. *Dundee Petrosea Ltd*, 1980 SC 351; *Morrison* v. *Panic Link Ltd*, 1993 SLT 602.

[185] *The Harvest Trader* case, HR, 28 Oct. 1988, [1989] NJ 765.

[186] *Kurz* v. *Stella Musical Veranstaltungs GmbH* [1992] Ch. 196; followed in *Gamlestaden* v. *CDS* [1994] 1 Lloyd's Rep. 433.   [187] See below, pp. 200–1.

Under Swiss private international law it is accepted that a non-exclusive jurisdiction clause will not be given exclusive effect. This is apparent from the Swiss Private International Law Statute of 1987 which provides that 'Unless otherwise provided by the agreement, the choice of jurisdiction is exclusive.'[188]

(c) A VALID AGREEMENT

It is an obvious requirement that the agreement must be a valid one. This has two aspects. First, a valid agreement must have been created. An agreement may be invalid under United States law because of fraud or overreaching.[189] Similarly, under French law, a jurisdiction clause will not give exclusive competence to the designated court when there is fraud. Secondly, even where the normal requirements for formation of a valid agreement have been satisfied, a statutory provision limiting the effectiveness of choice of jurisdiction clauses may render the agreement invalid. This second aspect will be examined later.[190]

Difficult choice of law questions can arise regarding the law governing the validity of the agreement. In certain common law (for example, England) and civil law (for example, Belgium) jurisdictions, it is not entirely clear whether the courts should apply the *lexi fori*, the law applicable to the jurisdiction agreement, or some other law, to issues of validity.[191]

(d) FORMAL REQUIREMENTS

The best known of these are to be found in Article 17 of the Brussels and Lugano Conventions which requires that the agreement must be (i) in writing or evidenced in writing, or (ii) in a form which accords with practices which the parties have established between themselves, or (iii), in international trade or commerce, in a form which accords with a usage of which the parties are or ought to have been aware and which in such trade or commerce is widely known to, and regularly observed by, parties to contracts of the type involved in the particular trade or commerce concerned.

The requirement of writing is to be found elsewhere, for example under Swedish law[192] and Italian law (in non-Convention cases). Also Article 5(1) of Switzerland's Private International Law Statute states that:

---

[188] Art. 5(1).   [189] *The Bremen*, n. 170 above.   [190] Below, pp. 55–6.
[191] For England see Dicey and Morris, *The Conflict of Laws*, n. 38 above, 422–3; for Belgium, see below, p. 112.
[192] The analogy is drawn of Ch. 10, s. 16 of the Code of Judicial Procedure.

'The agreement may be made in writing, by telegram, by telex, telecopier or any other means of communication which permits it to be evidenced by a text.'

Japanese law is more flexible in relation to formalities in international cases than it is in internal cases involving venue provisions. It is enough if a court of a State is expressly designated on the document prepared by either of the parties, and if the existence of such an agreement between the parties and its contents are made explicit.[193]

A German court will apply the German *lex fori derogati* to ascertain whether a foreign forum selection clause is formally valid. If, however, the foreign court (on which jurisdiction is conferred) holds the prorogation invalid by applying its own law, then as a matter of construction the derogation of the German courts also ceases to have effect.

(e) OTHER REQUIREMENTS

There is a wide range of other requirements laid down by different States for an effective choice of jurisdiction agreement. For example, under French law there must be an international dispute. Article 17 of the Brussels and Lugano Conventions requires, for an agreement to give exclusive jurisdiction, that one of the parties must be domiciled in a Contracting State.[194] Italian law (in non-Convention cases) imposes very strict restrictions in relation to foreign choice of jurisdiction agreements. There is no ouster of the Italian courts' jurisdiction unless the parties to a dispute are foreign nationals, or a foreign national and an Italian subject neither resident nor domiciled within the territory of the Italian State.[195]

(f) NO NEW AGREEMENT

A new choice of forum agreement may supersede the original agreement. This is the position under Quebecois law.[196] Swiss law provides that an unconditional appearance is equivalent to a new choice of forum agreement. German law is to the same effect, and if a defendant argues on the merits without attacking the derogated court's lack of jurisdiction, this constitutes a new agreement. The same line has been followed under the Brussels Convention. The European Court of Justice had held that the

[193] Sup. Ct. judgment of 28 Nov. 1975, *Koniglike Java China Paletvaat lijnen BV Amsterdam (Royal Interocean Lines)* v. *Tokyo Marine and Fire Insurance Co* (1976) 20 Japanese Annual of International Law 106.

[194] If this condition is not satisfied Art. 17(2) operates to deny jurisdiction to other Contracting States unless the court chosen has declined jurisdiction.

[195] Art. 2, Code of Civil Procedure 1942.   [196] See Art. 3148, Civil Code.

defendant's submission to the courts of a Contracting State under Article 18 of the Brussels Convention overrides an agreement conferring jurisdiction under Article 17.[197]

3. LIMITATIONS ON EFFECTIVENESS

Even if a valid choice of jurisdiction agreement has been created by the parties, that agreement may be ineffective. Many States impose limitations on the effectiveness of foreign choice of jurisdiction agreements. However, the nature of such limitations does vary very much from one State to another and, indeed, some States impose many more limitations than others.

Before looking at examples of limitations on effectiveness, it is important to make one general point, by way of introducing some balance into the discussion. The parties have the freedom to choose to have their dispute tried before the courts of a State with which there is no connection. Thus French, German, and English law respect the parties' interest in having trial in a neutral forum. Indeed, many cases tried in the Commercial Court in London involve parties, neither of whom is English, who have agreed on trial in England.

(a) FORUM NON CONVENIENS

Common law jurisdictions, by operating a discretionary rule in relation to foreign choice of jurisdiction agreements, are actually imposing a *forum non conveniens* limitation on the effectiveness of the agreement of the parties. Thus, under United States law, there is a limitation on the effectiveness of the agreement, in that it will not be enforced where it would be unreasonable and unjust to do so.

(b) PUBLIC POLICY/ORDRE PUBLIC

The leading Japanese case in this area has held that an exclusive jurisdiction agreement should be valid in principle unless this would lead to an unacceptable result which violates public policy.[198] The Finnish doctrine of *ordre public* enshrines the principle that any clause of a contract may be adjusted on grounds of inequity.[199] Under United States law there is likewise a rather imprecise restriction on foreign choice of jurisdiction agreements, in that they must not contravene an important public policy of the forum.[200]

[197] Case 150/80 *Elefanten Schuh GmbH* v. *Jacqmain* [1981] ECR 1671.
[198] Sup. Ct. judgment of 28 Nov. 1975, n. 193 above.   [199] Contract Act, s. 36.
[200] *The Bremen*, n. 170 above.

(c) NEGOTIATING POWERS

Under Argentinian law the courts will pay special attention to the negotiating powers of the parties in the situation in which a neutral forum has
been chosen.

(d) ABUSIVE DEPRIVATION OF PROTECTION

Article 5(2), of the Swiss Private International Law Statute provides that:
'A choice of jurisdiction is ineffective if a party is abusively deprived of
protection at a place of jurisdiction provided by Swiss law.' This provision
is concerned to ensure that a person is not deprived of a Swiss forum by
means of unfair stipulations or terms of trade.

(e) AN INACCESSIBLE FOREIGN FORUM

A Swiss court can still base jurisdiction on necessity in cases where the
court on which jurisdiction has been conferred is inaccessible because of
war, catastrophe, or similar disaster.[201] The position appears to be similar
under German law where, in very special circumstances, frustrated choice
of jurisdiction agreements will be corrected.

(f) SPECIFIC CONTRACTS

(i) Carriage by Sea

The Swedish Maritime Act of 1994 restricts in certain respects the parties'
freedom to confer jurisdiction on a State in cases involving contracts for
the carriage of passengers and luggage by sea.[202] In England an exclusive
jurisdiction clause has been held, by the House of Lords,[203] to be null and
void and of no effect by virtue of the Hague–Visby Rules, which have
been implemented by the Carriage of Goods by Sea Act 1971. New
Zealand law is similar, and the courts cannot give effect to an agreement
purporting to oust their jurisdiction in respect of a bill of lading relating to
carriage of goods by sea to or from New Zealand.[204]

(ii) Employment Contracts

These involve a weaker-party relationship, and a number of States provide special protection for the employee in this situation. Greek law
contains a special provision which renders a foreign choice of jurisdiction
agreement null and void in cases where Greek citizens are employed by

---

[201] Art. 3 of the Swiss Private International Law Statute of 1987.
[202] Ch. 21, s. 4 of the Swedish Maritime Act of 1994.
[203] *The Hollandia* [1982] 1 AC 565.   [204] S. 11A, Carriage of Goods Act 1940.

enterprises, with a seat or doing business in Greece, to work in Africa or Asia.[205]

Article 17 of the Brussels Convention states that:

In matters relating to individual contracts of employment an agreement conferring jurisdiction shall have legal force only if it is entered into after the dispute has arisen or if the employee invokes it to seise courts other than those for the defendant's domicile or those specified in Article 5(1) [special jurisdiction in matters relating to a contract].[206]

Article 17 of the Lugano Convention is much more restrictively worded and gives the agreement conferring jurisdiction legal force only if it is entered into after the dispute has arisen.

Swedish case law in non-Lugano Convention cases contains an important exception to the freedom of the parties to oust the Swedish courts' jurisdiction in employment cases. Thus the Swedish Labour Court has refused to be bound by a foreign choice of jurisdiction clause in a case involving an employment contract between a Swedish employee working in Sweden and her Swiss employer.[207] In order that her interests could be protected, the employee had to be able to sue in Sweden.

(iii) Consumer Contracts

These, too, involve a weaker-party relationship, with a number of States providing special protection for the consumer. Thus Article 114(2) of the Swiss Private International Law Statute provides that: 'the consumer may not waive in advance the jurisdiction at his domicile or his habitual residence.' A similar provision is to be found under Quebecois law.[208] Article 15 of the Brussels and Lugano Conventions sets out restrictions on when the special jurisdictional rules for consumer contracts contained in Articles 13 and 14 may be departed from by an agreement.

(iv) Insurance Contracts

Article 12 of the Brussels and Lugano Conventions sets out restrictions on when the special jurisdiction rules for insurance contracts contained in Section 3 may be departed from by an agreement.

(v) Non-financial Disputes

German law has a very wide restriction on ouster of local jurisdiction, in that this is not allowed in non-financial disputes.[209]

---

[205] See ss. 1 and 2 of art. 4 of Act 1429/1984 in [1984] Kodex No B 327 ff.

[206] This provision was added by the Spanish/Portuguese Accession Convention of 1989, which has yet to be ratified by Belgium, Denmark, and Germany.

[207] *Hapimag* v. *Mona Mårtensson* [1976] AD 101.

[208] Art. 3149, Civil Code. This provision protects workers as well as consumers and states that 'the waiver of . . . jurisdiction by the consumer or worker may not be set up against him'.

[209] S. 40, II 1 ZPO.

(g) EXCLUSIVE JURISDICTION

A commonly found restriction on the effectiveness of a foreign choice of jurisdiction agreement is that it cannot oust the forum's jurisdiction when this is exclusive. Thus Article 17(3) of the Brussels and Lugano Conventions provides that the courts which have exclusive jurisdiction under Article 16 cannot be deprived of it by an agreement under Article 17, and any agreement which purports to do so shall have no legal force. Germany, The Netherlands, Sweden, and Finland all, seemingly, appear to give priority to the jurisdiction of the forum when this is exclusive, even in non-Convention cases. The same is true under Japanese and Argentinian law. According to the *Première chambre civile* in *Cie de signaux et d'entreprises électriques (CSEE)* v. *Soc Sorelec*,[210] under French law one of the conditions which a foreign jurisdiction clause has to comply with is that it does not deny application of the mandatory territorial competence of a French court.

Contrast the position under Greek law, where foreign choice of jurisdiction agreements are upheld even if they oust an exclusive Greek jurisdiction.

4. FORUM CHOICE OF JURISDICTION AGREEMENTS

(a) A DISCRETION TO DECLINE JURISDICTION

In common law jurisdictions the forum court can decline jurisdiction, using its discretionary powers, even though the parties have agreed on trial in the forum. A New Zealand court on which exclusive jurisdiction has been conferred by the parties will normally exercise such jurisdiction. However, a defendant may obtain a dismissal or stay if he can show strong cause why trial in New Zealand is not in the interests of the parties and of the ends of justice.[211] Likewise, in the United States, forum-selection is binding on the parties unless the defendant can show that its enforcement would be unreasonable, unfair, or unjust.[212] The position is similar in England, although it would be unusual for an English court to decline jurisdiction on the ground of *forum non conveniens* in a case involving an English choice of jurisdiction clause.[213] Nor would it normally refuse to allow service of a writ out of the jurisdiction under Order 11 of the Rules of the Supreme Court in such a case. According to Israeli law, the defendant has an unusually heavy burden to convince the court to decline jurisdiction on the basis of *forum non conveniens* in the situation where there has been prior contractual consent to jurisdiction in Israel.[214]

---

[210] N. 171 above. The other requirement is that the dispute must be an international one.
[211] See *Bramwell* v. *The Pacific Lumber Co Ltd* (1986) 1 PRNZ 307 at 311–2.
[212] *The Bremen*, n. 170 above.   [213] Cheshire and North, n. 38 above, 225.
[214] *Multi-lock Inc* v. *Rav-bariach, Ltd*, 36(3) PD 272 (1982).

More interestingly, in some civil law jurisdictions the courts may decline jurisdiction. Thus, a Swiss court may decline to accept jurisdiction under a Swiss jurisdiction clause, although this is subject to a number of provisos, such as there being no international convention or statute preventing this.[215] Similarly, under Dutch law there is a discretion whether to try a case if there is an agreement conferring jurisdiction on a Dutch court.[216]

(b) NO DISCRETION

The alternative approach towards forum choice of jurisdiction agreements is to adopt a compulsory rule whereby such agreements confer jurisdiction and there is no discretion to decline this. The best example of this is contained in Article 17 of the Brussels and Lugano Conventions. An agreement that meets the requirements of Article 17 confers jurisdiction, there being no power to refuse to try the case. An English court has held that even an English non-exclusive jurisdiction agreement confers jurisdiction on the English courts under Article 17.[217]

VI
ARBITRATION AGREEMENTS

1. EFFECT OF THE AGREEMENT

When it comes to arbitration agreements, the position is very different from that in cases involving choice of jurisdiction agreements. Even in common law jurisdictions, it is only in very limited circumstances that a court will exercise a discretionary power to stay proceedings. Normally what happens is that a court must decline jurisdiction when faced with an arbitration agreement. The provisions which require this will be examined first, and then attention will turn to the limited circumstances in which discretionary powers to decline jurisdiction operate in the context of arbitration agreements.

(a) MANDATORY DECLINING OF JURISDICTION

For the very many States which have implemented either the New York Convention on the Recognition and Enforcement of Foreign Arbitral

---

[215] Art. 5(3) of the Swiss Private International Law Statute of 1987 provides that 'The court chosen may not decline jurisdiction: (a) if one of the parties has its domicile, habitual residence, or business establishment in the canton of the chosen court, or (b) if this Statute declares Swiss law applicable to the case.'

[216] *The Piscator* case, HR, 1 Feb. 1985, [1985] NJ 698, [1989] NILR 59.   [217] N. 186 above.

Awards of 1958 or the UNCITRAL Model Law on International Commercial Arbitration of 1985, the position is clear. A court, when faced with an arbitration agreement, must decline jurisdiction. All the States represented in the National Reports are, in fact, parties to either the New York Convention or, less commonly, the UNCITRAL Model Law.

(i) The New York Convention

Many common law jurisdictions have implemented this Convention. Thus England has substantially given effect to Article II of the New York Convention,[218] as have Australia, New Zealand,[219] Israel, and the United States.[220] This Convention has also found favour outside common law jurisdictions in Argentina, Belgium, Finland, France, Germany, Greece, Italy, Japan, The Netherlands, and Sweden. Switzerland[221] and France[222] have enacted provisions which are similar, albeit not identical, to those contained in the Convention.

Article II(3) of the Convention states that:

The court of a Contracting State, when seized of an action in a matter in respect of which the parties have made an agreement within the meaning of this article, shall, at the request of one of the parties, refer the parties to arbitration, unless it finds that the said agreement is null and void, inoperative or incapable of being performed.

(ii) The 1985 UNCITRAL Model Law

Scotland has given effect to this Model Law,[223] with certain modifications. Likewise, all Canadian jurisdictions (including Quebec) have enacted it to govern international arbitration. In New Zealand the Law Commission has prepared a draft Arbitration Act, the intention being that it shall provide for application of the principles of the Model Law to both international and domestic arbitrations.

The Model Law has a provision which is very similar to Article II(3) of the New York Convention. Article 8 states that:

(1) A court before which an action is brought in a matter which is the subject of an arbitration agreement shall, if a party so requests not later than when submitting his first statement on the substance of the dispute, refer the parties to arbitration unless it finds that the agreement is null and void, inoperative or incapable of being performed.

---

[218] S. 1, Arbitration Act 1975.
[219] The Arbitration (Foreign Agreements and Awards) Act 1982.
[220] Ch. 2 of the Federal Arbitration Act.
[221] See Art. 7 of the Swiss Private International Law Statute of 1987.
[222] See Art. 1458, New Code of Civil Procedure.
[223] Law Reform (Miscellaneous Provisions) (Scotland) Act 1990.

(2) Where an action referred to in paragraph (1) of this article has been brought, arbitral proceedings may nevertheless be commenced or continued, and an award may be made, while the issue is pending before the court.

(b) A DISCRETION TO STAY

Some common law jurisdictions still exercise a discretionary power to stay proceedings in certain limited circumstances. Under English law this power exists in the case of a domestic arbitration agreement.[224] It is exercised on the same principles as apply in relation to foreign jurisdiction agreements.[225] New Zealand law is to the same effect.[226] Under Australian law, although the power to stay is discretionary in relation to domestic arbitration agreements, the court will almost always grant the stay. Moreover, the English courts have an inherent discretionary power, exercised on the same principles, to stay proceedings brought before them in breach of an agreement to decide disputes by an alternative method (in the leading case by a dispute-resolution agreement), even if this is not an effective agreement to arbitrate.[227]

Under Scots law if the arbitration agreement does not come within the scope of the Model Law,[228] then the Scots courts have a discretion to decline to exercise jurisdiction.

Under United States law the mandatory stay of proceedings under legislation giving effect to the New York Convention requires a determination from the court that an agreement to arbitrate was made and breached; prior to this determination a court can dismiss a petition to compel arbitration on *forum non conveniens* grounds.

2. THE AGREEMENT

Some of the more commonly found requirements, needed before the agreement can have the above effect, are as follows:

(a) AN ARBITRABLE DISPUTE

The agreement must relate to an arbitrable dispute. The UNCITRAL Model Law requires that the arbitration must be a commercial one.[229] Argentinian law has a requirement to the effect that only pecuniary matters are arbitrable, thereby excluding such matters as divorce or custody. Swedish law imposes certain restrictions on what is arbitrable,

---

[224] See s. 4(1), Arbitration Act 1950. A domestic arbitration agreement is defined under s. 1(4), Arbitration Act 1975.

[225] N. 165 above, at 100.   [226] Arbitration Act 1908.

[227] *Channel Tunnel Group Ltd* v. *Balfour Beatty Construction Ltd* [1993] AC 334.

[228] Or s. 1, Arbitration Act 1975.   [229] Art. 1(1).

for instance regarding disputes between business enterprises and consumers.

(b) A VALID AGREEMENT

It is an obvious requirement that the arbitration must be a valid one. This has been spelled out under the New York Convention and the UNCITRAL Model Law; the mandatory declining of jurisdiction by a court is subject to the identical proviso, i.e. unless it finds that the agreement 'is null and void, inoperative or incapable of being performed'.[230] Under Italian law an arbitral agreement is inoperative where the award resulting from the proceedings will not be recognized and enforced in Italy as the territory of the State where recognition of the ousting effect of the agreement is sought. In common law jurisdictions the agreement must be valid according to the law that is applicable to it. However, in some other States, for example, Greece, the prevailing view is that this is a matter for the *lex fori.*

(c) IN WRITING

Both the New York Convention and the UNCITRAL Model Law require an agreement in writing. The former states that this 'shall include an arbitral clause in a contract or an arbitration agreement, signed by the parties or contained in an exchange of letters or telegrams'.[231] The UNCITRAL Model Law provision is similar.[232]

(d) INTERNATIONAL

It is a requirement under the UNCITRAL Model law that the arbitration be international.[233] Simiarly, under the English legislation implementing the New York Convention it is required that the agreement be a non-domestic one.[234] Argentinian law requires that the dispute be of an international nature.

(e) RAISED AS A DEFENCE

It is a requirement under the law of a number of States such as Germany, Greece, and The Netherlands that the agreement must be raised as a defence by a party, rather than being considered *ex officio* by the court.

---

[230] Art. II, para. 3, of the New York Convention; Art. 8(1) of the UNCITRAL Model Law.
[231] Art. II, para. 2.   [232] Art. 7(2).   [233] See Art. 1(1).
[234] S. 1(2)(4), Arbitration Act 1975.

3. Limitations on Effectiveness

Once a valid agreement on arbitration has been created, there are very few circumstances in which it will be ineffective. None the less, a few examples can be found. Under Dutch law, a party must be acting in accordance with requirements of reasonableness and equity in holding the other party to the agreement. These requirements were not met where in a small claims dispute, in order to enter arbitration, the plaintiff had to pay 5,000 guilders in advance.[235] Similarly, under the law of Finland an arbitration clause may be adjusted on grounds of inequity. Finally, under German law, in exceptional cases a party's reliance on an arbitration agreement can be malicious and without effect if that party is not able to meet the costs of the arbitration proceedings.

VII
FORUM-SHOPPING ABROAD

1. Introduction

So far, what has been considered is the forum declining its own jurisdiction. A very different problem is that of how the forum should react in the situation where there is a trial abroad, when this involves forum-shopping and injustice to the defendant in the foreign proceedings. There are two alternative ways in which a State could deal with this problem. It could either restrain the foreign proceedings or refuse to recognize and enforce the foreign judgment. The first method seeks to solve the problem directly; the second indirectly.

The first method involves the exercise by the court of a discretion, and it comes as no surprise to find that, by and large, States which have adopted a doctrine of *forum non conveniens* have also adopted this method for dealing with forum-shopping and injustice abroad. At the same time, there is a great difference between a court declining its own jurisdiction and seeking to restrain foreign proceedings. Although in common law jurisdictions the restraint is carried out by means of an injunction,[236] which operates *in personam* (against one of the parties), this is, nonetheless, an indirect interference with the jurisdiction of the foreign court. It is for this reason that any power to restrain foreign proceedings is exercised with caution. It also has to be admitted that there are practical problems with

---

[235] Kantongerecht Zierikzee, 19 Feb. 1988, [1988] Praktijkgids 2870, 268.

[236] Compare the position in Argentina where there are some procedural rules which allow the courts to restrain foreign proceedings, but there is no discretionary power to restrain by injunction.

this method. If the defendant is out of the jurisdiction and has no assets within it, proceedings for contempt of court for breach of the injunction become meaningless.

It also comes as no surprise to find that States which have not adopted a doctrine of *forum non conveniens* have dealt with the problem of forum-shopping and injustice abroad at the stage of recognition and enforcement of the foreign judgment.

2. RESTRAINING FOREIGN PROCEEDINGS

A similar pattern emerges to that observed in relation to *forum non conveniens*. Britain has taken a lead, which has been followed in other Commonwealth States. The United States have their own distinctive criteria for restraining foreign proceedings. Quebec and Japan have adopted criteria which are different from each other and from those adopted in the common law jurisdictions.

(a) BRITAIN AND SOME OTHER COMMONWEALTH STATES

Under English law a distinction is drawn between, on the one hand, the situation where there are two or more available fora for trial (one of which is England) and, on the other hand, the situation where the only available forum is abroad. The former situation is far more common and will be concentrated on in this Report. At one time, the English courts applied essentially the same criteria for restraining foreign proceedings as for staying their own proceedings.[237] The *Spiliada* case changed all that. The *Spiliada* criteria, if unthinkingly applied to the area of restraining foreign proceedings, would have led to English courts restraining foreign proceedings on the mere basis that the natural forum for trial was England. In the leading case of *Société Nationale Industrielle Aérospatiale* v. *Lee Kui Jak*,[238] the Privy Council held that what needs to be shown, as a general rule, is that England is the natural forum for trial *and* that it would be oppressive or vexatious to permit the defendant to continue with the proceedings abroad. The reference to the natural (or clearly appropriate) forum is interesting because of the importance attached to this concept under the English doctrine of *forum non conveniens*. It can therefore be seen that there is still some overlap in the criteria used for staying local proceedings and those for restraining foreign proceedings. It looks to be wrong in principle for an English court to grant an injunction restraining foreign proceedings in another Western European State, when that State has been allocated jurisdiction under the Brussels or Lugano Convention.[239] The

---

[237] *Castanho* v. *Brown and Root (UK) Ltd* [1981] AC 557.
[238] [1987] AC 871.   [239] See Cheshire and North, n. 38 above, 250–1.

English Court of Appeal has recently granted an injunction restraining Greek proceedings; however, this was in the situation where the English courts had exclusive jurisdiction under Article 17 of the Brussels Convention.[240]

A Scottish court in *Pan American World Airways* v. *Andrews*[241] has followed the *Société Nationale Aérospatiale* case, as well as earlier Scottish authority.

In New Zealand the law on restraint of foreign proceedings is identical to that in England, since the *Société Nationale Aérospatiale* case is accepted as being a binding precedent.

That case has also been followed in Australia[242] and in Singapore.[243]

The Supreme Court of Canada in *Amchem Products Inc* v. *British Columbia (Workers Compensation Board)*[244] were very much influenced by the *Société Nationale Aérospatiale* case, and the principles it sets out were taken as the foundation for the test to be applied in Canada. However, there are three clear differences between the Canadian and English doctrines.

First, in Canada the courts ask whether the foreign forum is *forum non conveniens*, rather than whether the local forum is the natural forum for the trial.

Secondly, when it comes to the trial abroad, the language of vexation and oppression is not used in Canada. An injunction will only be granted if the foreign court's assumption of jurisdiction was inequitable, i.e. an injustice results to a litigant or would-be litigant before the Canadian courts.

Thirdly, in examining the question of injustice, the domestic court should weigh up the loss of advantage to the foreign plaintiff if the injunction is granted, against the loss of advantage to the defendant if the action is tried abroad.

(b) THE UNITED STATES

A United States court will grant an injunction restraining a person from proceeding with an action abroad if it is satisfied that a refusal to grant the injunction will cause irreparable harm to the person seeking the injunction and will not impose undue hardship on the person against whom the injunction is sought.[245]

---

[240] *Continental Bank NA* v. *Aeakos Compania Naviera SA* [1994] 1 WLR 588. See the criticism by Bell, (1994) 110 *LQR* 204; Rogerson, (1994) 53 *CLJ* 241.

[241] 1992 SLT 268.

[242] See e.g. *National Mutual Holdings Pty Ltd* v. *Sentry Corporation* (1989) 87 ALR 539.

[243] *Djoni Widjaja* v. *Bank of America National Trust and Savings Association* [1993] 3 SLR 678.

[244] (1993) 102 DLR (4th) 96.

[245] See *Laker Airways Ltd* v. *Pan American World Airways*, 559 F. Supp 1124, 1129 (DDC 1983).

This doctrine is the same in many respects as the English one. Different criteria are applied for restraining foreign proceedings from those adopted for a stay of local proceedings. Likewise, comity is an important consideration, and an injunction will not lightly be granted. It is not enough to base the injunction on simple convenience; the foreign action must be shown to be frivolous or vexatious. Under both United States and English law, bringing an action abroad in breach of a valid choice of jurisdiction clause is in itself likely to lead to an injunction restraining the foreign proceedings.[246] On the other hand, in the United States the public interest must be taken into account. There is a difference, too, in the role that the doctrine of restraining foreign proceedings plays in the United States when compared to its role in other common law jurisdictions. The doctrine is seen in the United States as the prime method of stopping parallel proceedings.[247] Finally, an English court will, in rare cases, grant an injunction even though the substantive issue can only be decided by the foreign court.[248] An American court will not.[249]

(c) QUEBEC

In Quebec the criteria for restraining foreign proceedings are not entirely clear, but appear to be based on case law and to be similar to, but not identical with, the Quebecois *forum non conveniens* criteria. Two key elements under both sets of criteria are the general balance of inconveniences and abuses of procedure. As a result, a court could, using these criteria, reject a plea of *forum non conveniens* by one party but grant an injunction restraining the foreign proceedings in favour of the other party. In practice though, the power to grant an injunction restraining foreign proceedings has been very rarely used. The problem of forum-shopping has been dealt with at the stage of recognition of the judgment.

(d) JAPAN

There is a lack of Japanese case law on this topic. However, it is suggested[250] that it is in theory possible for a Japanese court to order someone not to continue to litigate in a foreign State, although the criteria to be adopted when deciding whether to make such an order are not clear.

---

[246] For the US see below, p. 425. For England see *Sohio Supply Co* v. *Gatoil (USA) Inc* [1989] 1 Lloyd's Rep. 588 (CA). For the situation where there is an arbitration agreement see *The Angelic Grace* [1994] 1 Lloyd's Rep. 168.

[247] See below, p. 418.

[248] See e.g. *Midland Bank plc* v. *Laker Airways Ltd* [1986] QB 689 (CA).

[249] See Hartley, (1987) 35 *Am. J Comp. Law* 487.   [250] See below, p. 318.

3. Refusing to Recognize and Enforce the Foreign Judgment

(a) THE UNDERLYING THEORY

The adoption of very narrow and restrictive rules on the recognition and enforcement of foreign judgments acts to discourage forum-shopping abroad. If there is little or no connection with the foreign place of trial there may also be a problem of enforcing the judgment in that State, and a successful plaintiff may have to seek enforcement abroad. Some States refuse to recognize or enforce foreign judgments altogether in the absence of a treaty obligation. Many other States require a strong connection with the judgment-granting State. This means necessarily that recognition and enforcement will not be accorded to a foreign judgment where this has been obtained as a result of forum-shopping.

This approach is not entirely satisfactory as a means of stopping forum-shopping abroad, since it may be possible for a plaintiff who has been forum-shopping abroad to find assets in the judgment-granting State or to enforce the judgment in some other State which has wide rules on recognition and enforcement of foreign judgments. Nor does this method stop parallel proceedings, while restraining foreign proceedings does. There are, though, the rules on *lis alibi pendens* to stop parallel proceedings.

(b) STATES ADOPTING THIS APPROACH

In France, Germany, and Switzerland the rules on recognition and enforcement of foreign judgments are seen as being the means of dealing with forum-shopping abroad in an incompetent forum. None of these States has adopted a doctrine of *forum non conveniens*, and, accordingly, one would not expect them to adopt a discretionary power to restrain foreign proceedings. More interestingly, each of these States uses a recognition prognosis to deal with problems of *lis alibi pendens*, at least in cases outside the Brussels and Lugano Conventions. The French, German, and Swiss reporters see the requirement that the foreign court must have indirect jurisdiction as the most important provision on recognition and enforcement when it comes to dealing with forum-shopping abroad. Under French law, for recognition and enforcement of a foreign judgment it is also required that the French courts did not have exclusive jurisdiction.[251] French law is particularly opposed to the power to restrain foreign proceedings, seeing this as an intolerable interference with the foreign court.

[251] Cass. Fr., 1ère ch. civ., 6 Feb. 1985, [1985] *Simitch, Rev. crit. de dr. internat. pr.* 369 with art. by Ph. Francescakis, at 243; [1985] *Journal du droit international* 460, note A. Huet; [1985] Dalloz 469, note Massip, and report at 497, observ. Audit; Ancel and Lequette, *Grands arrêts de la jurisprudence française de droit international privé*, n. 171 above, n°. 66.

In Sweden and Finland foreign judgments are normally unenforceable and forum-shopping abroad is seen as being pointless. In these two States there are also suggestions that a recognition prognosis should be used to deal with *lis pendens*.

Italian law provides litigants with a particularly potent weapon, which could be used to deal with forum-shopping abroad, in that the mere institution of proceedings in Italy, before a foreign judgment becomes final, effectively prevents recognition of the foreign judgment there.[252]

Even in States which have a power to restrain foreign proceedings, the question of enforcement of the foreign judgment does have some relevance. Thus in the United States, there is a tendency in commercial cases to let the parallel proceedings continue and refuse to restrain the foreign proceedings, in the knowledge that the rules on enforcement deny this to a foreign judgment which is irreconcilable with a judgment granted in the United States.

Under Quebecois law, it is accepted that certain of the rules on recognition and enforcement (e.g. the public policy rule) could be used to stop forum-shopping abroad. Moreover, the rules on recognition and enforcement contained in the Civil Code may be regarded as being formulated so as to control forum-shopping. A foreign court's jurisdiction is only recognized 'to the extent that the dispute is substantially connected with the country whose authority is seised of the case'.[253] Elsewhere in Canada, in the common law jurisdictions, the rules on the recognition and enforcement of foreign judgments are such that the judgment of a foreign State which is *forum non conveniens* is unlikely to be recognized.

VIII
CONCLUSIONS

1. By and large, States share the same concerns. If local courts are to try the case, this should be on the basis that the local forum is the appropriate, or an appropriate, one for trial. Parallel proceedings at home and abroad are undesirable and should not be allowed to continue. Effect should be given to the wishes of the parties as set out in choice of jurisdiction and arbitration clauses. Trial abroad in an unconnected foreign forum is a matter of concern to a local forum.

2. Common law jurisdictions deal with these concerns by means of discretionary rules, not only in relation to declining jurisdiction under the doctrine of *forum non conveniens* but also in relation to *lis pendens*, choice of jurisdiction agreements, (in limited circumstances) arbitration agree-

---

[252] Art. 797(1), n°. 6, Code of Civil Procedure.   [253] Art. 3164.

ments, forum-shopping abroad, and restraining foreign proceedings. In marked contrast, civil law jurisdictions show a consistent pattern of using non-discretionary rules in relation to all these areas of concern. The hybrid jurisdiction of Quebec adopts a mixture of approaches for, while it has a doctrine of *forum non conveniens*, in cases of *lis pendens* resort may be had to a (non-discretionary) recognition prognosis approach.

3. There is a group of States (France, Germany, Italy, Switzerland, Sweden, and Finland), which see the answer to at least some of these concerns in terms of rules on recognition and enforcement of foreign judgments. Thus it is the same States that use a recognition prognosis in cases of *lis pendens*, as use restrictive rules on recognition and enforcement of foreign judgments to discourage forum-shopping abroad.

4. When it comes to *forum non conveniens*, there is a major dichotomy between States which have such a doctrine, and this is not always precisely the same doctrine, and those which do not. Perhaps the most important single reason for this dichotomy can be found in the relationship between the concepts of *forum conveniens* and *forum non conveniens*. Many States do not have a doctrine of *forum non conveniens* because of their perception that they only have jurisdiction in the first place when the local forum is *forum conveniens*. Conversely, in common law jurisdictions the power to decline to exercise jurisdiction on the basis of *forum non conveniens* is used when the jurisdiction that undoubtedly exists is not based on *forum conveniens*.

5. As regards *lis pendens*, there is general agreement that, in certain circumstances, this should be dealt with by declining jurisdiction or by suspending local proceedings. The major exception is the United States where the solution to the problem is seen in terms of restraining the foreign proceedings. However, there is no agreement on the basis for declining jurisdiction/suspending local proceedings. This may be on the basis of *forum non conveniens*, or a mechanical rule which gives priority to the State which is first seised of the proceedings, or a recognition prognosis. Common law jurisdictions (with the exception of the United States) favour the first basis. With non-common law jurisdictions, though, there is no clear pattern. Thus many civil law States, while often adhering to a recognition prognosis, may also take into account the matter of which court was first seised of the proceedings (thus combining the two approaches). At the same time, civil and common law jurisdictions in Western Europe in Brussels/Lugano Convention cases will only apply the first-seised rule.

6. With foreign choice of jurisdiction agreements there is much more uniformity of approach than with *lis pendens*. There is a consensus among States that effect should be given to the wishes of the parties and that the local forum should not try the case. This may involve declining jurisdiction (in common law jurisdictions) or acknowledging that there is no

jurisdiction (in civil law jurisdictions), but the result will be the same. Of course, common law jurisdictions do have a power not to decline jurisdiction but, instead, to allow trial to continue despite the presence of a foreign choice of jurisdiction agreement. However, as a general rule jurisdiction is declined in this situation.

7. There is even more uniformity of approach among States when it comes to arbitration agreements. Jurisdiction must be declined in cases where there is a valid arbitration agreement. This uniformity comes about because of the influence of the New York Convention and the UNCITRAL Model Law. The result is that even common law jurisdictions operate a mandatory rule requiring them to decline jurisdiction, rather than a discretionary rule, in cases coming within the Convention or Model Law.

8. When it comes to forum-shopping abroad the fundamental difference in approach between common law and other jurisdictions in relation to discretionary powers resurfaces. For it is only in the common law jurisdictions that the courts have a discretionary power to restrain foreign proceedings. In fact, the adoption of this power is less widespread than the adoption of the doctrine of *forum non conveniens*. Thus Japan, while having a 'special circumstances' doctrine which bears a resemblance to a doctrine of *forum non conveniens*, has no power to restrain foreign proceedings. In this State, as in other non-common law jurisdictions, the problem of actions being brought in an unconnected forum abroad is dealt with at the stage of recognition and enforcement of the ensuing judgment.

9. Multilateral conventions have had a considerable impact on this whole area. The conventions in question have not been Hague Conventions on Private International Law,[254] which, so far, have had very little direct impact in this area; they are the New York Convention and the Brussels/Lugano Conventions.[255] The impact of the former has already been mentioned. The latter have harmonized the law for Western European States, not only in relation to *forum non conveniens* (the Conventions contain no *forum non conveniens* provision), but also in relation to *lis pendens* and foreign choice of jurisdiction clauses. The impact of the Brussels and Lugano Conventions has been most profound on the United Kingdom, where implementation of these Conventions, which are based on civil law concepts, has meant the loss of discretionary powers in cases coming within them.[256]

---

[254] i.e. the Hague Convention on the choice of court, concluded in 1965 (which has never come into force); the Hague Convention on the Recognition and Enforcement of Foreign Judgments in Civil and Commercial Matters, concluded in 1971 (ratified by Cyprus, The Netherlands, and Portugal).

[255] However, the work of the Hague Conference has had a considerable impact on the development of the Brussels Convention. See Arts. 1, 2, 5(2), 17, 20 of the Brussels Convention, and the Jenard Report, [1979] OJ C59/1.

[256] This is subject to *Re Harrods (Buenos Aires) Ltd*, n. 37 above.

Recent developments at the Hague Conference on Private International Law raise the possibility of a multilateral convention which could have an equally profound effect on *forum non conveniens, lis pendens,* and related rules in any State throughout the world which ratifies it. Following the Seventeenth Session of the Hague Conference on private international law, a Special Commission met in June 1994[257] which concluded that it would be advantageous to draw up a convention on jurisdiction, recognition, and enforcement of foreign judgments in civil and commercial matters. The Special Commission agreed that this convention should establish rules on judicial jurisdiction at the stage of the initial litigation. There was much discussion whether a judge who has jurisdiction should be able to decline this on the basis of *forum non conveniens.* This was bound to be a difficult matter, given the clear dichotomy between States which have such a doctrine and those that do not. However, it seems that there is a possibility of a compromise being reached:

allowing a limited possibility for application of the theory of *forum non conveniens* in specific cases to be determined and on the condition that a mechanism of coordination be instituted in the convention. The essence of this mechanism would be that, where the court of a Contracting State considers that the court of another Contracting State is better placed than it is to judge the case pending before it, under circumstances which might be set out in the convention, it would stay proceedings before it until that other court has declared itself to have jurisdiction. If this second court refuses to exercise jurisdiction, the first court would then have to decide the case on the merits.[258]

This opens up the possibility not only of common law jurisdictions using a new and more limited doctrine of *forum non conveniens* but also, more interestingly, of civil law jurisdictions operating a doctrine of *forum non conveniens* when this has not hitherto been the case. The proposed convention would also deal with the problem of *lis pendens,* thereby producing a measure of harmonization in an area which is well known for the variety of different solutions to the problem.

---

[257] See *Conclusions of the Special Commission of June 1994 on the Question of the Recognition and Enforcement of Foreign Judgments in Civil and Commercial Matters,* Prelim. Doc. No. 1 of Aug. 1994 for the attention of the Special Commission on general affairs and policy of the Conference.
[258] *Ibid.* 21.

2

Argentina

MAUREEN WILLIAMS

Professor of Law, University of Buenos Aires*

CONTENTS

I
FORUM NON CONVENIENS

1. Is There a Doctrine of *Forum Non Conveniens*?

Unlike common law countries, the Argentine Republic does not have any such doctrine. Be that as it may, Argentine courts and tribunals do have in

* The author is grateful to Griselda Capaldo de Nolfi and Paula Galante for their most helpful contribution.

mind the existence of more appropriate fora to deal with a given case. To claim the existence of a more suitable forum is a possibility—albeit infrequent in Argentine case law—open to the defendant. One of the very rare occasions on which a court spoke of a convenient forum was in *Elbert Clemens* v. *Buque Pavlo*.

2. Why There is no Doctrine of *Forum Non Conveniens*

Perhaps the Argentine has not grown enough yet to create the right situation for a doctrine of this nature to gain ground. An incipient trend in this direction may be perceived, given the present conditions of a free market economy which had not been the case for the last fifty years (with very brief exceptions).

Similarly, the dynamics of Argentine federalism show a progressive inclination to increase the power of the central government. For this reason, there is an ever-growing number of laws which are enforceable in the whole national territory. This situation, even though it may affect the autonomy of the provinces, creates, at the same time, a legislative uniformity which avoids internal forum-shopping. In other words, the parties to a dispute will not find different advantages depending on the jurisdiction in which legal action is taken.

In addition, there are other procedural mechanisms by which the interests and the rights of the defendant are protected. The country has very strict rules concerning the jurisdiction of the courts. These restrictions are related to territory, to the parties, to the claim, and to the matter.

3. Other Procedural Mechanisms

There are some effective procedural mechanisms in cases of doubt concerning the impartiality of judges or with a view to assuring that justice is really done. These mechanisms are:

— a motion to challenge or decline jurisdiction: the defendant asks the judge seised of the case to declare himself incompetent.

— a motion to request the dismissal of the case: the defendant requests the judge he considers competent to declare himself so and accordingly notify the judge who is hearing the case so that he may abstain from further action.

— a motion to dismiss: it may be resorted to by the defendant once he has been notified of the existence of a claim against him. This motion absorbs the motion to challenge jurisdiction.

— a motion for recusation: both plaintiff and defendant may employ this with the intention of disqualifying the judge when there are doubts concerning self-interest or prejudice.

— a motion for *recusal sua sponte*: it is similar to the previous one except that it is the judge himself who requests to be disqualified.

In general, Argentine law establishes in advance which will be the competent court in each situation. Moreover, the law envisages an alternative jurisdiction which normally coincides with the defendant's domicile. Because of the very slim margin left by the law for choosing jurisdiction, the practice of forum-shopping in Argentina is neither frequent nor a problem.

4. A Flexible Position

Courts have taken a rather flexible position. The power to stay or dismiss actions may be exercised, depending on the case, by the defendant, the plaintiff, or the judge (either *ex officio* or at the request of a party). This possibility is envisaged in all the Argentine Procedural Codes, both federal and provincial, and should be invoked after the submission of the claim within very short time-limits. Should there be no resort to these possibilities, then the law considers that the parties have accepted the competence of the court. This mechanism is based on the 'principle of preclusion' which applies to all legal procedings (except criminal). According to this principle the procedure is divided into several phases within which different actions should be taken. These actions are dismissed if brought outside the time-limit laid down by the law.

5. The Role of the Power to Decline Jurisdiction

Its aim is to protect the interests and legitimate expectations of the parties to a dispute and to assure a more direct relationship between the judge, the evidence provided, and the objective of the claim. The idea is that the judge should be in the best situation to settle the dispute in all fairness.

6. Forum-shopping

As said before, the Argentine law does not allow a wide margin for choosing jurisdiction. Therefore, forum-shopping is not an issue over which Argentina is concerned.

7. Relationship with Bases of Jurisdiction

Recourse to the legal remedies explained under 3., above, has no jurisdictional restrictions. It is widely applied as it covers all subjects and every forum.

II
LIS ALIBI PENDENS

In Argentine law there is an express defence called *litispendencia* which shall be taken into account by the judge at the request of either of the parties when proceedings are pending in two different fora at the same time, against the same defendant, and for the same reason. This rule applies to domestic proceedings. Interesting, because of its implications, is the fact that the Argentine National Procedural Code lays down a rule whereby a foreign judgment shall not be recognized if it conflicts with a previous or simultaneous one given by an Argentine court.

1. CONDITIONS FOR USING THE DEFENCE

The objective of the *litispendencia* defence is to avoid the same claim being adjudicated twice and contradictory judgments. The conditions for employing this defence are as follows:

— the first proceedings must be pending in another competent forum;
— the claim brought in the first proceedings should have been already notified;
— both proceedings should be apt to be continued in a similar manner, and
— the parties should appear in the same capacity in both proceedings.

2. DIFFERENCES FROM *FORUM NON CONVENIENS*

Both are legal remedies intended to ensure a better administration of justice, but they differ from the procedural mechanisms listed under 3., above, in that the purpose of the latter is to dismiss the judge seised of the case for reasons of incompetence or partiality, whereas the remedies described under *lis pendens* seek to avoid the same claim being judged twice with resulting contradictory judgments.

3. *LITISPENDENCIA* BY IDENTITY AND CONNEXITY

Litispendencia is one of the defences at the defendant's disposal. It may be of two different kinds, namely:

— By identity, when two pending proceedings are absolutely identical (same parties, same object, and same cause). In this case the judge will order filing of the second proceedings.

— By connexity, when one of those three elements are not identical (parties, object, or cause). In this situation the judge will order the accumulation of the proceedings. *Litispendencia* may be declared *ex officio* at any stage of the proceedings prior to the definitive judgment. The purpose of this defence is to save useless effort.

III
FOREIGN CHOICE OF JURISDICTION CLAUSES

According to Argentine law all international disputes may include a foreign choice of jurisdiction clause, provided there is a pecuniary interest involved. Very recent case law has confirmed the exclusive jurisdiction of the selected forum and it is expected that this trend will continue (Cf. decision of the Argentine Court of Appeal for Commercial Matters in *Quilmes Combustibles* v. *Vigon SA*, 15 March 1993). Argentina is a party to the 1889 and 1940 Montevideo Treaties on International Civil Law which embody rules on international jurisdiction. These Treaties envisage the 'extension of jurisdiction' which, again, is only allowed for pecuniary matters.

This power only gives way when it conflicts with a question of public order. The choice of jurisdiction cannot be exercised, for example, when such a possibility is ruled out by a national law or when Argentine courts have exclusive jurisdiction. Argentine courts generally take good faith into account in the choice of a given jurisdiction and when a neutral forum, alien to the transaction, has been chosen, special attention will be given to the differing powers of negotiation of the parties.

In Argentina there is no non-discretionary rule that requires the courts to decline jurisdiction in cases involving a foreign choice of jurisdiction clause except, as observed earlier, when some question relating to Argentine public order is involved.

IV
ARBITRATION AGREEMENTS

Under Argentine law, any dispute may be submitted to arbitration, even when the arbitral tribunal sits outside the country, provided the dispute is of an international nature and involves a pecuniary claim. Thus, questions relating, *inter alia*, to divorce or custody would not be included. In addition, Argentina is a party to the New York Convention on Enforcement of Arbitral Awards and, therefore, all the provisions of that Convention apply. When it comes to the power to stay court proceedings where arbitration proceding between the parties is in force, there are conflicting interpretations. However, the normal course of action would be that, since arbitration implies an exclusive jurisdiction, should a party begin proceedings before a domestic court, the other party would be able to obtain an order staying the proceedings.

There are separate rules in respect of domestic and non-domestic arbitration agreements. Recent case law has established that Argentine law is not applicable to international commercial arbitration disputes.

These rules are not mandatory but allow for discretion. Argentine courts are inclined to accept arbitration clauses in international contracts, particularly nowadays with the wave of privatizations in this country. Yet, the local courts would not decline jurisdiction automatically but would listen to the arguments of the parties concerning jurisdiction.

V
RESTRAINING FOREIGN PROCEEDINGS

1. NO DISCRETIONARY POWER

Under Argentine law there is no discretionary power to restrain foreign proceedings by means of an injunction. However, Argentine law has certain rules of procedure which permit the restraining of foreign proceedings when one of the parties to the dispute feels that some other court in the country should have jurisdiction. However, Argentine courts are extremely cautious in interfering with foreign proceedings. Thus, restraining foreign proceedings is a very rare possibility.

2. RECOGNITION AND ENFORCEMENT AND
FORUM-SHOPPING ABROAD

Under Argentine law foreign judgments are recognized and enforced if and when the following conditions are met:

— the judgment is final in the jurisdiction where it was given and should be granted by a court competent in accordance with Argentine laws concerning conflict of laws and jurisdiction. It should have resulted from a personal or *in rem* action with regard to personal, as opposed to real, property which property was transferred to Argentina during or after the prosecution of the foreign action; and

— the defendant against whom the enforcement is sought has been personally served with the summons in accordance with due process of law and an opportunity to defend has been given to him;

— the judgment is valid in the jurisdiction in which it was given and must be authentic in accordance with Argentine laws;

— the judgment must not be in breach of the principles of public order; of Argentine law.

— the judgment should not be contrary to a previous or simultaneous judgment of an Argentine court on the same matter.

The above requirements are listed in the National Procedural Code of Argentina. The list is exhaustive and judges do not look for any additional reasons.

3

Australia

JUDD EPSTEIN
Faculty of Law, Monash University

CONTENTS

I

INTRODUCTION—JURISDICTIONAL BACKGROUND

Australia has derived its rules for declining to exercise jurisdiction in civil and commercial matters from the United Kingdom,[1] with very minor

---

[1] This ch. is written on the basis that the reader is familiar in broad outline with the English developments set out in Ch. 10. The sources of law in Australia and the divergences from the English model will be highlighted in this ch.

modifications. In 1988 the Australian High Court declared that Australian courts may exercise a general discretion to decline jurisdiction. The Court, however, rejected the reforms in the United Kingdom and found its own path. The Australian developments in *forum non conveniens*, while *sui generis*, fall within the mainstream of Commonwealth law. In other areas of declining to exercise jurisdiction, e.g. *lis pendens*, foreign jurisdiction clauses, and arbitration clauses, Australia's rules are heavily influenced by decisions in the United Kingdom.

There has been marked evolution, if not revolution, in two areas which affect the rules for declining to exercise jurisdiction. Within Australia, each of the component States of the Federation had traditionally been regarded as a foreign-law area. The rules in this area regulating international proceedings were more or less identical to those regulating intra-Australian proceedings. Since 1987 legislation has reflected the view that Australia's component States and Territories should be regarded as parts of a common nation rather than as separate law nations.[2] The second major development within the last twenty years has been a broadening of the bases of jurisdiction. The range of situations in which originating process from Australian courts can be served upon defendants outside the Commonwealth of Australia has markedly increased. There has been an even more pronounced opening of the possibility of inter-State service within Australia.

1. MEANS OF EFFECTING SERVICE *EX JURIS*

The rules for declining to exercise jurisdiction have greater prominence where the forum facilitates service upon an out-of-jurisdiction defendant. The power to serve originating process on defendants outside the Commonwealth of Australia is found in the rules of each of the Supreme Courts of the various States and Territories. It has been broadly modelled on the English Order 11. This means of obtaining jurisdiction has widened over the last twenty years. Jurisdiction based upon a cause of action sounding in tort in the State of Victoria is illustrative. Throughout much of this century, in order to serve process on a foreign defendant based on an alleged commission of a tort, it had to be shown that the tort was committed within the State of Victoria. The intending plaintiff had to obtain leave from the court prior to serving Notice of the Writ outside Australia. The onus of proving that the claim fell within the relevant sub-heading set out in the rule lay upon the plaintiff, who had to show a good arguable case,

---

[2] Service and Execution of Process, Report 40, The Law Reform Commission—Australia (1987), see e.g. paras. 12, 13.

though the intending plaintiff was not required to prove the ground as if it were an issue to be proved at trial.[3]

Eventually it was deemed unnecessary for an intending plaintiff to present oral submissions to a Master in order to determine whether leave should be granted. For a time written materials were presented to the registry of the court and read by a Master who, on the written submissions alone, determined whether or not to grant leave. Today, as in most Australian States and Territories,[4] 'originating process may be served out of Victoria without order of the court'. Another development was the broadening of the nexus provisions by which a defendant could be commanded into the territory. For example, in addition to the tort being committed in Victoria, by Rule 7.01(1)(j) originating process may be served where 'the proceeding is brought in respect of damage suffered wholly or partly in Victoria and caused by a tortious act or omission wherever occurring'. The mere fact of going for medical treatment in the State after an injury anywhere else in the world is sufficient to endow the court with jurisdiction.

The development of these broader bases of jurisdiction, together with the abolition of prior leave for service outside Australia by an intending plaintiff, has resulted in a broader cross-section of cases coming before the court for scrutiny. A consequence of this has been the need to review the rules for declining to exercise jurisdiction in order to ensure fairness to intending Australian plaintiffs and foreign defendants.

2. SERVICE *EX JURIS* WITHIN AUSTRALIA

The rules of service *ex juris* reflected the traditional view that each Australian State and Territory was treated as a 'foreign country'. In most States the near equivalent of the English Order 11 of the Rules of the Supreme Court regulated service on both international and inter-State defendants. The Service and Execution of Process Act (Cth.) 1901 was an additional method of authorizing service *ex juris* within Australia. Two new developments—the institution of the cross-vesting scheme and the passage of the Service and Execution of Process Act 1992 (Cth.)—have replaced the old. The cross-vesting scheme consists of mirror legislation in the Commonwealth and in each of the States and Territories.[5] The *raison d'être* of the scheme, designed by the Standing Committee of Attorneys General, was to eliminate jurisdictional conflicts between the Federal

[3] Per Dean J in *W. A. Dewhurst & Co Pty Ltd* v. *Cawrse* [1960] VR 278 at 281.

[4] E.g. Queensland, Ord. 11; South Australia, Rule 18; Victoria, Ord. 7.

[5] See Jurisdiction of Courts (Cross-Vesting) Act 1987 (Cth.) and, e.g., Jurisdiction of Courts (Cross-Vesting) Act 1987 (NSW). The operation of the scheme is the subject of a recent report: Moloney and McMaster, *Cross Vesting of Jurisdiction: A Review of the Operation of the National Scheme* (Australian Institute of Judicial Administration, 1992).

Court and the State Supreme Courts, between the various State Supreme Courts, and between each of those courts and the Family Court of Australia. By the Acts the jurisdiction of each of those courts is cross-vested upon each of the other courts so that, for example, the Supreme Court of Tasmania now has all the jurisdiction of the Federal Court and of the Supreme Court of Victoria (and vice versa). A civil proceeding which a potential plaintiff previously had to initiate in two separate courts, because neither court had jurisdiction to hear all of the matters raised, may now be brought in either court. The system is structured in such a way as to ensure, as far as practicable, that proceedings which would have been entirely or substantially within the jurisdiction of any particular court are still instituted and determined in that court, while allowing the determination by one court of all Federal and State matters.[6] Service outside a particular State may now be instituted by means of writs endorsed under the cross-vesting legislation. In most of the State Supreme Courts, rules have been passed to permit service outside the particular State pursuant to prior leave from the issuing court.[7] In each case leave will be granted if the court is satisfied that it 'may be, having regard to the relevant cross-vesting law, an *appropriate* court to hear and determine the proceeding'.[8]

The second feature which has facilitated inter-State service of originating process is the passage of the Service and Execution of Process Act 1992 (Cth.). Pursuant to section 15 of that Act an initiating process issued in one State may be served in another State. There is no longer any requirement that prior leave of court be obtained in order to serve initiating process, and the nexus provisions which characterized the previous Service and Execution of Process Act have been eliminated. The contest over jurisdiction occurs after service. At that stage the person served may apply to the court of issue for an order staying the proceeding or for an order transferring the proceedings to a court of a different Australian jurisdiction.

II
FORUM NON CONVENIENS

Australia has a doctrine of *forum non conveniens*. Until very recently Australia has closely followed the English rules for stays of proceeding. The leading case decided by the High Court of Australia was *Maritime Insurance Co Ltd* v. *Geelong Harbour Trust Commissioners*.[9] In that case the plaintiff, Geelong Harbour Trust Commissioners, had brought an action in the Supreme Court of Victoria against the Maritime Insurance Co Ltd to

---

[6] See Preamble, Jurisdiction of Courts (Cross-Vesting) Act 1987 (Cth.).
[7] See e.g. Tasmania, r. 68.06(5); Victoria, Ch. II, r. 13.07.
[8] E.g. Vic., Ch. II, r. 13.07(3).   [9] (1908) 6 CLR 194.

recover a sum in respect of a policy of insurance upon a dredger which was lost during a voyage from Durban in Natal, South Africa, to Geelong. The defendants sought a stay on the ground that the action was vexatious and oppressive. The stay was refused using the test propounded in *Logan v. Bank of Scotland (No 2)*,[10] in that an injustice would be occasioned to the plaintiff by a stay. In cases involving service out of the jurisdiction in both England and Australia *forum conveniens* factors have always been relevant.[11] The 1936 rule announced by Scott LJ in *St Pierre v. South American Stores (Gath and Chaves) Ltd*.[12] was often cited in Australian cases. The Australian courts also drew a distinction based upon whether the jurisdiction had been obtained *ex juris* and with prior leave of the court or whether it had been obtained 'as of right', that is, through good personal service or its analogue or within its admiralty jurisdiction.

The Australian inferior courts were also aware of and regularly applied the developments in the United Kingdom from 1972 onwards.[13] Cases such as *The Atlantic Star, Rockware Glass v. MacShannon, The Abidin Daver*, and *Spiliada Maritime Corp v. Cansulex Ltd*, were all cited extensively within Australian court judgments.[14]

The final word on the principles in this area and, it was expected, the adoption of the English rules awaited the decision of the High Court of Australia. That occurred in 1988 with the case of *Oceanic Sun Line Special Shipping Co Inc v. Fay*.[15] In that case Dr Fay, the plaintiff, was seriously injured in a trap-shooting incident on board a ship owned by the defendant, Oceanic Sun Lines, during a cruise in Greek territorial waters. Dr Fay, alleging that he had sought and obtained hospital treatment within New South Wales, invoked the jurisdiction of the court by dint of damage having been suffered within the jurisdiction as a result of a tort committed elsewhere. The principal issue for the High Court was whether the Australian courts were to follow the doctrine of *forum non conveniens* which prevailed in the United Kingdom and similarly followed throughout the Commonwealth. By a three to two majority the court decided that it would reject the United Kingdom developments. The members of the majority were not themselves united on a particular test to apply; that had to await another day.

In what has become the leading judgment, Deane J held that the Australian position was dictated by legal principle, precedent, and policy. With regard to legal principle he stated: 'It is a basic tenet of our jurisprudence that, where jurisdiction exists, access to the courts is a right.'[16] With

---

[10] [1906] 1 KB 141.   [11] Collins (1991) 107 *LQR* 182 at 184.
[12] [1936] 1 KB 382.
[13] See e.g. *Ranger Uranium Mines Pty Ltd v. BTR Trading (Qld) Pty Ltd* (1985) 34 NTR 1; *Garseabo Nominees Pty Ltd v. Taub Pty Ltd* [1979] 1 NSWLR 663.
[14] *The Atlantic Star* [1974] AC 436; *MacShannon v. Rockware Glass Ltd* [1978] AC 795; *The Abidin Daver* [1984] AC 398; *Spiliada Maritime Corp v. Cansulex Ltd* [1986] 3 WLR 972.
[15] (1988) 79 ALR 9.   [16] *Ibid*. 49.

regard to precedent he invoked the *Maritime Insurance Co* case, stating that
it was a decision of a unanimous court and has stood as authority for
almost eighty years. With regard to policy the position was not so clear.
He adverted to the public interest including the costs of the administration of justice, limited judicial resources, congested court lists, over-
worked judges, and delayed justice. These factors point toward adoption
of the English position, but he also considered that such factors are not
usually taken into account by Australian judges. There were also to be
considered the private convenience of the litigants and notions of international comity. In Deane J's considered opinion the policy leaned towards acceptance of the principle in the *Spiliada* case, but he found this to
be persuasive but not compelling. Deane J endorsed the oppressive and
vexatious test, more or less as modified in *The Atlantic Star.* ' "Oppressive"
should, in this context, be understood as meaning seriously and unfairly
burdensome, prejudicial or damaging, while "vexatious" should be
understood as meaning productive of serious and unjustified trouble and
harassment.'[17]

Brennan J in the same case found that the *forum non conveniens* doctrine
was too arbitrary and capricious in its result: 'the English law can be seen
to have moved from a discretion confined by a tolerably precise principle
to a broad discretion to be exercised according to the judge's view of what
is suitable "for the interests of all the parties and the ends of justice".'[18] He
preferred the time-honoured view of Scott LJ that the words 'oppressive' and 'vexatious' should be understood according to their ordinary
meaning.

The third member of the majority, Gaudron J, drew a distinction between cases where foreign law applied and those where the substantive
rights were governed by the law of the forum. Where local law applied,
the slightly liberalized view of Deane J was acceptable; otherwise the full
orthodoxy of Brennan J should apply.

In the *Oceanic Sun* case jurisdiction had been obtained *ex juris*. The court
drew no particular distinction on the basis by which jurisdiction had been
acquired and utilized rules which, within the United Kingdom before
Spiliada, would have been inappropriate for the decision of proceedings
which were based upon service *ex juris*. The case did not avoid academic
and professional criticism.[19]

1. VOTH v. MANILDRA FLOUR MILLS PTY LTD

As the majority decision in the *Oceanic Sun* did not yield a precise and
authoritative statement of the principles that should be applied in dealing

---

[17] Dean J, *ibid*. 45.   [18] *Ibid*. 38.   [19] See e.g. Pryles (1988) 62 *ALJ* 774.

with an application to stay proceedings, the case was viewed as giving insufficient guidance to inferior courts.[20] It therefore required a definitive decision of the High Court of Australia in order to finalize the rules for stays of proceedings. Those rules were contained in a joint majority opinion in *Voth* v. *Manildra Flour Mills Pty Ltd*.[21] In *Voth* two New South Wales corporations sought to bring proceedings in the Supreme Court of New South Wales against an accountant practising in Kansas City, Missouri, as part of the partnership of Deloite Haskins and Sell. It was alleged that the accountant had failed to advise a United States corporation, part of the plaintiff's group, to deduct tax on interest owed by it to the operating company. As a result of this omission the United States company had to pay withholding tax and a penalty. This resulted in the parent company being deprived of tax losses, and making a decision to distribute dividends which should not have been paid. The plaintiff obtained leave to serve based upon damage suffered within New South Wales. The High Court announced that, within Australia, a stay of proceedings should be granted only when the forum chosen by the plaintiff was clearly inappropriate. The power to stay should be exercised only in a clear case where the continuation would be vexatious and oppressive. It would have to be shown that there was an appropriate foreign tribunal which had jurisdiction and which would exercise it. The factors indicated as relevant by Lord Goff in the *Spiliada* case would be of assistance in determining whether the forum chosen was clearly inappropriate. The court in this case was sensitive to the difference between cases in which jurisdiction had been acquired *ex juris* and those in which it had been acquired within the jurisdiction. The joint judgment stated: 'applications for leave to serve process outside the jurisdiction must be governed by the same principles as apply to applications for a stay on inappropriate forum grounds'.[22] The test of clearly inappropriate forum should apply to both. However, in those cases in which jurisdiction had been acquired through service *ex juris*, the onus would be upon the plaintiff to establish that the chosen jurisdiction was not a clearly inappropriate forum.

The issue of where the burden lies in the forum appropriateness enquiry may well be critical.[23] In the English context the onus was said to depend upon whether the jurisdiction was obtained through exorbitant means. Lord Diplock in *Amin Rasheed*[24] stated that exorbitant jurisdiction is 'one which, under general English conflict rules, an English court would not recognize as possessed by a foreign court in the absence of some treaty

---

[20] See Wilson and Toohey JJ in *Oceanic Sun Line Special Shipping Co* v. *Fay*, n. 15 above, at 25.

[21] *Voth* v. *Manildra Flour Mills Pty Ltd* (1990) 97 ALR 124. The majority judgment was that of Mason CJ, Deane J, Dawson J, and Gaudron J.

[22] *Ibid.* 140, *per* Mason CJ *et al.*   [23] Garner, (1989) 38 *ICLQ* 361 at 367.

[24] *Amin Rasheed Shipping Corp* v. *Kuwait Insurance Co* [1984] AC 50 at 65.

providing for such recognition'. It was later invoked by Lord Goff in the *Spiliada* case, where he stated: 'I myself feel that the word "exorbitant" is, as used in the present context, an old-fashioned word which perhaps carries unfortunate overtones: it means no more than that the exercise of the jurisdiction is extraordinary.'[25]

In the Australian context leave is now rarely required for service *ex juris*. This includes cases in which, on the one hand, the defendant has had a presence in the jurisdiction. Sometimes it may even include a defendant that left for the purpose of avoiding the issue of the writ. On the other hand, there is the non-resident, non-trading defendant that may never have had any presence within the jurisdiction and is amenable only by reason of wide clauses such as 'damage suffered within the jurisdiction by the plaintiff'. The connection with the forum may also be tenuous in instances of good personal service. A classic example is service on a transient whose presence in the jurisdiction is fleeting.

In factual situations, both where service is within the jurisdiction and *ex juris*, where the defendant has had a meaningful presence within the jurisdiction, there is no reason why the burden for seeking the stay should not fall upon that defendant. On the other hand, where the exercise of jurisdiction is exorbitant, in the sense of commanding a defendant with no meaningful contact with the jurisdiction, then properly the plaintiff ought to justify the choice of the tribunal. Unfortunately that distinction may not be clear until an analysis of supporting data clarifies the connection of the intended defendant with the jurisdiction. In any event in Australia the burden falls upon the plaintiff where the service has been *ex juris*. 'In such cases the onus [is] on the plaintiff irrespective of whether the proceedings involved an ex parte application by the plaintiff for leave or a subsequent application by the defendant to set aside service out of the jurisdiction.'[26] The burden remains upon the defendant where jurisdiction has been effected within the jurisdiction.

The situation for the foreseeable future is that, in Australia, the plaintiff-protective test reminiscent of the 1936 rule has been modified to resemble the position achieved in the United Kingdom after the decision in *The Atlantic Star*. One commentator concluded that 'the effect [in Voth] is to shift the balance in favour of plaintiffs suing defendants outside the jurisdiction further than in any other Commonwealth country.'[27]

2. The Factors

The factors to be considered by a court in determining whether to stay a proceeding in Australia are the same as those outlined by Lord Goff of

---

[25] *Spiliada Maritime Corp* v. *Cansulex Ltd*, n. 14 above, at 990.
[26] Pryles, (1991) 65 *ALJ* 442 at 447.   [27] Collins, n. 11 above, at 187.

Chieveley in the *Spiliada* case. These include private interest factors, such as the location or residence of each of the parties, where the cause of action arose, which law will apply, and whether other parties are involved in the proceedings. Further factors outside the individual interests of the litigants, such as the location of the witnesses and of the subject matter itself, may also be relevant in any given case. What of public interest factors? In the United States, it is said that the workload of any given court, the state of its calendar and of the overall administration of justice, and the increased flow of litigation into the courts are taken into account. In the opinion of Deane J, public interest factors should not be taken into account in the application of the Australian doctrine.[28] The use of the 'clearly inappropriate forum' test also avoids the necessity of considering in any detail the appropriateness of an alternative forum. As long as its existence is posited, then it is simply a matter of whether, on the connecting factors listed above, the forum chosen by the plaintiff can be said to be clearly inappropriate or otherwise.

Why did Australia choose to strike out on its own in this matter? Certain conditions in England which may have been relevant in shaping the developments there, such as its membership of the European Union, are inapplicable within Australia. Yet that hardly seems an adequate explanation. The Australian position appears unique in the Commonwealth. Australia has reaffirmed its adherence to the basic principle that a plaintiff's choice of forum ought not to be lightly disturbed. Though modern theories of civil procedure now suggest that equal prominence ought to be given to the views of the plaintiff, the defendant, and the court itself, the Australian position may not be wholly inconsistent with that view. Australian judges have been at some pains to explain that the difference between the doctrine in *Spiliada* and that of Australia will play a role in only a small minority of cases. Only in those cases where it can be said that the Australian forum is appropriate but that there is an even more appropriate forum will the difference between the two standards be outcome-determinative. The Australian position may be said to encourage forum-shopping. But the doctrine is likely to be applied with respect for the courts and legal systems in other countries and an adherence to the principles of international comity.[29] The Australian doctrine is intended to minimize the necessity of evaluating the quality of justice in the competing forum, or engaging in a complex comparative law exercise.

3. The Search for the Appropriate Court within Australia

The rules for declining to exercise jurisdiction in civil and commercial matters within Australia, that is, in matters involving competing jurisdic-

---

[28] *Oceanic Sun Line Special Shipping Co Inc* v. *Fay*, n. 15 above, at 50.
[29] See Garner (1989) 38 *ICLQ* 361.

tion between the courts of different States within the federal system or between the Federal Court, the Family Court, and the State Supreme Courts, have been radically altered by the cross-vesting scheme introduced in 1987. Service outside the jurisdiction, but within Australia, may be arranged pursuant to the Jurisdiction of Courts (Cross-Vesting) Act 1987 or through the Service and Execution of Process Act 1992 (Cth.). In superior State courts, as well as in the Federals Court or the Family Court, if a proceeding is instituted in a court that is not the appropriate court the cross-vesting system provides a transfer to the appropriate court.[30] The court of issue will, upon the motion of any party or upon its own motion, decide whether it is appropriate that the case remain within the issuing court or whether it should be transferred to another, more appropriate, court. The principal grounds upon which the court makes a decision to transfer include *lis alibi pendens*[31] and whether it is in the interests of justice that the issuing court transfer the relevant proceeding to another court.[32]

The issue of when a transfer is in the 'interests of justice' has been the topic of much litigation and debate within Australia. There is no definitive view of the appropriate test for determining the 'interests of justice'. This is due, in great part, to section 13 of the Cross-Vesting Act, which provides that an appeal does not lie from a decision of a court in relation to the transfer of a proceeding. The debate has centred upon whether the rules of private international law with regard to stays of proceedings are relevant to this area. The views advanced in the reported cases may be divided into three broad groupings: what may be called the broad view, the narrow view, and the 'case-by-case view'. The broad view was first developed by the New South Wales Court of Appeal in the case of *Bankinvest AG v. Seabrook*.[33] In the leading judgment Rogers AJA held that the goal stated by Lord Goff in the *Spiliada* case was the same as that sought by the legislation, that is, the interests of justice. In his opinion, the correct test to apply in deciding whether to transfer a proceeding was to determine which of the two courts was the more appropriate. The factors discussed

---

[30] Preamble, pt. (c), Jurisdiction of Courts (Cross-Vesting) Act 1987 (Cth.).

[31] To be discussed below, pp. 90–2.

[32] There is a third ground which is considerably less used. That is, pursuant to subsection 5(1)(b)(ii): '(A) whether, in the opinion of the first court, apart from this Act and any law of a State relating to cross-vesting of jurisdiction and apart from any accrued jurisdiction of the Federal Court or the Family Court, the relevant proceeding or a substantial part of the relevant proceeding would have been incapable of being instituted in the first court and capable of being instituted in the Federal Court or the Family Court; (B) the extent to which, in the opinion of the first court, the matters for determination in the relevant proceeding are matters arising under or involving questions as to the application, interpretation or validity of a law of the Commonwealth and not within the jurisdiction of the first court apart from this Act and any law of a State relating to cross-vesting of jurisdiction; and (C) the interests of justice.'

[33] (1988) 14 NSWLR 711.

within the *Spiliada* case were the same factors which would be relevant in the determination of that question. He further pointed out that, since the court may, of its own motion, examine the question of a transfer regardless of the desires of the parties, it would be inappropriate to impose an onus upon either of the parties. Street CJ, in the same case, indicated that the decision whether to transfer or to retain the case ought to be a matter of administration rather than of profound judicial contemplation.[34] The *Bankinvest* decision is binding upon the judges within New South Wales and provides guidance for judges in the other States and Territories.

A second view, designate the 'narrow view', was developed within the Australian Capital Territory by Kelly J in *Waterhouse* v. *Australian Broadcasting Corporation*[35] and followed by judges in Western Australia. In the opinion of those that adhere to this view the Australian rules of stays of proceedings developed in the international context are relevant in determining whether or not to transfer within the internal scheme. The clearly inappropriate forum test developed by the High Court of Australia in the *Voth* case applies. The judges following this view believe that the burden falls upon the defendant who is seeking a transfer to show that the forum chosen by the plaintiff is a clearly inappropriate forum. This view gives credence to the proposition that the lawful choice of forum by the plaintiff ought not lightly to be disturbed.

The third view, the case-by-case approach, was developed by Nicholson CJ of the Family Court of Australia in *Re Chapman and Jansen*.[36] He stated 'In my view, the expression "the interests of justice" is not one which should be narrowly defined and indeed it may not be particularly helpful to attempt to define it at all . . . The interests of justice will vary from case to case, and I think that, in general, in considering applications under this legislation, a broad approach is the approach to be preferred.'[37]

All judges are more or less agreed that the ones from the *Spiliada* case are the relevant factors to consider. These include the usual private litigation factors. But in this area of law, unlike the international arena, the public interest factors such as the state of the court calendar, delays in justice, speed of hearing, and the like are taken into account more often. In late October 1993, the Special Committee of Solicitors-General confirmed that *Bankinvest* represents the original intention of the drafters of the scheme. The Solicitors-General's report recommends a clarifying amendment to 'make it clear that there is no onus on an applicant for a transfer, and that what is required is a dispassionate inquiry to determine what is appropriate in the interests of justice'.[38]

---

[34] *Ibid.* 714.   [35] (1989) 86 ACTR 1.
[36] (1990) 13 Fam. LR 853.   [37] *Ibid.* 861.
[38] Special Committee of Solicitors-General, *Report to SCAG* on AIJA Review of Cross-Vesting of Jurisdiction (19 Oct. 1993), para. 12.

III
LIS ALIBI PENDENS

1. INTERNATIONAL

Within Australia there is a discretionary power to stay or dismiss proceedings in case of *lis alibi pendens*. *Lis pendens* is not regarded as a discrete area of law, but rather as a particular application of the Australian form of the doctrine *forum non conveniens*. There has been no High Court of Australia decision on *lis alibi pendens* since the *Oceanic Sun* and *Voth* cases were decided. Prior to those cases, the Australian courts exercised their discretion in accordance with the rationale underlying the decision in *The Abidin Daver*.[39] 'Certainly Australian cases decided before the High Court decision in *Oceanic Sun* applied a more liberal *forum non conveniens* test to determine whether a foreign pending action, taken together with other circumstances of the case, justified a stay of proceedings.'[40]

The true situation of *lis alibi pendens*, where the parties, the cause of action, and the relief requested are identical, is one in which the need to stay one of the proceedings, in order to avoid the risk of conflicting judgments and unnecessary duplication of costs and inconvenience, manifests itself clearly. More often presented is the situation of related proceedings in which there is some or a substantial overlap of facts and law, but not identical parties, causes of action, or remedies. As one leading text has stated: 'It is clear that the diverse situations which can be presented make it unwise to apply the test for staying actions in a rigid way ... In cases where there is a foreign action already pending, then there is an additional factor that the court should be slow to permit a multiplicity of proceedings.'[41]

Judges no longer have to choose between immediately exercising jurisdiction or, instead, staying proceedings indefinitely. This area has witnessed considerable judicial creativity. One method of avoiding the risk of conflicting decision or multiplicity is by granting a motion for a

---

[39] N. 14 above.

[40] Sykes and Pryles, *Australian Private International Law* (3rd edn., 1991), at 91, citing *Muller* v. *Fencott* (1991) 37 ALR 310 (Fed. Ct.) and *In the Marriage of Takach* (1980) 47 FLR 441.

[41] Sykes and Pryles, n. 40 above, at 95. The additional factor of the multiplicity of actions is not decisive in and of itself. E.g. contrast the decision in *Coloundra Boat Yard Pty Ltd* v. *The Ship Almonta* [1968] SASR 325, where a stay of proceedings was ordered, with *Clutha Developments Pty Ltd* v. *Marion Power Shovel Co Inc* [1973] 2 NSWLR 173, where a stay of proceedings was refused. In *Sentry Corp* v. *Peat Marwick Mitchell & Co* (1990) 95 ALR 11 at 36, Lockhart J stated: 'If, however, the defendant is able to establish that he is "doubly vexed" ... or that it is oppressive, vexatious or an abuse of process for the action to continue ... the Court may stay the Australian proceeding.'

temporary stay or lengthy adjournment of a case. For example, Rogers J in *Entrad Ltd*[42] was faced with a dispute in which proceedings had been commenced first in California by three plaintiffs against Arthur Anderson & Co, a United States accounting firm, and then later in November 1985 by four additional Australian plaintiffs joining with the United States plaintiffs in a proceeding against the New South Wales partnership of Arthur Anderson in the New South Wales Supreme Court. Rogers J granted a non-permanent stay of proceedings in the New South Wales court in order to monitor the progress of the proceedings in the California court. Lockhart J granted a similar order in *Sterling Pharmaceuticals Pty Ltd* v. *The Boots Co (Australia) Pty Ltd*[43] where a parallel proceeding was pending in New Zealand. He pointed out that there is a 'substantial difference between a motion for a permanent stay or dismissal of a proceeding and a motion for a temporary stay or lengthy adjournment of a case'.[44] In the latter category of order, the rules in the *Voth* case have no application.

Gummow J in the Federal Court granted an order 'that the motion itself, together with the proceeding, be stood over until later this year, the expectation being that the award in arbitration will by then have been handed down'.[45]

2. INTRA-AUSTRALIA

The issue of related proceedings pending in two different courts is handled within the States and Territories of Australia through the cross-vesting scheme. Subsection (5)(1)(b) provides that, where a proceeding is pending in the Supreme Court of a State or Territory and it appears to that court that the relevant proceeding arises out of, or is related to, another proceeding pending in the Federal Court or the Family Court and it is more appropriate that the relevant proceeding be determined by the Federal Court or the Family Court, the first court shall transfer it to the Federal Court or the Family Court, as the case may be.[46] The same rules, with necessary modification, apply where the proceedings are pending in any superior State or Territory court or the Federal Court. The cross-vesting scheme has, by section 5, provided a legislative solution not only for *lis pendens*, properly so-called, but also for cases which are

[42] *Entrad Ltd* v. *Blaikie* (unreported, SC NSW 24 Dec. 1985), Rogers J.
[43] (1992) 34 FCR 287.   [44] *Ibid.* 294.
[45] *D. A. Technology Pty Ltd* v. *Discreet Logic Inc* (unreported, Fed Ct. of Australia, 10 Mar. 1994), Gummow J, at 21.
[46] Jurisdiction of Courts (Cross-Vesting) Act 1987 (Cth.), s. 5(1)(b).

related, even if they lack identical parties, causes of action, or remedies. The grounds for transfer or non-transfer embrace the *Spiliada* doctrine rather than the High Court's 'clearly inappropriate forum' test.

The cases interpreting the subsection have been principally concerned with the meaning of 'arises out of, or is related to'. The view has been expressed that the phrase 'arises out of' imports a 'causal relationship', whereas 'related' involves some sort of nexus or association.[47] In order to invoke the section there merely has to be some relationship between the two pending proceedings. For example, in *Perpetual Holdings Pty Ltd*[48] O'Loughlin J had to decide whether a proceeding pending in the Supreme Court of South Australia and another in the Federal Court were within the ambit of the subsection. In the proceedings in the Supreme Court of South Australia, Leviathan, as plaintiff, brought the proceedings alleging misrepresentation, negligence, and misleading or deceptive conduct under the Trade Practice Act 1974. In the Federal Court, the defendant in the Supreme Court was the plaintiff and was bringing its proceedings against Leviathan, the plaintiff in the South Australian Supreme Court, as well as two other defendants, D'Allesandro and Newmark, concerning the causes of action alleged in the South Australian case as well as breaches of contract and the Fair Trading Act. The court held that those two were sufficiently related to fit within the ambit of the subsection.

The decision whether or not to transfer, pursuant to the cross-vesting scheme, is to be taken by whichever court first receives an application pursuant to section 5. That application may be made by the parties to the proceedings or by the court of its own motion. As in all cases of whether to transfer or not, the decision is not appealable pursuant to section 13 of the Act. Under the Act any transfer involves the complete transmission of the file from the transferor court to the transferee court, saving all steps that have been performed up until the time of transfer. No stays of proceedings are any longer available in the intra-State Australian context, other than where an inferior court of a particular State is the court of issue and it is decided to stay its proceedings and allow the parties to commence in a more appropriate court.[49]

---

[47] *Per* Beaumont J in *Re Hamilton-Irvine and the Companies Act 1985* (1990) 94 ALR 428.

[48] *Perpetual Holdings Pty Ltd* v. *Leviathan Pty Ltd* (1991) 30 FCR 524.

[49] Service and Execution of Process Act 1992 (Cth.), s. 20 provides that the person served may apply to the (inferior) court of issue for an order staying the proceeding. Subs. (4) states that the issuing court is to determine whether the court of another State is the appropriate court for the proceeding. Factors are listed which include the usual *Spiliada* considerations. The s. concludes by stating that the fact that the proceeding was commenced in the place of issue is not a factor to be considered in the court's determination.

IV
FOREIGN CHOICE OF
JURISDICTION CLAUSES

In Australia there is a discretionary power to stay or dismiss proceedings in cases involving a foreign choice of jurisdiction clause. In the absence of a definitive High Court of Australia decision on the considerations and grounds for staying proceedings, the English decisions of *The El Amria*[50] and *The Eleftheria*[51] provide the guidelines for stays in this area. There has been a relatively consistent approach in this area dating back to at least 1966[52] where it was said that the courts will approach an application for a stay based upon a foreign jurisdiction clause 'with a strong bias in favour of maintaining the special bargain and holding the parties to their contract'.[53] Kirby P in the *Oceanic Sun* case at the New South Wales Court of Appeal affirmed 'courts of this and like countries will normally hold parties to any such agreement which they enter'[54] and, at the High Court level, Brennan J in the same case stated: 'Where the parties to a contract agree that the courts of a foreign country shall have exclusive jurisdiction to decide disputes arising under the contract . . . the courts of this country . . . will, in the absence of countervailing reasons, stay proceedings brought here to decide those disputes'.[55] In the latest decision available, Beazley J in the Federal Court, in a closely reasoned judgment, stated: 'The position, therefore, is that there is no decision binding on me as to the appropriate test to apply in the case where there is a foreign jurisdiction clause. There are longstanding and persuasive authorities that the proper test is that, prima facie, effect is to be given to a foreign jurisdiction clause'.[56] The plaintiff then must adduce evidence of special circumstances that overcome the general rule.[57] The burden is even heavier when the foreign jurisdiction clause is an exclusive one.

Australian courts cannot give effect to clauses purporting to oust their jurisdiction in certain circumstances. For example, subsection 11(2)(b) of the Carriage of Goods by Sea Act 1991 (Cth.) provides (in part): 'An agreement (whether made in Australia or elsewhere) has no effect so far as it purports to: (b) preclude or limit the jurisdiction of a court of the

---

[50] *Aratra Potato Co Ltd v. Egyptian Navigation Co (The El Amria)* [1981] 2 Lloyd's Rep. 119.
[51] *The Eleftheria; Owners of Cargo Lately Laden on Board Ship or Vessel Eleftheria v. The Eleftheria (Owners)* [1969] 2 All ER 641.
[52] *Lewis Construction Co Pty Ltd v. M. Tichaeur Société Anonyme* [1966] VR 341.
[53] *Ibid.* 347, per Hudson J.
[54] *Oceanic Sunline Special Shipping Co Inc v. Fay* (1987) 8 NSWLR 242 at 257.
[55] *Oceanic Sun Line Special Shipping Co Inc v. Fay*, n. 15 above, at 28, relying upon the dictum in *Huddart Parker Ltd v. The Ship Mill Hill* (1950) 81 CLR 502 at 508.
[56] *Leigh-Mardon Pty Ltd v. PRC Inc* (1993) 44 FCR 88 at 99.
[57] E.g. *Alfred v. Australian Building Industries Pty Ltd* (1987) 48 NTR 59.

Declining Jurisdiction

Commonwealth or of a State or Territory in respect of a bill of lading or of a document.'

V
ARBITRATION AGREEMENTS

1. INTERNATIONAL

The courts in Australia have an obligation to stay court proceedings in cases where the parties have agreed to arbitration. Pursuant to subsection 7(1) of the International Arbitration Act 1974 (Cth.), where, pursuant to an express term of an agreement or law of a Convention country, there is an agreement to submit to arbitration and the proceedings involve a matter capable of settlement by arbitration, the court shall, upon such conditions as it thinks fit, stay the proceedings and refer the parties to arbitration.[58] Australia is a Contracting State to the New York Convention.

In addition to this statutory basis, more modern authority within Australia inclines to the view that the court has an inherent power to stay proceedings on account of an arbitration agreement. That proposition was considered, though no final decision was taken, in *Commonwealth* v. *Adelaide Steamship Industries Pty Ltd*.[59] This inherent power, if it exists, would be especially important for oral submissions as the statutory provisions apply only to written agreements.

2. DOMESTIC

The States and Territories of Australia agreed to pass mirror legislation resulting in, for example, the passage of the Commercial Arbitration Act 1984 (Vic.). Since that time minor differences have crept into the legislation of the various States and Territories. It is typical of all States, however, that, if a party brings proceedings in court in respect of a matter subject to arbitration, the other party may apply to stay and that court, 'if satisfied (a) that there is no sufficient reason why the matter should not be referred to arbitration in accordance with the agreement; and (b) that the applicant was at the time when the proceedings were commenced and still remains ready and willing to do all things necessary for the proper conduct of the arbitration—the court may make an order staying the proceedings and may further give such directions with respect to the future conduct of the arbitration as it thinks fit.'[60]

---

[58] International Arbitration Act 1974 (Cth.), s. 7(1) and (2).
[59] (1974) 24 FLR 97.   [60] E.g. Commercial Arbitration Act 1984 (Vic.), s. 53.

While the power to stay is expressed in mandatory terms when the agreement is international, and discretionary when the agreement is domestic, in almost all circumstances where the conditions are met, the court will grant the stay of proceedings. The litigation involving these sections has usually raised issues of whether there is a contract, whether the clause applies to the particular dispute, and whether the agreement to arbitrate was waived.[61] An additional ground of contention for the application of the legislation is whether Australian rules or the rules of another nation apply. The choice of law rules may refer to the law of another country. 'It is now established that an arbitration agreement is a separate contract distinct from the substantive agreement in which it is usually imbedded.'[62]

VI
RESTRAINING FOREIGN PROCEEDINGS

1. INTERNATIONAL

In Australia there is a discretionary power to restrain foreign proceedings by means of an injunction.

The courts of Australia have followed the views of the Privy Council in the *Lee Kui Jak* case.[63] The Australian courts view the granting of an injunction to restrain proceedings abroad as highly intrusive. The person seeking the injunction bears the burden of showing the court that allowing the opponent to proceed abroad would be vexatious and oppressive with regard to the person seeking the injunction. 'Account must be taken not only of the injustice to the defendant if the plaintiff is allowed to pursue the foreign proceedings, but also of injustice to the plaintiff if he is not allowed to do so.'[64] '[A]s a general rule, the court will not grant an injunction if by doing so, it will deprive the plaintiff of advantages in the foreign forum of which it would be unjust to deprive him.'[65]

The object of the injunction is to allow the court to protect its own process and proceedings. A recent Australian example is provided in *Re Siromath (No 3)*[66] in the New South Wales Supreme Court, Equity Division. The applicant asked that a Pennsylvania resident, physically present in New South Wales, be restrained from prosecuting proceedings commenced by it in Pennsylvania. The court, *per* McLelland J, held that:

---

[61] See e.g. *QBE Insurance Ltd* v. *Mercantile Insurance Co Ltd* (unreported, SC NSW, 15 Aug. 1986), Rogers J.

[62] Pryles (1990) 64 *ALJ* 470.

[63] *Société Nationale Industrielle Aérospatiale* v. *Lee Kui Jak* [1987] AC 871.

[64] *Ibid.* 896.   [65] Williams, *Civil Procedure Victoria* (vol. 1), at 3432.

[66] *Re Siromath Pty Ltd (No. 3)* (1991) 25 NSWLR 25.

'In civil matters . . . this Court has jurisdiction over a defendant if he is effectively served with the court's process'.[67] The court derived its jurisdiction through service outside Australia of a Notice of Motion. The validity of the service was then confirmed by the court. The power to enjoin a party from prosecuting proceedings in a foreign court, where sufficient cause is shown, is clearly recognized in major common law jurisdictions. In *Siromath* the court posed this issue: 'The question is whether the applicant for such an injunction has an equity sufficient to justify the court preventing the enjoined party from exercising its legal right to institute or continue proceedings in the foreign court.'[68] In the particular matter before it the court held that the effect of the joinder of the New South Wales liquidators in the proceedings in Pennsylvania appeared to be intimidatory and oppressive. The court, as is usual in these matters, mentioned that the power to enjoin prosecution of proceedings should be exercised with great caution.

2. INTER-STATE

The decision where to litigate within Australia, in Superior Courts, is reached through the operation of the cross-vesting scheme. An application is made for transfer. The power to grant an injunction to restrain proceedings where there are concurrent proceedings in the Supreme Courts of two of the States is recognized but 'it should be exercised with great caution and it is hoped that the occasion for its exercise will not arise'.[69]

VII
CONCLUSION

Australia has witnessed a major change in the philosophy of jurisdiction and the use of its courts in the past twenty years. Previously, the State provided the forum and left decisions to party initiative after that. The plaintiff chose the forum and, with rare exceptions, if valid jurisdiction could be established, that choice was final. In the last two decades there has been a recognition that the State itself has an interest in determining who has access to its tribunals. It has been further recognized that a defendant should be accorded some say as to which court is appropriate to hear the proceedings. Another major development has been the increasing recognition that the component States of Australia form part of a

---

[67] *Re Siromath Pty Ltd (No. 3)* (1991) 28.   [68] *Ibid.* 29.
[69] Rogers AJA in dictum, *Beecham (Australia) Pty Ltd* v. *Roque Pty Ltd* (1987) 11 NSWLR 1 at 6.

nation and ought not to regard each other's courts as foreign courts. Finally, the means to acquire jurisdiction over persons outside Australia have been broadened.

All these developments have meant that the rules for declining to exercise jurisdiction now operate in a very different procedural setting. In Australia, courts have been slower to give up the plaintiff preference rules than elsewhere in the common law world, at least with regard to *forum non conveniens* cases. With intra-Australian proceedings, the rules now favour allowing the most appropriate court to exercise jurisdiction, with the plaintiff, the defendant, and the court itself all able to advance submissions. Three important developments—the cross-vesting scheme, the Service and Execution of Process Act 1992, and the *Voth* case—have had a profound impact upon these rules in the last seven years. In some ways, they fit together uneasily and reflect diverse philosophies. The final chapter in the rules for declining to exercise jurisdiction in Australia has not yet been written.

4

Belgium

MARC FALLON

Professor, Faculté de Droit, Université catholique de Louvain

CONTENTS

I
INTRODUCTION

This chapter aims to determine whether the so-called doctrine of *forum non conveniens*, as applied in certain countries following the common law tradition, is to be found in Belgian private international law. In practical terms, this technique allows a judge to dismiss an action when it is considered more appropriate that a judge from another State should hear the case. One notes that the theory has an essentially negative effect, since it seeks to isolate the cases where the national court is 'not convenient'[1]

---

[1] A French term could be *For inapproprié*. On this issue, see e.g. Fallon, [1988] *Rev Trim. Dr. Fam.* 125–8; Gaudemet-Tallon, [1991] *Rev. Crit. Dr. Int. Pr.* 491–524.

rather than to specify the cases where this court can be considered as 'convenient'. It implies also the fulfilment of two conditions: the national judge declines jurisdiction only if the jurisdiction of the court of another State is established; the court seised would normally have jurisdiction according to the *lex fori*, subject to the possibility of a foreign court having jurisdiction under foreign law.

As such, the doctrine of *forum non conveniens* seems to imply a number of factors in favour of its development. On the one hand, it calls for a certain discretion on the part of the judge with regard to his own competence. On the other hand, it presupposes that there is a silence in the international context, which is characterized by the absence of common rules regarding the division of State competence. It thereby simultaneously aims at a fair practical objective in protecting the litigant from the consequences of the excessive rigidity of divergent national solutions, and in realizing a theoretical presupposition according to which a rule, whereby jurisdiction can be designated to a State, must fulfil such a principle of division, implicitly formulated. The judge seised will therefore be called upon to compensate for the inadequacies of the supreme legislature (as expressed through a treaty) and sometimes has to be an idealist.

Doubtless, a treaty including rules on international jurisdiction is supposed to aim at an appropriate distribution of international jurisdiction. Normally, it then becomes pointless—unless the treaty provides differently—to add to the fixed rules a corrective mechanism of a *forum non conveniens* discretion. If such a mechanism were to be considered as still available when a treaty exists, it would then be a kind of 'escape clause', i.e. a directing principle from which the conventional rules would be derived and which would prevail in case of discrepancies with such principle.[2] Today, this problem is well known in the conflict of laws field and it is not absolutely certain that, for the application of a treaty which expresses a fundamental connecting factor—such as the principle of proximity[3]—by way of fixed rules, the court of the forum could, if it seems convenient, invoke an escape clause not included in the treaty.

At first sight, Belgian law is unable to admit the doctrine of *forum non conveniens* since it lacks the above-mentioned features, subject to the application of a treaty. Indeed, the legislature has fixed international jurisdiction into a rather stiff corpus of rules without any apparent intention of coping with the problem of the possible concurrent jurisdiction of a foreign court. After a closer analysis, however, it seems that Belgian law contains a series of revealing indications of the concept underlying the doctrine of *forum non conveniens*.

---

[2] On the escape clause, see e.g. Mosconi, [1989] V *Hague Recueil* 9–214.
[3] As defined by Lagarde, [1986] III *Hague Recueil* 9–238.

II
INTERNATIONAL JURISDICTION IN GENERAL

A distinction must be drawn between two hypotheses, depending on whether or not the case is contentious.

1. CONTENTIOUS ISSUES

Since the second half of the nineteenth century, Belgian legislators have created proper rules on international jurisdiction, in addition to those related to internal territorial jurisdiction. This has a double effect. On the one hand, the determination of international jurisdiction is based on a set of written rules. On the other hand, the content of these rules is specially adapted to the problems of international jurisdiction. It is worth noting that this method does not normally allow for transposing an internal jurisdiction rule into an international one. As will be seen, this has nevertheless been done for certain matters.

(a) GENERAL PRESENTATION OF THE INTERNATIONAL JURISDICTION RULES

Subject to international jurisdiction rules perhaps provided for in special acts or in treaties ratified by Belgium, the general rules are set out in Articles 635, 636, and 638 of the *Code judiciaire*. Furthermore, Article 15 of the *Code civil* allows, in a manner similar to the corresponding provision of the French *Code civil*, a Belgian to be sued before the Belgian courts. These rules are clearly different from those determining the internal jurisdiction in Articles 624 to 634 of the *Code judiciaire*.

The list in Articles 635, 636, and 638 is exhaustive. Furthermore, it contains rules of an alternative nature. This means that Belgian courts are enabled to exercise jurisdiction if, and only if, the case fits within one of the criteria set out in the list laid down by the legislature.

This list sets out three types of provision. The first is a general one: it allows a plaintiff to proceed in Belgium if the defendant is domiciled or resides in Belgium (Article 635, 2°). A second set of provisions allows a plaintiff to proceed in Belgium according to a territorial factor which varies from one type of case to another, such as the place of creation or the place of performance of an obligation (Article 635, 3°), or the place where an immovable is located (Article 635, 1°). Such list is similar in nature to the provisions of Article 5 of the Brussels Convention. A third provision is subsidiary. When jurisdiction cannot be based on any of the above-mentioned rules, the plaintiff can bring an action in Belgium if he has a domicile or a residence in that country (Article 638). However, the defendant is allowed to reject this jurisdiction subject to certain conditions detailed below (Article 636).

As will be seen, according to their nature these rules have different aims, although they are all based on the common principle of the jurisdictional protection of the foreign defendant.

The special provisions in the second category tend to determine the most appropriate court according to the cause of action, following the example of Article 5 of the Brussels Convention. It is worth noticing the absence of any excessively wide basis of jurisdiction, such as the location of seizable goods.

This assessment should probably be clarified with regard to the criterion of the place of the immovable 'en matière immobilière' (in cases concerned with immovables). The merits of the rule are certainly beyond question. Thus, Article 16 of the Brussels Convention even gives to it the status of a rule of exclusive jurisdiction. All the same, the Belgian rule, taken in combination with the universality principle, apparently allows actions to be brought in Belgium regarding assets, the majority of which are mainly situated abroad. This is often the case in matters of succession. Is the Belgian judge, then, the most appropriate one to deal with the whole of the assets? The doctrine of *forum non conveniens* would allow a more flexible approach to the legal rule, according to the circumstances.

One could also wonder whether a foreign court would be inappropriate, according to Belgian law, to adjudicate upon an immovable located in Belgium, or if a Belgian court would be inappropriate to adjudicate upon an immovable located outside the country. It is uncertain whether the answer would be positive. Indeed, the above-mentioned rules do not create any exclusive jurisdiction in favour of the Belgian courts. Their presence in a list of alternatives confirms that, in the case of immovables abroad, a Belgian court could not possibly declare itself as inappropriate since, as an example, the defendant could be domiciled in Belgium. In fact, it is for the plaintiff—or at least his counsel—to assess which is the most appropriate forum, taking into account all the factual circumstances, such as the risk that the eventual Belgian decision may not be recognized in the foreign State where the immovable is located, on grounds that, as far as the foreign law is concerned, the courts of that country enjoy exclusive competence.

Belgian private international law also recognizes special rules of exclusive international competence. This is rather unusual, at least if one accepts that there is no automatic transposition of an internal rule of competence into an international rule of competence of the same nature.[4] It can be

---

[4] The same question is asked in related matters: see Rigaux and Fallon, *Droit international privé*, vol. II (Brussels, 1993), no. 1076.

found in bankruptcy cases where the internal jurisdictional rule of Article 631 of the *Code judiciaire* has been transposed into an international jurisdictional rule, not only because of its exclusive character but also because the choice of law rule has been brought into line with the jurisdictional rule. Indeed, the factor of the establishment of the bankrupt is used to determine international jurisdiction as well as the law to be applied to the case.[5] The exclusive character of such jurisdiction implies that, when the appropriate factor is not located on Belgian territory, the Belgian court shall declare *ex officio* that there is no jurisdiction, without any discretionary power.

This reluctance necessarily to transpose every exclusive jurisdiction rule into an international one can be based on a consideration in favour of the most appropriate forum. Indeed, while the attribution of an exclusive jurisdiction is understandable when it involves a distribution of jurisdiction between courts of the same legal system, this method presents far more risks in international matters, except when it happens by means of a treaty. Indeed, in the absence of any common rule on jurisdiction, the rigidity of assigning exclusive jurisdiction could raise negative conflicts and, thus, a denial of justice.

The general provisions of the first and third categories—forum of the defendant's domicile and forum of the claimant's domicile—are based on two aims which appear to be inconsistent but are in fact inspired by a common principle.

The defendant's forum, included in Article 635 of the *Code judiciaire* among other factors without any apparent priority, must naturally be linked to the principle included, for example, in Article 2 of the Brussels Convention. The choice of this forum perhaps does not correspond to the most appropriate forum given the nature of the case, but it rests on a principle of protection: it is in the country of his own domicile that the defendant must expect to be sued and where he enjoys the best conditions for his defence. In fact, the system of fixed rules laid down by the legislature rests as a whole on such a principle of protection. Initially, the legislature was preoccupied with strictly defining the different means by which a defendant of foreign nationality could be summoned before a Belgian court.[6] In other words, it must be considered fair to bring an action in Belgium under one of the heads set out in the legal text and thus inequitable to bring an action without the consent of the defendant in a case not provided for in the text. It is significant, for example, that the legislature only admits factors of a territorial nature against a foreign defendant. Indeed, since 1948, it has repealed the factor of the nationality of the claimant stipulated by the former Article 14 of the *Code civil*, a

---

[5] See Rigaux and Fallon, n. 4 above, nos. 1254 ff.
[6] For more details concerning this theory, see Fallon, [1986] JT 245–51.

factor more generally termed as exorbitant by Article 3 of the Brussels Convention.

It is equally significant to notice that the criterion of the plaintiff's domicile or residence, established by Article 638 of the *Code judiciaire*, is accompanied by a limitation in favour of the defendant. This is to say that, in principle, he cannot be sued in Belgium by virtue of this criterion without his consent. Moreover, the legislature assumes that non-appearance means he contests jurisdiction. This right to decline is, however, limited. It exists only if, reciprocally, the Belgian party hypothetically sued abroad would enjoy a similar right according to the foreign law. This mechanism, the enforcement of which is extremely complicated, seems to be original. It aims to lead to dismissal of the action when bringing the action in the forum State seems unfair to the foreign defendant, but this right to decline does not depend on the more appropriate character of a foreign court. The control by the court of the forum is purely formal, being based on the existence of a reciprocal condition set out in the law of the defendant's origin.

This concern of the Belgian legislature for a foreign defendant does not apply to nationals. Indeed, we have seen that, according to Article 15 of the *Code civil*, a Belgian may always be sued in Belgium. Thus, the court does not have to determine whether bringing an action in Belgium is or is not fair to the defendant. This rule arises from a sovereignty principle and reveals the special link between the sovereign and his subjects.

However, the existence of an exhaustive list of rules laid down by the legislature has not prevented Belgian case law from creating a *forum conveniens* when it would be unfair to oblige the individual to bring an action in a foreign country. Acting as a forum of necessity, this mechanism has been used in favour of Belgian plaintiffs in family law cases. In some ways it has the same effect as a rehabilitation of Article 14 of the *Code civil*, abolished by the legislature. The reasoning is linked to the choice of law rule. Indeed, it seems inconsistent to impede the individual from applying to his 'natural' judge, at least when this judge would apply Belgian law to the case.[7]

Hitherto, this solution prevailed in the field of divorce.[8] Indeed, the Belgian legislature has enacted a special choice-of-law rule of an exclusively unilateral character. This rule aims at applying Belgian law whenever a party to the case has Belgian nationality (Article 2 of the Act of 27 June 1960).

One could equally ask oneself if a forum of necessity ought not to be allowed each time an applicant raises the effects of a right which is valid

---

[7] Rigaux, *Droit international privé*, vol. II (Brussels, 1979), no. 784.

[8] Brussels, 22 May 1985, [1986] JT 251, note Fallon; 2 June 1987, [1988] *Rev. Trim. Dr. Fam.* 115, note Fallon.

by the private international law rules of the forum, but not by the law of the country which, at the time of litigation, would have jurisdiction because of the relevant connecting factors. This certainly somewhat hypothetical case can be relevant in the context of so-called limping family relations. As an example, Moroccans concluded a civil marriage in Belgium at the time they were residing in that country, in accordance with the rules of Belgian private international law, but their marriage is void according to Moroccan private international law. If one of the spouses asks for maintenance in Belgium but none of the connecting factors laid down on which to base jurisdiction exists, it is impossible to imagine how the Belgian court could refuse to hear the case. The same question could be asked about an action relating to maintenance after a divorce between an Irish couple in Belgium.

Finally, a forum of necessity could be allowed when the Belgian choice of law rule designates Belgian law as to the substance and the Belgian courts do not have jurisdiction by virtue of the set of rules on international jurisdiction, while the corresponding rule of internal jurisdiction designates, for internal cases, in an exclusive way a court following a connecting factor located on the territory. Such rule would then be transposed into one on international jurisdiction but without its exclusive character which would be contrary to the needs of international jurisdiction as set out above. Thus, in internal cases a claim relating to parenthood has to be made to the court of the residence of the child, which has exclusive jurisdiction by virtue of Article 331 of the *Code civil*. If the plaintiff is a Belgian child residing in Belgium and the defendant is a foreigner domiciled abroad, it seems appropriate to allow the jurisdiction of the Belgian court, which will apply Belgian law to the substance following Article 3 of the *Code civil*, while Article 15 of the *Code civil* and Articles 635 to 638 of the *Code judiciaire* would normally imply a denial of international jurisdiction in that case.

(b) THE POWER OF BELGIAN COURTS TO GRANT AN INJUNCTION

The civil courts are more and more often asked to order or to enjoin certain acts by an individual and to attach a fine to this should he not comply. In Belgian law, this hypothesis is confirmed by the progressive recognition of the *action en cessation* (a periodic payment by way of penalty). Other more traditional types of intervention of the civil courts can be compared with this new type of action, such as the making of provisional or protective measures or, in a rather different way, an order for attachment.

This chapter, focused as it is on the discretionary power left to the court as to its own jurisdiction with regard to the concurrent jurisdiction of a foreign court, is unable to deal with all the problems relating to such measures. It is sufficient to mention here the very axiomatic doctrinal assumption of absolute territoriality which is largely admitted and the doubts one may express about it, expecially in relation to the evolution of case law.[9]

One of the things that the territoriality principle implies is precisely the possibility of having recourse to the doctrine of *forum non conveniens*. It is, moreover, on the basis of a consideration of this kind that the criterion of the place where property is situated has surfaced in certain judicial systems, such as France, at a time when the idea prevailed that national courts had no jurisdiction over foreign defendants. The recourse to this territorial criterion appeared to be a broadening of the jurisdiction, which practice had come to require.[10] This forum was therefore considered appropriate. Today it must be admitted that the recourse to the territorial criterion does not flow from any precise requirement of public international law—at least to the extent that the judge seised will not purport immediately to order restraining measures on goods or persons situated abroad without the intervention of the competent local authorities— and that it may therefore be complemented by other jurisdictional criteria, for example those which allow the judge to rule on the substance of the litigation. From this perspective, it would seem judicious to limit such a power of intervention where it may have an extraterritorial effect, by giving the judge a discretionary power as to the appropriateness of his intervention, for instance, for the designation of an expert or the hearing of a witness. In the case of summary procedure for example, as in the so-called *référé* in Belgian law, the emergency condition can be used to this end; and in its decision, the court will normally keep in mind the necessity to submit the possible measure to an enforcement procedure abroad in order to ensure that it has all the effectiveness required abroad. The requirement of such a formality may, according to the circumstances of the case, lead to the following question: is it not preferable that the measure being requested should be ordered by a foreign court?

2. NON-CONTENTIOUS ISSUES

By way of contrast to contentious matters, the Belgian legislature has not laid down general rules on international jurisdiction for requests not directed against a defendant (the so-called *matière gracieuse*). Special rules are the exception. As an example, Article 350 of the *Code civil*, relating to

---

[9] On this issue see Collins, [1992] II *Hague Receuil* 9–238; Fallon, [1993] *Revue de droit de l'ULB* 43–94.

[10] See, especially, Batifol and Lagarde: *Droit international privé*, vol. II (Paris, 1983), no. 671.

adoption, may be cited. This allows the making in Belgium of an application for approval when the person who is adopting, or one of the adopting spouses, resides in Belgium or, if this is not the case, when the adopted child or one of the adopted children resides in Belgium or, if not, when one of the parties has Belgian nationality.

In the absence of general rules, one may think it fit to transpose the internal jurisdictional rules into international ones.[11] Depending on the matter in question, this method would lead to the retention of a territorial criterion, such as the residence of a minor for the organization of guardianship, or even party autonomy. By definition, this method ignores the nationality of one or all of the parties as a factor. It seems, none the less, that the forum of necessity used in contested cases should also be of value in uncontested cases, thus permitting a Belgian to obtain, in Belgium, an authorization in every family law matter which concerns him, at least whenever the Belgian judge would be applying Belgian law to the substance.

In uncontested matters, Belgian case law has, exceptionally, had recourse to a mechanism which closely resembles the theory of *forum non conveniens*. This technique, which relates to the control of *fraude à la loi*, comes under the conflict rules. Therefore, upon an application for divorce by mutual consent made in Belgium by a British man and an Italian woman, the Belgian judge verified that, in coming before the Belgian courts, the parties had not intended to escape the law which would normally be applied by a foreign court.[12] In the event, the fact that the couple were living in Belgium seemed to be sufficient to rule out such a risk.

III
LIS ALIBI PENDENS
IN AN INTERNATIONAL CASE

Neither the Belgian legislature nor Belgian case law has accepted the international *lis alibi pendens* exception, except within the limits of international treaties.

1. *Lis Alibi Pendens* in the Treaties

It would be superfluous to describe here the content of Article 21 of the Brussels Convention. This provision does not seem to have given rise to significant difficulties in Belgian case law.

---

[11] Born and Fallon, [1983] JT 214.   [12] Brussels, 23 Mar. 1977, [1978] JT 647.

The two bilateral conventions on international jurisdiction which Belgium concluded respectively with France on 8 July 1899 and with The Netherlands on 28 March 1925 contain provisions on *lis alibi pendens*. Other bilateral conventions on the enforcement of judgments also contain a provision of this kind which the court must keep in mind when examining its jurisdiction. This is the case when examining Article 14 of the Belgo–Italian Convention of 6 April 1962, Article 15 of the convention with Germany dated 30 June 1958, or Article 10 of the convention signed with Switzerland (29 April 1959).

Under the Belgo–German Convention, declining jurisdiction in a *lis alibi pendens* case may only occur subject to a condition: the prospective foreign judgment must be liable to be recognized in the forum State. This condition, which affords the court some discretionary power, can be understood as an examination of the appropriateness of the decision not to proceed, hand-in-hand with the jurisdiction of the foreign court. Indeed, among the conditions of recognition, the Convention provides for a control of the jurisdiction of the court of the State of origin.

Article 4(1) of the Franco–Belgian Convention states that the courts of one of the Contracting States will, at the request of one of the parties, refer to the courts of the other country disputes brought before them when these disputes are already pending or when they are connected to other disputes brought before those courts. Only disputes involving the same cause or the same object may be deemed to be connected. Article 6(1) of the Belgo–Dutch Convention contains the same provision. Applying this to a divorce between Italians where the defendant resided in Italy but had chosen a Belgian domicile, the court of first instance of Liège declined jurisdiction in favour of the Italian court, after having established the jurisdiction of the Belgian courts under Article 635 of the *Code judiciaire*.[13] In an obiter dictum, the court added that in any case 'the Italian judge appears to be the natural judge to decide a dispute between an Italian couple, married in Italy and where one of the spouses and their child live in Italy'. This point shows the link which can be established between the exception of international *lis alibi pendens* and the doctrine of *forum non conveniens*, which was implicitly applied by the court. However, those two notions should not be confused. Rather mechanically, the one acts in favour of the court first seised whilst the other rests on an objective evaluation of the case.

The application of the provisions of the conventions concluded with France and The Netherlands to divorce cases has turned out to be a rather delicate matter.

[13] 3 Oct. 1985, [1988] *Rev. Trim. Dr. Fam.* 123, note Fallon.

In one case, decided by the Brussels Court of Appeal on 7 November 1988, the Belgian court was asked to decide upon provisional measures in relation to a divorce: it referred the case to the Dutch courts to which the same application had been made.[14] This reference seemed in accordance with the *lis alibi pendens* rules. However, the Dutch courts had already declined jurisdiction, arguing that a request to take measures had been brought before a Belgian court at an earlier date. But this request sought measures between the spouses in a procedure that was unrelated to the divorce proceedings. The decision of the Brussels Court of Appeal not to proceed overlooked the fact that declining jurisdiction is only feasible if the foreign court first seised has jurisdiction. In this case, a lack of jurisdiction had been established, rightly or wrongly, by the Dutch court itself. In fact, it was for the Belgian court to recognize the Dutch judgment declining jurisdiction and to find afterwards that one of the conditions for applying the exception was not fulfilled.

The same Court of Appeal had to decide a rather complex case, in its judgment of 26 April 1990, about the guardianship of a child living in France.[15] An application for divorce had been made in Belgium and the Belgian court awarded guardianship of the child to the father. A French order gave the guardianship to the mother. After that order the Belgian measure was recognized in France and the French order was recognized in Belgium as well. The Brussels Court of Appeal, called upon to uphold the Belgian measure, held that the French court should have decided not to proceed, according to the above-mentioned provision of the Franco–Belgian Convention on *lis alibi pendens*. It is uncertain whether this criticism was justified. Indeed, the requested guardianship measure had a provisional nature and, in such a case, the Convention preserves the right to take such measures as are available under the law of each State.

2. *LIS ALIBI PENDENS* UNDER DOMESTIC LAW

It is impossible to deny that Belgian case law categorically rejects the exception of *lis alibi pendens* in international cases, but it is possible to hold that this exception should be admissible, under certain conditions, as a corollary to the principle of the recognition of foreign judgments without any special procedure being required (*reconnaissance de plein droit*). It is doubtless worth noticing that most international treaties establishing such a principle admit this exception, even if they do not establish common direct jurisdictional rules.

In fact such a principle implies that, when proceedings are brought in Belgium, the exception of *res judicata* in a foreign country may be raised as

---

[14] [1989] II Pas. Belge 108.   [15] [1990] *Rev. Trim Dr. Fam.* 368.

a defence without a process of preliminary control according to the authority given to the foreign judgment at the day stated by the law of the State of origin. The result will then be very close to that of the *lis alibi pendens* exception. The only difference is that the latter favours the court first seised whereas the recognition mechanism benefits the judgment *given* first, even if the proceedings in the State of origin were brought after the application was made in the State of the forum.

So it appears that the system of recognition without any special procedure runs the risk of encouraging forum-shopping in the absence of a *lis alibi pendens* exception and of leading the parties towards a race to commence proceedings with the first judgment as winner.

It must be conceded that the acceptance of an international *lis alibi pendens* exception in the absence of a treaty may be delicate. That is why French case law takes a lot of precautions. Among them, the doctrine of *forum non conveniens* may afford the forum court the discretion necessary for the implementation of such an exception in an international context.[16]

IV
FOREIGN CHOICE OF
JURISDICTION CLAUSES

Under Belgian private international law, the only statutory provision defining the status of a jurisdiction clause is Article 17 of the Brussels Convention. Neither the bilateral Conventions respectively concluded with France (8 July 1899) and with The Netherlands (28 March 1925) nor the domestic law even hint at it. The only exception is the new Act of 14 July 1991 on commercial practices and the information and protection of the consumer, whose Article 32(20) qualifies as unfair a term of a contract signed with a consumer giving jurisdiction to a court other than the one provided for by Article 624 of the *Code judiciaire*, subject to the application of the Brussels Convention. The wording of this provision is awkward, since it refers to a provision of the *Code judiciaire* defining only internal jurisdiction and not international, even though the legislature intended, to be consistent, to include international contracts, as the reference to the Brussels Convention clearly shows.

This observation is not valid in relation to arbitration clauses. On the one hand, the legislature has limited, through special acts, the extent to which one may rely on an arbitration clause written before the beginning

---

[16] Cass. civ, 6 Feb. 1985, *Simitch*, [1985] *Rev Crit dr int pr* 369, note Francescakis, 243 ff. The Court is required to verify whether the dispute in the State of origin had a strong connection (*se rattache de manière caractérisée*) with that State and whether there was no fraud when referring to a foreign court.

of the dispute in question. On the other hand, Belgium has ratified the Geneva Convention of 21 April 1961 on international commercial arbitration; however, it applies only to transactions concerning parties residing or established in the territory of a Contracting State at the time that the clause was drafted.

To tell the truth, the evaluation of the scope of a choice of jurisdiction clause by a Belgian court is proving extremely delicate. It seems necessary to distinguish between the effect of a rule of a procedural nature, i.e. the *principe dispositif* or *ultra petita* principle—according to which the court is not allowed to decide on more than the object of the application, unless public policy is at stake—and the evaluation of the validity of the clause.

1. THE EFFECT OF THE *ULTRA PETITA* PRINCIPLE

At first sight one could deduce from the silence of the legislature that a jurisdiction clause is void. Indeed, we have seen that, in Belgium, the international jurisdiction rules rest on a closed system, defined in an exhaustive list of grounds of jurisdiction. Thus, there seems no place left for any kind of prorogation or waiver decided by the parties.

Nevertheless, such a deduction would overlook an element which determines international jurisdiction, which stems from the general rules governing the judge's verification of his own jurisdiction. The judge will not undertake such an examination unless the jurisdiction under consideration is of a public policy nature. In such a case the examination is *ex officio* and, if it appears that the statutory conditions required by law on which to base jurisdiction are not fulfilled in the case, the court shall decline jurisdiction without having any other discretionary power.

However, it is very unusual for rules of international jurisdiction to relate to public policy. To show this, it is enough to mention those rules establishing an exclusive jurisdiction in favour of the Belgian courts. We have seen that Belgian law contains no formal provision of this kind, but that it has been possible to transpose internal jurisdictional rules into international ones. That is certainly so in bankruptcy matters. When this condition is fulfilled, the Belgian court seised, notwithstanding a clause conferring jurisdiction on foreign courts, must reject that clause.

For all matters not subject to exclusive jurisdiction, the parties are normally allowed to prorogate the jurisdiction of the Belgian courts or to derogate from it. This freedom does not have to be expressly stated. So, there is a valid prorogation when a Belgian court is seised in a case where jurisdiction is not derived from a statutory provision, if the defendant does not contest jurisdiction. Generally it is not possible for the court to decline jurisdiction merely because the case has an insufficient connection with the forum and is obviously more closely connected with a foreign

State. We have seen, however, the extent to which the fraud argument has been used to determine the jurisdiction of the court in non-contentious matters.[17]

2. EVALUATION OF THE ADMISSIBILITY OF THE CLAUSE

It is not necessary here to explain Article 17 of the Brussels Convention. On the whole Belgian case law has applied it honestly and has not hesitated to refer to the European Court of Justice relevant questions of interpretation, especially those asking whether national law may add a new requirement of validity to the conditions set out by the provision,[18] or concerning the definition of 'party' to a jurisdiction clause in a bill of lading.[19]

Under domestic law the question of the law applicable to the jurisdiction clause is a controversial one.[20] In fact, this problem does not directly affect the subject of the present chapter since the potential power of the court to decline its own jurisdiction in favour of the concurring jurisdiction of a foreign court depends less on the way of determining the applicable law—the law of the forum or a foreign law designated by the conflict of laws rule governing contractual obligations—than on the substantive content of the applicable law.

It seems more useful to comment on three case law methods used to evaluate the admissibility of a jurisdiction or arbitration clause. These present an interesting variation if we consider the discretionary power left to the court seised. The different cases all concern the situation where the legislature has enacted rules designed to protect one of the contracting parties, deemed to be the weaker. Such rules are generally mandatory: they are not of a public policy character, so that they are not applied *ex officio* by the court; it is for the protected person to assert his statutory rights. These matters concern, amongst others, employment contracts, exclusive distribution agreements, and the protection of a third party to a bill of lading.

The first method is to respect what is laid down by law, without affording any discretionary power to the Belgian court seised despite a clause conferring jurisdiction on foreign courts.

This method is illustrated by the Act of 27 July 1961 on the unilateral termination of exclusive distribution agreements.[21] Under section 6, 'the provisions of the present act apply notwithstanding any contrary

---

[17] See above, at II, 2.

[18] Case 150/80, *Elefanten Schuh GmbH* v. *Jacqmain* [1981] ECR 1671.

[19] Case 71/83, *Partenreederei MS Tilly Russ* v. *Haven en Vervoebedrijf Nova NV* [1984] ECR 2417.

[20] Rigaux and Fallon, n. 4 above, no. 1321 ff.   [21] *Moniteur Belge*, 5 Oct. 1961.

convention signed before the termination of the contract granting the concession'. An international jurisdictional rule using the connecting factor of the place of the effects of the agreement is linked to this prohibition (section 4).

Thus, any person who is given a concession for Belgian territory knows he may rely on the fact that a contract term conferring jurisdiction on foreign courts cannot be invoked, even if he has accepted this term. So one sees that, even if the foreign court has jurisdiction owing to a valid contractual term, the Belgian court also has jurisdiction by virtue of the will of the legislature. It is enough for the protected person to invoke this protection to his own advantage.

In a way, the Belgian legislature has considered it appropriate to allow the distributor to proceed in Belgium, if a special statutory criterion is fulfilled. This method is the one used, for example, in the Brussels Convention for the protection of the insured party or the consumer (Articles 12 and 15).

A second method is to interpret the content of the law applicable to the clause to find in it a special substantive rule for international cases.

This approach has been used by the Brussels Court of Appeal in relation to jurisdiction terms inserted in employment contracts, especially those of pilots working for a foreign airline.[22] It consists in applying the nullity sanction set out in Article 630 of the *Code judiciaire* when the clause is written before the beginning of the dispute, only if the situation presents enough connections with the Belgian legal system, and this evaluation is left to the appreciation of the court. The method can be understood in two different ways. First, the Belgian court applies the sanction only when the Belgian mandatory rules protecting the employee apply to the substance of the dispute. Secondly, after having decided that the law of the forum applies to the admissibility of the term, the court holds that the sanction foreseen by the legislature is only valid for internal contracts and not for international ones, the latter being defined by way of their degree of proximity to the legal order of the forum.

What is original about this case law is that it lays down—though not expressly—a substantive rule of private international law[23] according to which the non-invocability rule does not apply to certain international contracts. The definition of 'international' is a question of fact, which considers the degree of proximity of the situation to the forum. This method may be seen as an implicit illustration of the doctrine of *forum non conveniens*, since it may lead the Belgian court, which normally has jurisdiction in the absence of a jurisdiction clause, to refuse to accept it in favour of the foreign court chosen by the parties, after a process of

[22] Born and Fallon, [1987] JT 482.
[23] On this notion, see Rigaux, *Droit international privé*, vol. I (Brussels, 1987), no. 266.

reasoning based on the appropriateness of instituting proceedings in the forum State.

A third method links the validity of the clause to the application of Belgian law by the foreign court chosen. This method has been accepted by the Supreme Court in cases involving bills of lading and exclusive distribution agreements. These cases concern respectively public policy rules and mandatory rules. The authority of the case law of the Supreme Court leads naturally to the conclusion that this method prevails over the first and second methods.

When a Belgian court is seised in respect of one of these matters, despite a clause conferring jurisdiction on a foreign court, and when the substantive protection rules of Belgian law express their will to be applied to the case, the case will not be dismissed if it appears that the clause 'tends towards and results in the application of a foreign law' and shows 'the desire to escape from the application of Belgian law'.[24] On the other hand, the Belgian court will decline jurisdiction if the term conferring jurisdiction on a foreign court states that that court must apply the Belgian protection rules and if it does not appear that foreign law will prevent the foreign court from applying such rules. To contest the clause it would not really be enough to invoke the fact that the foreign court would apply foreign law if this is uncertain or would adopt a different interpretation of Belgian law than is usual in Belgium.[25]

This method is distinctive in that it requires the court to determine its international jurisdiction, anticipating the decision on the substance of the case. This anticipation relates to a simulation of the reasoning that the foreign court, and not the forum court, will adopt. This can also be seen as an illustration of the doctrine of *forum non conveniens*, since the forum court, which normally has jurisdiction, gives way to the foreign court, which also has jurisdiction. This method is based on a determination grounded on foreign private international law, the forum court simulating the reasoning the foreign court would adopt in order to determine which law is to be applied to the case. It neglects any procedural consideration consisting of evaluating the difficulties the protected person might face in being party to proceedings in a foreign country. From this point of view, it is not certain that this method is sufficient effectively to protect certain persons such as the consumer. It is worth noticing that every case brought before the Supreme Court related to a dispute between tradesmen.

[24] Cass. civ., 28 June 1979, *Audi v. N.S.U.*, [1979] I Pas. Belge 1288; the court also denounced a fictitious localizing of the place of performance abroad by the terms of the contract and stated that such localizing, being artificial, could be controlled by the doctrine of *fraude à la loi*.

[25] Cass. civ., 2 Feb. 1979, *Bibby Line*, [1979] I Pas. Belge 634.

V
RESTRAINING FOREIGN PROCEEDINGS

Consideration by the Belgian courts of the possibility of instituting proceedings in a foreign country can take place at two distinct stages. The classical one is at the stage of the enforcement of a foreign judgment. More unusually, the court may seek to limit an injunction power the foreign court derived from its own law.

1. CONTROL OF THE JURISDICTION OF THE COURT OF THE STATE OF ORIGIN

A distinction emerges depending on whether the foreign judgment was granted by the courts of a State with which Belgium has concluded a treaty on the enforcement of judgments in civil and commercial matters. Apart from the Brussels Convention, a number of bilateral treaties must be cited.[26]

As is well known, the Brussels Convention strictly limits control over the jurisdiction of the court of the State of origin. This verification may only take place if the court has failed to consider one of the exclusive or mandatory grounds of jurisdiction established by the Convention (Article 28(1)). Besides, the bilateral conventions concluded, for example, with the United Kingdom (2 May 1934), with Germany (30 June 1958), or Italy (6 April 1962), while concerned only with enforcement (without containing any jurisdictional rule), contain a rather complex set of rules on indirect jurisdiction to be applied only by the courts to which an application is made for enforcement. Thus, even though their object is strictly limited to the enforcement of judgments, these treaties set out indirectly to influence the exercise of jurisdiction. This process is attractive but artificial, and the method stated by the Brussels Convention is to be preferred. Within the framework of these bilateral conventions, the court to which an application is made for enforcement is allowed to determine whether the court of the State of origin really was the appropriate one.

When the foreign judgment was given by a court of a State with which Belgium has not concluded a treaty, it is necessary to consider the conditions set out in Article 570 of the *Code judiciaire*. According to that provision, the Belgian courts refuse to enforce a foreign judgment if it appears that the court of the State of origin has only been able to base its jurisdiction on the plaintiff's nationality. When providing for such control, the legislature confirms that this criterion is exorbitant. One notices,

[26] See a list in Rigaux and Fallon, n. 4 above, no. 758; see also the Luxembourg Convention of 20 May 1980 concerning guardianship.

though, that Belgian case law did not hesitate to found the international jurisdiction of Belgian courts on this criterion, on the basis of a forum of necessity.[27]

Presumably, the Belgian court will also refuse to enforce a foreign judgment by virtue of Article 570 of the *Code judiciaire*, on grounds of public policy, when the court of the State of origin has assumed jurisdiction in a case within the exclusive jurisdiction of the Belgian courts. An example would be the case of a judgment pronouncing the bankruptcy of a tradesman established in Belgium.[28] Another control allowed by Article 570 of the *Code judiciaire* is the review of the substance of the foreign decision. This is however excluded in family law matters.[29] If such a verification does not affect, at first sight, the evaluation of the appropriateness of the foreign court's intervention, it is not the same when the control by the Belgian court in respect of the substance of the decision concerns the law applied by the court of the State of origin. This is the case when the refusal intervenes whenever the foreign court has applied a different law from the one which the Belgian judge would have applied if he had been seised.[30] This control is thus rather close to that allowed by the Supreme Court in relation to the admissibility of jurisdiction clauses.[31]

2. RESTRAINING THE INJUNCTION POWER

Strictly speaking, Belgian private international law has no provision similar to the 'anti-suit injunction' of the common law which would allow a Belgian court to prohibit the institution of proceedings before a foreign court. This does not mean, however, that Belgian law does not seek to prevent such foreign action in certain circumstances. This happens whenever Belgian courts have exclusive jurisdiction, be it territorial or relating to the substance of the matter. Though, as we have seen, the remedy for such a prohibition is nothing less than a refusal to enforce the foreign judgment. Thus, at a time when repudiations took place on Belgian territory before foreign diplomatic authorities, the refusal to enforce the act was very firmly grounded in Belgium on the violation of an exclusive jurisdiction attributed to the Belgian courts when the act was performed on Belgian territory. This remedy was sufficient to put an end to the practice.[32]

---

[27] See above, at II, 1(a).

[28] See e.g. Comm. Brussels, 15 Mar. 1988, [1988] Rev prat soc. 234.

[29] Cass. civ., 23 Jan. 1981, *Lupo* v. *Castilla*, [1981] I Pas. Belge 547.

[30] This solution was applied to divorce proceedings before the adoption of the Act of 27 June 1960. See Cass. civ., 4 Oct. 1956, *Closset*, [1957] I Pas. Belge 88. This Act facilitates the application of Belgian law.

[31] See above, at IV, 2.   [32] Rigaux and Fallon, n. 4 above, no. 1050.

Two cases illustrate the possibility of an intervention aimed at preventing the institution of proceedings before a foreign court or the continuation of proceedings abroad.

The first method is to ensure the enforcement of the order by a periodic payment by way of a penalty. This was ordered in a case already mentioned under *lis pendens* and relating to the guardianship of a child in Belgium by the father where the mother had been afforded a similar measure in France.[33] The Belgian court upheld the measure in favour of the father and ordered the other party to pay a daily fine of 20.000 BFr. for delay. This is certainly not the same as preventing a person from commencing an action in a foreign country. Nevertheless, by subjecting the defendant to a financial threat if he does not respect the decision and render up the child, this process implies *a fortiori* that any contrary proceedings abroad would be excluded since such an initiative would illustrate a desire to oppose the Belgian decision.

If the policy of the daily fine were to become general, it would effectively prevent the other party from afterwards applying to a foreign country. Furthermore, obtaining a foreign decision is not enough to expunge the Belgian decision since, if there is an application for the enforcement of the foreign decision in Belgium, the Belgian court can oppose it—on the grounds of public policy under Article 570 of the *Code judiciaire*—as this judgment is irreconcilable with the first one. In other words, it is not necessary to order a daily fine to obviate the effects of a further foreign decision. The fine is intended rather to prevent an application abroad by the losing party.

Another way of obtaining an injunction is to apply to a Belgian court as a counter-measure against a foreign injunction prohibiting the commencement of proceedings in Belgium.

An order of the President of the Brussels first instance court dated 18 December 1989 tackled this issue.[34] An action (on the merits) was brought in Belgium against an American defendant, domiciled in the United States, for non-performance of a sportsman's employment contract concluded in Belgium and to be performed in the territory of several European countries. The defendant obtained an anti-suit injunction in the United States. The Belgian party brought an action in Belgium against this injunction. The court heard the case and prohibited the American defendant from pursuing abroad any proceedings tending to impede the functioning of Belgian courts, under penalty of a fine of 1.000.000 BFr. for each violation shown. In support of its decision, the court invoked a number of arguments: the foreign injunction was inconsistent with Article 6 of the European Convention on Human Rights, but also, and more

---

[33] See above, at III, 1.   [34] [1990–1] RW 676.

significantly, the Belgian court had jurisdiction to decide on the substance of the dispute under the unconditional provisions of Article 635 of the *Code judiciare*.[35]

More generally, one cannot exclude the possibility that a party could obtain an injunction in Belgium in order to limit further damage that could result from an application abroad. It seems difficult to imagine that the context of such proceedings could be that of one of the special Acts which have introduced this type of injunction, such as the Act of 14 July 1991 on commercial practices and the protection of the consumer. However, it could concern an issue in relation to a tortious dispute, where the injured party tries to establish that instituting proceedings abroad is vexatious and would risk causing particular damage such as the blocking of goods located in a foreign country or the payment of the costs of the proceedings.

In a divorce case where proceedings were brought both in Belgium and in the United States, the Belgian court refused to grant a so-called 'provision *ad litem*' to cover the costs of the proceedings in the United States.[36] This application was made by the party who was the applicant for a divorce in Belgium and the defendant in the same dispute in the United States. It was aimed at providing the 5,000 dollars necessary to take part in the foreign proceedings. If it is true, as the court held, that the rules of the forum on access to justice, such as judicial assistance, make sense only in respect of an application on the substance made in the forum, requiring the spouse applying abroad to pay the costs incurred by the other spouse when the probability that the foreign decision will be enforceable in Belgium is slight, this could help to prevent the introduction of purely vexatious proceedings in a foreign country.

VI
CONCLUSION

Subject to the application of international treaties, Belgian law is characterized by a statutory list containing an exhaustive set of rules on international jurisdiction. However, there is no statutory provision relating to international *lis pendens* or to the validity of jurisdiction clauses. Case law excludes the first and admits the second, on certain conditions.

This assessment implies at first sight that there is no place for the doctrine of *forum non conveniens*, since the court has no power to decline statutory jurisdiction. This finding is based not only on the existence of

---

[35] On this Art., see above, II, 1(a).
[36] Prés. Civ., Brussels (réf.), 23 July 1990, [1991] JT 353.

written rules on international jurisdiction, but also on the legislature's intention to maintain the jurisdiction of Belgian courts within reasonable bounds. Indeed, the criteria laid down are supposed to be appropriate ones and their exhaustive nature prevents a foreigner from being sued without his consent in cases other than those provided for by statute.

Such assessment does not mean, however, that the Belgian court has no discretionary power at all when its jurisdiction is contested. Significantly, Article 636 of the *Code judiciaire* is supposed to limit the exorbitant nature of the claimant's domicile criterion employed by Article 638. Such power depends, however, on a statutory policy upon which the jurisdiction of the Belgian court is dependent. It is more obvious when it comes to the validity of jurisdiction clauses. But it underlies also other mechanisms common to continental legal systems, such as the sanction of fraud (*fraude à la loi*), especially in non-contentious issues, the exception of international *lis pendens* or the conditions limiting the power of injunction of foreign courts, and of national courts as well, namely as regards provisional measures or the so-called *action en cessation*.

It is worth noticing that the introduction of such a discretionary power does not only permit the dismissal of actions. In several cases, this power has been invoked to grant the Belgian courts a jurisdiction that the legislature did not foresee. It is likely that the evaluation of the appropriateness of this kind of jurisdiction depends on the application by a foreign court of Belgian law to the substance of the dispute.

In a way, the proper choice of the most appropriate forum is a matter for the parties. The plaintiff, adequately advised by his counsel, has to evaluate this by working out what the likely result will be of bringing the proceedings in different countries. Indeed, the appropriateness of the forum does not depend only on jurisdiction. Other procedural aspects ought to be considered, namely the service of judicial documents, the taking of evidence, hearings, and language, but also the choice of the law applicable to the substance of the dispute and the necessity of obtaining a judgment on the best conditions. It would be paradoxical to condemn this practice as forum-shopping when its omission and the resulting choice of an inappropriate forum would most certainly engage a lawyer's professional liability.

Thus it seems likely that a discretionary power for the judge to evaluate the inappropriateness of the court's jurisdiction could only act as a rather exceptional adjustment mechanism since it is unable to hide the relativity which permeates the treatment of an international case in the absence of a treaty.

5

Canada
(Common Law Jurisdictions)

JOOST BLOM
Professor, Faculty of Law, University of British Columbia

CONTENTS

I
INTRODUCTION: BASES FOR JURISDICTION

This chapter concerns the rules for declining jurisdiction as applied in the common law jurisdictions of Canada, that is, the twelve Canadian court systems whose law is derived from English law. These include the courts of the nine provinces other than Quebec, the courts of the Yukon and Northwest Territories, and the Federal Court of Canada.

The rules for declining jurisdiction must be seen in the context of the rules determining when a court may take jurisdiction. As under English law (leaving aside the changes made by European Community law), the grounds for jurisdiction are implicit in the rules for service of process. In Canada these are contained in the rules of court of each province and territory, and the Federal Court Rules. The relevant provisions differ considerably from each other as well as from their English model.[1] To begin with that model, the traditional English rules for actions *in personam* distinguish between service on a defendant who is present[2] in the territory of the forum country, and service on a defendant who is outside the country (service *ex juris*). Jurisdiction over a person in the forum country is said to be 'as of right' because the right to serve that person with process is unqualified (although the defendant may apply to have the court decline jurisdiction on discretionary grounds). Jurisdiction over a person outside the forum country, or 'assumed' jurisdiction, has traditionally been seen as exceptional because the sovereign had no inherent right to extend her judicial process to persons outside her realm. This was reflected in the English rule that service *ex juris* requires leave of the court, which can only be sought in certain types of cases. The list of these cases includes proceedings that may appropriately be brought in England because of the remedy sought (such as an injunction against something to be done or not done in England),[3] the subject-matter of the claim (such as immovable property in England),[4] or the facts on which the claim is based (such as a breach of contract or a tort committed in England).[5] Leave to serve *ex juris* can be obtained only by showing, first, that the claim in question falls under one of the listed heads, and, secondly, the case is a proper one to be heard in England. The latter requirement is, in effect, that the plaintiff show that the court is *forum conveniens*.

The rules in the Canadian jurisdictions fall into four groups, based on the ways in which they have modified this scheme. First, two provinces have retained the English requirement of leave for service *ex juris*, with only some minor changes to the list of cases in which leave may be sought.[6] Secondly, five provinces[7] and the two territories[8] have retained the list of cases, again with some changes, but permit service *ex juris* without leave in these cases. Most of these jurisdictions' rules

---

[1] The English model is mainly found in O. 11 of the Rules of the Sup. Ct. (England), dealing with service *ex juris*. For commentary on the current version of O. 11, see Cheshire and North, *Private International Law* (12th ed., 1992), 191–213, Dicey and Morris, *The Conflict of Laws* (12th ed., 1993), 298–349.

[2] At common law a foreign-incorporated company was considered to be present for this purpose if it carried on business in the forum country through a more or less fixed place of business or a resident agent. See Dicey and Morris, n. 1 above, 298–310; Cheshire and North, n. 1 above, 183–8.

[3] Rules of the Sup. Ct. (Eng), O. 11, r. 1(1)(b).

[4] *Ibid.*, r. 1(1)(g).

[5] *Ibid.*, r. 1(1)(e) and (f).

[6] Alberta Rules of Ct., r. 30; Newfoundland Rules of the Sup. Ct., 1986, r. 10.01 ff.

[7] British Columbia Rules of Ct., r. 13(1); Saskatchewan Rules of Ct., r. 31(1); Manitoba Ct. of Queen's Bench Rules, r. 17.02; Ontario Rules of Civ. Proc., r. 17.02; New Brunswick Rules of Ct., r. 19.01.

[8] Northwest Territories Sup. Ct. Rules, O. 5, r. 38. The Yukon Territory uses the British Columbia Rules of Ct. (Judicature Act, RSY 1986, c. 96, s. 37).

further permit service *ex juris* with leave in any case that is not on the list.[9] Thirdly, two provinces's rules[10] permit service *ex juris* without leave in a case of any kind, provided that the defendant is resident in Canada or the United States. A defendant elsewhere may only be served with leave, but there is no restriction as to the types of case in which this may be done. Fourthly, the rules of the Federal Court require leave to serve *ex juris* but do not confine such service to particular types of cases.[11]

The stage of the proceedings at which questions of *forum non conveniens* and *lis alibi pendens* can be raised depends on whether or not leave is required for service. When the defendant can be served in the jurisdiction or the rules permit service *ex juris* without leave, the defendant must apply to the court to set aside the service.[12] When the plaintiff must obtain leave to serve the defendant *ex juris*, issues of *forum conveniens* or *lis alibi pendens* are relevant to the court's discretion to give leave and must be addressed by the plaintiff. If, however, leave is given on an *ex parte* application, as will often be the case, the defendant's arguments on these matters will be raised if he or she applies to have the service set aside on the ground that leave should not have been given. An important question, which will be addressed in the next section, is the extent to which these procedural differences, as to how and when the issues are raised, entail

---

[9] British Columbia Rules of Ct., r. 13(3); Manitoba Ct. of Queen's Bench Rules, r. 17.03; New Brunswick Rules of Ct., r. 19.02; Ontario Rules of Civ. Proc., r. 17.03; Saskatchewan Rules of Ct., r. 31(2). Northwest Territories, Sup. Ct. Rules, O. 5, r. 39, allows for leave only in actions on foreign judgments, and for alimony or maintenance.

[10] Nova Scotia Civ. Proc. Rules, r. 10.07–10.08; Prince Edward Island Civ. Proc. Rules, r. 10.07–10.08.

[11] Fed. Ct. Rules, r. 307.

[12] Although most provinces' rules refer only to setting aside the service *ex juris*, British Columbia's rules contemplate the alternative of a declaration that the court has no jurisdiction or declines jurisdiction: Rules of Ct., r. 13(10) (setting aside service *ex juris*) and r. 14(6)(c) (declaring that the court should decline jurisdiction). A further alternative order in any jurisdiction is a stay of proceedings, which may be useful if it is contemplated that circumstances may change in such a way as to justify lifting the stay and letting the plaintiff proceed after all: see e.g. *Gauthier* v. *Swain* (1989) 100 NBR (2d) 173 (QB). For obvious reasons, most rules of court provide that a party may raise arguments against jurisdiction without, by doing that very thing, being taken to submit to the court's jurisdiction: Alberta Rules of Ct., r. 27; British Columbia Rules of Ct., r. 14(8); Manitoba Ct. of Queen's Bench Rules, r. 17.06(4); New Brunswick Rules of Ct., r. 19.05(3); Newfoundland Rules of the Sup. Ct., 1986, r. 10.05(2); Nova Scotia Civ. Proc. Rules, r. 11.05; Ontario Civ. Proc. Rules, r. 17.06(4); Prince Edward Island Civ. Proc. Rules, r. 11.05. It will be too late, however, to raise such arguments if the party has taken other steps that do amount to an acceptance of the court's jurisdiction: *Catalyst Research Corp* v. *Medtronic Inc* (1981) 120 DLR (3d) 159 (FCTD), aff'd. [1982) 131 D.L.R. (3d) 767n (FCA); *Frey* v. *Heintzl Estate* (1988) 24 BCLR (2d) 25 (SC); *Lucas-California Co* v. *Charlottetown Metal Products Ltd* (1982) 134 DLR (3d) 438 (PEI CA). Compare *Nationale Nederlanden Financing Co BV* v. *Jones* [1985] 1 WWR 664 (Sask. QB), where a stay was granted two years after a statement of defence had been filed.

substantive differences in the nature of the court's discretion to decide for or against taking jurisdiction.

II
GROUNDS FOR DECLINING JURISDICTION

1. Forum Non Conveniens

(a) THE SOURCES AND NATURE OF THE DISCRETION

In Canada the doctrine of *forum non conveniens*[13] is used in deciding jurisdictional issues that arise because of the interprovincial or international elements in a case.[14] Ever since the mid-nineteenth century, when the English courts were first given jurisdiction over certain actions against defendants served outside the territory of England, the question of *forum conveniens* (although the Latin label has not always been attached to it in this context) has always been central to the discretion that English and Canadian courts have exercised in giving leave to serve *ex juris*. The question was approached on the basis that service on a person in another country was 'an interference with the exclusive sovereignty of a foreign power and that that interference should be the subject of an exceedingly careful exercise of the discretion'.[15] The court would consider many matters in exercising its discretion, including the issue of *forum conveniens*. That issue was usually put in terms of whether the forum was 'the most convenient place to try the issues raised'.[16] It was clear, however, that, besides 'convenience' in the sense of the parties' interests, a judge exercising the discretion to give leave to serve *ex juris* should give weight to considerations of policy relating to the legal system, such as avoiding a multiplicity of suits.

---

[13] The evolution of the Canadian law on *forum non conveniens* can be traced in Granger, (1972–4) 6 *Ottawa L Rev*. 416; Edinger, (1982) 16 *UBCL Rev*. 1 (hereinafter 'Discretion'); Edinger, (1986) 64 *Can. Bar Rev*. 283 (hereinafter 'MacShannon'); Feldman and Vella, (1988–9) 10 *Adv. Q*. 161.

[14] It is sometimes referred to in cases that concern the allocation of litigation as between the courts of a province and the Fed. Ct., where these have concurrent jurisdiction, but the discretion of one court to decline in favour of the other is usually exercised more on the basis of the courts' respective constitutional roles and subject-matter expertise: *Reza* v. *Canada* (9 June 1994), File No. 23361 (unrep. at time of writing) (SCC); *Sannes* v. *Canada* (10 Feb. 1994), Vancouver Reg. No. A934697 (unrep. at time of writing) (BCSC).

[15] *Singh* v. *Howden Petroleum Ltd* (1979) 100 DLR (3d) 121 at 124 (Ont. CA), citing McRuer CJHC in *Empire-Universal Films Ltd* v. *Rank* [1948] OR 235 at 242 (HCJ), who in turn was summarizing the English position.

[16] *Singh*, n. 15 above. See also *Talbot* v. *Pan Ocean Oil Corp* (1977) 3 Alta. LR (2d) 354 (CA); *Consumers Co-operative Refiners Ltd* v. *Taylor Instrument Companies of Canada Ltd* (1979) 102 DLR (3d) 337 (Sask. QB).

Traditionally under Anglo-Canadian law, the discretion exercised in service *ex juris* cases was sharply distinguished from the discretion to decline jurisdiction where the jurisdiction existed 'as of right'. The substantive difference in the basis of jurisdiction was reinforced by the procedural difference that, instead of the plaintiff seeking leave to serve the defendant, the defendant was seeking a stay of proceedings after being served, which meant the source of the discretion was different. In service *ex juris* cases the source was the rule that required the court's leave, coupled, in the case of the English rules, with an express direction that leave should not be granted unless 'it shall be made sufficiently to appear to the Court that the case is a proper one for service out of the jurisdiction'.[17] In cases of service in the jurisdiction the source of the court's discretion was not a specific rule but the court's inherent power to control its own process.[18] In these cases, until the mid-1970s, a stay was granted only in extreme circumstances. In order to succeed, a defendant had to show, first, that the continuance of the action in the forum would be oppressive or vexatious to the defendant or an abuse of process in some other way; and, secondly, that the stay would not cause an injustice to the plaintiff.[19] Although occasionally in Canada this was referred to as a *forum non conveniens* test,[20] the fact that the defendant had in effect to show that the plaintiff's choice of forum was an abuse of the court's process made it quite a different form of discretion from the one exercised in service *ex juris* cases. In England, beginning in 1973,[21] the House of Lords moved progressively further away from the strict requirement that the defendant show vexation, oppression, or some other form of abuse of process, until in 1984 it declared[22] that the discretion in its modern form was correctly described as *forum non conveniens*, a doctrine that had long been applied in the Scottish courts. The reconciliation between the discretion in cases of service in the jurisdiction, on the one hand, and in cases of service *ex juris*, on the other, was completed

[17] Sup. Ct. Rules (Eng.), O. 11, r. 4(2).

[18] *Rogers* v. *Bank of Montreal* (1984) 4 D.L.R. (4th) 507 at 522–3 (BCCA); *Singh*, n. 15 above at 132; *Magnolia Ocean Shipping Corp* v. *The 'Soledad Maria'* (30 Apr. 1981) (FCTD) (unrep.), quoted in Harrington, '*Forum Non Conveniens* in the Quebec and Federal Courts—Rigidity or Flexibility', in *Meredith Memorial Lectures*, 1986, Faculty of Law, McGill University: *Current Problems in Maritime Law* (Toronto, 1987), 257 at 263.

[19] *St Pierre* v. *South American Stores (Gath & Chaves) Ltd* [1936] 1 KB 382 at 398 (CA). The Canadian case usually cited as adopting this test is *Empire-Universal Films Ltd* v. *Rank* [1947] OR 775 (CA).

[20] *McKeeman* v. *Canadian Pacific Ltd* (1972) 33 DLR (3d) 379 (Alta. TD); *Van Vogt* v. *All-Canadian Group Distributors Ltd* (1967) 60 WWR 729 (Man. QB), rev'd. 9 DLR (3d) 407 (Man. CA); *Moreno* v. *Norwich Union Fire Ins. Society Ltd* (1970) 16 DLR (3d) 247 (Ont. HCJ); *Sittler* v. *Conwest Exploration Co* (1972) 31 DLR (3d) 201 (Y. Terr. Ct.); see Edinger, 'Discretion', n. 13 above, at 22–3.

[21] *The Atlantic Star* [1974] AC 436 (HL).

[22] *The Abidin Daver* [1984] AC 398 at 411 (HL).

in *Spiliada Maritime Corp* v. *Cansulex Ltd.*[23] In both situations, according to Lord Goff who gave the main judgment, the question is in which forum 'the case may be tried more suitably for the interests of all the parties and the ends of justice'.[24] The difference between the two is simply as to which party bears the burden of persuasion. Where the case is one of service in the jurisdiction, the defendant must 'establish that there is another available forum which is clearly or distinctly more appropriate than the English forum'.[25] Where service is to be *ex juris*, 'the burden is, quite simply, the obverse of that applicable where a stay is sought of proceedings started in this country as of right',[26] namely, the plaintiff must persuade the court that England is clearly the appropriate forum for the trial of the action when compared with the alternatives. In either type of case, even if the grounds for declining jurisdiction otherwise exist, the court may refuse to do so on the ground that it is unjust to deprive the plaintiff of a legitimate personal or juridical advantage that he or she has in England compared with the alternative forum; but the burden of proving such an advantage is always on the plaintiff.[27]

The Canadian courts have followed the English trend towards assimilating the discretion in cases of service in the jurisdiction to that in cases of service *ex juris*. This process was probably helped by the fact that in many provinces service *ex juris* became possible without leave. It was now the defendant who had to ask the court to decline jurisdiction, thus increasing the similarity between the *ex juris* cases and cases of jurisdiction 'as of right'.[28] Except in those jurisdictions where the rules of court expressly provided for it,[29] the discretion to decline jurisdiction in service *ex juris* cases now had to be derived, not, as under the former rules, from the fact that leave was required, but from the court's inherent right to control its process.[30]

---

[23] [1987] AC 460 (HL).

[24] *Ibid*. 476.

[25] *Ibid*. 477.

[26] *Ibid*. 481.

[27] *Ibid*. 476, 478. The question of legitimate advantage is further discussed below, nn. 64 to 76 and accompanying text.

[28] The burden of proof may nevertheless still be different. See below, nn. 36 to 42 and accompanying text.

[29] As they do in (BC), Rules of Ct., r. 14(6)(c); Manitoba, Ct. of Queen's Bench Rules, r. 17.06(2)(c); New Brunswick Rules of Ct., r. 19.05(2)(c); Ontario Rules of Civ. Proc., r. 17.06(2)(c); Saskatchewan Rules of Ct., r. 33(3).

[30] Some courts at first said that the abolition of the leave requirement had also removed any discretion to decline jurisdiction in *ex juris* cases: *Selan* v. *Neumeyer* (1959) 29 WWR 542 (Man. QB), affd. (*sub nom. Belan* v. *Neumeyer*) (1960) 33 WWR 48 (Man. CA); *John Ewing & Co Ltd* v. *Pullmax (Canada) Ltd* (1976) 13 OR (2d) 587 (HCJ). But *Singh*, n. 15 above, clearly established that the discretion survived.

The successive decisions of the House of Lords were followed in Canada,[31] albeit with occasional hesitations.[32] The culmination of the recent Canadian developments was the Supreme Court of Canada's decision in *Amchem Products Inc* v. *British Columbia (Workers' Compensation Board)*.[33] This was a case on the power of a British Columbia court to issue an injunction against legal proceedings in Texas, and will be discussed on that point below, but the court's reasoning was based in part on the doctrine of *forum non conveniens*. Sopinka J, speaking for the court, noted that the Canadian cases on *forum non conveniens* had not been consistent in their approach,[34] and sought to restate the doctrine. He did so in the same terms as the House of Lords had done in the *Spiliada* case, namely, that the essential question is the 'appropriateness' of the local forum compared with alternatives elsewhere.[35] On two significant matters, however, the Supreme Court differed from the House of Lords. One, discussed immediately below, was the question of the relationship between cases of service in the jurisdiction and those of service *ex juris*, as far as the discretion to decline jurisdiction was concerned. The other, discussed later, was the relevance of a 'legitimate advantage' enjoyed by the plaintiff in the local forum compared with the alternative forums.

(b) SERVICE IN THE JURISDICTION, SERVICE *EX JURIS*,
    AND THE BURDEN OF PROOF

Even more than the House of Lords in the *Spiliada* case, the Supreme Court downplayed the significance, for the *forum non conveniens* discretion, of the place where the defendant was served. 'It seems to me',

---

[31] *Skagway Terminal Co* v. *The 'Daphne'* (1987) 42 DLR (4th) 200 (FCTD); *Saint John Shipbuilding Ltd* v. *The Eldir* [1991] 1 FC D–34; *United Oilseed Products Ltd* v. *Royal Bank of Canada* [1988] 5 WWR 181 (Alta. CA); *Paterson* v. *Hamilton* (1991) 115 AR 73 (CA); *Avenue Properties Ltd* v. *First City Devt Corp* (1986) 32 DLR (4th) 40 (BCCA); *First City Invt Inc* v. *Shrum Liddle & Hebenton* (1988) 26 BCLR (2d) 46 (CA); *Patseas* v. *Costelo* (1988) 54 DLR (4th) 573 (BCCA); *Ecco Heating Products Ltd* v. *J. K. Campbell & Assoc Ltd*, [1990] 5 WWR 687 (BCCA); *Bushell* v. *T. & N. plc* (1992) 92 DLR (4th) 228 (BCCA); *Burt* v. *Clarkson Gordon* (1989) 62 DLR (4th) 676 (Man. CA); *Kornberg* v. *Kornberg* (1990) 76 DLR (4th) 379 (Man. CA); *McElheran* v. *Great Northwest Insulation Ltd* [1989] NWTR 160 (SC); *Halifax Grain Elevator Ltd* v. *Cargill Ltd* (1990) 96 NSR (2d) 234 (TD); *693663 Ontario Inc* v. *Deloitte & Touche Inc* (1991) 109 NSR (2d) 295 (CA), aff'ng. (1990) 102 NSR (2d) 376 (TD); *Owen* v. *Tinmouth* (1992) 116 NSR (2d) 245 (TD); *Bonaventure Systems Inc* v. *Royal Bank of Canada* (1986) 32 DLR (4th) 721 (Ont. Div. Ct.); *Middle East Banking Co SAL* v. *Al-Haddad* (1989) 70 OR (2d) 97 (HCJ); *Thorpe Bros Ltd* v. *Saan Stores Ltd* (1990) 89 Sask. R 106 (QB).
[32] Even fairly recently a judge still treated the change from an 'oppressive or vexatious' test to a *forum non conveniens* test, in cases of service in the jurisdiction, as an oper question: *Jepson Estate* v. *Westfair Foods Ltd* (1989) 61 Man. R (2d) 56 (QB).
[33] [1993] 1 SCR 897, 102 DLR (4th) 96 (hereinafter *Amchem*, cited to DLR).
[34] *Ibid*. 109, citing Hayes, (1992) 16 *UBCL Rev*. 41 at 42–3.
[35] N. 33 above, at 108–11.

Sopinka J said, 'that whether it is a case for service out of the jurisdiction or the defendant is served in the jurisdiction, the issue remains: is there a more appropriate jurisdiction based on the relevant factors'.[36] Whether the defendant *resides* out of the jurisdiction was a relevant factor, but that was true whether the defendant was served in or out of the jurisdiction. Sopinka J noted:[37]

The special treatment which the English courts have accorded to *ex juris* cases appears to be based on the dictates of O. 11 of the English rules which imposes a heavy burden on the plaintiff to justify the assertion of jurisdiction over a foreigner. In most provinces in Canada, leave to serve *ex juris* is no longer required except in special circumstances and this trend is one that is likely to spread to other provinces.

It is unclear to what extent this remark indicates disagreement with the clear distinction that was drawn in the *Spiliada* case between the two types of service for the purposes of the burden of proof. The quoted comment, together with the court's express approval of the proposition 'that the existence of a more appropriate forum must be *clearly* established to displace the forum selected by the plaintiff',[38] could be read as laying down the general rule that, in Canada, regardless of whether service was effected in the jurisdiction or *ex juris*, the defendant must persuade the court to decline jurisdiction on the ground of *forum non conveniens*. But Sopinka J also said:[39]

Whether the burden of proof should be on the plaintiff in *ex juris* cases will depend on the rule that permits service out of the jurisdiction. If it requires that service out of the jurisdiction be justified by the plaintiff, whether on an application for an order or in defending service *ex juris* where no order is required, then the rule must govern.

Taking these passages together, the court's view seems to be that there is no general principle that the burden of proof must be on the plaintiff in *ex juris* cases. It is just a question of construction of the rules of court.

In the cases where a plaintiff must have leave to serve *ex juris*, the Canadian courts have assumed on the basis of tradition, rather than any express reference to this issue in the rules of court, that the plaintiff has the burden of persuading the local court that it is *forum conveniens*.[40] Where

---

[36] N. 33 above, at 111.

[37] *Ibid*. The court also referred to *Voth* v. *Manildra Flour Mills Pty Ltd* (1990) 65 ALJR 83 (Aust. HC), as supporting the idea that the test should be the same irrespective of whether service was in or out of the jurisdiction. The High Ct. did, however, draw a distinction as to the burden of proof between service in the jurisdiction, and service *ex juris* that requires leave: *ibid*. 92–3.

[38] *Amchem*, n. 33 above.   [39] *Ibid*.

[40] See e.g. *Antares Shipping Corp* v. *The Ship 'Capricorn'* [1977] 2 SCR 422, 65 DLR (3d) 105 (hereinafter *The 'Capricorn'*, cited to DLR); *Paterson* v. *Hamilton* (1991) 79 Alta. LR (2d) 111

the requirement of leave has been removed, so that service *ex juris* is available as of right, it is arguable that the burden of proof has been altered as well, so that it is for the defendant who challenges such service to show that the court is *forum non conveniens*. A number of Canadian courts have assumed that that is so,[41] but the British Columbia Court of Appeal held the contrary, namely, that even where *ex juris* service was authorized without leave, it was for the plaintiff to show the court was *forum conveniens* if the defendant raised the issue.[42] Very recently the Ontario Court of Appeal went the same way, but with a possibly significant change. Apparently taking Sopinka J's point in *Amchem* that the defendant's residence, rather than the place of service, was the important factor in deciding which court was the appropriate forum, Arbour JA said:[43]

[W]hen the plaintiff chooses a forum in which jurisdiction exists 'as of right', in the sense that the defendant *is a resident* of that jurisdiction, the defendant has the burden of showing that another forum is the convenient one. If the plaintiff chooses to bring a *foreigner* into the jurisdiction, *typically* in the case of service *ex juris*, the burden will be on the plaintiff to establish that Ontario is the appropriate forum if the choice of forum is challenged by the defendant. This, in my view, accords with the principles of comity upon which the doctrine of *forum non conveniens* rests.

This seems to shift the criterion from whether service is in the province or *ex juris* to whether the defendant resides (according to whatever definition may be adopted) in the province or is a 'foreigner'. It thus raises the possibility that, by contrast with the traditional approach, a non-resident served in the jurisdiction can insist that the plaintiff show the court is an appropriate forum, and, a rarer case, a resident of the province who is served *ex juris* will have the burden of displacing the plaintiff's choice of jurisdiction.

(CA); *United Oilseed Products Ltd* v. *Royal Bank of Canada*, n. 31 above, at 191; *Davidson* v. *The Anchorage Inc* (1980) 23 BCLR 352 (SC).

[41] *Cranston* v. *Ville de Hull* (1983) 62 NSR (2d) 343 (TD); *Witham* v. *Liftair Int'l (1985) Ltd* (1992) 114 NSR (2d) 43 (TD); *Pindling* v. *National Broadcasting Corp* (1984) 14 DLR (4th) 391 (Ont. HCJ); *Newgrade Energy Inc* v. *Kubota America Corp* (1991) 95 Sask. R 304 (QE), leave to appeal refused (1991) 97 Sask. R 32 (CA).

[42] *Bushell* v. *T. & N. plc*, n. 31 above.

[43] *Frymer* v. *Brettschneider* (1994) 19 OR (3d) 60 at 85 (Ont. CA) (emphasis added). The confusion stemming from Sopinka J's equivocal remarks in *Amchem* is apparent from the fact that two first instance judges in Ontario took them to mean that the burden was now on the defendant: *Upper Lakes Shipping Ltd* v. *Foster Yeoman Ltd* (1993) 14 OR (3d) 548 (Gen. Div.); *Applied Processes Inc* v. *Crane Co* (1993) 15 OR (3d) 166 (Gen. Div.). In *Frymer* the court attached no importance, as far as the burden of persuasion was concerned, to the wording of r. 17.06(2)(c) of the Ontario Civ. Proc. Rules, which says that where service is effected *ex juris* without leave, the court should set it aside if 'the court is satisfied that . . . Ontario is not a convenient forum for the hearing of the proceeding'. The same rule is found in Manitoba, Queen's Bench Rules, r. 17.06(2)(c).

All this said, it is easy to overestimate the importance of the issue of burden of persuasion. It is only decisive if a judge thinks that the question of the appropriate forum is more or less evenly balanced, which, given the nature of the test, it seldom is.

(c) THE APPROPRIATE FORUM: FACTORS TO BE TAKEN
    INTO ACCOUNT

Whichever party has the burden of proof, resolving the question of *forum conveniens* may require the consideration of any factor that bears on the interests of the parties in obtaining the most success at the least cost, as well as on the interests of the administration of justice in the affected countries. The starting-point for any argument of *forum non conveniens* must be that there is in fact some alternative to the local forum. 'The overriding consideration', as the majority of the Supreme Court of Canada said in one case, 'must . . . be the existence of some other forum more convenient and appropriate for the pursuit of the action and for securing the ends of justice'.[44] That particular case, a Federal Court action against shipowners, had virtually nothing to do with Canada except that the defendants' ship had put into a Canadian port; but the court held that jurisdiction was properly taken.[45] The vessel was the principal defendant's only asset and, if the Federal Court declined jurisdiction, all that would have been achieved was to compel the plaintiff to bring new proceedings against the vessel in another country that might or might not have a greater connection with the litigation.[46] In non-maritime cases the mere presence of the defendant's property in the jurisdiction is unlikely to be enough to support the exercise of jurisdiction, if for no other reason than that the rules of court of most provinces do not permit service *ex juris* on that ground alone.[47] But where the litigation has at least a minimal

---

[44] *The 'Capricorn'*, n. 40 above, at 123.

[45] The plaintiff needed leave to serve *ex juris*.

[46] Laskin CJC dissented on the ground that, since the plaintiff's claims were *in personam* only, the presence of the vessel in Canada was an insufficient basis for taking jurisdiction. The Federal Court was held to be *forum conveniens* in similarly completely foreign cases, in *Kuhr* v. *The 'Friedrich Busse'* [1982] 2 FC 709, 134 DLR (3d) 261 (TD); and *Yasuda Fire & Marine Ins. Co Ltd* v. *The 'Nosira Lin'* [1984] 1 FC 895 (TD). Compare *Elesguro Inc* v. *Ssangyong Shipping Co Ltd* [1981] 2 FC 326, 117 DLR (3d) 105 (TD). See Oland, in *Meredith Memorial Lectures*, n. 18 above, at 319–20.

[47] See *Tortel Communications Inc* v. *Suntel Inc* [1994] 4 WWR 746 (Man. QB). An exception is BC, Rules of Ct., r. 13(1)(m), which permits service *ex juris* without leave if the action is in contract and the defendant has assets in the province. It was recognized in *Northern Sales Ltd* v. *Government Trading Corp of Iran* (1991) 81 DLR (4th) 316 at 321 (BCCA), that assuming jurisdiction on that basis alone, with no real and substantial connection with the province, would offend 'international good manners or comity'. Some provinces' rules do permit service *ex juris* simply on the basis that the defendant has assets in the jurisdiction, where the action is to enforce a foreign judgment. See e.g. *Lebo Co* v. *Thatcher* (1989) 74 Sask. R 134 (QB), aff'd. (1989) 75 Sask. R 148 (CA).

connection with the local forum, the fact that the defendant has assets in the local forum and not in the—otherwise more appropriate—alternative forum will be a powerful argument against declining jurisdiction.[48]

Sometimes Canadian courts approach the question of *forum conveniens* on the basis of a broad 'centre of gravity' approach, cumulating the various connections that the litigation has with each possible forum.[49] More commonly, they weigh the appropriateness of the alternative forums by assessing the impact of specific facts on the parties' respective interests as well as on the administration of justice. Probably the factual circumstance most often discussed is the difficulty and expense each party will have in presenting its case before one or another forum. Consideration may be given not only to where each party's witnesses and documentary evidence must come from,[50] but also to whether a party has the means of compelling the attendance of its witnesses.[51] If one party is impecunious, that fact may be put into the scales when comparing the difficulty that each side may have in litigating in a particular court.[52]

Also often referred to is the law that applies to the merits of the dispute. Since proof of foreign law is seldom especially difficult, the fact that another jurisdiction's law will have to be applied is usually not a weighty factor is favour of declining jurisdiction.[53] Typically, the fact that the litigation concerns a contract or a tort that is governed by the law of a particular country is mentioned only as a supplementary reason for favouring the hearing of the action in that country.[54] Occasionally it may

---

[48] *Delbreuck & Co v. Muenzenberg* (1984) 54 BCLR 264 (SC); *Nemaha Energy Inc v. Wood & Locker Inc* (1985) 68 BCLR 187 (SC); *Canadian Imperial Bank of Commerce v. Rio-Mar Fisheries Ltd* (1985) 71 NSR (2d) 446 (TD); *Pace v. Synetics Inc* (1983) 145 DLR (3d) 749 (Ont. HCJ); *Polar Hardware Mfg Co v. Zafir* (1984) 43 CPC 156 (Ont. HCJ); *General Dynamics Corp v. Veliotis* (1985) 7 CPC (2d) 169 (Ont. HCJ); *Middle East Banking Co SAL v. Al-Haddad*, n. 31 above. See the section on 'legitimate advantage', below.

[49] *First City Invts. Inc v. Shrum, Liddle & Hebenton*, n. 31 above; *Ash v. Lloyd's (Corp of)* (1992) 94 DLR (4th) 378, supplementary reasons, 95 DLR (4th) 766 (Ont. CA), leave to appeal refused (8 Oct. 1992), [1992] 3 SCR v; *Lucas-California Co v. Charlottetown Metal Products Ltd*, n. 12 above. See also *Spiliada*, n. 23 above, at 478, referring to a 'real and substantial connection' test.

[50] A few examples are *United Oilseed Products Ltd v. Royal Bank*, n. 31 above; *P.W.A. Corp v. Gemini Group Automated Distribn. Systems Inc* (1992) 98 DLR (4th) 277 (Alta. QB): *First City Invt. Inc v. Shrum, Liddle & Hebenton*, n. 31 above; *Burt v. Clarkson Gordon*, n. 31 above; *Canadian Insulation Services Co Ltd v. Petro-Canada Explorations, Inc* (1981) 122 DLR (3d) 21 (NSTD); *Pandalus Nordique Ltée v. Ulstein Propeller A/S* (1991) 105 NSR (2d) 52 (TD); *Bonaventure Systems Inc v. Royal Bank of Canada*, n. 31 above.

[51] *Peterson v. AB Bahco Ventilation* (1979) 107 DLR (3d) 49 (BCSC); *Canadian Commercial Bank v. Carpenter* (1989) 62 DLR (4th) 734 (BCCA).

[52] *Monahan (guardian ad litem of) v. Trahan* (1992) 13 CPC (3d) 52 (NSTD).

[53] See e.g. *Discreet Logic Inc v. Canada (Registrar of Copyrights)* (19 Apr. 1994), Appeal No. A–622-93 (FCA) (unrep. at time of writing).

[54] *Westcoast Transmission Co Ltd v. Interprovincial Steel & Pipe Corp Ltd* (1982) 41 BCLR 103 (SC); *Canadian Insulation Services Co Ltd v. Petro-Canada Explorations Inc*, n. 50 above; *Jones v. Ontario White Star Products Ltd* (1979) 15 CPC 144 (Ont. HCJ); *Hein v. Linwell Wood Products*

be treated as a dominant factor, as in one British Columbia case, where the court upheld the plaintiff's choice of British Columbia as the forum, on the ground that the British Columbia statute on which the plaintiff relied had such complex ramifications that the courts of another province would be hard put to cope with it.[55] The governing law may also be a strong factor if it results from the express choice of the parties, even more so if the choice of law were combined with a clause accepting the court's jurisdiction.[56] It may also be that a party seeks to invoke a local law, usually a regulatory statute of some kind, that will be applied in the local courts but not in the alternative forum. The weight the courts give to such a 'legitimate advantage' will be discussed below.

A powerful argument in favour of a particular forum may be the avoidance of multiple lawsuits in different jurisdictions. Thus, courts have favoured the jurisdiction where the plaintiff's claim can be joined with those of others against the same defendants on similar facts,[57] or with other claims by the plaintiff against further defendants,[58] or with claims over by the defendant against third parties.[59] The avoidance of parallel actions between the same parties in different places is discussed in the section on *lis alibi pendens*, below.

The weight given to all the factors that the courts take into account in assessing a *forum conveniens* argument may depend to some extent on whether the case is interprovincial or international, but it is difficult to draw any firm distinctions between the two situations. It has been suggested from time to time that, if the choice of fora is between two Canadian provinces or territories, a plaintiff's choice of the local forum deserves greater weight, because a court can take jurisdiction without the risk of offending against the interest of a foreign sovereignty in having the matter heard in its courts.[60] That is true enough, but one can argue with equal force that in interprovincial cases the local forum should be readier

---

Ltd (1986) 11 CPC (2d) 57 (Ont. Dist. Ct.); *Nationale-Nederlanden Financing Co BV* v. *Jones*, n. 12 above.

[55] *Ecco Heating Products Ltd* v. *J. K. Campbell & Assoc. Ltd* [1990] 5 WWR 687 (BCCA) (builder's lien statute).

[56] *P.W.A. Corp* v. *Gemini Group Automated Distribn. Systems Inc*, n. 50 above. Of course, if the choice of jurisdiction is an exclusive one, it will usually be decisive; see the section on choice of forum clauses below.

[57] Cf. *Bushell* v. *T. & N. plc*, n. 42 above.

[58] *Neptune Bulk Terminals Ltd* v. *Intertec Internationale Technische Assistenz GmbH* (1981) 127 DLR (3d) 736 (BCCA).

[59] *Canadian Commercial Bank* v. *Carpenter*, n. 51 above; *Halifax Grain Elevator Ltd* v. *Cargill Ltd*, n. 31 above; *S. G. Ryle & Associates Ltd* v. *Resources Mgmt. Int'l Inc* (1988) 86 NSR (2d) 171 (TD); *Aanestad* v. *Saskatchewan* (1991) 101 Sask. R 103 (QB); compare *Patseas* v. *Costelo*, n. 31 above.

[60] *Re Wismer and Javelin Int'l Ltd* (1981) 132 DLR (3d) 156 (Ont. HCJ); *Jannock Corp* v. *R. T. Tamblyn & Partners Ltd* (1985) 58 DLR (3d) 678 at 688 (Ont. HCJ). A variant of this argument is given by Lord Goff in a dictum in *Spiliada*, n. 23 above, at 476.

to decline jurisdiction at the instance of the defendant, since by doing so it is relegating the plaintiff, not to an alien court, but to a court in the same nation.[61] One court has specifically rejected the idea that there is any *a priori* difference between declining jurisdiction in interprovincial cases and in international ones.[62] Obviously, however, the way certain factors are viewed will depend upon which type of case it is. Arguments based on difficulties of litigating in a distant forum, for instance, may carry less weight if the alternative forum is in Canada. Another example is language. Courts in English-speaking provinces have refused on more than one occasion to entertain the argument that a plaintiff would be subject to a disadvantage if the action were litigated in Quebec, on account of the fact that the proceedings were likely to be in French. The bilingual nature of Canada precluded such arguments.[63] But the language of the courts presumably could be considered a significant factor in a case where the alternative forum was in France.

(d) LEGITIMATE ADVANTAGE TO ONE PARTY IN A FORUM

The aspect of the *forum conveniens* discretion that has proved the hardest to cast in clear terms, both in England and Canada, has been the proper role to be given to an assertion by the plaintiff that the action should be allowed to proceed in the local forum because of a 'legitimate personal or juridical advantage' that the plaintiff would enjoy there by comparison with the alternative forum. The phrase was used by Lord Diplock in *MacShannon* v. *Rockware Glass Ltd*, when he framed the *forum non conveniens* test, for cases of service in England, in two stages:[64]

(a) [The] defendant must satisfy the court that there is another forum to whose jurisdiction he is amenable in which justice can be done between the parties at substantially less inconvenience and expense, and (b) the stay must not deprive the plaintiff of a legitimate personal or juridical advantage which would be available to him if he invoked the jurisdiction of the English court.

Most of the Canadian cases that applied this formula gave scant attention to the qualifier 'legitimate' when plaintiffs argued, for example, that only in the local forum would they have access to advantages like a longer limitation period,[65] a more generous rule for the assessment of

---

[61] Edinger, 'MacShannon', n. 13 above, at 305.
[62] *United Oilseed Products Ltd* v. *Royal Bank of Canada*, n. 31 above, at 190.
[63] *Bonaventure Systems Inc* v. *Royal Bank of Canada*, n. 31 above, at 731; *Monahan (guardian ad litem of)* v. *Trahan*, n. 52 above, at 58.
[64] [1978] AC 795 at 812 (HL).
[65] *Butkovsky* v. *Donahue* (1984) 52 BCLR 278 (SC); *Abus KG* v. *Secord Inc* (1992) 8 CPC (3d) 343 (Ont. Gen. Div.); *Vancouver Island Helicopters Ltd* v. *Robertshaw Controls Co* (1980) 116 DLR (3d) 716 (Ont HCJ).

damages, [66] or special legislation for the protection of investors.[67] In many of them, the plaintiff was someone who had a reasonable claim to the benefit of the local rule.[68] In others, the nature of the advantage was such as to give it overriding practical importance, such as the fact that the defendant only had assets in the local forum,[69] or that the plaintiff risked being thrown in jail if he travelled to the alternative forum.[70] Sometimes, however, the plaintiff's claim of a legitimate advantage has led courts to take jurisdiction too readily over actions that had little connection with the local forum.[71] In this type of case, to give decisive weight to the advantage claimed by the plaintiff is effectively to license forum-shopping. It was for this reason that Lord Goff, in *Spiliada*, took pains to modify the second part of Lord Diplock's formula. If a court were of the view that, apart from the asserted advantage, the plaintiff's action should not be brought in the local forum, the presence of that advantage should only make the difference if the circumstances are such that 'objectively, injustice can be said to have been done' if the plaintiff is denied access to the local forum.[72] Thus if, for example, the plaintiff's action were statute-barred in the alternative forum, the local court should not hesitate to decline jurisdiction if the plaintiff acted unreasonably in not commencing an action in time in the other forum.[73] On the other hand, if the local forum is otherwise appropriate, it is immaterial that the plaintiff sued there with the motive of obtaining an advantage that was not available in the other possible forum.[74]

In the *Amchem* case the Supreme Court of Canada went further in one respect than the House of Lords. The Supreme Court saw no merit in continuing to treat the question of legitimate advantage as a second-stage

---

[66] *Skagway Terminal Co* v. *The 'Daphne'*, n. 31 above; *Marchand (Guardian ad litem of)* v. *Alberta Motor Assn. Ins Co* [1994] 5 WWR 764 (BCCA) (higher limits on insurance); *Byers* v. *Higgin* [1993] 6 WWR 511 (BCSC); *Westcoast Transmission Co Ltd* v. *Interprovincial Steel & Pipe Co Ltd*, n. 54 above.

[67] *Avenue Properties Ltd* v. *First City Devt. Corp*, n. 31 above; *Westminer Canada Holdings Ltd* v. *Coughlan* (1990) 73 DLR (4th) 584 (Ont. Div. Ct.).

[68] Such as a local-resident plaintiff claiming the benefit of local investor protection legislation in respect of a purchase of out-of-province property, the plaintiff having been solicited locally by the out-of-province vendor: *Avenue Properties*, n. 31 above.

[69] See the cases cited above, n. 48.

[70] *Jaffe* v. *Dearing* (1988) 65 OR (2d) 113 (HCJ); *Jaffe* v. *Miller* (1989) 39 CPC (2d) 157 (Ont. SC (MC)).

[71] Examples are the *Butkovsky* and *Vancouver Island Helicopter* cases, above, n. 65, and *The 'Daphne'*, above, n. 31.

[72] *Spiliada*, n. 23 above, at 482.

[73] *Ibid.* 483–4. Lord Goff noted that, as an alternative to allowing the plaintiff's action to proceed in the local forum, it may be possible to stay the local proceedings on condition that the defendant concede the plaintiff the advantage in question, by waiving the defence of a limitation period, if the plaintiff sues in the alternative forum.

[74] *Marchand (Guardian ad litem of)* v. *Alberta Motor Assn. Ins Co*, n. 66 above.

inquiry, the answer to which may override the conclusion that the local forum is inappropriate. Sopinka J said:[75]

[T]here is no reason in principle why the loss of juridical advantage should be treated as a separate and distinct condition rather than being weighed with the other factors which are considered in identifying the appropriate forum . . . The weight to be given to juridical advantage is very much a function of the parties' connection to the particular jurisdiction in question. If a party seeks out a jurisdiction simply to gain a juridical advantage rather than by reason of a real and substantial connection of the case to the jurisdiction, that is ordinarily condemned as 'forum shopping'. On the other hand, a party whose case has a real and substantial connection with a forum has a legitimate claim to the advantages that that forum provides. The legitimacy of this claim is based on a reasonable expectation that in the event of litigation arising out of the transaction in question, those advantages will be available.

As far as practical results are concerned, there is probably not much difference between the Supreme Court's one-stage analysis and the House of Lords's two-stage analysis. The Supreme Court's version is perhaps preferable from the point of view of the structure of the test. Giving the plaintiff's legitimate advantage in the domestic forum the status of an independent consideration, even qualified in the way that *Spiliada* indicated, seems at odds with the obvious point that the plaintiff's advantage is the defendant's disadvantage, and that both parties' interests are presumably entitled to their fair weight in the overall assessment of which forum would be more appropriate. The Supreme Court's affirmation of the idea that the plaintiff should show a 'legitimate claim' to the advantage will also be helpful in moderating the potential for forum-shopping that earlier Canadian cases seemed to leave open.[76]

2. LIS ALIBI PENDENS

In Canadian, as in English, common law, *lis alibi pendens* is not a doctrine unto itself, but simply one of the situations that give rise to a court's discretion to decline jurisdiction. In the current law, therefore, it is a facet of the doctrine of *forum conveniens*. It is only under particular statutes that legal proceedings between the same parties in another court will preclude a court altogether from taking jurisdiction. The clearest example is the federal Divorce Act, under which either of two courts in Canada may have

[75] *Amchem*, n. 33 above, at 110. The one-step was applied in *Bank van Parijs en de Nederlanden Belgie NV* v. *Cabri* (1993) 19 CPC (3d) 362 (Ont. Gen. Div.).

[76] Some recent cases had already followed *Spiliada*'s lead in scrutinizing claims of legitimate advantage more carefully: see e.g. *Buchar* v. *Weber* (1990) 71 DLR (4th) 544 (Ont. HCJ); *Tomlinson* v. *Turner* (1991) 99 Nfld. & PEIR 288 (PEI TD).

jurisdiction in divorce, namely the courts of the two provinces or territories where the spouses have respectively been ordinarily resident for a year. The Act gives exclusive jurisdiction to the court of the province or territory where a petition is first presented.[77]

As a reason for exercising the discretion to decline jurisdiction, *lis alibi pendens* has been given the most weight in Canada when the same party is plaintiff in both the local and the foreign proceedings, although even in that situation there is no presumption that the local proceedings should be stayed.[78] The parallel proceedings may be justified on a range of grounds. The remedies being sought in each of them might be distinct;[79] the foreign proceedings might have been started just to protect against the expiry of a limitation period,[80] or to secure assets abroad against which an eventual Canadian judgment could be enforced;[81] or the foreign proceedings might involve additional defendants.[82] Or the local forum might be so clearly the appropriate one for the hearing of the action that even the presence of the parallel proceedings elsewhere should not prevent the court from taking jurisdiction;[83] but in such a case it may be appropriate to require the plaintiff to discontinue the other proceedings.[84] Where the local proceedings are a form of cross-action, with the plaintiff being the party who is defendant in the foreign proceedings, the *lis alibi pendens* argument is usually harder to make, because it is not a case of one party having commenced parallel actions in different fora. The *lis alibi pendens* argument may still succeed if the local court decides that the two cross-actions would be most appropriately heard together in the other forum.[85] The plaintiff may be able to show, however, that the local forum offers some advantage that he or she is properly

[77] Divorce Act, RSC 1985, c. 3 (2nd Supp.), s. 3(2). Although not strictly a rule of *lis alibi pendens*, the extra-provincial custody orders legislation in various provinces gives priority to custody proceedings already brought in another jurisdiction, provided, in most cases, that the child was habitually resident there when those proceedings were begun: see e.g. Children's Law Reform Act, RSO 1990, c. C. 12, ss. 41–3.

[78] *Canastrand Industries Ltd* v. *The 'Lara S'* [1992] 3 FC 398 (TD).

[79] *Hunter Engineering Co Inc* v. *Hunter Machinery (Canada) Ltd* (1978) 8 BCLR 115 (SC).

[80] *Neptune Bulk Terminals Ltd* v. *Intertec Internationale Technische Assistenz GmbH*, n. 58 above; *Churchill Falls (Labrador) Corp Ltd* v. *McGraw-Edison Co* (1985) 1 CPC (2d) 229 (Nfld. TD).

[81] *Canastrand Industries Ltd* v. *The 'Lara S'*, n. 78 above.

[82] *Dal Ponte* v. *Northern Manitoba Native Lodges Inc* [1990] 4 WWR 60 (Man. QB). Compare *Suncorp Realty Inc* v. *Reid* [1984] 3 WWR 219 (Man. CA), where the plaintiff took steps to remove from the foreign proceeding the defendants it was suing locally.

[83] *DiCarlo* v. *Toronto Gen. Hospital* (1989) 104 NBR (2d) 67 (QB); the plaintiff was not pursuing the other action.

[84] This was done in *May* v. *Greenwood* (1991) 85 DLR (4th) 683 (Ont. Gen. Div.), but the decision was reversed and the local action stayed in favour of the continuation of the proceedings in the other province: (1992) 96 DLR (4th) 581 (Ont. Div. Ct.).

[85] *Ibid.*; *Plibrico (Canada) Ltd* v. *Suncor Inc* (1982) 35 OR (2d) 781 (HCJ); *Sterling Software Int'l (Canada) Inc* v. *Software Recording Corp of America* (1993) 47 CPR (3d) 420 (Ont. Gen. Div.).

entitled to,[86] or just that the local court is a more appropriate forum for the plaintiff's claim than the court in which the defendant is proceeding.[87] In one case a defendant tried to argue that the Supreme Court of Canada's recent emphasis on comity as a paramount consideration in the conflict of laws, especially as between the courts of different Canadian provinces,[88] should lead to a greater willingness to decline jurisdiction in favour of a court in another province where parallel proceedings had been brought by the defendant. The Ontario judge held that comity, with respect to litigation already under way in a sister province, was not a reason to decline jurisdiction where Ontario was the natural forum for the action.[89]

3. CHOICE OF JUDICIAL FORUM AND ARBITRATION CLAUSES

(a) CLAUSES CHOOSING A JUDICIAL FORUM

Canadian courts in the common law jurisdictions have followed the English principle that a clause by which the parties agree to litigate their disputes exclusively[90] in a particular foreign court is not binding on a domestic court. Its jurisdiction cannot be ousted by private agreement.[91] But the domestic court will usually hold the plaintiff to the clause unless he satisfies it that there are strong reasons, from the point of view of convenience or the interests of justice, for allowing the action to proceed despite the clause.[92] Thus courts have permitted the plaintiff to sue in disregard of the clause where litigation in the foreign court would have

---

[86] *Avenue Properties Ltd* v. *First City Devt. Corp*, n. 31 above; *Zurich Indemnity Ins Co of Canada* v. *Reemark Lincoln's Hill Project Ltd* (1992) 73 BCLR (2d) 234 (SC).
[87] *Gerling Global Gen. Ins Co* v. *PCL Const. Ltd* (1986) 48 Alta. LR (2d) 375 (QB); *Hudson's Bay Co* v. *PCL Const. Ltd* (1984) 6 DLR (4th) 763 (Ont. HCJ); *Polar Hardward Mfg Co* v. *Zafir*, n. 48 above; *Galtaco Redlaw Castings Corp* v. *Brunswick Industrial Supply Co* (1989) 69 OR (2d) 478 (HCJ).
[88] See n. 112 below.
[89] *Guarantee Co of N Am.* v. *Gordon Capital Corp* (1994), Action No. 93–CQ-40684 (Ont. Gen. Div.) (unrep. at time of writing).
[90] A choice of forum clause that is not exclusive will obviously not be as strong a reason for the domestic court to decline jurisdiction, although it may still be relevant to the overall assessment of the *forum conveniens*: see *P.W.A. Corp* v. *Gemini Group Automated Distribn. Systems Inc*, n. 50 above.
[91] The suggestion to the contrary in *E. K. Motors Ltd* v. *Volkswagen Canada Ltd* [1973] 1 WWR 466 (Sask. CA), is an anomaly; see *Volkswagen Canada Ltd* v. *Auto Haus Fröhlich Ltd* [1986] 1 WWR 380 (Alta. CA); *Pirrana Small Car Centres* v. *Rumm* [1981] 5 WWR 79 (BCSC). Canadian and English cases on choice of forum and arbitration clauses are summarized in Oland, n. 46 above.
[92] *Burrard-Yarrows Corp* v. *The 'Hoegh Merchant'* [1982] 1 FC 248 (TD), aff'd. [1983] 1 FC 495 (CA); *Nissho Iwai Corp* v. *Paragon Grand Carriers Corp* (1987) 11 FTR 134 (FCTD); *Volkswagen Canada Ltd* v. *Auto Haus Fröhlich Ltd*, n. 91 above; *G. & E. Auto Brokers Ltd* v. *Toyota Canada Inc* (1980) 117 DLR (3d) 707 (BCSC); *Ash* v. *Lloyd's (Corp of)*, n. 49 above; *Anthes Eqpt. Ltd* v. *William Layner GmbH* (1986) 6 CPC (2d) 252 (Ont. HCJ); *Fairfield* v. *Low* (1990) 44 CPC (2d) 65 (Ont. HCJ); *Mithras Mgmt. Ltd* v. *New Visions Entertainment Corp* (1992) 90 DLR (4th) 726 (Ont. Gen. Div.); *Oulton Agencies Inc* v. *Knolloffice Inc* (1988) 48 DLR (4th) 545 (PEI CA).

led to a multiplicity of proceedings;[93] where the defendant seeking to hold the plaintiff to the clause was being sued in its own province and had no real interest in being sued in the agreed forum;[94] where the plaintiff could not have compelled its key witnesses to testify in the agreed forum;[95] and where the plaintiff was relatively impecunious and would have difficulty suing in the agreed forum.[96]

(b) ARBITRATION CLAUSES

Until fairly recently the position with respect to arbitration clauses was the same as for choice of forum clauses. The court had a discretion to permit a party to bring the action before the court, notwithstanding the arbitration clause, if there were sufficient grounds for doing so. If the plaintiff could not show such grounds, his or her action would be stayed. This was specifically provided in the arbitration statutes in the Canadian jurisdictions.[97] In the mid-1980s, however, all the Canadian jurisdictions (including Quebec) enacted the UNCITRAL Model Law to govern international commercial arbitrations.[98] This statutory regime will apply to any arbitration agreement that qualifies as both international and commercial.[99] Under Article 8 of the Model Law, if an action is brought before a court in respect of matters that are covered by such an arbitration agreement the court must stay the proceeding unless it finds that the agreement is null and void, inoperative, or incapable of being performed.[100] The

---

[93] *Neptune Bulk Terminals Ltd* v. *Intertec Internationale Technische Assistenz GmbH*, n. 58 above.   [94] *Pirrana Small Car Centres Ltd* v. *Rumm*, n. 91 above.

[95] *Corostel Trading Ltd* v. *Secunda Marine Services Ltd* (1990) 38 FTR 232 (FCTD).

[96] *Mountainbell Co Ltd* v. *VVTC Air Freight (HK) Ltd* (1988) 20 FTR 57 (FCTD); *Fleming* v. *Samuelsohn Ltd* [1991] 1 WWR 176 (BCSC).

[97] The current rules in these statutes, often much more restrictive of the court's discretion than the old ones, are summarized in J.-G. Castel, *Canadian Conflict of Laws* (3rd ed., 1994), 307–8. An example is the Arbitration Act, RSO 1990, c. A.24, s. 7.

[98] See e.g. Commercial Arbitration Act, RSC 1985, c. 17 (2nd Supp.); International Commercial Arbitration Act, SBC 1986, c. 14 as am.; International Commercial Arbitration Act, RSO 1990, c. I.9. A table of all the Canadian implementing statutes is given in Paterson and Thompson, *Uncitral Arbitration Model in Canada* (1987), 165–6.

[99] Model Law, Art. 1. Art. 1(3) defines as 'international' an arbitration where (a) the parties to the arbitration agreement have their places of business in different states; (b) the parties have their places of business in the same state but (i) the place of arbitration or (ii) the place where a substantial part of the obligations of the commercial relationship is to be performed is in, or the subject-matter of the agreement is most closely connected with, another state; or (c) the parties have expressly agreed that the subject-matter of the arbitration agreement relates to more than one state.

[100] Model Law, Art. 8(1). See Paterson, (1993) 10 *J Int. Arb.* 29 at 37–43. In *BWV Investments Ltd* v. *Saskferco Products Inc* [1993] 4 WWR 553 (Sask. QB), it was held that an arbitration agreement in a contract expressly governed by Swiss law was void within the meaning of this provision because holding the plaintiff to the clause would preclude it from enforcing a builders' lien, the right to which, according to the Saskatchewan builders' lien statute, could not be ousted by private contract. A contrary decision is *Kværner Enviropower Inc* v. *Tanar Industries Ltd* (14 July 1994), Action No. 9403–10106 (Alta. QB) (unrep. at time of writing).

Model Law does not contemplate a discretion to allow the litigation to continue.[101] This means, for all practical purposes, that the plaintiff's only escape from the arbitration agreement is to frame its action in such a way as to persuade a court that the dispute is not within the scope of the agreement. One example is an action claiming that the defendant fraudulently induced the plaintiff to enter into a contract; a British Columbia court held that such a dispute did not 'arise out of' the contract and so was outside the scope of the arbitration clause in the contract.[102] Such a narrowly literal approach to the arbitration clause is not typical. Other courts have given arbitration clauses a more generous interpretation, on the ground of pursuing the statutory policy that arbitration agreements should be enforced unless there is a clear ground for not doing so.[103] In one of these cases the suggestion that a type of *forum conveniens* discretion had survived was specifically rejected, the court observing that '[t]he *forum conveniens* test almost always would defeat arbitration because . . . it would invite "unseemly and mutually destructive jockeying" . . . [It would place] a leash on arbitration that is as short as the pleading of opposing counsel is long, which sacrifices certainty to wit'.[104] A party may lose the right to insist on the arbitration clause if it does not invoke it in a timely fashion, before taking any substantial step in the proceedings before the court.[105]

In most Canadian jurisdictions the courts are not obliged to give the same automatic deference to domestic arbitration agreements, to which the old law still applies, as they are to international commercial arbitration agreements falling under the Model Law. It is probably a sign of future trends, however, that British Columbia's domestic arbitration statute has adopted the Model Law's Article 8 and thus extended to domestic arbitration clauses the policy of giving judges only the narrowest grounds for pre-empting a right to arbitration.[106]

---

[101] This overrides any inherent discretion the court might otherwise have: *Nanisivik Mines Ltd* v. *FCRS Shipping Ltd* (1994) 113 DLR (4th) 536 (FCA). In *Gulf Canada Resources Ltd* v. *Arochem Int'l Ltd* (1992) 66 BCLR (2d) 113 (CA), the court said there was a discretion but only as to whether the court should negate the arbitration agreement on the ground that the dispute fell outside its scope or that the agreement was invalid on one of the grounds contemplated by the Model Law. The court thought that, unless the answer was clearly yes, the question should be left to the arbitrators to decide.
[102] *ODC Exhibit Systems Ltd* v. *Lee* (1988) 41 BLR 286 (BCSC). See also *Canmax Properties Corp* v. *Vancity Enterprises Ltd* (1992) 63 BCLR (2d) 231 (CA).
[103] *Kaverit Steel & Crane Ltd* v. *Kone Corp* (1992) 87 DLR (4th) 129 (Alta. CA); *Boart Systems AB* v. *Nya Stromnes AB* (1988) 41 BLR 295 (Ont. HCJ).
[104] *Kaverit*, n. 103 above, at 139.
[105] Art. 8 only applies if the party seeks a stay 'not later than when submitting his first statement on the substance of the dispute': see *Iberfreight SA* v. *Ocean Star Container Line AG* (1989) 104 NR 164 (FCA); *Stancroft Trust Ltd* v. *Can-Asia Capital Co* (1990) 67 DLR (4th) 131 (BCCA).
[106] Commercial Arbitration Act, SBC 1986, c. 3, s. 15, as am. by SBC 1988, c. 46, s. 11.

III
ENJOINING FOREIGN LEGAL PROCEEDINGS

Canadian courts, following English precedent, have asserted that a court has the power to make an *in personam* order to restrain a person engaged in legal proceedings elsewhere from pursuing that litigation. The *Amchem* case, which was discussed above in connection with what it said about *forum non conveniens*, now completely supersedes the rather thin earlier case law on this question.[107] The case concerned litigation undertaken in a Texas District Court by 194 individual claimants, the great majority of whom had received benefits from the Workers' Compensation Board of British Columbia, which was subrogated to their claims and was effectively in charge of the litigation. The claims all related to injuries said to have been suffered as a result of exposure to asbestos products manufactured by the defendants in the Texas proceedings, most of whom were incorporated in the United States and none of whom had any connection with British Columbia. Several of the defendants had their primary manufacturing facility, or their head office, in Texas; each of the rest carried on business in Texas to some degree. The defendants had failed to persuade the Texas court that it lacked jurisdiction, and their further argument that Texas was *forum non conveniens* had also been rejected, apparently because the doctrine had been statutorily abolished in that State. The defendant companies subsequently began an action in British Columbia, the principal claims being for a permanent injunction to restrain the claimants from further prosecuting the Texas action, and a declaration that the companies were not liable for the claimants' injuries. The companies also asked for an injunction to restrain the claimants who resided in British Columbia from obtaining any injunction in Texas to restrain the companies from prosecuting their proceedings in British Columbia. This last injunction (effectively an anti-anti-anti-suit injunction) was granted by the trial judge and upheld by the British Columbia Court of Appeal. The latter court took the view that British Columbia was the only natural forum for the claimants' actions. The claimants were British Columbia residents, the alleged wrongful acts and omissions by the defendants (such as negligent failure to warn of risks) had taken place in Canada, and the claimants' injuries were predominantly suffered as a result of exposure to asbestos in British Columbia. The only connection with Texas, for all but a few of the companies, was that they sold their products

---

[107] Injunctions were granted in *Canadian Home Assurance Co* v. *Cooper* (1986) 29 DLR (4th) 419 (NSCA), and *Allied-Signal Inc* v. *Dome Petroleum Ltd* [1989] 5 WWR 326 (Alta. QB). The power to grant them was confirmed, but the order was denied, in *Aikmac Holdings Ltd* v. *Loewen* (1989) 66 Man. R (2d) 295, 42 CPC (2d) 139 (CA); *Kornberg* v. *Kornberg*, n. 31 above; and *Greymac Trust Co* v. *BNA Realty Inc* (1985) 50 CPC 45 (Ont. HCJ).

there.[108] The Court of Appeal followed a 1987 decision of the Privy Council, *Société Nationale Industrielle Aérospatiale* v. *Lee Kui Jak*,[109] to the effect that an injunction against foreign legal proceedings should be granted if the plaintiff shows not only that the local forum is the natural forum for the dispute to be heard, but also that the continuation of the foreign proceedings would be oppressive or vexatious towards the plaintiff. To a large extent the Court of Appeal in *Amchem* found the oppression in the fact that the asbestos manufacturers were being forced into a court that would not even entertain the argument of *forum non conveniens*.[110]

The Supreme Court accepted largely the same principles as the Court of Appeal, but held that the principles had been incorrectly applied. Rather than put the first question in terms of the natural forum, the Supreme Court preferred to ask whether the Texas court—irrespective of whether it would entertain the plea of *forum non conveniens* in the Canadian or in any other sense—was in point of fact a *forum non conveniens* according to Canadian standards. At this point the Supreme Court elaborated its view of that doctrine, as outlined above.[111] Applying that notion of *forum non conveniens* to a foreign court meant that:

the domestic court as a matter of comity must take cognizance of the fact that the foreign court has assumed jurisdiction. If, applying the principles relating to *forum non conveniens* outlined above, the foreign court could reasonably have concluded that there was no alternative forum that was clearly more appropriate, the domestic court should respect that decision and the application should be dismissed. When there is a genuine disagreement between the courts of our country and another, the courts of this country should not arrogate to themselves the decision for both jurisdictions.[112]

---

[108] In the Sup. Ct. of Canada, Sopinka J said that most of the companies carried on business in Texas in the form of manufacturing plants (n. 33 above, at 99–100), but the CA ((1990) 75 DLR (4th) 1 at 19) and the judge at first instance ((1989) 65 DLR (4th) 567 at 583) refer only to certain of the companies' products being sold in Texas.

[109] [1987] AC 871 (PC).

[110] CA, n. 108 above, at 21.

[111] Nn. 33–42 above and accompanying text.

[112] N. 33 above at 119. The court's reference to comity reflects a strong element in its current thinking about the conflict of laws. In *Morguard Investments Ltd* v. *De Savoye*, [1990] 3 SCR 1077, 76 DLR (4th) 256 at 268 (hereinafter *Morguard*, cited to DLR), it described comity as 'the informing principle of private international law'. Comity was a practical response to the need 'to facilitate the flow of wealth, skills, and people across state lines in a fair and orderly manner', and the content of the notion of comity 'must be adjusted in the light of a changing world order' (at 269). The court quoted *Hilton* v. *Guyot*, 159 US 113 at 163–4 (1895), in *Morguard* at 269 and in *Amchem*, n. 33 above at 105, for the definition of comity as 'the recognition which one nation allows within its territory to the legislative, executive or judicial acts of another nation, having due regard both to international duty and convenience, and to the rights of its own citizens or of other persons who are under the protection of its laws'.

The Supreme Court agreed with the *Aérospatiale* case that, even if the domestic court concludes that the foreign court is in fact *forum non conveniens*, the injunction should be granted only if the foreign court's assumption of jurisdiction is inequitable in the sense that 'an injustice results to a litigant or "would-be" litigant in our courts'.[113] The court preferred 'injustice' to the Privy Council's 'oppressive or vexatious' formula, which, according to the court, had never been satisfactorily defined and added nothing to the analysis.[114] In deciding whether an injunction was required to avoid injustice, the domestic court should examine the advantages that each party has in the forum that he or she prefers: 'Any loss of advantage to the foreign plaintiff [if the injunction is granted] must be weighed as against the loss of advantage, if any, to the defendant in the foreign jurisdiction if the action is tried there rather than in the domestic forum'.[115]

In the *Amchem* case itself the Supreme Court held that the claim for an injunction failed at both stages of the inquiry. It could not be said that British Columbia was clearly a more appropriate forum than Texas for the claimants' actions. The asbestos companies had connections with Texas and none with British Columbia. The acts on which the claims were based were mostly done in the companies' conduct of their business in the United States. '[I]f some weight is given to the choice of forum by the plaintiff in the absence of related litigation pending elsewhere, the decision of the Texas court could be recognized having due regard for the principles of comity.'[116] Even if Texas could be considered a *forum non conveniens* the manufacturers were unable to show that they would be unjustly deprived of a legitimate advantage by having to defend actions in Texas rather than British Columbia. Various advantages that they had suggested they would have in British Columbia but not in Texas were insufficiently substantial. In any event they were not advantages that the manufacturers could reasonably have expected to have, based on the companies' previous connection to British Columbia.[117]

IV

RECOGNITION AND ENFORCEMENT OF FOREIGN JUDGMENTS: THE FOREIGN COURT AS *FORUM NON CONVENIENS*

Under the traditional Anglo-Canadian common law rules for the recognition of foreign judgments it could seldom arise that an enforceable

---

[113] *Amchem*, n. 33 above, at 120–1.   [114] *Ibid*. 119.   [115] *Ibid*. 120.

[116] *Ibid*. 122. The 'decision of the Texas court' must be the decision to accept jurisdiction. There is no doubt that an eventual decision on the merits of the litigation would be enforceable, given that the defendants would certainly defend the action.

[117] *Ibid*. 123.

foreign judgment could come from a court that, in Canadian eyes, was a *forum non conveniens*. The requirement that the defendant either have been served in the country where the judgment was given, or have submitted to the jurisdiction of the court, ensured that in the great majority of cases the original court was not an inappropriate forum. A *forum conveniens* issue could arise if the defendant were served in a country where he or she was only temporarily present, and indeed it was said in one Canadian case that the transitory presence of the defendant in the jurisdiction at the time of service might not be a sufficient ground at common law for recognizing a default judgment in the proceedings.[118] Besides this possibility, if the foreign court was egregiously a *forum non conveniens*, it could result in the judgment being refused recognition on the ground of a lack of natural justice, especially if the defendant were unable to make a proper defence.[119]

In 1990 the Supreme Court of Canada greatly expanded the common law rules for the recognition of judgments, at least within Canada, in *Morguard Investments Ltd* v. *De Savoye*.[120] A default judgment, given in an action against a defendant who was not served within the original province or territory, was declared to be enforceable if the original court was 'acting through fair process and with properly restrained jurisdiction'.[121] The essential jurisdictional requirement was that there must have been a real and substantial connection between the litigation and the country where the action took place.[122] The concept of *forum conveniens* is obviously present in this test to a considerable degree, particularly when the test is expressed in terms of whether the original court was a 'reasonable place for the action . . . to take place',[123] or whether there was 'the kind of connection . . . that makes it fair for the defendant to be required to defend the action' in the original country.[124] Nevertheless, there remains a considerable difference between the two doctrines. Nothing in *Morguard* or the cases that follow it suggests that a foreign default judgment will be recognized only if the foreign court were the most appropriate forum for the action. The question, rather, is whether it was an acceptable forum in the sense of having a sufficient, not necessarily preponderant, connection with the litigation.[125]

---

[118] *Re Carrick Estates Ltd and Young* (1987) 43 DLR (4th) 161 at 163 (Sask. CA).

[119] The defence of natural justice has rarely succeeded in Canada; see Castel, n. 97 above at 272–3; McLeod, *The Conflict of Laws* (1983), 616–20.

[120] N. 112 above.   [121] *Ibid.* 274.   [122] *Ibid.* 276–9.   [123] *Ibid.* 277.

[124] *Moses* v. *Shore Boat Builders Ltd* [1992] 5 WWR 282 at 287 (BCSC), aff'd. (1993) 106 DLR (3d) 654 (BCCA), leave to appeal refused, 3 Mar. 1994 (SCC).

[125] This point is reinforced by the Sup. Ct.'s later confirmation that the jurisdictional standards for the recognition of foreign judgments are, essentially, the constitutional standards for the valid assertion of jurisdiction by courts of a province: *Hunt* v. *T. & N. Plc* [1993] 4 SCR 289, 109 DLR (4th) 16 at 40–42 (*Hunt*, hereinafter cited to DLR). It is clear that these standards do not demand anything like a preponderant connection with the province, only enough of a connection that is sufficient to make the

It is not yet finally settled whether the *Morguard* ground for the recognition of default judgments extends to judgments from outside Canada. *Morguard* itself relied heavily on the argument that conditions within the Canadian federation demanded a common law 'full faith and credit' approach to the enforcement of judgments from elsewhere in Canada, which leaves open the argument that it is limited to intra-Canadian enforcement actions. The cases decided so far, however, are virtually unanimous that it is not so limited.[126]

V
CONCLUSION

The Canadian common law *forum non conveniens* doctrine, including its treatment of *lis alibi pendens*, is less an accessory to the rules of jurisdiction than a major—possibly *the* major component of those rules in practice. Given jurisdiction as of right over defendants who are served in the jurisdiction, and broad service *ex juris* rules, there are few occasions when a Canadian court is absolutely precluded from taking jurisdiction over an action.[127] The discretion to decline jurisdiction has therefore become the means by which disputes as to jurisdiction are most often resolved in the common law jurisdictions of Canada.

assumption of jurisdiction 'in accordance with the broad principles of order and fairness' (*ibid.* 42).

[126] The most important decision at the time of writing was *Moses* v. *Shore Boat Builders Ltd*, n. 124 above (BCCA). There are a considerable number of first instance decisions, nearly all in British Columbia and Ontario. The only dissenting case I found is *Evans Dodd* v. *Gambin Associates* (1994) 17 OR (3d) 803 (Gen. Div.).

[127] The constitutional validity of some of the wider service *ex juris* rules has never been squarely tested, but the Sup. Ct. of Canada has served notice that the constitution requires a province's jurisdictional rules to be based on 'reasonable grounds' that 'are grounded in notions of order and fairness to participants in litigation with connections to multiple jurisdictions': *Hunt* v. *T. & N. Plc*, n. 125 above.

6

Canada (Quebec)

GERALD GOLDSTEIN

*Professor, Faculty of Law, University of Montreal**

CONTENTS

* The author wishes to thank Me Betty Coups, of the Bar of Montreal, for her very able and valuable help in editing the text. He also wishes to express his gratitude to his colleague Jean-Maurice Brissen, of the Faculty of Law (University of Montreal), for his encouragement and his precious help gained in discussing some questions encompassed in this chapter.

I
INTRODUCTION

Quebecois law on international proceedings has been deeply modified by the recent adoption of the new Civil Code of Quebec, in force since 1 January 1994. Its Book X contains comprehensive legislation on private international law. It originates in part in case law, but mostly in the academic literature which brought to Quebec recent developments stemming from other legislation, such as the Swiss or the German private international laws, and from international conventions. Therefore, in this chapter we shall deal primarily with the new law, although reference will also be made to the pre-existing law.

II
FORUM NON CONVENIENS

1. Existence of a Doctrine of *Forum Non Conveniens*

In Quebecois law, the doctrine of *forum non conveniens* has been codified in the new Civil Code of Quebec (referred to below as CCQ). Its Article 3135 states: 'Even though a Quebec authority has jurisdiction to hear a dispute, it may exceptionally and on application by a party, decline jurisdiction if it considers that the authorities of another country are in a better position to decide.' Therefore, in Quebecois law, one can affirm that the doctrine of *forum non conveniens* means: first, a discretionary power given to the judges; secondly, to dismiss actions; thirdly, notwithstanding the existence of a positive basis of jurisdiction in favour of Quebecois courts; fourthly, on the basis of the proof of a more appropriate forum.

Discretionary power: the discretionary nature of this power is precisely the reason it has been difficult to accept the doctrine of *forum non conveniens* in Quebecois law. Since most of the case law dealing with the doctrine arose from cases relating to personal actions of a patrimonial nature, Article 68 of the Quebecois Code of Civil Procedure (referred to below as CPC), which was the source of the law before the new Civil Code,[1] was applied and states:

---

[1] The Quebecois rules as to bases of international jurisdiction have been created by the case law applying Art. 68 CPC—originally adopted to deal with local jurisdiction only—to private international law cases. As a result, the Quebecois bases of international jurisdiction were very similar, but not identical, to the local bases of jurisdiction until the adoption of the new Civil Code. See generally, for references to Quebecois private international law: Groffier, *Précis de droit international privé québécois* (4th edn., Montreal, 1990) and *Supplément au Précis de droit international privé québécois* (Montreal, 1993); Glenn, 'Droit international privé' in *La réforme du Code civil* (Presses de l'Université Laval, 1993), iii. 669–800; Castel,

... notwithstanding any agreement to contrary, a purely personal action may be instituted:

(I) Before the court of the defendant's real domicile or, ... before that of his elected domicile.

If the defendant has no domicile in Quebec but resides or possesses property therein, he may be sued before the court of his ordinary residence, before the court of the place where such property is situated, or before the court of the place where the action is personally served upon him.

Since this Article was considered to be of a public policy nature and left no room for discretion, most of the case law in civil and commercial matters prior to the new Civil Code refused to admit the plea of *forum non conveniens* without express legislative intervention.[2]

Power to dismiss actions: Quebecois civil law never considered any remedy other than a dismissal of the action when dealing with *forum non conveniens*. Moreover, such a dismissal is non-conditional, since it is granted on the positive proof that a foreign court would be more convenient than the Quebecois court, but it is not possible to come back to the Quebecois court afterwards, even when the 'more convenient' court has refused to exercise jurisdiction over the action. However, a stay of action was possible if a plea of *lis alibi pendens* was raised.

These different remedies provide serious grounds for the need to distinguish *forum non conveniens* and *lis alibi pendens* in Quebecois law. However, they have both been seen as a means to avoid the rendering of contradictory judgments and *forum non conveniens* has been presented as a 'logical counterpart of *lis pendens*'.[3]

This raises a serious question as to the logic of the approach followed in the new Civil Code. Under Article 3137 of the CCQ the conditions for granting a stay of action on a plea of *lis pendens* include the proof that another decision between the same parties, etc., is pending before a foreign authority, or has already been delivered, 'provided that the latter action can result in a decision which may be recognized in Quebec'. The existence of such a decision raises the threat of contradictory judgments. But in order to obtain a dismissal under article 3135 of the CCQ, it is only necessary to convince a Quebecois judge that a foreign court 'is in a better position to decide', even if, afterwards, such court actually refuses to exercise jurisdiction. In such a situation, there

'Commentaires sur certaines dispositions du Code civil se rapportant au droit international privé' (1992) 119 JDI 625; Talpis and Castel, 'Le Code civil du Québec. Interprétation des règles du droit international privé' in *La réforme du Code civil*, above, 801–933; Talpis and Goldstein, (1989) 91 *R du N* 293, 456, 606; Goldstein and Talpis, *L'effet au Québec des jugements étrangers en matière de droits patrimoniaux* (Montreal, 1991).

[2] *Southern Pacific Cy* v. *M. Botner & Sons Inc* [1973] RP 97 (CA); *Aberman* v. *Solomon* [1986] RDJ 385 (CA). See Groffier, n. 1 above (*Précis*), no. 248–51.

[3] Meyer, (1964) 25 *R du B* 565 at 597.

would be no contradictory judgments but the threat of a plain denial of justice!

If, in such circumstances, one party sues again in Quebec, one could argue that the decision which declined jurisdiction is not *res judicata* in Quebec, since it only held that another court was more convenient than the Quebecois court, which nonetheless had jurisdiction in the first place. As a result, a second Quebecois court could accept jurisdiction to avoid a denial of justice. Such a course that multiplies trial costs should be avoided but could rather easily happen.

In order to avoid such a result, justice, logic, and practicality require not a straight and final dismissal in case of *forum non conveniens*, but a conditional one, according to which the parties could still sue in Quebec if the 'better' foreign court refused to take jurisdiction over the action. Only then could *forum non conveniens* truly be seen as a logical counterpart of *lis pendens*.

It seems that Article 3136 of the CCQ, which provides for the adoption of the opposite doctrine of *forum conveniens* in Quebecois law, could not be used in such a case, since it only allows a Quebecois authority *having no jurisdiction* to hear a dispute 'where proceedings cannot possibly be instituted outside Quebec'. It could be argued that in such a case, although it refused it, Quebec *had* jurisdiction.

2. ORIGINS OF THE DOCTRINE OF *FORUM NON CONVENIENS*

In order to give a full account of the origins of the doctrine of *forum non conveniens* in Quebecois law, it is necessary to review some juridical developments predating the adoption of Article 3135 of the CCQ.

In Quebecois law, the inclusion in the new Civil Code of *forum non conveniens* has been the subject of a fierce debate because Quebecois academic literature favours its inclusion while the case law presents two contradictory tendencies.[4]

A few minority cases accepted the plea of *forum non conveniens*, thus following the academic point of view.[5] Professor P. Meyer (as then he was), argued, in a seminal article published in 1964,[6] that, notwithstanding Article 68 of the CPC,[7] Quebecois courts should apply the doctrine of *forum non conveniens* in order to avoid the consequences of accepting into

---

[4] See Groffier, n. 1 above (*Précis*), no. 248–51.
[5] See e.g. *Dans l'affaire de Canadian Javelin Ltd; Plam* v. *Sparling* [1979] CS 465; *Dominion Jubilee Corp Ltd* v. *Canadian Javelin Ltd* [1977] CS 786; *Ajit Singh* v. *General Merchandising Corp* [1977] CS 173; *Droit de la famille—550* [1988] RJQ 2575 (CS); *Cie nationale de transports aériens Royal Air Maroc* [1986] RDJ 24 (CS).
[6] N. 3 above; see also Normandin, (1987) 47 *R du B* 469.
[7] Art. 94 CPC at the time the art. by Meyer was written.

Quebecois law a wide (common law) basis of jurisdiction such as the *assets rule* (jurisdiction in personal matters based only on the situation of property within Quebec)[8] and the so-called *transient rule* (jurisdiction based on personal service on a foreigner even if not domiciled or resident in Quebec).[9]

Moreover, Prof. Meyer argued that, since common law rules apply to Quebec in matters of civil procedure,[10] Quebecois courts, as all courts in the common law system, possess inherent powers necessary to the exercise of their jurisdiction, such as the discretionary power to decline their jurisdiction in the presence of a more appropriate foreign forum (the doctrine of *forum non conveniens*, inherited from the law of Scotland and accepted everywhere in common law jurisdictions). The debate on *forum non conveniens* focused on Article 46 of the CPC which seems to codify exactly such a position: 'The courts and the judges have all the powers necessary for the exercise of their jurisdiction. They may, in the cases brought before them, even of their own motion, pronounce orders or reprimands, suppress writings or declare them libellous, and make such orders as are appropriate to cover cases where no specific remedy is provided by law.' While it was still possible logically to argue that the 'inherent powers necessary for the exercise of their jurisdiction' did not include the power to simply dismiss an action, a counter-argument to this was raised: dismissing an action can also be considered as part of exercising jurisdiction.[11]

Indeed, it has been recognized by Quebecois courts in domestic cases that Article 46 of the CPC allows for the dismissal of actions because of procedural abuses such as excessively long delays.[12]

Despite this Article and notwithstanding academic support, the major part of the case law, led by cases mostly decided by the Court of Appeal, was rather strongly opposed to the doctrine of *forum non conveniens*, since it considered that Article 68 of the CPC is of a public policy nature (as well as the other basis of jurisdiction, as in family matters of immovable property) and it affirmed that Quebecois judges have no 'equitable power' to

---

[8] Art. 94(4) CPC (before the new Code of Civil Procedure of 1965); Art. 68(1) CPC (since 1965).

[9] Art. 94(2) CPC (before the new Code of Civil Procedure of 1965); Art. 68(1) CPC (since 1965) does accept such a basis but only if the defendant has some property within Quebec. However, this condition of personal service in that case does not seem to have been extended to private international law instances.

[10] See Brisson, *La formation d'un droit mixte: l'évolution de la procédure civile de 1774 à 1967* (Montreal, 1986).

[11] See Harrington, 'Forum non conveniens in the Quebec and Federal Courts—Rigidity or Flexibility' in *Meredith Memorial Lectures*, 1986, Faculty of Law, McGill University, R. De Boo, 1987, 257, 268.

[12] Ferland, Emery, and Tremblay, *Précis de procédure civile du Québec* (Montreal, 1992), 50, citing several cases, n. 10.

derogate from clear-cut Articles.[13] Such opposition is clearly illustrated by the following citation confirmed by the Court of Appeal in 1986 in the leading *Aberman* v. *Solomon* case:

I have come to the conclusion that, as the law now stands, the doctrine of *forum non conveniens* has no application in the law of Quebec. Article 68 C. P. is clear and does not give rise to the exercise of judicial discretion, however desirable that may be. Clearly, . . . this is a case where a more convenient forum exists. But the Appelant [*sic*] has assets in Quebec, and the Superior Court is, therefore, obliged to accept jurisdiction. Neither Article 2, nor Article 20 of the Code of Civil Procedure opens the door to the exercise of what the Appelant calls the Court's 'inherent jurisdiction' to do what would appear to be 'the right thing.' These are proceedings based on the civil law of the province; they are not proceedings in equity, as that term is used in the common law, and while I may concede that in cases which call into aid the equitable jurisdiction of the court . . . it cannot come to the rescue of a defendant who is summoned to appear before the courts of this province, so long as the court's jurisdiction is based on a positive provision of the Code of Civil Procedure. To hold otherwise would, in effect, be to amend the law by judicial edict, and this would usurp the function of the legislature.[14]

As a result, in a subsequent case also confirmed by the Court of Appeal, *Aberman* v. *Solomon* did not receive application. Instead, the doctrine was applied since it was determined that the issue involved was not private or civil law, but a particular remedy stemming from a public federal statute,[15] thus establishing that part of the common law applied in Quebec.[16] From a technical perspective, even prior to the new Civil Code, Quebecois courts were already given a discretionary power to dismiss actions based on the doctrine of *forum non conveniens* in all the matters tried in Quebec that were subject to the common law, such as public law, or even, perhaps, in private law matters that belong to the federal jurisdiction, such as bankruptcy law, banking law, etc., unless, of course, statutory law specifically excluded such a power.

In any case, the Quebecois legislature responded to calls from both academic writers and the case law, adopted Article 3135 of the CCQ[17] and ended this sterile and costly debate.

---

[13] It could also be argued, not too logically though, that since no foreign judgment had *autorité de chose jugée* in Quebec because Art. 178 CPC allowed Quebecois courts to review the merits of the case, there was no point accepting the doctrine of *forum non conveniens*, because if a foreign judgment dealing with the cause of action that was presented previously in Quebec had somehow to be later recognized in that province, then that judgment could be rewritten by a Quebecois judge: see Peacock, (1987) 47 *R du B* 112 at 120.

[14] *Aberman* v. *Solomon*, n. 2 above, 391–2. See on this subject: Peacock, n. 13 above.

[15] Canada Business Corporations Act, S.C. 1974–75–76, c. 33, s. 234.

[16] *80890 Canada Ltd* v. *Franck B. Hall & Co Inc* [1986] RDJ 544.

[17] See: Groffier, n. 1 above (*Supplément*), no. 108; Glenn, n. 1 above, no. 73–4; Talpis and Castel, n. 1 above, no. 411–26.

3. Functions of the Doctrine of *Forum Non Conveniens*

Although it could be argued that the doctrine of *forum non conveniens* might be a way to free courts from an overload of work, this is clearly not the case for Quebecois courts: the number of private international law cases they must deal with is small.[18] Three basic ideas could explain the adoption of Article 3135 of the CCQ.

(a) *Forum non conveniens* as a means to avoid contradictory judgments

In some instances, the plea of *forum non conveniens* has been made in order to avoid the possible rendering of contradictory judgments, most likely to occur when, according to Quebecois rules, several courts have alternative jurisdiction.[19] For instance, a Quebecois court accepting jurisdiction and rendering a judgment contradictory to another judgment rendered in the Province of Ontario might very well be ineffectual, if the Quebecois judgment could or would not be recognized in Ontario, potentially the location of all the assets of the defendant. Such justification for the doctrine of *forum non conveniens* is identical to the one given to accept the doctrine of *lis alibi pendens*. However, this argument alone would probably not in the eyes of the courts be considered sufficient to dismiss the action if the action had a substantial connection with Quebec, as some courts had previously stated prior to the adoption of Article 3135 of the CCQ.[20] It is to be hoped that this trend will survive under the new law, since, as previously stated, *forum non conveniens* results in a non-conditional dismissal of the action without ensuring that the assumed 'better' court will accept hearing the case.

(b) *Forum non conveniens* as an antidote to wide bases of jurisdiction or to forum-shopping

Traditionally, *forum non conveniens* has been used to counteract the negative effects of having too broad a basis of jurisdiction that would encourage forum-shopping if, in addition, the law of the forum is particularly favourable to one type of litigant, as in consumer protection legislation, for instance. In the common law system, two specific bases of jurisdiction have been singled out as too wide to provide efficient justice in every case: the *asset rule* and the *transient rule*. In effect, by 1849, Quebecois law

---

[18] Annually, about 20 cases of this type come before the Quebecois courts.

[19] See e.g. *Aberman* v. *Solomon*, n. 2 above; *Ajit Singh* v. *General Merchandising Corp*, n. 5 above.

[20] *Droit de la famille—375* [1987] RDF 228, 229 (CS).

already accepted the *asset rule* and the *transient rule* may have been accepted as early as 1785.[21] When the Quebecois legislature modernized its Code of Civil Procedure in 1965 the *transient rule*, such as it was known, disappeared, since it could only be used in connection with the presence of assets belonging to the defendant within Quebec. The *asset rule* remained in force until the adoption of the new Civil Code in 1994, at which time it was disposed of because it was not generally considered to be a pertinent basis of jurisdiction in itself. Indeed, a considerable number of instances where the plea of *forum non conveniens* was raised dealt with cases where the defendant only had assets in Quebec, sometimes even of a very 'evanescent nature'[22] such as a disputed debt.[23] Given that this basis of jurisdiction disappeared from the Quebecois rules with the new Civil Code, one can wonder whether the adoption of the doctrine of *forum non conveniens* was necessary.

However, the new Quebecois law admits some other wide bases, such as Article 3148(3) of the CCQ, which states that Quebecois courts have jurisdiction in personal actions of a patrimonial nature if 'a fault was committed in Quebec, damage was suffered in Quebec, an injurious act occurred in Quebec *or* one of the obligations arising from a contract was to be performed in Quebec'. Therefore, it can be said that the doctrine will still perform its traditional role under the new Civil Code.

Moreover, it is conceivable that people will shop for a Quebecois forum because the new Quebecois private international law rules are very modern and allow for considerable flexibility, an element that is lacking in the traditional systems. For instance, Articles 3082 (*clause échappatoire*) and 3079 of the CCQ (similar to Article 7 of the Rome Convention, allowing a Quebecois judge to apply a foreign mandatory rule originating in a system not designated by the conflict rule) could very well attract some litigants to the Quebecois courts. Some decisions rendered before the new Civil Code were already dealing with forum-shopping in Quebec[24] although this situation has not been very frequent and to date, was not considered a serious problem.

(c) *FORUM NON CONVENIENS* AS A DISCRETIONARY RESERVE

Quebec's new private international law demonstrates its strong attachment to the general principle of the law having the closest connection to

---

[21] See Meyer, n. 3 above, 581.   [22] *Ibid.* 598.

[23] See e.g., the asset rule: *Southern Pacific Cy* v. *M. Botner & Sons Inc* [1973] RP 97 (CA); *Aberman* v. *Solomon*, n. 2 above; *Dominion Jubilee Corp Ltd* v. *Canadian Javelin Ltd*, n. 5 above; *The First National Bank of Boston* v. *La Sarchi Compagnie* [1961] QB 702. For cases where the Quebecois jurisdiction was based on the transient rule: see *Dans l'affaire de Canadian Javelin Ltd*; *Plam* v. *Sparling*, n. 5 above; *Lieff* v. *Palmer* (1937) 63 KB 278.

[24] See e.g. *Dans l'affaire de Canadian Javelin Ltd*; *Plam* v. *Sparling*, n. 5 above; *Lieff* v. *Palmer*, n. 23 above; *Gauthier* v. *Bergeron* [1973] CA 77; *Union Acceptance Corp Ltd* v. *Guay* [1960] BR 827.

the case, by adopting a general *clause d'exception* (or *clause échappatoire*), such as Article 4(5) of the Rome Convention. Article 3082 of the CCQ states: 'Exceptionally, the law designated by this Book [Conflict of Laws] is not applicable if, in the light of all attendant circumstances, it is clear that the situation is only remotely connected with that law and is much more closely connected with the law of another country. This provision does not apply where the law is designated in a juridical act.' Article 3135 of the CCQ is seen as a specific functional equivalent to such a clause in the case of a conflict of jurisdictions. The existence of Articles 3135 and 3082 of the CCQ indicate that the Quebecois legislature has been very much aware of the current academic ideas; it has totally changed its traditional approach and adopted a generalized system of flexible rules rather than a rigid Savignian one.[25]

4. DETERMINING THE APPROPRIATE FORUM

Given that Quebecois law accepts the plea of *forum non conveniens*, are the considerations determining which is the appropriate forum contained within a rigid framework or are they part of a flexible approach (a), and what are these considerations (b)?

(a) RIGID FRAMEWORK OF CONSIDERATIONS OR FLEXIBLE APPROACH?

When Quebecois courts refused to apply the doctrine of *forum non conveniens*, their opposition was based on the principle that they had no discretionary power since they were not allowed to extend their jurisdiction on an equitable basis.[26] Since Article 3135 of the CCQ (and Article 3082 of the CCQ) depart totally from this restrictive position, Quebecois judges will be able to use their discretionary power expressly given by these Articles and adopt a very flexible approach. Article 3082 of the CCQ (see text, above, at II 3(c)) states only that they should look into 'all the attendant circumstances', that it should be 'clear' that the situation is 'only remotely connected' with the normally applicable law, and that it is 'much

---

[25] See generally, on this new approach, Goldstein, 'L'interprétation du domaine d'application international du nouveau Code civil' in *L'interprétation et l'application du domaine du nouveau Code civil* (Montreal, 1992), 81 ff.

[26] See *Trower and Sons Ltd* v. *Ripstein* [1944] AC 254 at 262 (*per* Lord Wright): 'The [Quebec] court is strictly bound by the terms of these articles [of the Quebec Code of Civil Procedure]. It has no general power to proceed on what might be described as the 'equity' of the articles. . . . It has no discretionary power to go outside the terms of the articles merely because in its opinion it would be the forum conveniens'; *Southern Pacific Cy* v. *M. Botner & Sons Inc*, n. 2 above, at 107 (Deschênes J): 'The jurisdiction of the Quebec courts does not depend on a case-by-case approach, but is based on objective criteria clearly defined by the law and to which the courts must give effect when the conditions that give rise to jurisdiction are met.'

more closely connected' with the law of another country. These are not rigid limits and call for a free interpretation. Moreover, Article 3135 of the CCQ only states that the Quebecois court *must* consider that the authorities of another country are in a 'better' position to hear the case. When the case law accumulates, then the usual rules as to precedents in civil law will apply. Each case will only be as good law as its reasoning but the application of Article 3135 of the CCQ will merely consist in dealing with a set of facts so that the judges will keep the rule 'open'.

But, here again, Article 3135 of the CCQ gives no insurance to the parties that the foreign court alleged to be in a better position to hear the case will actually want to do so. Hence the importance of carefully determining the (theoretical) more appropriate forum. What are the considerations that hitherto were given regard to in Quebecois law?

(b) CONSIDERATIONS DETERMINING THE APPROPRIATE FORUM

According to what just been said, it will be useful to study the previous case law to get a good idea of which considerations are likely to prevail in the future. The framework within which these *forum non conveniens* considerations have been examined is very flexible. These considerations, designed to decide whether or not a foreign court would be more appropriate than the Quebecois court, include:

1. Residence or domicile of the parties;[27]
2. Presence of witnesses or proof in Quebec;[28]
3. Enforceability of the Quebecois judgment abroad;[29]
4. Assets in Quebec in order to indemnify a victim;[30]
5. Abuses of procedure;[31]
6. Availability of an alternative forum;[32]
7. Interests of the parties or of the child;[33]

---

[27] See e.g. *80890 Canada Ltd v. Franck B. Hall & Co Inc*, n. 16 above.

[28] *Southern Pacific Cy v. M. Botner & Sons Inc*, n. 2 above; *Dans l'affaire de Canadian Javelin Ltd; Plam v. Sparling*, n. 5 above; *Cie nationale de transports aériens Royal Air Maroc*, n. 5 above; *Aberman v. Solomon*, n. 2 above; *Holt Cattle Cy v. Centennial International Inc* [1985] CS 559.

[29] *Dominion Jubilee Corp Ltd v. Canadian Javelin Ltd*, n. 5 above; *Ajit Singh v. General Merchandising Corp*, n. 5 above; *contra: Holt Cattle Cy v. Centennial International Inc*, n. 28 above, at 563; *Droit de la famille—375*, n. 20 above, at 230.

[30] *Southern Pacific Cy v. M. Botner & Sons Inc*, n. 2 above; *Olympia and York Development Ltd v. Peerless Rug Ltd* [1975] CA 445.

[31] *Olympia and York Development Ltd v. Peerless Rug Ltd*, n. 30 above; *Aberman v. Solomon*, n. 2 above.

[32] *Aberman v. Solomon*, n. 2 above; *Dominion Jubilee Corp Ltd v. Canadian Javelin Ltd*, n. 5 above; *Dans l'affaire de Canadian Javelin Ltd; Plam v. Sparling*, n. 5 above; *contra: Droit de la famille—375*, n. 20 above, at 230.

[33] *Droit de la famille—550*, n. 5 above; *Southern Pacific Cy v. M. Botner & Sons Inc*, n. 2 above; but see *Holt Cattle Cy v. Centennial International Inc*, n. 28 above, at 563 (it is not enough that the other court is merely more practical).

8. Forum familiar with the substantive law involved.[34]

Finally, it is clear from the case law that Quebecois courts will make their decisions after an analysis of the general balance of inconveniences or advantages to the courts and to the parties, taking into consideration all these factual elements.[35] It is to be hoped that the realistic availability of an alternative forum will play a prime role in this analysis and that, more generally, Quebecois judges will only in exceptional circumstances apply the doctrine, as Article 3135 of the CCQ urges them to do.

5. OTHER FUNCTIONAL EQUIVALENTS TO *FORUM NON CONVENIENS*

In order to avoid negative conflicts of competence and a denial of justice, Article 3136 of the CCQ provides for the adoption in Quebecois law of the doctrine of *forum conveniens*, but only 'if the dispute has a sufficient connection with Quebec, where proceedings cannot possibly be instituted outside Quebec or where the institution of such proceedings outside Quebec cannot reasonably be required'. Moreover, the doctrine of 'jurisdiction by necessity' is more specifically codified in Article 3140 of the CCQ which states that Quebecois courts, otherwise without jurisdiction, 'may take such measures as they consider necessary for the protection of the person or his property in Quebec' in 'cases of emergency or serious inconvenience'. Both these discretionary powers, based on a strong connection with Quebec, also apply so as to give jurisdiction to foreign courts in the same circumstances.[36]

These Articles can be seen as complementary powers giving exceptional jurisdiction to Quebecois courts or to foreign courts as a more appropriate forum—*forum conveniens*—than the one selected by the normal basis of jurisdiction. Normally, both Articles could be used in favour of foreign courts, at the recognition stage of a foreign decision. In this situation, there would be no direct question concerning Quebecois jurisdiction. But Article 3140 of the CCQ might also be used in order to raise a *lis pendens* argument in favour of a foreign court that had no jurisdiction otherwise. But, here again, such a plea does not aim at taking away the jurisdiction of a Quebecois court: its function lies in giving a foreign court a jurisdiction

---

[34] *Cie nationale de transports aériens Royal Air Maroc*, n. 5 above; *Dominion Jubilee Corp Ltd v. Canadian Javelin Ltd*, n. 5 above; *Clakson, Gordon, Peat, Marwick, Mitchell & Co v. Yufe* [1986] RDJ 393 at 394 (CA); *contra: Holt Cattle Cy v. Centennial International Inc*, n. 28 above, at 563.

[35] *Aberman v. Solomon*, n. 2 above; *Cie nationale de transports aériens Royal Air Maroc*, n. 5 above; *Olympia and York Development Ltd v. Peerless Rug Ltd*, n. 30 above; *Southern Pacific Cy v. M. Botner & Sons Inc*, n. 2 above, at 107; *Holt Cattle Cy v. Centennial International Inc*, n. 28 above, at 563; *80890 Canada Ltd v. Franck B. Hall & Co Inc*, n. 16 above; *contra: Clakson, Gordon, Peat, Marwick, Mitchell & Co v. Yufe*, n. 34 above.

[36] Art. 3164 CCQ bilateralizes the Quebecois basis of jurisdiction as a general and residual rule.

it did not have in the first place, according to Quebecois law. Therefore, in no way, could these Articles—if invoked in favour of a foreign court— take away the jurisdiction of a Quebecois court and allow it to dismiss the action, as would be possible when a plea of *forum non conveniens* is raised.

6. Discretionary Power to Dismiss Actions and Mandatory or Exclusive Bases of Jurisdiction

Article 3135 of the CCQ does not limit its domain in any way other than a discretionary finding that another court would be in a better position to judge. In this context, it is possible that a litigant might try to plead *forum non conveniens* in a situation where the Quebecois court would have exclusive jurisdiction over the matter, according to Quebecois law, so that no other court would presumably have jurisdiction. This situation could normally happen if the subject-matter were of vital importance to Quebec. Then, presumably, the exclusive jurisdiction would also be imperative. One such case could be realized if a litigant tried to avoid Quebecois exclusive jurisdiction to hear actions based on liability for damage suffered in or outside Quebec as a result of exposure to raw materials originating in Quebec (Articles 3151 and 3129 of the CCQ). It is highly improbable that a Quebecois court would agree to dismiss an action on a *forum non conveniens* plea in such a situation.

It would also seem that application of Article 3140 of the CCQ, giving exceptional jurisdiction to Quebecois courts in cases of emergency or 'serious inconvenience' to protect someone or his property in Quebec, would logically exclude the plea of *forum non conveniens*. If a Quebecois court considered itself sufficiently concerned to take this exceptional jurisdiction, it would not be ready to dismiss it easily. Indeed, in such circumstances, it would be very difficult to convince a Quebecois judge that there might be a more appropriate forum somewhere in the world. However, since Quebecois law introduced the mirror principle through Article 3164 of the CCQ, Article 3140 of the CCQ could be invoked in favour of a foreign court not designated by the normal rule as to jurisdiction. If, in that case, the other party invoked the *forum non conveniens* theory in order to avoid the application of Article 3140 of the CCQ and to give jurisdiction to the court normally designated, it is doubtful that the Quebecois court would apply Article 3135 of the CCQ.

Another situation where the doctrine of *forum non conveniens* might not work would occur if the parties to a contract agreed to give jurisdiction to a foreign court. Although Article 3135 of the CCQ does not specify it, one could argue that this rule implicitly stems from the limitation given to Article 3082 of the CCQ, which states that the *clause échappatoire* will not be used when the parties to an act have chosen the applicable law. It is also possible to argue that, contrary to Article 3082 of the CCQ, Article 3135 of the CCQ does not specify this limitation so the limitation should not be made. The new Code strongly favours party autonomy, as long as public policy or mandatory rules are not concerned. Articles 3165(2) and 3165(3) of the CCQ qualify jurisdiction given by a contractual clause to a foreign court as an *exclusive* basis of jurisdiction.[37] Given that it should not be qualified as a *mandatory* or *imperative* jurisdiction, it seems that *forum non conveniens* could be successfully pleaded in such a situation (see section IV).

III
LIS ALIBI PENDENS

1. Existence of the Doctrine

A primary motive for refusing the plea of *lis alibi pendens*[38] in Quebec was that it was public law and therefore governed by English law.[39] English law held that a foreign suit pending in another country was no ground for staying the action in England because there was no presumption that the multiplicity of judgments was vexatious: there could very well be good reason to take suit in two countries.[40] For instance, the situation might be analysed differently, the applicable rules might be different, and the defendant might have assets in different countries that do not recognize a certain type of judgment.

In Quebecois law the plea of *lis alibi pendens* has also been linked with *res judicata*.[41] Only a decision leading to *res judicata* between the same parties in actions stemming from the same cause and having the same object could realize a situation where two contradictory decisions would have to be implemented, leading to deep disrespect for the administration of justice. Only a decision leading to *res judicata* can be a motive to plead *lis alibi pendens*. Indeed, the case law repeatedly held that the conditions of the latter were the same as those of the former.[42] In cases of international

---

[37] Art. 3165: 'The jurisdiction of a foreign authority is not recognized by Quebec authorities in the following cases: . . . (2) where by reason of the subject matter or an agreement between the parties, Quebec law recognises the exclusive jurisdiction of another foreign authority; (3) where Quebec law recognises an agreement by which exclusive jurisdiction has been conferred upon an arbitrator.'

[38] See generally on the doctrine Groffier, n. 1 above (*Supplément*), no. 110; Glenn, n. 1 above, 745–6, no 75; Talpis and Castel, n. 1 above, no. 427–32.

[39] Whether that motive was justified or not (*contra: Toulon Construction Inc* v. *Rusco Industries Inc* [1973] RP 138 (CA)), it was invoked by the courts.

[40] The *Howard Guernsey Manufacturing Co* v. *King* (1894) 5 CS 182 at 183–4.

[41] On that point, see Goldstein and Talpis, *L'effet au Québec des jugements étrangers en matière de droits patrimoniaux* (Montreal, 1991), 40–52.

[42] *Cargill Grain Co* v. *Foundation Co of Canada* [1965] RCS 594.

disputes, the reasoning was different, since foreign judgments could not be treated as *res judicata* in Quebec without exemplification here. In addition, there was no possibility of contradictory judgments because it was still possible to judge on the merits of the case in these proceedings. *Res judicata* was expressly denied by Articles 178 to 180 of the CPC. Therefore, if an actual decision could not be *res judicata* in Quebec, how could mere proceedings abroad—not even a decision being *res judicata* there—be a basis of *lis pendens*?[43]

As a consequence, since judgments coming from other Canadian provinces could be *res judicata* in Quebec under some conditions, the courts accepted (in theory) the staying of Quebecois actions until the conclusion of those proceedings when the conditions allowing *res judicata* were met.[44]

Under the new Civil Code, Quebecois judges cannot review the merits of a foreign decision.[45] As a consequence, Article 3137 of the new Civil Code states now, as a general rule applicable to all foreign decisions alike, whatever their origin:

On the application of party, a Quebec authority may stay its ruling on an action brought before it if another action, between the same parties, based on the same facts and having the same object is pending before a foreign authority, provided that the latter action can result in a decision which may be recognised in Quebec, or if such a decision has already been rendered by a foreign authority.

While still linking *lis pendens* and *res judicata*—given that a foreign decision unlikely to be recognized in Quebec and thus a poor candidate for *res judicata* in Quebec, cannot be a motive to raise a plea of *lis pendens*—the new law seriously tries to cope with the specific nature of *lis pendens* in international situations, since its conditions are similar, but not identical, to those imposed on local litigation. This point will be developed next.

2. What are the Determining Considerations to Stay an Action in Cases of *Lis Pendens*?

Of course, the new law (Article 3137 of the CCQ) admits that only those foreign decisions susceptible to being treated as *res judicata* in Quebec

---

[43] The *Howard Guernsey Manufacturing Co v. King*, n. 40 above, at 183; *Unger v. Rosenfeld* [1972] CS 673 at 675–6.

[44] See *Blackwood v. Percival* (1903) 23 CS 5; *Canadian Acceptance Corp v. West* (1932) RP 6; *Canadian Conveyors v. Heakes* (1950) CS 416; *Olympia and York Development Ltd v. Peerless Rug Ltd*, n. 30 above; *Geocon Ltd v. Commonwealth Holiday Inns of Canada Ltd*, CA Quebec, 1976/02/06, no. 09-000140-756, in Reid and Ferland, *CPC annoté du Québec* (Montreal), iii. 366; *Warez Building & Investment Corp v. Bank of Montreal*, CS Montréal, 30/10/1981, no. 500-05-011 627-87, JE 81-1154; *St Georges International Inc v. Heuga Canada Ltd*, CS Montréal, no. 500-05-002580-833, 1983/07/15, JE 83–833; *St John Shipbuilding Ltd v. Groupe Mil Inc*, CA Quebec, no. 200-05-002271-919, 1991/07/16, JE 91-1351. See Groffier, n. 1 above (*Précis*), no. 249.

[45] Art. 3158 CCQ.

provide the condition *sine qua non* to *lis pendens*. Therefore, according to Quebecois rules, in order to allow the plea of *lis pendens*, the foreign court where the suit is already pending has to have international jurisdiction.

For both local and international *lis pendens*, evidence must be provided that the two suits, first, concern the *same parties* and, secondly, have the *same object*. Contrary to Article 2848 of the CCQ (local rule as to *lis pendens* and *res judicata*), Article 3137 of the CCQ does not require proof that the two suits stem from the same cause of action, but, thirdly, merely from the *same facts*. This difference comes as a consequence of the fact that the Supreme Court of Canada has recently and thoroughly tried to define *lis pendens* in local situations, to the extent that its elements do not fit international situations.

(a) SAME PARTIES

In most cases, this condition does not cause any problem but it should be noted that in *Roberge* v. *Bolduc*,[46] the Supreme Court of Canada has accepted a wide notion of identity of parties. It was held that the notion included not only a successor *ut universi*, but also a 'successor by particular title', such as the buyer, or the creditors, or a debtor, so that only persons not representing the parties can be considered genuine third parties in terms of *res judicata* and thus in terms of *lis alibi pendens*. If this concept is applied in international cases, it might greatly increase instances of *lis pendens* pleadings. There is no reason why it should not.

(b) SAME OBJECT

In *Rocois Construction Inc* v. *Quebec Ready Mix Inc*,[47] the Supreme Court of Canada held that what should be considered as the object is the right or immediate legal benefit sought by one party,[48] such as compensation for a prejudice, whatever its qualification under one legal regime or another. It also held that the identity of what is claimed in each action does not have to be absolute[49] for the condition to be fulfilled: for instance, the amounts claimed may differ, but this fact does not alter the nature of the object.[50] Quebecois case law clarified the following points: what has to be considered is the principal object of the action. Even if additional amounts are claimed as accessory damages in the second suit, there will still be identity of object. It is also not necessary for the two suits to seek the identical

---

[46] [1991] 1 RCS 374; see Royer, 'Développements récents en matière de litispendance et d'autorité de la chose jugée' in *Développements récents en droit civil (1992)* (Montreal, 1992), 21–32.

[47] [1990] 2 RCS 440; see Royer, n. 46 above.   [48] N. 47 above, 452.   [49] *Ibid.*

[50] *Cargill Grain Co* v. *Foundation Co of Canada* [1965] RCS 594 at 597.

conclusion; there will still be *res judicata* when the object of the second action is implicitly included in the object of the first.[51] Indeed, this is precisely where most of the difficulty lies: it is often not easy to be sure that the object of the second suit is not already implicitly included in the object of the first.[52] None the less, it is easier to check this condition in the case of *res judicata* because a decision has already been rendered. In the case of *lis pendens*, the only available documents concern the proceedings.

It has also been said that the correct test is to ask whether the second court would have no other alternative but to confirm or reverse the decision of the first court.[53] The usefulness of such a test is doubtful in international cases, since courts from different countries would normally apply different rules unless they had the same local law or the same conflict of laws rules. Even then, the end result could be very different from one country to another because the interpretation of such rules may vary.

This situation affects all the more the 'credibility' of a plea of *lis pendens* when, as in Quebecois law, it is not necessary to verify that both actions stem from the same cause but only from the *same facts*, so that the main analytical effort involves the identity of object.

(c) SAME FACTS

In *Rocois Construction Inc* v. *Quebec Ready Mix Inc*,[54] the Supreme Court of Canada held (in purely local litigation) that what should be considered as the cause of action, or the source of the obligation, or the principle giving rise to the right claimed, is neither the facts of the case, nor the applicable rules by themselves, but the characterization—required by the potentially applicable rule—given to the facts. It is only when the essential characterization of the alleged facts is identical under an applicable rule x in court X and under rule y in court Y that there can be identity of cause.[55]

According to the Court, a two-stage analysis is necessary to determine whether this condition is fulfilled. Since a characterization resulting from a rule of law depends first on the legal principle the rule is based on, then: 'two provisions based on different legal principles cannot give rise to identical causes since the fact regarded as the source of liability will necessarily be different: the legal characterisation of the factual situation will similarly be different'.[56] It is only when the two provisions are based

---

[51] Mignault, *Le droit civil canadien* (Montreal, 1902), vi. 105; *Droit de la famille—75*, CS Québec, 200-12-020578-796, 1983-08-09, JE 83-883.

[52] *Droit de la famille—75*, n. 51 above, at 6 (citing Planiol and Ripert, *Traité pratique de droit civil français* (2nd edn., Paris), vii: n. 1559, 1030).

[53] Nadeau and Ducharme, *Traité de droit civil du Québec* (Montreal, 1965), ix. no. 577, 480; *Hertel Construction Inc* v. *Cayor Investment Ltd*, CS St-Hyacinthe, no. 750-05-00046882, 23-02-1984, JE 84-336.

[54] N. 47 above, at 454–6.   [55] *Ibid*. 456.   [56] *Ibid*.

on the same legal principle that an identity of cause is possible. But, then 'it is then necessary to examine the potential result of applying these provisions to the facts under consideration. If . . . the effect produced by applying the provision relied on in the second action corresponds to the effect produced by applying the provision relied on in the first, it should be concluded that there is an identity of causes'.[57] While it seems very accurate to look after the essence of the characterization of the situation under each system of law in private international law cases in order to determine whether there is identity of cause, it is obvious that the two-stage test adopted by the Supreme Court does not fit at all with all aspects of such cases. In most of the cases, the basic principles of the applicable rules will be different and, if not, then the results will be, since this is precisely the reason somebody is shopping for a forum. Hence, the impossibility of accepting a plea of *lis pendens* in international situations.

Therefore the Quebecois legislature decided to broaden its definition of *lis pendens* by requiring in Article 3137 of the CCQ only that both suits pertain to the *same facts*. In doing so, though, it deprived Quebecois judges of a very important consideration and traded it against a vague condition referring to elements that are meaningless by themselves. As a consequence, in international litigation the whole weight of the analysis will only rest on the identity of object, this being itself a very delicate task implying a good grasp of comparative law.

If, of course, the second action is based on facts that happened after the first was introduced, then there is no identity of facts.[58]

3. How are These Considerations Different from Those Employed under the Doctrine of *Forum Non Conveniens*?

By themselves, the general considerations that determine when to stay an action in a case of *lis pendens* are different from those used in a case of *forum non conveniens* because the pleas do not have the same effects (stay / dismissal) and because the situations are different. *Forum non conveniens* has already been pleaded to cover some cases where a foreign court was seised first. Moreover, essentially, both pleas have the same ultimate goal, which is to avoid the rendering of conflicting judgments. Finally, as will be seen in the next paragraph, Quebecois courts seem to have received a discretionary power to administer the rule as to *lis pendens*. It is then possible that they use the same criteria as the ones used when they decide to dismiss a claim in a case of *forum non conveniens*, but it will only be an

---

[57] *Ibid.* 457.
[58] See *Protection de la Jeunesse—183*, TJ, Montréal, no. 500-41-000157-852, 1985-94-12, JE 86-129. It is also possible to argue in such a case that there is no identity of object: see *Richard-Laporte* v. *Donati*, CS Montréal, 500-05-009 600-808, 28-10-1980, JE 80-1071.

antidote to the vagueness or ambiguity of the conditions of *lis pendens*, namely, to the somewhat problematic comparison of the objects of each suit.

4. Discretionary Power or Mechanical Rule to Decline Jurisdiction in Cases of *Lis Pendens*?

Article 3137 of the CCQ merely states that a court may stay its ruling in a case of international *lis pendens*. Therefore, one can argue that it is not a mechanical rule so that, even if all the above conditions are met, a court would not be forced to apply the doctrine. In any case, it is a discretionary power, since it must be shown that the foreign decision is susceptible to recognition in Quebec. If a Quebecois judge considers that the foreign court, although having jurisdiction according to the regular rule as to its jurisdiction, is nonetheless *forum non conveniens*, then it would not be recognized and there would be no stay for *lis pendens*.[59]

This discretionary power could be explained simply as a vestige of the traditional Quebecois attitude towards foreign judgments. It could also be better justified by the general principle of 'adaptability' adopted in its new Civil Code that underlies its whole new private international law. Practically speaking, again it may be an antidote to the vagueness of the conditions of Article 3137 of the CCQ, particularly since the whole weight of the decision will probably lie on a very delicate appreciation of whether the object of each suit is the same.

Hitherto we have studied the general provisions dealing with *lis pendens* in all international cases. Are these specific provisions contained in treaties?

5. Specific Provisions Contained in Bilateral Treaties?

Canada has signed a bilateral convention with the United Kingdom concerning the reciprocal recognition of their decisions.[60] Article IV(2)(b) of the convention provides that each State has the right to refuse to enforce or recognize a judgment rendered by a court having jurisdiction if another judgment has been previously rendered on the same cause of action by another court also having jurisdiction in accordance with the convention. This convention is not in force in Quebec, but Article 3137 of the CCQ covers the same type of situation and Article IV(2)(b) would now probably be useless for Quebecois courts.

[59] See Glenn, n. 1 above, no. 75, 746.
[60] *Loi sur la Convention Canada-Royaume-Uni relative aux jugements en matière civile et commerciale*, LRC (1985), c. C–30 (sanctioned on 29 June 1984).

6. OTHER RULES DEALING WITH CASES THAT DO NOT FIT WITHIN THE DEFINITION OF *LIS PENDENS*

Since a definition of *lis pendens* is codified in Article 3137 of the CCQ, a solution had to be found for situations that fell outside such definition but which nevertheless could give rise to irreconcilable judgments. When either the objects or the parties of the two suits are different but none the less linked, so that it would be difficult to decide one separately from the other, Article 3139 of the CCQ provides that: 'Where a Quebec authority has jurisdiction to rule on the principal demand, it also has jurisdiction to rule on an incidental demand or a cross demand.' It is to be noted that Article 3165 of the CCQ allows a Quebecois court to invoke the same provision to justify the exceptional attribution of jurisdiction to a *foreign* court, if there is a connection between the action and such court.

Articles 46, 270, and 271 of the CPC might also be used in favour of Quebecois courts so as to allow joinders of actions in cases of *connexity*.[61] Such a situation, already defined as suits having such a close connection that the decision in the first will have a consequence on the second,[62] could exist even if the parties to the suits are not all the same (Article 271 of the CPC). The Court of Appeal has already accepted the plea that two suits in international litigation could be joined for connexity reasons where there is no ground for *lis pendens*.[63]

IV

FOREIGN CHOICE OF JURISDICTION CLAUSES AND ARBITRATION AGREEMENTS

Article 3148 of the CCQ provides:

In personal actions of a patrimonial nature, a Quebec authority has jurisdiction where: . . . However, a Quebec authority has no jurisdiction where the parties, by agreement, have chosen to submit all existing or future disputes between themselves relating to a specified legal relationship to a foreign authority or to

---

[61] Originally, connexity was expressly included in Art. 3139 CCQ, but was taken out during the final drafting.

[62] *Lachapelle* v. *Thériault* [1968] RP 30 at 32 (CS); cf. *Filion* v. *Dahme* [1965] BR 126 at 128.

[63] *York-Hannover Developments Ltd* v. *Commonwealth Insurance Co*, CA, Montreal, no. 500-09-000871-913, 1991-05-14, JE 92-297. See Glenn, n. 1 above, no. 75, 746. For purely local situations: see *Les Héritiers du feu Gérard Paquin* v. *Escorap Ltée*, CA, Montreal, no. 200-09-000054-798; *Nudleman* v. *Nudleman* [1971] CS 485 at 488; *Gnat* v. *Stanley Castle Building Ltd* [1968] BR 466; *contra*: *Deschamps* v. *Durand* [1966] RP 1 at 11 (CS) (stating that the conditions for connexity should be the same as those of *lis pendens*).

an arbitrator,[64] unless the defendant submits to the jurisdiction of the Quebec authority.

This provision does not seem to allow for any discretionary power; whenever the parties have agreed in such a manner as provided for in Article 3148 of the CCQ, the courts have no jurisdiction. Moreover, Article 3165(2) and (3) of the CCQ apply the same principle to foreign jurisdictions whenever the parties have agreed to such clauses.

Obviously, the choice of jurisdiction clause or the arbitration clause must be valid to be applied, and there should not be any agreement superseding it (Article 3148 of the CCQ, last paragraph). A choice of jurisdiction clause will be valid if contained in a valid agreement according to the law governing it under Article 3111 (express or implied choice by the parties) or 3112 CCQ (the law with which the act is most closely connected in the absence of such choice or if the law so chosen invalidates the agreement). An arbitration clause will be valid according to the law governing such a clause, even if the agreement that contains it is invalid, according to Article 16 of the 1985 UNCITRAL Model Law, which is part of the law of Quebec[65] (Article 940.6 of the CPC).

Article 3165 of the CCQ specifies that Quebecois law grants an *exclusive* jurisdiction to the court, Quebecois or foreign, chosen by the parties, 'by reason of an agreement'. Implicitly, it seems that this will only be the case when *the agreement itself* provides that the jurisdiction given is exclusive. In the case of a non-exclusive jurisdiction clause, then a Quebecois judge could consider himself competent notwithstanding the agreement. In the case of an arbitration clause, Article 3165-3° of the CCQ stipulates more clearly that the agreement itself gives an exclusive character to the jurisdiction, since it provides that 'The jurisdiction of foreign authorities is not recognized . . . 3) where Quebec law recognizes an agreement by which exclusive jurisdiction has been conferred upon an arbitrator.'

None the less, exclusive jurisdiction is not equivalent to *mandatory* or *imperative* jurisdiction,[66] so that, here again, the general rules as to jurisdic-

---

[64] See generally on arbitration in Quebec law: Brierley, (1987–8) 13 *Can.Bus. Law J* 58; (1987) 47 *R du B* 259; Prujiner, (1987) *Rev. Arb.* 425; Cohen, (1987) 47 *R du B* 435; Groffier, n. 1 above (*Supplément*), no. 125, 141; Thuilleaux, *l'Arbitrage commercial au Québec. Droit interne—Droit international privé* (Montreal, 1991). On arbitration under the new Civil Code: see Brierley, 'De la convention d'arbitrage. Articles 2638–2643' in *La réforme du Code civil* (Presses de l'Université Laval, 1993), ii. 1067–92.

[65] LQ 1986, c. 73, Art. 2.

[66] But see *Zodiac International Productions Inc* v. *The Polish People's Republic* [1983] RDJ 277 (SCC), where the Sup. Ct. of Canada qualified jurisdiction given by an arbitration clause as *ratione materiae* (293–4), therefore being of an imperative nature in local cases, at least. But this case was decided before the adoption of Art. 3165 CCQ. Anyway, it is arguable whether to classify such an international situation as jurisdiction *ratione materiae* or even *ratione loci*. This local classification does not properly fit international litigation. See Groffier, n. 1 above (*Précis*), no. 269, 264.

tion might apply,[67] rules such as Article 3135 (*forum non conveniens*), 3137 (*lis pendens*), 3138 (exceptional jurisdiction to grant a provisional order or conservatory measures), 3139 (jurisdiction on incidental demands or on a cross action), and 3140 of the CCQ (exceptional jurisdiction in case of emergency or serious inconvenience to take necessary measures for the protection of a person or of his property in Quebec). Therefore, even in the light of such clauses, Quebecois courts will still possess the discretionary powers given by these rules and all the considerations taken into account in applying these rules will come into play. Since they have been studied elsewhere in this chapter, we will not deal with them again here.

However, in the case of arbitration clauses, Quebec has enacted the 1985 UNCITRAL Model Law,[68] and since its Article 8(1) states that 'a court before which an action is brought in a matter which is the subject of an arbitration agreement shall, if a party so requests . . . refer the parties to arbitration unless it finds that the agreement is null and void, inoperative or incapable of being performed', all the Quebecois general rules such as *forum conveniens* or *forum non conveniens* do not apply, so that Quebecois judges have lost any discretionary power in this matter. Of course, if the arbitration agreement does not come within the scope of the Model Law, or is null, etc., then the Quebecois courts regain their discretionary powers.

Finally, under Quebecois law, employment and consumer contracts are subject to specific protective rules. Article 3149 of the CCQ states: 'A Quebec authority also has jurisdiction to hear an action involving a consumer or a contract of employment if the consumer or worker has his domicile or residence in Quebec; the waiver of such jurisdiction by the consumer or worker may not be set up against him.'

So far, we have seen that a Quebecois court has rather wide and flexible powers to decline its own jurisdiction if a foreign court seems to be more convenient, in case of *lis pendens*, or when the parties have agreed on a choice of foreign jurisdiction or on an arbitration clause. But how could it deal with an action being taken abroad involving forum-shopping?

V
RULES ON RESTRAINING FOREIGN PROCEEDINGS

In Quebecois law, the discretionary power to grant injunctions (permanent, provisional, or interlocutory) has its origin in the common law.[69]

---

[67] See also Glenn, n. 1 above, no. 120, 773; n. 127, 778.
[68] See Arts. 940–974(4) CPC (especially Art. 940(6) CPC).
[69] *Côté* v. *Morgan* (1877–83) 7 RCS 1; *Dilmont Inc* v. *Charlebois* [1988] RJQ 2805 (CS); *Enterprises Omnipac Inc* v. *De Serres* [1988] RJQ 1951 (CS).

Article 752 of the CPC, inspired by the common law principles, provides that: 'An interlocutory injunction may be granted when the applicant appears to be entitled to it and it is considered to be necessary in order to avoid serious or irreparable injury to him, or a factual or legal situation of such a nature as to render the final judgment ineffectual.' In Quebecois private international law, there is no specific rule giving a discretionary power to restrain foreign proceedings by means of an injunction, but Article 3138 of the CCQ states that a Quebec authority 'may order provisional or conservatory measures even if it has no jurisdiction over the merits of the dispute'. Moreover, Article 46 of the CPC (cited above, at II, 2) can very well be invoked as the real source of such a power. Article 758 of the CPC provides that an order for an injunction can in no way be granted to restrain legal proceedings, but the Quebecois Court of Appeal held in *Johns-Manville Corp* v. *Dominion of Canada General Insurance Cy*[70] that Article 758 of the CPC did not apply to foreign legal proceedings. Thus, it was legal to use the discretion belonging to the court, a discretion that belongs to all courts in the common law system, to grant an injunction restraining a Californian proceeding which itself purported to restrain a legal proceeding in Quebec.[71]

The court did not go into the details of the criteria that were to be followed in the case of an injunction restraining foreign procedure, but Rousseau-Houle J referred to the recent common law cases[72] and stated that, first, a court should be convinced that such an injunction does not purport to avoid the application of mandatory laws of the place where the foreign proceedings have been introduced; secondly, that the injunction should not deprive the defendant of the advantages of his natural forum; and, thirdly, that this forum offers the least inconvenience to the parties.[73]

It is submitted that Quebecois courts will first apply the general test used where a permanent, provisional, or interlocutory injunction is sought in a local proceeding, then they may add the criteria referred to by Rousseau-Houle J in *Johns-Manville Corp*. This general test is threefold.[74] First, the court has to be convinced that the proceeding is not *frivolous or vexatious*, so that there is a 'serious question' to solve. It will provisionally adjudicate on the merits to determine whether the party seeking the

---

[70] [1991] RDJ 616 (CA).   [71] *Ibid.* 619 (McCarthy J).

[72] *Ibid.* 623, citing *Laker Airways* v. *Sabena, Belgian World Airlines,* 731 F. 2d 909 (1984) (DC CA); *Société Nationale Aérospatiale* v. *Lee Kui Jak* [1987] 1 AC 871 (HL); *Spiliada Maritime Corp* v. *Cansulex Ltd* [1987] 1 AC 460 (HL).

[73] N. 70 above, at 623.

[74] *Manitoba (AG)* v. *Metropolitan Stores Ltd* [1987] 1 RCS 110; *Algonquins of Barrière Lake* v. *Bacon* [1990] RJQ 1144 (CS); *Syndicat professionnel des infirmières et infirmiers de Chicoutimi* v. *Hôpital de Chicoutimi Inc* [1990] RJQ 141 (CS); *Jules Beauchesne Inc* v. *S. M. du revenu du Québec* [1989] RDFQ 259 (CS); *Aluminerie Alouette Inc* v. *Société Radio-Canada* [1991] Com. Accès Infor. 326 (CS).

injunction shows an apparent right. Secondly, the court has to decide whether or not that party would suffer an irreparable loss—that is to say not susceptible to be compensated for by a sum of money—if the injunction was not granted. Thirdly, the court has to weigh all the inconveniences in order to determine which party will suffer the greatest prejudice if the injunction is or is not granted.

As can be seen from these developments, these criteria are somewhat similar, but not identical, to the ones used when determining whether to grant a dismissal for *forum non conveniens* reasons (Article 3135 of the CCQ), or a stay of proceedings in case of *lis pendens* (Article 3137 of the CCQ), or when taking jurisdiction for *forum conveniens* reasons (Article 3136 of the CCQ). The *general balance of inconveniences* and *abuses of procedure* are two key elements of these analyses. Also, the necessity of showing that there is a 'serious question' to solve is closely connected with the condition under Article 3137 of the CCQ showing that the foreign decision is apparently susceptible of recognition in Quebec. For instance, a court may use these criteria in order to decide whether to accept a plea of *lis pendens* or of *forum non conveniens*, as requested by one litigant, or to reject them and grant an injunction restraining foreign proceedings, as requested by the other. Although the granting of an injunction restraining foreign proceedings seems to be accepted in Quebecois law, hitherto these means have very rarely been used and, almost always, the problem of a foreign suit being in an unconnected forum has been dealt with at the stage of recognition of the judgment.

Generally speaking, at the stage of recognition, even if, according to Article 3157 of the CCQ, such recognition may not be refused on the sole ground that the foreign court applied a law different from that that would be applicable under Quebecois conflict of laws rules, Quebecois courts could take into account the fact that there was foreign forum-shopping by several means.

First, Article 3164 of the CCQ (which states: 'The jurisdiction of a foreign authority is established in accordance with the rules on jurisdiction applicable to Quebec authorities . . . , to the extent that the dispute is substantially connected with the country whose authority is seised of the case') can easily be understood as an express rule against forum-shopping.

Furthermore, a Quebecois court could also take account of forum-shopping either, first, by means of public policy, if the result of the decision were against international public policy—but it might be difficult to imagine a situation where Quebecois public interests could be so concerned with forum-shopping—or, secondly, if the proceedings abroad had been violating the fundamental principles of procedure (Article 3155 of the CCQ), or, more easily, thirdly, by refusing to consider that a foreign court had jurisdiction because it was *forum non conveniens* or, fourthly, because Quebecois courts had exclusive and imperative jurisdiction (Articles 3165, 3151 of the CCQ).

VI
CONCLUSION

As we have seen in this chapter, the new Quebecois law adopts an open-minded and modern approach to international litigation, very much in favour of international co-operation, providing not only rules as to *forum conveniens, forum non conveniens,* and *lis pendens,* but also more specific rules such as Articles 3139 (jurisdiction on incidental demands or on a cross-action) and 3140 of the CCQ (exceptional jurisdiction in case of emergency or serious inconvenience to take necessary measures for the protection of a person or of his property in Quebec). All of these new rules involve wide discretionary powers but, given that Quebecois case law has had little experience to date with any of them, at least in the case of international litigation, comparative law will be of prime importance to their application.

7

Finland

HANNU TAPANI KLAMI

Professor of Jurisprudence and Private International Law,
University of Helsinki

CONTENTS

I
GENERAL REMARKS

Private international law has traditionally been a matter rather neglected by the Finnish legislator, and this is even more so for international procedural law.[1] Neither has judicial practice developed clear rules. For this reason it is relatively easy to write the Finnish chapter, and I will in the discussion follow the agenda set forth by Professor Fawcett.

II
NO *FORUM NON CONVENIENS* DOCTRINE

In spite of the lack of a doctrine of *forum non conveniens* similar reasoning is to a certain extent employed by using different concepts.

---

[1] See, however, Hannu Tapani Klami, *Suomen kansainvalinen yksityisoikeus,* Jyvaskyla, 1986; an abridged English version; Hannu Tapani Klami, *Private International Law in Finland,* Turku, 1986; Juhani Walamies, *Tuomioistuimen yleistoimivalta siviiliprosessissa* (with a German summary: *Die internationale Zustandigkeit im Zivilprozess*), Vammala, 1982; Juhani Walamies, *Kanainvalinen prorogaatiosopimus* (with an English summary: *International Jurisdiction Agreement*), Vammala, 1988.

A Finnish court may take up a case, if:

(1) Finland has jurisdiction over the case, i.e. the Finnish legal order has so-called general competence, as it is called in Finland;
(2) The court can base its jurisdiction upon a forum norm. This is also called special competence.

Now, as there are virtually no rules whatsoever about general competence, it is in most cases inferred from the forum norms. But they are rather old and include *forum apprehensionis*: catch where you can, a venue norm with a bad reputation in the international context. Moreover, the norm about property of the defendant in Finland as a basis for Finnish jurisdiction is interpreted in an extensive manner. In a recent decision the Finnish Supreme Court considered a counterclaim of a Danish defendant to constitute 'property' in this sense, and for this reason Finland had jurisdiction over the case.

Although general competence is sometimes mentioned in the courts' decisions, this is not used in order to exclude jurisdiction, but rather to back up it. Why is this so?

The Finnish forum norms were codified in the then Swedish–Finnish Code of 1734, The Procedural Part, Ch. 10, and are still in force with certain amendments. They express a clear homeward trend: it was important to have a jurisdiction as broad as possible in order to serve the interests of the country's own citizens. *Forum apprehensionis* was, under such circumstances, fully understandable.

It should be added that until 1988 Finland followed a very restrictive policy as far as recognition and enforcement of foreign judgments were concerned: apart from foreign arbitration awards, only Nordic civil verdicts were recognized and enforced. But in 1988 Finland concluded a bilateral treaty with Austria to the effect that judgments recognized and exigible in Austria were also accepted in Finland. And as Austria has similar treaties with, among others, the EC States, this meant that a great number of relevant foreign judgments became exigible in Finland. Before that it was reasonable to allow Finnish jurisdiction on rather weak grounds, since foreign judgments were not recognized in Finland. This possibility was not misused: forum-shopping has never been a problem in Finland, and if a (usually Finnish) plaintiff chose to sue a foreign defendant in Finland, he presumably had good reasons for doing so, e.g. the expectation that there could—at least in the future—be in Finland such rights and/or property that could be used for execution.

All this means that Finnish courts do not have practically any discretion at all: if there is at least some connection with Finland (general competence) and a venue norm, the case will be taken up.

The situation is somewhat different in criminal procedure. Here reasoning about *forum (non) conveniens* plays a certain part, if the crime or offence was committed abroad. In such a case an order by the Chancellor of Justice is required for prosecution in Finland. The discretion here resembles the reasoning on *forum (non) conveniens*. One is taking into account such issues as the nationality, domicile, and residence of the defendant and the victim, the availability of evidence, and the probability of a (fair) trial abroad.

III
LIS ALIBI PENDENS

Since Finnish law has been very restrictive as far as the recognition and execution of foreign judgments are concerned, it is fully understandable that *a maiori ad minus* the *lis pendens* effect has been minimal, too. Statutory basis is lacking even here, except for Nordic judgments and trials that, as a rule, are recognized in Finland, and for certain issues of family law, especially divorce cases. This seldom applicable statutory basis expresses a principle that the Finnish court seised second should as a rule decline jurisdiction in favour of the court seised first, if the judgment of the first court ought to be recognized and/or enforced in Finland. The principle is, however, not unconditional, because the question about recognition and enforcement presupposes reasoning about general competence and this, again, comes rather near to the *forum non conveniens* doctrine. It is, however, very difficult to say what arguments should be used in this context. As has been said, the statutory basis is vague, and there are no relevant precedents. If I—as the author of the current textbook on Finnish private international and procedural law—am allowed to express my own opinion, I would like to refer to the *ordre public* clause in the relevant statutes and Conventions and to the *fair trial* principle (the European Human Rights Convention, Article 14(_)). This means that the choice between two parallel trials should be made so that (1) neither party would be subject to extreme injustice in the role of defendant and (2) the net sum of inconvenience and costs to the parties is minimized.

A judgment based only upon *forum deprehensionis* is unenforceable between the Nordic states.

Finland is applying for a membership in the EC. I do not anticipate any problems in relation to EC norms.

There are no separate rules about 'quasi-*lis pendens*'.

IV
FOREIGN CHOICE OF JURISDICTION CLAUSES

If the parties have agreed upon foreign jurisdiction, this prevents the Finnish courts from dealing with the case. Of course it is assumed here that this agreement does not contravene the mandatory forum norms of Finnish law (*forum rei sitae*, e.g., is mandatory, if the subject of the dispute is immovable property in Finland). Moreover, any clause of a contract may be amended on grounds of inequity (Contract Act, s. 36). This adjustment principle belongs to the Finnish notion of *ordre public*, both in substantive and procedural law. This means that a Finnish court may take up the case in Finland, if litigation abroad would involve extreme injustice and cost for the Finnish party.

The dismissal of the action on the basis of a foreign choice of jurisdiction clause presupposes an objection by the defendant before answering the principal claim, except for the situations where Finnish jurisdiction is mandatory according to Finnish law. In such cases the court *ex officio* takes the issue into consideration.

V
ARBITRATION AGREEMENTS

The situation is also very much the same for arbitration, whether Finnish or foreign. Finland has joined the New York Convention and recognizes foreign arbitration awards. Thus, if there is a *per se* valid arbitration agreement or clause, the action is dismissed by the Finnish court, provided that the defendant refers to it and the issue can be subject to arbitration according to the Finnish law. There are few exceptions:

(1) An arbitration clause may be amended on grounds of inequity. In this connection it should be noted that arbitration clauses are usually invalid in sales to Finnish consumers.

(2) If arbitration has already resulted in an invalid judgment, the way to the courts is open. As for foreign arbitration awards this means that recognition in Finland has been sought but without success.

In the first case the court may have some discretion. Otherwise the dismissal of the action is mandatory, provided that the defendant at the beginning of the trial refers to the arbitration clause.

There may, however, be situations where it is more advisable to stay the court proceedings instead of immediately dismissing them. If the validity of the arbitration clause is subject to a dispute between the parties, the arbitrators should in the first place decide about its validity and the competence of the arbitration tribunal. In that case the court should wait for the decision of the arbitrators.

VI
RESTRAINING FOREIGN PROCEEDINGS

Finnish law has no general injunction. The existing types cannot be used for restraining foreign proceedings.

As for forum-shopping abroad, there is not much case law in Finland, since foreign judgments have as a rule been unenforceable in Finland. But if recognition and enforcement do come into question, the issue is examined in summary written proceedings before an administrative court that is responsible for execution issues.

POSTSCRIPT

After I finished the present paper, the Lugano Convention was incorporated into Finnish legislation. Its well-known provisions on the recognition of foreign judgments need not be analysed in the present context. The Convention contains several conditions of recognition with respect to jurisdictional issues. No Finnish forum norms were, however, amended in this context. So, it remains to be seen how this *prima facie* conflict between the Finnish forum norms and the Convention will be solved by Finnish courts.

8

France

HÉLÈNE GAUDEMET-TALLON

Professeur à l'Université de Paris II*

CONTENTS

I

INTRODUCTION

The theme approached herein is disconcerting for any French lawyer: *a priori*, the French legal system determines whether the judge has jurisdiction or not. If he has jurisdiction, he must rule and cannot 'decline to exercise his jurisdiction'.[1] The expression *forum non conveniens* is extraneous to the French legal system; however, the latter knows about *exceptions de litispendance* (pleas of *lis pendens*) and *connexité*[2] (related actions), both of which provide almost the only bases whereby the court may decide not to proceed with the case. It will be seen, though, that the plea is the object of definite conditions in domestic and private international law.

---

* This Report, originally written in French and published in [1994] *Rev. Int. de Droit Comparé*, 423–35, has been translated into English, for the purpose of this book, and with the authorization of Prof. Drago, Sec. Gen. of the *Académie Internationale de Droit comparé*.

[1] *Refuser d'exercer sa compétence juridictionnelle.*

[2] There is *connexité* between two actions when they are so closely connected that there would be a risk of irreconcilable decisions should they be adjudicated upon separately. *Connexité* is also a condition for the admissibility of incidental pleas. For an English view of *connexité*, see Cheshire and North, *Private International Law* (12th edn., 1992), 329, on related actions.

Another power of the judge which is, in contrast, to decide the case even though he has no jurisdiction, is excluded from the scope of the study: this could be called *forum conveniens*; the judge settles the dispute, not by virtue of a legal rule empowering him to do so, but because judgment appears to be appropriate in view of the circumstances. In this sense, it is possible to mention the following two cases: first of all, both in domestic and private international law, the judge must declare that he has jurisdiction when the litigants would otherwise face a *déni de justice* (miscarriage of justice).[3] This assumption seems unlikely in domestic law: indeed, the set of principles relating to jurisdiction defines the proper court for any given case, although one could think of a *de facto* impossibility which would prevent the applicant from referring the matter to the competent court. In international law, on the one hand, since rules on conflict of jurisdictions emanate from different authorities, coherence may lessen. On the other hand, impediments of fact may be more frequent: there is a risk to the applicant of having no possibility, in fact or in law, of suing before a court admitting competence. In such cases, a French court may rule to avoid a *déni de justice*.[4]

The second situation, where the French judge has the power to regard himself *forum conveniens* when ordinary rules of competence do not give him jurisdiction, is the specific case where the object of the dispute referred to him deals with measures of execution to be performed in France. In accordance with a classic rule of French private international law he has clear jurisdiction. Furthermore, he then has the *option* to determine the existence of the debt which triggers attachment or distraint carried out in France, even if this question of law would normally fall within the competence of a foreign court.[5] It is a mere option, as the judge will assess if it is appropriate, 'convenient',[6] to do so.

The two cases above, which may be regarded as giving rise to a way of applying the theory of *forum conveniens*, are briefly mentioned as they do not come within the scope of the proposed topic: 'refusal to exercise legal competence'.

---

[3] There is *déni de justice* when any judge refuses to rule. See Art. 4 of the Civil Code.

[4] However, recent case law requires the applicant to show that no foreign court may be invoked, and that the dispute has a minimum connection with the French legal order. See TGI Paris, 1 Oct. 1976, [1977] D (Recueil Dalloz Sirey) 535, note Huet, [1977] JDI (*Journal de Droit International*) 878, observ. Kahn; Paris, 24 Feb. 1977, [1978] D 168, note Massip, [1978] (*Revue Critique de Droit International Privé*) RC 516, note Huet; 1 Cass. civ., 7 Jan. 1982, [1983] RC 87, note Ancel.

[5] See 1 Cass. civ., 6 Nov. 1979, *Nassibian*, [1980] JDI 95, report. Ponsard; [1980] RC 588, note Couchez; Ancel and Lequette, *Grands Arrêts de la Jurisprudence Française de Droit International Privé* (2nd edn., 1992), no. 58; 1 Cass. civ., 18 Nov. 1986, *Banque camerounaise de développement*, [1987] RC 773, note Muir-Watt; [1987] JDI 632, note Kahn; [1987] II JCP (*Semaine Juridique*) 20909, note Nicod.

[6] In English in the text.

As a matter of fact, the topic selected for the congress has little relevance as regards French law. Hence the hesitation of the *rapporteur* in the following discussion! Indeed, French lawyers are not familiar with the idea of refusing jurisdiction, and cases where such refusal is conceivable are scarce and strictly defined by law, as will be seen. This is very different from the common law concept whereby a court may refuse to rule because it is not *convenient*[7] to do so.

This difference is rooted in history: in France, it has always been thought that it was better to frame the power of legal authorities over questions of competence and of subject matter according to the famous saying: *Dieu nous garde de l'équité des Parlements.*[8] In contrast, in England the respect of the public towards judges and British pragmatism explain why the theories of *forum conveniens* and *forum non conveniens* have emerged without any major problem.

The plan will follow the questionnaire sent by J. J. Fawcett, Dean of the Law Faculty at the University of Leicester, general *rapporteur* on the subject, as it is very revealing about the differences in how common law and civil law countries deal with the matter. Thus, I shall deal successively with *forum non conveniens* (II), *lis pendens* (III), aspects of jurisdiction clauses (IV), arbitration clauses (V), and finally, the impossibility in French law of granting an injunction to stop proceedings started abroad (VI).

II
FORUM NON CONVENIENS

As mentioned earlier, this theory is unknown to French domestic and international law. This phenomenon may be explained by the following argument: since the Napoleonic era, and possibly as far back as Ancient Law,[9] legal competence, be it domestic or international, has been the object of substantive-law rules which state those cases where a French court is competent or, on an international level, if a French court has jurisdiction or not. In domestic law, these rules are found in the New Code of Civil Procedure, as amended in 1975: they form a complete set allocating disputes to the different legal authorities operating in France, in terms of competence of attribution and territorial jurisdiction. These principles were established with a concern for the requirements of the proper admin-

---

[7] In English in the text.
[8] 'May God preserve us from the fairness of the Parliaments'.
[9] See Holleaux, *Compétence du Juge Etranger et Reconnaissance des Jugements* (Dalloz, 1970); Hudault, 'Sens et Portée de la Compétence du Juge Naturel dans l'Ancien Droit Français', [1972] *RC* 27 and 249.

istration of justice and the interests of litigants. Therefore, there is no reason to grant the designated court the power to refuse to give a decision for the benefit of another legal authority. In international law, the principle is that rules relating to domestic territorial jurisdiction are transposed into the international order,[10] either as such,[11] or with slight adaptations.[12] Consequently, as is the case for domestic law, it is not generally appropriate to give the court recognized as being competent internationally the power to refuse to rule.

One could argue that Article 92 of the New Code of Civil Procedure allows the French judge to declare himself incompetent *ab initio* if 'the case . . . cannot be decided by French courts'.[13] However, there is no ground for this argument: when the judge avails himself of the option set up by Article 92, it is precisely because the French principles concerning international competence *do not give him jurisdiction*. Therefore, it is not for the court to renounce competence in favour of a foreign court considered to be the proper forum, but merely to acknowledge the fact that it has no jurisdiction.[14] Similarly in domestic law, Articles 92 and 93 of the New Code of Civil Procedure allow the judge to raise *ab initio* his 'incompetence' only where it is stated that he can do so. This is not in any way a power to stay proceedings by a judge declared competent, when he considers another court to be the proper forum.

Thus, it is certain that the theory of *forum non conveniens* is not part of French substantive law, and that a few cautious applications are found only in the specific cases of *lis pendens* and *connexité*, as will be seen in III.

The French chapter does not purport to deal specifically with the Brussels Convention of 27 September 1968 and the role it would or would not give to *forum non conveniens*. Unfortunately, the case (C–214/92 *Ladenimor SA* v. *Intercomfinanz SA*), which would have given the European Court of Justice the opportunity to decide whether or not to introduce *forum non conveniens* into the Brussels Convention, has been settled out of

---

[10] Cass. civ., 19 Oct. 1959, *Pelassa*, [1960] D 37, note Holleaux; [1960] RC 215, note Y.L.; 1 Cass. civ., 30 Oct. 1962, *Scheffel*, [1963] RC 387, note Francescakis; [1963] D 109, note Holleaux; *Grands arrêts*, n. 5 above, 38.

[11] E.g. the rule laid down by Art. 42(1) of the NCPC (New Code of Civil Procedure 1975) which declares competent the court of the defendant's domicile.

[12] E.g. Art. 45 of the NCPC, allocating jurisdiction in the case of a dispute to the court for the place where the inheritance occurred, cannot be transposed as such in international law, as it is valid only for inheritance of chattels. In the case of real property, the proper court is the one of the State where the real property is located.

[13] *L'affaire . . . échappe à la connaissance de la juridiction française.*

[14] In this sense, see Lagarde, [1986] I *Hague Recueil* 9, the author notes that 'Article 92 has been mostly sterilized by virtue of Article 18 of the Brussels Convention, which renders voluntary appearance by the parties who do not raise incompetence a satisfactory condition to give jurisdiction to the court invoked.'

court. All that can be said at this point is that French doctrine (academic authority) is not favourable to this introduction. As long ago as 1972, Droz wrote that it was necessary to *tuer dans l'œuf cette source de chicane*.[15] More recently, Huet strongly criticized a decision of the Cour de Paris of 17 November 1987 which had admitted that a French court, declared competent to order temporary measures pursuant to Article 24 of the Brussels Convention, could not proceed with the case in favour of an Italian court considered to be 'better placed than the French judge to rule on the temporary measures'.[16] In Huet's view, 'to state that the Italian judge is better placed amounts to sanctioning the theory of *forum non conveniens*, despite the fact that neither French private international law nor the Brussels Convention of 27 September 1968 gives any place to it [this theory] . . . ; if a French court has jurisdiction by virtue of the applicable law, it cannot declare itself incompetent on grounds of inappropriateness'.[17]

It should be added that Article 18 of the Brussels Convention, making the appearance of the defendant who does not contest competence a basis of jurisdiction, seems to be opposed to courts declaring themselves incompetent to rule on the dispute.

As far as non-Conventional French law is concerned, ignorance of *forum non conveniens* also entails that courts are not empowered to stay actions when the serving of a writ in a particular jurisdiction seems to be detrimental to the defendant. The idea is that, if rules regarding competence are respected, the defendant is not *a priori* liable to suffer any detriment because these rules have been established with due regard to his interests.

Finally, it has not been judged necessary in French law to have recourse to *forum non conveniens* in order to fight forum-shopping, which would give undue benefit to French courts: existing rules dealing with competence ensure that there is a strong link between the dispute and the French legal order. In cases where this link is missing, or the parties resort to fraud, the French court *has no jurisdiction*. This radical solution permits no application of *forum non conveniens* to escape forum-shopping.[18]

---

[15] 'Nip in the bud this source of quibbling' in *Compétence Judiciaire et Effets des Jugements dans le Marché Commun* (Dalloz, 1972), no. 206.

[16] Paris, 17 Nov. 1987, [1989] JDI 96, observ. Huet.

[17] In the same sense, see Duintjer Tebbens in Sumampouw *et al.* (eds), *Law & Reality—Voskuil Essays* (1992), 47; see also the article by the present author, [1991] RC 180; and North, 'La liberté d'apprèciation de la compétence (*Jurisdictional Discretion*) selon la Convention de Bruxelles', in *Nouveaue Itinéraires en Droit, Hommage à Fr. Rigaux* (Brussels, 1993), 373 ff.

[18] On the opposite case of forum-shopping exercised to the detriment of French courts in favour of foreign jurisdictions, see n. 33 below.

III

LIS PENDENS

In common law countries, *la litispendance*[19] is generally designated by the Latin terminology '*lis alibi pendens*' and treated as an aspect of *forum non conveniens*.

The position adopted by French law is very different: French law knows about the plea of *lis pendens* in domestic as well as international law, but the latter follows strict rules where discretionary powers have very little place. Furthermore, as the reader shall see, the decision not to proceed given by the court in international law, when it is second seised, does not depend on appropriateness or the 'convenient' character of the court first seised. Hence the spirit presiding over the plea of *lis pendens* is not akin to the English attitude towards the plea.

It is necessary to distinguish between three aspects of French law: *lis pendens* in domestic law (1), in ordinary international law (2), and the French reaction towards the attitude of the Brussels Convention and the European Court of Justice on *lis pendens* in the EC (3). Each case will also be seen in relation to the plea of *connexité*,[20] which is submitted to be relevant hereinafter.

1. In French domestic law, Article 100 of the New Code of Civil Procedure states that 'If the same dispute is referred to two jurisdictions of equal authority, equally competent to rule on the matter, the court last seised must decline to rule in favour of the other one if asked to do so by one of the parties. If not, it may do so of its own motion.' The consequence of this is that judges have no discretionary power when one of the parties raises the plea of *lis pendens*: when recording that a case which has a similar object and facts has already been laid before another French court, the judge must satisfy the party which has raised the plea and stay proceedings. Only silence by the parties gives him more latitude in decision-making: he *may* decide not to proceed but is not obliged to do so. In this very specific case, the decision given by the second court may be dictated by reasoning similar to what *forum non conveniens* allows.

Still within French domestic law, but with regard to the plea of related actions, Article 101 of the New Code of Civil Procedure provides that a court, facing a case judged *connexe* (connected) to another case referred to another French court, shall decide to stay proceedings only by request of one of the parties. This cannot be performed of its own motion, but, once established, the plea *forces* the judge not to proceed[21] if asked not to by one of the parties. However, when a party raises the plea of related actions

---

[19] In French in the text.   [20] See n. 2.
[21] 2 Cass. civ., 5 July 1978, [1978] 2 Gaz. Pal. (Gazette du Palais), 624.

(*connexité*), the judge retains a certain discretion in his power to ascertain the relation, and the Cour de Cassation clearly stated that this power falls within the full authority of the judge ruling on the merits.[22] The grounds are that *connexité* arises 'when several actions are so intricately connected that it is desirable to examine them together'.[23] This turn of phrase is vague and leaves freedom for interpretation: it is also possible to consider here that the process is akin to the theory of *forum non conveniens*. International law differs from this.

2. In ordinary French private international law, the plea of *lis pendens* did not force itself upon the legal order without some difficulty. For years, the French court second seised, when a competent foreign court was also involved, would refuse to stay actions in favour of the foreign court. Finally, strongly encouraged by academic thinking,[24] the Cour de Cassation admitted international *lis pendens* in the *Miniera di Fragne*[25] case. It is now established that the plea of international *lis pendens* is admissible before French courts. It must be noted that the decision laid down the very important principle that, in the case of international *lis pendens* (same dispute, French court competent in accordance with French rules, and foreign court competent under its own rules), the French judge *may* admit the plea and stay proceedings in favour of the foreign court *only if the decision given abroad is susceptible to being recognized in France*. Therefore, the French judge must forecast the legality of the decision rendered abroad. Should he consider that it will respect the conditions of legality required by French law so that it can be recognized in France, he has the power to stay proceedings. The power vested in the judge is important here: it is his task to evaluate whether or not the decision given abroad could take effect in France and, once he has done this, he is still free to adjudicate or not.[26] It is obvious that the decision taken by the French judge to stay actions does not depend on his evaluation of whether or not he is *forum non conveniens*, but is the consequence of the prognosis made on French recognition of a foreign judgment.

Again, it is necessary to make a comparison with the plea of international *connexité* (related actions): would a French court decide not to proceed with a related case in favour of a foreign jurisdiction? Substantive law is very scarce on this point: 'if the doctrine is favourable to stays of actions when there is international *connexité*, case law has no significant

[22] e.g. 1 Cass. civ., 20 Oct. 1987, [1987] IV JCP 400.
[23] Vincent and Guinchard, *Précis Dalloz de Procédure civile* (22nd edn., 1991), nc. 341.
[24] See Holleaux, 'La litispendance internationale,' [1971–3] *TCFDIP* (*Travaux du Comité Français de Droit International Privé*), 203.
[25] 1 Cass. civ., 26 Nov. 1974, [1975] RC 491, note Holleaux; [1975] JDI 108, note Ponsard; *Grands arrêts*, n. 5 above, no. 55.
[26] On the reception of the case of 26 Nov. 1974 in French case law, see our article in *Mélanges Dédiés à Holleaux* (Litec, 1990), 121 ff.

example to offer'.[27] It is possible to foresee a psychological resistance from courts to staying actions in favour of a foreign court, and they are reluctant to admit that it is desirable to have both cases laid before the foreign court. It is worth mentioning, though, that the Cour de Cassation is not opposed to the admissibility of related actions.[28] Should the distinction drawn by the Supreme Court be confirmed, the plea of internationally related actions would give judges important powers: to consider whether there is *connexité*, then decide whether to stay proceedings or not. We are fairly close to *forum non conveniens* here.

3. The most radical treatment of international *lis pendens* is found in Article 21 of the Brussels Convention.[29] We know that the text *forces* the second court to stay actions in favour of the court first seised in cases of *lis pendens*. It is compulsory to do so not only when a party raises the plea but also in the case of silence where the court does so *of its own motion*. No discretion is given to the judge here. The harsh character of the obligation is understandable in the sense that Article 21 concerns only courts of the EC Member States, and that the philosophy lying behind the Convention is that of reciprocal trust between courts. Moreover, since 1989 and the agreement admitting Spain and Portugal to the Brussels Convention, Article 21 requires that the jurisdiction of the court first seised must be established before the second court declines jurisdiction. Article 21 has been accepted by the French courts, but French academic writers were disturbed by the way that the European Court of Justice extensively interpreted the condition of object identity in the case of *Gubisch*:[30] the Court estimated that a request for the performance of an international sale of tangible property on the one hand, and for recission on the other hand, as well as cancellation of sale as an auxiliary plea, had the same object, entailing the justified application of Article 21. This unorthodox concep-

---

[27] Audit, *Droit International Privé* (Economica, 1991), no. 382.

[28] See 1 Cass. civ., 20 Oct. 1987, [1988] JDI 446, note Huet; [1988] RC 540, note Lequette: the decision dismissed the appeal on the basis that 'the admissibility of the exception of *connexité* remains a mere possibility for the courts'.

[29] Bilateral treaties ratified by France do not appear to offer any interest here: most of them deal with judicial co-operation and the recognition of judgments obtained abroad, and do not contain any provisions on *lis pendens*. This silence is normal, since agreement on *lis pendens* presupposes agreement on rules regarding direct jurisdiction. Although it is to be noted that Art. 19 of the Franco–Italian Convention of 3 June 1930, in spite of the fact that only one provision on direct jurisdiction is found in the Convention (Art. 30, setting aside Art. 14 Civil Code for contracts and torts), imposes an *obligation* to stay upon request of one of the parties in the case of *lis pendens* and *connexité* (although *connexité*, as defined in Art. 19, is equivalent to *lis pendens*). With regards to bilateral treaties on direct jurisdiction, only a few exist (Franco–Belgian Convention of 8 July 1899 and Franco–Madagascan Convention of 4 June 1973 for treaties having general effect; Franco–Polish Convention of 5 April 1967 and Franco–Yugoslav Convention of 18 May 1971 on family law), and they do not contain any provision on *lis pendens*.

[30] Case 144/86, [1987] ECR 4861, opinion of Mancini AG, [1988] JDI 537, observ. Huet, [1988] RC 374 note Gaudemet-Tallon.

tion of object identity was strongly criticized by French doctrine which noted that, in view of the context, the European Court of Justice should have considered both petitions as being *closely related (connexe)* so that Article 22 would have applied.

Article 22, dealing with related actions pending before courts of Member States, in paragraph (3) lays down a fairly precise definition of related actions: 'For the purpose of this Article, actions are deemed to be related where they are so closely connected that it is expedient to hear and determine them together to avoid the risk of irreconcilable judgments from separate proceedings.' The last two paragraphs give a certain flexibility to the court second seised when deciding its attitude: the court may stay proceedings of its own motion—Article 22(1); the court may stay upon request by one of the parties, should the conditions set out in Article 22(2) be met. The power to determine *connexité* is undeniable although 'framed' within the definition aforementioned. The flexibility examined here is far removed from the freedom of the judge in the application of *forum non conveniens*.

Thus, with regard to *lis pendens* (and related actions), French general private international law gives the judge a rather wide discretion and a rather loose comparison may be made with the doctrine of *forum non conveniens*. By way of contrast, the French judge has no real power under domestic law or the Brussels Convention. It must also be noted that French law remains impervious to *forum non conveniens* when it comes to jurisdiction clauses and arbitration clauses.

IV
JURISDICTION CLAUSES IN FAVOUR OF A FOREIGN COURT

In French domestic law, Article 48 of the New Code of Civil Procedure prohibits jurisdiction clauses except when arising between merchants. On the contrary, the Cour de Cassation in a decision on a matter of principle has allowed the use of such clauses within the international order. In *Cie de Signaux et d'Entreprises Electriques (CSEE)* v. *Soc. Sorelec*, the *Première chambre civile*, ending controversies which appeared just after the New Code of Civil Procedure appeared, stated that 'clauses which extend the scope of international jurisdiction are legal when dealing with an international dispute, and when the clause does not deny application of the mandatory territorial competence of a French court'.[31] As far as the

---

[31] [1986] D 265, observ. Audit; [1986] RC 537, note Gaudemet-Tallon; *Grands arrêts*, n. 5 above, no. 68.

present topic is concerned, this ruling entails that, in the presence of a jurisdiction clause in favour of a foreign court when the conditions set out in *CSEE* v. *Sorelec* are met, i.e. international dispute and no mandatory territorial competence (which rules out clauses in the field of personal status),[32] the French judge cannot oppose the application of the clause. His competence would only be triggered if the court were seised by the applicant with the consent or silence of the defendant, as it would be considered that the parties' attitude forms a new agreement and cancels the previous clause. Similarly in the absence of any jurisdiction clause, the serving of a writ abroad, when the defendant does not oppose it, is considered to be a tacit agreement between the parties to depart from French jurisdiction and extend foreign competence.

Hence in French law, the voluntary extension of jurisdiction resulting from a jurisdiction clause or absence of challenge to the competence of the court by the defendant gives exclusive jurisdiction to the designated court. The only cases where this is not applicable are: when the conditions set by *CSEE* v. *Sorelec* are not satisfied, when there is fraud,[33] and if the foreign court was referred to or a defence produced abroad in the case of emergency or necessity.[34]

French general international law is therefore very close to the scheme implemented by the Brussels Convention: Article 17 gives exclusive competence to the court of another State designated by the clause as long as the conditions of substance and form laid down are respected, and Article 18 gives rise to jurisdiction following uncontested appearance by the defendant. This is probably the reason French courts have applied these Articles without any problem.

To say that the theory of *forum non conveniens* has no place with regard to extension of jurisdiction should not be surprising. When the will of the parties has been expressed legally designating the competent court, it must be respected, as this would otherwise deny any significance to

[32] It is not always easy to know whether or not the rule allocating competence to French courts is mandatory, but this sensitive question is not relevant to this Ch. One could read the interesting comments from Ancel and Lequette on *CSEE* v. *Sorelec* in *Grands arrêts*, n. 5 above, 564–7; mention will be made that the French mandatory character of the jurisdictional rule relating to contracts of employment has been extensively discussed by academic writers and in case law, and that recent cases emanating from the Cour de Cassation (Chambre sociale and Première chambre civile) seem to be oriented towards easy admission of jurisdiction clauses in favour of a foreign jurisdiction with regards to international contracts of employment.

[33] On fraud with regards to personal status, see 1 Cass. civ., 1 Mar. 1988, *Senoussi*, [1989] RC 721, note Sinay-Cytermann; [1988] D 486, note Massip; 1 Cass. civ., 6 June 1990, *Akla*, [1991] RC 553, esp. note P. Courbe; [1990] D, Som.com. 263, observ. Audit.

[34] Cases where plea or defence abroad is made to avoid attachment or distraint. See French case law on the renunciation of Art. 14 or 15 of the *Code civil*: pleading abroad does not result in ouster of French jurisdiction if the litigant was forced to do so by circumstances or did not know about the privilege of jurisdiction pursuant to these Arts. (see the cases given by Audit, n. 31 above, no. 362).

jurisdiction clauses and their usefulness in the international order. It should be noted that in the United States, a country where *forum non conveniens* is well established, it appears that it is not applied in the presence of a voluntary extension of jurisdiction.[35] As Lagarde said, there is 'incompatibility between jurisdiction clauses and *forum non conveniens*'.[36]

V
ARBITRATION CLAUSES

The question asked by the *rapporteur général* about arbitration agreements is slightly different: the purpose is to know whether or not the judiciary has the power to *stay the proceedings*[37] when the parties have concluded an arbitration agreement (arbitration clause or compromise). Again, the solution adopted in France does not refer to *forum non conveniens*, but relies on the idea that the arbitration agreement entails *the incompetence* of the judiciary.

Article 1458 of the New Code of Civil Procedure, which is applicable to domestic and international arbitration[38] as laid down by the *décret*[39] of 12 May 1981, states that:

When a dispute, of which an arbitration tribunal is seised by virtue of an arbitration clause, is referred to a State court, the latter must declare itself incompetent. If the arbitration tribunal has not yet been seised, the court must equally refuse competence unless the arbitration agreement is patently null and void. In both cases, the court cannot raise incompetence of its own motion.

Thus, the text distinguishes between two situations.

In the first case, the arbitration tribunal has already been seised; if one of the parties refers the matter to a State court, the mere mention by the other party of the arbitration clause or compromise forces the court to stay proceedings. The court cannot rule on the validity of the arbitration agreement; the arbitration tribunal is the only one empowered to rule on this point, and should it declare itself as having no jurisdiction, the State court will be competent.

In the second case, the arbitration tribunal has not yet been seised. As in the first case, the State court cannot declare itself incompetent of its own motion: the defendant will have to raise a plea of incompetence by virtue

---

[35] See Lagarde, n. 14 above, at 147, the author quoting Dubler, *Les Clauses d'Exception en Droit International Privé* (1983), no. 253, 200 to support his views.

[36] N. 14 above.   [37] In English in the text.

[38] See Bellet and Mezger, [1981] *RC* 611 ff., spec. 626; M. de Boisséson, *Le Droit Français de l'Arbitrage Interne et International* (GLN July 1990), 79 and 516.

[39] More or less equal to the English s. 1 of the Arbitration Act of 1975, and to the New York Convention on the Recognition and Enforcement of Foreign Arbitral Awards of 1958.

of the arbitration agreement to *force* the State court to stay actions unless the arbitration agreement is 'patently null and void'. The turn of phrase implies no possible dispute on the nullity; should a dispute be possible, the arbitration tribunal would rule.

It should also be noted that deciding whether or not a dispute is within the scope of the arbitration agreement comes within the competence of the arbitration tribunal, even if the latter is not yet constituted, and not of State courts.[40]

Faced with an arbitration agreement, the State judge has very few powers indeed: he cannot stay proceedings of his own motion (if the parties remain silent, they forgo the agreement), and when a party puts forward the arbitration agreement, he *must* stay actions (with the exception of the marginal case where the arbitration tribunal has not yet been seised *and* the agreement is patently null and void). He cannot in any way rule on the appropriateness of a judge or an arbitrator concerning the case. This is very remote from *forum non conveniens*, as French law expresses the priority of arbitration competence over judicial competence, a priority reinforced by the well-known principle of the autonomy of an arbitration clause.[41]

VI
IMPOSSIBILITY OF OBTAINING AN INJUNCTION TO STOP PROCEEDINGS STARTED ABROAD

The position in French law on this point is totally the opposite of that under English law. The latter accepts the possibility of the judge granting an injunction to stop proceedings started abroad[42] while there is no such possibility under French law which would regard such an intervention as an intrusion in the functioning of the foreign legal system.

The consequence is not that French law is powerless against foreign decisions rendered by courts which the French legal system does not consider as being competent. The reasoning is totally different: French law will act only at the stage of recognition and enforcement of the foreign ruling and will refuse to give any effect to the ruling if the foreign court is regarded as having no 'indirect' jurisdiction. This refers to one of the

---

[40] 1 Cass. civ., 7 June 1989, [1992] Rev. Arbitr. 61, note Derains.

[41] M. de Boisséson, n. 38 above, 713, infers from this autonomy a real 'principle of validity of the arbitration clause'.

[42] See the English decisions in *British Airways Board* v. *Laker Airways Ltd* [1984] QB 142; reversed [1984] QB 142; on appeal [1985] AC 58; *Midland Bank plc* v. *Laker Airways Ltd* [1986] QB 689: Dicey & Morris, *The Conflict of Laws* (12th edn., 1993), 410–11.

conditions of the international validity of foreign judgments in French law: the foreign court must be regarded by the French legal order as having jurisdiction. The most recent expression of this control was formulated by the Cour de Cassation in *Simitch*:[43] the foreign court is considered competent when the French rule regarding the conflict of jurisdiction does not give exclusive competence to French jurisdiction, when the dispute has close connections with the foreign forum, and when the choice of jurisdiction is not fraudulent.

It is only when dealing with the indirect competence of the foreign court that French law offers the possibility of denying effect in France to a foreign decision for lack of competence of the court. This is in no way connected to the common law scheme, whereby the forum may grant an injunction staying proceedings abroad on the basis of *forum non conveniens*.

VII
CONCLUSION

The last point shows how different common law and French law are: French law, as without a doubt do other Roman- and German-based systems, ignores the theory of *forum non conveniens*. The concept is extraneous to our substantive law and arguably our mentality: to empower a French judge, while French law gives him jurisdiction, to determine that another court (French or foreign) is more appropriate, more 'convenient', would seem to open the door to arbitrariness or, at least, unpredictability, which would be detrimental to litigants. The rules we use when faced with *lis pendens* and *connexité*, which are both flexible and precise, seem to leave the judge sufficient discretion in these two particular circumstances. Actually, we have two conflicting concepts of judicial power: under French law, this power must be exercised within the framework of constraining and pre-existing rules (whether their origin is case law or statute law); under English law, the judge enjoys greater freedom which is apparent in the mechanism of *forum non conveniens*.

[43] [1985] RC 369 and art. by Francescakis, at 243; [1985] JDI 460, note Huet; [1985] D 469, note Massip and inf. rap. 497, observ. Audit; *Grands arrêts*, n. 5 above, no. 66.

9

Germany

DR HAIMO SCHACK

*Professor, Institut für Europäisches und Internationales Privat- und Verfahrensrecht,
Christian—Albrechts—University of Kiel**

CONTENTS

I
INTRODUCTION

It is hard for a judge to forgo exercising the international jurisdiction that
is extended to him by law: the plaintiff's expectations of domestic legal
protection will not be met. Moreover, the adjudication of the dispute will

---

* The author wishes cordially to thank his assistant Sebastian Kubis, LL.M. (Illinois), for
preparing a draft of the English translation. A German version of the German National
Report previously appeared in [1994] *Rabels Z* 40.

be left for a foreign judge to make and will sometimes differ in the result, because different procedural circumstances and often also different choice of law rules will govern the foreign forum. Renouncing domestic jurisdiction is therefore rather the exception than the rule, and needs specific justification. Whereas German law predominantly rejects the doctrine of *forum non conveniens* (below, II), it very generously respects the earlier pendency of a foreign action (below, III). Forum-selection agreements prorogating an exclusive foreign forum are also widely respected (below, IV, 1), as are arbitration agreements, if the defendant refers to them in time (below, IV, 2). German courts do not interfere with a foreign action by issuing antisuit injunctions (below, V); these conflicts can only be solved later by refusing to recognize the foreign judgment.

II
FORUM NON CONVENIENS

1. The German law of jurisdiction is distinguished by strict, clearly defined, statutory rules which generally do not give discretion to the judge. This is true without exception in so far as international jurisdiction is directly governed by statute, e.g. in § 606a of the Code of Civil Procedure (ZPO) concerning matrimonial affairs or in Articles 2 to 20 of the Brussels Convention (known in Germany as the GVÜ).[1] Often, however, the rules of German international jurisdiction are only indirectly derived from the statutory rules on venue (especially §§ 12 ff., ZPO). This 'double functionality' of the venue rules[2] allows a certain amount of flexibility and adaptation to the particularities of international jurisdiction. This leeway could be a possible starting-point for the doctrine of *forum non conveniens*;[3] but has not been used as such.

1. FORUM NON CONVENIENS SUBSTITUTES

(a) Considerations of *forum non conveniens* have not found their way into German law except in some narrowly defined areas of international non-contentious proceedings. So, pursuant to § 47 of the Code on Non-conten-

---

[1] In so far as the Brussels Convention is applicable, the doctrine of *forum non conveniens* does not apply! Kropholler, *Europäisches Zivilprozeßrecht* (3rd edn., Heidelberg, 1991), before Art. 2 GVÜ para. 19; Schlosser in [1983] *Praxis des Internationalen Privat- und Verfahrensrechts* (IPRax) 285; Jasper, *Forum shopping in England und Deutschland* (Berlin, 1990), 77 ff., 79; Schack, 'Rechtshängigkeit in England und Art. 21 GVÜ' [1991] IPRax 270, 273 ff.

[2] In this regard see Schack, *Internationales Zivilverfahrensrecht* (IZVR), (Munich, 1991), para. 236 ff.; Kropholler in *Handbuch des Internationalen Zivilverfahrensrechts* (Tübingen, 1982), i, ch. III, paras. 30 ff.

[3] Cf. Schumann in Stein/Jonas, *Zivilprozeßordnung* (20th edn., Tübingen, 1979), introduction, para. 760.

tious Proceedings (FGG), the guardianship court can refrain from placing a ward under its protection, if the ward's interests are better served by a foreign court's jurisdiction. Matters of *forum non conveniens* are also involved, where the principle of *perpetuatio fori* (§ 261, III, No. 2, ZPO, concerning contentious proceedings) is relaxed in non-contentious proceedings in the interest of the child. This happens particularly in adoption cases, when the adopting person(s) or the child changes his habitual residence to a foreign country (cf. § 43b FGG),[4] but recently also in custody cases (cf. Art. 1, Hague Convention of 5 October 1961, concerning the powers of authorities and the law applicable in respect of the protection of minors [MSA]; § 621, I, ZPO; §§ 35b, 43, FGG).[5]

(b) There are isolated attempts to introduce the idea of *forum non conveniens* indirectly by using the 'legitimate interest to take legal action' (*Rechtsschutzbedürfnis*) as an additional procedural requirement.[6] This legitimate interest may be lacking, if the plaintiff or petitioner abuses the judicial procedure.[7] That is certainly not the case, however, when the plaintiff only makes use of his right pursuant to § 35 ZPO to choose between several concurring jurisdictions.[8] Nor is the 'legitimate interest to take legal action' lost merely because the German judgment will not be recognized abroad.[9] The reason therefore is that nobody can say in advance where in the world the decision will later have effect. Besides, the decision will have to be enforced only if the debtor does not comply voluntarily. Thus, international jurisdiction cannot be limited by denying the plaintiff's legitimate interest in a domestic decision.[10]

---

[4] Kammergericht (KG), 4 June 1959 in [1958–9] *Die deutsche Rechtsprechung auf dem Gebiete des Internationalen Privatrechts* (IPRspr.), No. 209; Oberlandesgericht (OLG) Frankfurt/Main, 12 July 1973 in [1975] *Zeitschrift für Standesamtswesen* (StAZ) 98; OLG Zweibrücken, 30 Nov. 1972 in [1973] *Zeitschrift für das gesamte Familienrecht* (FamRZ) 479, 480; Amtsgericht (AG) Würzburg, 7 Aug. 1984 [1985] IPRax 111.

[5] OLG Frankfurt/Main, 15 Nov. 1982 [1983] IPRax 294, 295 with annotation by Schlosser, *ibid.* 285; OLG Hamburg, 7 May 1986 [1987] IPRax 319, 320; OLG Hamm, 13 June 1989 [1989] FamRZ 1109, 1110; Henrich, *Internationales Familienrecht* (Frankfurt/Main, 1989), 238 ff. Cf. Schack, *IZVR*, n. 2 above, para. 500, 394.

[6] In that sense especially Ulrich Wahl, *Die verfehlte internationale Zuständigkeit* (Berlin, 1974), 119 ff.; he is followed by Jayme, 'Zur Übernahme der Lehre vom "forum non conveniens" in das deutsche Internationale Verfahrensrecht', [1975] *StAZ* 91, 94. Cf. also Jayme, [1984] IPRax 121, 124; OLG Frankfurt/Main [1983] IPRax 294, 296.

[7] Cf. Stein/Jonas/Schumann (1986), before § 253, ZPO, paras. 101 ff., 117.

[8] Schack, *IZVR*, n. 2 above, paras. 501, 517; Geimer, *Internationales Zivilprozeßrecht* (IZPR) (Cologne, 1987), para. 1988.

[9] Bundesgerichtshof (BGH), 10 Dec. 1976 in [1977] Wertpapier-Mitteilungen (WM) 453, 455 ff.; OLG Munich 15 Feb. 1980 [1983] IPRax 120, 122; Kropholler, above, n. 2, paras. 213 ff.; Schack, *IZVR*, n. 2 above, para. 517. Cf. also, however, KG 16 Nov. 1989 [1991] IPRax 60: The court affirms the *Rechtsschutzbedürfnis* with respect to a German child-custody decision, because it is not completely impossible that this decision will be recognized at the child's residence in Saudi Arabia.

[10] Cf. Walchshöfer, 'Die deutsche internationale Zuständigkeit in der streitigen Gerichtsbarkeit' in (1967) 80 *Zeitschrift für Zivilprozeß* (ZZP) 165, 208 n. 181, with further references.

(c) Theoretically, the exercise of international jurisdiction may be refused if the plaintiff maliciously manipulated the circumstances on which the international jurisdiction is based. He might, for example, have pretended not to have a domestic residence, but really have established one, or he might have brought assets of the defendant into the forum State in order to sue there (§ 23 ZPO). Nevertheless, such a surreptitious obtaining of jurisdiction has in principle (apart from extreme cases) to be accepted because of the need for legal certainty. The court's jurisdiction is deliberately based on objective prerequisites; accordingly the plaintiff's motives are irrelevant and, in addition, difficult to ascertain.[11] Thus, the German Supreme Court (BGH) held that there is no abuse of process even in the extreme case of a plaintiff who changed his nationality in order to file a divorce suit with a German court sixteen days later.[12] Consequently, the malice defence in practice has no significance as a means of limiting jurisdiction.

(d) Under the term 'incompatible competence' (*wesensfremde Zuständigkeit* or *wesenseigene Unzuständigkeit*), cases are discussed in which the specific character of the dispute is said to take international jurisdiction away from German courts.[13] This is also called international non-competence *ratione materiae*.[14] If the applicable foreign law requires that the German court does something that is impossible, there is no German international jurisdiction. Of course, the applicability of foreign law alone does not justify the 'incompatible competence'.[15] The court is not allowed to escape the application of foreign law, even if it is difficult to ascertain. The required activity becomes incompatible only if a German court is in no way able to apply the foreign rule, even after adjusting, if necessary, German procedural rules.[16] Thus, a German court can, for example, declare a judicial separation by applying Italian family law, even though German law knows only a divorce *a vinculo matrimonii*.[17] Cases of true 'incompatible competence' are therefore very rare. Even actions on

---

[11] Cf. Kropholler, above, n. 2, para. 178; Schack, *IZVR*, n. 2 above, paras. 489 ff.

[12] BGH, 4 June 1971 [1971] FamRZ 519, 520 (on Art. 17, I, 2, Introductory Act to the Civil Code (EGBGB) in its current version).

[13] Schack, *IZVR*, n. 2 above, paras. 503 ff. with further references; recently Haunhorst, *Die 'wesenseigene (Un)Zuständigkeit' deutscher Gerichte* (Dissertation, Osnabrück, 1992).

[14] Riezler in *Festgabe Rosenberg* (Munich, 1949), 199 ff., and in *Internationales Zivilprozeßrecht und prozessuales Fremdenrecht* (Berlin, 1949), 230 ff.

[15] This is different with respect to decedents' estates cases, in which German courts consider themselves to have international jurisdiction only in so far as German inheritance law applies. This strict parallelism of jurisdiction and applicable inheritance law is misguided; Kegel, *Internationales Privatrecht* (6th ed., Munich, 1987), 665 ff.; cf. Heldrich in Palandt, *Bürgerliches Gesetzbuch* (53rd edn., Munich, 1994), Art. 25 EGBGB, para. 18, with further references.

[16] Cf. Heldrich, *Internationale Zuständigkeit und anwendbares Recht* (Berlin, 1969), 269 ff., 270; Schack, *IZVR*, n. 2 above, para. 506.

[17] BGH, 22 Mar. 1967 in 47 Entscheidungen des BGH in Zivilsachen (BGHZ) 324, 333 ff.

the existence of foreign patents and similar rights probably do not belong to this category.[18] In the last analysis, actions filed by foreign countries are only pertinent if they are based on foreign public laws, e.g. foreign tax laws.[19]

(e) An inverse example of *forum non conveniens* may be seen in the rare case of a negative conflict of competence, when the court asserts jurisdiction by necessity, if there is an urgent interest in granting domestic legal protection.[20] In this case the domestic forum has to be positively convenient.[21]

2. The Reasons Why There is No General Rule

A general rule of *forum non conveniens* which goes further than the single aspects described above is supported by some authors,[22] but did not prevail in Germany.[23]

(a) The argument most frequently raised in support of the doctrine of *forum non conveniens* is that it allows justice to be done in the particular case. Strict jurisdictional rules may miss the underlying legislative intent in some cases. Therefore, so the argument goes, the court should be free to take that into account by declaring itself a *forum non conveniens*. The decision will then be given by the court which has better access to the sources of evidence or whose substantive law is applicable, the decision of which has a better chance to prevail in practice, or which is in a general way better capable of economically dealing with the case. However justified these interests (access to sources of proof, applicability of the substantive law of the forum, effectiveness of the decision, economical proceeding) in theory may be, they often contradict each other and may also point to very different fora. Moreover, underlying the jurisdiction

---

[18] Schack, *IZVR*, n. 2 above, para. 509 with further references. *Contra* OLG Hamm, 20 June 1985 in [1986] Neue Juristische Wochenschrift, Rechtsprechungs–Report Zivilrecht (NJW–RR) 1047, 1048 (US trade mark); apparently also Geimer, *IZPR*, n. 8 above, para. 1005.

[19] Schack, *IZVR*, n. 2 above, paras. 510 ff.

[20] Schack, *IZVR*, n. 2 above, para. 397; Kropholler, above, n. 2, para. 192.

[21] Similar, but only with respect to venue, § 36, No. 3, ZPO; cf. Schack, *IZVR*, n. 2 above, para. 358.

[22] Especially Wahl, above, n. 6, 114 ff.; Jayme [1975] *StAZ* 94; Jochen Schröder, *Internationale Zuständigkeit* (Opladen, 1971), 486 ff., 489; Siehr in (1970) 34 Rabels Zeitschrift für ausländisches und internationales Privatrecht (RabelsZ) 585, 629; Wengler [1959] *NJW* 127, 130 (adoption).

[23] OLG Munich, 22 June 1983 [1984] IPRax 319; Geimer, 1, *IZPR*, n. 8 above, paras. 1075 ff.; *id.* in Zöller, *Zivilprozeßordnung* (18th edn., Cologne, 1993), *IZPR*, para. 56 and § 606a, ZPO, para. 32; Kropholler, above, n. 2, paras. 209, 212; Schack, *IZVR*, n. 2 above, para. 502; Schütze, *Deutsches Internationales Zivilprozeßrecht* (Berlin, 1985), 39; Reus, 'Die "forum non conveniens-doctrine" in Großbritannien und den USA in Zukunft auch im deutschen Prozeß?' in [1991] *Recht der Internationalen Wirtschaft (RIW)* 542, 548 ff., 553. Also, rejecting the doctrine, Cohn (1975) in 175 *Archiv für die civilistische Praxis (AcP)* 372, 374 (book review Wahl).

statutes are fairly different jurisdictional interests, which often overlap.[24] The general forum at the defendant's residence (§ 13 ZPO, Article 2 of the Brussels Convention) already shows that none of the interests mentioned above is absolutely decisive. The basic principle of *actor sequitur forum rei* respects none of the following: the applicability of forum law, the access to sources of proof, and the economical proceeding. This is also true with respect to many of the specific fora. The legislative intent is unequivocal only in cases of internationally exclusive fora (e.g. § 24 ZPO, Article 16 of the Brussels Convention) which bind the parties as well as the court.

(b) It is therefore questionable whether the doctrine of *forum non conveniens* really serves justice better in the particular case. Anyway, there are several weighty reasons against this doctrine. First, the constitutional commandment of Article 101, I, 2, GG (Grundgesetz, German Constitution) to guarantee the legally competent judge (*gesetzlicher Richter*) requires a predictable jurisdiction which cannot be manipulated under any circumstances whatsoever. This commandment would not necessarily hinder the adoption of the doctrine of *forum non conveniens*, if it were possible to make the decisive criteria precise enough so that an unequivocal determination of jurisdiction for every case would be possible in advance of the litigation.[25] But exactly that seems impossible, when one looks at the variety of factors which, for example, in the United States may influence the discretionary decision of the judge.[26] This chaos is insupportable, especially if the litigation of jurisdictional questions unfolds through several instances.

Legal certainty requires clear and foreseeable jurisdictional rules. Adopting the doctrine of *forum non conveniens* into the German system, which rests on statutorily standardized jurisdictional interests, would be paramount to breaking that system.[27] Such an 'appreciation of uncertainty'[28] is hardly enticing. The majority view therefore emphasizes correctly the high value of legal certainty.[29] Adhering to the statutorily defined jurisdiction nips in the bud capricious decisions by a judge; he is not given a tool that allows him to get rid of troublesome foreign cases in the name of justice in the particular case. The binding force of '*statute* and law' (Article 20, III, GG)[30] cannot be overcome by the 'law':[31] the doctrine of *forum non*

---

[24] Discussed extensively by Schack, *IZVR*, n. 2 above, paras. 199 ff.
[25] That should be possible according to Schröder, above, n. 22, 490, and Georg Graf, *Die internationale Verbundszuständigkeit* (Munich, 1984), 82 ff.
[26] Along these lines see also Reus [1991] *RIW* 551.
[27] Kropholler, above, n. 2, para. 208: *ein aliud.*
[28] Wahl, above, n. 6, 111.   [29] Cf. the citations in n. 23 above.
[30] Particularly emphasized by Geimer, *IZPR*, n. 8 above, para. 1075; cf. also OLG Munich [1984] IPRax 319.
[31] *Contra* Graf, above, n. 25, 84 ff.

conveniens does not contain so much justice, if any at all, that it could supersede the written statutes.

This is especially true, since the refusal of international jurisdiction on grounds of *forum non conveniens* would increase considerably the risk of a 'negative conflict of competence'.[32] As soon as the plaintiff runs the risk of losing any legal protection at all, he must be helped by allowing jurisdiction by necessity.[33]

3. CONSTRUCTION OF STATUTES

In Germany, the doctrine of *forum non conveniens* therefore cannot deliberately be used as a means of protection against single, maybe too broadly formulated, jurisdictional rules. Nevertheless, considerations of appropriateness may, to a certain degree, influence the *construction* of jurisdictional statutes. In this manner, the notorious, but sensible, forum based on the presence of the defendant's property in § 23 ZPO can be mitigated by a reasonable construction of the term 'property'.[34] Recently, one Senate of the BGH[35] read a new prerequisite into § 23 ZPO: the requirement of a 'sufficient connection' between the litigation and the forum State. In doing so, the BGH went beyond the limits of permissible statutory construction. Therefore, the decision met strong and justified opposition in the literature.[36] The insertion of such an uncertain legal term as 'sufficient domestic connection', which the BGH does not even define in its decision, can in practice lead to the introduction of the doctrine of *forum non conveniens* through the back door of statutory construction.[37] It is to be hoped that the BGH decision, which may cause considerable uncertainty and unnecessary jurisdictional disputes, will not find too many followers,[38] and that the Greater Senate for Civil Matters (§ 132 GVG (*Gerichtsverfassungsgesetz,* Courts Organization Act)) will soon have an opportunity to reclarify the law.

---

[32] Schack, *IZVR*, n. 2 above, para. 497; Reus [1991] *RIW* 552.   [33] See above, 1(e).

[34] Cf. Schack, 'Vermögensbelegenheit als Zuständigkeitsgrund—exorbitant oder sinnvoll?' (1984) 97 ZZP 46, 55 ff., 67; Schack, *IZVR*, n. 2 above, paras. 323 ff.

[35] BGH, 2 July 1991 (XIth Civil Senate), 115 BGHZ 90.

[36] Annotations by Geimer [1991] *NJW* 3072; Schütze in [1991] *Deutsche Zeitschrift für Wirtschaftsrecht (DWiR)* 239; Schack in [1992] *Juristenzeitung (JZ)* 54; Fischer [1992] *RIW* 57; Lüke (1992) 105 ZZP 321. Agreeing, Schlosser, [1992] IPRax 140 and apparently also Fricke [1992] *NJW* 3066.

[37] This connection is mentioned by Fischer [1990] *RIW* 794, 796 (with respect to the lower court's decision (OLG Stuttgart)); *id.* in [1992] *RIW* 57; Geimer [1991] *NJW* 3074; Schütze [1991] *DWiR* 240, 242 ff.; Schlosser [1992] IPRax 143. Thode in *Entscheidungssammlung zum Wirtschafts- und Bankrecht (WuB)*, VII, A., § 23, ZPO, 2.91, rightly fears the 'chaos of *forum non conveniens'.*

[38] OLG Munich, 7 Oct. 1992 [1993] IPRax 237, 239 (with dissenting annotation by Geimer, *ibid.* at 216, 217) follows all too willingly the BGH decision.

4. Forum-Shopping

Forum-shopping may be disliked in a particular case;[39] generally, however, it is perfectly legitimate.[40] Pursuant to § 35 ZPO (and also the Brussels Convention), the defendant is allowed to choose freely from among several competent courts. His considerations of appropriateness are paramount; the judge is not allowed to replace them with his own ideas of a convenient forum. The existence of several optional fora is generally desirable, because it potentially realizes the jurisdictional interests (not only those of the plaintiff!) far better than the rule of *actor sequitur forum rei*, which unilaterally favours the defendant.[41] Instead of condemning forum-shopping or, equally wrong, trying to discourage it by applying the doctrine of *forum non conveniens*, we should focus on reducing the differences between the national legal systems which may attract plaintiffs to a particular forum. That is why the international efforts to unify, in the first place, the choice of law rules are so important.

III
LIS ALIBI PENDENS

1. The Provisions

In German international civil procedure the pendency of a claim has the conclusive effect (pursuant to § 261, III, No. 1, ZPO) that a judge has *ex officio* to dismiss a second action between the same parties on the same cause of action. Here, too, the judge has no discretion. Respecting an otherwise pending action avoids potentially conflicting judgments from the beginning. Moreover, the court saves work and the defendant does not have to answer again on the merits.

The same arguments apply to the law of international jurisdiction.[42] It is therefore common practice also to recognize the earlier pendency of a foreign claim by analogy to § 261, III, No. 1, ZPO,[43] if the foreign proceeding will presumably lead to a judgment entitled to recognition ('recog-

---

[39] Cf. 115 BGHZ 90, 98.

[40] Siehr, '"Forum shopping" im internationalen Rechtsverkehr' in [1984] *Zeitschrift für Rechtsvergleichung (ZfRV)* 124, 139 ff., 142; Schack, *IZVR*, n. 2 above, paras. 220 ff., 228 ff. with further references.

[41] See above, 2, a. [42] Cf. Schack, *IZVR*, n. 2 above, paras. 747 ff.

[43] E.g., BGH, 16 June 1982 [1982] FamRZ 917; BGH, 10 Oct. 1985 [1986] NJW 2195; Schumann, 'Internationale Rechtshängigkeit' in *Festschrift für Winfried Kralik zum 65. Geburtstag* (Vienna, 1986), 301, 306, with further references. Contrast Schütze, above, n. 23, 177; *id.*, 'Die Wirkungen ausländischer Rechtshängigkeit in inländischen Verfahren' (1991) 104 *ZZP* 136, 147, 149, who supports a solution in the particular case with abuse of process as an argument.

nition prognosis'). Only then are the foreign proceedings equivalent to the domestic with respect to the aim of legal protection.[44] The prerequisites for recognition are found in the applicable treaties, otherwise in § 328, ZPO. Article 21 of the Brussels and Lugano Conventions, however, categorically requires respect for an action pending in another Contracting State, regardless of whether the future judgment will or will not be entitled to recognition.[45] So the pendency of an action in another Contracting State is recognized directly, as in the internal German law.

There are, however, time limits: the pendency blockade must cede when effective legal protection in the foreign forum is no longer guaranteed because of overly long proceedings. The BGH acknowledged such an exceptional case in an Italian divorce action pending for four years at first instance.[46] The defence of *lis alibi pendens* was rejected, however, in a property case, although the action had already been pending for ten years in a Turkish first instance court.[47] Thus, the non-observance of the foreign pendency of an action is limited to very extreme, exceptional cases.[48]

2. The Consequences of *Lis Alibi Pendens*

In German law the consequence of *lis alibi pendens* is usually the dismissal of the claim as inadmissible. Considering, however, the uncertainty always inherent in the recognition prognosis, a more flexible approach is desirable in order to ensure that the plaintiff in the foreign action will not suffer disadvantages, for example, by missing deadlines, if due to unforeseen circumstances the judgment cannot be recognized later. Therefore, in recent years the courts began to change their practice and now often only suspend the later German proceeding by analogy to § 148, ZPO.[49] This procedure corresponds to the new rule in Article 21(1) of the Brussels Convention in the version of the Accession Treaty of 1989 (Article 21(1)

[44] Schack, *IZVR*, n. 2 above, para. 754.
[45] Cf. Kropholler, above, n. 1, Art. 21 GVÜ, para. 12; Schack, *IZVR*, n. 2 above, para. 761.
[46] BGH, 26 Jan. 1983 [1984] IPRax 152, 154 ff. with dissenting annotation by Luther, *ibid.* 141, 143.
[47] BGH, 10 Oct. 1985 [1986] NJW 2195, 2196. Cf. also OLG Munich, 31 Oct. 1984 [1986] RIW 815, 816 (8 years, Italy); OLG Frankfurt/Main, 15 June 1989, [1989] IPRspr. No. 210b (5 years, Italy).
[48] Geimer, 'Beachtung ausländischer Rechtshängigkeit und Justizgewährungsanspruch' [1984] *NJW* 527, 529; Schumann [1986] IPRax 14, 15; Schack, *IZVR*, n. 2 above, para. 759. Special caution is appropriate with respect to Art. 21 of the Brussels and Lugano Conventions: cf. Isenburg-Epple, *Die Berücksichtigung ausländischer Rechtshängigkeit nach dem [GVÜ]* (Frankfurt/Main, 1992), 99 ff.
[49] Today this is probably the majority view: OLG Karlsruhe, 15 Dec. 1969 [1970] FamRZ 410, 412; Geimer, *IZPR*, n. 8 above, para. 2181; Schack, *IZVR*, n. 2 above, para. 764, with further references; narrower Lüke in *Münchener Kommentar zur ZPO (MünchKomm)*, (Munich, 1992), i, § 261, ZPO, para. 77. Left open in BGH [1986] NJW 2195, 2196. Disagreeing, e.g. Schumann, above, n. 43, 311.

of the Lugano Convention). Accordingly, the domestic claim should be dismissed only if the plaintiff definitely no longer has a need for domestic legal protection.[50] It is important to note that the judge's only discretion is with respect to dismissal or suspension of the claim. He is definitely not free to continue the domestic proceeding and disregard the earlier foreign pendency once the recognition prognosis is positive![51]

3. SPECIAL RULES

Special rules on the recognition of a foreign pendency exist in maritime law[52] and in several bilateral treaties.[53] All the nine pertinent treaties require a positive recognition prognosis[54] (above, III, 1), but they vary considerably with respect to the legal consequences. Some treaties[55] provide for the possibility of suspension of the proceedings instead of a dismissal;[56] others contain the obligation to respect an earlier pendent lawsuit, not *ex officio*, but only on a party's motion.[57] That should, however, not prevent the German court from going further and recognizing the foreign pendency *ex officio* (as otherwise in German law),[58] because avoiding unnecessary work and conflicting judgments is not only in the defendant's, but particularly in the public interest.

4. THE BRUSSELS AND LUGANO CONVENTIONS

The generous recognition of a foreign pendency (Article 21 of the Brussels and Lugano Conventions has practically no prerequisites) is, from the German viewpoint, very problematic in one respect.[59] In German civil procedure, pursuant to §§ 261, I, and 253, I, ZPO, the pendency of a claim (*Rechtshängigkeit*) takes effect very late, i.e. at the time the complaint is

---

[50] Schack, *IZVR*, n. 2 above, para. 764.

[51] OLG Cologne, 13 Dec. 1990 [1992] IPRax 89, 90 with annotation by Isenburg-Epple, *ibid.* 69, 71 on Art. 21 of the Brussels Convention.

[52] § 738a I HGB (Commercial Code), cf. Geimer, *IZPR*, n. 8 above, para. 2175; Schack, *IZVR*, n. 2 above, para. 749.

[53] The German recognition treaties are listed in Schack, *IZVR*, n. 2 above, para. 55; texts can be found *inter alia* in MünchKomm-Gottwald, *ZPO*, (Munich, 1992), iii, IZPR, 1820–1936; Stein/Jonas/Schumann (1988), § 328, ZPO, paras. 580 ff. Only the treaties with Switzerland and Great Britain do not contain rules on the recognition of a foreign pendent action.

[54] Cf. Geimer in Geimer/Schütze, *Internationale Urteilsanerkennung* (Munich, 1984), i/2, § 215, I, 1. The same is true for Art. 31, II, of the 1956 Convention on the Contract for the International Carriage of Goods by Road (CMR).

[55] The treaties with Greece (Art. 18), The Netherlands (Art. 18), and Austria (Art. 17) do not differ from internal German law.

[56] Israel (Art. 22), Norway (Art. 21), Spain (Art. 21), Tunisia (Art. 44).

[57] Belgium (Art. 15), Israel (Art. 22), Italy (Art. 11), Tunisia (Art. 44).

[58] Geimer [1984] *NJW* 528; Schack, *IZVR*, n. 2 above, para. 763; MünchKomm-Lüke, above, n. 49, § 261, ZPO, para. 74.

[59] Critical of the following especially Linke [1982] IPRax 229 ff.; Schack, *IZVR*, n. 2 above, paras. 756 ff., 760.

served on the defendant. In international proceedings a lot of time may pass between filing the complaint with the court (*Anhängigkeit*) and serving the defendant with process. In Germany, the majority opinion still determines the moment of the (foreign) pendency in accordance with the respective *lex fori*;[60] and the European Court of Justice also leaves it to the Member States to define the term 'pendency' as they think fit.[61] Consequently, those states have an advantage[62] which define the pendency at a very early moment, usually when the complaint is filed with the court. It therefore happens quite often that foreign proceedings are filed with the court later than the German, but that pendency results earlier according to the foreign law. If, in that case, the German proceedings had to give way to the foreign, the latter profiting by the technically 'earlier' foreign pendency, the result would be an open contradiction to a uniform application of the Brussels Convention as well as to a good international administration of law. There is no reason to let the necessarily time-consuming international service of process work to the disadvantage of the plaintiff in the German proceedings. It is therefore overdue for the European Court of Justice to give the term 'pendency' in Article 21 of the Brussels Convention an autonomous construction, i.e. for it to decide, in accordance with the practice in most countries, the moment of filing the claim with the court.[63]

5. RELATED ACTIONS

Unlike Article 22 of the Brussels and Lugano Conventions, German law does not allow for suspension of the domestic proceedings because of their connection with a foreign pending action. If the parties or the cause of action are not identical, the mere connection has no relevance to jurisdiction.[64] Only if the decision in the action depends on the outcome of

[60] BGH, 18 Mar. 1977 [1989] IPRax 104, 105 with annotation by Siehr (agreeing), *ibid.* 93, [1987] *NJW* 3083 with annotation Geimer (disagreeing); BGH 12 Feb. 1992 [1992] NJW-RR 642 ff.

[61] *Zelger* v. *Salinitri* [1984] ECR 2397 at para. 15.

[62] Until recently, that was true, e.g., for England; cf. Schack, 'Rechtshängigkeit in England und Art. 21 GVÜ' [1991] IPRax 270, 271, with further references. However, in *Dresser* v. *Falcongate* [1992] 2 WLR 319, 336 ff. (with annotation by Huber [1993] *IPRax* 114, 116) the Court of Appeal clearly opted for the moment of the service of process instead of the issue of the writ. See also *Neste Chemicals SA* v. *DK Line SA (The Sargasso)* [1994] 3 All ER 180 (CA).

[63] Rauscher, 'Rechtshängigkeit nach dem EuGVÜ' [1985] IPRax 317, 319, and [1986] *IPRax* 274, 276 ff.; Schack, *IZVR*, n. 2 above, para. 760 and in [1991] IPRax 271 ff. Independently from that, the German legislature should abolish the severe disadvantage for the German proceeding by changing § 253, I, ZPO so that filing the complaint with the court constitutes the pendency of the claim!

[64] Cf. § 147, ZPO and Schack, *IZVR*, n. 2 above, paras. 766 ff.

other pending proceedings (which may be foreign)[65] does § 148, ZPO permit the suspension of the domestic proceedings.

IV
FORUM-SELECTION AND ARBITRATION AGREEMENTS

1. Forum-selection Agreements

In the same way that a judge is not allowed to disregard the jurisdictional decision of the legislature (above, II), he has no discretion to respect or not to respect a forum-selection agreement prorogating a foreign forum. If the agreement is valid the derogated German court must dismiss the action for lack of jurisdiction (below, IV, 1 (c)). The court examines only[66] whether the derogation is admissible under the German *lex fori derogati*,[67] especially whether it is formally valid.[68] The derogation of jurisdiction is never permitted, if the law postulates an exclusive forum for the action.[69] In German autonomous law, derogation agreements are also disallowed in non-financial disputes[70] or in cases where the parties lack the capacity to enter into forum-selection agreements.[71] A sufficient connection with the prorogated foreign forum, however, is no prerequisite for a valid derogation.[72]

(a) The prorogation of a foreign forum implies the derogation of the German forum only if the parties have agreed that the prorogated forum should have *exclusive* jurisdiction. Article 17 of the Brussels Convention

---

[65] OLG Frankfurt/Main, 12 Nov. 1985 [1986] NJW 1443; Stein/Jonas/Roth (21st edn., 1994), § 148, ZPO, para. 140; more reluctant Geimer [1987] *NJW* 3085 ff.

[66] Notwithstanding the validity of the agreement. This question of substantive law is determined by the *lex causae*; BGH, 29 Feb. 1968, 49 BGHZ 384; Schack, *IZVR*, n. 2 above, paras. 432, 444.

[67] OLG Nürnberg, 28 Nov. 1984 [1985] NJW 1296; Geimer, *IZPR*, n. 8 above, paras. 1757, 1675; Schack, *IZVR*, n. 2 above, paras. 448, 436; *id.* [1990] IPRax 19 ff.; Hausmann in Reithmann/Martiny, *Internationales Vertragsrecht* (4th edn., Cologne, 1988), paras. 1244 ff.

[68] § 38, ZPO, Art. 17(1) and (2) Brussels and Lugano Conventions. § 38, ZPO, applies not only to prorogation, but by analogy also to derogation agreements: BGH, 20 Jan. 1986 [1987] IPRax 168, 169, with annotation by G. H. Roth, *ibid.* 141; Schack, ZVR, n. 2 above, para. 450.

[69] § 40, II, 1, ZPO, Art. 17(3) of the Brussels and Lugano Conventions. In addition, the BGH sometimes checks whether forum-selection agreements are abusive as violating German public policy. This is methodologically wrong (Schack, *IZVR*, n. 2 above, paras. 451 ff., 453 with further references) and clearly inadmissible where Art. 17, Brussels Convention, applies, because for the Brussels Convention only the ECJ has the power to define uniform standards for 'abusive' agreements: cf. *id.*, para. 475; and also Kohler [1983] IPRax 265, 270 ff.

[70] § 40, II, 1, ZPO; criticized by Schack, *IZVR*, n. 2 above, paras. 450, 440.

[71] Pursuant to § 38, I, ZPO, only merchants are allowed to prorogate without restrictions (differently from Art. 17, Brussels and Lugano Conventions)!

[72] Hausmann, above, n. 67, paras. 1263 ff. Cf. below, (d), on prorogations.

contains a (rebuttable) presumption to that effect.[73] In autonomous German law, however, the assumption in case of doubt is that the parties intended only a simple prorogation, i.e., an agreement on an additional forum, so that an otherwise existing German jurisdiction still holds.[74] In that case German law disregards the fact that a prorogation clause may be construed differently abroad, i.e., that the prorogated foreign forum deems itself exclusive.[75]

(b) If the parties have reached a valid agreement on the exclusive competence of a foreign court, they will be held to their agreement, even if the expected foreign judgment cannot later be recognized in Germany.[76] Frustrated forum-selection agreements will be corrected by German courts only in very special circumstances, e.g., if the administration of justice in the country of the prorogated forum has broken down and the plaintiff risks being deprived of his day in court.[77] If, however, the foreign court holds the prorogation invalid by applying its *lex fori prorogati*, the parties can be helped by construing their forum-selection agreement: as the prorogation of the foreign court has no effect, the derogation of the German courts also ceases to have effect.[78]

(c) The valid derogation of the German courts leads to mandatory and *ex officio*[79] dismissal of the claim as inadmissible, unless the defendant has argued on the merits of the case (§ 39, ZPO) without attacking the derogated court's lack of jurisdiction. Quite differently, Article 18 of the Brussels Convention already treats it as submission if the defendant argues on procedural points other than the jurisdictional question.[80]

---

[73] MünchKomm-Gottwald, *ZPO* iii, IZPR, Art. 17 GVÜ, para. 55, with further references.

[74] This is the majority opinion; Kropholler, above, n. 2, para. 584; Schack, *IZVR*, n. 2 above, para. 458. *Contra* Wirth [1978] *NJW* 460, 463.

[75] Differently, of course, in the scope of Art. 17(1) and (3), Brussels and Lugano Conventions, which results in a uniform treatment of the derogation aspect between the Contracting States; Kropholler, above, n. 1, Art. 17, Brussels Covention, para. 11 ff.

[76] BGH, 13 Dec. 1967, 49 BGHZ 124, 129; OLG Koblenz, 26 May 1983 [1984] IPRax 267 with annotation by Schütze, *ibid.* 246, 247 (agreeing); Kropholler, above, n. 2, paras. 552 ff., 558; Schack, *IZVR*, n. 2 above, para. 449, both with further references.

[77] Bundesarbeitsgericht (BAG), 29 June 1978 [1979] JZ 647 with annotation by Geimer (Lebanon); Landesarbeitsgericht (LAG) Hamburg, 21 Sept. 1979 [1990] IPRspr. No. 137A (Iran); LAG Frankfurt/Main, 10 June 1981 [1981] IPRspr. No. 163 (Iran). Cf. also Kropholler, above, n. 2, para. 570. Correspondingly for an arbitration agreement on Belgrade, LG Kassel, 2 Apr. 1992 [1993] RIW 239.

[78] Kropholler, above, n. 2, paras. 561 ff., 566 with further references; Schack, *IZVR*, n. 2 above, para. 448.

[79] Art. 20(1) of the Brussels and Lugano Conventions; cf. also § 331, I, 2, ZPO.

[80] Cf. Schack, *IZVR*, n. 2 above, para. 487. It is disputed whether the duty of the Amtsgericht to instruct the defendant on the legal consequences of defending himself without attacking the jurisdiction (§ 39, 2nd sentence, § 504, ZPO) is also applicable (a) with respect to international jurisdiction and (b) in cases where Art. 18 of the Brussels Convention applies; rightly in the affirmative Linke, *Internationales Zivilprozeßrecht* (Cologne, 1990), para. 194, with further references.

(d) The validity of a *prorogation* of a German court does not depend on a sufficient connection between the dispute and Germany.[81] On the contrary, German law respects the parties' interest in a neutral forum. This is the only way forum-selection agreements can fulfill their function to provide legal certainty to the parties. Here, considerations of *forum non conveniens* contradicting the expressed intentions of both parties would be particularly inappropriate.

2. ARBITRATION AGREEMENTS

The same holds with respect to *arbitration agreements*. Whether they are valid is examined by the invoked State court in application of its *lex fori derogati*,[82] including the relevant treaties.[83] The court in particular has to examine whether the subject matter can be arbitrated (§ 1025, I, ZPO; Article II, 1, UNÜ) and whether the agreement is formally valid (§ 1027, ZPO; Article I, 2, a, EuÜ; more restrictive Article II, 2, UNÜ). The common opinion that the *favor validitatis* rule of Article 11, I of the EGBGB is applicable to the form of an arbitration agreement[84] cannot—at least in the context of § 1027a, ZPO—be reconciled with the procedural warning function of the formal requirements in § 1027 of the ZPO which parallels § 38 of the ZPO: the circumstances under which the parties may waive judicial protection are always determined by the *lex fori derogati*.[85] As the directly applicable substantive rules of Article II, 2 of the UNÜ and Article I, 2, a of the EuÜ take priority over § 1027 of the ZPO, this problem, however, is not very important in practice.[86]

---

[81] *Zelger* v. *Salinitri* [1980] ECR 89, para. 4 (on Art. 17, Brussels Convention); Geimer, *IZPR*, n. 8 above, paras. 1745 ff.; Schack, *IZVR*, n. 2 above, paras. 442, 450; Kropholler, above, n. 2, para. 545; Hausmann, above, n. 67, para. 1257 ff. Wrong LG Hamburg, 6 Aug. 1975 [1976] RIW 228. Cf. also above, 1 (at n. 72) on the derogation; on the jurisdiction based on the presence of property, cf. above, II, 3.

[82] Hausmann, above, n. 67, para. 1382; Rahmann, *Ausschluß staatlicher Gerichtszuständigkeit* (Cologne, 1984), 42. The substantive-law question of the validity of the arbitration agreement is again controlled by the *lex causae*; BGH, 28 Nov. 1963, 40 BGHZ 320, 322 ff.; cf. above, n. 66.

[83] The most important treaties are the New York UN Convention on the Recognition and Enforcement of Foreign Arbitration Awards of 10 June 1958 (UNÜ) and the Geneva European Convention on the International Commercial Arbitration of 21 Apr. 1961: [1964] II Bundesgesetzblatt (BGBl.) 426 (EuÜ).

[84] E.g. Peter Schlosser, *Das Recht der internationalen Schiedsgerichtsbarkeit* (2nd edn., Tübingen, 1989), para. 363; Schütze in Schütze/Tscherning/Wais, *Handbuch des Schiedsverfahrens* (2nd edn., Berlin, 1990), para. 561.

[85] As in the text Hausmann, above, n. 67, para. 1391; Rahmann, above, n. 82, 41; cf. also Mann, 'Schiedsrichter und Recht' in *Festschrift für Werner Flume zum 70. Geburtstag* (Cologne, 1978), i. 593, 608. It might be consistent with this view, later in the enforcement proceeding (§ 1044 ZPO) to apply the law governing the arbitration agreement to the question of its formal validity, as does BGH, 9 Mar. 1978, 71 BGHZ 131, 137.

[86] On the priority of these rules, Schlosser, above, n. 84, para. 370.

Pursuant to § 1027a of the ZPO, the German court has to dismiss a claim as inadmissible if the defendant pleads a valid arbitration agreement. Unlike a forum-selection agreement,[87] the arbitration agreement is not given effect to *ex officio*, but only if it is raised as a defence. The defendant must raise it before he litigates on the merits of the claim (§ 282, III, ZPO). Delayed motions will be rejected by the court (§ 296, III, ZPO), if the defendant has insufficient excuse for the delay. Article II, 3 of the UNÜ also requires a motion to refer the case from the State court to the arbitration tribunal. National law (here again § 1027a, ZPO) determines the moment up to which this defence can be raised.[88]

Considerations of *forum non conveniens* again play no role in the due respect for arbitration agreements.[89] In exceptional cases, the defendant's reliance on the agreement can be malicious and without effect if he is not able to meet the costs of the arbitration proceeding.[90]

V
PROHIBITION OF FOREIGN ACTIONS

A German court cannot secure its international jurisdiction by prohibiting a party to the action from continuing its action abroad. A German judge's authority does not include such discretionary power.[91] The judge could prohibit conducting the continuation of an action only if one party has a cause of action, based on the substantive law, for an injunction against its adversary. In theory, such a cause of action can arise out of contract as well as tort.

Some authors want to perceive an obligation to sue only in the prorogated court in the very agreement to an exclusive jurisdiction.[92] The *lex fori prorogati* is said to determine whether a forum-selection agreement contains such an obligation of substantive law.[93] However, this view is

---

[87] See n. 76 above.

[88] Stein/Jonas/Schlosser (20th edn., 1986), app. to § 1044, ZPO, para. 13; MünchKomm-Gottwald, *ZPO*, iii, IZPR, Art. II, UNÜ, para. 19. Art. VI, 1, EuÜ directly corresponds to § 1027a, ZPO.

[89] Cf. also Schlosser, above, n. 84, paras. 401, 248.

[90] BGH, 12 Nov. 1987 [1988] NJW 1215.

[91] He probably also lacks this power when ordering temporary security measures pursuant to § 938, II, ZPO. Cf. Schütze in Wieczorek, *Zivilprozeßordnung und Nebengesetze* (2nd edn., Berlin, 1976), § 938, ZPO, para. B, II, 1.

[92] Schröder, 'The Right not to be Sued Abroad' in *Festschrift für Gerhard Kegel zum 75. Geburtstag* (Stuttgart, 1987), 523, 531 ff.; Kurth, *Inländischer Rechtsschutz gegen Verfahren vor ausländischen Gerichten* (Berlin, 1989), 60 ff., 67; Jasper, above, n. 1, 126; Schlosser, *Der Justizkonflikt zwischen den USA und Europa* (Berlin, 1985), 37.

[93] Schröder, n. 92 above, 534; Kurth, n. 92 above, 70; Jasper, n. 92 above, 127.

hardly correct: interpretation goes by the *lex contractus*, i.e. by the chosen law for the forum-selection agreement, and this law does not always coincide with the *lex fori prorogati*.

In contrast, most scholars generally and rightly deny any obligatory character of common forum-selection agreements.[94] Rather, these agreements immediately alter the court's jurisdiction: they dispose of jurisdiction without containing an obligation.[95] If a judge applying his *lex fori derogati* finds that the forum-selection agreement is void, he will not refrain in any way from hearing the action only because the *lex fori prorogati* holds the agreement to be valid. A German court does not allow itself to be dictated to by a foreign court as to when it may conduct court proceedings.[96] Likewise, a German court does not try to influence the conduct of an action abroad. Accordingly, the German courts, in connection with forum-selection agreements, to date have not granted any antisuit injunctions.[97] In any case, within the Brussels and Lugano Conventions, antisuit injunctions are clearly impermissible, because they would destroy the Conventions' system of fixed jurisdiction and ensuing recognition and would also undermine in particular Articles 17 and 21 of the Brussels and Lugano Conventions.[98]

Thus, German law counters forum-shopping abroad not through antisuit injunctions, but instead later at the stage of recognition of judgments. Recognition, *inter alia*, requires that the foreign court had international jurisdiction in its mirror-image use of German jurisdictional rules (§ 328, I, No. 1, ZPO; *Anerkennungszuständigkeit*).[99] By this means, forum-selection agreements which are invalid according to the German *lex fori derogati* may be rendered harmless, as they are incapable of establishing the jurisdictional requirement for recognition. However, even this final method of combating forum-shopping fails if international treaties, such as Article 28(3) of the Brussels and Lugano Conventions, categorically forbid the verification of the judgment-granting court's jurisdiction; in this respect, the recognizing State cannot even invoke the public policy excep-

---

[94] Schack, *IZVR*, n. 2 above, paras. 771 ff.; Kropholler, above, n. 2, para. 168; Geimer, *IZPR*, n. 8 above, para. 1717; de Lousanoff (1992) 105 *ZZP* 111, 114 (book review Kurth).

[95] Generally Rosenberg/Schwab/Gottwald, *Zivilprozeßrecht* (15th edn., Munich, 1993), § 37, I, 8.

[96] Cf. Schack, *IZVR*, n. 2 above, para. 773, with further references. Cf. also above, IV, 1, a.

[97] The only case of a prohibition against the conducting of another action concerned the obligation (based on § 826, BGB (Civil Code)) of a husband to retract his divorce suit in Latvia: Reichsgericht (RG), 3 Mar. 1938, 157 Entscheidungen des Reichsgerichts in Zivilsachen (RGZ) 136, 140. The background was that the RG did not want to tolerate the non-application of German divorce law, which at that time was based on the principle of fault. Therefore, this dubious decision does not lend itself to generalization. In any case, § 826, BGB, seriously blurs the borderline to legitimate forum-shopping (see above, II, 4); cf. Kropholler, above, n. 2, para. 170.

[98] MünchKomm-Gottwald, above, n. 53, Art. 21, Brussels Convention, para. 13.

[99] Cf. e.g. Schack, *IZVR*, n. 2 above, paras. 828 ff.

tion of Article 27(1) of the Brussels and Lugano Conventions. Consequently, we in Europe do forum-shop and must live with forum-shopping. Occasionally it might be troublesome, but the disadvantages are more than counterbalanced by a system of fixed and predictable jurisdictional rules and the corresponding recognition of judgments.

10

Great Britain

PAUL BEAUMONT

*Faculty of Law, University of Aberdeen, Scotland**

CONTENTS

I

FORUM NON CONVENIENS

This chapter examines the recent case law on *forum non conveniens* in England, but first of all examines its origins in Scotland. It is arguably one of the Scottish legal system's most successful exports.[1] It was originally referred to in Scotland as *forum non competens*, but in the latter half of the nineteenth century the modern wording was adopted, as it better reflected

* The author wishes to thank Professors Sandy Anton and James Fawcett for their insightful comments on an earlier draft of this chapter. An earlier version of this chapter was published in *United Kingdom Law in the Mid-1990s*, ed. by Bridge, Banakas, Gardner, and Carey Miller (1994), 549–75.

[1] See e.g. its adoption in the US, discussed in Braucher, (1947) 60 *Harv. L Rev.* 908, 909, and its adoption in England discussed in this ch. On *forum non conveniens* generally, see Barma and Elvin, (1985) 101 *LQR* 48; Slater, (1988) 104 *LQR* 554; Fawcett, (1989) 9 *OXJLS* 205; Cheshire and North, *Private International Law* (12th edn., 1992), 220–34; Dicey and Morris, *The Conflict of Laws* (12th edn., 1993), 395–419; Anton with Beaumont, *Private International Law* (2nd edn., 1990), 212–8.

the true nature of the plea.[2] It is today a plea of general application in Scotland and England except where its application is inconsistent with the Brussels and Lugano Conventions.[3]

The meaning of the plea has not always been free from doubt. Some authority supports a very restricted scope for *forum non conveniens* whereby the Scottish courts would sist (stay) the proceedings only if an 'unfair disadvantage'[4] or a 'real unfairness'[5] would result for the defender if the action were held there. Another narrow interpretation of the plea is that it only applies when it is in the 'interests of all the parties' that the case should be tried in a forum other than Scotland.[6] Given that the pursuer has chosen to litigate in Scotland, this is never likely to be the case, and such an approach effectively gives the court no discretion to decline to exercise jurisdiction.[7] At the other end of the spectrum, one can find some backing for the proposition that the aim of the plea is to find the 'best and most suitable forum for trying the case', which gives no weight to the forum chosen by the pursuer.[8]

The most persuasive authorities, however, advocate an 'ends of justice' test or an 'appropriateness' test. The former can be traced to a dictum by Lord President McNeill saying that the plea applied in 'cases in which the Court may consider it more proper for the ends of justice that the parties should seek their remedy in another forum'.[9] The idea of seeking the

---

[2] See e.g. Lord Deas in *Longworth* v. *Hope* (1865) 3 M 1049 at 1058: 'Although questions like the present are ranged in our books under the head of *forum competens* or *forum non competens*, the plea is really not that the one forum is incompetent, but that the other forum ought to be preferred. Where there are two competent forums, the question is, do the ends of justice require that an action brought in the one should be sisted in order that proceedings may be taken or go in the other?'. For the first comprehensive analysis of the Scottish plea of *forum non conveniens*, see Anton, *Private International Law* (1967), 148–54.

[3] See s. 49 of the Civil Jurisdiction and Judgments Act 1982. The breadth of the plea's application is illustrated by its use in the context of an application for judicial review in *Sokha* v. *Secretary of State for the Home Department*, 1992 SLT 1049.

[4] See the dicta of Lord Deas in *Longworth* v. *Hope*, n. 2 above, at 1057, and the approach of Lord Kissen in *Balshaw* v. *Balshaw*, 1967 SC 63 at 73.

[5] Lord Shaw of Dunfermline in *Société du Gaz de Paris* v. *La Société anonyme de navigation 'Les Armateurs Français'*, 1926 SC (HL) 13 at 17.

[6] See the dictum of Lord Justice-Clerk Inglis in *Clements* v. *Macaulay* (1866) 4 M 583 at 592 and the statement by the learned judge at 593 that 'In cases in which jurisdiction is competently founded a court has no discretion whether it shall exercise its jurisdiction or not.' Lord Inglis subsequently significantly softened this position, when Lord President in *Martin* v. *Stopford Blair's Executors* (1879) 7 R 329 at 331, saying of *forum non conveniens* 'the plea really means that of two courts having jurisdiction to try a question it is more expedient to try it in one than in the other'. None the less his no-discretion approach was quoted approvingly by Lord Kinnear in *Sim* v. *Robinow* (1892) 19 R 665 at 668; Lord Shaw of Dunfermline in *Société du Gaz*, n. 5 above at 19; and by Lord Avonside in *Stenhouse London Ltd* v. *Allwright*, 1971 SLT (Notes) 84 at 85.

[7] Lord Sumner recognized the futility of trying to satisfy the interests of all the parties in *Société du Gaz*, n. 5 above, 22.

[8] See Lord Justice Clerk Moncrieff in *Williamson* v. *North Eastern Railway Co* (1884) 11 R 596 at 598. See also Lord Justice-Clerk Alness asking the question 'where can the case best be tried?' in *Sheaf Steamship Co Ltd* v. *The Compania Transmediterranea*, 1930 SC 660 at 667.

[9] *Longworth* v. *Hope*, n. 2 above, at 1053.

forum which is most likely to secure the ends of justice was combined with that of seeking the best interests of all the parties,[10] but the latter aim was discredited by Lord Sumner in the leading Scottish case on *forum non conveniens*.[11] In that case the *'conveniens'* element of the plea was interpreted as 'appropriate' by Lord Chancellor Cave and Lord Dunedin.[12] The temptation to stir all the elements together into a composite definition can be seen in Lord Jauncey's view that the plea applies where 'the interests of the parties can more appropriately be served and the ends of justice can more appropriately be secured in that other court'.[13]

Against this background of varied interpretations of the plea of *forum non conveniens* in Scotland, it is fortunate that the House of Lords in a series of landmark judgments in the 1970s and 1980s gradually moved towards the adoption of the Scottish plea.[14] It is undoubtedly advantageous to Scotland to have the benefit of a very clear and authoritative judgment by Lord Goff in the case where the recognition of the English adoption of the Scots doctrine was consummated.[15] That judgment focuses on the two key elements of 'appropriateness' and 'justice' and gives a clearer framework as to their interrelation.

1. THE *SPILIADA* CASE

Lord Goff gave a six point summary of the plea of *forum non conveniens*:[16]

[10] See the authorities cited in n. 6 above.

[11] See n. 7 above and Lord Guthrie in *Argyllshire Weavers Ltd* v. *A. Macaulay (Tweeds) Ltd*, 1962 SC 388 at 403. Lord Prosser recently quoted the combined test of declining to exercise jurisdiction in favour of a competent court in another jurisdiction where it is in the 'interests of and for the ends of justice' as still being a correct statement of the law, *Sokha*, n. 3 above, at 1052–1053. He went on, however, to note that 'It does not appear to me that the prospects of either party can be determinative of the appropriate forum, since any advantage of this kind to one party is correspondingly a disadvantage to the other.'

[12] *Ibid*. 17 and 18. Lord Dunedin repeated this in *Robinson* v. *Robinson's trustees*, 1930 SC (HL) 20 at 24 and his opinion was concurred in by Lords Warrington and Tomlin. See also the support for this idea by all three judges in the Inner House in the *Argyllshire Weavers* case, n. 11 above, at 400–1, 403, and 405. The idea that even though the Scottish courts have jurisdiction it may not be 'appropriate' for the court to exercise jurisdiction was suggested by Lord Ardmillan in *Longworth* v. *Hope*, n. 2 above, at 1059.

[13] *Crédit Chimique* v. *James Scott Engineering Group Ltd*, 1979 SC 406 at 410.

[14] *The Atlantic Star* [1974] AC 436; *MacShannon* v. *Rockware Glass Ltd* [1978] AC 795; *The Abidin Daver* [1984] AC 398. In the process the English courts abandoned a very pro-plaintiff position which declined to exercise jurisdiction which was competently founded in England only if it would be 'oppressive or vexatious' to the defendant, or would be an abuse of the court, and if a stay would not cause 'an injustice to the plaintiff': see the *Spiliada* case, n. 15 below, Scott LJ in *St Pierre* v. *South American Stores* [1936] 1 KB 382 at 398. See also the earlier cases of *McHenry* v. *Lewis* (1882) 22 Ch.D 397; *Peruvian Guano Co* v. *Bockwoldt* (1883) 23 Ch.D 225; *Hyman* v. *Helm* (1883) 24 Ch.D 531 and *Thornton* v. *Thornton* (1886) 11 PD 176.

[15] *Spiliada Maritime Corp* v. *Cansulex Ltd* [1987] AC 460. The reasoning of Lord Goff was helpful to the application of *forum non conveniens* in *Morrison* v. *Panic Link Ltd*, 1993 SLT 602, in the *Sokha* case, n. 3 above, and in *PTKF Kontinent* v. *VMPTO Progress*, 1994 SLT 235. Also the related decision of the House of Lords adopting *forum non conveniens* in the context of matrimonial proceedings, *De Dampierre* v. *De Dampierre* [1988] AC 92 was followed by the Inner House in *Mitchell* v. *Mitchell*, 1993 SLT 123.

[16] N. 15 above, at 476–8. This ch. does not consider the controversial question whether the

(a) A stay of proceedings will only be granted where the court is satisfied that there is some other available forum, having competent jurisdiction, which is the appropriate forum for the trial of the action.

(b) In general the burden of proof rests on the defendant to persuade the court to exercise its discretion to grant a stay. However, once the defendant has made a *prima facie* case that another forum is more appropriate, the burden shifts to the plaintiff to show that justice requires the case to be tried in England.

(c) If jurisdiction is founded as of right in England, rather than leave to serve the defendant out of the jurisdiction being required, then the defendant has to show that there is another forum which is clearly or distinctly more appropriate than the English forum.

(d) In determining the appropriateness of a forum the court will determine how real and substantial is its connection with the dispute. In doing so it will consider a number of connecting factors, including the convenience of witnesses, the law governing the issue, and the places where the parties reside or carry on business.

(e) If there is no clearly more appropriate forum then no stay will be granted.

(f) If, however, the court decides that there is a *prima facie* more appropriate forum it will grant a stay unless the plaintiff can show that there are circumstances by reason of which justice requires that a stay should nevertheless not be granted.

Lord Goff then explained the difference in the application of the plea in cases where the court exercises its discretionary power to grant leave to serve out of the jurisdiction. In these cases the burden of proof rests on the plaintiff to persuade the court to exercise its discretion to grant leave to serve the defendant outwith the jurisdiction. If the jurisdiction so exercised might be regarded in international terms as an 'exorbitant jurisdiction',[17] then the burden of proof rests on the plaintiff to show that England is clearly the appropriate forum for the trial of the action.

plea of *forum non conveniens* is competent when a court in the UK has jurisdiction under Art. 2 of the Brussels or Lugano Convention. The English CA considers that *forum non conveniens* is a competent plea in these circumstances provided the parties are not connected with another Contracting State and the alternative forum is a non-Contracting State: see *Re Harrods (Buenos Aires) Ltd* [1992] Ch. 72 and *The Po* [1991] 2 Lloyd's Rep. 206. The former case was later referred to the ECJ by the HL: see Case C–314/92 *Ladenimor SA* v. *Intercomfinanz* but then settled before the Court could give a ruling. The decision of the CA has been extensively analysed: Briggs, (1991) 107 *LQR* 180; Kaye, [1992] *JBL* 47; Gaudemet-Tallon, (1991) 80 *Rev. crit. dr. internat. privé* 491; and Duintjer Tebbens in Sumampouw *et al.* (eds), *Law and Reality* (1992), 47–61.

[17] Lord Goff, n. 15 above, at 481, disliked the word 'exorbitant' and preferred 'extraordinary'. He cautioned that not all cases where the defendant has to be served out of the

The advantage of Lord Goff's approach is a clear separation of the consideration of 'appropriateness' from that of 'justice'. Judges are directed to consider the question whether another competent forum is more appropriate to hear the case before they consider whether any exceptional reasons of justice constrain them to hear the case in England. Although Lord Goff did not attempt to define 'justice', he gave it a relatively narrow focus by referring back to Lord Diplock's consideration of the word in *The Abidin Daver*.[18] Lord Diplock's dictum is worth quoting:

> The possibility cannot be excluded that there are still some countries in whose courts there is a risk that justice will not be obtained by a foreign litigant in particular kinds of suits whether for ideological or political reasons, or because of inexperience or inefficiency of the judiciary or excessive delay in the conduct of the business of the courts, or the unavailability of appropriate remedies.

The emphasis here is on the avoidance of bias, a basic level of judicial competence, and the court process not taking an unduly long time. It will be a rare case where a judge says that foreign courts do not meet these basic criteria of natural justice.[19] The question of the unavailability of appropriate remedies in the *prima facie* more appropriate forum would appear to give some more discretion to English courts to retain jurisdiction on grounds of justice. However, Lord Goff, in the *Spiliada* case, said that the fact that damages in England are awarded on a higher scale, that there is a more complete procedure of discovery, and that interest can be awarded when it cannot be in the other forum are normally not good reasons to retain jurisdiction and repel a plea of *forum non conveniens* relying on the 'justice' exception.[20] Lord Goff did concede that, if the limitation period has expired in the more appropriate forum and the

jurisdiction are in any sense extraordinary, the defendant's place of residence abroad may be no more than a tax haven.

[18] Lord Goff's reference is at 478 of *Spiliada* to *The Abidin Daver*, n. 14 above, at 411.

[19] One such case is *The 'Al Battani'* [1993] 2 Lloyd's Rep. 219, where Sheen J decided that Egypt was clearly a more appropriate forum for the trial of the action than England but declined to stay the proceedings on 'justice' grounds. He decided that the 'financial burden of litigating in Egypt' would be 'so heavy that justice requires a stay should not be granted' (224). Sheen J emphasized that there would be a five-year delay in the litigation in Egypt, that no costs other than court fees could be recovered there, and that interest on damages is only awarded as from the date of the final judgment on appeal. He also mentioned the high cost of translating the contract and other documents from English into Arabic.

[20] N. 15 above, at 482–3. This restrictive approach to this aspect of the 'justice' exception was followed by Lord Prosser in *Sokha* v. *Secretary of State for the Home Department*, n. 3 above, at 1054. Sokha was being detained in prison as an illegal immigrant pending a decision to deport him. He argued that it was easier to obtain a conditional release in Scotland than in England, and that therefore it would be unjust for the Scottish court to decline to exercise jurisdiction on the basis of *forum non conveniens*. England clearly was the more appropriate forum as Sokha had no connection with Scotland and was being detained in England. Lord Prosser was satisfied that, even if Sokha would be deprived of a juridical advantage if the Scottish court declined to exercise jurisdiction, substantial justice would still be done in England. On the other hand, 'justice' may not be available in a foreign forum where the

plaintiff acted reasonably in litigating in England, and did not act unreasonably in failing to commence proceedings in the more appropriate
forum before the limitation period expired, then justice would require
allowing the plaintiff to continue with the action in England or requiring
the defendant to waive the time bar in the foreign jurisdiction.[21]

2. Relevant Factors

Given the relatively narrow focus of the justice exception, it is critical to
establish what factors the courts will consider in deciding on the relative
appropriateness of different fora. In the *Spiliada* case, Lord Templeman
made the observation that: 'The factors which the court is entitled to take
into account in considering whether one forum is more appropriate are
legion. The authorities do not, perhaps cannot, give any clear guidance as
to how these factors are to be weighed in any particular case.'[22] With this
cautionary note in mind an attempt will be made to isolate some of the
factors that have been influential in *forum non conveniens* cases since the
Spiliada case.

(a) the applicable law

In several cases the applicable law has been a very significant factor in
determining the appropriate forum. In the *Spiliada* case itself Lord Goff
regarded the fact that English law was the putative governing law of the
contract as being 'by no means an insignificant factor'.[23] The alternative
forum was a Canadian one, and it appeared that the judges there took a
different view of the effect of the bill of lading contract and there was a
dispute as to the obligations under the contract in respect of what is
usually called dangerous cargo. In *Banco Atlantico SA* v. *British Bank for the
Middle East*,[24] the Court of Appeal overturned the decision of the judge at
first instance. The latter had granted a stay of proceedings in favour of the
case being heard in the United Arab Emirates. The Court of Appeal was
particularly influenced by the fact that, under English choice of law rules,
Spanish law was applicable to the case. In the United Arab Emirates the
courts would apply their own law and the plaintiff would have had no
prospect of succeeding, whereas the English courts would apply Spanish
law. In *Charm Maritime Inc.* v. *Kyriakou* and *Mathias*,[25] the Court of Appeal
was not confident that certain issues of English trust law would be
handled appropriately in Greece, given the lack of trust law in that country and the potential for distortion when two parties present conflicting

pursuers do not have a right to have their case reviewed by a judicial body, see *PTKF
Kontinent* v. *VMPTO Progress*, n. 15 above, at 239.

[21] N. 15 above, at 483–4.   [22] *Ibid.* 465.   [23] *Ibid.* 486.
[24] [1990] 2 Lloyd's Rep. 504.   [25] [1987] 1 Lloyd's Rep. 433.

evidence of what the foreign law is. Thus, even though the plaintiff and the first defendant were Greek, the fact that English law was applicable and that the plaintiff could only sue the non-Greek second defendant in England meant that Greece was not clearly and distinctly a more appropriate forum than England.

In *Du Pont* v. *Agnew*,[26] the Court of Appeal was dealing with a leave-to-serve case where it was necessary for the plaintiff to show that England was clearly and distinctly a more appropriate forum than Illinois. Du Pont was a Delaware Corporation which had paid punitive damages to Mr Chelos as a result of having administered a drug to him in Illinois which led to his leg having to be amputated below the knee. Du Pont sought to recover the damages from its insurers in the English courts. The American defendants sought to have leave to serve them out of the jurisdiction set aside. Du Pont chose the English courts because, under Illinois law, if the senior management of the company is held to be personally at fault it cannot recover from its insurers any punitive damages that it has been required to pay. This would seem to be a clear case of forum-shopping but for the fact that the Court of Appeal construed the lead insurance policy as being a Lloyd's policy governed by English law. This was the key factor in determining that England was clearly more appropriate than Illinois, because the English courts would have to determine a difficult and seemingly novel question as to whether English public policy would deny indemnity to a company against which an award of punitive damages has been made and, if so, under what circumstances. However, this is possibly a circular argument. The Illinois courts construed the lead insurance policy as being governed by Illinois law, and therefore questions of English law and public policy were, from their point of view, irrelevant to the case.

There are cases where the courts have given relatively little weight to the applicable law in determining the appropriate forum. In *Re Harrods (Buenos Aires) Ltd (No. 2)*,[27] the Court of Appeal acknowledged that, under English choice of law rules, English law was the governing law because the company was incorporated in England. Not much significance was given to this fact because the incorporation in England was an 'anomalous historical survival',[28] the company had its commercial base and management in Argentina, and under Argentine law it was an Argentine

---

[26] [1987] 2 Lloyd's Rep. 585. See further nn. 126–8 below.

[27] [1991] 4 All ER 348. In *The 'Varna'* (*No. 2*) [1994] 2 Lloyd's Rep. 41 at 48–9, Clarke J did not regard the fact that under English choice-of-law rules the contract was governed by English law as a significant factor in deciding the natural forum. The plaintiffs could have sought to rely on English law in the Bulgarian proceedings but did not do so, and it had not been demonstrated that there was any difference between Bulgarian and English law in relation to the merits of the claim.

[28] N. 27 above, at 367.

company. Bingham LJ made the point that the situation was not 'closely analogous with that in which parties to a contract deliberately choose to subject their bargain to the provisions of a given law'.[29] In *Morrison* v. *Panic Link Ltd*,[30] Lord Sutherland did not regard the English forum as clearly and distinctly more appropriate, notwithstanding that in their franchise agreement the parties had given the English courts non-exclusive jurisdiction and had made English law applicable. The defender had not averred in what way the English law was different from Scots law and therefore the assumption was made that it was the same. Lord Sutherland was particularly influenced by the fact that the agreement related to the operation of a franchise in Scotland, and the majority of the contractual obligations which were the subject of the action were to be performed in Scotland.

If the parties have chosen the law governing their dispute or the same law would be applicable to the case under either potential forum, this is an objective factor that should be weighted in determining which forum is the most appropriate to determine the case. Clearly if the legal issues are complex and disputable, it will be a strong factor in favour of choosing the forum that would be applying its own law. The alternative forum would have to prove the law by use of expert evidence, and in such cases conflicting evidence would be provided. The judge would have to determine the meaning of the foreign law as an issue of fact and, at least in the United Kingdom, this would not be subject to appeal.

If, however, the applicable law has not been agreed by the parties and the potential fora would apply different laws, the applicable law under Scots or English choice-of-law rules should not be considered a significant factor in determining the appropriate forum. It is unwise to assume that the law applicable according to English or Scottish choice-of-law rules is the appropriate law to govern the dispute. It may be that in an extreme case the law selected by the choice-of-law rules of the alternative forum may be so unrelated to the case that it would be contrary to 'justice' to stay the proceedings. Such matters should be considered under the justice exception, and not in an analysis of appropriateness.

(b) LITIGATION IS PENDING ELSEWHERE (*LIS PENDENS*)

Bingham LJ said that, with regard to concurrent proceedings between the same parties on the same issues in different jurisdictions 'The policy of the law must . . . be to favour the litigation of issues only once, in the most appropriate forum.'[31] The reason the courts disapprove of such concurrent proceedings was stated by Lord Brandon in *The Abidin Daver*: 'one or other of two undesirable consequences may follow: first, there may be two conflicting judgments of the two Courts concerned; or, secondly, there

---

[29] *Ibid.*   [30] N. 15 above.   [31] *Du Pont* v. *Agnew*, n. 26 above, at 589.

may be an ugly rush to get one action decided ahead of the other, in order to create a situation of *res judicata*, or issue estoppel in the latter'.[32]

If the two actions started about the same time, then priority will matter very little in determining the appropriate forum. In *Du Pont*, Bingham LJ did not think that the fact that the English proceedings began a month before the Illinois proceedings should affect the outcome of the plea of *forum non conveniens*.[33] On the other hand, if proceedings are commenced in two fora at about the same time but have reached a much more advanced stage in one rather than the other, so that 'they have had some impact upon the dispute between the parties,'[34] then this is a factor in favour of the action being allowed to proceed in that forum. It is not, however, determinative. This was precisely the case in *Meadows* v. *ICI*, where the action in Ireland was much closer to coming to trial than in England but Hirst J decided that Ireland was not clearly and distinctly the more appropriate forum, because otherwise the case had no connection with Ireland, the case had a real and close connection with Guernsey and England, the convenience of witnesses favoured Guernsey and England, and , most significantly, England was the only forum in which all three parties, Meadows, ICI, and ICB, were before the court in one single action.[35]

In *Cleveland Museum of Art* v. *Capricorn Art*,[36] Hirst J was influenced to grant a stay of the English proceedings in favour of proceedings in Ohio by the fact that the latter proceedings had been commenced just over eighteen months before the former and was ready for trial in Ohio. If a stay was not granted substantial costs would be wasted in the Ohio proceedings, and substantial delay would occur before the English courts could resolve the dispute. In this case most of the other factors favoured

---

[32] N. 14 above, at 423. Quoted with approval by Bingham LJ in *Du Pont*, n. 26 above, at 589.

[33] N. 26 above, at 593. In *Irish Shipping Ltd* v. *Commercial Union* [1991] 2 QB 206 at 232, Sir John Megaw gave 'no weight' to the fact that Belgian proceedings were instituted four months before the English proceedings. However, he was influenced by the fact that the defendants who were arguing for the case to be heard in Belgium had not acted in good faith because for a long time they had relied on a non-existent confidentiality clause in the contracts of insurance. In the absence of such lack of good faith, the fact that the action in Belgium was commenced four months earlier than the English action would have had no more than 'little weight' in determining where the action should be heard. In *Banque Paribas* v. *Cargill International SA* [1992] 1 Lloyd's Rep. 96, the fact that the Swiss proceedings were commenced about a month earlier than the English proceedings did not outweigh a variety of factors pointing to England as a clearly and distinctly more appropriate forum, including the fact that several key issues were governed by English law. The decision was affirmed by the CA in [1992] 2 Lloyd's Rep. 19, 25.

[34] Lord Goff in *De Dampierre* v. *De Dampierre*, n. 15 above, at 108, quoted with approval by Hirst J in *Meadows* v. *ICI* [1989] 1 Lloyd's Rep. 181 at 189.

[35] N. 34 above, at 189–90. Hirst J's decision was upheld by the CA [1989] 2 Lloyd's Rep. 298 at 305. This case was decided before Ireland acceded to the Brussels Convention.

[36] [1990] 2 Lloyd's Rep. 166. In *The Varna (No 2)*, n. 27 above, the proceedings in Bulgaria were already at an advanced stage and some of the questions had been decided. Clarke J regarded this as a particularly significant point in favour of regarding Bulgaria as the more appropriate forum and he stayed the English proceedings.

Ohio; it was more convenient for witnesses and Ohio law was the proper law of the loan agreement. The principal factor favouring England was to ensure the participation of the second defendant, Rogers & Co., in the same proceedings as the other two parties. This was clearly outweighed by the several factors favouring trial in Ohio.

The English courts give much greater weight to concurrent proceedings commenced elsewhere when the English proceedings are simply an attempt to obtain a negative declaration. This is disapproved of as being an example of 'forum-shopping'.[37] The case of *FNBB* v. *UBS* illustrates the point.[38] The Court of Appeal overturned the decision of the court of first instance and granted a stay in favour of the proceedings in Geneva. The Union Bank of Switzerland (UBS) claimed $5.3 million from First National Bank of Boston (FNBB) in proceedings in Geneva, and then FNBB brought proceedings against UBS in London for a declaration that it was under no such liability. In the English proceedings FNBB sued four other defendants, alleging a conspiracy between them to extract $5.3 million from the banking system as between FNBB and UBS, the sum that UBS was claiming from FNBB in Switzerland. Steyn J was heavily influenced by the fact that FNBB's claims against the four defendants other than UBS could only be brought in England and decided not to stay the English proceedings, even though Geneva was the appropriate forum to resolve the dispute between UBS and FNBB. The Swiss courts were the appropriate forum because Swiss law governed and the case had a closer connection with Switzerland than anywhere else. The Court of Appeal made some important observations about actions for negative declarations and relied on Lord Wilberforce's dictum in *Camilla Cotton Oil Co* v. *Granadex SA*, that:

The declaration claimed is of a negative character and as Lord Sterndale himself had said 'a declaration that a person is not liable in an existing or possible action is one that will hardly ever be made'. He went on: 'Hardly ever' is not the same as 'never' but the words warn us that we must apply some careful scrutiny. So I inquire whether to grant such a negative declaration would be useful.[39]

In the instant case a negative declaration against UBS would not have been useful, as it would not have prevented the continuance of the Swiss proceedings and any judgment there in favour of UBS could have been enforced against FNBB in Switzerland. In relation to the importance of being able to sue the other four defendants together with UBS the Court of

---

[37] See *The Volvox Hollandia* [1988] 2 Lloyd's Rep. 361 at 371; *Sohio Supply Co* v. *Gatoil* [1989] 1 Lloyd's Rep. 588 at 593; and *FNBB* v. *UBS* [1990] 1 Lloyd's Rep. 32 at 38, 39.

[38] N. 37 above.

[39] [1976] 2 Lloyd's Rep. 10 at 14. The quotaton from Lord Sterndale is from a decision when he was still Pickford LJ in *Guaranty Trust Company of New York* v. *Hannay & Co* [1915] 2 KB 536 at 564–5. The quotations were made by Sir Michael Kerr in *FNBB* v. *UBS*, n. 37 above, at 36–7.

Appeal pointed out that, if FNBB were to obtain its negative declaration against UBS, then its claims against the other four defendants would fall. Those claims would have had a chance of succeeding only if it was discovered that FNBB was liable to give UBS $5.3 million. Therefore allowing a negative declaration action against UBS to proceed in England would have had no utility in relation to the action against the other four defendants unless it failed. Sir Michael Kerr concluded that: 'To allow FNBB's claim for a declaration of non-liability to proceed against UBS would be contrary to the spirit of comity between our Courts and the Swiss Courts'.[40]

(c) CONVENIENCE OF WITNESSES

The convenience of witnesses is usually a relevant factor in determining the appropriate forum to hear a case, but has rarely, if ever, been determinative. In *CMA* v. *Capricorn Art*,[41] it was one of several factors pointing towards Ohio as the more appropriate forum, and the English proceedings were stayed. It seems likely that the facts that considerable time and expense had already been incurred in relation to the Ohio action and that Ohio law governed the loan agreement were of more significance than the convenience of witnesses. Jet travel reduces the level of inconvenience involved in witnesses giving evidence in a foreign forum and, if travel is not possible, the evidence can usually be taken on commission. Certainly in *Du Pont* v. *Agnew*,[42] the Court of Appeal did not regard the fact that Illinois was more convenient for the bulk of the witnesses than London as creating a substantial advantage in favour of Illinois as the appropriate forum. Indeed this advantage to Illinois was outweighed by the view of the Court of Appeal that the insurance policies were governed by English law.

If the witnesses will give oral evidence in a foreign language and the bulk of the written evidence is in that language then this constitutes a more significant factor in favour of the English proceedings being stayed. In *Re Harrods (Buenos Aires) Ltd (No 2)*, Stocker LJ noted that the bulk of the witnesses would give evidence in Spanish, that the documents were in Spanish, and thus a lot of translation would be required. He concluded that: 'The difficulties of a trial in this country are such that it is not easy to see how such a trial is to be conducted. At the very least, it will present a formidable task for a trial judge.'[43]

[40] N. 37 above, at 38. His reasoning was concurred in by Russell LJ and Sir Stephen Brown, P.

[41] N. 36 above, at 173.   [42] N. 26 above, at 594. Discussed further at nn. 31 and 59.

[43] N. 27 above, at 364. Bingham LJ pointed out that the fact that the bulk of the witnesses spoke Spanish was a 'significant matter in an action where credibility is very much in issue' (at 367).

(d) CONVENIENCE OF THE PARTIES

Often convenience of the parties is a factor which cancels itself out, in that one forum is more convenient for one party and the alternative forum is more convenient for the other. However, if the defendant is sued in his home court, then this is a factor against granting a stay of the proceedings. Bingham LJ has said that: 'It must be rare that a corporation resists suit in its domiciliary forum. Rarely would this Court refuse jurisdiction in such a case.'[44]

Where the alternative forum is the plaintiff's home base, then this is a factor in favour of upholding a plea of *forum non conveniens*. In *Cleveland Museum of Art* v. *Capricorn Art*, Hirst J decided that Ohio was a more appropriate forum than England and was significantly influenced by the fact that the Cleveland Museum of Art is situated there.[45]

The courts may be willing to look behind the nominal parties to the insurers who are financing the litigation. In the *Spiliada* case, Lord Goff took account of the fact that the shipowners' insurers, who were managed in England, financed the litigation and were *dominus litis*, as a factor against granting a stay of the English proceedings even though the nominal parties had Greek, Liberian, and Canadian connections.[46]

(e) REAL AND CLOSE CONNECTION BETWEEN THE FORUM
    AND THE DISPUTE

This factor may be linked to the convenience of the parties in that it focuses on the place where the parties' dispute is centred, and this is often where one or both of the parties reside. In *Meadows* v. *ICI*, Hirst J concluded that London was the place which had the most real and close connection with the dispute, partly because the parties had offices in London and the bulk of the important transactions took place there.[47] Likewise in *Morrison* v. *Panic Link Ltd*, Lord Sutherland was influenced by the fact that Scotland was 'the country which has the clearest connection with the subject matter of the action'.[48] He reached this conclusion on the basis that the majority of the contractual obligations were due to be performed in Scotland, because the agreement concerned the operation of a franchise there. This connection with Scotland was strengthened by the fact that the pursuer was domiciled there.

[44] *Banco Atlantico*, n. 24 above, at 510. Bingham LJ may take a different view where the company is registered in England but simply has a 'ghostly legal existence' there carrying on all its business in another country: see *Re Harrods (Buenos Aires) Ltd (No 2)*, n. 27 above, at 367.
[45] N. 36 above, at 173.
[46] N. 15 above, at 486. He cited in support of this approach Lord Sumner in *Société du Gaz*, n. 5 above, at 20.
[47] N. 34 above, at 190.
[48] N. 15 above, at 604. The decision was affirmed by an Extra Division, 1994 SLT 232.

(f) ACTIONS FOR NEGATIVE DECLARATIONS

The importance of this factor is considered above under '(b) Litigation Pending Elsewhere'. If an action is pending elsewhere and the defendant in that action brings proceedings in England for a negative declaration, this is usually regarded as forum-shopping and the courts in Great Britain may decline to exercise jurisdiction.[49] Similarly, if a plaintiff brings proceedings in England for a negative declaration in an attempt to pre-empt a positive action against them in another forum, the English courts may well refuse to grant such a declaration.[50]

(g) THIRD PARTY/MULTIPLE DEFENDANTS

If the plaintiff is able to sue all the defendants in England or join a third party to the action there, but this is not possible in the alternative forum, then this is a significant factor in favour of the English court retaining jurisdiction.[51] It is not, however, a conclusive factor. In the *Cleveland Museum of Art* case, the second defendant, T. Rogers & Co., could be sued together with the first defendants only in England, and yet Hirst J decided to stay the English action against the first defendants, Capricorn Art, in favour of the already pending proceedings in Ohio. In this case several factors favoured Ohio and only the 'Rogers' factor pointed towards England.[52]

(h) RELATED PROCEEDINGS ('THE *CAMBRIDGESHIRE* FACTOR')

In the *Spiliada* case,[53] a significant reason why the English courts declined to stay the proceedings was the existence of related litigation in England concerning *The Cambridgeshire* and involving the same defendants, Cansulex Ltd. Fifteen counsel were engaged in the *Cambridgeshire* case and each had seventy-five files. Staughton J, who was hearing both cases, in the *Spiliada* case (later supported by the House of Lords) thought it would be 'wasteful in the extreme of talent, effort and money if the parties to this case were to have to start again in Canada'.[54] It is wise to take into account the loss of the specialist knowledge gained by the lawyers, experts, and judges in related proceedings in the same forum when deciding whether or not to stay a case.

---

[49] See nn. 37–40 above.

[50] Nn. 37–40 above and *Midland Bank Plc* v. *Laker Airways Ltd* [1986] QB 689. If the negative declaration is being sought in the alternative forum then this is a factor against staying the English proceedings: see *Sohio* v. *Gatoil*, n. 37 above, 593.

[51] See *Charm Maritime* v. *Kyriakou*, n. 25 above, at 448 and 451; *Meadows* v. *ICI*, n. 34 above, at 190.

[52] N. 36 above.   [53] N. 15 above.

[54] *Ibid*. 471. See the comments of Lord Goff at 485–6 about the steep 'learning curve' where lawyers and experts grapple with difficult scientific questions in protracted litigation.

(i) RES JUDICATA

If a foreign judgment may be *res judicata* in relation to the proceedings
pending in the United Kingdom, then this is a factor in favour of staying
the proceedings to allow the question of *res judicata* to be determined in
the foreign forum.[55] In *Charm Maritime* v. *Kyriakou*,[56] it was not clear if the
Greek judgment was *res judicata*, and to determine this question in
England would involve a good deal of evidence from Greek lawyers.
Therefore this was a strong factor pointing towards the case being heard
in Greece. Nonetheless, the Court of Appeal gave greater weight to other
factors pointing towards England, in particular the need to determine
questions of trust law unfamiliar in Greece[57] and the ability to sue the
second defendant, Mathias, in the English courts.[58]

(j) PUBLIC POLICY

In *Du Pont* v. *Agnew*[59] the Court of Appeal decided that the contract was
governed by English law and that the question whether the plaintiffs
could be indemnified by the insurers against the punitive damages
awarded against them in Illinois was an open one to be determined by
English public policy. Bingham LJ seemed to be saying that, when a novel
question of English public policy is in issue, the English courts must not
decline to exercise jurisdiction:

If English public policy is to be held to deny the right to indemnity in these
circumstances, then this Court and no other must so hold. I do not regard this as
a question capable of fair resolution in any foreign court, however distinguished
and well instructed . . . The primary question, as I regard it, is the effect of this
contract as a matter of English public policy, and that is a question which I do not
think any foreign Judge could conscientiously resolve with any confidence that he
was reaching a correct answer.[60]

(k) EXPENSE AND TIME

The trial judge in *Irish Shipping Ltd* v. *Commercial Union*,[61] refused to grant
a stay of the English proceedings. He decided that both the English and
Belgian courts were appropriate fora but 'The advantage of this jurisdiction appears to be that it will probably lead to a resolution of the dispute
more quickly than Belgian process and at less expense, because the issues
on the plaintiffs' title to sue are more complex in Belgium.'[62] This view
was affirmed by the Court of Appeal.

[55] See *Charm Maritime* v. *Kyriakou*, n. 25 above, at 447 and 451.   [56] *Ibid.*
[57] *Ibid.*   [58] See nn. 25 and 51 above.   [59] Nn. 26, 31, and 42 above.
[60] *Ibid.* 594–5.   [61] [1991] 2 QB 206.   [62] *Ibid.* 246.

II
LIS ALIBI PENDENS

The existence of another action involving the same parties and the same cause of action in a foreign jurisdiction is one factor to be taken into account when considering a plea of *forum non conveniens*.[63] When the case falls within the scope of the Brussels or Lugano Convention then the courts in the United Kingdom cannot apply *forum non conveniens*[64] and must apply the *lis pendens* rule established in Article 21 of those Conventions. The European Court of Justice case law on Article 21 is discussed elsewhere.[65]

The critical question in the application of Article 21 is determining when each court was 'first seised', as priority in time is the sole factor in deciding which court should exercise jurisdiction. The European Court has not given a Community answer to the question, but rather leaves it to be determined in accordance with the national law of each of the courts concerned.[66] In England, in the *Dresser* case, the Court of Appeal stated that: 'In the ordinary, straightforward case service of proceedings will be the time when the English court becomes seised.'[67] Sheen J subsequently included within the compass of an 'ordinary, straightforward case' one where leave to serve the writ out of the jurisdiction was being sought.[68]

Earlier authority had pointed to the issue of the proceedings as being the time when the English courts are first seised,[69] but the Court of Appeal has opted for the later date of service of the proceedings. In the *Dresser* case, *obiter* remarks indicated that there would be exceptions to the rule, for example when the exercise of jurisdiction precedes service because the Court operates on an *ex parte* basis, as in the granting of a Mareva injunction, or the making of an Anton Piller order, or the arrest of a vessel. However, in the *Neste Chemicals* case, the Court of Appeal rejected these *obiter* remarks and affirmed the date of service rule with no exceptions.[70]

---

[63] See nn. 31–40 above.

[64] See s. 49 of the Civil Jurisdiction and Judgments Act 1982.

[65] See O'Malley and Layton, *European Civil Practice* (1989), 629–37; Cheshire and North, n. 1 above, 326–9; Dicey and Morris, n. 1 above, 413–9; and Beaumont, *Anton and Beaumont's Civil Jurisdiction in Scotland: Brussels and Lugano Conventions* (2nd edn., 1994), ch. 7.

[66] See Case 129/83 *Zelger* v. *Salinitri* [1984] ECR 2397 at 2409.

[67] *Dresser UK Ltd* v. *Falcongate Ltd* [1992] 1 QB 502 at 523 (Bingham LJ).

[68] *The Sargasso* [1993] 1 Lloyd's Rep. 424 at 427. This decision was affirmed on appeal, see [1994] 3 All ER 180, n. 70 below.

[69] See Hirst J in *Kloeckner* v. *Gatoil* [1990] 1 Lloyd's Rep. 177 and the Schlosser Report, [1979] OJ C59 at 125, which stated the law in England and Ireland as being that 'proceedings become pending as soon as the originating document has been issued'.

[70] See *Neste Chemicals SA and Others* v. *DK Line SA and Another (The Sargasso)* [1994] 3 All ER 180.

The interpretation of Article 21 has not yet been the subject of case law in Scotland. The position may be consistent with the one taken by the Court of Appeal in England. The Schlosser Report took the view that in Scotland 'proceedings become pending only when service of the summons has been effected on the defender'.[71]

In *Polly Peck International Ltd* v. *Citibank NA and others*,[72] Vinelott J. declined to decide when a case becomes definitively pending in Zürich until the courts there had determined that issue. This necessitated an adjournment in the English proceedings. This case, the uncertainty about the position in Scots law, and the change in English law all highlight the problems in leaving it to the national law of the courts concerned to determine when a case is definitively pending before them. In the long term the matter will be clearer once each country has developed a body of case law on the application of Article 21.

Article 21 applies only if the two proceedings have the same 'cause of action'. The European Court has placed a construction on the Article which requires concurrence of 'subject matter' as well. It has, however, given a wide ambit to the notion of same subject matter in deciding that it covered an action to enforce a contract for the sale of corporeal movable property and an action for its rescission or discharge.[73] This liberal approach to the interpretation of Article 21 has been followed by the English courts in deciding that in admiralty proceedings the same cause of action can exist even though one action is *in rem* and *in personam* and the other *in personam*, and the remedies are different.[74]

Article 22 of the Brussels and Lugano Conventions provides rules for declining jurisdiction in favour of a related action pending in another jurisdiction. The English courts have considered this Article on several occasions.[75] A broad discretion is given to courts, other than those first seised of related proceedings, to decide to continue hearing the case and risk creating irreconcilable judgments or to decline to exercise jurisdiction in favour of the court first seised. It would seem that an English court will be reluctant to stay the proceedings if it considers that the parties

---

[71] Schlosser Report, at 125. See also the *Report of the Scottish Committee on Jurisdiction and Enforcement* (the Maxwell Report) (Edinburgh, 1980), 99–100 and Lord Hunter in *Argyllshire Weavers Ltd* v. *A. Macaulay (Tweeds) Ltd*, n. 11 above, 394.

[72] Judgment of 14 Oct. 1993, *The Times*, 20 Oct. 1993.

[73] Case 144/86 *Gubisch Maschinenfabrik* v. *Palumbo* [1987] ECR 4861 at 4876–7.

[74] See *The Kherson* [1992] 2 Lloyd's Rep. 261 at 266; *The Deichland* [1989] 3 WLR 478 at 500; and *The Nordglimt* [1988] 1 QB 183 at 202. Cf. *Republic of India and another* v. *India Steamship Co Ltd (Indian Endurance and Indian Grace) (No 2)*, *The Times*, 9 June 1994. For a non-admiralty case, see *Kinnear and Others* v. *Falconfilms NV and others* [1994] 3 All ER 42 at 50–3.

[75] *Dresser UK Ltd* v. *Falcongate Ltd*, n. 67 above; *IP Metal Ltd* v. *Ruote* [1993] 2 Lloyd's Rep. 60; *The Maciej Rataj* [1991] 2 Lloyd's Rep. 458 (later referred to the ECJ by the CA, see Case C–406/92); and *Owens Bank Ltd* v. *Bracco* [1991] 4 All ER 833 (later referred to the ECJ by the HL, see Case C–129/92 [1994] ECR I–117).

have prorogated their jurisdiction within the terms of Article 17 of the Convention.[76]

Article 23 of the Brussels and Lugano Conventions states that: 'Where actions come within the exclusive jurisdiction of several courts, any court other than the court first seised shall decline jurisdiction in favour of that court.' This Article is designed to deal with cases where more than one court has exclusive jurisdiction under the provisions of Articles 16 and 17 of the Conventions. It has not, as yet, given rise to any points of note in United Kingdom cases.[77]

III
FOREIGN CHOICE OF JURISDICTION CLAUSES

Where the Brussels and Lugano Conventions are not applicable, the courts in England have a discretion to decline to exercise jurisdiction where the parties have previously agreed that a foreign court should have exclusive jurisdiction over their disputes.[78] The principles governing this exercise of discretion were set out by Brandon J in *The Eleftheria*:

(2) The discretion should be exercised by granting a stay unless strong cause for not doing so is shown. (3) The burden of proving such strong cause is on the plaintiffs. (4) In exercising its discretion the court should take into account all the circumstances of the particular case. (5) In particular, but without prejudice to (4), the following matters, where they arise, may properly be regarded: (a) In what country the evidence of the issues of fact is situated, or more readily available, and the effect of that on the relative convenience and expense of trial as between the English and foreign courts. (b) Whether the law of the foreign court applies and, if so, whether it differs from English law in any material respects. (c) With what country either party is connected, and how closely. (d) Whether the defendants genuinely desire trial in the foreign country, or are only seeking procedural advantages. (e) Whether the plaintiffs would be prejudiced by having to sue in the foreign court because they would: (i) be deprived of security for their claim;[79] (ii)

---

[76] See *IP Metal Ltd*, n. 75 above.

[77] In Case C–129/92 *Owens Bank Ltd* v. *Bracco*, the HL sought a ruling from the ECJ on the interpretation of Arts. 21 to 23 of the Brussels Convention. Lenz AG delivered his Opinion on 16 Sept. 1993 and advised the Court to reply as follows: 'The Brussels Convention . . . is not applicable to proceedings concerning the recognition and enforcement of judgments in civil and commercial matters given in noncontracting States, nor to issues arising in such proceedings.' This approach was followed by the Sixth Chamber of the Court: see n. 75 above.

[78] See Cheshire and North, n. 1 above, 234–9; Dicey and Morris, n. 1 above, 419–37; and Briggs, [1984] *Lloyd's Maritime and Commercial Law Quarterly* 227 at 241–8.

[79] In the context of admiralty proceedings this is no longer a relevant factor as s 26 of the Civil Jurisdiction and Judgments Act 1982 empowers the English courts to stay the proceedings but make an order that 'the property arrested be retained as security for the satisfaction

be unable to enforce any judgment obtained; (iii) be faced with a time-bar not applicable in England; or (iv) for political, racial, religious or other reasons be unlikely to get a fair trial.[80]

The learned judge, having become a Lord Justice, affirmed these principles in *The El Amria*.[81] The principles have been followed in several cases[82] and confirmed by the House of Lords.[83]

The fundamental principle stated in (2) above gives strong weight to freedom of contract and recognizes that it is an 'exceptional case'[84] where the English courts do not stay proceedings where there is a foreign exclusive jurisdiction clause. There is some similarity to the plea of *forum non conveniens* where the plaintiff is seeking leave to serve the defendant out of the jurisdiction. In both situations the burden of proof is on the plaintiff. In the leave-to-serve cases where the ground of jurisdiction could be described as 'exorbitant' the plaintiff has to show that England is clearly the more appropriate forum for the trial. Where the parties have previously given exclusive jurisdiction to a foreign court, then the plaintiff is trying to exercise an exorbitant jurisdiction by litigating in England. The English courts are conscious of this and will only do so where 'some strong reason' can be shown for overriding the 'parties' contractual intentions'.[85]

It should in principle be easier for the plaintiff to convince the court to allow the action in England to proceed when the clause conferring jurisdiction on the foreign court is a non-exclusive one.[86] The question whether or not the agreement is an exclusive one is a matter for the law governing the agreement.[87] If the parties say that the agreement is to be governed by

of any award or judgment' which may be made in the foreign jurisdiction: see *The Havhelt* [1993] 1 Lloyd's Rep. 523 at 524–6.

[80]   [1970] P 94 at 99–100.   [81]   [1981] 2 Lloyd's Rep. 119 at 123–4.

[82]   Some of the cases are as follows: *The 'Christos'* [1977] 1 Lloyd's Rep. 109; *Carvalho v. Hull Blyth (Angola) Ltd* [1979] 3 All ER 280; *The 'Panseptos'* [1981] 1 Lloyd's Rep. 139; *The 'Indian Fortune'* [1985] 1 Lloyd's Rep. 344; and *The 'Ruben Martinez Villena'* [1988] 1 Lloyd's Rep. 435. The exclusive jurisdiction agreement can be an oral one: see *The 'Nile Rhapsody'* [1992] 2 Lloyd's Rep. 399.

[83]   See *The Sennar (No 2)* [1985] 1 WLR 490 at 500. See also the PC in *The Pioneer Container* [1994] 2 All ER 250.

[84]   See Brandon J in *The 'Makefjell'* [1975] 1 Lloyd's Rep. 528 at 536, where he told counsel that Lord Denning had abandoned a greatest connection-style test: see *The Fehmarn* [1958] 1 WLR 159 at 162, in favour of the view that it would be an 'exceptional case' in which the English courts did not grant a stay: see *YTC Universal Ltd. v. Trans Europe* [1973] 1 Lloyd's Rep. 480.

[85]   See Lord Wilberforce in *Trendtex Trading Corp and another v. Crédit Suisse* [1982] AC 679 at 695; [1981] 3 All ER 520 at 525. In *The Pioneer Container*, n. 83 above, the PC did not allow the plaintiff to proceed in Hong Kong in defiance of a Taiwanese exclusive jurisdiction clause even though the case was time-barred in Taiwan. The plaintiffs had deliberately allowed the time-bar to elapse in Taiwan.

[86]   See *Evans Marshall and Co Ltd v. Bertola SA* [1973] 1 WLR 349 at 361.

[87]   This is a matter governed by the common law conflict rules as 'agreements on the choice of court' are excluded from the scope of the Rome Convention (Art. 1(2)(d), [1980] OJ L266/1).

English law and combine this with a phrase like 'under the jurisdiction of the English court'[88] or 'the courts of law in England shall have jurisdiction to entertain any action in respect hereof',[89] the courts will construe this as granting exclusive jurisdiction to the English courts. The argument is that there is no point in specifically conferring non-exclusive jurisdiction on the English courts when by choosing English law such a jurisdiction has already been conferred.[90] Even if the court decides that the clause does not create exclusive jurisdiction it will take 'strong reasons' not to hold the parties to the jurisdiction agreed between them.[91]

In Scotland, the leading case is *Elderslie Steamship Company, Ltd* v. *Burrell & Son*.[92] Here the parties agreed that the owners of the salving vessel could choose to bring any action between them 'in any Court in England or Scotland'. The owners of the salved ship attempted to bring the case before the Scottish courts. The Court of Session decided that, as the owners of the salving vessel had the right to select any courts in England or Scotland and had chosen the admiralty court in the former, the Scottish action should be dismissed. Lord Trayner, emphasizing freedom of contract, said: 'I am for keeping the petitioners strictly to the bargain which they made and giving the respondents the opportunity of bringing their claim before the English Courts.'[93]

A non-exclusive jurisdiction clause conferring jurisdiction on a foreign court is only one factor to be weighed in a plea that Scotland is *forum non conveniens*. In *Scotmotors (Plant Hire) Ltd* v. *Dundee Petrosea Ltd*,[94] two Scottish companies had agreed the following clause in their contract: 'Proper law. This agreement shall be governed and construed in accordance with the laws of England, and the parties thereto submit to the jurisdiction of the English courts.' The Court of Session construed this as a non-exclusive jurisdiction clause and declined to sist the proceedings:

It does not provide that the parties agree that all disputes must be submitted to the jurisdiction of the English Courts. Nor does it mean that the parties agree to

---

[88] *Sohio Supply Co* v. *Gatoil*, n. 37 above.

[89] *British Aerospace Plc* v. *Dee Howard Co* [1993] 1 Lloyd's Rep. 368.

[90] *British Aerospace*, n. 89 above, at 374 (but contrast the decision of Hobhouse J in *Cannon Screen Entertainment Ltd* v. *Handmade Films (Distributors) Ltd*, 11 July 1989, discussed in *British Aerospace* at 374–5). This point is not applicable in Scotland as choice of Scots law to govern the contract does not by itself confer jurisdiction on the Scottish courts: see *Blasquez (Raymond)* v. *Levy and Sons* (1893) 1 SLT 14.

[91] See *Berisford Plc* v. *New Hampshire Insurance* [1990] 2 QB 631 at 638 and 646; and *Standard Steamship Owners Protection & Indemnity Association (Bermuda) Ltd* v. *Gann* [1992] 2 Lloyd's Rep. 528 at 533.

[92] (1895) 22 R 389. See the analysis by Graupner, (1943) 59 *LQR* 227 at 239–41.

[93] *Ibid.* 396. See also Lord Young at 394 and the Lord Justice-Clerk at 396. In *WAC Ltd* v. *Whilloch*, 1990 SLT 213, Lord Cameron of Lochbroom decided that a clause giving exclusive jurisdiction to the courts in Northern Ireland did not prevent the Scottish courts from having jurisdiction to interdict a threatened wrong in Scotland. His view was upheld by the Second Division: see 219.

[94] 1980 SC 351.

abandon their right to resort to the otherwise obvious jurisdiction of Scottish Courts. Had it been intended to give exclusive jurisdiction to the English Courts, that could easily have been clearly specified.[95]

In *Morrison* v. *Panic Link Ltd*,[96] the parties agreed that: 'Any proceedings arising out of or in connection with this agreement may be brought in any Court of competent jurisdiction in England.' Morrison, nonetheless, commenced proceedings in Scotland. Lord Sutherland decided that the clause did not confer exclusive jurisdiction on the English courts, because such a conferment must be done 'expressly and not be left to ambiguous implication'.[97] Lord Sutherland subsequently refused the plea of *forum non conveniens*, notwithstanding the choice of English law and agreement to give non-exclusive jurisdiction to the English courts.[98] Lord Sutherland's decision and reasoning were subsequently affirmed by an Extra Division of the Inner House of the Court of Session. It seems that, in deciding on a plea of *forum non conveniens*, less weight is given to non-exclusive jurisdiction clauses in the Scottish courts than in the English courts. However, it may be significant that the English cases have involved clauses conferring jurisdiction on the English courts, whereas the Scottish cases have concerned clauses giving jurisdiction to foreign courts. A certain acquisitiveness of jurisdiction may be in evidence.

If Article 17 of the Brussels or Lugano Convention is applicable, then the courts of a Contracting State must decline jurisdiction in favour of the courts of the Contracting State chosen in the exclusive jurisdiction clause. The scope of Article 17 and the European Court's case law on it are too extensive to consider here.[99] One of the undecided questions is whether a non-exclusive jurisdiction clause comes within the scope of Article 17. In the *Kurz* case,[100] Hoffman J accepted that parties could confer non-exclusive jurisdiction on the English courts, under Article 17 of the Brussels Convention, in addition to the jurisdictions otherwise applicable under the Convention. If this is the case then it is not consistent with the wording of Article 17, which states that the jurisdiction is an 'exclusive' one.[101] Clearly the courts in other Contracting States exercising jurisdiction under one of the other heads of jurisdiction in the Convention should not be

---

[95] 1980 SC 355.   [96] N. 15 above. Aff'd. by an Extra Division, 1994 SLT 232.
[97] *Ibid*. 603.
[98] *Ibid*. 604. In addition the defenders were domiciled in England. For the reason no sist was granted, see above, n. 48.
[99] See Cheshire and North, n. 1 above, 314–22; Dicey and Morris, n. 1 above, 424–31; and Beaumont, n. 65 above, paras. 7.23–7.26.
[100] *Kurz* v. *Stella Musical GmbH* [1992] Ch. 196.
[101] The ECJ has accepted that Art. 17 is applicable even when the parties agree that a party can choose to bring proceedings in one of a number of specified courts: see Case 22/85 *Anterist* v. *Crédit Lyonnais* [1986] ECR 1951 at 1962. The jurisdiction in such cases is still an 'exclusive' one in the sense that it excludes the normal grounds of jurisdiction found elsewhere in the Convention.

obliged to decline to exercise jurisdiction in favour of a court chosen on a non-exclusive basis.

Another issue which has caused some concern in the English courts is the interrelationship between Articles 17 and 21 of the Brussels Convention. In *Kloeckner* v. *Gatoil*,[102] Hirst J concluded that whenever Article 17 is applicable the chosen courts are not bound by Article 21 to stay proceedings pending the outcome of litigation in a court in another Contracting State, seised earlier of the same cause of action between the same parties. The Court of Appeal reached the same conclusion in *Continental Bank NA* v. *Aeakaos Compania Naviera SA and Others*.[103] These opinions seem to be inconsistent with the broad interpretation given to Article 21 by the European Court in *Overseas Union Insurance* v. *New Hampshire Insurance*.[104] The court second seised must decline jurisdiction or stay the proceedings unless it claims to have exclusive jurisdiction under Article 16 of the Convention.

If parties who are domiciled in one or more Contracting States to the Brussels or Lugano Convention decide to give exclusive jurisdiction to a non-Contracting State, and one of the parties attempts to litigate in England, then the English courts are free to apply their own conflict rules to the determination of whether or not to decline jurisdiction.[105] In such circumstances the courts are likely to follow the principles established in *The Eleftheria*.[106]

IV
ARBITRATION AGREEMENTS

The English courts are obliged by section 1(1) of the Arbitration Act 1975[107] to grant a stay of any proceedings brought before them in respect of any matter agreed to be referred to arbitration by an arbitration agreement.[108] Limited exceptions to this mandatory stay are provided by section 1(1)

---

[102] N. 69 above.

[103] [1994] 1 Lloyd's Rep. 505 at 510–11. See the critique by Bell, (1994) 110 *LQR* 204.

[104] [1991] ECR I–3317 at 3349–51. This was the consensus view recorded in the synthesis of discussions at the colloquium on the interpretation of the Brussels Convention at Luxembourg in Mar. 1991: *Civil Jurisdiction and Judgments in Europe* (Butterworths, 1992). 266.

[105] See the Schlosser Report, n. 69 above, at 124.

[106] See those principles at n. 80 above. Hobhouse J noted that the courts would be free to apply those principles in this context in an obiter dictum in *Berisford Plc* v. *New Hampshire Insurance*, n. 91 above, 643.

[107] The 1975 Act was passed to implement the New York Convention on the Recognition and Enforcement of Arbitral Awards of 1958 and s. 1(1) of the 1975 Act closely follows the terms of Art. II(3) of the Convention.

[108] See Mustill and Boyd, *Commercial Arbitration* (2nd edn., 1989), 462–83; Cheshire and North, n. 1 above, 239–41; Dicey and Morris, n. 1 above, 573–600; Anton with Beaumont, n. 1 above, 355–70.

where the court is satisfied that the 'arbitration agreement is null and void, inoperative or incapable of being performed[109] or that there is not in fact any dispute between the parties with regard to the matter agreed to be referred'.[110] The section does not apply to 'domestic arbitration agreements' which are defined as follows:

an arbitration agreement which does not provide, expressly or by implication, for arbitration in a State other than the United Kingdom and to which neither (a) an individual who is a national of, or habitually resident in, any State other than the United Kingdom; nor (b) a body corporate which is incorporated in, or whose central management and control is exercised in, any State other than the United Kingdom; is a party at the time the proceedings are commenced.[111]

In relation to domestic arbitration agreements, the English courts have a discretion whether or not to stay court proceedings concerning a matter covered by the agreement.[112] The discretion is exercised in a similar way to that applicable to cases where the parties had given exclusive jurisdiction to a foreign court.[113]

Even if an agreement between the parties falls short of an arbitration agreement, but is a dispute-resolution agreement which is not quite an immediately effective agreement to arbitrate, the English courts have an inherent power to stay their proceedings in a way similar to that applicable where the parties have given exclusive jurisdiction to a foreign court.[114]

In Scotland, the Law Reform (Miscellaneous Provisions) (Scotland) Act 1990 gave effect to the UNCITRAL Model law on International Commer-

---

[109] These exceptions are the ones provided for by Art. II(3) of the New York Convention: for their application see *Astro Valiente Compania Naviera SA* v. *Pakistan Ministry of Food and Agriculture (No 2)* [1982] 1 WLR 1096; *The 'Marques de Bolarque'* [1984] 1 Lloyd's Rep. 652. See also *Harbour Assurance Co (UK) Ltd* v. *Kansa General International Co Ltd* [1992] 1 Lloyd's Rep. 81.

[110] These words were inserted into earlier arbitration legislation by the Arbitration Foreign Awards Act 1930 and retained in the 1975 Act, although not contained in the New York Convention: see *Hayter* v. *Nelson* [1990] 2 Lloyd's Rep. 265 at 269–70. The words are very difficult to understand but for some elucidation see the *Hayter* case and *Channel Tunnel* v. *Balfour Beatty Group* [1993] AC 334 at 355–7; [1993] 1 Lloyd's Rep. 291 at 302–3 (*per* Lord Mustill). Only if it is readily and immediately demonstrable that the party seeking to invoke the arbitration agreement has no good grounds at all for disputing the claim before the court should that party be deprived of his contractual right to arbitrate: see Saville J in the *Hayter* case at 271.

[111] S. 1(4) of the 1975 Act.

[112] S. 4(1) of the Arbitration Act 1950. This provision is not applicable to Scotland, see s. 34 of the 1950 Act.

[113] See *Bulk Oil (Zug) AG* v. *Trans Asiatic Oil Ltd SA* [1973] 1 Lloyd's Rep. 129 at 135–6 where Kerr J adopted the principles set out in *The Eleftheria*, n. 80 above, 100. Cf. *Home and Overseas Insurance Co Ltd* v. *Mentor Insurance Co (UK) Ltd* [1989] 1 Lloyd's Rep. 473.

[114] See *Channel Tunnel* v. *Balfour Beatty Group* [1993] AC 334 at 355–7, [1993] 1 Lloyd's Rep. 291 at 300–2 (*per* Lord Mustill).

cial Arbitration of 21 June 1985, with certain modifications to adapt it for application in Scotland.[115] The Model Law applies to 'international commercial arbitrations' and gives definitions of these terms.[116] In order for the agreement to come within the scope of the Model Law it must meet the following condition:

(a) the parties to an arbitration agreement have, at the time of the conclusion of that agreement, their places of business in different States; or (b) one of the following places is situated outside the State in which the parties have their places of business: (i) the place of arbitration if determined in, or pursuant to, the arbitration agreement; (ii) the place where a substantial part of the obligations of the commercial relationship is to be performed or the place with which the subject matter of the dispute is most closely connected.[117]

The Model Law provides for a mandatory stay of court proceedings in relation to matters covered by an arbitration agreement, in a very similar way to the New York Convention. Article 8(1) states:

A court before which an action is brought in a matter which is the subject of an arbitration agreement shall, if a party so requests at any time before the pleadings in the action are finalised, refer the parties to arbitration unless it finds that the agreement is null and void, inoperative or incapable of being performed.[118]

If the arbitration agreement does not come within the scope of the Model Law, or of section 1 of the 1975 Act, then the Scottish courts have a discretion to decline to exercise jurisdiction.[119]

V
RESTRAINING FOREIGN PROCEEDINGS

In the leading case, the decision of the Privy Council in *Société Nationale Industrielle Aérospatiale* v. *Lee Kui Jak*,[120] Lord Goff helpfully set out certain basic principles about the law relating to injunctions restraining a party

[115] See s. 66 of and Sched. 7 to the Act. The model law as adapted for Scotland is set out in Sched. 7. See generally *Davidson, International Commercial Arbitration: Scotland and the UNCITRAL Model Law* (Edinburgh, 1991).
[116] An arbitration agreement must be in writing and this is further defined in Art. 7, Sched. 7. 'Commercial' is defined as including 'matters arising from all relationships of a commercial nature, whether contractual or not' (Art. 2(d), Sched. 7).
[117] Art. 1(3), Sched. 7, of the 1990 Act.
[118] The words retained by the 1975 Act, s. 1(1) which are not in the New York Convention (see n. 110 above) have not been included in the 1990 Act.
[119] The courts are likely to grant a sist of the proceedings: cf. *Hamlyn & Co* v. *Talisker Distillery* (1894) 21 R (HL) 21 at 25; *Robertson* v. *Brandes, Schonwald & Co* (1906) 8 F 815; *Howden & Co* v. *Powell Duffryn Steam Coal Co Ltd*, 1912 SC 920; *Sanderson & Son* v. *Armour & Co*, 1922 SC (HL) 117; *Motordrift A/S* v. *Trachem Co Ltd*, 1982 SLT 127.
[120] [1987] AC 871.

from commencing or pursuing legal proceedings in a foreign jurisdiction.[121] First, the jurisdiction is to be exercised when the 'ends of justice' require it. Secondly, where the court decides to grant an injunction restraining proceedings in a foreign court, its order is directed not against the foreign court but against the parties so proceeding or threatening to proceed. Thirdly, an injunction will only be issued restraining a party who is amenable to the jurisdiction of the court, against whom an injunction will be an effective remedy. Fourthly, the jurisdiction is one which must be exercised with caution.[122]

The Privy Council departed from an earlier House of Lords decision[123] in rejecting any symmetry between the principles applicable for staying proceedings initiated in England with those applicable to restraining a party from proceeding abroad. The reason for this change of view was the further liberalization of the English rules for staying proceedings adopted in the *Spiliada* case.[124] The consequence of symmetry would be that, if England were the natural forum for the trial and 'justice' did not require that the action should nevertheless be allowed to proceed in the foreign court, an injunction would be granted. The Privy Council decided that such an approach would be contrary to comity and was strengthened in its rejection of symmetry between the principle of *forum non conveniens* and the restraining of foreign proceedings by noting that it does not apply in Scotland or the United States of America.[125] Instead the Privy Council revived the old English case law referring to restraining proceedings in the foreign court if such pursuit would be 'vexatious or oppressive'.[126] Thus to succeed in getting an injunction the plaintiff needs to show, as a general rule, that England is the natural forum and that it would be oppressive or vexatious to permit the defendant to continue with the foreign proceedings.

On the facts of the case the Privy Council decided that Brunei was clearly the natural forum and that it would be vexatious and oppressive to allow Lee Kui Jak to continue with the proceedings in Texas. The principal reason for the decision was that Société Aérospatiale, the first defendant in the Brunei proceedings, may well have been unable to claim over against Bristow Helicopters Malaysia in the Texan proceedings, whereas it would have been able to do so in Brunei, where Bristow was the second

[121] See Hartley, (1987) 35 *AJCL* 487–511; Cheshire and North, n. 1 above, 241–51; and Dicey and Morris, n. 1 above, 408–11.

[122] *Ibid.* 892.

[123] See *Castanho* v. *Brown & Root (UK) Ltd* [1981] AC 557 at 574–5; and the obiter remarks of Lord Brandon in *South Carolina Insurance Co* v. *Assurantie Maatschappij 'De Zeven Provincien' NV* [1987] AC 24 at 40.

[124] N. 15 above.   [125] N. 120 above, at 895–6.

[126] *Ibid.* 897. See *McHenry* v. *Lewis*, n. 14 above; *Peruvian Guano Co* v. *Bockwoldt*, n. 14 above; *Hyman* v. *Helm*, n. 14 above.

defendant. If Société Aérospatiale were held liable to Lee Kui Jak in the Texan proceedings, it may have had to bring a separate action against Bristow in Brunei, in which it may have had to establish its own liability to Lee Kui Jak before it could be entitled to claim contribution from Bristow. The Privy Council was concerned about the risk of inconsistent conclusions on the issue of liability between the Texan and the Brunei courts. Furthermore, no injustice would be done to Lee Kui Jak by granting an injunction restraining her from proceeding in Texas, because Société Aérospatiale gave an undertaking providing letters of credit to cover the potential damages and costs that might be awarded against it in the Brunei courts, to allow for the documents obtained in the Texan discovery process to be used in the Brunei courts, and to assist in the admission of Lee Kui Jak's American lawyers who had developed an expertise in the case as ad hoc members of the Brunei Bar.[127]

The clear difference between the principles applicable in the plea of *forum non conveniens* test and in seeking an injunction restraining foreign proceedings is illustrated by the *Du Pont* case. The English Court of Appeal rejected the insurer's plea of *forum non conveniens* on the ground that Illinois was not a clearly more appropriate forum than England,[128] and subsequently refused to grant an order to Du Pont restraining the insurers from continuing with the proceedings in Illinois.[129] The principal reason why the Illinois and the English courts differed as to which was the more appropriate forum to hear the case was that they each regarded their own law as the proper law of the contract. The Court of Appeal denied an injunction restraining the Illinois proceedings because it followed the Privy Council's rejection of the symmetry between these cases and those involving *forum non conveniens* and noted that no reasons had been put forward as to why it would be vexatious or oppressive to allow the proceedings in Illinois to continue.[130]

Where the foreign proceedings have been brought in defiance of an English exclusive jurisdiction clause then the English courts may well regard the continuance of those proceedings as in itself vexatious and oppressive and may grant an injunction.[131]

In *Pan American World Airways* v. *Andrews*, Lord Kirkwood decided that the Court of Session can 'interdict a party who is subject to the jurisdiction of the Scottish courts from raising proceedings in a foreign country or from continuing with such proceedings if they have already been commenced, and that interdict can be granted even though no proceedings are

---

[127] N. 120 above, at 897–904.   [128] N. 26 above.   [129] [1988] 2 Lloyd's Rep. 240.
[130] *Ibid*. 244 and 249.
[131] See Staughton LJ in *Sohio Supply Co* v. *Gatoil*, n. 37 above, 592. Cf. *The Lisboa* [1980] 2 Lloyd's Rep. 546. In relation to an arbitration clause see *The Angelic Grace* [1994] 1 Lloyd's Rep. 168.

currently before the Scottish courts'.[132] Relying on earlier Scottish authority and on the Privy Council decision in *Société Aérospatiale*, Lord Kirkwood concluded that the power to grant such an interdict is one which should be 'exercised with caution'.[133]

Pan American Airways were seeking an interim interdict preventing the respondents, who were on the ground in Lockerbie when a Pan Am aircraft crashed there, from claiming damages in the United States for emotional distress. Lord Kirkwood refused the motion for interim interdict. He was influenced by the facts that the proceedings before him were *ex parte* and that Pan American Airways could plead *forum non conveniens* in any American court in which the respondents might bring their case.

VI
CONCLUSION

Given the propensity for States to arrogate to themselves extensive jurisdiction in civil and commercial cases, it seems highly appropriate to employ *forum non conveniens* as a means of declining to hear cases which would clearly be better heard in another forum. The alternative mechanism of *lis pendens*, employed in the Brussels and Lugano Conventions, does not concern itself with which is the more appropriate forum to hear the case, but rather with which party launched its action first. An arbitrary first-come, first-served rule may be necessary and acceptable in the context of these Conventions where the grounds of jurisdiction are clearly circumscribed and an almost automatic system of recognition and enforcement of judgments is created. Outwith such a tight-knit framework, its arbitrariness becomes unacceptable. The benefit of certainty is outweighed by the fact that it encourages parties to rush to be the first to initiate proceedings, including purely defensive actions for negative declarations, in a forum which is so inconvenient for the other party that it is designed to deter that party from pursuing its positive remedy.

The availability of the plea of *forum non conveniens* does increase the uncertainty about whether or not a particular court will exercise its jurisdiction. This in turn increases the risk of fruitless litigation simply trying to establish whether a court will hear the case. None the less, the alterna-

---

[132] 1992 SLT 268 at 271.

[133] *Ibid*. The Scottish cases are *Young* v. *Barclay* (1846) 8 D 774; and *Dawson's Trustees* v. *Macleans* (1860) 22 D 685. For a recent case exemplifying the 'caution' exercised by the Scottish courts before granting interdict and for the importance of comity in these matters: see *Shell UK Exploration and Productions Ltd* v. *Innes*, judgment of Lord Abernethy on 29 June 1994, 1994 GWD 28–1717 and of the 1st. Div. on 6 July 1994, 1994 GWD 27–1633.

tives of always exercising even the most exorbitant of jurisdictions or of operating a *lis pendens* rule create too many opportunities for injustice. The recent developments in the plea of *forum non conveniens*, particularly its adoption by the House of Lords in the *Spiliada* case, have greatly clarified its scope and increased the certainty of its application in an individual case. One reason for that enhanced certainty is the large number of cases decided on the plea since its adoption in England. Such a volume of precedent could never be established in the much smaller jurisdiction of Scotland. It has to be acknowledged that the analysis of the various factors considered in these cases to determine the 'appropriate' forum shows that different weight can be given to different factors in different circumstances. A trial judge can find some guidance from these cases, but still has considerable discretion in determining the appropriate forum. It will be a very rare occasion when the plea is denied on the ground of 'justice', even though there is clearly a more appropriate forum.

It is consistent with respect for freedom of contract to give great weight to a freely entered-into foreign exclusive jurisdiction clause or foreign arbitration clause and to readily decline to exercise jurisdiction. The British courts must decline to exercise jurisdiction in relation to international arbitration agreements and will exercise a discretion to do so, in all but exceptional cases, in relation to foreign exclusive jurisdiction clauses.

Finally, the courts in Great Britain exercise caution before ordering a party not to litigate abroad. This is consistent with due respect for the jurisdiction of foreign courts and the principle of comity.

11

Greece

PANAGIOTIS KARGADOS

Professor, Faculty of Law, University of Thrace*

&

ELINA MOUSTAIRA, DR JUR.

Staff Lawyer of the Hellenic Institute of International and Foreign Law

CONTENTS

* The first author wrote the first two sections; the second author the remaining three sections.

I
INTRODUCTION

1. The Jurisdictional Background

As it is an old, well known, and well respected principle of international law that every State has the power autonomously to determine its own international jurisdiction,[1] Greece was early on confronted with the problem of whether and on what conditions Greek courts should have the power to decide international, i.e. Graeco–foreign private law disputes.

However, it was some time (1835–1968) before Greek citizenship ceased to be the determinative factor of our international jurisdiction.[2] First in 1940, and then more clearly in 1968, Greek citizenship gave way, as such a factor, to the principle of overlapping international and territorial jurisdiction. According to Article 3 of the Code of Civil Procedure of 1968,[3] Greek courts have international jurisdiction when they have territorial jurisdiction.[4]

---

[1] Cf. Fragistas, 'Problèmes resultant du Conflit de règles sur la compétence internationale' in *Aktuelle Probleme des Internationalen Rechts* (Berlin, 1957), i. 102 ff. (Legal Studies, Sakkoulas, Athens, 1987, Tome III, 801 *et seq*); *id*., (1961) III *Hague Recueil* 165; Maridakis, *Private International Law* (Athens, 1968), (in Greek), ii. 185 ff. *id*., *Execution of Foreign Judgments according to Greek Law* (3rd edn., 1970) (in Greek), 56; Kerameus, *Civil Procedural Law, General Part* (1968) (in Greek), 1 ff.; Wengler, *Völkerrecht II* (1964), ii. 1123; Schlosser, *Zivilprozessrecht* (1983) i. No. 115 (69).

[2] Arts. 27 and 28 of our previous Code of Civil Procedure of 1834, raising Greek nationality to the main factor of our international jurisdiction, had their model in French civil law (Fragistas, n. 1 above Studies, 674, 696. 805; *idem.*, *Jurisdiction in International Private Law Disputes* (Thessaloniki, 1934) (in Greek), 26 ff.). The corresponding arts. 14 and 15 of the French Civil Code, granting the French courts, even today, international jurisdiction, when only the plaintiff or defendant have French citizenship, are subject, particularly today, to harsh criticism internationally. They are blamed for extending French international jurisdiction too far, making it exorbitant, excessive, inappropriate, etc. S. Ilka Karen Mössle, Internationale Forderungspfändung . . . Schriften z. Internat. Recht, Band 54, Berlin 1991, 181 ff. 184 ff. Cf. also Art. 3 of the Brussels Convention (nn. 9–11 below).

[3] Arts. of our Code of Civil Procedure (CCP) of 1968 refer to its version of 1971. The initial text (a German translation of which is published by Baumgärtel and Rammos in C. Heymanns Verlag 1969 under the title *Das griechische Zivilprozess-Gesetzbuch mit Einführungsgesetz*) in 1971 took a new form as a result of strong legislative intervention immediately after its promulgation.

[4] On this evolution: Fragistas in ERMAK = Interpretation of the Greek Civil Code, Art. 126 to the Introductory Act to Civil Code 1950 (in Greek); Rammos, *Elements of Greek Civil Procedure* (1961), 146; Mitsopoulos, *Civil Procedure* A (1972), 138 ff.; Delikostopoulos-Sinaniotis, *Commentary on CCP* A (1968), Art. 3; Beys, *Civil Procedure* (1973), i. Art. 3; Kerameus, n. 1 above; Evrygenis, *Private international law in the Greek Judicature* (Thessaloniki, 1964), 409 ff.

However, this rule does not always ensure an appropriate court on the international level, as is indicated by some important breaches of the rule:

Greek citizenship always remains a connecting factor for some very personal matters. Greek courts have international jurisdiction over matrimonial causes; parent and child cases; cases where only one of the parties has Greek citizenship; and petitions for appointment of a guardian for incompetent Greek citizens living abroad.[5] The serious consequences of the decision over the status of the parties make our courts appear to us, as far as Greeks are concerned, equally appropriate[6] even if our fellow citizens have never been here before and the subject matter is not connected with Greece at all.

The Greek Code of Civil Procedure (CCP) has left it too, in a certain measure, to the parties to decide whether a court in Greece is also the appropriate forum for them. Foreign forum choice agreements, referring to disputes arising out of property rights, have priority over legal territorial jurisdictions, even if exclusive, even for future disputes.[7]

In order to prevent our legislature from keeping our country in isolation our Constitution declares autonomous Greek law as subsidiary to international conventions (Article 28). Accordingly, international conventions on jurisdiction and on enforcement of foreign judgments have priority over autonomous Greek law.[8] But international conventions may also contribute information on international standards. They may show that internal autonomous law does not always correspond to international criteria, that territorial jurisdiction is not always a good criterion of international jurisdiction. A recent example is the Brussels Convention of 27 September 1968.[9] According to Greek autonomous law Greek courts have international jurisdiction in relation to actions arising out of property rights only when the defendant has (any) property in the country,[10] i.e. even if the subject-matter does not have any connection at all with Greece. The Brussels Convention (Article 3) declares explicitly

---

[5] Arts. 512, 622, 803 CCP. A change of the proceedings for some of these disputes (by s. 5 of Act 733/1977 and s. 38 of Act 1329/1983) has not touched international jurisdiction; cf. Athan. Pouliades, *Armenopoulos* 46 (1992), 994 with full particulars on the pertinent literature and case law.

[6] See below, text relating to n. 32.

[7] Arts. 3, 42–44 CCP and permanent case law; see newly Areopag 4/1992 NoB (1992) 40 Legal Tribune 707; see also below, text relating to n. 34 and to nn. 41 and 42. Our courts must, however, dismiss an action if their alleged jurisdiction is based on an agreement referring to real property abroad (Art. 4 CCP).

[8] Cf. Areopag 440/1990 [1992] Dike 816; Piraeus CA 176/1989 [1992] Dike 819 with remarks by KEB, (826).

[9] Cf. Act 1814/1988, [1988] Kodex NoB 1135 ff.; Kerameus in Kerameus, Kremlis, and Tagaras, *The Brussels Convention, Commentary* (1989) (in Greek), 1; Gessiou-Faltsi in Tome, *Civil Procedure; From Theory to Practice* (1993) (in Greek), 17, 24.

[10] Arts. 3, 40 CCP.

that this provision is inapplicable. From its point of view, international jurisdiction based only on the location of the defendant's property is considered inappropriate or exorbitant.[11] The Brussels Convention also diverges from Greek autonomous law in so far as it allows foreign forum-selection agreements to the extent described above.[12] And the 'real' meaning of some jurisdictional rules of our autonomous law could go further than, or not so far as, parallel provisions of the Brussels Convention.

2. ARE THERE EXCEPTIONAL CASES?

The question now is whether the principle of overlapping international and territorial jurisdiction is subject to some further[13] curtailment. Furthermore, can this general rule be broken by our courts for one reason or another in some peculiar cases not always known in advance? This could be the case if international jurisdiction were not always to be regulated exhaustively and 'appropriately' in advance.

Two questions appear to be of practical significance here.

   (i) Are there cases in which our courts could ever decide on the merits in spite of the fact that they do not have international jurisdiction? At first sight this seems impossible.[14] Nevertheless in some cases[15] of a negative conflict of international jurisdiction, when the plaintiff is threatened by a denial of justice on the international scale, some consideration of the need for an emergency jurisdiction can be found in our legal literature. But our law does not explicitly recognize an 'emergency international jurisdiction' and our case law does not easily offer examples of our courts having practised some kind of 'international jurisdiction by necessity'.

   (ii) Secondly, it is necessary to ask directly whether we have in our country a doctrine of *forum non conveniens*. Have our courts, their international jurisdiction being obvious, a discretionary power to deny a decision on the merits on the grounds that a foreign court has more appropriate jurisdiction?

[11] Cf. Fragistas, 'Les compétences exorbitantes dans les travaux de la conférence de droit international privé de la Haye,' (1968) 12 *Revue Roumaine de sciences socialies, Sciences Jurid* 176; Kerameus, 'International Jurisdiction over maritime law disputes in the Continent, esp. in Greece' (1983) 31 *NoB* 28ff., 32 (VI). The German BGH having already formally considered the corresponding provision of § 23 ZPO as exorbitant and undesirable in international commerce ruled recently (2 July 1991) that it is—also beyond the scope of Art. 3 of the Brussels Convention—only applicable, when, besides assets of the defendant in the land, the case presents sufficient connection with it: BGH [1991] NJW 3092, (1992) 105 ZZP 314 with comment by Lüke, 321).

[12] Above, text relating to n. 7. Cf. Arts. 3, 42 CCP, to Arts. 16, 17(3), of the Brussels Convention.

[13] Cf. above.   [14] Cf. Arts. 3, 4, 22 ff., CCP.

[15] Very rare indeed, cf. Fragistas, 'La compétence internationale aux conférence de la Haye de droit internationale privé' in *Festschrift für Jean Spiropoulos*, (1959), 139–40.

II
FORUM NON CONVENIENS
(AND FOREIGN CHOICE OF
JURISDICTION CLAUSES)

1. No Doctrine of *Forum Non Conveniens*

The doctrine of *forum non conveniens* as a basis for dismissals of actions is, however, not recognized in Greece at all. The following reasons, legal and pragmatic, seem responsible for this.

First, our law is quite clear on the following point. If a court has international jurisdiction (and if there are also, all other 'procedural prerequisites'), then it must make a decision on the merits. And if it does not have one of these prerequisites, e.g. international jurisdiction, then it must dismiss the action with what is called 'a decision on procedural issues only'. It seems as strange that a court, recognizing its jurisdiction (and the existence of all other procedural prerequisites), could ever come to deny a decision on the merits, as it seems unusual that a court realizing the lack of its jurisdiction would ever permit the action. Such an attitude, even if not necessarily contradictory, seems contrary to the law, the jurisdictional system, some basic procedural principles, and our Constitution. The latter demands clearly that the competent court for every dispute must always be determined by the law in advance ('legal judge'; Article 8), which implies that the determination of the jurisdiction of the courts should never be left to their own discretion. It is also a principal procedural rule of ours that the procedural prerequisites are examined by the courts *ex officio*.[16] Such an obligation of the courts is considered now to exist because they must decide only on the merits and always when such prerequisites exist.

Our CCP also offers a plethora of jurisdictions. Very many and very narrow-based jurisdictions seem to make up a complete jurisdictional system providing for the appropriate court for almost every possible case.[17] Thus, the abundance and speciality of our jurisdictional rules seem to ensure that our law, by setting them up, has taken into account and finely balanced all public and private interests involved;[18] that, in any

---

[16] Cf. Arts. 4, 73 CCP.

[17] The same could be said for the jurisdictional systems in other countries on the Continent. But Austria seems to surpass them all, cf. Fasching, 'Österreich und das "Europäische Zivilprozessrecht"' (1992) 105 ZZP 460 ff. The Brussels Convention has covered only a few of our jurisdictional rules.

[18] To such interests from the Greek point of view see Rammos, *Der Gerichtsstand des Vermögens und das Ausländerforum nach vergleichendem Recht* (1930); Fragistas, n. 1 above; Mitsopoulos, n. 4 above. Cf. Heldrich, 'Die Interessen der internationalen Zuständigkeit' in *Festschrift für Ficker* (1967), 205 ff.

case, in so far as jurisdictional rules are good for internal (territorial) jurisdiction, they must be good enough also for international jurisdiction.[19] Apparently, it is believed, too, that when a national law by determining international jurisdiction takes account of the country not as a nation but as a region, then it does provide good rules, from an international point of view of course; therefore there is no room and no need for a judicial discretion to regulate, here or there, the international jurisdiction otherwise, i.e. 'better'. Besides, a discretion is generally considered to go against legal certainty.

Our courts, of course, come quite often to decide whether they have or have not international jurisdiction. And procedural dismissals of the action in cases with foreign elements (refusal of the courts to decide on the merits because of lack of international jurisdiction) are very frequent, too. But the matter in question is always whether there is or is not a legal connecting factor. And then, whatever the answer may be, the question of international jurisdiction is resolved definitely or automatically. One is likely to think that our jurisdictional rules do not let our international jurisdiction become a matter of conscience for our courts, that our connecting factors are so perfect that they fulfil all demands of justice as regards the appropriate forum in every possible international private law dispute.[20] On the other hand, special circumstances, able to lead our courts into the temptation of breaking our jurisdictional rules, do not seem to appear before them frequently.

Greek courts do not seem often to be confronted with situations that might lead them to deny their own jurisdiction in favour of a foreign court in the name of justice. Simple passing through or ephemeral, for one day only stay in the country or mere service on the defendant in Greece cannot establish Greek international jurisdiction. We never have had a 'transient' jurisdiction, our courts never have had the chance to resist it. Our courts are also not excessively attractive to foreigners. Quick judgments in civil and commercial proceedings, technical facilities, discovery, cross-examination, generous compensation, punitive damages, or some other Greek benefits package are not to be expected from them. And an applicable foreign substantive law (*lex causae*), very unlike our own, is not likely to be applied by our (internationally competent) courts.[21] Our courts have never been exposed, either, to a massive migration of claims from foreign lands. And as they did not have to protect themselves from overload consisting of claims coming from abroad and also somehow connected with Greece, they did not have to think of methods for remitting such claims to a more appropriate court according to their discretion or overload.

---

[19] Cf. Mitsopoulos, *Revue Hellénique de Droit International* (1977), 2 (II.3).
[20] Cf., too, above, text relating to nn. 16–19.   [21] Cf. Art. 33 of the Civil Code 1940.

A spirit of judicial discipline also seems to have played a similar role. Our courts are rather unwilling to search for a more appropriate court abroad, when the law has already decided on their international jurisdiction, such maxims as *judex non debet lege chementior esse* and *judex non facile recedere debet* seem to have made a strong impression on them. They would rather decide a difficult Graeco–foreign case falling within their jurisdiction than let themselves be exposed to the criticism that they only wanted to get rid of a troublesome case, that they favoured the defendant who would feel at home before foreign courts, that they exposed the plaintiff to the risk of a denial of justice etc., or that they suffer from some kind of xenophobia.

Also a spirit of strict legality seems to be a hindrance. A few years ago there came into question whether a Greek court, whose jurisdiction was established by the arrest of the debtor's ship, could now determine the case upon its merits, even after the defendant had offered a bank guarantee and the ship was thereupon set free by the same court.[22] The opposing views on the point were concentrated on (made dependent on) the issue whether the bank guarantee was or was not to be regarded as an asset of the defendant located in our territory.[23] The question whether according to our relevant jurisdictional rule, interpreted on the basis of international criteria, property of the defendant in the country is (in)sufficient to establish our international jurisdiction even if the case is not connected with it at all, was peacefully set aside. It is thought that, when our law gives our courts territorial jurisdiction, their international jurisdiction is always a postulate of justice or it is improper to ask whether a foreign court has more appropriate jurisdiction.[24]

2. FORUM-SHOPPING

It is perhaps because our courts have not had a discretionary power to decline to exercise their jurisdiction in favour of a more appropriate court abroad, that 'forum-shopping' (and perhaps also 'arbitration-shopping') has not been a problem in our country at all.

If the plaintiff prefers our courts, then it does not concern us why he does so, as long as they have international jurisdiction. In such a case he can prefer the courts which are more convenient to him, as long as the foreign jurisdiction is not exclusive according to our law. Only when he exercises unfairly such a right of his (to choose between the Greek and a foreign jurisdiction) could our courts refuse to decide on the merits.[25]

[22] Cf. Mitsopoulos, 'Internationale Zuständigkeit der griechischen Gerichte...' in *Festschrift für Heinrich Nagel* (1987), 267 ff.

[23] See Arts. 3, 40, 705 CCP.

[24] See, however, above, text relating to n. 11 and below, text relating to nn. 39 and 40.

[25] See below, text relating to nn. 28–47.

If the plaintiff prefers the foreign courts which then permit the action, our courts cannot deny recognition or execution only on the grounds of forum-shopping which is not considered as an obstacle to recognition or execution by our law.[26] Only when forum-shopping can lead to a foreign judgment infringing our public policy can our courts deny recognition or execution.[27] For the rest, they would be more willing to neutralize immediately provisions of our substantive or procedural law, making them unjustifiably attractive than defy their international jurisdiction based on traditional connecting factors on the grounds that, according to their own discretion, a foreign court has more appropriate jurisdiction.

3. Abusive Exercise of Rights

There is, however, a point of view from which such a discretionary power could be regarded as possible or even necessary. Our Constitution explicitly forbids the 'abusive exercise of (any) rights' (Article 25). Also our Civil Code prohibits the exercise of civil law rights against good faith and morality (Article 281). But our CCP also asks the parties to behave in litigation in accordance with the demands of good faith and *bonos mores*.[28]

Our legal literature and our courts now agree to a great extent to the following. Subject to this prohibitory rule are also 'procedural rights'; the sanction for disobeying such a basic prohibition is, as far as procedural rights are concerned, inadmissibility or, when appropriate, a bar to the action. And, last but not least, the courts have to take into consideration the legal consequences of such behaviour *ex officio*.[29] The latter could mean now that the decision on the assumption of such a sanction is left in some measure to the discretion of the courts. As the prerequisites of these sanctions are to a certain measure indefinite, since they rely very much upon the circumstances of the case, it seems necessary to leave their final determination (exact formulation and further development of the concept of 'improper exercise of rights') to the discretion of the court. Already on the internal level the plaintiff is not always considered to be absolutely free to choose any of the concurrent territorial jurisdictions within Greece which our jurisdictional system offers him generally. He must not establish a territorial jurisdiction with unfair methods and he should not always ignore the situation of the other party when exercising his right to

---

[26] Cf. Art. 323 CCP.

[27] Cf. Art. 323(5) CCP. Whether our *ordre public* would suffer from the execution of a US court's judgment awarding immense punitive damages to a plaintiff having chosen those courts (forum-shopping) because of their world-famous generosity, is not yet decided in Greece. (The attitude of the BGH in Germany towards a similar problem is set out in its judgment of 4 June 1992 (1993) 106 ZZP 79–103 with remarks of Schack, *ibid.*, 104 ff.)

[28] Art. 116 CCP.

[29] Cf. Klamaris, *The abusive exercise of rights in civil procedural law*, (1980) (in Greek), B. 495 ff.

choose between concurrent jurisdictions.[30] Thus, when it comes about that the court considers that, in view of the particular circumstances of the case, the plaintiff abuses his right, he must be ready to take the consequences.

The same can be said at the international level. There are many cases where the plaintiff can choose between a Greek and a foreign court. The prevailing opinion in Greece for instance considers Greek international jurisdiction based upon Greek citizenship[31] as not being exclusive.[32] And there is, of course, Greek international jurisdiction based upon the territorial jurisdiction of a Greek court or upon a forum-selection agreement competing with foreign jurisdictions. But the question whether a procedural right is properly exercised is raised not only by concurrent but also by exclusive[33] Greek international jurisdiction, e.g. on the basis of an exclusive forum-selection clause. According to our law, in case of doubt the forum selected shall be deemed exclusive, both at the national and international level.[34] And what Article 17 of the Brussels Convention now prescribes as the effect of such an agreement was already part of our internal law before that. Thus, if a forum-selection clause is valid, according to our internal law our courts must dismiss the action. However, they do not always have to enforce such a clause. A Greek court having, for instance, exclusive international jurisdiction on the grounds of a foreign forum-choice clause could dismiss the action not only when such a clause has come into existence through unfair behaviour of the plaintiff, but also when he exercises his rights, arising out of a legally founded agreement of this kind, under circumstances that make his behaviour now appear unfair.[35]

The crucial question is, of course, more specific. Under what circumstances, in practice, is the resort to our (concurrent or exclusive) international jurisdiction to be regarded as abusive?

One is likely to find here the notion that the action is to be dismissed as 'abusive' when the litigation does not show any connection with the Greek court invoked and the plaintiff seeks to achieve 'improper' aims or aims other than those allowed by the jurisdictional rules or by the forum-selection clauses as all these are to be interpreted under the principles of good faith and morality. Such an answer is of course a generalization

---

[30] Cf. Klamaris, n. 29 above, 440 ff.   [31] See text relating to nn. 5–6 above.

[32] See Beys, *Civil Procedure* (1979), xii. Art. 612(4), Art. 622(2), (1992), xviii. Art. 803(3.1); Sinaniotis, *Special Proceedings* (2nd edn., 1984) (in Greek), 32, 33, 115.

[33] Cf. Fragistas, 'La compétence internationale exclusive en droit privé' in *Studi in onore di Antonio Segni* (Milan, 1967), ii. 199 ff.

[34] Cf. Mitsopoulos, n. 4 above, 256; Areopag 196/1974 (1974) 22 NoB 1063–64; Piraeus Court (Sole Judge) 40/1992 [1992] Piraeus Judicature 203 ff.

[35] Cf. Doris, *Contractual freedom restrictions in exclusive foreign forum selection clauses* (1988) (in Greek), 71 ff.

again. But we do not have a rich casuistry which could take its place. Our courts have not, one could say fortunately enough, had very often to prevent a plaintiff from employing Greek international jurisdiction 'unfairly'. Then otherwise they would have made, of course, use of those instruments our legislation and academic writing offer them for enforcing good faith and morality and some more characteristic cases would have appeared in our case law. However, as far as this chapter is concerned, it seems rather unfortunate that a wealth of dismissals of this sort is not available. Only by observing real cases could we compare on a pragmatic basis our 'abusive exercise of rights dismissals' with dismissals based in some other countries on the doctrine of *forum non conveniens* and find out the real similarities and differences between the two. Nevertheless, a difference seems obvious: it is only in our dismissals that the refusal of the courts to pass judgment on the merits seems based on the lack of any international jurisdiction.[36]

4. Dismissals/Jurisdiction Clauses

Taking now account of the reasons why our courts denied, during the last decades, their (having) international jurisdiction 'for the rest', i.e. on the basis that the plaintiff 'does not have a right to resort to the Greek courts from the beginning',[37] an important difference appears between our dismissals and *forum non conveniens* dismissals.

When it comes to our dismissals 'for the rest' our courts had never had a discretionary power and never exercised a discretion. The reasons for this have been mentioned above.[38] Here they only need to be emphasised. Our courts faithfully follow our legal jurisdictional system and avoid taking an initiative as being forbidden (illicit) or superfluous (since the law provides the appropriate forum for every case). Indeed, the idea, that territorial jurisdiction cannot cover the functions of international jurisdiction in some further cases than those already recognized as exceptions to the rule of overlapping international and territorial jurisdiction,[39] is not yet quite widespread.[40]

The same can be said with regard to our foreign forum-selection clauses dismissals. Here too, our courts faithfully follow our law which does not give them any discretionary power. It rather gives some initiative to the parties[41] or takes it all itself. This was the case, too, with a recent statutory

---

[36] *Fraus omnia corrumpit*. Cf. Klamaris, n. 29 above, A, 161 ff.; M. Planiol, *Traité élémentaire de droit civil* (6) ii. no. 871: 'le droit cesse où l' abus commence'.

[37] i.e. not on the basis that 'he exercises such a right of his unfairly', Cf. text relating to nn. 28–36 above.

[38] See text relating to nn. 16–24 above.   [39] See text relating to nn. 20–4 above.

[40] See text relating to nn. 22–4 above.

[41] See text between nn. 21 and 22 above.

prohibition on such clauses in a special area. The explicit 'ratio' of our Act. 1429/1984 is to protect from (foreign law and) foreign forum-choice clauses Greek citizens employed by some enterprises (with a seat or also doing business in Greece) to work in Africa or Asia. Foreign forum-choice agreements excluding Greek jurisdiction in relation to disputes arising out of such employment are declared null and void. Only agreements establishing an Asian or African jurisdiction as parallel to a Greek one are here allowed.[42]

The fact that our courts now follow faithfully all 'legally valid' foreign forum-choice clauses, that they do not inquire whether another court is to be considered as more appropriate in the particular case, seems to operate in favour of the jurisdiction of foreign courts, in contrast to what seems to happen when our courts truly follow our international jurisdiction rules based upon territorial jurisdiction and Greek citizenship.

At any rate our courts seem, however, to have been much more hospitable to foreign forum-selection clauses than is the case by recognizing new exceptions to the principle of overlapping international and territorial jurisdiction. Indeed our courts have always been ready to enforce foreign forum-choice clauses, even if they exclude absolutely Greek jurisdiction or establish an exclusive foreign one, even if they abolish an exclusive Greek jurisdiction,[43] even if they appear in a standard-form contract, as in the printed terms of a bill of lading,[44] even if the bill of lading refers (explicitly) to such a clause appearing in the contract of carriage (or affreightment),[45] even if the bearer of the bill of lading is not the 'contracting party' but only a 'third person'.[46] Lately our Supreme Court resolved a long-standing dissent in a sense again favouring enforcement of foreign forum-selection agreements. Such a clause is valid even if it does not determine in advance and by name the exact court of the foreign country selected. It is enough that the clause allows the foreign court to be determined, later on, on the basis of the relevant procedural rules of the foreign country whose courts have been chosen.[47]

---

[42] See s. 4(1) and (2) of Act 1429/1984 in [1984] Kodex NoB 327 ff. and the analysis of Doris, n. 35 above, 82 ff.

[43] See n. 5 above for a legal exception.

[44] See for a recent instance the decision of the Piraeus Court (Sole Judge) No. 40/1992 [1992] Piraeus Judicature 202 ff.

[45] Even for foreign arbitration clauses, see the Areopag decision (Plenum) No 236/1966 (1966) 17 Review of Commercial Law 290 ff. As to some terms, set up by this decision cf. Kerameus, n. 11 above: two purposely vague restrictions able to assure adaptation to the circumstances of the case (36), i.e. compliance with the demands of justice as to the appropriate forum on the international level and perhaps similar results to those to be achieved by application of the doctrine of *forum non conveniens* (38).

[46] See e.g. the Piraeus Court (Sole Judge) judgment No 620/1989: even against the insurer as substitute for the bearer of the bill of lading [1989] Piraeus Judicature, 600 at 601–2.

[47] See the Areopag judgment No 4/1992 (1992) 40 NoB 707.

5. FUTURE PROSPECTS

Is there a chance in the (near) future for a doctrine of *forum non conveniens* in Greece?

Our academics and our courts have long since recognized that it is not possible, even if desirable, to have everything regulated in advance by the legislature; that courts also create law.[48] Besides, our courts also prepare themselves for the aspired European Single Market, now largely a reality. In any case *forum non conveniens* dismissals, practised in England[49] as a European Community country, or outside the EC, even on the other side of the Atlantic in the United States,[50] have a chance in Greece today on the basis of the creative function of courts and of 'comparative judicature'.[51]

For the courts of a civil law country in Europe,[52] however, to proceed in this way, it is necessary that they are aware of some old and new findings. Also national rules on international jurisdiction are often incomplete, contain gaps etc. And also by determining the 'proper forum' for international private law disputes substantial justice demands that all the special

---

[48] Cf. Ligeropoulos, *Judicature as a factor for evolution of private law* (Athens, 1933) (in Greek). On the grounds of a widespread recognition of such a creative role of the judicature at the European level, judges and courts were recently asked for their contribution to the desired unification of civil procedural law: cf. Storme, 'Rechtsvereinheitlichung in Europa, Ein Plädoyer fur ein einheitliches Prozessrecht' (1992) 56 *Rabels Z* 291 at 296; 'Überall dasselbe Prozessrecht?' in *Festschrift für Franz Matscher* (Wien, 1993), 496 at 500; as to the possibilities and limits of a unification of the procedural law cf. Kerameus, 'Procedural Unification. Necessity and Restraints' in *Charistia Ioanni Deliyanni*, (Thessaloninca, 1992), pt. III, iii. 315 ff. As to the extent of such a creative role of the courts in other countries it is interesting to read in Taitz, 'Unity of civil procedural law and its national divergencies', paper presented to the International Symposium of Civil Procedural Law (held in Lublin, Poland, 22–25 Aug. 1993), that 'It has been held by some South African Supreme Courts that in the exercise of their inherent jurisdiction they may not create substantive law,' that the inability, however, to discern any clear distinction between substantive and procedural law 'affects the judicial constraint placed on the court's inherent jurisdiction' (1 ff.).

[49] Also taken into account have been, among others, the following treatises Herzog, 76 *Revue crit dr intern pr* 1 ff. Wahl, 'Die verfehlte internationale Zuständigkeit, Forum non conveniens . . .' Schriften z. Prozessrecht, Band 34, 1974.

[50] See Kerameus, 'Institutionenschutz und Fallgerechtigkeit in der zivilprozessualen Zuständigkeitsordnung' in *Tome to honour G. Rammos* (Athens 1979) i. 396; Moustaira, 'Forum non conveniens . . .' in (1993) 24 *Dike*, Athens 86 ff. Cf. recently, too, Carrington, 'International Litigation in the courts of the USA', paper presented to the International Symposium on Civil Justice in the Era of Globalization, organized by the Japanese Association of the Law of Civil Procedure in Tokyo 22–24 Aug. 1992 (9f).

[51] To the functions and methods of such a *vergleichende Rechtsprechung* reports recently Storme, n. 48 above, *Rabels Z* at 296, and *Matscher* at 500.

[52] Desires (e.g. Wengler, (1965) 165 *AcP* 368: 'Es wäre zu wünschen . . . möge . . .') that some healthy practical legal institutions of the USA and the general clause of *forum non conveniens* make an entry into Europe (see Wengler, *ibid.*) have not yet been fulfilled. (The majority of opinions, e.g. in Germany, are still against such a doctrine as being opposed to continental understanding of legal stability etc. Cf. e.g. Gottwald, *Münchener Kommentar zur ZPO* (1992), iii. IZPR EuGVÜ, Art. 1(5), 1004.) In Greece the question has not yet been raised in discussion: see above, text relating to nn. 16–24.

circumstances of the case are taken into account. Besides an absolute 'right not to be sued abroad'[53] when one can only be sued in the local forum does not exist. After all, 'comparative judicature' has an important role to play in relation to the unification and harmonization of European law[54] as well as for the amelioration of law generally.

III
LIS ALIBI PENDENS

1. Preliminary Remarks

All issues concerning the litispendence objection are characterized—by Greek law as well as by most other national laws—as procedural, and, according to a universally recognized international customary rule, they are governed by the law of the State of the adjudicating judge.[55] However, it is accepted, as a rule, that the moment at which the foreign proceedings become pending, as well as that at which they are no longer considered as pending, is determined in accordance with that foreign court's law, since, in that case, the second (Greek) judge does not apply the provisions of the foreign law concerning litispendence, but simply takes them into account.[56] Consequently, resort to either unilaterally the Greek law, or to both laws (*Doppelqualifikation*) must be excluded.[57]

During the time when the former Code of Civil Procedure, of 1834, was in force (from 25 January 1835 to 15 September 1968), both case law and theory, by a majority, denied the recognition of the foreign litispendence in Greece,[58] emphasizing the independence of national legal systems, as

---

[53] See Geimer, 'Rechtsschutz in Deutschland künftig nur by Inlandsbezug?' [1991] *NJW* 3072 ff (3074).

[54] Cf. Storme, nn. 48 and 51 above.

[55] See Vrellis, *Private International Law* (1988) (in Greek), 210.

[56] See Krispis, 'Legal opinion' (in Greek) (1973) 21 NoB 1290 at 1291.

[57] See Nikas, *The litispendence objection in civil proceedings* (1991) (in Greek), 145. Also, Sahpekidou, 'Problems of the compound and related proceedings in Brussels Convention on Jurisdiction and the Enforcement of Judgments' [1990] *Elliniki, Epitheorissi Europaïkou Dikaiou* 683, 710 & n. 95, who points out that this fact—of not taking into account the regulations of the second court—is important for such institutions as e.g. the plea of compensation during the trial or the notification of the trial, which are not uniformly regulated by the various national laws, as far as the moment at which the action becomes pending is concerned. E.g., according to the Greek law, by pleading compensation the compensated claim becomes pending—Art. 222(II) CCP.

[58] See Kerameus, 'Rechtsvergleichende Bemerkungen zur internationalen Rechtshängigkeit', in *Festschrift Schwab* (1990), 257 at 262; *id.*, 'Problemi attuali della litispendenza internazionale nel processo civile', [1990] *Rivista di Diritto Processuale* 1001 at 1010. In favour of the recognition of the foreign litispendence was Fragistas, *Jurisdiction in international litigation* (1934) (in Greek), 140 at 144.

well as the fact that there is no superior authority which would be competent to resolve conflicts of jurisdiction.[59]

2. DOMESTIC AND FOREIGN LITISPENDENCE

Article 222 of the current Code of Civil Procedure,[60] in force since 16 September 1968, regulates, basically, domestic litispendence. According to it:

1. After the commencement of the litispendence and during the time it lasts no new proceedings are permitted before any other court, for the same dispute between the same parties having the same status.

2. If during the litispendence another action, counteraction or interpleading summons is instituted or a plea of compensation is raised for the same dispute, its adjudication is stayed *ex motu proprio* too until the first proceedings are terminated.

In Greek positive law there is no provision which explicitly requires foreign litispendence to be taken into account. The formulation of Article 222 of the CCP does not make it clear whether that should happen. For that reason it was attempted to base the recognition of foreign litispendence on other law provisions. It was emphasized, for example, that it would be inconsistent with domestic law if the consequences of the institution of an action in a foreign jurisdiction where the defendant has his (her) domicile—which (action) is permitted under the Greek general provisions on territorial jurisdiction (Articles 22 and 23 of the CCP)—are not recognized in Greece.[61]

Some exceptions apart, most Greek scholars are of the opinion that foreign litispendence must be recognized under certain conditions.[62] The case law, however, is divided.[63] According to the prevailing theoretical

---

[59] But see Klamaris, *The right to judicial protection according to art. 20 I of the Constitution* (1989) (in Greek), 195, who points out that public international law imposes mutual respect of national legal orders.

[60] Influenced by central European laws, especially German and Austrian, see Kerameus, 'Judicial Organization and Civil Procedure' in *Introduction to Greek Law* (2nd rev. edn. 1993), 265 at 266.

[61] See Sinaniotis, 'Legal opinion' (in Greek) (1971) 21 *Nomiko Vima*, 313 ff.

[62] See Maridakis, *Enforcement of foreign decisions according to the law prevailing in Greece* (1970) (in Greek), 95–96; Bedermacher-Geroussis, 'Legal opinion' (in Greek) (1974) 22 *Nomiko Vima* 168; Georgiadis, 'Recognition and enforcement of foreign decisions' [1974] *Harmenopoulos* 599, 606; Sahpekidou, *Elliniki Epitheorissi Europaikou Dikaiou* (1990), 683, 717 n. 123. According to Varsami, 'Recognition of the foreign litispendence according to Greek law and the Brussels Convention' (1988) 19 *Dike* 344, an intense disagreement still prevails with respect to this issue.

[63] For a detailed presentation of the various views in theory and in case law see Nikas, n. 57 above, 69–70, nn. 280–1. The decision of the Athens CA 13671/88 [1989] *Elliniki Dikaiossini* 358–9, which recognized the foreign litispendence is deemed commendable. Areios Pagos has not yet delivered any judgment in relation to this issue, see Kerameus,

view, the foreign and the domestic proceedings are equivalent: therefore, the foreign proceedings should be respected by our courts. Besides, it must be noted that this evolution—towards the recognition of foreign litispendence—is to a large extent due to jurisprudential influences.[64] Extending the argument on the inadmissibility of a second action concerning the same dispute between the same parties, in the international field, it is generally accepted that the basic reasons which impose this position are two-fold. First, the need to eliminate the risk of conflicting judgments, and, second, the need to spare time, and procedural expense. It is also maintained that the inadmissibility of the second action because of (domestic) litispendence is justified mainly by the singularity of the claim for judicial hearing and protection, which leads to the prohibition of the multiplicity of the means for the obtaining of this protection. This argument, though, cannot be extended to the international field.[65] To start with, it is maintained that he whose rights are affected has as many claims for judicial hearing and protection as the States the courts of which are internationally competent to try his case. Choosing to bring an action in one State out of several, having parallel international jurisdiction, it is possible to render inactive the international jurisdiction of the other States' courts, either by an autonomous national legal provision or by a rule established on the basis of a bilateral or multilateral convention. The universality of justice requires the foreign litispendence to be recognized. Besides, another argument which appears very interesting is that, according to the dictates of logic the foreign litispendence must be recognized. Thus, one can also cope indirectly with the conflict which is the consequence of the conflux of more than one basis of international jurisdiction.[66]

The former arguments are mainly based on the generally accepted connection between recognition of the foreign *res judicata* and recognition of foreign litispendence. The *res judicata* which will come into play where the (foreign) court first seised pronounces a judgment on the merits will render the action brought in the second (Greek) court inadmissible (Article 323 of the CCP).[67] Thinking along the same lines, one reaches the

Schwab, n. 58 above, 260; *id.*, [1990] *Rivista di Diritto Processuale* 1006; *id.*, 'Das EuGVÜ innerhalb einer Vielzahl von Rechtsquellen: Griechische Erfahrungen und Perspektiven' in *Ein internationales Zivilverfahrensrecht für Gesamteuropa* (Heidelberg, 1992), 383, 387.

[64] See Sahpekidou [1990] *Elliniki Epitheorissi Europaikou Dikaiou* 705.

[65] See Beys, 'Inadmissibility because of litispendence before a foreign court' (1991) 22 *Dike* 140, 142.

[66] See Nikas, n. 57 above, 80.

[67] According to this Art., there are five requirements for foreign judgments to be recognized, that is to be given *res judicata* effect in Greece: (1) the judgment must have *res judicata* effect under the law of the state of origin; (2) the foreign court must have had international jurisdiction according to Greek law; (3) the losing party must have had the same rights of defence and participation in the proceedings as have the nationals of the state of origin; (4)

conclusion that raising the plea of litispendence, too, must have the consequence of staying an action, so that the *res judicata* aims are achieved sooner, albeit temporarily.[68] In conformity with this teleological connection of the foreign litispendence with the foreign *res judicata*, the conditions set forth by Article 323 of the CCP for the recognition of foreign *res judicata* must be fulfilled in the case of foreign litispendence too.[69] What is required, basically, is a positive recognition prognosis. However, it must be noted that it has been proposed that the plea of foreign litispendence should only be accepted if the conditions of Article 222 of the CCP are fulfilled; that is, without inquiring about the possibility of recognition or enforcement of the foreign decision in Greece.[70]

Since the rule is the recognition of foreign *res judicata*, it is the party opposing the recognition of the foreign litispendence who has the burden of proving that the conditions set forth in Article 323(1) and (3)–(5) of the CCP are not fulfilled.[71] Where there is conflict between foreign and a domestic *res judicata*, it is the domestic that prevails, even if it is subsequent to the foreign (Article 323(4) of the CCP). This fact does not render the recognition of the foreign litispendence unnecessary, since it is not impossible that, before the internal decision becomes *res judicata*, the foreign decision is already recognized in Greece; that would have as a result the risk of irreconcilable *res judicata*.[72]

The ruling of Article 222 of the CCP according to which the second action is stayed—and not dismissed as inadmissible[73]—is praiseworthy,[74] as much in the case of domestic as in the case of foreign litispendence. This

---

the judgment must not be inconsistent with a Greek judgment (either subsequent or prior) on the same issue and having a *res judicata* effect between the same parties; (5) the judgment must not be contrary to morality or (and) to Greek public policy. See Kozyris, 'Conflict of Laws, Nationality, International Jurisdiction and Recognition and Enforcement of Judgments and Awards' in *Introduction to Greek Law*, 313, 314.

[68] A 'justified expectation' (*begründete Erwartung*) is sufficient, see Varsami (1998) 19 *Dike* 347.

[69] See Kerameus, 'International litigation (Legal opinion)' (in Greek) (1988) 29 *Ellinike Dikaiossini* 1537, 1538.

[70] See Georgiadis, *Harmenopoulos* (1974), 606–7. Besides, by that time, this view is supported by many scholars in various States.

[71] See Sinaniotis, 'Recognition in Greece of the litispendence before foreign courts' (in Greek) in *Anamnistikos Tomos Em. Michelakis* (1973), 585 at 591–592. *Contra*, Nikas, n. 57 above, 92, who supports the view that, under Greek law, it is the party asking for recognition of the foreign judgment who has the objective burden of proof of the requirements for recognition.

[72] See Maridakis, n. 1 above, 96 n. 24, 97 n. 25, 99 n. 30, Fragistas, 'Domestic proceedings and foreign judgments' (in Greek) in *Eranion Maridakis III* (1964), 627 at 644–6. The same solution was adopted by the Brussels Convention, Arts. 21 and 27(3). See Kerameus, *Schwab*, n. 48 above; 264. *id.*, [1990] *Rivista di Diritto Processuale* 1012 n. 54.

[73] Since the inadmissibility of the action may be temporary and not definitive, when e.g. the first (foreign) action is withdrawn or dismissed on procedural prerequisites.

[74] For many reasons, especially the maintenance of liens, the avoidance of the risk that the statute of limitations has run out, the avoidance of usucaption, etc.

holds true particularly in the second case, because in this way the judicial protection of the plaintiff in the second (domestic) proceedings is rendered more efficient, where the foreign decision is not recognized in Greece.

3. SOME SPECIFIC ISSUES

For the litispendence objection to be admissible it is not necessary that the second (Greek) court lacks jurisdiction. Furthermore, the typical perfection of the document initiating the second proceedings and the fulfilment of the procedural requirements of the second (Greek) proceedings do not constitute necessary conditions for the foundation of this objection.

According to the prevailing view, in spite of the fact that bringing an action for a negative declaratory judgment creates litispendence, because it renders the disputed right subject to litigation, nevertheless it cannot prevent the hearing of a subsequently brought action for performance having the same subject matter. However, the opposite view is right to point out that, in the international context, this position is undermining the claim for efficient judicial protection of the plaintiff. And this is so, because the defendant to the action for a negative declaratory judgment would be able, by bringing an action for performance before a foreign court, to neutralize the plaintiff's right to choose the forum, and thus indirectly to ensure that the provisions of the law that he considers disadvantageous do not apply; he would be able, perhaps, to 'exclude' the application of the Brussels Convention. Therefore, according to the same view, this danger is avoided only by applying Article 249 of the CCP[75] that is, by staying the second proceedings.[76]

As far as the issue of the period of time during which the second (Greek) proceedings should be stayed is concerned, the correct view is that they should be stayed until the first (foreign) court's decision becomes final—and this will be determined by the law of that court. This has the consequence that, if the foreign court reaches a final judgment on the merits, the action before the Greek court will have no meaning, and if the litigants proceed to the hearing of their case, the action will be dismissed on the basis of the *res judicata* objection; and if the foreign court reaches a final judgment dismissing the action on procedural prerequisites, the stay of the action, ordered by the Greek court, will no longer be valid, and the (Greek) court will proceed to the hearing of the action brought before it.

[75] Which provides for the staying of the proceedings until another related civil or administrative proceeding is over.
[76] See Nikas, n. 57 above, 211–2.

4. Prerequisites

The conditions for domestic litispendence must be fulfilled in the case of a foreign litispendence too.

With respect to the issue of identical disputes, a necessary prerequisite for a successful plea of (international) litispendence, opinions are divided on whether it should be governed by the law of the second (Greek) court[77] or of the first (foreign) court;[78] or, perhaps, by both procedural laws. The last view seems the better one because, in this way, a uniformity of solutions is achieved; especially since this uniformity constitutes one of the aims of international procedural law.[79]

According to the prevailing theoretical view—not, however, always in case law as well—there is also litispendence between two procedures when, even though both actions involve the same parties and subject matter, the parties have the reverse status in those two proceedings. The same must also be said about the foreign litispendence. However, according to that (correct) view, the reversal of the litigants' status must be coupled with a reversal of petitions.

Under Greek procedural law, the prevailing view is that, inside the State, the subjective limits of the litispendence objection correspond to those of *res judicata*. As far as the issue of the subjective limits of the foreign litispendence are concerned, various views are put forward; it seems that the better one is that according to which the procedural laws of both courts should govern this issue.

5. The Brussels Convention

Since 1 April 1989, Greece has been a party to the Brussels Convention on Jurisdiction and the Enforcement of Judgments in Civil and Commercial Matters, of 1968, as amended.[80] Under Greek procedural law, proceedings

---

[77] According to the prevailing view, under Greek law there is identity of subject-matter not only when the subject-matter of both proceedings is absolutely the same, but also when the subject-matter of the second proceedings is included in the subject-matter of the first. The legal protection asked for by the first action renders the second action unnecessary: see Kondylis, *Res judicata according to the Code of Civil Procedure* (in Greek) (1983), 161 ff. As far as the question whether litispendence covers interlocutory issues is concerned, both positive and negative answers are supported. In the first case it is necessary for interlocutory issues to be covered by *res judicata* under the conditions of Art. 331 CCP: see Beys, 'Die objektiven Grenzen der Rechtskraft im griechischen Recht' in *Festschrift Habscheid* (1989), 11, 18. For a negative answer, see Kerameus, *Res judicata on interlocutory issues* (in Greek) (1967) 127 ff., 155 ff.

[78] See Gasis, 'Litispendence in international transactions' (in Greek) [1939] I *Symmikta* 377 at 386.

[79] According to Nikas, n. 57 above, 272–3, the preclusion of parallel proceedings should be deemed one of the most important principles of public policy.

[80] Ratification of the Accession Convention of Spain and Portugal, San Sebastian, 26 May 1989, by Greece, on 7 Apr. 1992; entry into force on 1 July 1992.

are considered pending from the time the action is filed before a court, under the condition that, subsequently, the defendant will be lawfully served with a copy of the complaint (Articles 215(I)(1), 221(I)(a) of the CCP). That is, litispendence, by a legal fiction, takes effect from a moment preceding the fulfilment of the last required condition. Thus, according to one opinion, for Article 21 of the Convention to apply and problems to be avoided, proceedings will be considered as pending as from the moment the last condition is fulfilled.[81] The opposite view is also supported[82] according to which, the corrective interpretation of Article 221(I) CCP should be excluded. If not, the manner of application of this Article would be dependant on whether the Brussels Convention is or is not applicable to the case being litigated.[83] The first opinion seems better, as it is the only appropriate way to cope with the problems which might be created due to the lack of uniformity of the relevant regulations. Furthermore, problems might also be created owing to the different rules on the termination of litispendence. Under many national laws, litispendence is terminated at the moment the decision of the first court becomes final. In Greece, many scholars take this position but, according to the case law, litispendence is terminated at the moment the first instance judgment is issued, and revives by the lodging of an appeal.[84]

6. The Germano-Greek Convention

It is obvious that the fact of the absence in Greek law of an express legal provision which would sanction the successful entertainment of the litispendence objection contributes a great deal to the risk of conflicting judgments—foreign and domestic—on the same dispute and between the same parties; at the expense, that is, of the correct administration of justice and, consequently, of the citizens' confidence in the infallibility of the court's judgment. At the time of the conclusion of the bilateral convention between Greece and Germany of 4 November 1961[85] on the recognition and enforcement of judgments, this reason was deemed very important; thus, a special provision was inserted (Article 3(1)), which permits the refusal of recognition of the foreign judgment[86] if a first instance judgment

---

[81] See Kerameus, Kremlis, and Tagaras, n. 9 above, Art. 21, para. 10.

[82] The argument put forth is that proceedings, under Art. 222 CCP. are considered as pending, by the filing of the action, even when the defendant has not been served with a copy: see Beys, n. 32 above, Art. 222 (in Greek), 999; *id.*, 'Issues created by the way of filing an action according to the new law' (in Greek) (1971) 2 *Dike* 746 at 752.

[83] See Sahpekidou, [1990] *Elliniki Epitheorissi Europaikou Dikaiou* 709.

[84] See Yessiou-Faltsi and Kaissis, *Civil trial in motion* (1985) (in Greek), i. 56–7; Kerameus, *Civil procedural law* (1986) general part (in Greek), 216.

[85] Ratified by Act 4305 of 22 May 1963, entered into force on 30 May 1963.

[86] It is the party opposing the recognition who has the burden of proof: see Piraeus Court of Appeals 537/1981 [1982] Elliniki Dikaiossini 315. See also Fragistas and Yessiou-Faltsi,

on the same dispute has already been issued in Greece. We notice that the litispendence is provided, not as a reason for lack of international jurisdiction or for a stay of other proceedings, but as a reason for potential refusal of recognition of a judgment already issued.[87]

7. Related Actions

In Greek law, the exclusive jurisdiction of connexity (*forum connexitatis*) is provided for. According to Article 31 of the CCP auxiliary claims are tried before the courts having jurisdiction over the main claim; main claims related between them are submitted to the exclusive competence of the court first seised. In contrast, the Brussels Convention does not establish a *forum connexitatis*.[88] It only provides that, where related actions are brought in the courts of different Member States, any court other than the one first seised may stay its proceedings or decline its jurisdiction (Article 22). Since Greek law only permits the consolidation of several actions if they are pending before the same court, or the staying of the proceedings until other proceedings, civil or administrative (Article 249 of the CCP) or penal (Article 250 of the CCP), are terminated, Greek courts, as far as the application of Article 22 of Brussels Convention is concerned, will only be able to stay the proceedings and not to decline jurisdiction in favour of another Member State's courts.[89]

IV
ARBITRATION AGREEMENTS

1. The Provisions

According to Articles 263b and 870(I) of the CCP, in order that the dispute be referred from the State court to arbitration, the defendant must plead the arbitration agreement specifically, and before the court proceeds to examine the merits of the case;[90] that is, *in limine litis*, where the agreement

International conventions in civil procedural law, (1976) (in Greek), 33 n. 32; Yessiou-Faltsi, 'Die Anerkennung und Vollstreckung deutscher Gerichtsurteile aus der Sichts eines griechischen Juristen' (1983) 96 *ZZP* 75–6; Pouliadis, *Die Bedeutung des deutsch-griechischen Vertrages vom 4.11.1961 für die Anerkennung und Vollstreckung deutscher Entscheidungen in der griechischen Praxis* (1985), 21–22 n. 21.

[87] See Kerameus, Kremlis, and Tagaras, n. 9 above, para 2, note 4.
[88] See Kerameus, Kremlis, and Tagaras, n. 9 above, art 23. para. 10; Makridou, 'Interpretatory Issues of the jurisdiction bases of "tort" and "quasi-tort" of art. 5 (3) of the Brussels Convention' [1990] *Harmenopoulos* 1165 at 1169.
[89] See the Evrigenis and Kerameus Report, [1986] OJ C298/1, 19.
[90] See Mainas, 'The proceeding's impeding objections, of art. 272 CCP.' (in Greek) (1969) 17 *Nomiko Vima* 607 at 609.

was concluded before the action is brought before the court. The court cannot raise the plea of arbitration of its own motion. This leads to the conclusion that, by bringing an action before the arbitral tribunal, litispendence does not come into play,[91] because the objection of submitting the dispute to arbitration may always be raised before the State court.[92] Consequently, if the interested party does not plead the arbitration agreement before the State court, it is a case—the only one in Greek law—of tacit waiver of the objection.[93]

When an international (or foreign) arbitration agreement[94] is pleaded before the Greek court before which the action has been brought—in accordance with Article 264 of the CCP which applies, regardless of whether the arbitration agreement is domestic or international[95]—the court must stay the proceedings before it[96] and refer the case to arbitration, if the agreement is valid.[97] In that case, too, the arbitration agreement must be pleaded by the interested party *in limine litis*.[98] According to the view prevailing in Greek case law as well as in theory, the adjudicating court judges the validity of the international arbitration agreement in conformity with the provisions of Greek law, regardless of the international

[91] France is the only State to have codified an *exception de litispendance arbitrale* in its Civil Procedure Code, Art. 1458(1).

[92] See Areios Pagos 816/1983 (1984) 32 Nomiko Vima 638, Athens CA 12086/1979 (1983) 14 Dike 33. Also see Krispi Nikoletopoulou, 'Arbitration in private international law' (in Greek) (1985) 25 *Ephimeris Ellinon Nomikon* 505 at 510; Kerameus, n. 1 above, 216. *Contra*, Foustoucos, *L'arbitrage—interne et international—en droit privé hellénique* (1976), 76 according to whom the proceedings before an arbitral tribunal have litispendence as a consequence. See also Kaissis, *Setting aside arbitral awards* (in Greek) (2nd edn., 1989), 81 n. 101, that only the bringing of the same dispute before another arbitral tribunal would have litispendence as a consequence.

[93] See Foustoucos, n. 92 above, 76.

[94] For a definition of international (and foreign) arbitration by Greek scholars, see: Fragistas, 'Arbitrage étranger et arbitrage internationale en droit privé' [1960] *Rev. Crit. Dr. Int. Pr.* 1 ff.; Karympali-Tsiptsiou, 'Problems of international arbitration' (in Greek) [1979] *Harmenopoulos* 634 at 637; Dimolitsa, 'The advantages of foreign arbitral awards' (in Greek) (1981) 29 *Nomiko Vima* 230; Kalavros, *The concept of foreign arbitral award* (in Greek) (1984), 87; Papassiopi-Passia, *New tendencies of private international law in the field of contractual obligations* (in Greek) (1985), 155; Verveniotis, *International commercial arbitration* (in Greek) (1990), 25; Foustoucos 'International arbitration and foreign decision' (in Greek) (1992) 40 *Nomiko Vima* 253 ff.

[95] See Maridakis, n. 62 above, 125 n. 40.

[96] All the consequences of the institution of the action are preserved: see Areios Pagos 816/1983 (1984) 32 Nomiko Vima 638. See also Kaissis, n. 92 above, 82.

[97] See Kerameus, 'International jurisdiction on disputes of maritime law in continental countries and especially in Greece' (in Greek) (1983) 31, *Nomiko Vima* 28 at 35, that Greek courts always consider foreign arbitration agreements as valid, without examining whether the solution of dispute by arbitration or the place of the arbitration's conduct abroad would, in that very case, be convenient for all the parties, in respect to the subject matter of the litigation. See also, Foustoucos, 'Conditions of the validity of the arbitration agreement' (in Greek) (1988) 36 *Nomiko Vima* 1370 ff.

[98] A regulation corresponding to those of the Geneva Protocol (Art. 4), of the New York Convention (Art. II(3)), and of the European Convention 1961 (Art. 6).

element and, therefore, not applying a rule of private international law. This view is criticized vehemently, on the basic argument that, according to Article 903 of the CCP, when the enforcement of a foreign arbitral award is sought, the court judges the validity of the arbitration agreement in conformity with its *lex causae*.[99] Therefore, the supporters of this view believe that one should aspire to a uniform solution of these two cases. Also from the point of view of substantive law, this solution is deemed preferable, in order for the Greek legal system not to be accused of a denial of justice. This would happen in the situation where a Greek court, before which an action is brought in spite of an arbitration agreement, holds itself incompetent if under Greek law that agreement is valid, and rejects the petition for the enforcement of a subsequent foreign arbitral award because the agreement in invalid according to its *lex causae*.[100]

As far as the issue of who is competent to rule on the arbitrators' competence is concerned, that is, whether it is the arbitrators themselves or the Greek court, Greek law recognizes the competence of the arbitrators, by a *lois d'application immediate* (Article 887(II) of the CCP)[101] to all abitrations, both domestic and international.

2. Provisional Measures

The arbitration agreement does not prevent the parties from asking the court to order provisional measures, since, according to Article 685 of the CCP, no arbitration agreement about provisional measures is valid.[102] According to this Article, the parties may, either before or after the arbitration proceedings are commenced, submit a petition to the one-member first instance court asking it to order provisional measures, without running the risk of their act (petition) being considered as a waiver of the arbitration. On the other hand, according to Article 889(I) of the CCP, completing the above-mentioned provision, the arbitrators may not order, modify, or revoke provisional measures. This Article 'compels' the petitioner who obtained an injunction ordering provisional measures to do whatever is necessary for the arbitration proceedings to commence in a fixed period of time. If that period of time is over and the petitioner remains inactive, the provisional measures are suspended *ipso facto* (Articles 693(II), 715(IV)(b), 729(IV)(b) of the CCP).

---

[99] On recognition and enforcement of a foreign arbitration award in Greece, see Foustoucos, 'La reconnaissance et l'exécution en Grèce des sentences arbitrales étrangères après la récente réforme du droit de l'arbitrage' [1974], *Revue de l'arbitrage* 265 ff.; Kerameus, 'Arbitrage, international et ordre juridique hellenique' [1987] *Revue de l'arbitrage* 35 at 38.

[100] See Foustoucos, n. 92 above, 209.

[101] According to which the arbitrators, if nothing else is provided in the abritration agreement, judge their own competence themselves.

[102] Consequently, if the parties introduce such a clause into the arbitration agreement concluded by them, that clause will not be valid; however, this fact will not influence the validity of the rest of the agreement.

In theory as well as in case law in Greece, it is admitted that the court has the power to order provisional measures in disregard of an arbitration agreement, even when that agreement is international. As far, now, as the above-mentioned provisions are concerned, according to which the parties cannot either agree to have recourse to arbitration for the ordering of provisional measures, or order, modify, or revoke provisional measures, they are deemed provisions of the Greek courts' international jurisdiction, valid not only in a domestic, but also in a foreign or international, arbitration. According to the better view,[103] this solution does not lead to a conflict between judicial and arbitral jurisdiction, but to their coexistence which aims at the protection of the same private rights, although from a different perspective. Provisional measures, being measures of the enforcement of decisions inside the (Greek) State, ensure that those rights remain until a judgment in the litigation is reached.

V
RESTRAINING FOREIGN PROCEEDINGS

According to the prevailing view, our civil courts are internationally competent to order provisional measures only if these measures are to be enforced in Greece.[104] The main reason for this limitation is that the decision which orders the provisional measures is an administrative act and, as a consequence, its enforcement in another State would offend the sovereignty of that State.[105] The same thinking is to be found in the Graeco–German Convention of 1961, according to which the Convention does not apply either to arrests (Article 17(1)(2)) or to decisions ordering provisional measures (Article 17(II)).

It is worth noting that, according to the wording of Article 238(I) of the draft Code of Civil Procedure, presented by the Constituent Committee: 'After the commencement of the litispendence and during the time it lasts, no new proceedings are possible between the same parties having the same status before the same or another domestic or foreign court.' However, the reference to the foreign court was considered as an interference with the civil procedure of the other States, inadmissible since the *lex fori* governs issues of international procedural law. Thus, the former formulation was replaced by the one in Article 225(I) of the CCP 1968, and, after the amendment of the Code of Civil Procedure by legislative decree 958/71, by the formulation of the actual Article 222 of the CCP.

---

[103] See Foustoucos, n. 92 above, 213.
[104] See Beys, *Proceedings before the one-member court of first instance* (1970) (in Greek), 285; Vrellis, n. 55 above, 214.
[105] See Beys, n. 32 above, *(1), General principles and articles' interpretation* (in Greek) (1973), 149.

12

Israel

STEPHEN GOLDSTEIN
*Professor, Faculty of Law, The Hebrew University of Jerusalem**

CONTENTS

I
INTRODUCTION

Israel does not have separate courts for commercial matters. Nor does Israeli procedural law generally distinguish between civil and commercial matters. Thus in this chapter we will not so distinguish and will consider commercial matters merely as a type of civil matter.

The appropriateness and, indeed, necessity, for a court to have the authority to decline jurisdiction on a discretionary basis is, of course, related to the law of international jurisdiction, i.e., the authority of a State's judicial system to assert jurisdiction over defendants, of the given

---

* The Israeli National Report was previously published by the Harry and Michael Sacher Institute for Legislative Research and Comparative Law, The Hebrew University of Jerusalem, in *Israeli Reports to the XIV International Congress of Comparative Law*, ed. Rabello (Jerusalem, 1994), 107.

State. The greater the international jurisdiction, and, in particular, the more that such international jurisdiction is not based on a significant connection between the transaction or event on which the action is based and the forum State, the greater the need for the courts to have discretionary authority to decline jurisdiction.

The Israeli law of international jurisdiction is based on the English, and thus premises jurisdiction, *inter alia*, on proper service of process on the defendant. A defendant found within the territorial limits of the State may be served with process, thereby seising the Israeli courts with international jurisdiction. This is so even if he is only temporarily in the State and the action itself has no connection with Israel.

It should also be noted that owing to special regulation in this regard, for purposes of service of process the territorial limits of the State include the territories administered by the State since the 1967 Six Day War.

Thus, it would be expected that discretionary declining of jurisdiction would long have been a part of Israeli law. This is not so, however, since until 1979 there was little need for such a doctrine. Until that year, the two typical cases in which such a doctrine would be necessary were solved by another means, i.e., the absence of venue (or local jurisdiction as it is termed in Israeli law). These two typical cases were (1) the service of process on a defendant who is only temporarily in Israel, including those who are tourists, relating to a claim that also has no relation with Israel; and (2) litigation between two residents of the Administered Territories (today the West Bank and Gaza Strip) who are not Israeli citizens, relating to a claim which also originated in the Administered Territories.

As to the first case there was, and is today, jurisdiction over the person of the defendant by reason of service of process within the confines of the State of Israel. As to the second case there also was, and is, jurisdiction over the person of the defendant, a resident of the Administered Territories, by virtue of the Special Regulations, noted above, which provide, in essence, for service of process in such Territories *as if* they were within the borders of the State of Israel. However, in both of these situations, until 1979 no Israeli court was properly seised with internal territorial jurisdiction, or venue, and thus, if the defendant properly raised the defence of lack of venue, the case would be dismissed. In 1979, the Israeli Rules of Civil Procedure were amended to provide that, if an Israeli court has jurisdiction over the person of the defendants but there is no venue pursuant to the venue rules, there is residuary venue in the Jerusalem courts. Thus, the lack of venue was removed as an impediment to maintenance of an action in Israel.

This new situation raised, for the first time, the true issues involved in entertaining actions where an Israeli court has jurisdiction over the person by virtue of service of process, but Israel is clearly an inappropriate forum for the action. At this point, the author of this chapter wrote an article advocating the adoption of the doctrine of *forum non conveniens* for such cases.[1] Until that time, the very limited Israeli case law in this regard had referred primarily to the traditionally very restricted English doctrine concerning staying actions in which the court had jurisdiction, which allowed such stays only when the plaintiff's choice of England as a forum was deemed 'vexatious' or 'oppressive' to the defendant.

In the article referred to above, we advocated the need for the adoption of the doctrine of *forum non conveniens*, as developed in the United States. We also pointed out that in England, itself, the case law was moving in the direction of the American doctrine.

Since 1980, as will be discussed below in greater detail, Israeli case law essentially has accepted our thesis in the above article and has adopted the doctrine of *forum non conveniens*.[2] Indeed, while a full discussion of this matter is beyond this chapter on Israel, so indeed, has English case law.[3] In the next section of this chapter we will discuss the doctrine of *forum non conveniens* as it has developed in Israel since 1929.

In the third and final section we will discuss a related, but different, area of law concerning the discretionary denial of jurisdiction: that related to the consent of the parties. That is, discretionary denial of jurisdiction in cases in which the parties, through contractual forum-selection clauses, have consented to jurisdiction in Israel, yet Israel is clearly not an appropriate forum, as well as reverse situations, i.e., cases in which Israel is clearly an appropriate forum, yet the parties have agreed to exclusive jurisdiction in another State.

II
FORUM NON CONVENIENS

1. Relation to *Lis Alibi Pendens*

While the issue has not been determined definitively, it appears that Israeli law does not recognize an independent doctrine of *lis alibi pendens*. Rather, the existence of litigation in another jurisdiction on the same subject matter as that pending in Israel serves as a factor—indeed a major factor—in determining whether an Israeli court will refuse to entertain the matter on grounds of *forum non conveniens*.

---

[1] See Goldstein (1980) 10 *Mishpatim* 409 (Hebrew).

[2] See e.g. *Atiyah* v. *Arbatisi* (1985) 39(1) PD 365; *Abu-Ghichla* v. *The East Jerusalem Electric Co Ltd*, 30 Dec. 1993 (not yet published) and cases cited therein.

[3] See *Spiliada Maritime Corp* v. *Cansulex Ltd* [1987] AC 460; [1986] 3 All ER 843 (HL).

2. General Principles of *Forum Non Conveniens*

In its recent, and as yet unpublished, decision in December 1993, in the case of *Abu-Ghichla* v. *East Jerusalem Electric Co Ltd*, the Supreme Court set out the governing principles of *forum non conveniens* in Israel.[4] Since this case concerns the Administered Territories we will also discuss it in the following section of the chapter. We will concentrate herein, therefore, on the general principles of *forum non conveniens* set out in this decision.

In its opinion, the Supreme Court surveyed the latest developments in both English and American law as to *forum non conveniens* and, in essence, accepted a synthesis of those developments as also representing Israeli law. Thus, the Court stated that a defendant who raises a defence of *forum non conveniens* must convince the court that, despite the existence of international jurisdiction, there is another forum which very clearly has the majority of contacts, or has the most substantial connection, with the matter in dispute. Among those contacts are the place of the occurrence, transaction, or the event which is the subject of the action, and the citizenship, domicile, and residence of the parties. It should be noted in this regard that the defendant's technical Israeli citizenship was not given great weight by the Court. Additional factors are the residence of the witnesses as well as the ease or difficulty to the various parties of conducting the litigation in the different fora under discussion.

The Court noted, however, that this comparison of fora does not start with a *tabula rasa*. Rather, the facts that the plaintiff has brought his action in Israel and Israel has international jurisdiction over the defendant create a strong presumption against relinquishing jurisdiction, and another forum will be determined to be the preferred or 'natural' one only when the balance of the above factors is strongly against an Israeli forum in the matter in question. Once, however, the court determines that another forum is the 'natural' one and Israel is *prima facie* the *forum non conveniens*, the matter is not necessarily closed. Rather, the plaintiff still has the opportunity to show that dismissing the action in Israel would, on the facts of the case, cause him 'injustice'. As to the question of what constitutes such an injustice, the Court adopted the view current both in England and the United States that differences in the law that might be applied, including questions of the amount of damages or aspects of relief that would be awarded, between Israel and the natural forum do not, in and of themselves, constitute such an 'injustice'.[5]

In this respect, the Court discussed at length the special problem of limitations, i.e. situations in which, by the time that an action is dismissed

[4] N. 2 above.
[5] As to the US, see *Piper Aircraft Co* v. *Reyno*, 454 US 235 (1981); as to England, see *Spiliada Maritime Corp* v. *Cansulex Ltd*, n. 3 above.

on grounds of *forum non conveniens*, it may be time-barred in the foreign, natural forum. Under the English rule, in effect until the 1986 decision of the House of Lords in the *Spiliada* case,[6] this would be a controlling factor preventing a stay of the action on grounds of *forum non conveniens*. In changing the general English rule as to differences in law between the fora, the House of Lords (Lord Goff), left open the possibility of still considering the situation as presenting a reason for not staying an English action. However, this was specifically limited to a situation in which a 'plaintiff did not act unreasonably in failing to commence proceedings (for example, by issuing a protective writ) in that [the natural] jurisdiction within the limitation period applicable there'.[7]

Moreover, Lord Goff noted that 'as the applicable [new principles] became more clearly established and better known, it will, I suspect become increasingly difficult for plaintiffs to prove lack of negligence in this regard'.[8] Finally, even if the plaintiff was not negligent, it may be appropriate not to refuse to stay the proceedings in the forum State; but in the words of Lord Goff, 'the appropriate order, where the application of the time-bar in the foreign jurisdiction is dependent on its invocation by the defendant, may well be to make it a condition of the grant of a stay . . . that the defendant should waive the time-bar in the foreign jurisdiction; this is apparently the practice in the United States of America'.

And that, indeed, is the American approach.[9]

In the *East Jerusalem Electric Co Ltd* case, because of the shorter limitation period in the Administered Territories than in Israel, the plaintiff's action was time-barred in the Territories, before he filed his action in time (under Israeli law) in Israel. Dismissal of the action on *forum non conveniens* grounds would mean, of course, that the action could not be maintained in the natural forum (the Administered Territories), if the defendant raised the limitations defence.

In addressing this issue, the Court noted that the defendant had agreed not to raise the issue of limitations against an action that would be filed in the Administered Territories if such action were filed within two months following the *forum non conveniens* dismissal in Israel. The Court accepted this agreement of the defendant as sufficient to dispose of the problem of limitations. It noted that 'this solution is consistent with the spirit of the Anglo-American law' on this problem.[10] Thus the Court was not required to—and did not—determine what it would have done had the defendant not so agreed. It is curious that, despite its extensive references to both English and American law as to this problem, the Court did not refer at all to Israeli precedent on this point. This precedent, while not concerning

---

[6] N. 3 above.   [7] *Ibid.* 860 (All ER).   [8] *Ibid.*   [9] *Ibid.* 860–1.
[10] See e.g. Scoles and Hay, *Conflict of Laws* (1982), 363; *Brewers v. American Home Products*, 99 App. Div. 2d 949 (NY 1984).

forum non conveniens per se, does concern an analogous situation, discussed below in this chapter, of dismissal of an action because of a contractual provision between the parties providing for exclusive jurisdiction in another forum.

In a 1990 case in this regard, the Israeli Supreme Court rejected the plaintiff's argument that the Israeli action should not be dismissed because, during the appeal before the Supreme Court, it had become time-barred in Germany, the State of exclusive jurisdiction pursuant to the contract. In so holding, the Court stated:

> The danger of an action being time-barred is not an event that happens at one point in time; rather as to any period of limitations, it is possible to know at any point prior to it ending, to what extent we are approaching that critical time, when the defendant may plead a limitations defence, and to act accordingly to prevent it from happening. Thus it is in the case before us. Despite the fact that the limitations period in German law passed only during the stage of the appeal before us, there is substance to the argument of the respondent [defendant] that the appellant [plaintiff] should have taken action at an earlier stage, when he could still control the situation.[11]

The Court also cited with approval the following quotation from a similar case in 1965:

> The appellant [plaintiff] knew in advance that the respondent [defendant] is insisting on enforcing the exclusive jurisdiction clause providing for such jurisdiction in an Amsterdam court and despite that, and without any fault on the part of the respondent [defendant] delayed filing his action (in the Israeli Court) until after two-thirds of the limitation period [in the Netherlands] had run. If, as a result of this delay, he suddenly finds that he has not sufficient time to file an action in Amsterdam during the limitations period, he has no one to blame but himself.[12]

Finally as regards our discussion of the general principles of *forum non conveniens* as they were discussed and applied in the *East Jerusalem Electric Co Ltd* case, we must note the discussion on the application of the American principles concerning 'public factors' to be considered in determining whether Israel is, indeed, a *forum non conveniens* in a given case. In its opinion in this case, the Court, speaking through President Shamgar, noted that under American law if the factors discussed above as to the interests of the parties, i.e., the place of the occurrences, citizenship, domicile, and residence of the parties, residence of the witnesses, etc., are in equilibrium, an American court will then consider public factors. Such

---

[11] *Adrat Shomnon Ltd* v *Hollingswort GmbH* (1990) 44(3) PD 600 at 615.

[12] *'Tsion', Insurance Co Ltd* v. *Koninklijke Nederlandsche Stoomboot-Maatschappij NV* (1965) 19(1) PD 303 at 305–6. See also, the rejection of a new hearing in this case: (1965) 19(2) PD 625.

public factors, include, *inter alia*, the concern that continuation of the adjudication in the current forum will put an undue burden on a society that has no connection with the litigation, the fact that the forum has no public interest (or minimal interest) in the litigation; or that substantive law that would be applied in the forum is foreign law with which the court is not familiar.

In an earlier decision in *Atiyah* v. *Arbatisi*,[13] Barak J had expressed 'serious doubts' whether the Israeli courts should adopt the complete American doctrine of *forum non conveniens* because of the use of such public factors in this doctrine. He stated that:

pursuant to the American approach, the court must consider, in addition to factors of justice between the parties, also public factors concerning the court itself, the amount of its work and the expenditure of its public funds, and in a case where the factors of justice [between the parties] are in equilibrium, the public factors will determine the issue. I am doubtful whether it is justified to give such great weight to public factors. However, as stated above, I would request to leave this matter to future decisions, since there is no need to determine it herein, since the factors concerning the parties themselves are not in equilibrium.[14]

In the *East Jerusalem Electric Co Ltd* case, Shamgar P also stated that he need not determine whether to consider public interests, as in American law, since also in this case the parties' interests were not in equilibrium but clearly favoured dismissal. However, he went on to note that:

despite that, I wish to note that *prima facie*, I see no reason why, in Israel, it is not appropriate to consider public interests and even to give them weight, when the party interests are in equilibrium. It is possible to ask: why should the Israeli judicial system—an arm of the society—bear the heavy cost of actions and the administration of litigation which have no connection with it, particularly since these costs would be relatively greater than those of ordinary litigation, in light of the difficulties of proving foreign law that will naturally be the *lex causae* and in bringing witnesses who cannot be summoned in the usual way.

Thus, at least in theory, this issue remains open in Israeli law with conflicting indications expressed by Barak J and Shamgar P. However, in our view, this issue is more semantic than real. This is so since, except for the difficulties of the court in applying foreign law, the public factors noted above are not really factors, i.e., independent variables that vary from case to case. Rather, they are part of the justification for the doctrine of *forum non conveniens* and will always be subsumed as part of the private, or party, factors.

[13] N. 2 above.
[14] *Ibid*. 386. In referring to the use of public factors in the American doctrine, Barak J refers expressly to *Pain* v. *United Technologies Corp*, 637 F. 2d 775 (DC 1980), which, indeed, accurately sets forth the principles of American law in this regard as derived from the leading Supreme Court case: *Gulf Oil Corp* v. *Gilbert*, 330 US 510 (1947).

Thus when there is no real contact with the forum, the costs of the litigation may be seen to be an undue burden on such forum; when there is such real contact, they will not be. It is not coincidental, therefore, that neither Barak J in *Atiyah* nor Shamgar P in *East Jerusalem Electric Co Ltd* found it necessary to resort to public factors.

Nor does English doctrine find it necessary to discuss such factors explicitly.

Moreover, as to the one factor that may, indeed, be an independent variable, i.e. the need to apply foreign law, there is universal agreement that the difficulty involved in applying foreign law is a factor weighing in favour of a *forum non conveniens* dismissal. In Israel all the judges who have considered the issue, including Barak J in *Atiyah* and Shamgar P in *East Jerusalem Electric Co Ltd*, agree. Moreover, so does American and English academic literature. However, one need not resort to 'public interests' in order to reach this result, since the difficulty in litigating pursuant to foreign law is clearly also a private- or party-interest consideration. Indeed, this is the view of English law on this point.

We should, however, note one qualification in this regard. The unanimous agreement mentioned above as to the effect of the need to apply foreign law is clear. This, however, does not mean that, in every case, an Israeli court faced with a *forum non conveniens* defence must determine what substantive law will apply to the litigation as part of its resolution of the motion to dismiss.

In the *Atiyah* case, Barak J quite correctly suggested that, at this preliminary stage of the proceedings, the court should not get involved in difficult issues of choice of law in order to determine which law will apply. As Barak J so aptly stated: 'Indeed, the forum that determines the issue of *forum non conveniens* is itself a *forum non conveniens* for determining complex questions of choice of law.'[15] Simply put, the advantage in knowing what law will apply does not outweigh the time and energy involved in determining difficult choice-of-law issues. Thus, the court should consider the question of what law will apply only when this matter is clear.

As noted above, we will return to other aspects of the *East Jerusalem Electric Co Ltd* case, and the *Atiyah* case in our discussion of the unique problems concerning the Administered Territories. Before we do so, however, we should mention two other decisions, not concerning the Administered Territories, that preceded the *East Jerusalem Electric Co Ltd* case.

The first case, *Pollak* v. *Bijou d'Etoile*,[16] involved an action brought by Canadian creditors against a debtor resident in Canada concerning a

---

[15] N. 2 above, at 386.

[16] (1979–80) (1) PM 353. While this decision was that of a DC, not of the Sup. Ct., its precedential importance is greater than that of a usual DC opinion. This is so since its author,

transaction that took place in Canada. The debtor-defendant held dual citizenship—both Canadian and Israeli—since his family had emigrated to Canada from Israel when he was a child. He had, however, lived almost all his life in Canada, and was only visiting temporarily in Israel when he was served with process. This was, then, a classic case for the application of *forum non conveniens*, despite the fact that the defendant was an Israeli citizen, and, indeed, the court stayed the action on *forum non conveniens* grounds.

However, the main issue in this case was a different one. The plaintiffs argued that, despite the fact that Israel was not a 'natural forum' for the adjudication, an Israeli court should not stay the action since the defendant, in fleeing from Canada, was attempting to avoid his creditors and frustrate the possibility of bringing an action against him. In such a case of a debtor who is fleeing from jurisdiction to jurisdiction in order to avoid litigation, argued the plaintiffs, any jurisdiction in which the defendant is 'caught' should permit the litigation against him even if such jurisdiction has no real connection with either the parties or the transaction.

The Israeli court suggested strongly that it was sympathetic to this argument. However, on the facts of the case before it, the plaintiffs had not proven that defendant was, indeed, attempting to avoid his creditors by fleeing from jurisdiction to jurisdiction.

In terms of the allocation of the burden of proof, this opinion is in accord with the later authoritative decision in the *East Jerusalem Electric Co Ltd* case. That is, the issue of a defendant trying to escape from his creditors arises as an argument of 'injustice' raised by the plaintiffs—and as to which the burden of proof is on them—after the defendant has successfully borne his original burden of persuading the court that Israel is a *forum non conveniens*, since Canada is the natural forum for this litigation.

In this case, the plaintiffs did not succeed in meeting this burden, i.e., proving that the defendant was, indeed, fleeing from jurisdiction to jurisdiction in order to avoid litigation. As noted above, however, had the plaintiffs met their burden, the clear implication of the opinion is that the court would not have stayed the action.

Such a principle about fleeing debtors seems to us to be correct if, and only if, the *forum non conveniens* in which the debtor is trapped cannot act so as to ensure that the defendant will be subject to jurisdiction in the natural forum, in this case, Canada. If it can so ensure that adjudication is possible in the natural forum it should do so, and then decline jurisdiction in favour of such natural forum, even if it is convinced that the defendant has been fleeing from jurisdiction to jurisdiction in order to avoid litigation.

Levin J, has since been elevated to the Sup. Ct. and is considered a leading expert on civil procedure in Israel.

In the *Pollak* case, the court did, in fact, make sure that Canada had jurisdiction in the matter. Following service of process on the defendant, he was also prevented from leaving the State of Israel, pursuant to Israeli procedure by which courts regularly prevent civil defendants from leaving the State.[17] We will discuss this procedure further below. Suffice it to note now that, due to the continued enforced presence of the defendant in Israel, the plaintiffs could serve him with Canadian process in Israel after receiving permission to serve process out of the jurisdiction from the appropriate Canadian court. The court expressly noted that, despite the stay of the proceedings which would ordinarily terminate the order preventing the defendant from leaving the country, the defendant had agreed that such order 'would remain in force for a further 45 days in order to allow the filing of an action in Canada and the effecting of service [pursuant to such action] in Israel'.

Under these circumstances, in our view, it is irrelevant whether or not the defendant had prior to this time been trying to avoid litigation by fleeing from jurisdiction to jurisdiction. We would also submit that our view is in accord with the decision of the Supreme Court in the *East Jerusalem Electric Co Ltd* case, both as to its specific disposition of the issue of the limitation period and as to its approving discussion of American precedents which have conditioned *forum non conveniens* dismissals on the defendant agreeing, *inter alia*, to submit to the jurisdiction of the natural forum.[18]

In another case, *Korpol* v. *Export Credit Corporation*,[19] the Supreme Court refused to dismiss the action on *forum non conveniens* grounds despite the fact that neither the plaintiff, an American corporation, nor the defendant, a resident and citizen of Mexico, was a resident or citizen of Israel and the action involved obligations under bonds issued by the defendant in Mexico. This decision is in our view problematic. Nevertheless, the defendant did have some connection with Israel beyond the fact that he was served with process while temporarily present in the State. This connection concerned the defendant's involvement, through shares in his wife's name, in a major Israeli hotel country-club development. In addition to the monetary value of this investment, the shares in this development entitled the defendant's family to use two suites in the hotel, for certain periods of time, which they in fact did from time to time. Moreover, without discussing the issue at length it appears from the opinion that the Court did, indeed, believe that, by opposing adjudication in every jurisdiction, the defendant was, indeed, trying to use procedural devices in order to frustrate the legitimate claims of his creditors.

---

[17] See Goldstein (1985) 20 *Israel Law Review* 18.

[18] See e.g. the approving references in this regard to the American case of *Brewers* v. *American Home Products*, n. 10 above.

[19] (1979) 34(1) PD 741.

The Court also referred affirmatively to the argument of the plaintiff that the investment in the Israeli development, despite the fact that it was in the name of the defendant's wife, might be an asset which could be reached in satisfaction of a judgment against the defendant, without stating precisely the relevance of that fact.

In examining such relevance we should note that Israeli law includes generally accepted principles of private international law, pursuant to which a party may enforce a foreign judgment by bringing an action on it in Israel and then enforcing the subsequent Israeli judgment against a defendant's assets in the State. Thus bringing an Israeli action initially is not a *sine qua non* for enforcing against a defendant's assets in Israel. Of course, the process is simpler and, perhaps, quicker and less expensive if the original action is, indeed, maintained in Israel.

Even more significant, however, is the fact that the assets in Israel can be attached prior to judgment, in order to prevent a defendant transferring or dissipating them only if the action is brought in Israel. Israeli law does not allow for pre-judgment attachment of a defendant's assets as interim relief incidental to an action pending abroad. In a later case, the Israeli Supreme Court recognized expressly that the possibility of attaching a defendant's assets at the beginning of the proceedings was a factor weighing against dismissing an action on grounds of *forum non conveniens*.[20]

In concluding this discussion of the *Pollak* and *Korpol* cases, we should note that in *Korpol*, as in *Pollak*, the court had issued an order preventing the defendant from leaving the country and, indeed, one of the express purposes of the defendants in the *Korpol* case in attempting to have the action dismissed on *forum non conveniens* grounds was to have this order lifted.

It appears to us that a significant inducement for plaintiffs to bring actions in Israel when Israel is clearly not the natural forum is the fact that Israeli law allows plaintiffs easily to burden defendants by preliminary remedies, particularly the draconian one of preventing them from leaving the country.[21]

[20] *Ra'ad* v. *Chai* (1986) 40(2) PD 453 at 464. For discussion of the extensive use of preliminary attachments in Israel, see Goldstein, n. 17 above, at 24–5.

[21] For a full discussion of the traditional widespread use of this device in Israel, see Goldstein, n. 17 above. The criticism of this use as expressed in the above article did not result in any changes in the Israeli Rules of Civ. Proc. concerning this remedy. However, in recent years there appears to be a growing sensitivity to the issues involved, particularly in the case of the Sup. Ct. Moreover, in Mar. 1992, the Knesset adopted a new Basic Law: The Dignity and Liberty of Man, which includes a provision guaranteeing the right to leave the country. As a formal matter of law, this new Basic Law does not affect the status of the current Rules concerning preventing a defendant from leaving the country, since it provides that none of its provisions shall affect existing legal rules, which, as defined, included the Rules of Civ. Proc. However, the adoption of this new Basic Law, which includes the right to leave the country, has increased the already growing sensitivity to the issue and, indeed, the Sup. Ct. has held, recently, that when implementing this remedy, a court must give great weight to the right to leave Israel as expressed in the Basic Law: *Bintin* v. *State of Israel*, 14

3. THE SPECIAL CASE OF THE ADMINISTERED TERRITORIES

As noted in the introduction, since 1979 there has been no jurisdictional impediment to bringing an action in an Israeli court when all the parties and the transaction or occurrence on which the action is based are concerned exclusively with the Administered Territories. In such situations, when the parties are not Israeli settlers in the Administered Territories, the Israeli courts have been unanimous in declining jurisdiction on *forum non conveniens* grounds.

The jurisprudence in this situation is summarized in the recent leading case of the *East Jerusalem Electric Co Ltd*, discussed in the previous section. This case involved a tort action brought by an Arab, West Bank, resident against the *East Jerusalem Electric Co Ltd*, based on an accident that had occurred in the West Bank. It should be noted that the defendant electric company was owned and licensed to supply electricity during the British mandate and continued under Jordanian rule to supply electricity to East Jerusalem and the West Bank. Its continuing licence to supply electricity in the West Bank was maintained by order of the Israeli military government in the West Bank. However, since, under Israeli law, East Jerusalem, as distinguished from the West Bank and Gaza Strip, is part of the State of Israel, the defendant electric company was also registered as an Israeli corporation and supplied electricity to East Jerusalem pursuant to an Israeli licence. This 'Israeli' status of the defendant led the Magistrate's Court to reject a *forum non conveniens* dismissal. This, however, was overturned on appeal to the District Court, the decision of which was upheld on a further appeal to the Supreme Court.

In its opinion the Supreme Court stressed that, despite the defendant corporation's nominal Israeli status, all the relevant connections were with the West Bank. Moreover, most of the defendant's activities were in the West Bank, not in East Jerusalem, and the litigation in question was based on such West Bank activity.

This Supreme Court decision in the *East Jerusalem Electric Co Ltd* case is consistent with that of the Court's prior decision in the *Atiyah* case, also discussed above. In this latter case, an action based on an accident occurring in the West Bank was dismissed on *forum non conveniens* grounds, despite the fact that one of the defendants, an insurance company, had an office in East Jerusalem, and that, following the work accident in the West Bank, the plaintiff was treated in an Israeli hospital. Moreover, in *Atiyah* the Court also rejected the argument that the plaintiff's desire to have

Dec. 1993 (not yet published); *Lev* v. *The Regional Rabbinic Court*, 10 Feb. 1994 (not yet published). It remains to be seen whether this will, indeed, affect the practice of trial courts. For an English translation of this Basic Law, as well as a discussion of its terms, see Kretzmer, (1992) 26 *Israel Law Review* 238.

expert evidence from Israeli physicians justified maintaining the action in Israel.

Returning to *East Jerusalem Electric Co Ltd*, in that case the Supreme Court also rejected the plaintiff's argument that, despite the fact that the West Bank was the natural forum, the action should not be dismissed in Israel since there were special circumstances which would make it 'unjust' to require him to litigate his action in the Administered Territories. We have already discussed the issue of limitations in this regard and will not repeat that discussion herein. However, we should note herein three other 'injustice' arguments made by the plaintiff. The first two were that the standard of care (in terms of negligence) applicable in the West Bank is less than in Israel and that the level of damages that would be awarded in the West Bank is less than that in Israel.

In rejecting the first argument the Court noted that the standard of care applicable in the West Bank, even if, *arguendo*, it is less than that in Israel, is the standard by which all the parties have acted. Moreover, even if the action were to be maintained in Israel, it is reasonable to assume that Israel would apply the West Bank standard, since this was the *locus causem* and expectation of the parties. In any event, the argument of standard of care is merely a form of arguing as to different legal norms, and the Court had, consistently with both American and English precedent, rejected this as a basis for an 'injustice' claim.

Similarly, the argument as to the level of damages that would be awarded was rejected. Such a difference does not *per se* constitute an injustice.[22]

The third argument is, however, most interesting and unique to the situation of the Administered Territories. It is based on the fact that the '*intifada*', the Arab uprising in the Gaza Strip and West Bank, has seriously affected the local judicial system in those territories. Thus, as quoted by the Supreme Court, the plaintiff argued that 'the present situation in the territories will burden the proper administration of the case. As a result of the *intifada*, cases wait a long time [before trial and decision] and there are clear difficulties in the execution [of judgments]'. In response to this argument the Court stated:

This argument is of little weight, relatively, when it is set forth between parties who are before us in this matter, even if we ignore the fact that it has not been

---

[22] Compare the *Atiyah* case, n. 2 above, in which the plaintiff argued that the action should not be dismissed in Israel since in the West Bank a statutory limitation on damages would apply in the situation of a work accident. In rejecting the argument, Barak J stated: 'Indeed, it may be that in a foreign [West Bank] court the plaintiff will be awarded lesser damages than he would be awarded in an Israeli court, that determines the matter pursuant to Israeli law, yet this factor is not determinative, since it does not make the Israeli forum a natural one for the adjudication (see Piper Aircraft Co., *supra*), but rather only emphasizes the artificiality of filing the action in an Israeli forum.' N. 2 above, at 386.

proven. As to the execution of the judgment—the same objective difficulties will be present as to execution in the West Bank, even if the action is maintained in Israel [citation omitted, S.G.], and if the appellant [plaintiff] will want to execute a judgment of a West Bank court in Israel, he will be able to avail himself of para. 5(a) of the Order Concerning Judicial Aid, which allows the execution of a judgment from the Administered territories through the regular [Israeli] Executive Authority.

This judicial response as to the argument of difficulties in enforcement seems clearly correct. However, the response to the difficulties in bringing and maintaining an action in the Administered Territories, which difficulties are well known, is more problematic. Is it sufficient to say, in relation to an argument against dismissing an action in Israel in favour of its being brought in the West Bank, that the argument as to difficulties 'is of little weight', since it is being raised in litigation between parties, both of whom are West Bank Palestinian entities? We should also note that, although not raised in this case, in earlier cases concerning the Administered Territories, plaintiffs have argued against a *forum non conveniens* on grounds, *inter alia*, that they wished to present medical expert evidence of Israeli physicians who are reluctant to testify in West Bank or Gaza courts. These arguments have been uniformly rejected.[23].

However, these latter cases preceded the *intifada*, which has not only seriously affected the operation of the local judicial systems in the Administered Territories, but has also had the effect of discouraging Israeli travel to the territories, which may affect the willingness of, for example, Israeli physicians to agree to testify in the local courts in the territories. We should also note that, at the time of writing, Israel and the PLO are negotiating the implementation of the 13 September Declaration of Principles concerning the Gaza Strip and Jericho as a first step toward Palestinian autonomy in the territories. It is to be expected that such implementation will include determination of issues concerning international jurisdiction and *forum non conveniens* as between the courts of Israel and the autonomous areas.

4. Raising the Defence of *Forum Non Conveniens* and the Results of its Determination

In general, Israeli law requires that preliminary defences concerning jurisdiction be raised at the earliest possible opportunity, either by a preliminary motion or, at the latest, at the time the defendant files an answer to the plaintiff's complaints.[24] It would appear that these principles should apply also to the defence of *forum non conveniens*.

[23] See e.g. *Atiyah* v. *Arbatisi*, n. 2 above, at 383–4.
[24] See Israeli Rules of Civ. Proc., R. 502(b); *Root* v. *Fisher* (1965) 19(2) PD 148.

A corollary to the obligation of a defendant to raise issues of lack of international jurisdiction and *forum non conveniens* at an early stage of the proceedings is that the court will determine these issues at such early stage.[25] It would also seem to follow that such a judicial determination should be final and not subject to change at a later stage of the proceedings. The whole purpose of doctrines of international jurisdiction and *forum non conveniens* is to determine whether given litigation should be conducted on the merits in the forum State. It is highly inefficient, if not, indeed, illogical, to conduct adjudication on the merits and then dismiss the action on grounds of lack of international jurisdiction or *forum non conveniens*.

On the other hand, the basic rule of Israeli law is that interim trial court decisions are not final and can be re-examined and changed at any time until judgment. *Prima facie* this rule should apply also to decisions rejecting motions to dismiss the action on grounds of lack of international jurisdiction or *forum non conveniens*. However, in the leading 1986 case of *Ra'ad* v. *Chai*,[26] the court held that, for the reasons stated above, a trial court's rejection of a motion to dismiss an action for lack of international jurisdiction is final, despite the fact that it is an interlocutory decision. Moreover, the trial court cannot change such a decision even if it purported expressly to reserve the authority to do so in its original decision. If this is so as to international jurisdiction it should equally be so as to *forum non conveniens*. And, indeed, the Supreme Court in *Ra'ad* noted that the result as to *forum non conveniens* should follow *a fortiori* from its decision as to international jurisdiction.

And thus the Supreme Court in *Ra'ad* stated that, as a matter of general legal principle, a trial court must determine an issue of *forum non conveniens* at the outset of the proceedings. This determination is final. However, since it was reluctant to overrule expressly a prior Supreme Court decision that had suggested otherwise, the Supreme Court in *Ra'ad* refused to reject the possibility that, under unusual circumstances, a trial court might be justified in postponing a decision on a motion to decline jurisdiction on *forum non conveniens* grounds until a later stage of the proceedings.

In terms of the result of the court accepting a defence of *forum non conveniens* and thus declining jurisdiction on such grounds, the Israeli case law is not uniform as to the terminology used in such declining. Most of the cases use the English-derived terminology, 'stayed'. On the other hand, other cases use the American terminology, i.e., the proceedings are 'dismissed without prejudice'. In our view, the American terminology is preferable as it more adequately describes what occurs. On the other

[25] Compare *Ra'ad* v. *Chai*, n. 20 above.   [26] N. 20 above.

hand, it must be emphasized that the difference is purely semantic. Whichever terminology is used, the result is a final judgment which terminates the proceedings in Israel.

III
DISCRETIONARY DECLINING OF JURISDICTION BASED ON CONSENT OF THE PARTIES

1. JURISDICTION BASED ON CONSENT

Under Israeli law, a party's consent to international jurisdiction in Israel thereby confers such jurisdiction on Israeli courts. This is an independent alternative form of conferring jurisdiction, in addition to serving the party either within or outwith Israel, as discussed above. This consent may be expressed beforehand, as is typical in contractual forum-selection clauses, or once adjudication has begun. In the latter case, the consent need not even be expressed. Rather, a defendant may be taken to have 'consented' to international jurisdiction or waived his defence of lack of international jurisdiction if he does not raise such a defence at the required time and in the proper manner.

In the first case, i.e. prior contractual consent to international jurisdiction in Israel, at the time of the litigation the defendant may attempt to raise the doctrine of *forum non conveniens*. In such a case, Israeli case law does not completely reject the possibility of employing the doctrine of *forum non conveniens* so as to decline jurisdiction. However, the Supreme Court has held that the defendant has an unusually heavy burden in convincing the court to decline jurisdiction. This is so, since, in addition to the usual burden on the defendant to justify a discretionary declining of existing jurisdiction, in this case the defendant has himself *consented* to such jurisdiction and only in a most extreme case will a court enable him to violate his contractual agreement.[27]

2. EXCLUSIVE FORUM-SELECTION CLAUSES THAT PURPORT TO DENY JURISDICTION TO ISRAELI COURTS

It is quite common in international transactions for the parties to provide for exclusive jurisdiction in a given State as to any disputes arising out of the transaction. The issue then arises of the effect of such a clause providing for exclusive jurisdiction in another State when an action is brought in

---

[27] See *Multi-lock Inc* v. *Rav-bariach Ltd* (1982) 36(3) PD 272.

Israel, in apparent violation of such exclusive forum-selection clauses. The assumption is, of course, that, except for the existence of such a clause, the Israeli courts have jurisdiction and would not otherwise dismiss the action on grounds of *forum non conveniens.*

Under these circumstances Israeli law provides first that an ambiguous contract clause is presumed not to confer exclusive jurisdiction on the other State. A clause should be interpreted as one of exclusive forum-selection only if it expressly so states or that is clearly the necessary intent of the parties. And, indeed, in at least one case, the Israeli Supreme Court really strained to interpret such a clause as not conferring exclusive jurisdiction on another State.[28] Once, however, it is clear that the clause involved must be interpreted as conferring exclusive jurisdiction on another State the following rules apply:

    (a) The clause itself does not oust the jurisdiction of the Israeli courts since the parties cannot deny jurisdiction that the Israeli law has conferred;

    (b) However, except in cases of exceptional circumstances, an Israeli court will nevertheless dismiss the action as a matter of judicial discretion, as it will not allow a party to violate its agreement.

Thus, in effect, the situation comes down to a question whether in a given case there are special circumstances which justify not dismissing the action despite the forum-selection clause providing for exclusive jurisdiction in another State. The burden of proving such special circumstances is on the plaintiff, and the situation is analogous to that discussed above where the plaintiff argues that there are special circumstances which should prevent a dismissal on *forum non conveniens* grounds, despite the fact that the defendant has proven that Israel is not a 'natural forum'. Thus the discussion above as to the effect of differences in the law that would be applied in Israel as compared with the other State on the issue of *forum non conveniens* is equally applicable to exclusive forum-selection clauses.

The clearest, albeit rare, case of such special circumstances is where the other State is one in which the plaintiff will not be allowed to bring his action at all or will be faced with clearly demonstrable discrimination. Such, indeed, occurred where such other State for the Israeli plaintiff was Iraq, the contract having been entered into before the plaintiff emigrated to Israel from that State.[29]

More common contentions as to special circumstances involve joinder of parties. In the leading 1945 case, *Narrom Roumanian Maritime and Fluvial Navigation* v. *Ha'sneh, Israel Insurance Co Ltd*,[30] involving a subrogation action by an Israeli insurance company against a Roumanian shipping

---

[28] *Korpol* v. *Horowitz* (1979) 34(1) PD 260.
[29] *Oneon Insurance Co Ltd* v. *Moshe* (1963) 17 PD 646.   [30] (1965) 19(2) PD 159.

company for damage to cargo carried by the defendant, it was argued that the forum-selection clause providing for exclusive jurisdiction in Roumania should not prevent the litigation in Israel since the plaintiff had joined in the action additional Israeli defendants in relation to whom there was no such clause. This joinder of defendants was pursuant to the liberal joinder-of-parties rule applicable in Israel which provides that a plaintiff 'may join in one action all defendants against whom he seeks any relief—whether jointly, severally, or jointly and severally—due to one act or transaction or a series of acts or transactions, or as a result of any of these, and if separate actions were initiated against them there would have arisen a common question, either of law or fact'.

This rule and the parallel one discussed below as to joinder of plaintiffs reflect the desire of Israeli law to enable plaintiffs to determine in one action all the aspects of any given transaction with the resultant procedural convenience that such joinder creates. Thus, the plaintiff argued that this norm of Israeli procedure concerning joinder should prevail over the exclusive forum-selection clause, as upholding such clause in favour of the Roumanian defendant would mean that the Israeli plaintiff would be forced to litigate against this defendant in Roumania and against the other defendants, all of which were Israeli companies, in Israel. Moreover in this case, the damage to the cargo was discovered in Israel and the witnesses to such damage were all Israeli inhabitants. In holding that the joinder of such additional Israeli defendants should not prevent the dismissal of the action as to the Roumanian defendant that enjoyed the forum selection clause providing for exclusive jurisdiction in its home State, the Supreme Court noted that it is most common in international transportation transactions for there to be other local companies that could be joined with the foreign international carrier, and thus acceptance of such joinder as a basis for not honouring the exclusive forum-selection clause would effectively avoid such clauses. Moreover, the question of the witnesses was merely a matter of convenience which should not prevent enforcement of the exclusive forum selection clause.

However, in a 1969 case this ruling on joined defendants was distinguished from the case of joined plaintiffs.[31] As to the latter, the Supreme Court held, albeit in a dictum, that the joinder of plaintiffs did represent a reason for not enforcing an exclusive forum-selection clause which was in effect only as to one of the joined plaintiffs. It should be noted that the Israeli rule as to the joinder of plaintiffs is parallel to that quoted above as to defendants. It provides that 'there may be joined as plaintiffs in one action all who claim relief—whether joint, several, or joint and several—due to one act or transaction or a series of acts or transactions, or as a

---

[31] *Vizra Israeli Automotive Co Ltd* v. *Volkswagenwerk AG* (1969) 23(1) PD 581.

result of any of these, and if they had initiated separate actions there would have arisen a common question, either of law or fact'.

The distinction drawn by the Court between joined defendants and joined plaintiffs was based on the fact that, whereas upholding the exclusive forum-selection clause in the case of joined defendants completely exempted the defendant protected by the clause from having to litigate in Israel, this was not so in the case of joined plaintiffs. In the latter situation, even if the exclusive forum-selection clause were to be enforced, the defendant would still have to litigate in Israel as to the other joined plaintiffs, as to whom there was no such clause.

Moreover, despite the liberal joinder-of-parties rule in Israel, joinder of plaintiffs as with joinder of defendants still requires a minimal connection among the joined parties as quoted above. Thus, said the Court, it is also in the interest of the defendant that such joinder not be severed because of the exclusive forum-litigation clause applicable to one of the plaintiffs. While one might question the correctness of the paternalism involved in the Court telling the defendant what is for the latter's own good, it is true that, because of the necessary connection among the joined parties, enforcing an exclusive forum-selection clause as to joined plaintiffs benefits less the defendant than does its enforcement as to joined defendants.

While this difference is merely a matter of degree, it could support a difference in result. This is so since, as discussed above, dismissal of a case because of an exclusive forum-selection clause is viewed as a discretionary dismissal, not one compelled by the clause itself. In such a case, the court could rightly weigh the harm caused to the norm of Israeli law which seeks to allow plaintiffs to join all relevant parties in one proceeding and the procedural convenience attained thereby against the need to enforce the contractual commitments.

In such an overall determination a difference as to the benefit to the protected defendant such as that involved in the cases of joined defendants, whereby the protected defendant is exempted completely from litigation concerning the transaction or occurrence in Israel, and that concerning joined plaintiffs, where the protected defendant must still litigate in Israel against other plaintiffs involved in the common act or transaction, could well tilt the balance in different directions.

13

Italy

NICOLO TROCKER

Professor, Dipartimento di diritto comparato,
Università degli Studie di Firenze

CONTENTS

I
INTRODUCTION:
THE PROBLEM OF PARALLEL PROCEEDINGS

Expansive contemporary notions of jurisdiction, both to prescribe and to adjudicate, often make it possible for the courts of more than one country to hear a civil dispute. Concurrent jurisdiction causes concurrent litigation.[1]

Differences in procedure and substantive law between available fora give private parties strong incentives to litigate in one country rather than another. 'Forum-shopping'—it has been said—'is a dirty word; but it is only a pejorative way of saying that, if you offer a plaintiff a choice of jurisdictions, he will naturally choose the one in which he thinks his case can be most favourably presented: this should be a matter neither for surprise nor for indignation'.[2]

In some cases parties to a civil dispute will find it advantageous to start litigation in the courts of more than one nation, with each party seeking resolution of the dispute in what is perceived to be the forum most favourable to it. Strategies of this kind may assume a variety of forms. There are situations in which one party seeks declaratory relief in one forum and the opponent asks for affirmative relief with regard to the same legal relationship in another forum; and there are situations where the same parties, although in a different position, file the same suit in different fora.

Lawyers are familiar with cases of parallel actions, protective or reactive, where a suit is started in a domestic or foreign forum and the defendant to that action seeks to institute proceedings as plaintiff elsewhere, notably before a court within the boundaries of the State of his domicile or residence, or before one with whose organization and function he is familiar. Parallel actions are instituted in a growing number of civil disputes having an international or transnational character, arising in fields of law such as international sale of goods, product liability, antitrust, family affairs, etc.

The questions are whether and to what extent proceedings in one country have the effect of barring proceedings in another; whether and to what extent a given legal system simply ignores any overlap of its jurisdiction with that of a foreign country; whether and to what extent parallel proceedings in different fora are found inherently undesirable or are allowed to go forward to judgment. We are, or course, familiar with the general rule in domestic law that an action must be dismissed (or stayed) if it is shown that another action, involving the same parties and the same claim (or another related action), has previously been instituted and is still pending in a court of the same jurisdiction. Will a suit filed in a domestic

---

[1] The problem of parallel proceedings has received increasing attention in recent times. See, in Italian writing Di Blase, *Connessione e litispendenza nella Convenzione di Bruxelles* (1993); La China, 'La connessione nel diritto processuale civile internazionale' in [1988] *Rivista di diritto processuale* 344; Franchi, 'La competenza giurisdizionale tra convenzioni internazionali e diritto interno' in [1987] *Rivista trimestrale di diritto e procedura civile* 237. For the common law, in particular for the US scenario, see e.g. Teitz, (1992) 26 *Int. Lawyer* 21.

[2] Lord Simon of Glaisdale in *The Atlantic Star* [1974] AC 436 at 471.

court be similarly treated if the same (or a related) suit is already pending in the courts of a foreign jurisdiction?

Closely related to these questions is the problem of the impact which agreements between parties to devolve litigation for resolution to a foreign jurisdiction or to arbitrators who render their decisions abroad have upon the exercise of jurisdiction on the part of national courts. Will pending or prospective litigation in the domestic jurisdiction be barred by such agreements? Do the national courts have a duty to decline jurisdiction by force of the effects given to contractual choices of foreign fora?

Lastly, there is the question of the kind of power with which courts faced with issues of parallel proceedings should be vested: should they be able to exercise discretion in deciding the issue, or should there be a clear-cut non-discretionary rule? Is the 'first-filed' rule, according to which courts must 'automatically' give way to the forum applied to first, an adequate response to the problems under consideration or should preference be given to an individualized search for the most appropriate forum?

This chapter examines these questions and issues in the light of Italian law and practice.

We shall start with a description of the rules of *lis pendens* in the domestic setting. Following this is an analysis of the provisions and doctrines elaborated on the subject of *lis pendens* in international relations. Next, the problem of the effect of forum-selection and arbitration agreements in 'ousting' or 'staying' the jurisdiction of national courts will be considered. Finally, the paper will deal with the doctrine of *forum non conveniens* and the reasons it has traditionally been excluded under the Italian system.

II
LIS PENDENS IN DOMESTIC LAW

The domestic law of many countries of the civil law tradition considers the problem of parallel proceedings primarily with regard to disputes involving the *same* parties and the *same* cause of action. Conceptually the doctrine of *lis pendens* (*litispendenza*) has been tailored for this kind of situation.[3]

An express statutory provision on the subject is contained in Article 39 of the Italian Code of Civil Procedure, the first paragraph of which reads as follows: 'When the same case has been brought before different courts,

---

[3] For a comparative analysis see Pålsson, 'The Institute of Lis Pendens in International Civil Procedure' in (1970) XIV *Scandinavian Studies in Law* 65; Kerameus, 'Problemi attuali della litispendenza internazionale nelprocesso civile' in [1990] *Rivista di diritto processuale* 1001.

the court second seised shall at any stage of the proceeding and even on its own motion, decline jurisdiction and order the case before it to be stricken from the docket.' Which court becomes first seised for the purpose of the present provision is determined by the third paragraph of Article 39. The 'first seised' court is the one before which the requirement for proceedings to become definitively pending are first fulfilled, i.e. where service on the defendant of the document initiating the proceeding (stating the factual and legal bases of the plaintiff's claim and the remedy or remedies requested) first occurs.

Factors relevant to the application of the *lis pendens* rule in domestic law are: (a) the *principle of priority*, according to which preference is given to the action first started, and (b) the *principle of identity* pursuant to which the parallel actions must involve the same parties and the same subject matter.[4] Where cases are more loosely related, different principles apply.

As to the effect of *lis pendens*, Article 39 requires the court second seised to dismiss the action without trial on the merits, either on its own motion or on objection raised by the defendant. This is the only solution available. The *lis pendens* rule is not confided to the court's discretion; nor can the court simply stay the pending action until the action in the other forum is resolved. The solution is somewhat mechanical: considerations of convenience or equity in favour of maintaining the action in the second rather than in the first court, or in favour of staying rather than dismissing the second action, are not included. In addition, except for the case where the court second seised has exclusive 'competence', the second court may not itself examine the 'competence' of the first court.[5] The principle of priority prevails over the rules of competence.[6]

The objectives of the *lis pendens* rule are: avoidance of separate adjudications on the same subject matter; protection of the defendant from the costs of a second action; prevention of the delivery of conflicting judgments by different courts of the same country.[7]

Since the *lis pendens* rule is confined to situations of identity of parties and issues in the two actions, a separate statutory provision, Article 39(2), considers the case of what has been labelled 'partial lis pendens',[8] i.e. the case of two actions pending between the same parties having the same

---

[4] The question of what constitutes the same action is the subject of elaborate discussion and rich case law. For detailed references see Mandrioli, *Corso di diritto processuale civile* (1993), i. 223; Monteleone, 'Litispendenza' in *Enciclopedia Giuridica Treccani* (1990), xix. See also Consolo, 'Domanda giudiziale' in *Digesto delle Discipline Giuridiche, Sezione Civile* (1991).

[5] For the meaning of the terms 'jurisdiction' (*giurisdizione*) and 'competence' (*competenza*), see generally, Cappelletti and Perillo, *Civil Procedure in Italy* (1965), 80.

[6] There is a special procedure for contesting decisions rendered on the issue of *lis pendens*, called *Regolamento di competenza* (Art. 42 of the Code of Civil Procedure). The attack has to be taken directly to the Corte di Cassazione.

[7] See Mandrioli, n. 4 above, at 225.   [8] Cappelletti and Perillo, n. 5 above, at 107.

causa petendi, but one with a broader *petitum* than the other. The situation is defined in Italian law as *continenza*: one case is contained within another. This may be illustrated by the following example: a suit for an unpaid loan instalment is contained within a case for the recovery of the entire loan.[9]

According to Article 39(2), where a situation of *continenza* occurs, the court first seised is the proper forum, if that court is competent also to hear the case with the broader *petitum*. Otherwise, the proper forum is that before which the second case with the more encompassing *petitum* has been instituted. Preference is given not to the action started first but to the court in which, in accordance with the applicable rules of competence, both actions may be heard. Despite the inconvenience which may be involved for the parties, the action before the 'improper' forum is stricken from the docket and must be 'transferred' to the proper court.

Various other provisions of the Italian Code of Civil Procedure deal with joinder and consolidation of related actions (Articles 31–6, 103–4, 273–4) and with the stay of proceedings in situations of claims involving collateral issues (Article 295).[10] The objectives of these provisions are not dissimilar to those pursued by the *lis pendens* rule of Article 39: conservation of judicial resources, procedural economy, uniformity of judgments.

In brief, in Italian law a multiplicity of statutory provisions provides guidance for situations where parallel proceedings are involved, where the same or related disputes are litigated before more than one court of the forum. The powers conferred upon the courts by these provisions are inherently not discretionary. When the requirements for *lis pendens*, joinder, consolidation, etc. have been met, the courts have a duty either to decline to adjudicate (and direct the parties to the competent court) or to stay proceedings. Little space is left for an inquiry into the circumstances of the individual case and for a balancing of interests approach.[11]

---

[9] It is worth noting that according to certain case law the principle of *continenza* also applies in situations where the same parties, although in a different position, are engaged in two legal proceedings which are based on the same contractual relationship; where, e.g., a creditor sues his debtor for a performance judgment and the debtor sues the creditor for a judgment declaring the non-existence of the debt in question, or declaring the invalidity of a contract clause: Corte di Cassazione (Cass.), 22 Feb. 1984, no. 5341 [1985] I Foro It. 796. For further indications see Mandrioli, n. 4 above, at 226; Balbi, 'Connessione e continenza nel diritto processuale civile' in *Digesto delle Discipline Giuridiche, Sezione Civile* (1988), 457.

[10] For a more detailed account see Cappelletti and Perillo, n. 5 above, at 102.

[11] See, however, Arts. 103, 274, 279 of the Code of Civil Procedure which attribute to the courts a discretionary power to consolidate or separate proceedings involving related actions. For an extensive treatment of the subject see Tarzia, 'Connessione di cause e processo simultaneo' in [1988] *Rivista trimestrale di diritto e procedura civile* 409.

III
LIS PENDENS IN
INTERNATIONAL RELATIONS

1. The Traditional Rule of Non-recognition of Foreign *Lis Pendens*

Legal systems vary greatly in their approach to the issue of what influence upon the exercise of domestic jurisdiction should be attributed to the pendency of concurrent litigation in a foreign country. Some take the view that no significance should be attached to the existence of foreign proceedings; others give deference to foreign litigation when certain requirements are fulfilled (such as the existence of jurisdiction to adjudicate of the foreign court or the possibility of recognition of the foreign judgment in the forum); others again tend to apply to international *lis pendens* rules and principles developed with regard to the domestic setting.[12] In general it can be said that the attitude of a legal system toward the effect of *lis alibi pendens* is strictly related to the attitude taken with regard to the issue of recognition of foreign judgments. Where foreign judgments are refused recognition in a country, the foreign *lis pendens* cannot be recognized either. Rules of *lis pendens* have a rational sense only in so far as the expected judgment is capable of acquiring legal force in the forum.

At the beginning of this century, when the issue of whether the institution of an action in a foreign court could have the effect of barring the exercise of national jurisdiction became the subject of elaborate discussions in Italian legal writing, different opinions were expressed. Some held that the pendency of an action abroad could not be used as an adequate defence to an action involving the same parties and the same subject matter in Italy; others expressed some doubts on the appropriateness of this rule from the viewpoint of international co-operation and suggested the possibility of recognizing a *lis alibi pendens* doctrine in transnational cases under certain conditions.[13]

The most restrictive of these views found its way into the Code of Civil Procedure which was enacted in 1940 and came into force in 1942. Included in the Code was an express provision on the subject (Article 3),

---

[12] For a comparative discussion see Pålsson, n. 3 above, at 68; Kerameus, n. 3 above, at 1003; Habscheid, 'Zur Berücksichtigung der Rechtshängigkeit eines ausländischen Verfahrens' in (1967) 31 *Rabels Zeitschrift für ausländisches und internationales Privatrecht* 254; Schütze, 'Die Wirkungen ausländischer Rechtshängigkeit in inländischen Verfahren' in [1991] *Zeitschrift für Zivilprozess* 136; Schlesinger, Baade, Damaska, and Herzog, *Comparative Law* (1988), 413, and *Supplement 1994*, 112.

[13] See Ottolenghi, 'Un nuovo procedimento per l'esecuzione delle sentenze straniere' in [1919] I *Rivista di diritto commerciale* 607; Ghirardini, 'La litispendenza nel diritto processuale civile internazionale' in [1907] *Rivista di diritto internazionale* 229 at 318.

reading that 'Italian jurisdiction is not excluded by the pendency of the same case or another connected with it, before a foreign court.' The existence of foreign proceedings is therefore disregarded, both in cases where the actions are the same and in those where the actions are merely related.

Various reasons can be suggested to explain this rule. One point of view often underlined is the lack, at the international level, of clear limits on the exercise of adjudicatory jurisdiction. As it is put by scholars ard court decisions, in an international community of sovereign states, each State, as *superiorem non recognoscens*, has the authority to decide for itself under which conditions jurisdiction to adjudicate will be granted. National jurisdiction cannot be barred by the assertion of jurisdiction of a foreign country.[14]

A closely related explanation of the rule embodied in Article 3 of the Code can be found in the desire of the Italian codifiers of 1940 to assert the jurisdictional power of the State in order to safeguard Italian citizens' access to Italian courts, and to safeguard the State's legal order. The same idea is obvious in the provision of Article 2 of the Code of Civil Procedure which prevents any derogation from the jurisdiction of Italian courts.[15] In order to understand the rule of Article 3 it is also important to recall Italian law's approach to foreign judgments. In principle such judgments have no effect in Italy until they have been validated by an Italian court (Articles 796 ff. of the Code of Civil Procedure).[16] It thus appeared natural to establish that courts have a duty to decline jurisdiction only *after* a proceeding to validate a foreign judgment rendered on the same or on a connected claim had been initiated.

On the other hand, it did not seem wise to anticipate the preclusive effect of foreign litigation and to consider the likelihood of the foreign judgment being recognized and capable of enforcement in Italy. According to the position taken by leading authors in support of the solution adopted by the Code on the topic of foreign *lis pendens*, if the effect of *lis alibi pendens* were to be made subject to the condition of the expected recognition of the foreign judgment in Italy, the courts would be required to make a *prediction* whether the judgment would be recognized or not.

---

[14] Carbone, 'Il regime della litispendenza nelle Convenzioni dell'Aja e di Bruxelles' in [1968] *Rivista di diritto internazionale privato e processuale* [RDIPP] 8; Scarpa, 'Diritto processuale interno e Convenzione di Bruxelles. Instaurazione della litispendenza' in [1985] *Giustizia civile* 5. Corte di Cassazione, 4 Mar. 1978, no. 1092 [1979] RDIPP 711. Corte di Cassazione, 20 Dec. 1978, no. 6111 [1980] RDIPP 64; Tribunale di Genova, 23 July 1983, [1985] RDIPP 421. For further references see *Rassegna di giurisprudenza sul Codice di procedura civile*, ed. by Stella Richter (1967) i. 7, 27.

[15] See e.g. La China, n. 1 above, at 355. Corte di Cassazione, 12 June 1969, no 2078 [1969] I Foro It. 2158.

[16] See Cappelletti and Perillo, n. 5 above, at 367; Carella, 'Sentenza civile straniera' in Enciclopedia del Diritto (1989), xli. 1272.

Such predictions, however, cannot be made with any certainty and completeness. It might be feasible to assess some of the requirements for recognition (e.g. the jurisdiction of the foreign forum) as soon as the question of *lis pendens* arises; others, in particular the public policy clause which recurs in the rules on recognition of foreign judgments, can only be fully ascertained *after* the foreign judgment has been delivered.[17]

Modern legal writers advocate a more liberal approach to recognition of foreign *lis pendens*. The rule contained in the provision of Article 3 of the Code of Civil Procedure is criticized as 'nationalistic', unreasonable, and contrary to the needs of judicial co-operation in these days.[18] Proposals to amend the provision are at present under discussion.[19]

At the same time it must be stressed that the traditional Italian response to litigation in multiple fora is to allow parallel proceedings to (be started and to) continue simultaneously in the courts of two or more countries. Article 3 of the Code of Civil Procedure simply ignores any overlap of jurisdiction with foreign courts; it is not designed to foreclose (parallel) proceedings in foreign fora.[20] In Italian law dual litigation cannot be restrained by means of injunctive relief designed to halt an action in a foreign nation in order to maintain the action exclusively in the domestic court.[21]

Italian courts do not assert any power to enjoin parties from bringing or continuing (reactive or protective) proceedings in the courts of another country while proceedings on the same matter are pending in Italy. The authority to grant antisuit injunctions (which exists in common law countries) is not part of the Italian tradition.

[17] Morelli, *Diritto processuale civile internazionale* (1954), 168; Vitta, *Corso di diritto internazionale privato e processuale* (4th edn., 1991), 22.

[18] See Sorace, *Litispendenza, Enciclopedia del Diritto* (1972), xxiv. 879; Gaja, 'La Convenzione di Bruxelles del 1968 e la riforma delle norme italiane sulla giurisdizione e sul riconoscimento delle sentenze straniere' in *La Convenzione giudiziaria di Bruxelles e la riforma del processo civile italiano* (1985), 23; Starace, 'La disciplina dell'ambito della giurisdizione italiana nel progetto di riforma' in [1992] *Rivista di diritto internazionale* 8; Di Blase, n. 1 above, at 80.

[19] See the new rule recognizing foreign *lis pendens* included in Art. 7 of the *Disegno di legge presentato il 29 aprile 1993 dal Ministro di grazia e giustizia di concerto col Ministro degli affari esteri e col Ministro dell'interno*, in *La riforma del diritto internazionale privato e processuale*, Gaja (ed.) (1994), 401 at 407. For a critical appraisal of the proposed solution see Starace, *La disciplina dell'ambito della giurisdizione italiana nel disegno di legge*, ivi, 271; Carbone, *In tema di valore del diritto straniero, deroga alla giurisdizione, litispendenza e disciplina dei contratti internazionali*, ivi, 297, 303.

[20] See La China, n. 1 above, at 355.

[21] It should be noted, however, that pursuant to Art. 4(2) of the Code of Civil Procedure the litigation of one dispute before an Italian court may form the basis for jurisdiction over another related dispute. Therefore, if related claims are being pursued, consolidation of all litigation may be sought in Italy (as the moving party's preferred forum). E.g., an alien guarantor may be called into a case if a case is pending between the parties in privity, although the guarantor may not otherwise be subject to the jurisdiction of the Italian courts: see Cappelletti and Perillo, n. 5 above, at 88–9.

2. Domestic *Lis Pendens* as a Bar to Recognition of Foreign Judgments

A powerful instrument to bar foreign proceedings, not at the stage of their institution and their unfolding, but at the stage of their conclusion is offered to litigants by another principle of Italian law which considers the pendency of a domestic suit to be preclusive of the recognition of foreign judgments, irrespective of whether the domestic or the foreign suit was started first. Recognition may be paralysed where the foreign suit has been instituted in disregard of domestic *lis pendens*, as well as where the domestic suit has been initiated in disregard of foreign *lis pendens*.

An express provision to this effect exists in the Code of Civil Procedure (Article 797(1), no. 6): 'If an action is instituted in Italy before the foreign judgment becomes final, no proceeding may be brought to validate the foreign judgment'. The rule—an expression of the marked preference given to the domestic jurisdiction—clearly provides litigants with a kind of 'enjoining weapon'. If jurisdiction to adjudicate can be established in Italy, a party who fears losing the foreign suit or who has already been defeated in the foreign action, by bringing an action in Italy on the 'same matter' before the foreign judgment becomes final in the foreign State, can effectively prevent recognition and/or enforcement of the foreign judgment in Italy.[22]

In applying Article 797(1), no. 6, courts do not investigate the purpose for which the action was started—whether it is 'vexatious' or unjust to the defendant, or constitutes an abuse of the court's jurisdiction in some way. The doctrine of abuse of judicial process developed and used in other procedural contexts is not applied here. Established case law emphasizes that the only assessment courts have to make with regard to the provision at hand concerns the 'objective fact' of the pendency of an action in Italy prior to a final decision by the foreign court.[23]

This is consistent with the idea (laid down in Article 3) that foreign litigation is immaterial and no deference is owed to foreign courts before they deliver a final decision. The implications of the rule could be avoided only by abandoning the actual principle which demands observance of the forum's *lis pendens* irrespective of the institution of a suit abroad.

3. Foreign *Lis Pendens* under Bilateral Conventions

Exceptions to the traditional rule of non-recognition of foreign *lis pendens* are provided by bilateral conventions with certain countries on recog-

[22] This rule is criticized by some scholars: see Cappelletti and Perillo, n. 5 above, at 378; from a comparative perspective Pålsson, n. 3 above, at 81. For the rule to operate there must be an identity of parties but not of the 'legal basis' of the claim.

[23] Pertinent judicial decisions are CA, Milan, 10 May 1968, in [1968] *Giustizia Civile, Repertorio*, voce *Delibazione*, n. 29; Cass., 9 Dec. 1979, no. 6595, in [1979] Foro Padano 361.

nition and enforcement of judgments, in particular by the treaties with France, Germany, Switzerland, and Austria which contain express provisions on the subject.[24]

It may be stressed at the outset that, by establishing a rule of international *lis pendens*, the conventions seek to prevent conflicting and incompatible decisions being given by the courts of the Contracting States and thereby to improve the recognition and enforcement of judgments. Little consideration is given to other aspects related to the phenomenon of parallel proceedings, in particular to the problem of forum-shopping. In addition, the provisions on the subject give no uniform answer to the issues of the extent to and the conditions under which proceedings in a foreign court have the effect of *lis pendens* in a domestic suit.

While, pursuant to Article 19 of the bilateral convention between Italy and France of 3 June 1930, a new action in the domestic forum is barred by the pendency of the same action, as well as by the pendency of another action 'connected' with it, before the foreign court,[25] the rules contained in the conventions between Italy and Germany of 9 March 1936 (Article 11) and between Italy and Austria of 16 November 1971 (Article 12) are narrower in their scope. They are concerned only with cases where the co-existing proceedings involve the *same* parties and the *same* cause of action.[26]

Differences also exist in so far as some of the provisions—Article 19 of the Italo–French Convention, Article 11 of the Italo–German Convention and Article 8 of the Italo–Swiss Convention of 3 January 1933—subordinate the effect of the *lis pendens* rule to an application by one of the parties, whereas Article 12 of the Italo–Austrian Convention seems to confer on the courts the power to attach significance to the existence of foreign proceedings.[27] Article 12 of the Italo–Austrian Convention differs from the

---

[24] See Di Blase, n. 1 above; Perassi, 'Il regolamento della litispendenza in alcune convenzioni internazionali' in [1953] *Rivista di diritto internazionale* 357.

[25] Art. 19 reads as follows: 'les juridictions de l'un des Etats contractants dovent, si l'une des parties le demande, se dessaisir des contestations portees devant elles quand ces contestations sont déjà pendantes devant les juridictions de l'autre pays, ou quand elles sont connexes à d'autres contestations déjà pendantes entre les mêmes parties devant ces juridictions, sous réserve que celles-ci soient compétentes selon les règles du présent Titre'. For comments see Perassi, 'Su l'art. 19 della Convenzione tra l'Italia e la Francia sull'esecuzione delle sentenze' in [1935] *Rivista di diritto internazionale* 392; Arangio and Ruiz, *Litispendenza e competenza del giudice del luogo di conclusione o di esecuzione del contratto nella convenzione italo-francese del 1930* ivi (1957), 419; Franchi, 'Domande reciproche di separazione coniugale tra italiani in Francia e Italia e rilevanza della connessione' in (1966) I *Giurisprudenza Italiana* 1, 607.

[26] See La China, n. 1 above, 375; Perassi, n. 24 above, at 358

[27] See Matscher, 'La nuova Convenzione italo-austriaca per il riconoscimento e l'esecuzione delle sentenze in materia civile e commerciale' in [1975] RDIPP 253. As to the solution adopted by the earlier conventions, see Perassi, n. 24 above, at 359.

provisions expressed in the other conventions also in as much as it makes recognition of foreign *lis pendens* subject, not to the sole condition that the foreign court has jurisdiction under the rules of the Convention, but to the positive assessment of all other factors affecting the recognition of the expected foreign judgment.[28]

As to the legal consequence of *lis alibi pendens*, the rules found in the bilateral conventions show a common core by resorting to an *abstention doctrine*. The court second seised is required to 'abstain' from deciding the dispute brought before it, thereby permitting the court first seised alone to hear the case. The operational boundaries of this doctrine deserve some further analysis.

4. Recognition of Foreign *Lis Pendens*: Time Factor or Proper Court?

In principle, according to the provisions of the bilateral conventions the obligation on any court other than the court first seised to abstain from hearing a case, of its own motion or on objection raised by the defendant, is compulsory in nature. Article 19 of the Italo–French Convention clearly states that 'Les jurisdictions de l'un des Etats contractants *doivent* . . . se dessaisir des contestations portées devant elles'; similarly Article 11 of the Italo–German Convention provides that 'The judicial authorities of one of the two States *shall* abstain from hearing disputes brought before them'.

In Italian legal writing and case law it is held that the only form this reaction may take is the *dismissal* of the pending suit. The abstention rule seems not to be intended to allow the more flexible form of staying the pending action until an action in another forum is resolved.[29] It is also argued that, when dealing with matters of litispendence, courts are asked to carry out an investigation conceived largely as mechanical. In order to retain or decline jurisdiction courts need only to assess certain prerequisites which are defined in an objective manner and leave no space for subjective appraisal. The prerequisites include the following factors: (a) priority of the action initiated abroad; (b) identity of or connexity between the concurrent actions; (c) jurisdiction to adjudicate of the foreign court or expected recognition of the foreign judgment in the forum. Where these

---

[28] Matscher, n. 27 above, at 254. See also Art. 14 of the Italo–Belgian Convention of 6 Apr. 1962. The same standpoint of recognizing foreign *lis pendens* where the expected decision in the foreign proceedings will be entitled to recognition in Italy is adopted by Art 7 of the proposed Italian conflict of laws statute: n. 19 above.

[29] Cass., 17 Mar. 1983, no. 1917 [1984] RDIPP 345 at 349. This is also due to the fact that according to the common view the *lis pendens* rule operates only where identical claims are pursued in two forums. In the case of related claims Art. 3 of the Code of Civil Procedure applies. See La China, n. 1 above, at 373.

requirements are met, dismissal of the action seems to be the only solution available.

In principle, courts are not allowed to go beyond this inquiry and to evaluate factors different from those listed by the statutory provisions. In particular they are not supposed to take into consideration whether or not the foreign forum appears to be 'in a better position' to decide the dispute, whether or not the foreign proceedings offer satisfactory guarantees of fair trial, or whether or not the foreign action has been instituted simply with a view to preventing litigation in the domestic forum.[30]

In recent years, however, a different trend has also made itself felt in judicial decisions. Opinions rendered by Italian courts, in particular with regard to Article 11 of the Italo–German Convention, seem to favour a softening of the traditional view. According to these opinions, in order to allow a defence of foreign *lis pendens* the fact that an action has been instituted abroad is not sufficient. The *lis pendens* effect cannot be attached to the purely objective fact of the initiation of proceedings in another jurisdiction. Attention has to be given to the handling and development of the case.[31] The rule recognizing foreign *lis pendens*—emphasizes a decision of the Tribunale di Milano—is not intended to provide the basis for dilatory tactics or other disloyal manœuvers by the party who started an action first. The purpose of Article 11 of the Convention is to co-ordinate the jurisdiction of the two Contracting States and to secure the enforcement of judgments, not to allow or to favour strategies that are an abuse of the judicial process in some way.[32]

German courts have gone even further in qualifying the application of Article 11 of the bilateral Convention. It has been held that an action for divorce in Germany is not barred by an action concerning the same subject matter first started in Italy by the defendant to the German suit, if under the circumstances of the case it is shown that the foreign (Italian) court will render a decision with *unreasonable delay*. In the view of the German Bundesgerichtshof courts have the power to not recognize the preclusive effect of the action pending abroad, if the dismissal of the action brought in the forum would deprive the plaintiff of his legitimate expectations of a speedy decision and an effective protection of his rights.[33] The principle of good faith also applies to the rules of procedure. In situations of

---

[30] For extensive information see Franchi, *La litispendenza* (1963). A more flexible approach echoing the *forum non conveniens* doctrine is advocated by some modern writers. See Carbone, n. 19 above, at 303.

[31] See generally Bariatti, 'L'efficacia delle sentenze in materia civile e commerciale ai sensi della Convenzione italo-tedesca del 1936' in [1981] RDIPP 638.

[32] Tribunale, Milan, 17 Mar. 1975, in [1976] RDIPP 805.

[33] BGH, 26 Jan. 1983, in [1983] NJW 1269. For a critical appraisal of the decision see Luther, 'Die Grenzen der Sperrwirkung einer auslandischen Rechtshangigheit' [1984] IPRax 141; Tortorici, 'Licet iniuriam iniuria repellere?' in [1983] *Il Diritto di famiglia e delle persone* 528.

excessive delay such as the one at hand—the Court concluded—the recognition of foreign *lis pendens* would cause unreasonable hardship for the plaintiff.[34]

This trend deserves consideration in so far as it shows that the time factor (the principle of priority) cannot always be the key to determining whether foreign *lis pendens* should or should not have effect. Exceptions to the priority principle need to be introduced when either party endeavours to delay court proceedings or impede a judgment from becoming conclusive by unjustifiable tactics. To decide otherwise would encourage (unfair) races to commence proceedings.[35] After all, forum-shoppers are well aware that the differences between litigating in different jurisdictions are much greater than litigating in different courts of the same jurisdiction.

5. Lis Pendens and the Brussels Convention: The Principle of Identity Revisited

In domestic law, according to a widely accepted rule, the doctrine of *lis pendens* applies only to cases of *identity* between actions successively brought in different courts. Article 39 of the Italian Code of Civil Procedure reflects this attitude by referring to situations where the 'same case' is involved. Other rules offer guidance for the cases where related or 'connected' actions are involved (II, above).

Identity of claims is also usually required under the bilateral conventions recognizing the effect of foreign *lis pendens*. Only Article 19 of the Italo–French Convention extends the abstention rule to parallel proceedings in which related actions are simultaneously litigated before courts of the two Contracting States. The question of what constitutes 'identity of claims' therefore becomes crucial to the operation of the *lis pendens* rule in international relations.

In general, it can be said that there is consensus that the requirement of *subjective identity* is satisfied even where the position of the parties is not the same in the two concurring suits. This situation is most common in transnational divorce cases—with one party petitioning for divorce in country A and the other party asking for divorce in country B in order to react to litigation in country A, and in contractual disputes where the seller sues the buyer for the goods sold in a domestic court and the buyer sues for reduction in purchase price abroad.[36]

---

[34] A similar approach can be found in Art. 9 of the new Swiss Private International Law Statute of 1987 which requires dismissal of the Swiss action brought second if it is to be anticipated that the foreign court will render, *within* a reasonable time, a decision that will probably be recognized in Switzerland.

[35] See also OLG Frankfurt, 8 Dec. 1986 [1988] IPRax 24.

[36] See generally Sawaki, 'Battle of Lawsuits. Lis Pendens in International Relations' (1979–80) 23 *Japanese Annual of International Law* 26.

Greater difficulties arise when it comes to defining the *objective identity* of the two actions. In theory the answer is simple: two cases involve the same subject-matter when they have the same *petitum* (relief sought) and the same *causa petendi* (factual and legal basis of the claim). In practice, however, the application of these concepts is not easy to handle and often results in diverging outcomes. For reasons of space, this point cannot be further developed here. For present purposes it is sufficient to note that there is a tendency within Italian courts to interpret the terms 'the same subject-matter' and 'the same cause of action' restrictively with regard to transnational cases. A lack of identity of claims has been seen even in a situation which might appear to be a typical example of *lis alibi pendens*: i.e. where the creditor sues for performance of the contract in *his* domestic forum and the defendant sues for a declaratory judgment of non-existence of the contractual relationship in *his* domestic forum.[37] The obvious consequence of this restrictive attitude is that the abstention rule laid down in the bilateral conventions has a limited scope of operation, thereby offering an inadequate response to the problem of parallel proceedings in transnational cases. Conflicting results, piecemeal litigation, and some duplication of judicial effort are unavoidable if parallel disputes that are not identical but related in some looser way are allowed to be pursued without co-ordination in different fora.[38]

The concepts used to determine litispendence in domestic law and in cases falling within the subject-matter scope of the bilateral conventions were initially also applied to Article 21 of the Brussels Convention.

Italian courts in their earlier decisions held that Article 21 did not apply where one action was a seller's claim against a buyer for the price of goods sold, defended on the basis that the goods were defective, and the other action was the buyer's claim for a reduction in purchase price and for damages on the basis of the same defects.[39] They have also reasoned that a case where, in relation to the same contract, one party applies to a court in a Contracting State for a declaration that the contract is inoperative (or in any event for its discharge), while the other institutes proceedings before a court of another Contracting State for its enforcement, did not fall within the scope of the *lis pendens* provision embodied in Article 21.

---

[37] Cass., 23 Mar. 1983, no. 2022, in [1984] RDIPP 331; Cass., 17 Mar. 1983, no. 1917, ivi, [1984] RDIPP 345 affirms with regard to Art. 12 of the Italo–Austrian Convention that cases of 'partial *lis pendens*' (*continenza*) and cases of related actions pending in the courts of the two Contracting States do not fall within the scope of that provision and are governed by the general rule of Art. 3 of the Code of Civil Procedure.

[38] A more expansive notion of *lis pendens* also covering situations of related claims is adopted by the provision of Art. 7 of the proposed Italian Conflict of Laws Statute, where the purpose of avoiding the risk of conflicting judgments is pursued by allowing a court other than the court first seised to stay its proceedings: see n. 19 above.

[39] Tribunale, Bassano del Grappa, 13 Feb. 1976, in [1978] RDIPP 74. A similar position has been taken by Pretura, Parma, 17 June 1980, ivi, [1982] RDIPP 86.

From the standpoint of Italian domestic procedural law the relief sought by the plaintiff—*the petitum*—in the two cases differed widely in its scope and in its effects.[40]

A different view prevails in more recent case law following the well known judgment of 8 December 1987 of the European Court of Justice, according to which the concept of the 'same cause of action' in Article 21 is to be interpreted liberally and not restricted to cases of formal identity of the claims.[41] In matters falling under the Convention *lis alibi pendens* has been recognized between multiple proceedings pending in two different Contracting States based on the *same legal relationship*, even though the requests mutually made by the parties were not formally identical, as in the case of a request for damages for the breach of an agency contract and the request for cancellation of the same contract proposed, respectively, in France and Italy.[42]

The new 'European' concept of 'identity of claims', which modifies a long-standing notion of national procedural law, is obviously in accord with the objectives of the Brussels Convention to avoid conflicts between decisions which might result from parallel proceedings before the courts of different Contracting States; and to preclude, in so far as is possible and from the outset, the possibility of such a situation arising as that referred to in Article 27(3) of the Convention.

With respect to this the European solution avoids the shortcomings of the narrower approach adopted by Italian courts with regard to the bilateral conventions. One point, however, still needs to find a satisfactory response. As Advocate General Mancini pointed out in the above-mentioned European case, the broad interpretation of Article 21 does not only provide advantages when it is linked to a rigid principle of priority. If jurisdiction to adjudicate rests with the court first seised, in contractual disputes, for example, it will be sufficient to challenge the validity of the contract first in order to paralyse, by raising an objection of *lis pendens*, any subsequent action brought on the basis of that contractual relationship before the courts of another State (as a forum considered less favour-

[40] See the decision of the Tribunale, Rome, in *Gubisch Maschinenfabrik AG v. Palumbo*. The case was subsequently submitted for a preliminary ruling to the ECJ.

[41] Case 144/86 *Gubisch Maschinenfabrik KG v. Palumbo* [1987] ECR 4861. It should be noted that, in its written observations submitted to the ECJ, the Italian Government maintained that Art. 21 must be interpreted literally and in its technical sense; i.e. as requiring for *lis pendens* to arise the institution of multiple actions with the same subject-matter and the same cause of action. For a critique of the ECJ's decision see Broggi, 'Sui rapporti tra litispendenza e connessione alla stregua della Convenzione giudiziaria di Bruxelles' in [1988] I *Giustizia civile* 2166.

[42] Cass., 12 Dec. 1988, no. 6756, in [1990] RDIPP 134. For a comment see Campeis and De Pauli, 'La nozione di litispendenza europea e l'impossibilita della notifica all'estero come condizione per esperire il rito residuale' in *La nuova giurisprudenza civile commentata* (1989), 389.

able).[43] This lays too much importance on being the first to sue and thereby favours the 'race to the court house'.

IV
LIS PENDENS, LACK OF JURISDICTION TO ADJUDICATE, AND FORUM-SELECTION AGREEMENTS

1. *Lis Pendens* and Forum-selection Agreements: A Preliminary Remark

Lis alibi pendens is not the only situation where a national court may be required to decline jurisdiction. Agreements stipulating foreign courts for dispute resolution and agreements to take controversies to arbitration to be performed abroad may produce the same effect. A distinction, however, must be made between the two situations.

A recent opinion of the Italian Corte di Cassazione emphasizes the point. Where an action has been instituted in a foreign court on the ground of a prorogation agreement or where a dispute had been taken to arbitration abroad on the basis of an agreement to arbitrate, and a new action between the same parties and involving the same subject matter is brought in a court of the forum, the issue is not properly one of *lis alibi pendens* but rather one of lack of jurisdiction.[44] Italian legal writing and case law tend to keep the question of recognizing foreign *lis pendens* separate from that of the jurisdiction of the forum. In fact, in situations such as the one mentioned the reason a new action may not be entertained lies in the prorogation or arbitration clause validly entered into by the parties and in the derogation of the forum's jurisdiction expressed or implied therein, not in the fact of a suit pending in a foreign country. That this is the correct way of looking at the phenomenon under consideration is clear from the fact that, in cases of valid prorogation or arbitration agreements, an action in the forum is also barred where no prior action has been brought in the foreign country. The problem may therefore be formulated as one of validity (operative character or capability of being performed) of the forum agreements 'ousting' the jurisdiction of domestic courts, not as one of recognition of foreign *lis pendens*.

---

[43] See the Opinion of Mancini AG delivered in *Gubisch Machinenfabrik KG* v. *Palumbo*, n. 41 above.

[44] Cass., 24 Feb. 1986, no. 1092, in [1987] RDIPP 539. See also Tribunale, Rome, 26 Feb. 1968, ivi, [1969] RDIPP 450.

2. The Effect of Forum-selection Agreements:
The Traditional Restrictive Attitude of Italian Law

The attitude of national law to an agreement to refer disputes to the courts of another country or to arbitration abroad varies considerably. Many courts give effect to such agreements, at least in certain circumstances, but there are important differences even between countries possessing broadly similar legal systems.[45]

The attitude taken in this respect by Italian law has traditionally been a very restrictive one. The basic rule concerning the subject was embodied in Article 2 of the Code of Civil Procedure of 1942, which prevents any derogation from the jurisdiction of Italian courts in favour of a foreign forum or arbitration to be performed abroad, unless the parties to a dispute are foreign nationals, or a foreign national and an Italian subject neither resident nor domiciled within the territory of the Italian State.[46]

This extremely restrictive rule seems to have been brought about as a consequence of particular theoretical positions, according to which the jurisdiction of courts is inherently universal in character, and courts have the power to adjudicate on disputes that may be brought to them on the ground of statutory provisions irrespective of the nature of the link existing between any such dispute and the jurisdictional power of the State. According to the nationalistic conceptions prevailing at the time when the Code was enacted, the possibility of resorting to Italian courts was further viewed as an essential safeguard for Italian citizens. The position expressed by Italian law in this regard was therefore inherently unfavourable to foreign instruments for settlement of disputes.[47] As far as arbitration agreements are concerned, it is also worth recalling that, according to the view prevailing in Italian legal literature and case law, arbitration is considered as an equivalent of judicial proceedings (rather than a phenomenon of a contractual nature); consequently the treatment in Article 2 of the Code of Civil Procedure as well as in Article 3 of the Code of Foreign Arbitration and of Foreign Judicial Proceedings is the

---

[45] For a comparative survey see Pryles, (1976) 25 *ICLQ* 542.

[46] In addition the forum agreement must be in writing and is permitted only in cases of (pecuniary) obligations. For an account of this provision see Perillo, (1964) 13 *Am. J Comp. L* 165. In contrast, Italy favours prorogation clauses. Art. 4, no. 1 of the Code of Civil Procedure classifies consent as one of the grounds upon which jurisdiction may rest. In addition, the parties may in their contract elect domicile in Italy. Such an election is an additional basis of jurisdiction.

[47] Luzzatto, (1977) II *Hague Recueil* 34; Vitta, n. 17 above, at 20; Ballariro, *Diritto internazionale privato* (1982), 125, Many decisions reflecting these views are collected in Capotorti and Starace, *La giurisprudenza italiana di diritto internazionale privato e processuale* (1991), and in Capotorti, Conforti, Ferrari Bravo, and Starace, *La giurisprudenza italiana di diritto internazionale privato e processuale* (1967).

same as their effects upon the exercise of the jurisdiction of the Italian courts.[48]

3. Forum-selection Agreements and Their 'Ousting Effect': The Impact of International Conventions

The traditional restrictions and obstacles connected with the particular attitude of Italian law towards prorogation and arbitration agreements have been removed by the conclusion and ratification of international conventions which impose upon the Italian State as Contracting Party the obligation to decline jurisdiction, upon application of one of the parties or on the court's own initiative, with regard to disputes which the parties wish to take or have taken to a foreign forum or to arbitration abroad by virtue of agreements validly entered into.

As far as agreements stipulating foreign courts for dispute resolution are concerned, the most important step toward the possibility of achieving the above purpose (acceptance of the effectiveness of such agreements) was taken when the Brussels Convention on Jurisdiction and the Enforcement of Civil and Commercial Judgments was signed and came into force in Italy.

The Convention, which replaces across a wide range of civil and commercial cases the conflicting national provision of Article 2 of the Code of Civil Procedure, gives binding effect to prorogation agreements involving a party domiciled in a Contracting State, subject to certain exceptions (the exclusive jurisdiction provisions of Article 16) and qualifications (set out in Articles 12 and 15). 'If the parties ... have agreed that a court or the courts of a Contracting State are to have jurisdiction to settle any disputes which have arisen or which may arise in connection with a particular legal relationship, that court or those courts shall have exclusive jurisdiction (Article 17).'

The provision in question—as is well known—has given rise and continues to give rise to many problems, particularly with regard to the determination of the formal requirements which need to be satisfied for the validity of the prorogation agreement. These problems cannot be examined here.[49] The rule contained in Article 17 is clear with respect to the effectiveness of forum-selection agreements; i.e. with regard to the obligation assumed by the contracting parties to allow forum-selection

---

[48] Luzzatto, 'Arbitrato commerciale internazionale' in *Digesto delle Discipline Giuridiche, Sezione Commerciale* (1991), 192.

[49] For recent accounts see Di Blase, 'Deroga alla giurisdizione' in *Digesto delle Discipline Giuridiche, Sezione Civile* (1992), 304; Bariatti, 'La Corte di Cassazione Italiana e la Convenzione di Bruxelles del 1968' in [1992] RDIPP 855; Carbone, 'La disciplina comunitaria della "proroga della giurisdizione" in materia civile e commerciale' in [1986] *Diritto del commercio internazionale* 362.

agreements to fulfil their purpose without being frustrated by the intervention of domestic courts acting on the basis of their national rules.

A rich national case law deals with the effects of forum agreements in 'ousting' or 'staying' the jurisdiction of national courts. There is consensus that prorogation agreements preclude the exercise of concurrent jurisdiction on the part of national courts over disputes having the same object, which the parties have agreed to bring before a court of another Contracting State for resolution. Once an agreement to submit disputes to a foreign jurisdiction has been validly concluded and pleaded before the court, the 'derogated' forum must decline jurisdiction over the same disputes.[50] There is no inherent discretion of the courts under Article 17 of the Convention to entertain parallel proceedings brought before them by parties, notwithstanding the existence of a valid forum clause.

Also under the traditional rule embodied in Article 2 of the Code of Civil Procedure, courts have no power to disregard valid clauses for reasons of convenience or concerns about the ends of justice better served by a trial in the country itself. The courts must accede to an application to *decline jurisdiction* when the necessary conditions of a valid forum agreement are met.[51]

The jurisdiction-declining rule takes the form of staying the pending action when a related dispute constitutes the object of a forum agreement. Accordingly it has been held that the Italian judge competent to hear a claim on social security (not according to its Article 1(3), governed by the Convention) has to stay the proceedings in order to enable the foreign judge, competent under the jurisdiction clause duly entered into by the parties under Article 17 of the Convention, to decide the related issue concerning the employment contract.[52]

4. Arbitration Clauses as a Bar to the Exercise of National Jurisdiction

Italy is a party to the New York Convention which embodies, in Article II, rules concerning recognition of arbitration clauses that under Article 2 of the Code of Civil Procedure would be void or invalid. As a Contracting State it must give effect to an arbitral agreement provided it is 'in writing'

---

[50] See Campeis and De Pauli, *La procedura civile internazionale* (1991), 123. A prorogation agreement needs to be pleaded as a defence by the interested party. Courts are not required to take notice of such an agreement on their own motion. A court which would be required to decline jurisdiction may decide to stay its jurisdiction if the jurisdiction of the other court based on the forum agreement is contested: see Di Blase, n. 49 above, at 309, 312.

[51] There is discussion whether a forum selection agreement constitutes a ground for declining (or staying) jurisdiction only where the resulting judgment would be enforceable in Italy: see Gaja, *La deroga alla giurisdizione italiana* (1971), 68; Di Blase, n. 49 above, at 306; Campeis and De Pauli, n. 50 above, at 125.

[52] Tribunale, Florence, 7 May 1987 [1988] RDIPP 313.

and concerns 'a subject-matter capable of settlement by arbitration'.[53] The obligation thus imposed upon the State implies the duty not to entertain judicial proceedings upon the merits of the case covered by the terms of the arbitration clause. The judicial authorities, when seised of an action in matters where the parties have made a 'valid' arbitral agreement, shall refer the parties to arbitration.

The domestic courts are under a duty, and have no discretion, to bring the dispute to arbitration and to decline to proceed any further to adjudicate upon the case. This is not an innovation to the traditional approach prevailing in the Italian legal system where courts have generally not been vested with a discretionary power in this regard.[54]

As to the questions of what the 'operative character' and the 'capability of being performed', in relation to the arbitration agreement, in Article II, section 3, of the New York Convention actually mean, it is generally assumed that the provision wishes to make sure that the arbitral agreement can result in a valid arbitration and award under the rules applicable to the proceedings. It does not seem correct to refuse to give effect to an arbitration agreement in view of the fact that the dispute submitted to arbitration is related to another which is not.[55] This position adopted occasionally in Italian case law—with a view to principles of national law concerning the effects of 'connection' (*connessione*) between disputes as to 'competence' of arbitrators acting under domestic law[56]—has been severely criticized. However, more recent decisions state that in situations of the kind under consideration the procedure to be followed is to stay proceedings.[57]

---

[53] On the following see Luzzatto, n. 47 above, at 35. Italian courts have shown some reluctance in accepting that the rules of the New York Convention have deeply affected the pre-existing rules and standards adopted by domestic law with regard to the validity requirements of arbitral agreements. According to the dominant view a forum-selection agreement is characterized as a substantive and not a procedural matter and therefore not suject to the *lex fori*. See *Rassegna di giurisprudenza*, n. 14 above, App. 1986–90, at 6.

[54] In general it can be said that Italian law, like the law of other civil law countries, does not confer any power or duty on the courts to evaluate the fairness of the chosen forum. It tends to more formal solutions. The question of fairness of a forum is considered in a more abstract way by special provisions for certain categories of disputes or by special requirements as to the form of the jurisdiction agreement.

[55] Luzzatto, n. 47 above, at 43.

[56] See Tribunale, Milan, 22 Mar. 1976 [1977] Rivista di diritto processuale 556, critically annotated by Tamburini, *Efficacia dell'accordo arbitrale e connessione di cause con riferimento alla Convenzione di New York del 1958*. On the operation under domestic law of the so called *vis attractiva* in cases of related actions see Rubino and Sammartano, *n diritto dell'arbitrato interno* (1991), 141.

[57] In particular where collateral issues are involved in the parallel proceedings. Cass., 18 Mar. 1988, no. 2488 [1989] RDIPP 895. See also Cass., 9 Oct. 1984, no. 5028 stating that *un criterio di prevalenza (del giudice ordinario) e un effetto di attrazione non hanno modo di essere utilizzati*. For a comment see Sutti, *Giurisdizione italiana ed arbitrato estero: problemi di connessione*, ivi, (1990), 631. See also La China, n. 1 above, at 366.

The arbitral agreement is considered to be inoperative for the purpose of Article II(3)—or in general as not constituting a ground for dismissing or staying a court action—where the award resulting from the arbitral proceedings will not be recognized and enforced in Italy as the territory of the State where recognition of the ousting effect of the agreement is sought.

How deep an inquiry into the prospects of recognition of the award (which may still have to be rendered) there should be remains an open question. In principle it is maintained that the bar to the exercise of national jurisdiction is bound to cease once it is clear that the dispute cannot be settled by means of arbitration through an award that may be enforceable within the State where judicial proceedings have been stopped as a consequence of the arbitration agreement. According to this approach it would be unreasonable to prevent the jurisdiction of the State from being exercised or to stop it in any other way, whenever it becomes certain that the arbitral award resulting from arbitration proceedings will not be recognized and enforced in the country where the effects of the agreement are sought.[58]

V
CERTAINTY VERSUS FLEXIBILITY: JURISDICTION TO ADJUDICATE, *LIS PENDENS*, AND *FORUM NON CONVENIENS*

'When confronted with problems of jurisdiction to adjudicate the only investigation courts are supposed to make is the assessment of the specific conditions set forth in the statutory provisions determining their power to hear a dispute.'[59] This statement taken from a decision of the Italian Corte di Cassazione reflects the general attitude of Italian legal culture toward jurisdictional issues surrounding litigation in civil and commercial matters; an attitude widely shared by other civil law countries. Locating the proper court in a civil action is not a nuanced inquiry into the specific circumstances of a particular case, but depends on pre-established concepts (e.g. domicile of the defendant, performance of contracts, place of the wrongful conduct, etc.) and prefixed rules. Jurisdiction to adjudicate is perceived as a self-evident link stated on general lines, rather than a highly individualized structure of authority which safeguards in the individual case fairness, justice, and appropriateness of the forum. The main

---

[58] Luzzatto, n. 47 above, at 44.   [59] Cass., 20 Nov. 1976 [1977] II RDIPP 607.

purpose of the specific statutory provisions on the subject embodied in the Code of Civil Procedure is to allow a determination of the courts having jurisdiction on the basis of clear and sufficiently objective criteria, which can be applied uniformly by all courts and do not rely upon their subjective appraisal. The statutory regulation also ensures that jurisdiction is definitely granted if the conditions laid down in the statute are fulfilled.[60]

The doctrine of *forum non conveniens* is not part of the Italian tradition— as it is not part of the civil law tradition in general—nor is there any actual discussion about the need to introduce such a doctrine. Legal scholars remind us that 'whatever inconvenience may be involved, a court must hear any case that is brought before it in accordance with the applicable rules of jurisdiction'.[61] The legal system simply attempts to identify in advance an appropriate nexus for asserting jurisdiction in most cases, but with full awareness that such nexus may be less proper in some cases. This is a deliberate policy choice in favour of legal certainty and the speedy resolution of preliminary jurisdictional issues, at the expense, perhaps, of individual equity.

Should this approach be reconsidered? Should courts be authorized to deny or decline jurisdiction if in a specific case another forum seems more appropriate and closer to the cause of action?

It is certainly true that, in times of (expansion and) concurrence of international jurisdiction in different States, safeguarding an adequate solution for the exercise of judicial power in the individual case becomes a major concern; and it is equally true that in theory it is a desirable goal to place each transnational controversy that arises in the best possible forum for its solution. But are these also realistic goals?

In countries where the doctrine of *forum non conveniens* is recognized, experience shows that the doctrine is costly in terms of delay, expense, uncertainty, and a substantial loss of judicial accountability. Where jurisdictional rules are determined on an individual basis, parties to a dispute all too often have 'to litigate in order to determine where they shall litigate'.[62]

Doubts also exist whether a doctrine of *forum non conveniens* could fit into the structure of the Italian legal system.

A fundamental concept in that system is the right to adjudication before a court and judge predetermined by a general rule of law. Article 25(1) of the Italian Constitution says that 'no one shall be denied the right to be tried by his natural judge pre-established by statute'. The Constitutional

---

[60] Cappelletti and Perillo, n. 5 above, at 80–1, 107. For a comparative perspective Kerameus, (1987) 47 *Louisiana L Rev.* 495.

[61] Cappelletti and Perillo, n. 5 above, at 107.

[62] Lord Templeman in *Spiliada* [1986] 3 All ER 846. See generally Robertson, (1987) 103 *LQR* 398.

Court has repeatedly pointed out that the main function of this fundamental procedural guarantee is strictly to limit discretion in assigning particular judges to particular cases. The ideal of the natural judge principle—the Court argues—is that the adjudicating court be predetermined by general statutory rules which indicate in advance, in as unequivocal a fashion as possible, what court will be called to decide a particular dispute.[63] Broad jurisdiction-declining powers enabling the courts to evaluate the jurisdictional issue in a particular case on the basis of an ad hoc appreciation of the specific interests at stake could therefore hardly be reconciled with Article 25(2) of the Constitution. This does not mean that a doctrine of *forum non conveniens* could not assume the limited function of allowing a corrective flexibility in the application of strict rules of jurisdiction. Trends in this sense can already be found in some court decisions where *forum non conveniens*—type considerations are taken into account in order to attenuate the impact of the priority principle of the *lis alibi pendens* rule.[64] It is doubtful, however, whether other problems related to the phenomenon of concurrent jurisdiction and parallel proceedings, in particular the problems of improper fora and of excessive forum-shopping, can adequately be resolved by the means of a *forum non conveniens* doctrine. What seems to be needed are carefully structured rules of jurisdiction reflecting the idea of international due process[65] and carefully designed conflict-of-law rules attuned to the exigencies of inter-state and international justice.[66]

---

[63] For judicial decisions illustrating this view see Cappelletti and Cohen, *Comparative Constitutional Law* (1979), 359.

[64] See nn. 33 and 34 above.

[65] See in Italian legal literature, Gaja, n. 18 above, at 14, emphasizing the 'sufficient connection' requirement for jurisdictional rules. With regard to due process concerns see Schlosser, 'Jurisdiction in International Litigation. The Issue of Human Rights in Relation to National Law and to the Brussels Convention' in [1991] *Rivista di diritto internazionale* 1.

[66] Juenger, (1989) 63 *Tul. Law Rev.* 553 at 574.

14

Japan

MASATO DOGAUCHI

Professor adjoint, Faculty of Law, University of Tokyo

CONTENTS

I
INTRODUCTION

As there are no particular provisions for international jurisdiction in the Code of Civil Procedure, Japanese rules on this subject are governed by case law.[1] The leading case on international jurisdiction in civil and com-

---

[1] As an exception, there are several provisions in international treaties to which Japan is

mercial matters in Japan is the *Malaysian Airlines System* case[2] in 1981 which recognized wide international jurisdiction of Japanese courts. Since this judgment, rules for declining jurisdiction have been developed.

The rules on jurisdiction in general will be dealt with in Part II. Then, in Part III the rules for declining jurisdiction as a general tool for adjustment will be discussed. *Lis alibi pendens* and other related matters will be dealt with in Parts IV and V.

II
JURISDICTION IN GENERAL

1. MALAYSIAN AIRLINES SYSTEM CASE OF 1981

There was only a small number of cases on international jurisdiction in Japan before World War II. Keeping pace with the internationalization of Japan, international civil and commercial disputes have increased rapidly in the past fifty years.

In the *Malaysian Airlines System* case on 16 October 1981,[3] the Supreme Court set out the following general rules on international jurisdiction with regard to civil and commercial matters:

(1) There are no explicit statutory provisions on international jurisdiction in Japan;

(2) Therefore, international jurisdiction has to be decided in accordance with those principles of justice which would require that fairness be maintained between parties, and a proper and prompt trial be secured;

(3) Although the provisions on distribution of venue among the local courts as established in the Code of Civil Procedure are not concerned with international jurisdiction itself, they are believed to reflect the above principles. Thus, a defendant should be subject

a party, such as the Convention for the Unification of Certain Rules Relating to International Carriage by Air of 1929 (Art. 28(1)), the International Convention on Civil Liability for Oil Pollution Damage of 1969 (Arts. 5(3) and 9(1)), and so on.

[2] See the text accompanying n. 3 below.

[3] *Michiko Goto et al.* v. *Malaysian Airline System Berhad* (1983) 26 Japanese Annual of International Law 122. A Japanese wife and other family members living in Japan brought an action for damages against a foreign airline company which has an office in Japan for the death of the husband in an aeroplane accident in Malaysia which was where he purchased his ticket while on a short trip. The Nagoya Dist. Ct. dismissed the case for lack of international jurisdiction on 15 Mar. 1979. The Nagoya High Ct., however, reversed the judgment and admitted jurisdiction on 12 Nov. 1979. Following general discussion on international jurisdiction, the Sup. Ct. admitted the jurisdiction based upon Art. 4(3) which provides for venue where the local branch of the foreign company is situated.

to the jurisdiction of Japan when the conditions meet the provisions for intra-territorial jurisdiction set forth in the Code of Civil Procedure.

The purport of (1) above is currently recognized in general, while the legislators of the Code of Civil Procedure in the nineteenth century, and some judgments over sixty years ago, seem to have thought the contrary. As regards (2), indeed although there are some scholars who make a special point of protecting Japanese citizens, almost all commentators agree to such leading principles in deciding international jurisdiction.

However, there is criticism as regards (3). The issue at stake is whether all the provisions on intra-territorial jurisdiction in fact reflect the principles on international jurisdiction.

Regarding this point, before the *Malaysian Airlines System* case, the Supreme Court had established certain rules on international jurisdiction, which were different from the rules on intra-territorial jurisdiction, in its judgments on 25 March 1964 on international divorce[4] and on 28 November 1975 on the choice of forum in an international case.[5] In the latter judgment, for example, it was stated that the requirements for validity of the agreement on the choice of forum in a bill of lading for international carriage by sea should be determined in accordance with the principles of justice, and that Article 25 of the Code of Civil Procedure[6] was a mere guideline. The court held that the agreement on jurisdiction in an international case should not necessarily be in writing as required by Article 25, and that the formality for the agreement on international jurisdiction should be deemed to be satisfied if a court of a certain country is at least expressly designated on the document prepared by either of the parties, and if the existence of such an agreement between the parties and the contents thereof is made explicit. The reasons mentioned by the court were that the purpose of Article 25 was to preserve the clear intentions of the parties, that under the laws of many countries the agreement on jurisdiction was not necessarily required to be in writing, particularly that the signature of the shipper on the bill of lading was not required, and that it was important to secure the necessity of expedient processing of international transactions. In addition, the court clarified the requirements on the merits of the choice of international jurisdiction: (a) the case was not subject to the exclusive jurisdiction of Japan; (b) the designated foreign

---

[4] (1965) 8 Japanese Annual of International Law 175.

[5] *Koniglike Java China Paletvaat lijnen BV Amsterdam (Royal Interocean lines)* v. *Tokyo Marine and Fire Insurance Co* (1976) 20 Japanese Annual of International Law 106.

[6] Art. 25 of the Code of Civil procedure: '(1) In so far as only the first instance is concerned the parties may by agreement decide the court with jurisdiction. (2) The agreement referred to in the preceding paragraph shall not be valid unless it is made in writing and is made in respect to a suit based on particular legal relations.'

court had jurisdiction over such a case under its own law. Moreover, the court held that the agreement on exclusive international jurisdiction designating a foreign court should be valid in principle unless such a conclusion would lead to an unacceptable result which violates public policy, and that the choice of the Amsterdam court in the present case was valid.

In the light of such precedents, the formula for (3) in the *Malaysian Airlines System* judgment is simplistic, not only in that it deems all provisions of the Code of Civil Procedure as expressing the principle of justice in relation to international jurisdiction, but also in that it does not mention any proviso that can be applied to guarantee equitable results under specific circumstances.

2. LOWER COURT JUDGMENTS SINCE 1981

Since the above Supreme Court judgment in 1981, there have been approximately thirty lower court judgments on international jurisdiction. They can be divided into two types. One consists of those cases which were based upon the internal venue provisions of the Code of Civil Procedure itself, as decided by the *Malaysian Airlines System* judgment. The other group consists of those cases which denied several provisions of the Code of Civil Procedure because they were not adequate as criteria for international jurisdiction, although the basic structure of consideration is the same as in the Supreme Court judgment.

The latter cases seem to reflect the criticism by commentators of the *Malaysian Airlines System* judgment. Examples of the latter cases are discussed below.

The Tokyo District Court preliminary judgment on 15 February 1984[7] held that, although Article 5 of the Code of Civil Procedure provided for the forum where the obligation was to be performed in cases of pecuniary claims,[8] the court should reject assuming jurisdiction based upon Article 5 at least in international tort cases, because Article 15 of the Code specially allowed the *forum delicti* in cases of tort.[9]

The Tokyo District Court judgment on 1 June 1987[10] held the same. The Tokyo District Court judgment on 28 July 1987[11] held that it was not

---

[7] *Greenlines Shipping Company Ltd* v. *California First Bank* (1985) 28 Japanese Annual of International Law 243. As to the facts of this case, see the text accompanying n. 22 below.

[8] Art. 5 of the Code of Civil Procedure: 'A suit concerning a pecuniary claim may be brought before the court situated in the place where the obligation is to be performed.'

[9] Art. 15(1) of the Code of Civil Procedure: 'A suit relating to a tort may be brought before the court of the place where the act was committed.'

[10] *Kinyushojihanrei*, No 790, 32.

[11] *Nagan (Panama) SA and Shinwa Shipping Co Ltd* v. *Attica Shipping Co SA* (1989) 32 Japanese Annual of International Law 161.

reasonable, at least in cases of actions for a negative declaration of a debt in an international dispute, for the court to assume international jurisdiction based upon Article 8,[12] which provides for the *forum bonae rei sitae* (the place where the defendant kept his properties). The reason was that, if the court recognized Article 8 as a basis for jurisdiction in the action for a negative declaration of a debt as the place of assets location of the defendant creditor, that is, in the case of intangibles, the residence of the debtor, it would be permitting any debtor to file such action at the court of his own residence. The creditor, on the other hand, would be forced to appear at a forum in a country completely irrelevant to his business, and moreover the forum may have nothing to do with the claim at stake. These consequences would be absolutely contrary to the principle of fairness between the parties. The court also held that Article 21,[13] which provides for ancillary jurisdiction for actions joined together in one suit, unlike in cases of a purely domestic character, was not appropriate in principle as a basis for deciding international jurisdiction.

The Tokyo District Court judgment of 29 January 1991[14] held the same in relation to Article 21.

The Shizuoka District Court judgment of 15 July 1991,[15] holding that the last residence of the defendant in Japan could serve as the basis of international jurisdiction only if he has neither a residence nor a temporary residence in any country, added such a requirement to Article 2(2)[16] for international cases. Subsequently, the court denied its international jurisdiction.

Commentators who criticize the simple formula of (3) of the *Malaysian Airlines System* case place emphasis on such lower court judgments as mentioned above which denied some of the provisions of the Code of Civil Procedure as a basis for international jurisdiction. But they have not established which provisions can be referred to in deciding international jurisdiction and which can not. Furthermore, there has not been consensus

---

[12] Art. 8 of the Code of Civil Procedure: 'An action concerning a pecuniary claim, against a person who does not abide in Japan or whose residence is unknown, may be brought in the judicial district [in which] any seizable property of the defendant which is the object of a claim or security therefor is situated.'

[13] Art. 21 of the Code of Civil Procedure: 'When two or more claims are made in one action, it may be brought before any court which is competent to entertain one of the claims under Arts. 1 to 20.'

[14] *Masaki Bussan Corp* v. *Nanka Seimen Co* (1992) 35 Japanese Annual of International Law 171.

[15] *Hanreijiho*, No 1401, 98.

[16] Art. 2 of the Code of Civil Procedure: '(1) The general venue of a person [where he can be sued in any type of action] shall be determined by his residence. (2) Where there is no residence in Japan or his residence is unknown, the general venue shall be determined by his temporary residence. Where there is no temporary residence or his temporary residence is unknown, it shall be determined by his last residence.'

on the question whether any adequate rules on international jurisdiction other than the provisions of the Code of Civil Procedure exist.

III
DECLINING JURISDICTION

1. 'SPECIAL CIRCUMSTANCES' CONSIDERATION

The lower court judgments have developed a fourth step as a proviso in addition to the three steps set forth above (Part II, 1) by the Supreme Court judgment in the *Malaysian Airlines System* case of 1981. The fourth step is as follows:

> (4) Where, upon taking into account international aspects of the case, there are special circumstances which invoke a conclusion on the international jurisdiction derived from (3) that violate the principles of justice as set forth in (2), the conclusion will be altered.

This stage is called the 'special circumstances' consideration. Whereas the principle as set forth in (3) aims to bring about predictability on the issue of international jurisdiction, the proviso of (4) aims to attain equity in individual cases in a flexible way.

One example of this consideration is the Tokyo District Court judgment of 20 June 1986,[17] where the family members of the victim of an accident aboard a Taiwanese airline (Far Eastern Air Transport), which occurred in Taiwan, claimed damages against two American companies: one was the aeroplane manufacturer (the Boeing Co., Inc.) and the other was the airline company (United Air Lines Inc.) which had sold the aeroplane to the Taiwanese airline. The plaintiffs alleged that the defendants had manufactured the aeroplane with defects and had sold it knowingly. The defendants argued that the court lacked international jurisdiction and, regarding the merits of the case, provisionally, that the cause of the accident was improper maintenance on the part of the Taiwanese airline company.

The court held that:

if venue for local territorial competence provided for in the Code of Civil Procedure is located in Japan, it would be in accordance with the principles of justice and reason to sustain the jurisdiction of the Japanese court in general, unless special circumstances can be found. Such special circumstances exist where, in the light of the concrete facts of the case, sustaining the Japanese court's jurisdiction would result in contradicting the principles of securing fairness between the parties and maintaining the proper and prompt administration of justice.

---

[17] *Sei Mukoda et al.* v. *The Boeing Co Inc* (1988) 31 Japanese Annual of International Law 216.

Recognizing that Articles 4, 5, and 21 of the Code of Civil Procedure were to be the basis for international jurisdiction in the case, the court proceeded to the 'special circumstances' consideration.

The court considered the two dimensions separately. As to the proper and prompt administration of justice, it held that there was ample danger of producing results that would impede the above criteria for deciding international jurisdiction. The reason the court indicated was that the unavailability of evidence and witnesses for the Japanese court would make it extremely difficult to secure a fair and prompt trial in Japan. The crucial issue was the cause of the accident and important evidence and witnesses were located in Taiwan. Yet, it was not possible to obtain these from Taiwan by way of judicial assistance because no regular diplomatic relations existed between Japan and Taiwan.

Regarding the issue of fairness between the parties in the case of dismissal in Japan, the questions that the court considered were, first, whether the Taiwanese court should not dismiss the case on account of lack of international jurisdiction; secondly, whether the plaintiffs had enough money to bring an action again in Taiwan; thirdly, whether the Taiwanese court should not dismiss the claim on account of prescription; and fourthly, whether the plaintiffs could enforce the judgment they would obtain in Taiwan. Upon consideration of all the facts, the court held that dismissing the case would not unreasonably impede fairness between the parties even if the plaintiffs were obliged to bring an action in Taiwan.

Thus the court dismissed the case on the ground that there were special circumstances which made the assertion of the Japanese court's jurisdiction unreasonable.

2. COMPARISON WITH THE DOCTRINE OF *FORUM NON CONVENIENS*

The above 'special circumstances' consideration is generally similar to the doctrine of *forum non conveniens*. This method has developed as an antidote to excessively wide assertions under the formula established by the Supreme Court judgment of 16 October 1981 (*Malaysian Airlines System* case). There are, however, some differences.

First, while one of the indispensable prerequisites in applying the doctrine of *forum non conveniens* is the existence of other more appropriate forums, such a condition is not deemed indispensable in dismissing the case on the ground of Japan's 'special circumstances' consideration. Indeed, the Tokyo District Court on 20 June 1986, as cited above, did consider this condition when it dismissed the case, but there have been several cases in which the court did not mention the existence and availability of more convenient foreign courts. However, in fact, it can be said that there was no necessity in these cases to verify the existence of available foreign courts due either to the foreign residence of the defendant or to foreign pending litigation. If the defendant had argued for the availability of a foreign court, the court would have considered this problem deliberately. Therefore, this difference is not as significant as it might seem at first.

Secondly, whereas not only the private factors but also public factors play an important role in the doctrine of *forum non conveniens*, such as administrative difficulties caused by the number of cases, jury duty of the members of the local community, and local interest in having localized controversies decided at home,[18] the factors considered in the Japanese 'special circumstances' method are all private ones in accordance with the distinction between public and private in the doctrine of *forum non conveniens* in the United States, such as relative ease of access to source of proof, availability of compulsory process for attendance of unwilling witnesses, the cost of obtaining their attendance, the enforceability of a judgment, and other relative advantages and obstacles to a fair, proper, and prompt trial. However, in Japan a proper trial is understood to be an aspect of public interest in the judicial system.

Thirdly, although the American courts have wide discretionary powers, including the power to stay or to dismiss with suitable conditions, Japanese courts do not have such a discretion. The Code of Civil Procedure provides for a stay in such extraordinary situations as natural disasters or the unavailability of a party owing to illness and the like (Articles 220 and 221). Therefore, there are only two choices for the Japanese court in relation to the question of jurisdiction: either to exercise jurisdiction or to dismiss the case completely. This lack of options makes it difficult for the court to deal with cases in a flexible manner.

IV
LIS ALIBI PENDENS

1. GENERAL

With regard to *lis alibi pendens*, there is neither an explicit statutory provision nor established case law in Japan.

The court cases can be divided into three categories. First, there are some cases which ignored a foreign pending action entirely. Secondly, there is one case which dealt with *lis alibi pendens* under the 'special circumstances' consideration. Thirdly, there is a recent case which

---

[18] See *Gulf Oil Corp* v. *Gilbert*, 330 US 501 (1947).

adopted the German method, that is, to dismiss the case where the future foreign judgment is expected to be recognized in Japan.

The views of the critics are also divided. But the second method and the third method in particular have become popular among scholars.

2. Ignoring a Foreign Pending Action

The typical finding of the judgments classified in this category is that the word 'court' as described in Article 231[19] of the Code of Civil Procedure does not include a foreign court.[20] Commentators criticize this finding as lacking due consideration for international civil order.[21]

3. 'Special Circumstances' Consideration

The Tokyo District Court judgment of 15 February 1984[22] dealt with the situation of international concurrent litigation under the consideration of 'special circumstances' affecting the decision on international jurisdiction. The plaintiff in this case was a Panamanian shipping company, and the defendant a Californian bank which had a representative office in Japan. In connection with a divorce action between the president of the plaintiff company and his wife, the wife's attorney gave the defendant bank notice to freeze the account in the name of the plaintiff. On the same day, however, the plaintiff remitted about 3 million United States dollars out of the account to another bank account in Tokyo. The wife brought an action for damages against the defendant in California. The defendant paid approximately 1.2 million dollars and settled the dispute out of court. The defendant then arrested the plaintiff's ship in California, but this arrest was later cancelled by the California court. The plaintiff brought an action for damages in California against the defendant, alleging that the 'illegal' arrest caused a loss of profit. Finally, the plaintiff brought an action for damages against the defendant bank in Tokyo.

The court held that, while the defendant's office in Tokyo would fall within the meaning of 'office' in Article 4(3) of the Code of Civil Proce-

---

[19] Art. 231 of the Code of Civil Procedure: 'The parties cannot file another action when the same action is pending in the court.'

[20] The Tokyo High Ct. judgment of 18 July 1957, *Kakyusaibansho-Minji-Hanreisiu*, viii. No 7, 1282; Tokyo Dis. Ct. of 27 May 1965 (1968) 11 Japanese Annual of International Law 197; Osaka Dist. Ct. preliminary judgment of 9 Oct. 1973, *Hanreijiho*, No 728, 76; Tokyo Dist. Ct. preliminary judgment of 19 June 1989 (1990) 33 Japanese Annual of International Law 202.

[21] As to the Osaka Dist. Ct. preliminary judgment of 9 Oct. 1973 n. 20 above, and reactions of scholars to this judgment: see Sawaki (1979–80) 23 *Japanese Annual of International Law* 17.

[22] *Greenlines Shipping Co Ltd* v. *California First Bank* (1985) 28 Japanese Annual of International Law 243.

dure,[23] considering the actions pending in California, the facts of the case clearly showed that the courts in California would be the more appropriate forum, not only for the defendant, but also for the plaintiff, in terms of their collecting evidence and performing other procedural activities. Furthermore, the court noted that assuming jurisdiction would run the risk of delivering a judgment conflicting with those of the California courts, and that the concurrence of the actions would lead to a heavy burden upon the defendant. Thus, the court declined jurisdiction.

This is similar to the disposition of *lis alibi pendens* under the doctrine of *forum non conveniens*. While some Japanese scholars agree with this method, others disagree. One of the arguments of the latter group is that the problem of jurisdiction and that of *lis alibi pendens* are considered to be separate matters on different levels in domestic procedural law. Accordingly, the problem of *lis alibi pendens* should be considered after the establishment of the jurisdiction of the court. The basic structure of the Code of Civil Procedure should not be ignored so rashly even in international civil procedure. The second criticism on the part of those who are against the *forum non conveniens*-like method is that, if an action in an appropriate forum which started subsequently to an initial action were to be allowed to proceed under the scheme of international concurrent litigation, a defendant who was sued in an inconvenient forum would bring another action for a negative declaration in a more convenient forum. This means that international concurrent litigation, or the battle of fora, would be aggravated by this method. The third and most important criticism is that this method would spoil the objectives of the system of recognition of foreign judgments in accordance with Article 200 of the Code of Civil Procedure.[24] Accordingly, a foreign pending action can be said to be a premature foreign judgment, and the judicial policy of recognizing and enforcing a foreign judgment in order to maintain international legal order to a certain extent can be promoted by respecting a foreign pending action under adequate requirements.

[23] Art. 4 of the Code of Civil Procedure: '(1) The general forum of a legal person or any other association or foundation shall be determined by the place of its principal office or its principal place of business, or in case there is no office or place of business, by the residence of the principal person in charge of its affairs. (2) [omitted] (3) In regard to the general forum of a foreign association or foundation, the provision of paragraph 1 shall apply to the office, place of business or person in charge of the affairs thereof in Japan.'

[24] Art. 200 of the Code of Civil Procedure: 'An irrevocable judgment in a foreign court shall have its effect in so far as it satisfies the following conditions: i. the jurisdiction of the foreign court is not denied either by law or a treaty; ii. if the defeated defendant is a Japanese, the defendant was served summons or an order necessary for the commencement of the procedure other than by service by publication, or has voluntarily appeared without being served; iii. the judgment of the foreign court is not repugnant to the public policy in Japan; and iv. reciprocity is given.'

4. THE GERMAN METHOD

The Tokyo District Court judgment of 30 May 1989[25] represents the third category of case which adopted the German method of dealing with *lis alibi pendens*. Under this method, the case in Japan is dismissed where the future foreign judgment in a foreign court in which the same action is pending is expected to be recognized in Japan. The facts of and the findings in this case are as follows.

In October 1984, Miyakoshi Machine Tools Co. Ltd., a Japanese company manufacturing copper foil, entered into a contract with a small American company, Danver Technological Group Inc. (DTG), established by Dale C. Danver, a former employee of a large American company, Gould, Inc., also a manufacturer of copper foil. According to the contract DTG was to sell to Miyakoshi the technical data with respect to the surface treatment of copper leaf. However, Miyakoshi obtained the know-how at stake.

Gould became aware of these transactions and brought an action for damages and a restraining order under the Racketeer Influenced and Corrupt Organizations Act (RICO) and others in October 1985 in the United States District Court for the Northern District of Ohio against Miyakoshi, one other Japanese company (Mitsui Mining and Smelting Co. Ltd.), and two French companies, alleging that they had received trade secrets of Gould misappropriated by the former employee.

Instead of appearing in the Ohio court, Miyakoshi filed an action for a negative declaration of any liability against Gould in the Tokyo District Court as a countermeasure. According to Miyakoshi's claim, there was no wrongdoing, and thus it was not obliged to pay any compensation to Gould or even stop manufacturing copper foil. Gould disputed two issues on procedural points before arguing on the merits. One was the international jurisdiction of the Japanese court in this case, and the other was *lis alibi pendens*.

The Tokyo District Court sustained its international jurisdiction initially based upon the fact that Tokyo was the place of negotiation and conclusion of the contract on the transfer of technology and that the transfer itself was executed in Tokyo, that is, that Tokyo was the alleged *forum delicti*.

Then, the court proceeded to its discussion of the plea of *lis alibi pendens*. It held that, considering the objectives of Article 200 of the Code of Civil Procedure[26] on the recognition of foreign judgments, the second action in Japan shall be restricted as a rule in the case where it is expected with reasonable certainty that the first action in the foreign country will result in an irrevocable judgment which can be recognized in Japan. In this

---

[25] See n. 30 below.   [26] See n. 24 above.

particular case, however, the court did not dismiss the case because it was still uncertain whether the action in Ohio would come to a judgment on account of the dispute over the jurisdiction of the Ohio court raised by the co-defendant there. Additionally, the court held that it was too early to predict the possibility of recognition when the foreign proceedings were still at their starting-point, because the issue of procedural aspects which should be checked as one of the requirements for the recognition of a judgment could not be predicted. Therefore, the court rejected both pleas on procedural matters in this preliminary judgment.

Many commentators generally welcomed the approach taken by this judgment. However, if the likelihood of recognition of the future foreign judgment, as stated in this judgment, is expected to be high the statement in the general form would merely be lip-service. The reason the court required such a high degree of likelihood of recognition is that, once the plea of *lis alibi pendens* is sustained, the only possible disposal of the action brought in Japan is a complete dismissal. As stated above, the Japanese court has no power to stay or dismiss with adequate conditions. In practice it is said that the judges sometimes use a technique of not deciding a next hearing date and saying that the parties will be notified later. This technique may be useful in waiting for the development of an action pending in a foreign country until such time as the Japanese court can adjudicate upon the plea of *lis alibi pendens*, but this technique would ignore the right of the party in opposition who wants to proceed with the action quickly, for in this situation there is no way of appealing to a higher court.

There are some other problems to be dealt with when this method is to be utilized. First, how should the court act if the action brought in Japan is not exactly the same as that pending in a foreign country? In the case of the Tokyo District Court judgment of 15 February 1984, which is classified in the second category above,[27] there were several actions in California and one in Tokyo, though the Japanese one was not identical to any of the Californian suits. The most inflexible way to deal with the Japanese action is to dismiss only when the claims of the plaintiff in the action in Japan will be perfectly resolved by the future foreign judgment to be recognized in Japan. If this rigid system were to be adopted, the plaintiff in the Japanese action would easily escape from the regulation of international concurrent litigation simply by adding one claim not disputed in the pending foreign proceeding. Therefore, the second action must be regulated where a conflict between the foreign and domestic judgments can be anticipated. A definitive solution, however, has not yet been reached in deciding the plea of *lis alibi pendens* as to the degree to which the actions must be identical.

---

[27] See the text accompanying n. 22 above.

The second problem to be solved concerns provisional measures. Article 37 of the Civil Provisional Measures Act of 1989 provides that the court ordering the provisional measures shall, upon the plea of the defendant, order the plaintiff to bring an action on the merits of the case within an appropriate period. Even if the only assets of the defendant are situated in Japan, in the case where an action by a creditor is pending in a foreign country, the second action in Japan by the creditor is barred where the future foreign judgment is expected to be recognized in Japan. The only way for the creditor to secure his claim in Japan is to arrest the assets in Japan. Therefore, Article 37 of the above Act must be construed to include the action in a foreign country which is expected to be recognized in Japan. However, as the judge in the action on the merits of the case and the judge in the provisional measures action are not the same, it is possible that the expectation of the likelihood of recognition of the future foreign judgment might differ. Therefore, the difference in the decisions of the judges regarding the matter must somehow be reconciled.

The third problem concerns prescription. If the action had been dismissed because of *lis alibi pendens* on the assumption that a future foreign judgment would be recognized in Japan, but actually the enforcement of a foreign judgment is later rejected in Japan, not only have the costs and efforts of the creditor been wasted, but also, in certain circumstances, the claim itself may have expired in Japan. According to Japanese private international law, the problem of prescription is a matter for the *lex causae*, that is, in the case of a contractual claim, the law designated by the parties or the *lex loci contractus*. Therefore, the suspension of prescription is governed by the *lex causae*. Where that is Japanese law, the suspension by bringing an action for the claim shall not be effectuated in the case of dismissal or withdrawal of the action in accordance with Article 149 of the Civil Code. Keeping in line with this provision, it is reasonable to decide that bringing an action in a foreign country will not be sufficient to suspend the prescription when the judgment rendered in the foreign proceedings is not recognized in Japan. In order to rescue the creditor in such cases, a foreign proceeding will have to be deemed to be a reminder of the claim which continues during the pending foreign proceeding. According to this construction, the claim does not expire if the creditor brings an action within six months[28] of the date of the foreign judgment. Within this period, the creditor shall bring an action for the enforcement of the foreign judgment along with the provisional claim on the merits in case the enforcement of the foreign judgment is rejected. Next, where the *lex causae* is a foreign law, it is not always possible to construe it to rescue the creditor. Is it always possible to use the public policy clause (Article 33

[28] Art. 153 of the Civil Code provides that the suspension by the reminder shall cease to effective unless the creditor takes the judicial proceedings within six months.

of the Application of Laws (General) Act)? Furthermore, it is unclear what should be done, if there is no suspension of the time-bar under the *lex causae*. For example, under Japanese law,[29] no suspension of the time-bar is provided for in cases involving the claim of a buyer for either reducing the price or avoiding the contract against a seller of goods the title of which belongs to a third party. These problems have also not yet been answered.

V
OTHER RELATED TOPICS

1. Forum-shopping

Forum-shopping is one of the important factors to be considered in establishing the rules on international jurisdiction. However, once the rules are established, it is natural for parties to bring an action in the most advantageous court for themselves. Such behaviour cannot be condemned. Therefore, in the case of Japan, as the rules on international jurisdiction have not been established firmly, as stated in Parts II and III, making such rules as will always unduly favour a certain category of parties must be avoided.

One of the problems with Japanese rules on international jurisdiction is whether the *forum delicti* can be a basis for jurisdiction in the case of an action for a negative declaration of a debt brought by an alleged wrongdoer. Particularly where the plaintiff is a company which is alleged to have committed a wrong, such as in product liability cases, it would cause an undue burden on the defendant living in a foreign country who alleges that he is a victim if the court were to sustain jurisdiction on the grounds that it was the place where the tort was committed by the plaintiff. There has not been a case of product liability in the narrow sense in which a Japanese manufacturer brought an action for a negative declaration of a debt to a consumer, but there have been several judgments holding that the *forum delicti* could be a basis for a dispute concerning economic loss between a Japanese company and an American company.

A typical example is the Tokyo District Court judgment of 19 June 1989.[30] The court held as follows: 'The place of tort shall be the place where

---

[29] Art. 564 of the Civil Code provides for a one-year time-bar without suspension, which is *Ausschlußfrist* in German.

[30] *Shinagawa Hakurenga Co Ltd* v. *Houston Technical Ceramics Inc* (1990) 33 Japanese Annual of International Law 202. The same findings are in the Tokyo Dist. Ct. judgment of 27 May 1965 (1968) 11 Japanese Annual of International Law 197; Osaka Dist. Ct. of 9 Oct. 1973, *Hanreijiho*, No 728, 78; Tokyo Dist. Ct. of 30 May 1989, *Hanreijiho*, No 1348, 91, *Hanreitaimuzu*, No 703, 240.

the wrongful act has occurred. Because the goods in question were designed and manufactured in Japan, Japan is the place of tort in this sense,
and the jurisdiction of the Japanese courts in the tort case alleging defects
in the above goods can be admitted.' 'In this case, . . . the existence of the
defects in the goods . . . will be the issue to be disputed in the
action . . . There is no reason why the claim for a negative declaration of
liability to pay damages based upon tort should be allowed in this case.'

In contrast to the above findings, it is thought to be reasonable that the
rule of *forum delicti* is based on the premise that the plaintiff is a victim.
Indeed, the possibility of the existence of evidence about the alleged
wrongdoing also serves as a basis for the rule, but such grounds shall be
insufficient to admit the jurisdiction of the *forum delicti* in the action for a
negative declaration of the debt by the alleged wrongdoer against the
alleged victim. The minimum conditions for any rules on jurisdiction are,
in general, not to make it impossible or unreasonably burdensome for the
defendant to defend himself in the forum. In the case of the action for a
negative declaration, even this minimum condition may not be secured
because the presumed plaintiff, to whom the rules do not give minimum
protection, is actually the defendant. Therefore, unless a special rule on
jurisdiction is established for the action for a negative declaration, forum-
shopping by the wrongdoer may cause injustice to the tort victims. Such
injustice may be prevented by using the 'special circumstances' consideration as stated in Part III, 1, but it is considered necessary to make a special
category for the action for a negative declaration in order fully to protect
tort victims. The general rules on jurisdiction, as follows, shall only be
applied to these categories of cases: forum of the residence of the defendant, forum of agreed choice, forum of unconditional appearance of the
defendant, and forum of related claims.

2. Foreign Choice of Jurisdiction Clauses

With regard to the choice of a foreign jurisdiction, there are no explicit
provisions in Japan. Article 25 of the Code of Civil Procedure[31] is concerned only with an agreement of choice of forum within Japan. Therefore, this subject is governed by case law. The Supreme Court judgment
on 28 November 1975 is the leading case on the choice of foreign jurisdiction as stated in II, 1. above.[32] Incidentally, the framework in dealing with
this matter is not the 'special circumstances' consideration but, rather, the
regular structure of international jurisdiction in general. In other words,
choice of forum is one of the special rules on international jurisdiction like
forum rei sitae or *forum delicti* in Japan.

---

[31] See n. 6 above.   [32] See the text accompanying n. 5 above.

3. Arbitration Agreements

Japanese courts dismiss cases where the parties have agreed to go to arbitration. Although there is no statutory rule on this, it is generally recognized. The Code of Civil Procedure provides the requirements for the arbitration agreement to be valid. Regarding the issue of arbitrability, Article 786 provides that the arbitration agreement is valid only where the parties can settle the case concerned by themselves. There are no separate rules on international arbitration apart from domestic ones, but Japan is a party to some multilateral treaties and bilateral treaties which have a provision on arbitration agreements. For example, Article II(3) of the Convention on the Recognition and Enforcement of Foreign Arbitral Awards of 1958 (New York Convention) provides for referring the parties to arbitration unless the arbitration agreement is null and void, inoperative, or incapable of being performed. Dismissal in the case where the requirements are fulfilled is mandatory for the court.

4. Restraining Foreign Proceedings

There has been no case in Japan ordering a restraint of foreign proceedings or rejecting such an order. In contrast to the antisuit injunction in Anglo-American jurisdictions, it is generally thought that Japanese courts have jurisdiction to order a party to perform or not to perform an act only within the territory of Japan. Therefore, a Japanese court would deny a claim for restraining an opponent from continuing the action in a foreign court.

From a theoretical point of view, however, an order to perform or not to perform in a foreign country can be deemed to be a kind of extraterritorial application of law which prescribes the activity, not for everyone but for the party at stake. Thus, it can be considered possible for Japanese courts to order a person over whom Japan has jurisdiction to withdraw his claim in a foreign court. The problem is when such jurisdiction is vested in the Japanese courts. Indeed, international law is not certain on this subject, but there has to be an adequate connection between the party and the subject-matter at stake, on the one hand, and the country whose court is going to make the order, on the other. According to this criterion, Japanese courts may in certain cases order a party to refrain from disturbing its proceedings, that is, not to continue to perform in a foreign court.

VI
CONCLUSION

With the advance of international trade and interdependence, international disputes have rapidly increased in Japanese courts, a trend expected to continue into the future. The amendment of the Japanese Code of Civil Procedure currently under way (to be completed within three or four years) aims at making rules adapted to the globalization of civil disputes. Making reasonable new provisions on international jurisdiction and *lis alibi pendens* is recognized to be particularly important for Japan in the era of global interdependence. Still, there are many other problems to be dealt with in the Code, such as making more effective the collecting of evidence or making more efficient the procedure for small claims. Therefore, it is somewhat difficult on this occasion to make many explicit provisions to cover the problems relating to international civil procedure. Further projects on internationalization of Japanese law are necessary to clarify the rules on such matters as are discussed in this chapter.

15

The Netherlands

MIRJAM FREUDENTHAL
Faculty of Law, Utrecht University
and
FRANS VAN DER VELDEN
Ministry of Justice

CONTENTS

I
INTRODUCTION

Legal decisions are precious objects. They often decide a man's life in a drastic way and in most cases they cost the parties and the Treasury a lot of money. In civil and commercial cases each claimant or petitioner tries to find the court that is most willing to decide his or her case in an expectedly favourable way, positive and executable at a place where execution makes sense. Legislators for their part try to balance the interests of the parties and to reduce the costs of adjudication by reducing the workload of the courts.[1]

In general, two systems of controlling the number of cases by way of jurisdiction are available:

(1) The law of procedure strictly defines the cases in which the courts have jurisdiction, in principle leaving no room for judicial discretion. In this jurisdictional system two questions will arise: first, what to do in cases where two courts have jurisdiction at the same time in the same cause of action—to be answered by rules of *lis pendens*[2]—and, secondly, what should be done if no positive or negative rule of jurisdiction is given—to be answered by rules of *forum necessitatis*.[3]

(2) The law of procedure creates an open system of jurisdiction. In this case only broad and general rules of jurisdiction are formulated, leaving the courts with discretion whether to accept or decline jurisdiction. In this jurisdictional system *forum non conveniens* is of major importance to protect the parties from an action which, for reasons of equity or of effectiveness, could more appropriately have been heard in another court and to protect the courts from an overload. In this open system two courts may easily assume jurisdiction in the same case, and the situation must be corrected by rules of *lis pendens*. The general rules of jurisdiction and the wide discretion of the courts seem to make a *forum necessitatis* rule redundant.

This theoretical distinction of systems of jurisdiction may of course be

[1] In this ch. the following abbreviations will be used: Brussels Convention = Convention of 27 September 1968 on Jurisdiction and the Enforcement of Judgments in Civil and Commercial Matters (see n. 12); HR = Hoge Raad = Dutch Sup. Ct.; KG = Kort Geding = Interim Injunctions Reports (cases cited by year and number); *NILR* = *Dutch International Law Review*; *NIPR* = *Nederlands Internationaal Privaatrecht* = Dutch Private International Law Review (with extensive collection of published and unpublished cases, cited by year and number); NJ = Nederlandse Jurisprudentie = Dutch Law Reports (cases cited by year and number); OJ = Official Journal of the European Communities (cited by year, number and page); RvdW = Rechtspraak van de Week = Weekly Law Reports (cases cited by year and number); Trb = Tractatenblad = Bulletin of Conventions (cited by year and number); WBRv = Wetboek van Burgerlijke Rechtsvordering = Code of Civil Procedure.

[2] To be dealt with in Part XI.

[3] In the jurisdictional system here described, rules of *forum necessitatis* are mostly not provided for, since the system in principle covers all possible situations. The Dutch Codes of Procedure do not have *forum necessitatis* like 'hardship'—rules in case statutory rules are lacking. In reality, from time to time Dutch courts have to fill in gaps by extensive interpretation or by assuming jurisdiction as *forum necessitatis*: see e.g. HR, 26 Oct. 1984 [1985] NJ 696. In this case the HR overruled its previous decision in which it had decided that the rule of jurisdiction in succession cases (i.e. the court of the last domicile of the deceased person has jurisdiction) were *lex specialis* excluding the general rules of jurisdiction: *forum rei* and *forum rei sitae*. The main reason for this result was the necessity to decide a case in which the deceased had no domicile in The Netherlands, but had a major connection to The Netherlands, since the estate was located in The Netherlands and the heirs were domiciled there. See also Part XII of this ch.

refined by intermediary systems. Such a system is proposed in a Dutch draft Bill, amending the Code of Civil Procedure.[4] The draft introduces a *forum conveniens* in petition cases by providing that the Dutch courts will have international jurisdiction if the petitioner is domiciled in The Netherlands or the petition is collateral to a summons proceeding over which the Dutch court has jurisdiction or *the matter is in any other way closely connected to* the legal sphere of The Netherlands.

Legal practitioners, at least European legal practitioners, seem to favour a closed system, where courts have to apply statutory rules of jurisdiction and claimants do not have to face a denial of jurisdiction for reasons of *forum non conveniens*—particularly in international commercial conflicts where predictability of jurisdiction is of major importance. International contracts used to have provisions restricting the right to bring legal proceedings, often by using a limitation period of six or twelve months. Since on the one hand, parties do not start court proceedings directly after the dispute has arisen and, on the other hand, court proceedings from start to decision take at least several months, even if only on the question of jurisdiction, a negative decision on jurisdiction in reality is often a negative decision on the case itself. The requirement of certainty is also rooted in the Brussels Convention on Jurisdiction and the Enforcement of Judgments, as this Convention prohibits *forum non conveniens* relief.[5]

II
PROLEGOMENA

Before discussing the rules for declining jurisdiction in Dutch law, some general informative remarks on the Dutch law of civil procedure may be of value.

Our first remark is one on terminology. Jurisdiction as a general term is the power or authority of a court to take cognizance of matters put before it and to decide such matters. Rules of 'absolute' jurisdiction allocate cases to the courts on the basis of the subject matter or the value of the subject matter involved *ratione materiae*; this way of allocating will be discussed later. Rules of 'relative' jurisdiction distribute cases among courts enjoying the same absolute jurisdiction; distribution is mostly done by district. Absolute jurisdiction is out of the parties' discretion and therefore of no interest to our discussion.[6] In common law terminology relative jurisdiction is called venue. Therefore, to specify relative jurisdiction we will use the word 'venue'. Rules of 'international' jurisdiction determine whether

---

[4] See Pt. XII of this ch.   [5] To be discussed in Pt. IV.

[6] See Art. 156 WBRv. Parties can only escape from absolute jurisdiction by leap-frogging directly to the next highest court. As a consequence they lose their right of appeal: see Art. 157 WBRv.

Dutch courts have jurisdiction in international cases. In this chapter, the word 'jurisdiction' is often used as a synonym of 'international jurisdiction'.

Secondly, Dutch law does not distinguish between civil and commercial law. Commercial matters are decided according to rules of civil law. Although Dutch law still has a commercial code, its rules are not independent from, but are subordinate to, the Civil Code rules.[7] Civil procedure has no specific rules for commercial cases in general, and the Dutch court system has no specific courts for commercial litigation.

The third remark is that this chapter deals with the exercise of jurisdiction in civil and commercial matters. Administrative and criminal matters are excluded.[8] However, Dutch law has no impenetrable fence between these kinds of matters. In the relationship between civil and administrative jurisdiction the general rule is that the claimant must bring his administrative claim in an administrative court, and that only where there is no administrative court, or such court does not offer sufficient legal protection, may the claimant ask the civil court to provide supplementary protection on a civil law basis, especially in the form of damages.[9]

The fourth comment is that The Netherlands are in the middle of a thorough recodification of civil law and civil procedure.[10] Some major changes in the Code of Civil Procedure (WBRv) concerning jurisdiction in petition cases—including divorce and connecting claims petitions as well as petitions for provisional measures in divorce cases—entered into force on 31 December 1992. There are no court decisions yet interpreting these changes, so our remarks have to be restricted. Moreover, in April 1993, the Ministry of Justice published a draft of a bill to recodify the general rules of jurisdiction of the WBRv. This draft is open to public discussion; we will refer to it when appropriate.[11]

---

[7] As a consequence of the recodification of the civil law, matters formerly covered by the Commercial Code are more and more frequently transferred to the Civil Code. Note that in Dutch legal terminology 'civil law' is often used as a synonym for 'private law'.

[8] In general, administrative courts are competent only if the subject-matter of the dispute is an administrative decision made in an individual case. For a general survey see, J. B. J. M. ten Berge *et al.*, 'Civil and Administrative Procedures in the Netherlands: Comparison and Future Changes' in: *Dutch Reports to the Thirteenth International Congress of Comparative Law* (The Hague, 1990), 149 ff.

[9] Unless parties have agreed to exclude the jurisdiction of the civil courts: see HR, 5 Feb. 1993 [1993] RvdW 49.

[10] An important part of the Dutch Civil Code, consisting of the general rules of patrimonial law (Bk. 3), real rights (Bk. 5), the general part of the law of obligations (Bk. 6), and rules on (some) special contracts (Bk. 7, in part), entered into force on 1 Jan. 1992. This part of the Dutch Civil Code is translated into English and French: see P. P. C. Haanappel and Ejan Mackaay, *New Netherlands Civil Code/Nouveau code civil néerlandais—Patrimonial Law/le droit patrimonial* (Deventer/Boston, 1990).

[11] See Pt. XII.

In the fifth place, as are all the Member-States of the EC, The Netherlands is a party to the Brussels Convention on Jurisdiction and the Enforcement of Judgments.[12] Uniformity of interpretation is guaranteed by the interpretative decisions of the European Court of Justice in Luxembourg.[13] In many civil cases, for example those concerning contracts, torts, maintenance, the Brussels Convention rules the international jurisdiction of the Dutch courts—and frequently even the venue. This Convention has specific and strict rules; although it offers more then one competent forum in many a case, it does not have a *forum non conveniens*-like negative rule of jurisdiction. Except for a small number of court decisions it attributes full faith and credit to decisions of the courts of the Contracting States. An almost identical convention on jurisdiction and enforcement of judgments, the so-called Lugano Convention, is open for ratification by Member States of the EC and EFTA.[14] Hitherto the Lugano Convention has been ratified by a restricted number of States; it is in force between Finland, Norway, Switzerland, and Sweden—EFTA States—and France, Ireland, Italy, Luxembourg, The Netherlands, Portugal, and the United Kingdom—EC States.[15]

Our sixth observation is that, in accordance with Dutch rules of civil procedure, court proceedings commence with a petition or a writ of summons. The petition procedure is obligatory in all family cases and in a restricted number of other matters; the summons procedure is used in all other civil cases. As will be shown, this distinction is of importance to the *forum non conveniens* discretionary powers of the Dutch courts.[16]

Our last remark is on absolute jurisdiction. As a rule civil proceedings start at a District Court (rechtbank), but cases involving no more than Dfl 5,000 (approximately US$ 2,600), disputes between landlord and tenant and on agricultural tenancies, and labour disputes are heard by the sub-district courts (kantongerecht). Interim injunction proceedings can be lodged with the president of the District Court if the case urgently requires an interim decision in the short term. Appeals from the (fifty-six)

---

[12] Convention of 27 Sept. 1968 on Jurisdiction and the Enforcement of Judgments in Civil and Commercial Matters, as amended in 1978, 1982, and 1989. Consolidated version in: [1990] OJ C189/1; explanatory report to the 1968 text by Jenard in [1979] OJ C59/1, to the 1978 text by Schlosser in [1979] OJ C59/71, to the 1982 text by Evrigenis and Kerameus in [1986] OJ C298/1, to the 1989 text by Almeida Cruz, Desantes Real, and Jenard in [1990] OJ C189/35.

[13] 2nd Prot. to the Brussels Convention, published as an annex to the Convention: see n. 12.

[14] Text in [1988] OJ L319/9: explanatory report by Jenard/Möller in [1990] OJ C189/57.

[15] Date of enforcement: France: 1 Jan. 1992; Ireland: 1 Dec. 1993; Italy: 1 Dec. 1992; Luxembourg: 1 Feb. 1992; The Netherlands: 1 Jan. 1992; Portugal: 1 July 1992; Finland: 1 July 1993; Norway: 1 Apr. 1993; Switzerland: 1 Jan. 1992; Sweden: 1 Jan. 1993; and the United Kingdom: 1 May 1992.

[16] See Pt. V.

sub-district courts decisions are made to the (nineteen) District Courts; appeals from decisions of the District Courts and of the President of the District Court are made to the (five) Courts of Appeal (gerechtshof). However there is no appeal for claims less than Dfl 2,500 unless principal points of law are at stake, in which case cassation is open. Cassation from appeal decisions of the District Courts and of the Courts of Appeal are made to the Supreme Court (Hoge Raad). Cassation proceedings do not require leave; however, to reduce its workload the Hoge Raad may restrict its judgment solely to the operative part without disclosing its reasons, if the case is dismissed and if in the Hoge Raad's view it does not involve legal questions of relevance to the unity or development of the law. The authority of the Hoge Raad to give judgment without disclosing the (always unanimous) opinion was introduced in 1988. Since then approximately 16 per cent of the requests for cassation have been decided with an undisclosed opinion.

III
DUTCH LAW OF *FORUM NON CONVENIENS*

Dutch law of civil procedure—which includes procedure in commercial cases—has no general rule of *forum non conveniens*. In Dutch domestic cases *forum non conveniens* does not play a part; rules of absolute jurisdiction are exclusive, rules of venue are exclusive as far as sub-district courts are concerned, in other cases parties may deviate from the statutory rules of venue without intervention of the court.

In international cases Dutch law has two sets of specific rules of *forum non conveniens*, one statutory, one judge-made. As already indicated, rules of *forum non conveniens* are collateral to the international jurisdiction rules. In Dutch law, the general rule of international jurisdiction is that, unless conventional or statutory rules decide otherwise, the Dutch courts have jurisdiction if the rules of venue so indicate.

The supremacy of international conventions in Dutch law obliges us to discuss conventional jurisdiction rules first.

IV
CONVENTIONAL JURISDICTION RULES

We have to start our discussion with a reference to the international conventions on jurisdiction. International conventions have constitutional priority over domestic law.[17] In many proceedings international jurisdiction is based on international conventions. We have already indicated the most important ones, the Brussels Convention and the Lugano Convention. Both Conventions have compulsory rules of international jurisdiction; their main fields of application are international contracts and torts. In a restricted number of cases all indicated in Article 16 of the Convention, only one court, to the exclusion of all others, has jurisdiction. These cases deal, for example, with rights *in rem* in, or tenancies of, immovable property, with the validity, nullity, or dissolution of legal persons, with (public) registers; then the courts of the *situs* of the real property, of the seat of the legal person, of the register, and so on, have exclusive jurisdiction, which means that no other court can assume jurisdiction on whatever ground. In all other cases jurisdiction can be based on forum choice by the parties.[18] Forum choice complying with the formal requirements of Article 17 of the Brussels and the Lugano Conventions creates exclusive jurisdiction if one of the parties is domiciled in a Contracting State; the chosen court may not refuse to hear the case for *non conveniens* reasons.[19]

If no choice has been made, in most cases more than one national court will have international jurisdiction, based on the domicile of the defendant on the one hand (Article 2), on the other hand on the *locus contractus*, *locus delicti*, locus of a trust, etc. (Article 5). If more than one court has jurisdiction the selection of the forum lies with the plaintiff. Since both Conventions have no *forum non conveniens* rule, the court has no authority to refuse the plaintiff's selection on a *non conveniens* consideration.[20] A *lis pendens* rule (Article 21) prevents the unpleasant situation where at the same time two courts deal with the same matter between the same parties.[21]

The Netherlands are a party to several other conventions with rules of jurisdiction.[22] These jurisdictional rules also have priority over domestic rules of jurisdiction. They will be discussed where appropriate.

[17] Art. 94 of the Constitution of the Kingdom of The Netherlands reads as follows: 'Statutory regulations in force within the Kingdom shall not be applicable if such application is in conflict with provisions of treaties that are binding on all persons or of resolutions by international institutions.'

[18] Albeit restricted in some cases, involving insurance (Art. 17) and consumer contracts (Art. 15).

[19] If no party to the contract is domiciled in a Contracting State, Art. 17 obliges the courts of other states to stay proceedings until the court chosen refuses to hear the case, which may indeed be the case if municipal law denies jurisdiction.

[20] So e.g. President, RB, Arnhem, 1 Nov. 1990 [1991] NIPR 227: 'In the closed system of jurisdictions as ruled in the Brussels Convention it is inappropriate to the court to declare that it has no jurisdiction for lack of connection to the legal order of the country of the forum.'

[21] See Pt. XI.

[22] Hague Convention of 5 Oct. 1961 on Child Protection, Collection of Conventions (1951–

V
STATUTORY *FORUM NON CONVENIENS* IN PETITION CASES

As already mentioned above, cases are brought to trial by petition or by writ of summons.

Article 429c of the WBRv governs jurisdiction in proceedings that are initiated by a petition to the court.[23] Generally speaking, the petition procedure is used if the law so prescribes and in all cases which are not concerned with a legal relationship between the parties, unless the law prescribes otherwise. In more concrete words, all family cases including divorce, maintenance, and matrimonial property commence with a petition, as do many cases concerning the management of a legal person (like a corporation, association, or foundation) and of a condominium, disputes on the fixing of the rent of dwelling-houses, reduction of liability in transport and collision cases, requests for a court confirmation of a person's Dutch nationality, works councils' disputes, as well as a number of less important instances. In petition cases, in general, international jurisdiction is based solely upon the filing of a petition in a Dutch court. Venue is with the court of the domicile or the actual residence of the petitioner in The Netherlands. If such domicile or residence is lacking the District Court of The Hague has jurisdiction.[24] In case of procuration the permanent or actual residence of the procurator as well as that of the petitioner also vest relative jurisdiction, and in succession cases only the last residence of the deceased does so. A specific rule of venue in petition cases concerns venue in divorce cases. This will be discussed later.

These liberal rules of international jurisdiction in petition cases ask for discretionary authority in the courts to reduce the influx of cases with no or only a slight connection with The Netherlands. Therefore, Article 429c has an escape rule in section 11 that reads: 'A court has no jurisdiction if the petition is insufficiently connected with the legal sphere of The Netherlands.' At this moment this is the sole example of a written rule of *forum non conveniens* in Dutch law.

There is one major exception to the general rules of international jurisdiction in petition cases: that is the jurisdiction in international divorces and divorce-related matters. Divorce jurisdiction is governed by Article

88), X, edited by the Permanent Bureau of the Hague Conference on Private International Law (1988).

[23] Art. 429c Code of Civ. Proc. has been amended by Act of 1 July 1992 [1992] Stb 373, in force on 1 Jan. 1993.

[24] Art. 429c, s. 10 WBRv. In contrast to summons proceedings, petition cases often lack an opposing party. Therefore, jurisdiction based on the domicile of the opposing party was judged not useful in petition cases.

814 of the WBRv. This Article states that Dutch courts have jurisdiction in three instances: (1) the petitioner and the respondent are both Dutch nationals, (2) one or both of them have been domiciled in The Netherlands for a period of at least twelve months or (3) one or both spouses is a Dutch national and that spouse has been domiciled in The Netherlands for a period of at least six months.[25] As to *forum non conveniens* Article 814, section 2, of the WBRv expressly excludes the application of this doctrine in divorce cases, including divorce-related petitions like maintenance, child custody, and visiting rights.

Petition cases in which *forum non conveniens* is applied as a bar to international jurisdiction are numerous. An interesting example is Hoge Raad, 13 February 1987.[26] The case was complicated. The parties were German nationals when they married in Germany in 1948. In 1953 they emigrated to Canada and became Canadian citizens. From 1968 to 1975 the man worked and had residence in The Netherlands, while the wife stayed in Canada. He then petitioned for a divorce in The Netherlands. After the divorce he married an English woman and lived with her in the United Kingdom, although stating still to be domiciled in Canada. In 1984 he filed a petition in the District Court of Amsterdam to reduce his maintenance obligation to his former wife. The Amsterdam District Court decided accordingly. On the former wife's petition, the Court of Appeal overruled this decision, holding the Dutch courts to be *forum non conveniens* in this case.

In Cassation the man stated, as his first argument, that the mere fact that his petition concerned the revision of the decision of a Dutch court was in all cases a sufficient connection with the legal sphere of The Netherlands to justify the jurisdiction of the Dutch courts. The Hoge Raad rejected this argument. It referred to the general rule that, unless conventional or statutory rules decide otherwise, the Dutch courts have jurisdiction if the rules of venue so indicate, but that in petition cases they may refuse jurisdiction in case of insufficient connection as prescribed in Article 429c, section 11, of the WBRv. The mere fact that the revision of a Dutch court's maintenance decision was sought as such was an insufficient connection to justify jurisdiction.

However, as his second argument, the man contended that Canadian law, being the law of the domicile of the parties, could not confer jurisdiction on Canadian courts to revise maintenance decisions of foreign courts. For this very reason the Hoge Raad decided that the case could not

---

[25] Act of 1 July 1992 [1992] Stb 373, which came into force on 1 Jan. 1993. This Act amended the rules of divorce procedure by replacing the writ of summons as the introductory document of a divorce proceeding by a petition for a divorce. This amendment implied the applicability of the petition procedure of Arts. 429a to 429t WBRv.

[26] [1987] NJ 1014.

be considered insufficiently connected to the legal sphere of The Netherlands.[27]

A decision of the Hague Court of Appeal (gerechtshof) requires special attention.[28] In a petition case for the constitution of a fund in respect of claims subject to limitation, the District Court declared itself to have jurisdiction. One party involved appealed this decision on the basis that the case—a collision on the River Rhône—lacked sufficient connection with The Netherlands and that the court was *forum non conveniens*. However, the Court of Appeal rejected this argument, stating that *forum non conveniens* could not be invoked since the defendant/petitioner had its seat in The Netherlands, the ship was registered in The Netherlands, and redress was only possible in The Netherlands. Now that the court combines several reasons for denying *forum non conveniens*, it remains to be decided if the sole fact that the petitioner is domiciled in the court's district in any case excludes a *forum non conveniens* decision.[29]

VI
FORUM NON CONVENIENS IN
SUMMONS CASES

The jurisdictional rules of the Brussels Convention (and the Lugano Convention) apply in all cases not excluded by Article 1, if the defendant is domiciled in a Contracting State.[30] Article 1 contains two restrictions on the applicability of the Brussels Convention.

Excluded *ratione materiae* are disputes on the status or legal capacity of natural persons, on rights in property arising out of a matrimonial relationship, on wills and succession, as well as on bankruptcy, the winding-up of legal persons, judicial arrangements, compositions, and the like, on social security, and on arbitration.

Excluded *ratione personae* are cases that do not concern 'civil and commercial matters'. In its *Rüffer* decision,[31] the European Court of Justice

---

[27] Here the rules of *forum non conveniens* and of *forum necessitatis* go together: see n. 6.

[28] Hague Gerechtshof, 2 June 1987 [1987] S&S 135.

[29] In 1986 the same CA decided that there was international jurisdiction in cases of liability limitation funds if a Dutch port is the first called into after the collision which gave rise to the liability: see Hague Gerechtshof, 28 Nov. 1986 [1987] NIPR 455. This court declared itself *forum non conveniens* in a fund case, where none of the parties had residence in The Netherlands and Cadiz (Spain) was the first port after the collision, while the only connection with The Netherlands was the presence of the ship in a Dutch port: see Hague Gerechtshof, 22 Jan. 1991 [1991] S&S 50.

[30] With some exceptions. We have already mentioned Art. 16 of the Brussels Convention; see Pt. IV of this ch. Also to be mentioned is Art. 24 of this Convention dealing with jurisdiction in provisional measures.

[31] Case 814/79, *Netherlands* v. *Rüffer* [1980] ECR 3807.

decided that 'whilst certain judgments given in an action between a public authority and a person governed by private law may come within the area of application of the Convention, that is not the case if the public authority is acting in the exercise its public authority powers'.

The Brussels Convention has concurrent jurisdiction with jurisdictional rules of conventions on particular matters, like the Hague Conventions on maintenance.[32] This concurrency rule can be found in Article 57 of the Brussels Convention.[33]

Dutch domestic rules of international jurisdiction will apply once the application of the Brussels Convention and the Lugano Convention, and of any convention on a particular matter, is excluded. We have already discussed the rules of jurisdiction in petition cases. Civil and commercial cases which are not initiated by a petition start with a writ of summons. The plaintiff sends a 'writ of summons', drafted in the prescribed form, to the defendant, summoning him before a certain District or sub-district Court. As already described, writs of summons initiate court proceedings in most disputes over legal relationships between the parties, in cases that are called 'contentious'.[34]

VII
ACCEPTANCE OF JURISDICTION IN THE CASE OF CHOICE OF JURISDICTION AGREEMENTS

According to Dutch domestic rules of international jurisdiction the jurisdiction and lack of it of the Dutch courts are based in the first place on forum agreement of the parties. In Dutch civil procedure prorogation of jurisdiction in contentious cases was unknown until 1985, when the Hoge Raad decided the *Piscator* case.[35] Until 1985 the general rule of jurisdiction had been that, where jurisdiction was not based on convention or specific statutory provision, venue created jurisdiction; in other words, that the rules territorially distributing cases over the Dutch District Courts (the

---

[32] Hague Convention of 7 Oct. 1973 on the Law applicable to Maintenance Obligations; Hague Convention of 7 Oct. 1973 on the Recognition and Enforcement of Decisions Relating to Maintenance Obligations, Collection of Conventions (1951–88), Nos XXIII and XXIV, edited by the Permanent Bureau of the Hague Conference on Private International Law (1988).

[33] An exception is made for the Belgo–Dutch Convention on Jurisdiction and Enforcement 1925 which, for the major part, is set aside by the Brussels Convention: see Art. 55 of the Brussels Convention.

[34] We have mentioned the main exceptions to this rule: divorce cases and maintenance cases.

[35] HR, 1 Feb. 1985 [1985] NJ 698 JCS, [1989] NILR 59.

venue rules), for lack of a comprehensive statutory system of international jurisdiction, also allocate jurisdiction to Dutch courts. Since the Dutch rules of venue did not comprise forum-choice as a ground for venue, until 1985 it was generally held that the Dutch domestic law of jurisdiction did not recognize prorogation. Then the *Piscator* case was litigated. As for the jurisdiction decision, the facts were simple. The Maltese Transocean Towage Company was contracted by the Korean company, Hyundai Construction Co, to tow a dredger from the United Arab Emirates to Libya. During the journey the dredger sank in the Arabian Sea. The parties did not have any relationship with The Netherlands, nor did any other of the facts. The contract included (indirectly) a prorogation rule conferring jurisdiction on the Dutch courts in disputes arising out of the contract. The District Court and the Court of Appeal declined jurisdiction. They applied the 1940 decision of the Hoge Raad, holding that, in the absence of a specific jurisdictional rule in a convention or statute, the rules of venue allocate international jurisdiction, and that prorogation does not create jurisdiction since there is no rule allowing parties to create venue by agreement. Once the judgment was *res judicata* (finally adjudged), the Advocate General brought the case to the Hoge Raad and asked for a ruling on the interpretation of the domestic jurisdictional law.

In the so-called *Piscator* judgment the Hoge Raad held 'that subject to statutory or conventional provisions specifically regulating the jurisdiction of Dutch courts, parties are at liberty—in matters they may freely dispose of[36]—to confer jurisdiction on a Dutch court, unless a reasonable interest is lacking'.[37]

By this 'unless' proviso the Hoge Raad introduced a second rule of *forum non conveniens* into the domestic jurisdictional system of The Netherlands. In his statement of claim opening this 'cassation without prejudice to the parties'—procedure the Advocate General invited the Hoge Raad to allow prorogation of jurisdiction under certain restrictions.[38] His opinion is that in principle parties are entitled to confer jurisdiction on a Dutch court unless apparently there is no reasonable interest in such agreement. As illustrations of the reasonable interest in their selection of a Dutch forum he listed six examples: (a) the neutrality of the Dutch courts as fora of a State that objectively is not involved with the disputed legal relationship nor with the parties; (b) the (self-evident) expertise of the courts if Dutch law is applicable; (c) the expertise of the courts in the

---

[36] This restriction is rather vague. At least conflicts over marriage, divorce, custody, and over the devolution of a future succession are not at the parties' freedom to dispose by agreement.

[37] Translation taken from Betlem, *Civil Liability for Transfrontier Pollution* (Graham and Trotman, London, 1993).

[38] Requests for cassation 'in the interest of the law' may only apply to judgments which have been *res judicata* and shall not affect the judgment which gives rise to that request.

matter disputed; (d) the probability of execution of the other party's assets, e.g. if there is a bank-guarantee, in The Netherlands; (e) the susceptibility of a Dutch decision for execution outside The Netherlands; (f) the creation of legal certainty as to the applicable conflict rules and to the applicable substantive rules and to prevent forum-shopping in cases in which, without the selection of an exclusively competent forum, the courts of more than one State would have jurisdiction.

As an extra argument in support of his opinion the Advocate General referred to Articles 17 and 18 of the Brussels Convention, which allow forum agreements and even recognize the forum selection of the courts of a non-Contracting State. The reasonable interest test he proposed is unknown in the restricted area of the Brussels Convention; it has to function as a bar to the caprices of the parties, as a *forum non conveniens* escape rule.

The Hoge Raad decided as mentioned above. It used as its main arguments the awareness that the Dutch legal order is part of the international legal order and therefore has to take into account the interests of international legal practice.[39] This practice not only requires knowing in advance which court will decide disputes between the parties; it also needs the freedom to confer jurisdiction for the sole reason that both parties consider the agreed court as neutral or particularly expert.

Many forum contract cases have since been decided. The number of cases in which a jurisdiction agreement not governed by Article 17 vested jurisdiction in a Dutch court is not known. The number of disputed jurisdictional agreements, however, is exceptionally low.

As a result of the *Piscator* decision, since 1985 the general rule of jurisdiction in summons cases is that venue and forum-choice create jurisdiction, and that in cases of forum-choice the court has a *forum non conveniens* discretion, that is, a right to deny jurisdiction in case of insufficient connection between the dispute and the Dutch forum.

VIII
DECLINING JURISDICTION IN THE CASE OF A CHOICE OF FOREIGN JURISDICTION AGREEMENT

The above-stated general rule of jurisdiction in summons cases, that venue and forum-choice create international jurisdiction, left one important question open. That question was: does a Dutch court have international jurisdiction if the rules of venue so indicate but parties have

---

[39] This argument had been used already by the Rotterdam RB in its decision of 22 July 1983 [1983] NIPR 371.

agreed on the exclusive choice of a foreign forum? This point of law was the subject of the so-called *Harvest Trader* case.[40] In the light of the rule in the *Piscator* case, the decision of the Hoge Raad was easy to predict. Referring to Article 17 of the Brussels Convention and Article 1022 (1074) of the WBRv[41] the Hoge Raad decided:

> that if in matters they may freely dispose of[42] the parties have conferred exclusive jurisdiction on a foreign court, Dutch courts that would otherwise have had jurisdiction and that are asked to decide such matter in conflict with such agreement in principle must decline jurisdiction unless if and in as far as statutory or Conventional provisions specifically regulating the jurisdiction of Dutch courts do not allow such decision.

In this decision the 'in principle' proviso is not specified. By analogy to Article 17, exceptions to this principle may be found in cases of insurance contracts and consumer contracts, as well as in cases where courts other than the one agreed upon may claim exclusive jurisdiction.[43]

IX
DECLINING JURISDICTION IN INTERIM INJUNCTION PROCEEDINGS

If for reasons of urgency an immediate court decision is required, the claimant or petitioner may bring his or her case before the President of the District Court. This kind of action is called *kort geding*. The president then will grant (or refuse to grant) an interim injunction. Although interim injunctions are provisional measures, in practice (95 per cent) they end the dispute, since in most cases the President's interim decision is for an indefinite period of time and the parties seldom go for a final decision by instituting litigation in ordinary proceedings. *Kort geding* injunctions are fully enforceable. According to Dutch law the president has *kort geding* jurisdiction in all cases in which venue lies with the sub-district or the District Courts.[44] In addition to this general rule of jurisdiction, he also has

---

[40] HR, 28 Oct. 1988 [1989] NJ 765.   [41] See Pt. X.   [42] For this restriction see n. 36.

[43] Here, by analogy to Art. 16 of the Brussels Convention, a court excluded in the agreement might claim exclusive jurisdiction if the object of the proceeding were the ownership in or tenancies of real property, the constitution, nullity of dissolution of companies, legal persons or associations, or the decisions of their organs of such entities, or related to public registers or patents.

[44] Art. 289 s. 1, WBRv. The main requirement of *kort geding* is that an immediate interim decision is needed. In case law, requests for declaratory judgments and for the payment of money were adjudged not fit for interim decisions. For about ten years Presidents of some Dist. Cts. have accepted claims for the payment of money in *kort geding*; others continue to refuse such decisions.

special jurisdiction if the interim injunction is to be executed in his district.[45]

International jurisdiction in interim injunction proceedings is based in the first place on Article 24 of the Brussels Convention.[46] Article 24 reads as follows: 'Application may be made to the courts of a Contracting State for such provisional, including protective, measures as may be available under the law of that State, even if, under this Convention, the courts of another Contracting State have jurisdiction as to the substance of the matter.'

This comprehensive international and relative jurisdiction of the President invites restriction. However, there is no explicit conventional or statutory right for the President to find himself *forum non conveniens*. The restrictions are found in the first place by interpreting the very character of the *kort geding* procedure. In many cases the President declines jurisdiction by judging that the case is lacking in urgency, or that the question to decide is factually or legally too complex to decide in a short time by way of an interim decision. However, in recent cases District Court Presidents increasingly use a *forum non conveniens* consideration to deny jurisdiction. The decision of the President of the Amsterdam District Court of 26 March 1991 gives a fair example. Although one of the defendants had his domicile in The Netherlands, the President refused to grant an interim injunction since the injunction sought was mainly to force the French co-defendant to perform the disputed act.[47]

X
DECLINING JURISDICTION IN THE CASE OF ARBITRATION

The Dutch law of national and international arbitration was recodified in 1986.[48] Since then arbitration has been a special part of the Code of Civil Procedure. The relationship between court jurisdiction and arbitration is covered in Article 1022 of the WBRv—in the case of domestic arbitration—and by Article 1074 of the WBRv—in the case of international arbitration.

[45] This jurisdiction is based on a decision of the HR, 23 Nov. 1917 [1918] NJ 6.

[46] See for an extensive discussion of international jurisdiction in interim injunction proceedings, Betlem, *Civil Liability for Transfrontier Pollution* (Graham and Trotman, London, 1993) 146 ff. See, especially, his discussion about the semi-final character of these injunctions according to Dutch law. According to some District Court Presidents *kort geding* actions for the payment of money do not have an interim character and, therefore, may not constitute Art. 24 jurisdiction: see President, RB, Rotterdam, 16 Mar. 1993 [1993] KG 138.

[47] President, RB, Amsterdam, 26 Mar. 1991 [1991] KG 163.

[48] Act of 2 July 1986, s. 372, in force on 1 Dec. 1986.

These Articles provide that, in the case of a dispute governed by an arbitration agreement, the court has no jurisdiction to decide that dispute if one of the parties raises the agreement, unless it is void. However, an arbitration agreement does not preclude a party from asking the court for conservational seizure of the other party's assets or to seek an interim injunction from the President of the District Court.[49]

The rules of Articles 1022 and 1074 of the WBRv are not absolute. In a recent case, the sub-district court of Zierikzee did not apply this provision, because in its view the defendant was not acting in accordance with requirements of reasonableness and equity in holding the other party to the agreement. The main ground for this decision was that, as a condition for entering into the arbitration, the plaintiff had to pay Dfl 5,000 in advance with no possible reduction or legal aid for financially weak claimants. To hold the claimant to this provision was seen to be in conflict with the requirements of reasonableness and equity.[50]

XI
JURISDICTION AND *LIS ALIBI PENDENS*

Jurisdiction can be based on a number of grounds, like the domicile of the defendant, the forum-choice of the parties, the place of performance, or the *locus delicti*. Therefore, in many cases more than one court has venue or jurisdiction. If one party introduces proceedings into one competent court, the other party is not automatically barred from introducing the same dispute into another competent court. The eventuality of a dispute pending in more than one court is also possible in cases with more than one claimant/petitioner or more than one defendant. All legal systems try to prevent the involvement of more than one court in the same case by making rules on *lis alibi pendens*. In Dutch law rules of jurisdiction in the case of *lis alibi pendens* vary slightly in conventional cases and non-conventional cases.

In general, conventional cases of *lis alibi pendens* are covered by Articles 21 and 22 of the Brussels Convention. Article 21 obliges the court to stay proceedings if a dispute between the same parties involving the same cause of action has already been brought before the court of another Contracting State, and to decline international jurisdiction once the jurisdiction of that other court is certain. In case of closely related actions, i.e., where they are so closely connected that it is expedient to hear and

---

[49] Since 1992 sub-district courts have the same authority as the Presidents of the District Courts to give interim injunctions: see Art. 116 WBRv. Arts. 1022 and 1074 WBRv have to be interpreted accordingly: see Kantongerecht, Zaandam, 16 Apr. 1992 [1992] NJ 616.

[50] Kantongerecht, Zierikzee, 19 Feb. 1988 [1988] Praktijkgids No 2870, 268.

determine them together to avoid the risk of irreconcilable judgments resulting from separate proceedings, Article 22 allows the courts to stay proceedings and, on the request of one of the parties, to refer the case to the court first seised.

In both non-conventional summons and petition cases Dutch law does not oblige the court to stay proceedings if another court has been first seised with the same or a closely related action. In petition cases the court of its own motion or on the request of any of the parties involved may refer the case to the other court; in summons cases the court may refer only on request of the defendant.[51] As a rule, in the case of actions between the same parties on the same subject-matter, courts always refer to the court first seised. In the case of related actions courts use their discretion to refuse referment only if they consider the relationship between the actions too weak or if the proceedings in that other court are already in a too-advanced stage.

The mere fact that more than one court has international jurisdiction may raise questions of recognition and enforcement if one of these courts is a Dutch court. In that case the query is, does Dutch law recognize and allow enforcement of a foreign judgment if the same cause of action between the same parties has been decided or could have been decided in a Dutch court?

In the Brussels Convention, which is applicable in the main to contract and tort cases, the answer is given in Articles 27, 28, and 34. Apart from rules on public policy, due process, and exclusive jurisdiction, the Convention provides for a refusal of recognition and enforcement only in the case of a judgment of a court of another Contracting State if that judgment is irreconcilable with a Dutch judgment given in a dispute between the same parties.

A number of multilateral and bilateral conventions on recognition and enforcement contain similar provisions.[52]

The actual Dutch non-conventional rules on recognition and enforcement do not solve the problem of conflicting judgments. The Code of Civil

---

[51] Art. 158 WBRv in summons cases; Art. 429m WBRv in petition cases.

[52] Multilateral conventions on recognition and enforcement adopted by The Netherlands and containing rules on conflicting decisions in the courts of the state of origin and Dutch courts are: the Hague Convention on the recogition and enforcement of decisions relating to maintenance obligations to children 1958, and the Hague Convention on the recognition and enforcement of decisions relating to maintenance obligations 1973; see Hague Conference on Private International Law, Collection of Conventions. Nos VIII and XXIII. Bilateral Conventions on recognition and enforcement adopted by The Netherlands and containing rules on conflicting decisions in the courts of the state of origin and Dutch courts are the Italo–Dutch Convention on the recognition and enforcement of decisions relating to civil and commercial matters 1959 ([1959] Trb 137), and the Austro–Dutch Convention on the recognition and enforcement of decisions and authentic documents relating to civil law 1963 ([1963] Trb 51).

Procedure does not even contain a rule on recognition of foreign judgments. Case law provides that, unless conventions or statutes otherwise declare, foreign judgments may be recognized if they fulfill at least three conditions: (a) the deciding court had jurisdiction based on an internationally accepted ground, (b) due process was observed, and (c) recognition does not lead to consequences incompatible with the public order of The Netherlands.[53] The mere fact that a Dutch court has already decided in the same matter between the same parties is reason not to recognize a foreign judgment as against public order.[54]

XII
A DRAFT OF A NEW CODE OF
CIVIL PROCEDURE

A draft Bill to amend the Dutch Code of Civil Procedure has recently been published by the Ministry of Justice. It consolidates and codifies the Dutch law of international jurisdiction and related rules, adding some interesting new rules of jurisdiction. In this draft the salient features of the rules of international jurisdiction are the following:

(a) The rule that, unless conventional or statutory rules otherwise decide, venue will define jurisdiction is to be replaced by specific rules of international jurisdiction.
(b) Jurisdiction in petition cases is based on the domicile of the petitioner (or one of the petitioners), on the summons rules in cases where the petition is related to a summons case, or on the mere fact that the case is otherwise sufficiently connected with the legal sphere of The Netherlands. This last rule is new and creates a *forum conveniens* jurisdiction in petition cases.
(c) Divorce jurisdiction has specific rules based on nationality and residence. Where neither party is of Dutch nationality one or both must reside in The Netherlands for twelve months, where one party is a Dutch national he or she must reside for six months. Where both parties are Dutch nationals no residence is required.

---

[53] Here 'public order' is used as a synonym of the French *ordre public*, meaning the complex of written and unwritten principles which, in a given system of law, are considered fundamental and therefore require a denial of the effect of individual acts, foreign legislation, and foreign decisions in this system of law.

[54] As to the execution of foreign judgments, the Code of Civ. Proc. is clear: unless conventions or statutes otherwise declare, foreign judgments may not be executed in The Netherlands: Art. 431 WBRv. A Dutch court decision is needed. In this new decision the court is free to use the foreign judgment as it pleases. It may e.g. order the defendant to obey the foreign judgment, if that judgment was fit for recognition.

(d) Jurisdiction in summons cases is based on the same rules as provided for in the Brussels Convention, as e.g. domicile of the defendant, place of performance of the contractual obligation in question, domicile of the maintenance creditor, place of the harmful event in the case of torts, place of the real property in the case of rights *in rem* or tenancies, the seat of the company, legal entity, or association in questions of their constitution or dissolution, or of the decisions of their organs, the domicile of the trust if the trust fund is in dispute, or the domicile of the trustee if his or her rights or duties are questioned. Added to this list are rules of jurisdiction in succession cases if the estate is located in The Netherlands, as well as in cases involving bankruptcy or suspension of payment.

(e) In matters they may freely dispose of, the parties may agree on a choice of forum. If in such matters the parties appear without disputing the court's jurisdiction, they are supposed tacitly to have agreed on such a choice. However, the choice of forum will not vest jurisdiction if a reasonable interest therein is lacking. This *forum non conveniens* exception stems from the *Piscator* rule discussed in Part VII.

(f) *Forum necessitatis* is now explicitly mentioned as constituting jurisdiction. Two situations are covered. In the case where none of the previous rules of jurisdiction is applicable, Dutch courts nevertheless have jurisdiction if an action appears to be practically impossible in any other country. In the same case courts also have jurisdiction if the matter is sufficiently connected to the legal sphere of The Netherlands and either the plaintiff or the petitioner cannot reasonably be asked to submit the case to a foreign court that has jurisdiction.

(g) The general *forum non conveniens* rule in petition cases actually in force is to be abolished. The new rules on jurisdiction in petition and in summons cases are specific; the jurisdiction system is completed by a *forum necessitatis* provision acting as a hardship rule. As a result there is no role left for *forum non conveniens*.

The draft Bill is currently being discussed in legal circles. Whether it will be placed before Parliament, and what amendments and modifications might be added, is not clear at this moment. Notwithstanding this uncertainty, the subject will no doubt become increasingly important as the search for the creation of a modern code which can both accommodate the existing international provisions and the future developments of procedural law gathers momentum.

16

New Zealand

LAURETTE BARNARD

*Faculty of Law, University of Auckland**

CONTENTS

I
PRELIMINARY REMARKS

1. INTRODUCTION

New Zealand is a common law country. Its law on jurisdiction is derived partly from statute (which has overriding force) and partly from precedent. In the absence of a New Zealand statute or precedent in point the courts will refer to the case law of other common law countries and academic commentaries as persuasive authorities.

---

* The law in this report is stated as at 31 August 1994.

2. VESTING OF JURISDICTION

The New Zealand courts are generally[1] entitled to exercise jurisdiction *in personam* whenever the defendant has been validly served[2] or submits to their jurisdiction:

SERVICE IN NEW ZEALAND

Service can be validly effected whenever the defendant (or his or her authorized agent) is present in New Zealand,[3] however temporarily.[4]

---

[1] The general principles stated below are subject to the qualifications that NZ courts cannot: (a) exercise any jurisdiction where (i) the dispute principally concerns title to a foreign immovable (*Doulson* v. *Matthews* (1792) 4 TR 503), or (ii) in most instances where the parties have agreed to submit their dispute to a foreign arbitrator, and one party relies on that agreement to contest the NZ courts' jurisdiction (see text at n. 134 ff. below; (b) exercise common law jurisdiction (as opposed to admiralty jurisdiction: see *The Tolten* [1946] P 135) where the dispute concerns a tort involving a foreign immovable, regardless of whether title is in issue: *Doulson* v. *Matthews*, above, and cf. also *British South Africa Co* v. *Companhia de Moçambique* [1893] AC 602; *Hesperides Hotels Ltd* v. *Aegean Turkish Holidays Ltd* [1979] AC 508. (It should, however, be noted that this restriction will probably be overruled if the NZ courts are invited to reconsider it: the restriction is illogical and potentially productive of injustice, and the arguments advanced in support of it in *Hesperides Hotels* do not apply in the NZ context.); (c) exercise admiralty jurisdiction *in personam* (i) in respect of claims for damage, loss of life, or personal injury arising out of a collision between ships, a manœuvre to avoid a collision, or non-compliance with the Collision Regulations unless: the defendant ordinarily resides in NZ or has a place of business in NZ; the cause of action arose within NZ territorial waters; an action arising out of the same incident or series of incidents is proceeding in or has been determined by the NZ courts; or the defendant submits or has agreed to submit to the jurisdiction of the NZ courts (Admiralty Act 1973, s. 6(1) and (3)); or (ii) while foreign proceedings in respect of such claims are pending between the same parties and in respect of the same incident or series of incidents (Admiralty Act 1973, s. 6(2) and (3), as analysed by Myburgh, 'New Zealand' in Huybrechts (ed.), *International Encyclopaedia of Transport Law* (forthcoming), para. 213); see n. 110 below); (d) determine any action for damages arising out of carriage by air to which the Warsaw Convention 1929 (as amended by the 1955 Protocol and the Guadalajara Convention 1961) applies unless NZ was the destination; or the carrier ordinarily resides or has its principal place of business, or has an establishment by which the contract was made, in NZ (Carriage by Air Act 1967, Sch. I, art. 28(1)).

[2] *Johnson* v. *Taylor Bros & Co Ltd* [1920] AC 144 at 153.

[3] Mere presence is *all* that is required. The NZ courts will be vested with jurisdiction regardless of whether the cause of action arose in NZ, the parties have any connection with NZ, or the defendant has any assets in NZ. The presence requirement is generally satisfied in respect of: individuals, by physical presence; companies, by incorporation in NZ, registration as an overseas company under the Companies Act 1955, s. 39, or establishing a place of business in NZ; partnerships, by having a place of business in NZ or the physical presence of any partner; and unincorporated associations, by the physical presence of its president, chairperson, secretary, or any similar officer. See McGechan (ed.), *McGechan on Procedure: High Court Rules* (Brooker's, Wellington, 1988), paras. 192–212; Goddard, *Conflict of Laws— The International Element in Commerce and Litigation* (New Zealand Law Society Seminar, 1991), 7–10 for further information on service in NZ.

[4] Cf Dicey and Morris, *The Conflict of Laws* (12th edn., 1993), 298 ff.; Cheshire and North, *Private International Law* (12th edn., 1992), 182 ff. An exception is where the defendant has been enticed into NZ fraudulently or improperly to effect service: cf. Dicey and Morris, 300 n. 84; Cheshire and North, 184.

SUBMISSION

The courts will be vested with jurisdiction *in personam* where litigants over whom they would not otherwise enjoy jurisdiction submit to their jurisdiction. Submission can be express, such as where the litigants have incorporated a New Zealand forum clause in their contract. Submission can also be implied, such as where a litigant institutes proceedings, counterclaims locally, takes any procedural step which is necessary or useful only if the New Zealand courts have jurisdiction,[5] or appears to contest a case on the merits.[6] An appearance to protest jurisdiction does not constitute implied submission;[7] nor, probably, does an appearance to seek a stay on the ground that New Zealand is *forum non conveniens* or to apply for the setting aside of an order affecting property, provided that a protest to jurisdiction has previously been filed or is filed at the same time.[8]

SERVICE OVERSEAS

The High Court Rules[9] govern service overseas in civil and commercial proceedings. Rule 219 provides that service may be effected overseas without leave of the court in certain cases where the parties or the cause of action have a connection[10] with New Zealand or New Zealand law.[11] Furthermore, Rule 220 provides for service overseas with leave where the

[5] *Equiticorp Industries Group Ltd* v. *Hawkins* [1991] 3 NZLR 700 at 714–7.
[6] Cf. Dicey and Morris, n. 4 above, 310–4; Cheshire and North, n. 4 above, pp. 188–90.
[7] R. 131(2) of the High Ct. Rules; Judicature Act 1908, Sch. 2.
[8] Cf Dicey and Morris, n. 4 above, 311–2; Cheshire and North, n. 4 above, 188–90.
[9] N. 7 above. Note that R. 89 of the Dist. Ct. Rules prohibits the service of any process of a Dist. Ct. overseas. However, the High Ct. can direct and supervise such service: see the District Courts Act 1947, s. 55(2). The High Ct. will presumably deal with an application to serve Dist. Ct. proceedings out of NZ on the basis of RR. 219 and 220 of the High Ct. Rules. (The District Court Amendment Act 1989 will amend the principal Act to provide for overseas service of Dist. Ct. proceedings, but the relevant s. is not yet in force.) There is no provision for overseas service of Disputes Tribunal proceedings: see Goddard, n. 3 above, 17.
[10] This connection is not required to be significant—see text at n. 108 below.
[11] More specifically, R. 219 provides that service may be effected overseas without the leave of the court where: (a) the proceedings concern a claim for damages for any act or omission in NZ; (b) the contract in issue was made in NZ or through a NZ agent or was to be performed in NZ or is governed by NZ law; (c) the contract in issue was breached in NZ; (d) it is sought to compel or restrain an act in NZ; (e) the proceedings concern property in NZ or any document affecting property in NZ; (f) the person to be served is a trustee of a trust, the execution of which is governed by NZ law; (g) the defendant is domiciled or ordinarily resident in NZ; (h) the overseas person is a necessary and proper party to proceedings instituted against a person in NZ; (i) the proceedings concern the estate of a person who died domiciled in NZ; (j) the proceedings are brought under the Carriage by Air Act 1967 and the person to be served is not a High Contracting Party to a relevant Convention; (k) the proceedings are for matrimonial property relief and either party is domiciled in NZ; (l) the proceedings relate to marine pollution; or (m) the person to be served has submitted to the jurisdiction. See further McGechan, n. 3 above, para. 219; Goddard, n. 3 above, 11. On the interpretation of R. 219, see *Longbeach Holdings Ltd* v. *Bhanabhai & Co Ltd* [1994] 2 NZLR 28 at 34; *Biddulph* v. *Wyeth Australia Ltd*, unrep., 15 June 1994, High Ct., Wellington Registry, CP 500/86, 4–12.

court in its discretion considers New Zealand *forum conveniens*.[12] Both rules are also applicable in admiralty proceedings,[13] but in this context they are qualified by the operation of Rule 8 of the Admiralty Rules 1975[14] which provides that writs relating to certain admiralty claims *in personam* may be served overseas only by leave of the court, and then only if certain additional requirements are met.[15] Rule 8 does not specify which considerations the court should take into account in determining whether or not to give leave in the relevant instances; but the court is likely to grant leave only if it is *forum conveniens*.[16]

In rem jurisdiction remains relevant in the context of admiralty actions only.[17] The High Court will generally[18] be entitled to exercise admiralty jurisdiction *in rem* whenever a writ *in rem* can be validly served in accordance with the Admiralty Rules. Broadly put, service can be effected by: (a) physically attaching the writ to the ship (or, in some instances, a sister ship),[19] cargo, freight, or other property; (b) delivering the writ to a person

---

[12] R. 220 does not employ the concept *forum conveniens*. It provides that, in exercising its discretion, the court must consider the value of the property in dispute, the existence of a competent court in the place of residence of the person to be served, and the comparative cost and convenience of proceeding in NZ or in the place of residence of the person to be served. However, the factors mentioned in R. 220 are not exhaustive; an applicant must establish that NZ is *forum conveniens* on general principles before an application for leave to serve overseas will succeed: see *Oilseed Products (NZ) Ltd* v. *H. E. Burton Ltd* (1987) 1 PRNZ 313 at 317; McGechan, n. 3 above, para. 200.04.2.b; and see also *Society of Lloyd's and Oxford Members' Agency Ltd* v. *Hyslop* [1993] 3 NZLR 135 at 149. These principles are the same as those governing *forum non conveniens* cases (see text at nn. 42 ff. below), except that the court will assume that it is *not forum conveniens* until the *plaintiff* establishes the converse on clear evidence: cf *Spiliada Maritime Corp* v. *Cansulex Ltd* [1987] 1 AC 460 at 480–1. See further McGechan, n. 3 above, para. 220; Goddard, n. 3 above, 12–13.

[13] Myburgh, n. 1 above, para. 130. *Contra* Gresson and Barratt *Admiralty Actions* (Auckland District Law Society, 1990), 4.8.8, who state that service out of the jurisdiction is limited to the collision and limitation actions set out in R. 8 (see n. 15 below); their restrictive interpretation of R. 8 ignores R. 4 of the Admiralty Rules, which provides for the residual application of the rules and general practice of the High Ct. in admiralty proceedings.

[14] SR 1975/85.

[15] R. 8 provides that where the action is (i) instituted to enforce a claim *in personam* in respect of damage, loss of life, or personal injury arising out of a collision between ships, a manoeuvre to avoid a collision, or non-compliance with the Collision Regulations, or (ii) a limitation action, the court may grant leave to serve overseas if, but only if, the defendant ordinarily resides in NZ or has a place of business in NZ, the cause of action arose within NZ territorial waters, an action arising out of the same incident or series of incidents is proceeding in or has been determined by the NZ courts, or the defendant submits or has agreed to submit to the jurisdiction of the NZ courts.

[16] Cf. R. 4 of the Admiralty Rules, which provides for the residual application of the rules and general practice of the High Ct. in admiralty proceedings.

[17] An admiralty action *in rem* can be substituted by an admiralty action *in personam*, or (under R. 7(1) of the Admiralty Rules) can be continued concurrently with an admiralty action *in personam*, in which case the principles set out in the previous paragraph also apply.

[18] The High Ct. cannot exercise any admiralty jurisdiction where the parties have agreed to submit their dispute to a foreign arbitrator, and one party relies on that agreement to contest the NZ courts' jurisdiction: see text at n. 134 ff. below.

[19] Admiralty Act 1973, s. 5(2)(b).

in control of the cargo, freight, or other property; or (c) such other means as the court may order.[20] Where service can be effected by means other than physically attaching the writ, the cargo, or other property that is the subject-matter of the claim need not be located in New Zealand territory when the writ is served.[21]

Jurisdiction in probate proceedings, the administration of estates, matrimonial causes, and proceedings affecting status is governed by statute.[22]

3. PROTESTING JURISDICTION

Where proceedings are served in breach of the principles set out above, a defendant can appear to protest the New Zealand courts' jurisdiction under Rule 131 of the High Court Rules.[23] If the court is satisfied that it has no jurisdiction, it must dismiss the proceedings.[24]

An objection to jurisdiction cannot succeed if jurisdiction was validly founded as of right, i.e. is based on service within New Zealand or the defendant's submission to the jurisdiction. If service was effected overseas under Rule 219, an objection to jurisdiction will succeed if: (i) the service was invalid because none of the limbs of Rule 219 applied;[25] or (ii) the

---

[20] R. 10(1) provides that the writ in an action *in rem* must be served as follows: (a) upon a ship or upon cargo, freight, or other property on board a ship, by attaching a sealed copy of the writ for a short time to the main mast or the single mast or some other conspicuous part of the ship, and by leaving a copy of the writ attached to it or with the person apparently in charge of the ship; (b) upon cargo, freight, or other property not on board a ship, by attaching a sealed copy of the writ for a short time to that cargo or property and by leaving a copy of the writ attached to it; (c) upon freight in the hands of any person, by showing him or her a sealed copy of the writ and leaving a copy of the writ with him or her; (d) upon proceeds in court, by showing a sealed copy of the writ to the Registrar and by leaving a copy of the writ with him or her; (e) if access cannot be obtained to the cargo, freight, or other property on which the writ is to be served, by showing a sealed copy of the writ to any person appearing to be in charge of the same and leaving a copy of the writ with him or her; or (f) in such other manner as the court may order.

[21] In *Sembawang Salvage Pte Ltd* v. *Shell Todd Oil Services Ltd* (*The Sembawang*) [1993] 2 NZLR 97 at 103, cargo that was subject to a maritime lien was outside NZ territorial waters when the writ *in rem* was served on the solicitor of the company in charge of the cargo. The court considered this valid service under R. 10(1)(e).

[22] See the Family Proceedings Act 1980 (matrimonial causes and paternity disputes); the Guardianship Act 1968 (guardianship, custody, and access proceedings); the Adoption Act 1955 (adoption applications); the Protection of Personal and Property Rights Act 1988 (applications for personal care orders, property orders, and enduring power of attorney); the Administration Act 1969 (matters relating to the administration of the estates of deceased persons); the Insolvency Act 1967 (bankruptcy and insolvency proceedings); and the Companies Act 1955 (winding-up proceedings).

[23] See also R. 11(7) of the Admiralty Rules.

[24] R. 131(4)(a) of the High Court Rules.

[25] See n. 11 above. It will usually not suffice that the proceeding merely does not fall within the specific limb of R. 219 relied on by the plaintiff in the notice of proceeding. If the plaintiff can show that another limb of R. 219 applies, the court will generally not be inclined to

plaintiff's pleadings disclose no good arguable case;[26] or (iii) the court chooses to exercise its residual discretion to set aside service under Rule 219[27] (for example, because New Zealand is *forum non conveniens*).[28] An objection to jurisdiction where service was effected overseas under Rule 220 will succeed if: (i) leave to serve overseas should not have been granted (because the factors listed in Rule 220 had not been applied properly, or New Zealand is otherwise *forum non conveniens*);[29] or (ii) the plaintiff has no good arguable case.

II
DISCRETIONARY LIMITATIONS

The fact that a New Zealand court may be vested with jurisdiction does not necessarily mean that it will exercise that jurisdiction in a particular case. The New Zealand courts have an inherent jurisdiction, preserved by statute,[30] to regulate their own processes in the interests of justice.[31] Thus, the courts have a discretion to stay proceedings where litigation in New Zealand would be productive of injustice. In determining whether it should exercise this discretion in the applicant's favour, the court will take account of the following considerations:[32]

- whether the proceedings in New Zealand are vexatious, oppressive, or an abuse of the process of the courts;
- whether New Zealand is *forum non conveniens*;
- whether the New Zealand proceedings breach an exclusive foreign jurisdiction clause; and

require the plaintiff to go through the cumbersome and pointless ritual of filing an amended notice of proceeding and serving the papers a second time: see Goddard, n. 3 above, 23 and cf. *McConnell Dowell Constructors Ltd* v. *Lloyd's Syndicate 396* [1988] 2 NZLR 257 at 270.

[26] Jurisdiction will not be accepted if the plaintiff does not make out a good arguable case: *Society of Lloyd's*, n. 12 above, 148; Biddulph, n. 11 above, 16 at 20.

[27] The PC has confirmed that the High Ct. retains a residual discretion to set aside service effected overseas under R. 219. This residual discretion will be exercised on the same principles that governed the granting of leave to serve overseas and the setting aside of service before the introduction of R. 219 in 1986: see *Kuwait Asia Bank EC* v. *National Mutual Life Nominees Ltd* [1991] 1 AC 187 at 212.

[28] *Society of Lloyd's*, n. 12 above, 148.

[29] Goddard, n. 3 above, 26. There is nothing in NZ law analogous to the English procedure whereby the defendant may apply for service of the writ to be set aside: the defendant must rely on R. 131 as a challenge mechanism.

[30] Judicature Act 1908, s. 16.

[31] The inherent jurisdiction of the NZ courts is derived from the traditional inherent jurisdiction of the English courts, and is presumably similar in scope: *Dunedin Fire Board* v. *Arthur Barnett Ltd* [1964] NZLR 717 at 721. Both superior and inferior courts enjoy this inherent jurisdiction: see *McMenamin* v. *Attorney-General* [1985] 2 NZLR 274 at 276.

[32] The following list is not exhaustive: new considerations may be identified in future.

- in some instances, whether proceedings are instituted in breach of an arbitration agreement.

A recent Court of Appeal decision indicates that these considerations are not to be treated as separate and distinct grounds for a stay, but that the court will instead seek to arrive at a global assessment on a consideration of all relevant factors pleaded by the parties.[33]

1. ABUSE OF PROCESS

(a) COMMON LAW

The courts have an inherent jurisdiction to stay proceedings where the pleadings disclose no reasonable cause of action or the proceedings are frivolous, vexatious, or otherwise an abuse of process.[34] This inherent jurisdiction empowers the courts to stay not only domestic, but also transnational, litigation.[35] For example, the courts will stay an action if the *lex causae* does not provide for the cause of action relied on by the plaintiff, the proceedings are instituted in breach of a settlement,[36] or the plaintiff does not genuinely desire trial in New Zealand but instead seeks to put the defendant to unnecessary expense or to achieve an improper advantage.[37] The onus to prove abuse rests on the applicant.

(b) STATUTORY PROVISIONS

Rule 477 of the High Court Rules provides as follows:

477. **Summary stay or dismissal**—Where in any proceeding it appears to the Court that in relation to the proceeding generally or in relation to any claim for relief in the proceeding—

(a) No reasonable cause of action is disclosed; or
(b) The proceeding is frivolous or vexatious; or
(c) The proceeding is an abuse of the process of the Court, the Court may order that the proceeding be stayed or dismissed generally or in relation to any claim for relief in the proceeding.

[33] *Society of Lloyd's*, n. 12 above, 142–4, 148, 154. The Court did not address the issue of how this conflation of considerations might square with the fact that different rules on burden of proof apply in e.g. *forum non conveniens* and exclusive foreign jurisdiction cases respectively. Cf. also *Ariki New Zealand Ltd* v. *Anzac Enterprises LP*, unrep., 23 Dec. 1993, High Ct., Wellington Registry, CP 183/93, 8–9 where the court conflated the issues of *forum non conveniens* and breach of an exclusive jurisdiction agreement.
[34] Cf. McGechan, n. 3 above, para. 477.04, read with 186.04 passim.
[35] Cf. *St Pierre* v. *South American Stores (Gath and Chaves) Ltd* [1936] 1 KB 382 at 397–8.
[36] See e.g. *Kontvanis* v. *O'Brien (No 2)* [1958] NZLR 516.
[37] E.g. where the plaintiff institutes proceedings to intimidate a NZ defendant: cf. *Wallersteiner* v. *Moir* [1974] 3 All ER 217 (but note now the provisions on gagging writs in the Defamation Act 1992); and cf. generally *Atlantic Star (Owners)* v. *Bona Spes (Owner) (The*

Further, Rule 186 of the High Court Rules provides that pleadings may be struck out (a process which will in certain cases *de facto* terminate the proceedings) if they disclose no reasonable cause of action, are likely to be prejudicial, embarassing, or productive of delays, or are an abuse of process. Similar considerations will apply where an application to strike out a writ is brought under Rule 11(7) of the Admiralty Rules.[38]

The above statutory bases for a stay or dismissal fall within the broader framework of the courts' inherent jurisdiction with regard to abuse of process. As such, the authorities relating to the latter remain relevant to the interpretation of the statutory rules.

2. FORUM NON CONVENIENS

(a) INTRODUCTION

The doctrine of *forum non conveniens* was introduced into New Zealand law in 1987 when the Court of Appeal[39] adopted the *Spiliada* case.[40]

The doctrine of *forum non conveniens*, as understood in New Zealand law, provides that a New Zealand court will refuse to adjudicate on proceedings over which it enjoys jurisdiction if: (i) there is a foreign competent court; and (ii) the New Zealand court is persuaded that it would best serve the interests of all the parties and the ends of justice for that foreign forum to try the proceedings instead.[41]

(b) PRINCIPLES

The principles relevant to *forum non conveniens* may be summarized as follows:[42]

> (i) A stay will only be granted on the ground of *forum non conveniens* where the court is satisfied that there is some other available forum, having competent jurisdiction, which is the appropriate forum for the trial of the action, i.e. in which the case may be tried more suitably for the interests of all the parties and the ends of justice.

Atlantic Star) [1973] 2 WLR 795 at 804–5; *MacShannon* v. *Rockware Glass Ltd* [1978] AC 795 at 810.

[38] Cf. *The Sembawang*, n. 21 above, 98.

[39] *Club Méditerranée NZ* v. *Wendell* [1989] 1 NZLR 216 at 219.

[40] N. 12 above.

[41] *Club Méditerranée NZ*, n. 39 above, 219; *McConnell Dowell Constructors Ltd*, n. 25 above, 273.

[42] This exposition is based on that appearing in the *Spiliada* case, n. 12 above, 476, as adopted by the High Ct. in *Oilseed Products (NZ) Ltd*, n. 12 above, 316–7; *Gilmore* v. *Gilmore*, unrep., 3 May 1993, High Ct., Wellington Registry, M 109/93, 5–6; *Biddulph*, n. 11 above, 16; and more generally by the CA in *Club Méditerranée*, n. 39 above, 219; *McConnell Dowell Constructors Ltd*, n. 25 above, 273; *Longbeach Holdings*, n. 11 above, 35.

(ii) In general, the burden of proof rests on the defendant to persuade the court to exercise its discretion to grant a stay. This applies both where jurisdiction exists as of right (i.e. where the defendant is served in New Zealand or has submitted to the New Zealand courts' jurisdiction), and served where the courts may assume jurisdiction pursuant to service overseas under Rule 219[43] or 220[44] of the High Court Rules, or Rule 8(3) of the Admiralty Rules.[45]

(iii) The burden resting on the defendant is not just to show that New Zealand is not the natural or appropriate forum for the trial, but to establish that there is another available forum which is clearly and distinctly more appropriate.[46]

(iv) The appropriate forum is that with which the trial has the most real and substantial connection. Since the question is whether there exists some other forum which is clearly more appropriate for the trial, the court will first look to see what factors point to another forum, including: (i) factors affecting convenience and expense; and (ii) further factors, such as the law governing the transaction, and the places where the parties reside or carry on business.

(v) If the court concludes that there is no other available forum which is clearly more appropriate for the trial, it will ordinarily refuse a stay.

(vi) If, however, the court decides at this stage that there is another, clearly more appropriate, forum, it will ordinarily grant a

[43] *McConnell Dowell Constructors Ltd*, n. 25 above, 281; *Society of Lloyd's*, n. 12 above, 149 (but see n. 33 above); *Longbeach Holdings*, n. 11 above, 35; *Biddulph*, n. 11 above, 13. This view is criticized by Paterson, (1989) 13 *NZ Univ. LR* 337 at 364–9, who argues that the onus should be on the plaintiff, because a pro-plaintiff bias conflicts with the *Spiliada* principle that the courts should not lightly assume exorbitant jurisdiction.

[44] *Oilseed Products (NZ) Ltd*, n. 12 above, 317; *Cockburn* v. *Kinzie Industries Inc* (1988) 1 PRNZ 243 at 245, 248. Both are low-level precedents. They are criticized by Paterson: see n. 43 above. The CA did not enter into this issue in *Society of Lloyd's*, n. 12 above, 149, but merely affirmed that the applicant bears the onus when leave to serve overseas is first sought.

[45] See n. 16 above.

[46] In the *Spiliada* case, n. 12 above, the onus was variously stated as the defendant having to show that the foreign forum was 'more appropriate' (see Lord Templeman at 464, 465) and 'clearly and distinctly more appropriate' (see Lord Goff at 477, 478, 484). In *Club Méditerranée*, n. 39 above, 218, 220 and *Longbeach Holdings*, n. 11 above, 35, 36 the CA apparently proceeded on the basis that the defendant had to show that the foreign court was the 'more appropriate' forum; but in *McConnell Dowell Constructors Ltd*, n. 25 above, 276, 282 it employed the 'clearly more appropriate' formulation. The practice in the High Ct. has been to employ the 'clearly and distinctly more appropriate' formulation (see e.g. *Gilmore*, n. 42 above, 10; *Miracle Nail Ltd* v. *Backscratchers Nail Care Products Inc*, unrep., 31 May 1993, High Ct., Hamilton Registry, CP 134/91, 23; *Biddulph*, n. 11 above, 16; but see *New Zealand Insurance Co Ltd* v. *New Zealand Forest Products Ltd* (1994) 7 PRNZ 365 at 370, where the court adopted the expression 'more appropriate'.

stay, unless the plaintiff can establish on cogent evidence[47] that granting a stay would be unjust in all the circumstances of the case.

(c) APPLICATION OF THE PRINCIPLES

Although the issue before the court is stated as being whether New Zealand is the forum with 'the closest and most real' connection with the trial, the assessment is in practice relative rather than absolute. The court will consider whether New Zealand or the forum which the defendant invokes has the better claim to being *forum conveniens*. It will not *mero motu* consider the claims of other potentially interested foreign courts, even if there are indications that one of those courts has the closest and most real connection with the matter.[48]

There are two broad fields of inquiry in determining whether New Zealand is *forum non conveniens*.[49] The court will consider: first, the factors tending to show that the forum identified by the defendant has the closest connection with the case, can thus determine the dispute most expeditiously, and is therefore *prima facie* the appropriate forum; and, secondly, considerations militating against justice being done if the plaintiff is confined to proceeding in that foreign forum.

(i) **Factors Considered in Assessing the *Prima Facie* Case for a Stay**

In ascertaining whether New Zealand or a foreign jurisdiction has the closest and most real connection with the trial and is therefore *prima facie*

---

[47] This was described as an evidential burden in *Charm Maritime Inc* v. *Kyriakou* [1987] 1 Lloyd's Rep 433 at 447. Thus, the overall burden to establish that trial in NZ would not promote the ends of justice remains on the defendant. Cf. *Longbeach Holdings*, n. 11 above, 35.

[48] See *Van Dyck* v. *Van Dyck* [1990] 3 NZLR 624, 627 where the court declared NZ *forum conveniens* on the ground that it clearly had a closer and more real connection with the trial than did The Netherlands, the jurisdiction invoked by the defendant; but where the court indicated that its finding might well have been different had the defendant submitted that California was the *forum conveniens*.

[49] It is controversial whether the *Spiliada* case introduced a two-stage or a global analysis. The English CA stated in *Charm Maritime Inc*, n. 47 above, 447 that the *Spiliada* case introduced a global analysis requiring that issues of connection and issues of injustice be considered together. The High Ct. similarly adopted a global approach in the NZ cases involving questions of substantial injustice that have arisen to date (*Gilmore*, n. 42 above; *Wong* v. *Australian and New Zealand Banking Group Ltd* (1991) 4 PRNZ 451; *Biddulph*, n. 11 above. Cf. also *Longbeach Holdings*, n. 11 above, 36, where the CA expressed the issues requiring analysis in *forum non conveniens* applications in global terms; but note that the court did so without analysis, and that injustice was not in issue in the case before it. However, such an analysis seems inconsistent with the terms employed by Lord Goff in the *Spiliada* case. In *De Dampierre* v. *De Dampierre* [1988] 1 AC 92 at 108–209, Lord Goff clearly describes the approach in *forum non conveniens* cases as structured, and as involving a distinct assessment of connection and injustice. It is therefore submitted that a two-stage approach applies in England, and should apply in NZ, given its CA's acceptance of the HL's exposition of the principles governing *forum non conveniens*.

the appropriate forum, the court will consider a wide range of factors. These include:

- the location of documents and witnesses, the degree to which the various courts can obtain access to material evidence, and the respective costs of doing so;[50]
- whether the dispute concerns the conduct of a company incorporated in New Zealand (in which event only very clear and weighty considerations would justify finding New Zealand *forum non conveniens*);[51]
- the existence of litigation in the other jurisdiction between the same parties (*lis alibi pendens*), and the state of those proceedings;[52]
- the prospect of parallel litigation elsewhere;[53]
- whether all relevant parties are subject to New Zealand jurisdiction, so that all issues can be resolved in one hearing or set of hearings;[54]
- in highly complex cases,[55] whether factually related litigation already has been, or is being, conducted in the other jurisdiction, so that experienced teams of counsel and expert witnesses are available there;[56]
- the degree to which the outcome of litigation in the other forum between the defendant and other parties will affect the plaintiff's case;[57]
- the degree to which the relief sought by the plaintiff, if afforded, would affect third parties engaged in litigation against the defendant in the other forum;[58]
- procedural advantages, such as that the proceedings will be adjudicated more speedily or at less cost in one jurisdiction than in

---

[50] E.g. *Club Méditerranée NZ*, n. 39 above, 220; *McConnell Dowell Constructors Ltd*, n. 25 above, 274, 282; *Oilseed Products*, n. 12 above, 319 read with 317; *Johnston & Associates Inc* v. *Stewart*, unrep., 25 Feb. 1991, High Ct. in Admiralty, Auckland Registry, AD 551/90, 6–8; *New Zealand Insurance*, n. 46 above, 371; *Longbeach Holdings*, n. 11 above, 36; *Biddulph*, n. 11 above, 17.

[51] *Britannia Brands (Holdings) Pte Ltd* v. *Britannia Brands Holdings NZ Ltd*, unrep., 19 May 1993, High Ct., Auckland Registry, CP 7/93, 7–8, following *Banco Atlantico SA* v. *The British Bank of the Middle East* [1990] 2 Lloyd's Rep. 504, Cf. also *Air Nauru* v. *Niue Airlines* [1993] 2 NZLR 639 at 640.

[52] *McConnell Dowell Constructors Ltd*, n. 25 above, 275–6, 277–8; *Gilmore*, n. 42 above, 6, 8–9, 10–11; *Van Dyck*, n. 48 above, 627; *Carter Holt Harvey Timber Ltd* v. *Pacifico Timber Importers Ltd*, unrep., 25 May 1993, High Ct., Auckland Registry, CP 1066/92, 17, 18.

[53] *Primesite Outdoor Advertising Ltd* v. *City Clock (Australia) Ltd* (1991) 4 PRNZ 472 at 477–8.

[54] *McConnell Dowell Constructors Ltd*, n. 25 above, 274, 282. But see *Curnow Shipping Ltd* v. *National Bank of New Zealand Ltd* (1990) 2 PRNZ 67 at 70.

[55] *Société Nationale Industrielle Aérospatiale* v. *Lee Kui Jak* [1987] 1 AC 871 at 898.

[56] The *Spiliada* case, n. 12 above, 486.

[57] Cf. *Society of Lloyd's*, n. 12 above, 143.

[58] Cf. *Society of Lloyd's* n. 12 above, 143.

the other,[59] or that one jurisdiction appropriately disallows jury trials in the relevant kind of proceedings;[60]

- whether trial in New Zealand will deprive a litigant of a real juridical advantage available to him or her in the foreign forum;[61]
- localizing factors, such as the *situs* of the property in dispute,[62] the places where the parties and their representatives reside or carry on business,[63] the place of contracting and agreed performance,[64] and the place where the damage resulting from a breach of contract was experienced;[65]
- in which jurisdiction the judgment will need to be enforced (it will generally be more efficient to obtain judgment in the forum where enforcement will take place);[66]
- the degree to which a judgment given in one jurisdiction would be enforceable in the other;[67]
- the *lex causae*[68] (other things being equal, it is generally better for litigation to be conducted in the court whose law will be applied, as that court is best able to identify and apply the relevant rules correctly and as the scope for appeal on disputed points of law will be greater);[69]
- whether the dispute concerns public policy issues or the social conditions in a given country (it is generally better for the courts of that country to assess such issues);[70]

[59] *McConnell Dowell Constructors Ltd*, n. 25 above, 273–4; *Johnston & Associates Inc*, n. 50 above, 8; *Carter Holt Harvey Timber Ltd*, n. 52 above, 16, 18; *New Zealand Insurance*, n. 46 above, 370–1.

[60] *New Zealand Insurance*, n. 46 above, 370–1.

[61] *New Zealand Insurance*, n. 46 above, 371 (where the factors favouring a trial in NZ outweighed the loss of a cause of action available in California).

[62] *Gilmore*, n. 42 above, 8; *Ronstan International Ltd* v. *RC Marine Corp*, unrep., 16 Feb. 1993, High Ct., Auckland Registry, CP 422/92.

[63] The *Spiliada* case, n. 12 above, 478; *Longbeach Holdings*, n. 11 above, 35; *Biddulph*, n. 11 above, 17. The parties' common residence in NZ was considered a decisive factor in holding NZ to be *forum conveniens* in *Van Dyck*, n. 48 above, 627.

[64] *New Zealand Insurance*, n. 46 above, 370.

[65] *Longbeach Holdings*, n. 11 above, 36.

[66] *Crane Accessories Ltd* v. *Lim Swee Hee* [1989] 1 NZLR 221 at 231–2; *Auckland Receivers Ltd* v. *Diners Club* [1985] 2 NZLR 652 at 654; *Lloyd's Bank plc* v. *Barton*, unrep., 14 Feb. 1991, High Ct., Auckland Registry, CP 1534/90,11.

[67] *Johnston & Associates Inc*, n. 50 above, 90; *Van Dyck*, n. 48 above, 627–8; *Miracle Nail Ltd*, n. 46 above, 21–2; *Gilmore*, n. 42 above, 9–10; *New Zealand Insurance*, n. 46 above, 371.

[68] The *Spiliada* case, n. 12 above, 478; *Johnston & Associates Inc*, n. 50 above, 9; *Oilseed Products (NZ) Ltd*, n. 12 above, 319; *New Zealand Insurance*, n. 46 above, 370; *Longbeach Holdings*, n. 11 above, 35.

[69] *Club Méditerranée*, n. 39 above, 220; *Society of Lloyd's*, n. 12 above, 154; *Johnston & Associates Inc*, n. 50 above, 11; all approving *Owners of Cargo Lately Laden on Board the Ship or Vessel Eleftheria* v. *The Eleftheria (Owners) (The Eleftheria)*. [1970] P 94 at 105.

[70] *Partnership Pacific Ltd* v. *Mellsop* (1991) 5 PRNZ 619 at 623–4; *Air Nauru*, n. 51 above, 640.

- the extent to which a party's desire to proceed in a specific jurisdiction is genuine or is instead merely tactical;[71]
- the defendant's readiness to proceed in the other forum;[72]
- the strength of the plaintiff's case;[73]
- a foreign forum clause;[74]
- whether jurisdiction arises as of right or is exorbitant;[75]
- the degree to which courts in third and further countries regard the other forum as *forum conveniens*;[76] and
- general considerations of international comity.[77]

The courts will consider any factors regarded as relevant: the above list is not exhaustive

It will be noted that the above list includes factors relating to litigational convenience. This is not to suggest that convenience is the focus of the analysis: the issue is justice, not mere convenience. However, litigational convenience is factored into the analysis, as this may influence the justice of the outcome. For example, it may frustrate the ends of justice if a party is discouraged from defending an action because of disproportionate expense, or cannot compel witnesses whose evidence is material.

The weight accorded to the relevant factors depends on the circumstances of each case. However, there are certain guidelines that will be applied in making this assessment:

- If the New Zealand court is the only forum that can make the order sought, it will ordinarily be *forum conveniens*.[78]
- Great weight will ordinarily be attached to comparative comprehensiveness. If there is only one court in which all issues between all interested parties can be resolved, that court will ordinarily be the *forum conveniens*.[79]

[71] Gilmore, n. 42 above, 8; *Carter Holt Harvey Timber Ltd*, n. 52 above, 16, 18.

[72] Cockburn, n. 44 above, 249.

[73] Jurisdiction will not be accepted if the plaintiff does not make out a good arguable case: *Society of Lloyd's*, n. 12 above, 148, 149–54. See also *Oilseed Products (NZ) Ltd*, n. 12 above, 320, read with 317; *Pacific Fundraising Ltd* v. *Universal Australia Pty Ltd* (1990) 3 PRNZ 372 at 378.

[74] Whether valid under its proper law or not: *Society of Lloyd's*, n. 12 above, 154. However, the court must disregard a foreign forum clause in breach of the Sea Carriage of Goods Act 1940, s. 11A (or the Maritime Transport Bill 1994, cl. 208(1), when enacted): see text at n. 135 below.

[75] *Johnston & Associates Inc*, n. 50 above, 9.

[76] *Society of Lloyd's*, n. 12 above, 154.

[77] *Gilmore*, n. 42 above, 5.

[78] *Air Nauru*, n. 51 above, 639 (winding-up order against a NZ company sought in consequence of its alleged breach of contract). Cf. also *Apple Computer Inc* v. *Apple Corps SA* [1990] 2 NZLR 598 at 600 (removal of trade mark from NZ register sought). But see *Society of Lloyd's*, n. 12 above, 154 where NZ was considered *forum non conveniens* even though only a NZ court could exercise the discretionary power to grant relief under the Illegal Contracts Act 1970.

[79] *McConnell Dowell Constructors Ltd*, n. 25 above, 274, 282; *Society of Lloyd's*, n. 12 above, 154. But see *Longbeach Holdings*, n. 11 above, 36, where the CA refused a foreign supplier's

- Factors that are not material on the facts of the particular case will ordinarily not be accorded significance. For example, the foreign residence of witnesses will ordinarily be significant only if their evidence is disputed and is likely to be material.[80] Similarly, the fact that the other court's law is the *lex causae* will ordinarily be significant only if there is a dispute about the contents of the *lex causae*,[81] and then usually only in those instances where the *lex causae* and New Zealand law are sufficiently dissimilar to create the risk that a New Zealand court may misinterpret or misapply the *lex causae*.[82]
- The nature of the dispute and the amount involved have an impact on the weight to be given to the various factors. For example, where large sums are at stake in a commercial dispute, comparative costs will generally not be of great moment, whereas comparative efficiency will.[83]
- The court will consider the practical realities of the case. For example, where a contract was technically breached in one country but the real damage resulting from this was experienced elsewhere, the court will regard the place of damage as the cardinal factor.[84] Similarly, in subrogation claims the court will consider the interests of the respective underwriters who finance and control the litigation, even though the proceedings may be conducted in the assured parties' names.[85]
- Concurrent litigation is undesirable: it not only leads to additional expense and inconvenience, but also entails a risk of different outcomes and consequent complications regarding issue estoppel, *res judicata*, and enforcement.[86] The existence of proceedings elsewhere can therefore influence the question whether trial in New Zealand is appropriate. In assessing the relevance of this factor, a New Zealand court will have regard to the length of time for which the other court has been seised of the case and what stage the

application to stay an action in breach of contract, holding that the NZ purchaser was not to be prejudiced by the existence of any disputes between the supplier and its foreign subcontractors as to the quality of the merchandise manufactured.

[80] *Club Méditerranée NZ*, n. 39 above, 220; *Wong v. Ting*, unrep., 13 Sept. 1993, CA, CA 361/92, 7. See also *McConnell Dowell Constructors Ltd*, n. 25 above, 274.

[81] The *Spiliada* case, n. 12 above, 481; *Club Méditerranée NZ*, n. 39 above, 219, 220; *Miracle Nail Ltd*, n. 46 above, 22–3.

[82] Cf. *Society of Lloyd's*, n. 12 above, 143 (but see also 138); *Wong v. Ting*, n. 80 above, 5–6; *Wong v. Australian and New Zealand Banking Group Ltd*, n. 49 above, 458; *Carter Holt Harvey Timber Ltd*, n. 52 above, 16, 18.

[83] *McConnell Dowell Constructors Ltd*, n. 25 above, 274.

[84] *Longbeach Holdings*, n. 11 above, 36.

[85] The *Spiliada* case, n. 12 above, 486 (on which see also *Société Nationale Industrielle Aérospatiale*, n. 55 above, 898).

[86] *Gilmore*, n. 42 above, 10.

foreign proceedings have reached.[87] The court will generally not accord the *lis alibi pendens* factor much weight if the foreign proceedings have not passed beyond the stage of the initiating process. However, the position will be different if those proceedings have progressed to the stage where they have had some impact on the dispute between the parties, especially if that impact is likely to have a continuing effect.[88] The court will tend to disregard the *lis alibi pendens* factor if the foreign proceedings are not genuine, for example, where they were instituted merely for the purpose of demonstrating the existence of a competing jurisdiction.[89] The court will further consider whether the foreign court's exercise of jurisdiction is dependent on its being an appropriate forum (in which case considerations of comity may point towards a decision in harmony with that court's determination), or whether it exercises exorbitant jurisdiction (in which case no comity concern arises).[90] However, pre-existing litigation in the other forum is not decisive: a New Zealand court will not give priority to one party's rush to judgment,[91] and will not give way if it considers itself clearly the *forum conveniens*.[92]

- The court can accord greater weight to a given factor than a party has submitted it should bear.[93]
- In making its assessment, the court will consider the interests of all the parties, not simply those of the applicant.[94] It will also consider the broader demands of justice.

The courts will not, by rigid adherence to a framework of specific rules or criteria, unduly fetter their discretion or sacrifice their ability to respond flexibly. Their approach is to make a global assessment of the suitability of litigation in the competing jurisdictions.[95]

The weight to be accorded the various factors individually and in conjunction with one another is a matter for the trial judge. A court of appeal will not lightly interfere with the trial judge's assessment.[96]

[87] *Van Dyck*, n. 48 above, 627; *Carter Holt Harvey Timber Ltd*, n. 52 above, 17, 18. Foreign proceedings instituted after the NZ proceedings were disregarded in *Longbeach Holdings*, n. 11 above, 37.

[88] *De Dampierre*, n. 49 above, 108.   [89] *Ibid.*, 108.

[90] *McConnell Dowell Constructors Ltd*, n. 25 above, 277; *Gilmore*, n. 42 above, 5, 10–11. Cf. also *Primesite Outdoor Advertising Ltd*, n. 53 above, 478.

[91] *Gilmore*, n. 42 above, 8.

[92] *McConnell Dowell Constructors Ltd*, n. 25 above, 275–6, 277–8; *Gilmore*, n. 42 above, 10–11.

[93] *Johnston & Associates Inc*, n. 50 above, 9.

[94] *Club Méditerranée NZ*, n. 39 above, 220.

[95] *McConnell Dowell Constructors Ltd*, n. 25 above, 282; *Gilmore*, n. 42 above, 10; *Johnston & Associates Inc*, n. 50 above, 12; *Miracle Nail Ltd*, n. 46 above, 23.

[96] *Wong v. Ting*, n. 80 above, 3, following the *Spiliada* case, n. 12 above, 465, 486; *Longbeach Holdings*, n. 11 above, 36.

There are cases (for example certain transnational commercial cases, or cases involving collisions on the high seas) where no particular forum can be described as the natural forum. In such cases, the courts will ordinarily not stay proceedings instituted in New Zealand.

If the court determines that New Zealand has the closest and most real connection with the trial it will ordinarily refuse a stay. Conversely, it will ordinarily grant a stay if it determines that the other forum has the closest and most real connection with the trial. However, this is subject to whether other factors indicate that trial in the court having the closest connection with the case would be inappropriate.

(ii) Factors Tending to Rebut the *Prima Facie* Case

The *prima facie* case for a stay will be rebutted if the plaintiff can establish that justice nevertheless requires the trial to be conducted in New Zealand. The courts will therefore ordinarily not stay New Zealand proceedings if the plaintiff can establish on objective, cogent evidence that justice will not be done by the forum having the closest connection.[97] This would be the case if the foreign judicial system is deficient,[98] for example because the foreign judiciary is biased[99] or the foreign court will not adhere to a minimum standard of justice.[100] The courts will also refuse a stay where the administration of justice in the other country has been disrupted owing to war or civil unrest.[101] Other instances where justice would not be done abroad are where the foreign court would summarily dismiss the plaintiff's claim when New Zealand would regard him or her as having a good case under the *lex causae*, if there would be a delay of many years before the action would be tried abroad, or if the foreign court would impose a derisorily low limit on damages.[102]

As a general rule, the court will not be deterred from granting a stay simply because the plaintiff will be deprived of a real and legitimate personal or juridical advantage that he or she would enjoy if proceeding

---

[97] The *Spiliada* case, n. 12 above, 478.

[98] Considerations of comity dictate that the courts will not lightly refuse a stay on this ground: see Cheshire and North, n. 4 above, 229.

[99] *The Abidin Daver* [1984] AC 398 at 411.

[100] *Gilmore*, n. 42 above, 6.

[101] See also *Muduroglu Ltd* v. *TC Ziraat Bankasi* [1986] QB 1225 at 1248. *Gilmore*, n. 42 above, 8. In *Oilseed Products (NZ) Ltd*, n. 12 above, 320–1 the court refused to declare Fiji the *forum conveniens*, *inter alia* because a coup d'etat had disrupted the administration of justice in Fiji: its Sup. Ct. was not operational, the validity of the appointment of its new judges was uncertain, it was unclear when those judges would commence work, there would be a considerable backlog of cases once the court did become operational, and the disruption of Fiji's relationship with the Commonwealth and the PC meant that there was no longer any effective right of appeal from its judgments.

[102] Cheshire and North, n. 4 above, 226–7.

in New Zealand, provided that it is satisfied that substantial justice will be done in the foreign court. Thus, the court will generally grant a stay where the foreign court has the closest connection with the trial, even though, for instance, the latter's discovery procedures may be less generous, it may award damages on a less liberal scale, or the law it will apply may be less beneficial to the plaintiff. Broadly put, any factor advantaging the plaintiff which is counterbalanced by an equal disadvantage to the defendant will be disregarded. However, the position may be different where the plaintiff would obtain an advantage in New Zealand which would not entail a countervailing disadvantage to the defendant: in such a case, there may be substantial injustice in depriving the plaintiff of his or her advantage.[103] Other instances where justice may dictate that the trial should be in New Zealand are: first, where the action is time-barred abroad but not in New Zealand, and the plaintiff acted reasonably in commencing proceedings in New Zealand, and did not act unreasonably in failing to commence proceedings abroad;[104] and, secondly, where there is no effective right of appeal in the foreign country.[105]

(d) THE ROLE OF *FORUM NON CONVENIENS*

Before the mid-1980s the New Zealand courts enjoyed a potentially excessive jurisdiction: jurisdiction vested and was typically exercised whenever service could be effected on the defendant, however fleeting his or her presence in New Zealand, and regardless of any real connection between the parties or the cause of action and New Zealand or New Zealand law. Nevertheless, there is no evidence that forum-shopping[106] used to present a practical problem. This was partly because of New Zealand's geographic isolation, which reduced the possibility of service on a defendant whose presence in New Zealand was fortuitous and fleeting, and partly because most international contact occurred between New Zealand and other common law countries, which tended to reduce any comparative substantive, procedural, or remedial advantage in suing in New Zealand.

---

[103] Cheshire and North, n. 4 above, 229.

[104] As in *Biddulph*, n. 11 above, 17–18.

[105] *Oilseed Products (NZ) Ltd*, n. 12 above, as discussed in n. 101 above; *Wong v. Australian and New Zealand Banking Group Ltd*, n. 49 above, 456–8.

[106] This expression is here used to denote the case where a plaintiff selects a jurisdiction which has no real connection with the parties or the cause of action, rather than where a plaintiff by reason of comparative advantage elects to sue in one of several juridictions that are properly (albeit not necessarily equally) interested in the conduct and outcome of the proceedings. •

Forum-shopping became a real risk in 1986,[107] when the High Court Rules were amended to provide for service overseas without leave in a range of circumstances, including instances where the connection between the parties or the cause of action and New Zealand or New Zealand law was not necessarily significant.[108] The doctrine of *forum non conveniens* was adopted into New Zealand law the next year. However, this was not articulated as a judicial response to a perception that the risk of forum-shopping had materialized, or was likely to do so. Rather, the doctrine was adopted without analysis, seemingly simply because English law had done so.[109]

The doctrine of *forum non conveniens* is now available to combat unacceptable forum-shopping in those cases where it does arise.

3. LIS ALIBI PENDENS

Statute provides that the New Zealand courts cannot exercise admiralty jurisdiction *in personam* in respect of claims for damage, loss of life, or personal injury arising from a collision between ships, a ship's manœuvre, or omission to carry out a manœuvre to avoid a collision, or noncompliance with the Collision Regulations, while proceedings between the same parties in respect of the same incident or series of incidents are pending in any foreign court, unless the defendant submits or has agreed to submit to their jurisdiction.[110]

The above restriction aside, *lis alibi pendens* does not constitute a distinct ground affecting the exercise of jurisdiction. There is no principle to the effect that the New Zealand courts should decline to exercise jurisdiction simply because proceedings concerning the same matter have already been instituted abroad. However, *lis alibi pendens* may be a relevant factor when the courts consider staying an action on the ground that proceeding in New Zealand constitutes an abuse of process[111] or that New Zealand is *forum non conveniens*.[112]

---

[107] The Admiralty Rules 1975 provided for service overseas in certain instances before this date (see n. 15 above), but there is no evidence that this had led to forum-shopping.

[108] E.g. service can be effected overseas without leave on the ground that the contract was concluded in NZ, even though the issue concerns the interpretation of the contract under its foreign proper law: cf. *Johnston & Associates Inc*, n. 50 above. Cf. also *Biddulph*, n. 11 above, 17. See n. 11 above for the circumstances in which service can be effected overseas without the leave of the court.   [109] See *Club Méditerranée NZ*, n. 39 above.

[110] Admiralty Act 1973, s. 6(2) and (3). S. 6(2) provides in general terms that no action *in personam* be brought in the event of *lis alibi pendens*. However, it is clear from the context of the subsection and the Special Law Reform Committee on Admiralty Jurisdiction's *Report on Admiralty Jurisdiction* that the restriction in s. 6(2) was only intended to apply to those collision claims specified in s. 6(1): *Myburgh*, n. 1 above, para. 213.

[111] McGechan, n. 3 above, para. 477 *in fine*. See text at n. 34 ff. above.

[112] See *Kuwait Asia Bank EC*, n. 27 above, 208; *De Dampierre*, n. 49 above, 108; text at nn. 52, 89–92 above, and generally *McConnell Dowell Constructors Ltd*, n. 25 above.

4. JURISDICTION CLAUSES

(a) NON-EXCLUSIVE JURISDICTION CLAUSES

A clause[113] conferring non-exclusive jurisdiction on the New Zealand courts will enable them to exercise jurisdiction as of right, will facilitate service overseas in cases where leave would otherwise have been needed, and will improve the prospects of the New Zealand judgment being enforceable elsewhere. However, such a clause will not prevent a defendant from (i) objecting to New Zealand jurisdiction on the ground that there is no good arguable case or that New Zealand is *forum non conveniens*, or (ii) applying for a stay on the basis of *forum non conveniens*. The defendant's agreement to submit to the jurisdiction may be a relevant factor when considering whether or not New Zealand is *forum non conveniens*, but it will not be decisive.[114]

A clause conferring non-exclusive jurisdiction on a foreign court will not prevent a New Zealand court from exercising jurisdiction. Such a clause will be relevant in *forum non conveniens* applications to the extent that it establishes the existence of a foreign court of competent jurisdiction, but it cannot, in itself, be accorded much further weight.[115]

(b) EXCLUSIVE JURISDICTION CLAUSES

A clause conferring exclusive jurisdiction on a foreign court does not oust the jurisdiction of the New Zealand courts. There is an overriding public interest in the administration of justice, and individuals cannot, by their private stipulation, oust the courts of their jurisdiction in matters that properly belong to them.[116] Nevertheless, the courts are of the view that it generally does not serve the ends of justice to allow parties to renege on their undertakings: to do so would fail to give effect to parties' reasonable expectations and undermine certainty in international commerce.[117] The courts will therefore generally exercise their discretion to stay or dismiss proceedings instituted in New Zealand in breach of an exclusive jurisdiction clause, unless the plaintiff can show strong cause why the trial should proceed.[118]

---

[113] The proper law of the contract will determine the nature, scope, and interpretation of the jurisdiction clause.

[114] Goddard, n. 3 above, 31–2.

[115] Goddard, n. 3 above, 32–3.

[116] *The Fehmarn* [1958] 1 All ER 333 at 335.

[117] Cf. *Mackender* v. *Feldia* [1967] 2 QB 596 at 604–5; *Society of Lloyd's*, n. 12 above, 142.

[118] *Society of Lloyd's*, n. 12 above, 142; *KH Enterprises (cargo owners)* v. *Pioneer Containers (owners) (The Pioneer Container)* [1994] 2 All ER 250 at 267 (determined on appeal to the PC from the courts of Hong Kong, but considered a binding precedent under NZ precedent rules: see *Breuer* v. *Wright* [1982] 2 NZLR 77 at 83).

The applicable principles may be summarized as follows:[119]

- Where a plaintiff sues in New Zealand in breach of an agreement to refer the dispute to a foreign court only, and the defendant applies for dismissal or a stay, the New Zealand court (assuming the claim to be otherwise within its discretion) is not bound to dismiss the proceedings or grant a stay, but has a discretion whether to do so.
- The discretion should be exercised by granting a stay unless strong cause for not doing so is shown.
- The burden of proving strong cause is on the plaintiff.[120]
- In exercising its discretion the court should take into account all the circumstances of the particular case.
- In this regard, the court may consider factors indicating the extent to which New Zealand or the chosen forum respectively is the appropriate forum in which proceedings should be conducted in the interests of all the parties and for the ends of justice.[121]

Instances where a plaintiff may succeed in discharging the heavy burden of showing that a stay should not be granted are where he will be unfairly prejudiced by having to proceed abroad (for example, because the action is time-barred abroad and the plaintiff did not act unreasonably in failing to institute a foreign action timeously),[122] the chosen foreign forum cannot grant the relief sought,[123] or New Zealand is the country in which the great bulk of the material evidence is located and almost all the activities requiring examination occurred.[124]

Similarly, a clause conferring exclusive jurisdiction on the New Zealand courts will ordinarily ensure that they will exercise jurisdiction; but a defendant may nevertheless obtain a dismissal or a stay of the proceedings if he or she can show strong cause why trial in New Zealand would not serve the interests of all the parties and the ends of justice.[125] For example, an application for a stay has succeeded where the exclusive

---

[119] Based on *The Eleftheria*, n. 69 above, 99–100, which was adopted in *Apple Computer*, n. 78 above, 601; *Carberry Exports (NZ) Ltd* v. *Krazzy Price Discount Ltd* (1985) 1 PRNZ 279 at 283–4; *Kingsway Industries Ltd* v. *John Holland Engineering Pty Ltd* (1986) 1 PRNZ 286 at 290; *Pacific Fundraising Ltd*, n. 73 above, 375–6; and approved in *Society of Lloyd's*, n. 12 above, 142–3.

[120] But see n. 33 above.

[121] This paraphrases *The Eleftheria*, n. 69 above, 100, where the court called for a consideration of relative convenience and expense, the *lex causae*, the parties' connections with the respective countries, whether the defendant genuinely desires trial in the chosen forum, and whether the plaintiff would be substantially prejudiced by having to sue in the chosen forum. These factors correspond to those considered in *forum non conveniens* applications: see text at n. 50 ff. above.

[122] *The Pioneer Container*, n. 118 above, 267–8.

[123] *Apple Computer*, n. 78 above, 600; *Air Nauru*, n. 51 above, 637, 639–40.

[124] *Pacific Fundraising Ltd*, n. 73 above, 378.

[125] *Ariki New Zealand*, n. 33 above, 8–9.

jurisdiction clause and the plaintiff's residence represented the sole connections between the case and New Zealand, and all the other factors pointed to and favoured trial elsewhere.[126]

The foregoing general principles are subject to a restriction in the area of the sea carriage of goods. The courts cannot give effect to any stipulation or agreement purporting to oust or limit their jurisdiction in respect of any bill of lading or other document relating to the carriage of goods by sea to or from New Zealand.[127]

(c) FORUM NON CONVENIENS CLAUSES

Some contracts now contain clauses providing that neither party shall object to the chosen forum on the ground that it is *forum non conveniens*. There is no authority on the effect of such clauses. However, analogy with the decisions of the courts in relation to exclusive jurisdiction clauses indicates that such clauses should not prevent a party from successfully raising a plea of *forum non conveniens*. Although such clauses should be taken into consideration as an indication of the parties' reasonable expectations, they should not be decisive.[128]

5. ARBITRATION AGREEMENTS

(a) ARBITRATION IN NEW ZEALAND

Where proceedings are instituted in New Zealand in breach of an agreement to submit the matter in dispute to arbitration in New Zealand, the court enjoys a discretion to order a stay of the proceedings. This power is conferred by the Arbitration Act 1908, which provides as follows:

5(1) If any party to any submission, or any person claiming through or under him, commences any legal proceedings in any Court against any other party to the submission, or any person claiming through or under him, in respect of any matter agreed to be referred, any party to those legal proceedings may, at any time before filing a statement of defence or a notice of intention to defend or taking any other steps in the proceedings, apply to the Court in which the proceedings were commenced to stay the proceedings; and the Court may, if satisfied that there is no sufficient reason why the matter should not be referred in accordance with the submission, and that the applicant was at the time when the proceedings were

[126] *Bramwell* v. *The Pacific Lumber Co Ltd* (1986) 1 PRNZ 307 at 311–12.
[127] Sea Carriage of Goods Act 1940, s. 11A. This s. does not limit or affect agreements to submit disputes to arbitration in NZ or in any other country which is a party to an international convention or protocol relating to arbitration to which NZ is also a party: s. 11A(3). (The Maritime Transport Bill 1994, cl. 208 is to the same general effect, except that *all* arbitration agreements, not merely those providing for arbitration in NZ or its Convention partners, are saved.)
[128] Goddard, n. 3 above, 33.

commenced, and still remains, ready and willing to do all things necessary to the proper conduct of the arbitration, make an order staying the proceedings.

The court will generally order a stay unless the plaintiff can show strong reasons why this should not be done.

The court will not stay proceedings if it appears that there is no genuine dispute to be arbitrated. Thus, the court will not grant a stay where there is no dispute whatsoever, but merely a refusal to perform an undisputed obligation, or where the defence pleaded has no merit.[129] As a rule, a stay will be available only where the application for a stay is filed before or at the same time as any notice of opposition. There is conflicting authority on whether a stay can be granted where a notice of opposition was filed first but the arbitration clause was raised in it.[130]

The Arbitration Act applies to written submissions to arbitration only.[131] The courts' inherent jurisdiction should enable them to stay proceedings instituted in breach of oral arbitration agreements, should these occur.[132] If so, the principles on which a stay will be granted will correspond to those set out in the Act.[133]

(b) ARBITRATION ABROAD

(i) The Arbitration (Foreign Agreements and Awards) Act 1982

The Arbitration (Foreign Agreements and Awards) Act 1982 implements the 1958 New York Convention on the Recognition and Enforcement of Foreign Arbitral Awards. Section 4 of the Act governs a court's jurisdiction where a party seeks to institute legal proceedings in breach of an arbitration agreement to which the Act applies. It provides for a mandatory stay at the request of one of the parties:

4(1) If any party to an arbitration agreement to which this section applies (or any person claiming through or under that person) commences any legal proceedings in any Court against any other party to that arbitration agreement (or any person claiming through or under that other party) in respect of any matter in dispute between the parties which the parties have agreed to refer to arbitration pursuant to that arbitration agreement, any party to those proceedings may at any time apply to the Court to stay those proceedings; and the Court shall, unless the

---

[129] Cf. *Baltimar APS Ltd* v. *Nalder & Biddle Ltd*, unrep., 20 June 1994, CA 81/94, 7–8, 11.

[130] This possibility was denied in *McKee-Fehl Constructors Ltd* v. *Green & McCahill (Contractors) Ltd* (1988) 4 PRNZ 277 at 282–4, but supported in *Timberlands West Coast Ltd* v. *Nahanni Ward Helicopters*, unrep., 24 Mar. 1994, High Ct., Greymouth Registry, CP 2/94.

[131] See the definition of 'submission' in s. 2.

[132] The traditional view was that courts do not have the power to stay legal proceedings breaching an arbitration agreement unless a statute so provides or arbitration is a condition precedent to legal liability under the contract. However, there is some more modern English and Australian authority to the contrary. See Sykes and Pryles, *Australian Private International Law* (3rd edn., 1991), 163–4.

[133] Cf. Sykes and Pryles, n. 132 above, 163.

arbitration agreement is null and void, inoperative, or incapable of being performed, make an order staying the proceedings.

(i) Arbitration Agreements to which the Act Applies

A mandatory stay may be sought only if the litigation breaches 'an arbitration agreement to which [section 4] applies'. Analysis of the Act reveals that section 4 applies to an agreement which:

- provides that the parties will submit to arbitration all or any differences which have arisen or may arise between them in respect of a defined legal relationship, whether contractual or not, concerning a subject-matter capable of settlement by arbitration;
- is in writing, the term 'agreement in writing' to include an arbitral clause in a contract or an arbitration agreement, signed by the parties or contained in an exchange of letters or telegrams; and
- provides expressly or by implication for arbitration in any country other than New Zealand.[134]

The requirement that the arbitration agreement must apply in respect of a defined legal relationship has not yet been the subject of judicial comment. It is therefore not clear which legal system the court will use to decide whether or not the relationship between the parties constitutes a legal relationship.

The requirement that the subject matter of the dispute must be capable of settlement by arbitration apparently refers to legality. Thus, the mandatory stay provisions are not applicable where arbitration is illegal under the proper law of the contract, the law of the place of arbitration, or New Zealand law. An example of the last instance occurs in the context of sea carriage of goods. The New Zealand courts must disregard an arbitration agreement in a bill of lading or other document relating to the carriage of goods by sea to or from New Zealand which provides for arbitration in a country which is not a party to an international convention or protocol relating to arbitration to which New Zealand is a party.[135]

Section 4 applies only if the arbitration agreement is in writing, as defined. It has been held that section 4 consequently does not apply to an arbitration agreement in a bill of lading, as bills of lading are signed by the carrier or his or her agent only, rather than by 'the parties'.[136] It is submitted that this restrictive interpretation of the requirement of writing is incorrect.[137]

---

[134] S. 2 read with Art. II(1) of the Convention, as set out in the Sch. to the Act; s. 4(4).

[135] Sea Carriage of Goods Act 1940, s. 11A. (However, the Maritime Transport Bill 1994, cl. 280(2), will render such arbitration agreements legal: cf. n. 127 above.)

[136] *Air New Zealand Ltd* v. *The Ship 'Contship America'* [1992] 1 NZLR 425 at 434.

[137] This interpretation disregards the fact that the concept 'agreement in writing' is inclusively defined in the Convention. It is also difficult to reconcile with the legislative intention informing s. 11A(3) of the Sea Carriage of Goods Act 1940, inserted in 1985, which provides

The question whether an agreement expressly or impliedly[138] provides for arbitration elsewhere than in New Zealand should, on general principles, be governed by the proper law of the arbitration agreement, i.e. that system of law which the parties either expressly or impliedly chose to govern their contract or, failing such a choice, which has the closest and most real connection with the transaction.[139]

The Act does not apply to disputes to which the 1965 Washington Convention on the Settlement of Investment Disputes between States and Nationals of other States relates; such disputes are subject to special provisions.[140]

(ii) Persons Entitled to Apply for a Stay

A mandatory stay will be available only if the litigants are themselves party to the arbitration agreement or are claiming through or under a party to the arbitration agreement.

General principles indicate that the question whether a litigant is a party to a foreign arbitration agreement should be resolved on an application of the proper law of that agreement. However, the question whether a litigant is claiming 'through or under' a party to the arbitration agreement is determined on an application of New Zealand principles,[141] presumably because this is seen to concern the interpretation of the New Zealand statute. A litigant will be regarded as claiming through or under a party to the arbitration agreement if there is a sufficient relationship between them. This relationship may be legal; in this case, what is required is that the litigant succeeded to the relevant rights or duties of the party to the arbitration agreement, for example by assignment or subrogation.[142] Alternatively, a relationship which is so close on the facts that it is within the purview of the arbitration clause will suffice. An example of this would be where the litigant is the alter ego of the party to

that stipulations or agreements in bills of lading providing for arbitration in another country which is a member of an international convention or protocol to which NZ is also a party are not affected by the restrictions in s. 11A (see text at nn. 127, 135 above).

[138] In *Air Nauru*, n. 51 above, the arbitration clause provided for arbitration by an arbitrator to be appointed by the parties who was 'an expert, knowledgeable in aviation law and not a resident of Nauru, New Zealand, or Niue'. It is submitted that the court should have considered whether this constituted an implied submission to arbitration elsewhere than in NZ under the proper law (the law of Nauru), rather than simply to assume that the domestic Arbitration Act 1908 applied.

[139] *Bonython* v. *Commonwealth of Australia* [1951] AC 201 at 219.

[140] See text at n. 153 below.

[141] See *Mount Cook (Northland) Ltd* v. *Swedish Motors Ltd* [1986] 1 NZLR 720 where NZ principles were applied to determine whether the defendant was suing 'through or under' a party to a foreign arbitration agreement even though the proper law of the contract was that of Sweden.

[142] Cf. *Mount Cook (Northland) Ltd*, n. 141 above, 724, following *Shayler* v. *Woolf* [1946] Ch. 320; *The Leage* [1984] 2 Lloyd's Rep. 259; *Smith* v. *Pearl Insurance Co Ltd* [1939] 1 All ER 95.

the arbitration agreement, such as where a claim is instituted by a wholly-owned subsidiary company acting as its parent's selling agent.[143]

A stay will be refused where a litigant's claim is brought on an independent cause of action rather than through or under a party to the arbitration agreement. Thus, section 4 did not avail a manufacturer who had entered into an arbitration agreement with an intermediary distributor when sued by a supplier to whom it had given negligent advice, as the court held that the supplier's claim against the manufacturer sounded in the tort of negligence and was not brought through or under the distributor.[144]

The Contracts (Privity) Act 1982 modifies the common law privity rule by providing that a third party who is designated in a contract may enforce a promise for a benefit conferred on him or her in that contract.[145] 'Benefit' is defined sufficiently widely to encompass the factual advantages flowing from arbitration.[146] It is not clear what impact this Act should have on the extent to which a third party may rely on a foreign arbitration clause.

(iii) Scope and Effect

Section 4 will operate only if the litigation of which a stay is sought concerns a matter which the parties to the arbitration agreement have agreed to refer to arbitration.

Any issue concerning the interpretation, scope, and effect of an arbitration agreement or an arbitration clause will be governed by the proper law of the arbitration agreement or of the contract in which the arbitration clause appears.[147]

The Act lists a limited number of cases in which a court may refuse to grant a stay. Absence of a genuine dispute is not included in this list. The Court of Appeal has therefore held that the courts have no jurisdiction to assess the reality of the dispute between the parties. Thus, the courts cannot refuse a stay on the ground that the pleaded defence has no substance.[148] However, the Court of Appeal has indicated that there may be an exception where the applicant is merely refusing to perform an

---

[143] Cf. *Mount Cook (Northland) Ltd*, n. 141 above, 724–5, following *Roussel-Uclaf* v. *G. D. Searle & Co Ltd* [1978] FSR 95.

[144] *Mount Cook (Northland) Ltd*, n. 141 above, 724–5. See also *The Contship America*, n. 136 above, 434 where a stay was refused *inter alia* on the grounds that (i) the plaintiffs (the purchasers of cargo lost at sea) were not claiming under the bill of lading containing an arbitration provision or as consignees or through the shipper, but independently as owners in tort or bailment; and (ii) the defendant shipowner was not a party to the bill of lading.

[145] S. 4.   [146] S. 2.

[147] *Mount Cook (Northland) Ltd*, n. 141 above, 725 read with *Bonython*, n. 139 above, 219. See the text at n. 139 above concerning the assessment of the proper law.

[148] *Baltimar APS*, n. 129 above, 9–10, in effect overruling *Ariki New Zealand*, n. 33 above, 5–7.

undisputed obligation and his or her application for a stay constitutes an abuse of the court's process.[149]

(iv) Validity

Section 4 provides that the court shall not stay the proceedings if the foreign arbitration agreement is null and void, inoperative, or incapable of being performed. Neither the Act nor the Convention specifies which legal system will govern the issues listed. It is submitted that the common law conflicts rules in point remain applicable. Thus, the court will not order a stay if the arbitration agreement is invalid, inoperative, or incapable of being performed by its proper law.[150]

(v) Procedural Aspects

Section 4 provides that the application for a stay may be brought at any time. It has been held that filing an unconditional appearance ends the right to arbitration, and that a stay under section 4 will not be available in such a case;[151] but it is difficult to reconcile this restrictive interpretation with the clear wording of the Act.

The common law rules on onus apply. So, for example, the onus of proving that the dispute comes within the ambit of the arbitration clause rests on the party applying for a stay.[152]

(ii) The Arbitration (International Investment Disputes) Act 1979

The Arbitration (International Investment Disputes) Act 1979 gives effect to the 1965 Washington Convention on the Settlement of Investment Disputes between States and Nationals of other States. Section 8(1) provides as follows:

8(1) If any party to proceedings pursuant to the Convention (or any person claiming through or under him) commences any legal proceedings in any Court against any other party to the proceedings pursuant to the Convention (or any person claiming through or under him) in respect of any matter to which the proceedings pursuant to the Convention relate, any party to the legal proceedings may at any time apply to the Court to stay the legal proceedings; and the Court may, if satisfied that there is no sufficient reason why the matter should not be dealt with under the Convention, make an order staying the legal proceedings.

The effect of this section is that a New Zealand court will usually stay any litigation if there is a sufficient relationship or nexus between the domestic proceedings and the issues they raise, on the one hand, and the

[149] *Baltimar APS*, n. 129 above, 10.
[150] As explained in the text at n. 139 above. Illegality is addressed in the text at n. 135 above.
[151] *The Contship America*, n. 136 above, 434–5. The court did not give reasons for this restrictive interpretation.
[152] *Mount Cook (Northland) Ltd*, n. 141 above, 730.

Convention proceedings and the issues they raise, on the other. It is not necessary to persuade the court that the relevant dispute is within the terms of the arbitration agreement.[153] However, the court retains a residual discretion to refuse a stay for sufficient reason. A stay will be refused by way of exception only, where fundamental injustice overriding mutual disadvantage would otherwise result. The need to promote predictability and orderliness in international investment and the resolution of disputes arising therefrom will play a critical role in the court's overall assessment.[154]

(c) FUTURE DEVELOPMENT

The New Zealand Law Commission has prepared a draft Arbitration Act to replace the present Arbitration Act 1908 as well as the Arbitration (Foreign Agreements and Awards) Act 1982 and harmonize the provisions relating to domestic and foreign arbitrations[155] respectively. The intention is that the new Act should provide for the application of the principles of the 1985 UNCITRAL Model Law on International Commercial Arbitration to both international and domestic arbitrations.[156] The Commission's proposal is still awaiting Government consideration.

III
RESTRAINING FOREIGN PROCEEDINGS

The New Zealand courts are able to enjoin a party from commencing or pursuing legal proceedings in a foreign jurisdiction.[157] The court order is

---

[153] *Attorney-General* v. *Mobil Oil NZ Ltd* [1989] 2 NZLR 649 at 659, 663, interpreting s. 8(1) in the light of Art. 41 of the Convention, which provides that the arbitral tribunal shall be the judge of its own competence. The court found in the alternative that the parties' arbitration agreement embraced the dispute before it.

[154] *Mobil Oil NZ Ltd*, n. 153 above, 664, 666–8, following *Mitsubishi Motors Corp* v. *Soler Chrysler-Plymouth Inc*, 473 US 614 (1985) and *Scherk* v. *Alberto-Culver Co*, 417 US 506 (1974). *Mobil Oil* concerned the construction and application of the Commerce Act 1986, which the Government alleged retroactively invalidated an arrangement between it and the first defendant. The court granted a stay even though the dispute concerned novel and difficult questions of NZ law and legal policy on which the tribunal and the court might reach different conclusions, in which event the award would: (i) expose the Crown to claims for declarations, damages, and injunctions by the investor's competitors; or (ii) be unenforceable by the investor as being contrary to NZ law. The court held that the importance of certainty in international investment dealings outweighed these risks.

[155] Excluding arbitrations covered by the Arbitration (International Investment Disputes) Act 1979.

[156] NZ Law Commission Arbitration Report No 2 (R. 20, Wellington, 1991).

[157] The following discussion is based on *Société Nationale Industrielle Aérospatiale*, n. 55 above, 892 ff., except where otherwise indicated. Although this case was determined on appeal to the PC from the court of Brunei Darussalam, it constitutes a binding precedent under NZ precedent rules: see *Breuer* v. *Wright* [1982] 2 NZLR 77 at 83.

directed against the party who has instituted proceedings abroad or is proposing to do so, and an injunction will thus only be issued if the party sought to be restrained is amenable to the jurisdiction of the court. Breach of the injunction exposes the party proceeding abroad to punishment for contempt of court, i.e. to a fine and sequestration or imprisonment. The court will only issue an injunction if the party whom it is sought to enjoin is present in New Zealand or has assets here, so that an injunction is likely to be an effective remedy.

Although the injunction is not directed against the foreign court, it nevertheless indirectly affects that court; therefore, comity requires that a New Zealand court exercise caution when asked to enjoin foreign proceedings.

Foreign proceedings can be enjoined where:

- an estate is being administered, or a petition in bankruptcy has been presented, or winding-up proceedings have been commenced in New Zealand, and the respondent seeks to obtain the sole benefit of certain foreign assets by proceeding abroad;
- the respondent has commenced proceedings in respect of the same subject-matter both in New Zealand and abroad, the foreign proceedings are vexatious or oppressive,[158] and an injunction against proceeding abroad will not deprive the respondent of advantages in the foreign forum of which it would be unjust to deprive him or her;[159]
- the foreign proceedings are instituted in breach of an arbitration agreement or an exclusive jurisdiction agreement;[160] or
- the bringing of the suit in the foreign court is unconscionable.[161]

The above are instances only: the court may enjoin foreign proceedings whenever the ends of justice so require.

IV
GENERAL PROCEDURAL ISSUES

In certain cases it will be open to the defendant either to object to the New Zealand courts' jurisdiction or to apply for a stay on one of the discretionary grounds discussed above.[162] The former course is advis-

---

[158] The mere fact of multiplicity or of the institution of proceedings in an inconvenient jurisdiction does not lead to a presumption that the foreign proceedings are vexatious. It is not enough to demonstrate that the foreign court is *forum non conveniens*.

[159] *Société Nationale Industrielle Aérospatiale*, n. 55 above, 896.

[160] Cf. Cheshire and North, n. 4 above, 247–8 and cases cited there.

[161] Cf. Cheshire and North, n. 4 above, 248–50 and cases cited there.

[162] See e.g. text at nn. 28, 29 above.

able,[163] as there is a risk that the courts of some countries[164] may treat an unsuccessful application for a stay as implied submission and on that ground enforce the New Zealand judgment overseas.[165]

It is essential that a party who wishes to establish that trial should proceed in a given country because of its closer relationship should plead the materiality of the factors on which he or she relies. For example, it is not enough to plead that physical evidence is located in that country; it must be shown that the relevant evidence is both necessary and disputed.[166]

A party who wishes to establish that trial should proceed in a given forum should consider ways in which to neutralize the grounds on which the other side can rely. For example, if the plaintiff has obtained security abroad or the defendant has assets against which execution can be levied in the foreign country only, but the defendant desires trial in New Zealand, he or she can undertake to post security here or provide irrevocable letters of credit.[167] Undertakings can be given not to invoke remedies, defences, or procedures that are available in the foreign court.[168] Where physical evidence or witnesses are located abroad, ways in which the costs and inconvenience of obtaining that evidence can be reduced should be considered. Examples of how this can be done include arranging for evidence to be taken abroad,[169] or for the foreign witnesses to give evidence by teleconferencing or videolinking; making concessions that eliminate the need for some or all of the overseas evidence; and agreeing to meet some or all of the additional costs to the defendant of a trial in New Zealand.[170]

The court may issue its order in conditional terms.[171]

---

[163] Some High Ct. judgments have suggested that an issue of *forum non conveniens* can be raised under a R. 477 application only, but this approach was questioned by the PC in *Kuwait Asia Bank EC*, n. 27 above, 217.

[164] E.g. a Commonwealth court, following *Henry* v. *Geoprosco International Ltd* [1976] QB 726.

[165] See Paterson, n. 43 above, 366 n. 4; Goddard, n. 3 above, 24–6.

[166] Failure to plead the materiality of the foreign witnesses, evidence, and foreign *lex causae* scuttled the *forum non conveniens* application in *Club Méditerranée NZ*, n. 39 above: see at 220.

[167] Cf. *Société Nationale Industrielle Aérospatiale*, n. 55 above, 903.

[168] Cf. the *Spiliada* case, n. 12 above, 484; *Société Nationale Industrielle Aérospatiale*, n. 55 above, 899.

[169] Evidence can be taken abroad by: the NZ judge, acting as a commissioner; a court-appointed expert, including a foreign lawyer or retired judge, appointed under R. 324 of the High Ct. Rules; a referee, appointed under s. 15 of the Arbitration Act 1908; a court-appointed examiner, appointed under R. 369 of the High Ct. Rules; and a foreign court, in compliance with a letter of request issued by the NZ court under R. 369 of the High Ct. Rules. See *New Zealand Insurance*, n. 46 above, 371; Goddard, n. 3 above, 31.

[170] Goddard, n. 3 above, 31.

[171] Cf. the *Spiliada* case, n. 12 above, 484; *Société Nationale Industrielle Aérospatiale*, n. 55 above, 902.

17

Sweden

MICHAEL BOGDAN

Professor, Faculty of Law, University of Lund

CONTENTS

I
INTRODUCTION

This chapter deals, in a summary fashion, with some of the rather exceptional situations where Swedish courts are entitled, or even obliged, to decline to exercise the jurisdiction which they have under the normal Swedish jurisdictional rules. Not all such exceptional situations will be covered: among those omitted it is possible to mention those cases where the defendant enjoys jurisdictional immunity pursuant to the law of nations. Another self-imposed limitation on this chapter is that family law will not be dealt with here, since the nature and scope of the problem is very different in that field.

It must be pointed out that Sweden is a small jurisdiction with relatively few judicial decisions on this point. Together with the lack of comprehensive statutory regulation of the area under scrutiny, this leads to considerable uncertainty as to the state of the law. Many questions remain open and legal writers are often forced to resort to speculation and guesswork.

The jurisdiction of Swedish courts in civil matters is not exhaustively regulated by statute. The existing statutory jurisdictional rules deal mostly with rather special matters covered by the provisions on jurisdiction in international Conventions, e.g. the Warsaw Convention for the Unification of Certain Rules relating to International Carriage by Air. An important exception is the Lugano Convention on Jurisdiction and the Enforcement of Judgments in Civil and Commercial Matters of 16 September 1988,[1] which entered into force for Sweden on 1 January 1993, but not even this Convention contains a comprehensive regulation of the jurisdiction of Swedish courts.

In the absence of statutory regulation, the jurisdiction of Swedish courts depends, roughly speaking, on whether there is a locally competent Swedish court of first instance.[2] The main idea behind this principle seems to be that a legal dispute can be presumed to have a connection with Sweden sufficient for Swedish jurisdiction if it is connected to a particular Swedish court district in such a way that the district's court is locally competent to try the case. This means, in fact, that, by analogy, the rules concerning local competence are applied also to the question of Swedish jurisdiction in international cases. It must, however, be stressed that making such an analogy requires great care and must not be done mechanically, since deviations from the described principle are often justified. Swedish courts thus possess a substantial margin of discretion and they are not considered bound by the exact wording of the rules on local competence when these rules are by analogy applied to the question of Swedish jurisdiction.

The general rules concerning the local competence of Swedish district courts in civil actions are found in Chapter 10 of the Swedish Code of Judicial Procedure (*Rättegångsbalken*) of 1942 (as amended). Some of the most important rules deserve to be mentioned here.

According to Chapter 10, section 1 of the Code, the competent court for civil cases in general is the court for the place in which the defendant habitually resides. A corporation, partnership, co-operative association, foundation, or similar society or institution is considered to reside at the place in which the board has its permanent seat or, if the board has no permanent seat or there is no board, at the place from which the administration is carried out. When this rule is applied by analogy to jurisdiction, it means that Swedish courts have jurisdiction to try a dispute if the defendant has his habitual residence or seat in Sweden.

But even a defendant with no habitual residence or seat in Sweden (a non-domiciliary defendant[3]) can be sued here under certain conditions

---

[1] The full text of the Lugano Convention is found in, *inter alia* [1988] OJ L319/9.

[2] See Bogdan, *Svensk internationell privat- och processrätt* (4th edn., Stockholm, 1992), 107–23; Eek, *The Swedish Conflict of Laws* (The Hague, 1965), 72–84; Nial, *American-Swedish Private International Law* (Dobbs Ferry, 1965), 59–61. For a general analysis of Swedish jurisdiction, see Dennemark, *Om svensk domstols behörighet i internationellt förmögenhetsrättsliga mål* (Stockholm, 1961); Pålsson, *Svensk rättspraxis i internationell processrätt* (Stockholm, 1989), 19–128.

[3] In Swedish private international law, domicile (*hemvist*) normally equals habitual residence.

with regard to some special types of disputes. The most conspicuous of these grounds of jurisdiction is found in the first sentence of Chapter 10, section 3(1), of the Code: in disputes concerning debt obligations, a non-domiciliary may be sued at the place in which property belonging to him is located. In disputes involving a right to personal property, a non-domiciliary may be sued at the place at which the property in question is located (second sentence of Chapter 10, section 3(1)). A non-domiciliary who has entered into a contract in Sweden or who has incurred a debt in this country may be sued in a dispute concerning that contract or debt at the place in which the contract was formed or the debt was incurred (Chapter 10, section 4). Anyone engaged in farming, mining, manufacturing, handicrafts, commerce, or similar business with a permanent establishment in Sweden may be sued in an action arising directly out of the activity carried on at the establishment at the place in which the establishment is located (Chapter 10, section 5). According to Chapter 10, section 8, of the Code, an action for tort damages may be instituted in the court for the place in which the tortious act occurred or had its impact.

Whereas the above-mentioned bases of jurisdiction are optional as far as the plaintiff is concerned (they stipulate where the defendant 'may' be sued, without objecting to the plaintiff's choice of another forum), Chapter 10, section 10, of the Code is imperative: disputes about title to land, the use of land, or other right to land 'shall' be instituted in the court for the place in which the land is situated. This means, first of all, that such disputes can always be adjudicated on in Sweden if the real property in question is located here, but the provision is also interpreted to mean that there is in principle no Swedish jurisdiction if the dispute concerns real property abroad, regardless of the residence of the parties or the existence of other contacts with Sweden.

Since 1 January 1993 Sweden has been bound by the Lugano Convention, which means that the jurisdictional rules described above are, to a certain extent, modified in situations covered by the Convention. Since the Lugano rules are generally known, there is no need to describe them here. They will, however, be dealt with when their application in Sweden gives rise to specific problems related to the subject of this chapter.

II
FORUM NON CONVENIENS

It is uncertain whether, and to what extent, Swedish law recognizes the concept of *forum non conveniens*.[4] However, to the extent that Swedish jurisdiction is determined by mere application, by way of analogy, of the

---

[4] See Nial, n. 2 above, 62; Pålsson, n. 2 above, 54–6.

internal forum rules (see above), the courts have a substantial margin of discretion which can be used for the same purposes as the doctrine of *forum non conveniens*. When the case's connection with Sweden is very weak, Swedish courts may deviate from the exact wording of the internal forum rules in order to avoid Swedish jurisdiction, for example if it would be excessively burdensome to the foreign defendant. If, for instance, a contract were entered into by two American businessmen when they met in the transit lounge of Stockholm Airport, without there being any other relevant connection with Sweden, Swedish courts might decide to dismiss an action emanating from that contract despite the wording of Chapter 10, section 4, of the Swedish Code of Judicial Procedure (see above).[5] Such dismissal probably requires, however, that the defendant object to the jurisdiction of Swedish courts as being unreasonably burdensome for him.[6]

So far, Swedish courts do not seem to be popular among forum-shoppers. There are, however, some Supreme Court and appellate decisions indicating that an action might be dismissed if the 'Swedish connection', on which Swedish jurisdiction is based, had been created artificially for jurisdictional purposes, for example if the Swedish plaintiff had admitted owing a small sum to the foreign defendant or had refused to pay an undisputed debt to the foreign defendant in order to be able to claim that the defendant owned a claim in Sweden and was thus subject to Swedish jurisdiction on the basis of the first sentence of Chapter 10, section 3(1), of the Code of Judicial Procedure (see above).[7]

III
LIS PENDENS

Swedish statutory law does not contain any general rule providing that foreign proceedings constitute an obstacle to judicial proceedings in Sweden involving the same parties and the same cause of action. On the other hand, nor is there any statutory rule to the contrary.

For obvious reasons, the effect of *lis pendens* can normally be accorded only to those foreign proceedings that are expected to result in a foreign judgment that will be given effect to in Sweden. Since foreign judgments are, in principle, neither recognized nor enforced in Sweden unless there is a statutory rule requiring this (normally based on an international

---

[5] See, e.g., Dennemark, n. 2 above, 67–8 and 173–8.

[6] See Bogdan, n. 2 above, 113; Dennemark, n. 2 above, 67–8.

[7] See e.g. *Scandinavian Raw Materials* v. *Jung* Sup. Ct. [1962] NJA 354, and the decision of the Övre Norrland CA in *Polar Print Production* v. *Braillo Norway A/S* [1987] RH 25. Cf. *Landerholm* v. *Christensen* Sup. Ct. [1966] NJA 450.

treaty), proceedings pending in a foreign country are normally only considered a cause for dismissing or staying Swedish proceedings in such statute-governed cases. Most treaties in this field contain clauses dealing with the problem of *lis pendens*, the most important example being, of course, Article 21 of the Lugano Convention. These treaty-based statutory *lis pendens* rules are mandatory, obliging Swedish courts to dismiss or stay proceedings, without leaving them any discretionary powers.

Some international treaties oblige Sweden to recognize foreign judgments without containing any clause dealing with the *lis pendens* issue. It is reasonable to assume that the effect of *lis pendens* will be given to foreign proceedings in these cases too.[8]

If, and to the extent that, Swedish courts choose to abandon their present parochial and negative attitude to recognition and enforcement of foreign judgments, the recognition of the *lis pendens* effect of foreign proceedings will probably also be extended. Even today, foreign judgments can be given certain evidentiary value as to the facts of the case or the contents of the applicable foreign law. This requires no statutory provision, since Swedish procedural law considers practically all evidence as admissible. It is, therefore, submitted that, if proceedings pending abroad are expected to result in a foreign judgment of great value as evidence in Sweden, Swedish courts are free to stay proceedings in order to await the foreign judgment in question, unless the postponement would lead to excessive delay. The decision whether to stay the proceedings under these circumstances should, of course, be left to the discretion of the Swedish court.[9]

The Lugano Convention stipulates in Article 21 that, where proceedings involving the same cause of action and between the same parties are brought in the courts of different Contracting States, any court other than the court 'first seised' shall of its own motion stay its proceedings until such time as the jurisdiction of the court first seised is established and, when such jurisdiction is established, decline jurisdiction in favour of that court. It is thus of great importance to determine at what moment a court is 'seised'. This is not regulated in the Convention and the European Court of Justice has held, regarding the corresponding provision of the Brussels Convention,[10] that this issue is left to be decided by the domestic law of the

---

[8] This view is, e.g., supported *a contrario* by the Sup. Ct. in *Young* v. *Young* [1978] NJA 610, and is explicitly confirmed by statements in the Government Bill 1991/92:128, 155–6; Pålsson, n. 2 above, at 162.

[9] See Pålsson, n. 2 above, at 163–4. Cf. however, the decision of Svea CA in *Island Gem* v. *Skandia* [1982] RH 8.

[10] The case law of the ECJ regarding the Brussels Convention up to the time of signature of the Lugano Convention is *de facto* binding for the interpretation of the latter Convention as well, pursuant to Preamble to Protocol no 2 to the Lugano Convention.

court in question.[11] According to Chapter 13, section 4, of the Swedish Code of Judicial Procedure, a court is considered seised (the action is deemed initiated) when the summons is filed with the court or, if a summons is not necessary, when the claim is presented to the court. In many foreign countries, the decisive moment is instead when the document instituting the proceedings is served on the defendant. Such differences can, to some extent, be used by forum-shoppers. If, for example, an action is brought in a Contracting State where the court is not considered 'seised' until the document has been served on the defendant, the defendant, who knows about the action but has not yet been served, can avoid the courts of the State in question by quickly instituting an action in Sweden (provided, of course, that Swedish courts also have jurisdiction under the Convention). Since the Swedish court is considered seised at the moment when the summons is filed with the court, it will be seised before the foreign court, in spite of the fact that the action may have been filed in the foreign country before it was filed in Sweden. This result has been rightly criticized by Swedish writers.[12]

IV
CHOICE OF JURISDICTION CLAUSES

This part deals with agreements by means of which the parties, in a binding manner and *for the future*, agree to avoid the jurisdiction of the Swedish courts. This is a different issue from that arising where both parties are in agreement on avoiding Swedish courts at the time of the proceedings: such cases rarely present any problem, since the plaintiff will simply refrain from instituting an action in Swedish courts or he will withdraw it if already instituted.

The right of the parties to agree, in a binding manner, on a particular court being exclusively competent to deal with their existing or future disputes is, in principle, recognized in Swedish domestic law by Chapter 10, section 16, of the Code of Judicial Procedure: 'If a written contract stipulates that a controversy already in existence, or one that may arise in the future based upon a legal relationship detailed in the contract, may be instituted in a certain court, or that a certain court exclusively shall be competent, the stipulation is to be complied with unless otherwise stated by law.'

---

[11] See the judgment of the ECJ of 7 July 1984 in Case 129/83 *Zelger* v. *Salinitri* [1984] ECR 2397.

[12] See e.g. Göranson, 'Instämd i London vill hellre processa i Eksjö, in *Process och exekution: vänbok till Robert Boman* (Uppsala, 1990), 107–31; Pålsson, *Luganokonventionen* (Stockholm, 1992), 186.

Among the exceptions 'stated by law', one may mention those disputes for which a particular local court has exclusive competence, such as disputes concerning a right to real property (Chapter 10, sections 10 and 17, of the Code of Judicial Procedure).

The Principles of section 16 are applied, by way of analogy, to the question of Swedish jurisdiction as well, i.e. the jurisdiction of Swedish courts can be contracted out of by the parties if the foreign court selected by the parties (*forum prorogatum*) is willing to deal with the case and the dispute is not one of those subject to exclusive jurisdiction or other special restrictions.[13]

Since the limits of the freedom of the parties to agree on avoiding Swedish courts are based on a mere analogy, there is a margin of discretion, i.e. the courts are not totally bound by the exact wording of section 16. In fact, it seems that the freedom of the parties may be even greater when it comes to Swedish international jurisdiction than it is in internal cases where the choice is between two Swedish courts. In contrast to the wording of section 16, it appears that the parties may agree to entrust their disputes to the courts of a particular foreign country without ascertaining a particular court. The parties may even agree to avoid Swedish courts without saying anything about where they wish to have their disputes adjudicated.[14]

There is an important exception to the freedom of the parties to agree on avoiding Swedish jurisdiction in certain weak-party relationships, such as employment or consumer disputes.[15] Thus, the Swedish Labour Court in the case of *Hapimag* v. *Mona Mårtensson*[16] has refused to be bound by a choice of forum clause in an employment contract between a Swedish employee working in Sweden and her Swiss employer. According to the clause in question, all disputes had to be adjudicated by a court in Switzerland. The Labour Court held that the protection of the employee's interests would not be secured if she could not sue the employer in Sweden. The Labour Court held, furthermore, that the dispute involved the application of mandatory rules of Swedish labour law and that the employer–employee relationship's connection with Switzerland was relatively weak. As far as consumers are concerned, it is possible to mention, for example, Chapter 21, section 4, of the Swedish Maritime Act of 1994, restricting in certain respects the prorogation freedom in cases involving disputes emanating from contracts for the carriage of passengers and luggage by sea. With the exception of such statutory provisions, the exact

---

[13] See e.g. *Süddeutsche Motorenwerke* v. *William Stein AB* Sup. Ct. [1969] NJA 180; Dennemark, n. 2 above, 318–9; Pålsson, *Svensk rättspraxis i internationell processrätt* (Stockholm, 1989), 95–9.

[14] See Dennemark, n. 2 above, at 320–1.

[15] See Government Bill 1982/83:117, 23–4.   [16] [1976] AD 101.

limits of the freedom to avoid Swedish courts in weak-party relations are, however, far from clear.

The Lugano Convention, too, contains certain restrictions on prorogation of jurisdiction in weak-party situations, namely insurance disputes (Article 12), consumer disputes (Article 15), and employment disputes (Article 17(5)). On the other hand, the Lugano Convention is in some respects more liberal than general Swedish law. For example, Swedish law requires the choice of forum clause to be in writing, whereas Article 17 of the Lugano Convention, under certain circumstances, accepts unwritten prorogation agreements, provided that they are in a form which accords with practices which the parties have established between themselves or, in international trade or commerce, in a form which accords with an established usage.

V
ARBITRATION AGREEMENTS

A valid arbitration agreement constitutes a ground for dismissal of the case by Swedish courts, provided that the defendant objects to jurisdiction. The dismissal is mandatory, the courts having practically no discretionary power. Swedish and foreign arbitration agreements are basically treated in the same way in this respect, which makes it unnecessary to discuss here how the line between them is to be drawn. The arbitration agreement must, of course, be valid under the Swedish or foreign law that is applicable to it.[17] Even if the arbitration agreement is a foreign one, the dispute must be of a kind that is arbitrable under Swedish law, which contains certain conditions and restrictions.[18]

VI
RESTRAINING FOREIGN PROCEEDINGS

Swedish law does not make it possible for Swedish courts or other Swedish authorities to restrain foreign judicial proceedings by means of

[17] About the question of which legal system governs the validity of an arbitration agreement, see Bogdan, 'Some Arbitration-Related Problems of Swedish Private International Law' in *Swedish and International Arbitration: Yearbook of the Arbitration Institute of the Stockholm Chamber of Commerce* (1990), 70–9, at 70–4.

[18] For further details, see the Swedish Arbitration Act (1929:145) and the Act (1929:147) on Foreign Arbitration Agreements and Awards. An English translation of these statutes, together with a detailed commentary, is found in *Arbitration in Sweden* (2nd rev. edn., 1984) published by the Stockholm Chamber of Commerce. An official investigation commission recently submitted proposals for new Swedish legislation on arbitration: see SOU 1994:81.

an injunction. It is equally impossible for Swedish courts to forbid the plaintiff, who has obtained a foreign judgment, to apply for the enforcement of the judgment abroad, whether in the country where the judgment was made or in a third country. Furthermore, it has been suggested by writers that a foreign judgment on which execution has been carried out abroad should be recognized as conclusive in Sweden, in order to avoid an endless battle where payment secured by execution abroad could be reclaimed in Sweden and vice versa.[19]

The Swedish negative attitude towards recognition and enforcement of foreign judgments often makes forum-shopping meaningless. There are normally no reasons for the plaintiff, who needs a judgment that is valid in Sweden, to attempt to obtain a foreign judgment, since foreign judgments are, in principle, neither recognized nor enforced in Sweden without a statutory provision which is almost always based on an international treaty. Most of these treaty-based statutes contain indirect jurisdictional rules, discouraging plaintiffs from forum-shopping because the judgment obtained abroad will not be recognized and enforced in Sweden.

A partial exception is the Lugano Convention, which contains very few indirect jurisdictional rules. The Convention makes forum-shopping possible to a certain extent. Of particular importance in this respect is the last paragraph of Article 28 which, subject to certain exceptions, prohibits the review of the jurisdiction of the court of the State of origin of the judgment; not even the test of public policy (*ordre public*) may be applied to the rules relating to jurisdiction. The Convention's indirect jurisdictional rules are limited to some special cases, such as when the foreign judgment conflicts with the Convention's rules on exclusive jurisdiction or on jurisdiction over insurance or consumer contracts. The fact that the plaintiff has been forum-shopping abroad is, as such, normally not relevant for the application of these indirect jurisdictional rules, since most of them are mandatory and leave no room for discretion. The Convention also, however, contains some indirect jurisdictional rules that give the State in which recognition or enforcement is sought some discretionary power, for example Article 54B(3); within this power, the fact that there has been forum-shopping abroad can be taken into account.

---

[19] See Bogdan, n. 2 above, at 282; Nial, n. 2 above, at 69.

18

Switzerland

KURT SIEHR

Professor, Centrum für internationales Privatrecht, University of Zürich

CONTENTS

I
FORUM NON CONVENIENS

1. DOCTRINE OF *FORUM NON CONVENIENS*

(a) SOURCES

The Swiss law of civil procedure is not unified. There is one statute dealing with procedure in the Federal Court[1] whereas the procedure of the inferior courts is regulated by codes of civil procedure in every one of the twenty-six cantons.[2] None of these statutes provides proper rules for *forum non conveniens* (as to exceptions see below, at I, 3(c)) and legal theory has not developed such a doctrine.[3] Swiss literature on *forum non conveniens* is mainly limited to information about the doctrine of *forum non conveniens* as applied in foreign countries.[4] Efforts to introduce and codify such a doctrine have not been successful.[5]

(b) EXPLANATION FOR A MISSING DOCTRINE OF *FORUM NON CONVENIENS*

The Swiss system of jurisdiction, as in many other continental European legal systems, is based on at least two basic principles. First, the defendant has to be sued in the place with which he is most closely connected (normally his domicile or habitual residence). The physical presence of the defendant or his subjection to the power of competent courts is not decisive.[6] The other principle is that the plaintiff is more or less given the right to bring his cause of action in this place of principal jurisdiction.[7] The

---

[1] Federal Act of 4 Dec. 1947 on the Federal Civil Procedure *(Bundesgesetz über den Bundeszivilprozess), Systematische Sammlung des Bundesrechts*, No. 273.

[2] See e.g. the Statute of 13 June 1976 on Civil Procedure of the Canton of Zürich *(Gesetz über den Zivilprozess* (Zivilprozessordnung)), 46 Offizielle Sammlung der Zürcher Gesetze 139.

[3] See Guldener, *Schweizerisches Zivilprozessrecht* (2nd edn., Zürich, 1958); Habscheid, *Schweizerisches Zivilprozess- und Gerichtsorganisationsrecht* (2nd edn., Basel, 1990), 129; Schwander, *Einführung in das international Privatrecht, Allgemeiner Teil* (2nd edn., St. Gallen, 1990), 318 ff.; Vogel, *Grundriss des Zivilprozessrechts* (3rd edn., Bern, 1992), 89; Walder, *Einführung in das Internationale Zivilprozessrecht der Schweiz* (Zürich, 1989).

[4] Blum, *Forum non conveniens* (Zürich, 1979) (thesis); Bernasconi and Gerber, 'La théorie du forum non conveniens—un regard suisse,' [1994] *Praxis des Internationalen Privat- und Verfahrensrechts* 3–10.

[5] Keller/Siehr, *Allgemeine Lehren des internationalen Privatrechts* (Zürich, 1986), 573; Siehr, in *Freiburger Kolloquium über den schweizerischen Entwurf zu einem Bundesgesetz über das internationale Privatrecht* (Zürich, 1979), 86; see also Bernasconi and Gerber, n. 4 above, 10.

[6] As to this difference between basic attitudes in common law countries and civil law countries see Kropholler in *Handbuch des Internationalen Zivilverfahrensrechts* (Tübingen, 1982), i. 237 ff.

[7] As to this general right see Cappelletti, *The Judicial Process in Comparative Perspective* (Oxford, 1989), 215 ff.

Swiss law of civil procedure therefore tries to locate the forum at a place which has substantial contacts with the defendant, his liability, his property, or his conduct.

2. Substitutes for a Missing Doctrine of Forum Non Conveniens

(a) choice of jurisdiction clauses

Choice of jurisdiction clauses will be treated separately later (below, at I, 3(b)). Therefore this example of a substitute for a missing doctrine of *forum non conveniens* will be mentioned only briefly at this stage.

(b) power to stay or dismiss actions

(i) Jurisdiction based on Swiss Citizenship

There are several provisions which provide a subsidiary Swiss forum for Swiss citizens living abroad.[8] In these cases the cause of action (mainly in matters of family law) may be brought in Swiss courts if at least one Swiss citizen is involved (as spouse or parent) and if the action cannot be brought at its normal forum abroad (e.g. foreign courts are not accessible because of war or natural disasters) or if it cannot reasonably be demanded that the parties bring their action in these foreign courts (e.g. foreign courts are religious tribunals and will not be impartial). Where the possibility of a subsidiarily competent Swiss forum exists, the Swiss court may decide to argue that in fact it would not be possible or unreasonable to bring an action in the foreign court rather than in Switzerland. Such a dismissal is not primarily based on the intention of preventing injustice to the defendant. The court evaluates the situation abroad and construes the provisions on the exceptional Swiss forum restrictively and thereby also takes into account the defendant's situation.

Although case material is still lacking, a fictitious example may serve as an illustration. An Irishman is living with his Swiss wife (she is also an Irishwoman) in Dublin. The marriage breaks down and her husband wants to file a petition for divorce. As there is no divorce in Ireland and hence no jurisdiction for divorce cases, he may file his petition in the Swiss courts because Article 60 of the Swiss Statute of Private International Law (St. PIL) reads:[9] 'If a married couple is not domiciled in Switzerland and one of the spouses is Swiss, the Courts of the domicile of origin have jurisdiction in the proceedings for divorce or judicial separation if the said

---

[8] See Arts. 43(2), 47, 60, 67, 76, 80, 87 of the Swiss Statute of 18 Dec. 1987 on private international law, *Systematische Sammlung des Bundesrechts*, No. 291; English translation by Poncet in (1990) 29 *International Legal Materials* 1254.

[9] Translation by Poncet, n. 8 above, 1264.

action cannot be brought at the place of domicile of either spouse or if it is not reasonable to demand that it should be brought there.' As the double nationality of the Swiss wife is no obstacle to jurisdiction based on Swiss nationality (St. PIL, Article 23(1)[10]) and the spouses live abroad, either of them may file the petition for divorce in the Swiss courts. This may even be done by the Irishman against his Swiss wife domiciled in Ireland. The reason is that the Irish-Swiss couple's contacts with Switzerland are sufficient to provide a subsidiarily competent forum for their family matters. All other matters, such as service of a writ out of the jurisdiction, fair trial, and evidence, are governed by special rules dealing with international legal assistance and procedure.

(ii) Subsidiary Jurisdiction for Foreigners

Similar problems arise with cases of subsidiary Swiss jurisdiction in favour of foreigners. Here, too, the exceptional Swiss jurisdiction for matters concerning foreigners may be declined if certain prerequisites are not met. Article 3 of the St. PIL reads:[11] 'Where the present Act makes no provision for judicial competence in Switzerland, and it proves impossible for the proceedings to be taken abroad or it is unreasonable to demand such proceedings, the judicial or administrative Swiss authorities of the place with which the case is sufficiently connected, have jurisdiction.' The same test (impossibility or unreasonableness of proceedings abroad) may eventually result in a dismissal of an action because it would be more suitably brought in a foreign court.

A similar provision can be found in Article 88(1) of the St. PIL. If a foreigner dies domiciled abroad, leaving assets in Switzerland, and if the foreign probate court does not assume jurisdiction with respect to the Swiss assets, the Swiss authorities will be competent subsidiarily.

(iii) Dismissal because of Non-recognition of
Swiss Decisions Abroad

Under the pre-1989 conflicts statute, in divorce cases involving foreign citizens, Swiss courts quite often declined jurisdiction because a Swiss divorce decree would not be recognized in the State of the parties' nationality. Such interrelations have been reduced considerably and only some residual traces of this former policy can be found in the new Statute on private international law.

The best example is furnished by the law of adoption. According to Article 77(1) of the St. PIL adoption orders made in Switzerland are

---

[10] 'If a person has one or more nationalities over and above Swiss nationality, Swiss nationality shall be the sole criterion to determine the competence of the jurisdiction of the domicile of origin': translation by Poncet, n. 8 above, 1257.

[11] Translation by Poncet, n. 8 above, 1254.

governed by Swiss law. A caveat is, however, added in Article 77(2) of the St. PIL:[12] 'If it becomes evident that an adoption would not be recognized in the State of domicile or in the national State of the adopting party or spouses and the result would be highly prejudicial to the child, the authority shall also take into account the conditions imposed by the law of the State in question. If, despite this, the recognition does not seem to be assured, the adoption order must not be made.' Thus a limping adoption is avoided in the case where a Swiss adoption is likely not to be recognized in the foreign State with which the adopting parents have close contacts.

A similar provision can be found in Article 43(2) of the St. PIL with respect to the jurisdiction of Swiss authorities over the marriage of foreigners who are not domiciled in Switzerland. They may be permitted to marry in Switzerland if the Swiss marriage 'is recognized in their State of domicile or in their national State'.

Finally, although Swiss probate courts may be competent because the deceased had his last domicile in Switzerland, they have to decline jurisdiction in so far as immovable property is located abroad and the State in which it is located claims exclusive jurisdiction with respect to that part of the immovable estate: Article 86(2) of the St. PIL. In this case the Swiss authorities refrain from asserting jurisdiction because any Swiss decision concerning such immovable estate located abroad would not be recognized in that foreign State.

Apart from the cases mentioned, Swiss courts will not deny jurisdiction just because the Swiss judgment would not be recognized abroad at the place of the defendant's domicile or place of business. It is for the plaintiff to decide whether he will make use of competent local courts and run the risk of obtaining a judgment unenforceable abroad[13] or whether he will sue abroad. Only then may a claim be dismissed for lack of an interest as there is no possibility of enforcing it.

In 1939 the heirs of the German author, Jakob Wassermann, brought an action in Zürich for payment of overdue credits against his publisher, Bermann-Fischer, who had left Vienna as a refugee and was temporarily staying in Zürich. Jurisdiction was declined because a Swiss judgment would be enforceable neither in Switzerland, because of lack of assets, nor in Germany or Austria, because a Swiss judgment would not be recognized by these States.[14] It is interesting that the Swiss court was not at all concerned with whether there was a forum against Bermann-Fischer, he

---

[12] Translation by Poncet, n. 8 above, 1267.
[13] Obergericht Zürich, 17 Apr. 1968 (1969) 68 Blätter für Zürcherische Rechtsprechung 270 at 271.
[14] Kassationsgericht Zürich, 22 May 1939 (1940) 39 Blätter für Zürcherische Rechtsprechung 5.

being a refugee who later settled in Sweden. Today, jurisdiction would have to be declined because there is no Swiss forum at the defendant's mere residence in the forum State. Swiss courts do not decide whether a competent Swiss forum is less convenient than a foreign court which also has jurisdiction. Also in 1939 it could have been argued that Swiss courts had no jurisdiction and therefore had to decline taking the case.

(iv) Dismissal because of Closer Contacts with a Foreign State

Article 85 of the St. PIL refers to the Hague Convention of 1961 on Jurisdiction and the Law Applicable to the Protection of Minors.[15] Article 4(1) of this Convention provides a subsidiarily competent forum in the State of the minor's nationality. Normally the child should be protected by the courts and authorities at its place of habitual residence. Therefore it is the regular practice of Swiss courts and authorities to refuse to act on behalf of a Swiss child because the authorities at the child's place of residence are better informed and therefore provide a more convenient forum. In this case the Swiss courts will decline jurisdiction as *fora non convenientes*.

(c) INTERMEDIATE SUMMARY

There is no doctrine of *forum non conveniens* in Switzerland. The reason for this and the fact that substitutes for it are lacking is due to the constant effort to appoint an appropriate forum with enough contacts with the place for every type of case. There may be situations where Swiss courts might be inconvenient fora.

> If two Japanese car drivers driving different cars collide in Switzerland, the victim could sue the tortfeasor in Switzerland as the *locus delicti commissi* (Article 129(2) of the St. PIL) although a Japanese court might be more convenient. Swiss courts, however, cannot decline jurisdiction.

Hitherto there have been no cases brought in an inconvenient or less convenient Swiss forum. All cases with minimal contacts with Switzerland (either by simple residence or presence or by property located in Switzerland)[16] could be decided on the basis of the lack of normal jurisdiction.

3. FORUM-SHOPPING

(a) CHOICE OF STATUTORILY PROVIDED FORA

Apart from normal cases where parties choose one of several competent fora, there are three different types of cases in which forum-shopping may create problems.

---

[15] *Systematische Sammlung des Bundesrechts,* No. 0.211.231.01 and 658 UNTS 143.
[16] Obergericht Zürich, 12 Oct. 1939 (1940) 39 Blätter für Zürcherische Rechtsprechung 275.

(i) Types of Cases

Although Switzerland ratified the two 1980 Conventions on child kidnapping,[17] a Swiss parent in particular may abduct his child to Switzerland hoping to obtain a Swiss custody decree more favourable to him than that he would have obtained abroad at the place of matrimonial residence. This type of situation need not be described here because it is well known everywhere.

If a debtor is about to become insolvent or if he is unwilling to pay his debts, the creditor may try to obtain the debtor's assets and liquidate them. This happened in the case of *Tracomin* v. *Sudan Oil*.[18] Although the Swiss buyers (Tracomin) had stipulated for an arbitration clause conferring jurisdiction on the FOSFA arbitration tribunal in London, they attached the Swiss bank accounts of the Sudanese sellers and started proceedings in Switzerland for the validation of the attachment, arguing that the arbitration clause was invalid under Swiss law. This argument was not upheld by the Swiss Federal Court.[19]

Similarly in cases of marriage and divorce and other family law matters (such as abduction cases) Swiss courts may attract persons who, for some reason or another, seem to prefer a Swiss forum. This happened in the case of *Thyssen-Bornemisza* v. *Thyssen-Bornemisza*.[20] While Mr Thyssen's divorce suit was pending in the English courts, the wife commenced protection-of-marriage proceedings in Zürich and later on, also in Zürich, started divorce proceedings. Apparently the wife and her solicitors felt that Swiss courts, applying Swiss law, might be more favourable towards her.

(ii) Solution of Problems

As there is no doctrine of *forum non conveniens* in Switzerland, the problems created by forum-shopping must be treated in some other way if such behaviour is felt to be unfair or illegal.

In kidnapping cases (above, at 3(a)(i)), unless a certain period of time has elapsed since the abduction, Swiss courts will decline jurisdiction in respect of custody orders[21] because the abducted child is held not to have habitual residence in Switzerland. Applying the kidnapping Conventions of 1980[22] Swiss courts try to do their best to deter parents from abducting children to Switzerland.

[17] European Convention of 20 May 1980 on the Recognition and Enforcement of Decisions concerning Custody of Children and on Restoration of Custody of Children and Hague Convention of 25 Oct. 1980 on the Civil Aspects of International Child Abduction, *Systematische Sammlung des Bundesrechts*, Nos. 0.211.230.01 and 0.211.230.02.

[18] *Tracomin SA* v. *Sudan Oil Seeds Co Ltd* [1983] 2 All ER 129.

[19] Bundesgericht, 5 Nov. 1985 (*Tracomin SA* v. *Sudan Oil Seeds Co Ltd*). 111 Ib Entscheidungen des Schweizerischen Bundesgerichts 253.

[20] *Thyssen-Bornemisza* v. *Thyssen-Bornemisza* [1985] Family Law Reports 670.

[21] Bundesgericht, 9 Sept. 1991 (*JD.* v. *J.*), 117 II Entscheidungen des Schweizerischen Bundesgerichts 334; decisions of the lower courts in the same case in (1991) 90 Blätter für Zürcherische Rechtsprechung No. 22.   [22] N. 17 above.

Asset-hunting (above at I, 3(a)(i)) is not illegal. However, what may be forbidden is the commencement of validation proceedings at the place of attachment. Under the Brussels Convention such a validation forum is no longer available at the place of attachment.

In other cases (above, at I, 3(a)(i)) the rules on *lis alibi pendens* have to be applied to prevent several court proceedings between the same parties on the same subject-matter running concurrently and to avoid contradictory judgments (see below, at II).

(b) SWISS CHOICE OF JURISDICTION CLAUSES

Even though parties have chosen Swiss courts and conferred jurisdiction on them, and if no international treaty governs this choice of jurisdiction clause, Swiss courts may decline to accept this allocation. The codes of civil procedure of some cantons provide rules like § 11(2) of the Code of Civil Procedure of the Canton of Zürich. This provision reads: 'The court must exercise jurisdiction [conferred on it by a choice of jurisdiction clause] only if one party is domiciled in the Canton of Zürich or has its business establishment there, if one party is a Swiss citizen domiciled abroad or if the choice of jurisdiction clause is part of the terms of a loan offered for public subscription in the canton of Zürich.'

In all other cases the courts of Zürich could decline to exercise the jurisdiction conferred on them by choice of jurisdiction clauses if the Federal Statute on private international law did not restrict this freedom. Article 5 of the St. PIL dealing with choice of jurisdiction clauses reads in paragraph 3:[23]

> The chosen court may not decline its jurisdiction:
> a. if one party has its domicile, its ordinary residence, or a business establishment in the canton of the chosen Swiss court, or
> b. if, according to the Act, Swiss law governs the matter in dispute.

Only Article 5(3)(b) of the St. PIL is a barrier to declining to exercise jurisdiction. This provision does not indicate clearly whether the Swiss law governing the matter in dispute has to be objectively fixed by the conflict-of-laws rules of the St. PIL or whether a valid choice of Swiss law may also prevent a Swiss court from declining jurisdiction.

> A Swedish producer and a Polish wholesale-dealer choose Swiss law to govern their contract and confer jurisdiction on the commercial court of Zürich. According to § 11(2) of the Zürich Code of Civil Procedure the Zürich court could decline exercising jurisdiction. Is it prevented from doing so by Article 5(3)(b) of the St. PIL?

[23] Adapted translation from Thomann, Meyer-Hauser, Reber, and Insley, *Swiss Federal Act on International Private Law* (Zürich, 1989), 2.

Although no court decision on this problem has yet been handed down, it can be predicted that a valid choice of Swiss law is sufficient for Article 5(3)(b) of the St. PIL.[24] The reason for this liberal interpretation in favour of party autonomy is rather simple: Swiss conflict of laws does not limit party autonomy for contractual relations (Article 116 of the St. PIL), it should not close the doors to those courts in which Swiss law will be best applied.

(c) FREEDOM TO DECLINE JURISDICTION

If Swiss cantonal courts are not restricted by federal law or by international conventions from declining jurisdiction, then these courts are completely free to exercise their discretion. The courts of the canton of Zürich have either exercised this discretion[25] or under § 11(2) of the Zürich Code of Civil Procedure they declined jurisdiction because of the heavy burden of work imposed by domestic cases.[26] I have not found any court decision which rationalized its rejection with arguments of *forum non conveniens* and a more convenient foreign forum.

II
LIS ALIBI PENDENS

1. DOMESTIC RULE ON *LIS ALIBI PENDENS*

(a) BASIC RULE

Swiss courts have no discretionary power to stay or dismiss proceedings in cases of *lis alibi pendens*. They have to apply Article 9 of the St. PIL which reads:[27]

1. If a lawsuit on the same matter between the same parties is already pending abroad, the Swiss court must stay the proceedings if it is to be expected that the foreign court will, within a reasonable time, render a judgment recognizable in Switzerland.
2. A lawsuit becomes pending in Switzerland when the first act necessary to commence the lawsuit is performed. To commence the lawsuit it is sufficient to initiate conciliation proceedings.

---

[24] See Schnyder, *Das neue IPR-Gesetz* (2nd edn., Zürich, 1990), 24.
[25] Handelsgericht Zürich, 4 Apr. 1950, 51 Blätter für Zürcherische Rechtsprechung No. 206, 383.
[26] Obergericht Zürich, 13 Aug. 1954, 54 Blätter für Zürcherische Rechtsprechung No. 107, 218.
[27] Translation from Karrer and Arnold, *Switzerland's Private International Law Statute* (Boston, 1989), 35.

3. The Swiss court must dismiss a lawsuit without prejudice as soon as a foreign judgment recognizable in Switzerland is submitted to it.

As may be seen from Article 9(1) of the St. PIL this provision is very similar to Article 21 of the Brussels/Lugano Conventions. There are, however, three differences which can be explained easily: (1) because not all foreign judgments are recognized in Switzerland, Swiss courts have to evaluate the foreign proceedings and to give a prognosis on whether the foreign court will render a judgment which will be recognized in Switzerland; (2) if such a recognizable judgment will not be rendered within a reasonable time the Swiss court will not stay the local proceedings; (3) as the above-mentioned prognosis may turn out to be mistaken, the Swiss courts only stay proceedings *ex officio* and do not decline jurisdiction in favour of the foreign court. If, however, a foreign judgment has been rendered and if it will be recognized in Switzerland, the Swiss court has to dismiss the action pending in Switzerland: Article 9(3) of the St. PIL.

(b) COMMENCEMENT OF SWISS PROCEEDINGS

(i) Statutory Provisions

According to Article 9(2) of the St. PIL an action becomes pending in Switzerland 'when the first act necessary to commence a lawsuit is performed'. This has to be decided according to the Code of Civil Procedure valid in the canton of the Swiss forum unless federal law applies as indicated by Article 9(2)(2) of the St. PIL. According to this federal provision the initiation of conciliation proceedings is sufficient to commence the action. Such conciliation commences with the application for the issue of a summons to appear for conciliation before the justice of the peace (see § 94 of the Zürich Code of Civil Procedure). If there are no conciliation proceedings, the Swiss court proceedings are commenced by lodging a complaint and an application to issue a writ of summons (see § 103 of the Zürich Code of Civil Procedure).

(ii) Problems in Relation to Article 21 of the Brussels/Lugano Conventions

Recently a problem arose with respect to Article 9(2)(2) of the St. PIL and its relation to Article 21 of the Brussels/Lugano Conventions. 'In a case still pending conciliation proceedings by the justice of the peace in Zürich had been initiated one day before a writ of summons was issued in the High Court in London and served on the defendants the same day. The question arose whether the High Court has to decline jurisdiction because the Swiss justice of the peace was first seised.' In *Zelger* v. *Salinitri*[28] the

[28] Case 129/83, [1984] ECR 2397 at 2409.

European Court of Justice said with respect to Article 21 of the Brussels Convention: 'The court first seised "is the one in which the requirements for proceedings to become definitively pending are first fulfilled, such requirements to be determined in accordance with the national law of each of the courts concerned".' If the qualification 'definitively' is taken seriously as being a unified European prerequisite for a *lis pendens* and as superseding diverging national rules, the English court did not have to decline jurisdiction because the initiation of Swiss conciliation proceedings does not commence proceedings definitively. After the conciliation proceedings the justice of the peace has to issue a document which entitles the plaintiff to commence court proceedings in the competent tribunal within a fixed time-limit. If this is not done in time, the action is regarded as being withdrawn and the plaintiff had to start new conciliation proceedings.

The fact that an application for conciliation does not commence proceedings definitively is confirmed by the Court of Appeal of the Canton of Zürich.[29]

> In divorce proceedings the plaintiff applied for conciliation in Zürich on 6 April and the defendant started divorce proceedings in Austria on 11 April.

The Court of Appeal applied Article 9(2) of the St. PIL with respect to the commencement of proceedings in Switzerland but added:[30] 'This is a so-called temporarily restricted *lis pendens* which ceases to exist if the document [issued by the justice of the peace] is not submitted within three months to the county court according to § 101 Code of Civil Procedure.' As the *lis pendens* provision of the Swiss–Austrian Treaty (below, at II 2(b)(i)) does not require definitively pending proceedings; this kind of initiation of proceedings with the justice of the peace was sufficient. If, however, definitively commenced proceedings are required, as under Article 21 of the Brussels/Lugano Conventions, the Swiss 'temporarily restricted *lis pendens*' will not meet this requirement.

2. BILATERAL TREATIES

(a) SURVEY

There are five bilateral treaties which contain provisions on *lis alibi pendens*. Four of them are mentioned in Article 55 of the Lugano Convention as being superseded by this multilateral Convention. Only the treaty

[29] Obergericht Zürich, 25 July 1991, (1991) 90 Blätter für Zürcherische Rechtsprechung 193.
[30] Obergericht, n. 29 above, at 194.

with the Principality of Liechtenstein has not been affected by the Lugano Convention.

(b) TREATY PROVISIONS

(i) Swiss–Austrian Treaty of 1960

The Treaty of 16 December 1960 between the Swiss Confederation and the Republic of Austria on the Recognition and Enforcement of Judicial Decisions[31] reads in Article 8: 'If proceedings are pending in a court of one of the two States and if it is likely that the decision to be rendered on the subject matter of these proceedings will be recognized in the other State, the court of the other State seized later shall abstain from proceedings on the same subject matter between the same parties.' This provision is very similar to Article 9(1) of the St. PIL. It does not apply any more in cases covered by the Brussels/Lugano Conventions (Article 55 of these Conventions).

(ii) Swiss–Belgian Treaty of 1959

The Treaty of 29 April 1959 between Switzerland and Belgium on the Recognition and Enforcement of Judicial Decisions and Arbitral Awards[32] reads in Article 10:

(1) Upon the motion of one party the courts of each of the two Contracting States have to abstain from a decision in a litigation if proceedings on the same subject matter between the same parties are pending in a court of the other State, provided that this court has jurisdiction under this Treaty and could render a decision to be recognized in the other State.

(2) In urgent cases the provisional and protective measures provided by the legislation of Belgium and Switzerland may be applied for with the authorities of each of the two States no matter which court is seised with the merits of the case.

This provision expressly requires that a *lis alibi pendens* has to be pleaded. It does not apply any more in proceedings covered by the Brussels/Lugano Conventions (Article 55 of these Conventions).

(iii) Swiss–Italian Treaty of 1933

The Treaty of 3 January 1933 between Switzerland and Italy on the Recognition and Enforcement of Judicial Decisions[33] reads in Article 8: 'Upon the motion of a party the courts of one of the two States have to decline jurisdiction in disputes submitted to them if these disputes are already pending in a court of the other State, provided that this court has jurisdic-

---

[31] Systematische Sammlung des Bundesrechts, No. 0.276.191.632.
[32] Systematische Sammlung des Bundesrechts, No. 0.276.191.721.
[33] Systematische Sammlung des Bundesrechts, No. 0.276.194.541.

tion according to the provisions of the present Treaty.' This provision does not require a prognosis. It is sufficient if the court first seised has jurisdiction under the Treaty. Also this Treaty is mentioned in Article 55 of the Brussels/Lugano Conventions and no longer applies if these Conventions cover the litigation.

(iv) Swiss–Liechtenstein Treaty of 1968

The Treaty of 25 April 1968 between the Swiss Confederation and the Principality of Liechtenstein on the Recognition and Enforcement of Judicial Decisions and Arbitral Awards in Civil Matters[34] is drafted in Article 9(1) in the same manner as Article 8 of the Swiss-Austrian Treaty of 1960 (above, at II, 2(b)(i)). Article 9(2) adds: 'The provisional and protective measures provided by the legislation of Switzerland and Liechtenstein may be applied for with the authorities of each of the two States no matter which court is seized with the merits of the case.' This is very similar to Article 10(2) of the Swiss-Belgian Treaty (above, at II, 2(b)(ii)).

(v) Swiss–Swedish Treaty of 1936

The Treaty of 15 January 1936 between Switzerland and Sweden on the Recognition and Enforcement of Judicial Decisions and Arbitral Awards[35] reads in Article 7: 'The courts of one of the two States have to decline jurisdiction in disputes submitted to them if they know that these disputes are already pending in a court of the other State, provided that this court has jurisdiction according to the provisions of the present Treaty.' This Treaty, too, is mentioned in Article 55 of the Brussels/Lugano Conventions.

(c) INTERMEDIATE SUMMARY

(i) *Lis Pendens* and *Forum Non Conveniens*

Provisions on *lis alibi pendens* contained in bilateral treaties are rather mechanical rules which do not provide for any discretionary power to stay or dismiss proceedings by reason of a more convenient foreign forum.

(ii) Main Features of Bilateral Rules

There are four main features contained in these conventional *lis pendens* provisions:

(1) Two treaties (with Belgium and Italy) require that a motion of a party for any *lis alibi pendens* should be taken into consideration.

---

[34] Systematische Sammlung des Bundesrechts, No. 0.276.195.141.
[35] Systematische Sammlung des Bundesrechts, No. 0.276.197.141.

This is due to the domestic systems in Belgium[36] and Italy[37] where, according to domestic law, a foreign *lis pendens* is no defence in domestic proceedings commenced later.

(2) The treaties with Italy and Sweden do not require a prognosis as to whether the foreign judgment still to be rendered will be recognized. These instruments are satisfied with the jurisdiction of the foreign court under the respective treaty.

(3) All treaties make no exception for long trials abroad. Even if the foreign proceedings, commenced earlier than in the domestic court, are likely to last for a long period, the defence of *lis alibi pendens* is valid.

(4) All treaties are rather vague as to what kind of domestic reaction there will be to a *lis alibi pendens*. The domestic rules of civil procedure have to determine whether local proceedings will be stayed or the cause of action dismissed.

In these bilaterally stipulated rules on *lis alibi pendens* there is no Swiss case law which contributes anything further to what has already been mentioned in these provisions.[38]

(iii) Related Actions

There are no domestic rules which are similar to Article 22 of the Brussels/Lugano Conventions and extend the defence of *lis alibi pendens* to related actions. It may, however, happen that the parties agree to stay proceedings until a related cause of action has been decided by a foreign court seised of this cause of action.

III
FOREIGN CHOICE OF JURISDICTION CLAUSES

1. JURISDICTION CLAUSE

Article 5(1) and (2) of the St. PIL on jurisdiction clauses in general also covers the choice of a foreign forum. This provision reads:[39]

1. For an existing or future dispute of financial interest arising from a specific legal relationship the parties may agree on a place of jurisdiction. The agreement may be made in writing, by telegram, by telex, telecopier or any other means of

---

[36] See Van Hecke and Lenaerts, *Internationaal Privaatrecht* (Ghent, 1986), 33.

[37] See Art. 3. Italian Codice di procedura civile.

[38] See Dutoit, Knoepfler, Lalive, and Mercier, *Répertoire de droit international privé suisse* (Bern, 1983), ii. 240 (Italy), 261 (Sweden), 277 ff. (Belgium), 298 (Austria), and 321 (Liechtenstein).

[39] Translation from Karrer, n. 27 above, at 32.

communication which permits it to be evidenced by a text. Unless otherwise provided by the agreement, the choice of jurisdiction is exclusive.

2. A choice of jurisdiction is ineffective if a party is abusively deprived of protection at a place of jurisdiction provided by Swiss law.

As an exception to this rule with respect to consumer contracts, Article 114(2) of the St. PIL provides that the consumer may not waive in advance the jurisdiction at his domicile or his habitual residence.

2. Power to Stay or Dismiss

(a) general policy

If there is a valid foreign choice of forum clause, the domestic court has no discretionary power to stay or dismiss local proceedings. Normally the court has to dismiss the claim because it lacks domestic jurisdiction. Similarly to Article 17(1) of the Brussels/Lugano Conventions, the last sentence of Article 5(1) of the St. PIL provides that a validly chosen forum has exclusive jurisdiction unless otherwise provided in the choice of jurisdiction clause. As an exception to this a domestic court will postpone a final decision until the defendant has had the opportunity to object to the jurisdiction of the Swiss courts or to enter an unconditional appearance which, according to Article 6 of the St. PIL, is equivalent to a new choice of forum and supersedes the original choice of forum clause.

So long as the foreign chosen forum has not yet assumed jurisdiction conferred on it by the choice of jurisdiction clause, the domestic court may stay proceedings because of *lis alibi pendens* (Article 9 of the St. PIL) until a final decision on the jurisdiction issue has been rendered abroad.

(b) exceptions

Article 5(2) of the St. PIL formulates an exception to the general attitude towards foreign choice of forum clauses. There is no case law dealing with this provision. It is meant as a safety-valve for cases in which, by unfair stipulations or by doubtful means (terms of trade), a person has been deprived of his Swiss forum.

3. Operation of Article 5 of the St. PIL

(a) field of operation

A Swiss court will decline jurisdiction if a foreign court has been chosen by means of a valid choice of forum clause for pecuniary disputes and if that court accepts the choice.

(b) PARTICULAR PROBLEMS

Problems may arise if a foreign court has been chosen and this court is inaccessible because of war, catastrophe, or similar disaster. No such cases have yet arisen but Swiss courts may assume jurisdiction under the exception clause of Article 3 of the St. PIL which provides for Swiss jurisdiction of necessity with the following terms:[40] 'If this Statute does not provide for jurisdiction in Switzerland and if proceedings abroad are impossible or cannot reasonably be required to be brought, the Swiss judicial or administrative authorities at the place with which the facts of the case are sufficiently connected shall have jurisdiction.'

Article 5 of the St. PIL has not yet caused problems in relation to Article 17 of the Lugano Convention. The problems may lie with Article 17 of the Brussels/Lugano Conventions and, as soon as these problems are solved, Article 17 of the Lugano Convention takes precedence over the St. PIL.

IV
ARBITRATION AGREEMENTS

1. INTERNATIONAL ARBITRATION

International arbitration is dealt with in the Federal Statute on private international law. Article 7 of the St. PIL reads:[41]

> If the parties have concluded an arbitration agreement concerning an arbitrable dispute, the Swiss court invoked shall decline jurisdiction except where:
> a. the defendant has made an appearance in the proceedings without reservation;
> b. the court determines that the arbitration agreement is void, without effect, or cannot be fulfilled; or
> c. the arbitral tribunal cannot be constituted due to reasons for which the defendant in the arbitration proceedings is obviously responsible.

According to this provision the Swiss court seised of the case covered by an arbitration clause has no discretion to stay court proceedings. If one of the exceptions mentioned in a.–c. does not apply, the court must decline jurisdiction. It may, however, be argued that Article 7b. and c. gives discretion to the court in establishing one of the exceptions mentioned in this provision. In Swiss law, however, this would not amount to a power of discretion because, once an exception is either established or not, the court must either accept jurisdiction or decline it.

[40] Adapted version from LDIP (Loi fédérale suisse sur le droit international privé) (Français, Deutsch, Italiano, English) (Lausanne, 1989), 17.
[41] Translation from Thomann, n. 23 above, 3.

2. DOMESTIC ARBITRATION

For domestic arbitration Swiss cantons have entered into the Treaty (Konkordat) of 27 March 1969 on Arbitration.[42] All cantons except Lucerne are contracting parties to this Treaty.[43] It is well settled that a valid arbitration agreement fixes the exclusive jurisdiction of the arbitration tribunal[44] and that the defendant sued in State courts has to plead the arbitration agreement and object to the jurisdiction of the State court.[45] Once this plea has been made, the court has no discretion to stay the proceedings. The court has to decline jurisdiction.

V
RESTRAINING FOREIGN PROCEEDINGS

1. GENERAL ATTITUDE

Swiss courts do not have any power to restrain foreign proceedings by means of an injunction or any other device.

2. FORUM-SHOPPING AND RECOGNITION AND ENFORCEMENT OF FOREIGN JUDGMENTS

Apart from treaty obligations (e.g. Article 27 of the Brussels/Lugano Conventions), foreign judgments are only recognized and enforced in Switzerland if the foreign court had indirect jurisdiction (for purposes of recognition and not directly for actions brought in Swiss courts) according to Swiss principles of indirect jurisdiction. Article 25 a. and Article 26 of the St. PIL read:[46]

Article 25
  A foreign decision shall be recognized in Switzerland:
a. If the judicial or administrative authorities of the State in which the decision was . . . rendered had jurisdiction;
Article 26
  The foreign authorities have jurisdiction:
a. If a provision of this Statute so provides or, in the absence of such a provision, the defendant was domiciled in the State in which the decision was rendered;

---

[42] Systematische Sammlung des Bundesrechts, No. 279.
[43] See Rüede and Hadenfeldt, *Schweizerisches Schiedsgerichtsrecht* (2nd edn., Zürich, 1993), 7.
[44] Bundesgericht, 1 July 1970 ('Elan' *Hemijkska Industrija* v. *Tivoli Werke*), 96 I Entscheidungen des Schweizerischen Bundesgerichts 334 at 338.
[45] See Rüede and Hadenfeldt, n. 43 above, at 79.
[46] Translation from *LDIP*, n. 40 above, 39 and 41.

b. If, in the case of pecuniary claims, the parties have submitted by an agreement valid under this Statute to the jurisdiction of the authority that rendered the decision;

c. If, in the case of pecuniary claims, the defendant pleaded to the merits without objecting to jurisdiction; or

d. If, in the case of a counterclaim, the authority which rendered the decision had jurisdiction over the principal claim and there is a factual connection between the principal claim and the counterclaim.

Special provisions referred to in Article 26 a. are made for certain special subject matters. Also in these special cases the foreign court must have had jurisdiction according to Swiss standards unless the St. PIL makes an exception to this general attitude and recognizes the foreign decision if it is recognized in a non-Contracting State. To give an example, Article 65(1) of the St. PIL on the recognition of foreign divorce decrees reads:[47] 'Foreign decisions of divorce or separation shall be recognized in Switzerland if they were rendered in the State of domicile or habitual residence or in the State of citizenship of one spouse or if they are recognized in one of those States.' The last condition indicates such an exception. If the marriage of an American couple in New York, having no contact with Switzerland or with a Caribbean State, has been dissolved by a court in the Caribbean, and if such forum-shopping is recognized by New York, Switzerland will share the New York attitude and recognize the decision even though the court has no jurisdiction according to Swiss standards. In general it can be formulated as follows: if an action has been brought abroad in a forum having no indirect jurisdiction under Swiss standards, the decision of this forum will not be recognized unless the special exception mentioned in the St. PIL applies. In such cases of forum-shopping in an 'incompetent' forum, Swiss authorities will decline *ex officio* recognition and enforcement of a decision made by such a forum.

VI
CONCLUSION

Swiss law cannot be characterized as a cornucopia abundantly furnishing case law or statutory solutions for the present subject-matter. Such a negative statement is revealing because it shows at least two basic features which Swiss law may share with other systems of civil law: (1) a system of jurisdiction not being based on fortuitous events (simple presence, location of property) but on some closer connection of the parties to the forum State, does not furnish fertile soil for a corrective device such as

---

[47] Translation from *LDIP*, n. 40 above, 87.

forum non conveniens; (2) Swiss courts have less discretionary power to make exceptions to general principles. It may be claimed that is a common feature of those legal systems which are not dominated by case law, law-making tribunals, and attorneys.

19

United States of America

LOUIS F DEL DUCA

Professor, Dickinson School of Law, Pennsylvania*

and

GEORGE A ZAPHIRIOU

Professor, George Mason University, School of Law, Virginia†

CONTENTS

I

INTRODUCTION

This chapter deals with the difficulties that arise when courts in different territorial units assume or are about to assume jurisdiction to deal with the same matter between the same parties.[1] Conflicts, or in any case costly

---

* The research assistance of Elizabeth T. Dold, third-year law student at the Dickinson School of Law, is greatly appreciated. An earlier version of the American National Report has appeared in (1994) 42 *Am. J Comp. L* 245.

† This is to acknowledge with thanks the help of my research assistant, Anne-Marie L. Kagy, a third-year student at the George Mason University School of Law.

[1] Different territorial units may be two or more countries or two or more States or provinces in a federation. Although the main focus of this paper is on parallel proceedings

duplication, between the two proceedings are avoided when one of the multiple courts assumes jurisdiction while the other court stays or dismisses the same case. Ideally, the non-convenient jurisdictions will dismiss the case in favour of the most convenient forum. The factors which determine when a forum is not convenient are analysed in Part II of this chapter. When no court is prepared to decline jurisdiction by invoking the doctrine of *forum non conveniens*, and two or more courts proceed to judgment independently, we are faced with a *lis alibi pendens* situation (hereinafter referred to as *lis pendens*). *Lis pendens* will be dealt with in Part III of this chapter.

II
FORUM NON CONVENIENS

The doctrine of *forum non conveniens* is a discretionary one which attempts to balance the interests of the plaintiff, the defendant, and the forum. It permits a court to decline to exercise its jurisdiction if the court finds that it is a 'seriously inconvenient' forum and the interests of the parties and the public will be best served by remitting the plaintiff to another, more convenient, forum that is available.[2] Thus, it allows the court to exercise its jurisdictional power to dismiss a case when what is constitutional is not desirable.[3]

The doctrine has traditionally been applied by federal, admiralty, and State courts when a plaintiff chooses a forum not solely in search of justice but to 'vex, harass, or oppress' the defendant. In recent years, the doctrine has been applied with some frequency to deny foreign plaintiffs a forum where their chief purpose in pursuing the litigation is to benefit from a more favourable law.

The plaintiff's choice of forum is given great weight especially if it is his or her home forum. A court should not deprive a plaintiff of the chosen forum unless: (1) the facts establish such oppressiveness and vexation to a defendant as to be out of all proportion to a plaintiff's convenience, or (2) trial in the chosen forum would be inappropriate because of considerations affecting the court's own administrative and legal problems.[4]

---

in different countries, some reference will be made to parallel proceedings in sister-States in search of relevant analogies. Because of the lack of *transnational* or comparative interest, there will be no discussion of conflicts of jurisdiction between American federal and State courts. For a thorough treatment of this matter: see Comment, (1965) 32 *U Chi. L Rev.* 471.

[2] Russell J. Weintraub, *Commentary on The Conflict of Laws* (3rd edn. 1986), s. 4–33.
[3] *Ibid.*   [4] See e.g. *Gulf Oil Corp* v. *Gilbert*, 330 US 501, 508 (1947).

1. DEVELOPMENT OF *FORUM NON CONVENIENS* DOCTRINE IN THE UNITED STATES

(a) FEDERAL COURTS

The development of the common law of *forum non conveniens* in the federal courts can be traced by examining *Gulf Oil Corp* v. *Gilbert*,[5] *Koster* v. *Lumbermans Mutual Casualty Co*,[6] *Piper Aircraft Co* v. *Reyno*,[7] and *In re Union Carbide Corp Gas Plant Disaster at Bhopal, India in Dec. 1984*.[8]

In *Gulf Oil Corp*[9] a Virginia resident brought an action in the federal district court of New York to recover damages for the destruction of its Virginia warehouse and its contents by fire resulting from the defendant's negligence.[10] The defendant invoked the doctrine of *forum non conveniens*, claiming that Virginia was the appropriate place for trial because Virginia was where (a) the plaintiff lived; (b) the defendant did business; (c) all events in the litigation had taken place; (d) most of the witnesses resided; and (e) both State and federal courts were available to the plaintiff and able to obtain jurisdiction over the defendant.[11] Applying the *forum non conveniens* doctrine, the Supreme Court upheld the District Court's dismissal of the case.[12] The Court laid out both private and public factors to weigh in determining if a motion to dismiss on grounds of *forum non conveniens* is appropriate.[13] The private factors included: relative ease of access to sources of proof, availability and cost of obtaining witnesses, possibility of view of the premises, and all other practical problems that make a trial easy, expeditious, and inexpensive.[14] The public factors included: administrative difficulties from court congestion; local interest in having localized controversies decided at home; interest in applying familiar law; avoidance of unnecessary problems in conflicts of laws or in the application of foreign law; and the unfairness of burdening citizens in an unrelated forum with jury duty.[15]

In *Koster*,[16] as in *Gulf*,[17] the court applied the *forum non conveniens* doctrine to dismiss the case.[18] A New York citizen brought a derivative action in New York against an Illinois insurance company.[19] Since all the evidence and witnesses were located in Illinois and no convenience was established on behalf of the plaintiff for bringing the action in New York, the complaint was dismissed on grounds of *forum non conveniens*.[20] The court noted that a presumption in favour of a plaintiff's choice of forum

---

[5] *Ibid.*   [6] 330 US 518 (1947).   [7] 454 US 235 (1981).

[8] 809 F.2d 195 (2nd Cir. 1987), cert. denied, *sub nom. Executive Comm. Members* v. *Union of India*, 484 US 871 (1987).

[9] N. 4 above.   [10] *Ibid.* 502.   [11] *Ibid.* 503.   [12] *Ibid.* 512.   [13] *Ibid.* 508–9.

[14] *Ibid.* 508.   [15] *Ibid.* 508–9.   [16] N. 6 above.   [17] N. 4 above.

[18] N. 6 above, at 532.   [19] *Ibid.* 519.   [20] *Ibid.* 531–2.

exists, which will normally outweigh any inconvenience to a defendant.[21] Nevertheless, a clear showing that oppressiveness and vexation to a defendant is out of proportion to the plaintiff's convenience, or that the chosen forum burdens the court, will weaken the presumption and allow dismissal based on *forum non conveniens*.[22]

In *Piper*,[23] foreign plaintiffs had brought an action in the United States against American manufacturers for injuries suffered in an aeroplane crash in Scotland.[24] Although the court had jurisdiction, it dismissed the case under the doctrine of *forum non conveniens*.[25] The court continued to apply the factors set out in *Gulf Oil Corp* v. *Gilbert*,[26] but failed to recognize a strong presumption in favour of a plaintiff's choice of forum when the plaintiff or real party in interest is foreign.[27] The central purpose of any *forum non conveniens* inquiry is to ensure that a trial is convenient. Thus, a foreign plaintiff's choice deserves less deference,[28] since he cannot claim the forum is as convenient to him. In addition, the fact that substantive law in the alternative forum was less favourable to the plaintiff was not a sufficient basis to defeat dismissal on *forum non conveniens* grounds.[29]

In *Union Carbide*[30] the court followed the Supreme Court's standard, and dismissed the products liability case under the doctrine of *forum non conveniens*.[31] In Bhopal, India, lethal gas was released from a chemical plant operated by Union Carbide India Limited, killing over 2,000 people and injuring over 200,000.[32] The Indian Government, representing the victims, brought a class action in New York against the American parent company, Union Carbide Corp.[33] To determine if dismissal was appropriate under *forum non conveniens*, the court weighed a number of factors: (1) the majority of witnesses did not speak English and were located in India; (2) documentary proof of causation and liability was in India; (3) transportation costs for witnesses would have been substantial; (4) India had a strong interest in adjudicating the claims in its courts according to its standards rather than imposing foreign standards on them; and (5) United States interest was minor and the cases would overburden the court in both jury-hardship and heavy expenses.[34]

---

[21] N. 6 above, at 524.   [22] *Ibid.*   [23] *Piper Aircraft Co* v. *Reyno*, 454 US 235 (1981).
[24] *Ibid.*   [25] *Ibid.*   [26] N. 4 above; n. 23 above, at 257–61.
[27] N. 23 above, at 255. This is consistent with *Koster* where the strong presumption in favour of plaintiff's choice of forum was based on home jurisdiction: see *Koster* v. *Lumbermans Mutual Casualty Co*, n. 6 above, at 524.
[28] N. 23 above.
[29] *Ibid.* 247–61; *Canada Malting Co* v. *Paterson Steamships Ltd*, 285 US 413, 423 (1932).
[30] N. 8 above. Subsequent litigation arose out of the Bhopal incident in 1992, whereby the Dist. Ct. again dismissed the action on the grounds of *forum non conveniens* under federal law: *In re Union Carbide Corp. Plant Disaster* v. *Union Carbide Chemicals and Plastics Co Inc*, 1992 WL 36135 (SDNY 18 Feb. 1992).
[31] N. 8 above, at 206.   [32] *Ibid.* 197.   [33] *Ibid.* 197–8.   [34] *Ibid.* 199–202.

The court dismissed the case subject to Union Carbide agreeing to specified conditions in order to qualify India as an adequate alternative forum. Union Carbide was required to (1) consent to the jurisdiction of the courts of India and continue to waive defences based on the statute of limitations; (2) agree to satisfy any judgment rendered by an Indian court upheld on appeal, provided the judgment and affirmance 'comport with the minimal requirements of due process', and (3) subject itself to discovery under the Federal Rules of Civil Procedure of the United States.[35] The first condition was upheld on appeal; it was not unusual and had been imposed in a number of previous cases where a foreign court was not an adequate alternative in the absence of such conditions.[36] The Court of Appeals overruled the imposition of the second condition on the ground that it merely repeated New York law that a foreign country judgment was final, conclusive, and enforceable if the country had personal jurisdiction over the defendant and the judgment comported with requirements of due process of law.[37] The imposition of the third condition was also erroneous. The court reasoned that basic justice dictated that both sides be treated equally, with each having equal access to evidence.[38] Therefore, either both parties had to follow Federal Rules or both had to follow Indian limited discovery rules.[39]

(b) STATE COURTS

The majority of the States recognize the common law doctrine of *forum non conveniens*.[40] In Texas, although the Court of Appeals' finding in *Alfaro* v. *Dow Chem. Co*[41] seemed to reject the doctrine *forum non conveniens* entirely, the subsequent State Supreme Court finding made it clear that Texas continued to recognize the validity of the theory of *forum non conveniens* for all cases except those involving personal injury or death.[42] Moreover, Texas continues to apply the Supreme Court's standard whenever the doctrine is applicable.[43] In Louisiana, although the courts initially rejected *forum non conveniens* altogether,[44] the legislature enacted Article 123 of the

---

[35] *Ibid*. 198.   [36] *Ibid*. 203–4.   [37] *Ibid*. 204–5.   [38] *Ibid*. 205.   [39] *Ibid*. 206.
[40] See n. 46 below.   [41] 751 S.W.2d 208, 210–11 (Tex. App. 1988).
[42] See *Dow Chem. Co* v. *Alfaro*, 786 S.W.2d 674 (Tex. 1990), cert. denied, 498 US 1024 (1991); *Sarieddine* v. *Moussa*, 820 S.W.2d 837, 841 (Tex. App. 1991). S. 71.031 of the Civil Practice and Remedies Code has statutorily abolished the doctrine of *forum non conveniens* in wrongful death and personal injury actions arising out of an incident in a foreign state or country. *Dow Chem*., at 674–5.
[43] *Sarieddine* v. *Moussa*, n. 42 above (Texas courts have adopted the *Gulf Oil* factors in applying the doctrine of *forum non conveniens*).
[44] *Trahan* v. *Pheonix Ins. Co*, 200 So.2d 118 (La. App. 1967); *Kassapas* v. *Arkon Shipping Agency, Inc*, 485 So.2d 565, 566–7 (La. Ct. App.), writ denied, 488 So.2d 203 (La.), cert. denied, 479 US 940 (1986).

Code which provided for *forum non conveniens* dismissals in limited situations, which conform with the federal standard.[45]

In the past, the doctrine of *forum non conveniens* at the State level has sometimes varied from the Supreme Court's analysis, but the trend is leaning towards compliance with the federal standard.[46] Divergence in the State arena is illustrated by the California experience. In *Holmes* v. *Syntex Laboratories, Inc*[47] the British plaintiff brought an action in California against Syntex Laboratories, a California-based corporation, for a defective oral contraceptive drug that had disabled or killed women upon ingestion.[48] Syntex moved to dismiss on grounds of *forum non conveniens*, asserting that litigation should take place in Britain. The District Court granted the defendant's motion.[49] The California Court of Appeals overruled the dismissal, holding that the Californian forum was not inconvenient to the defendant.[50] The standard the court applied deviated from the federal standard in that it required that: (1) a foreign plaintiff's choice of forum should not be disturbed except for weighty reasons, and (2) the action would not be dismissed unless a suitable alternative forum were available to the plaintiff.[51] The court held that Britain was not a suitable alternative forum because Britain did not recognize a cause of action based upon strict liability.[52] Under the federal standard, there was no strong presumption in favour of the plaintiff's choice of forum when the plaintiff was foreign.[53] In addition, the fact that substantive law in the alternative forum was less favourable to the plaintiff was not a sufficient basis to defeat *forum non conveniens* dismissal.[54]

Stangvik v. *Shiley Inc*[55] overruled the *Holmes* approach, bringing California back in line with the Supreme Court standards.[56] In *Stangvik*,[57] families of Swedish and Norwegian patients who had died after heart-valve implants allegedly failed brought a product liability action in California against the Californian manufacturers. The defendant manufacturers

---

[45] LA Code Civ. Proc. Ann., Art. 123 (West Supp., 1989) Art. 123 provides that any defendant in a civil case filed in the district court of Louisiana in which the claim or cause of action is predicated solely upon a federal statute and is based upon acts or omissions originating outside of this state, when it is shown that there exists a more appropriate forum outside this state, taking into account the location where the acts giving rise to the action occurred, the convenience of the parties and witnesses, and in the interest of justice, the court may dismiss the suit 'if it is not brought pursuant to 46 USC S688 [the Jones Act, which covers recovery of injury or death of a seaman] or federal maritime law'.

[46] See Robertson and Speck, (1990) 58 *Tex. L Rev*. 937, 950 nn. 74–9. Until 1990, 32 States and DC seem to have adopted either the federal doctrine or something very similar. While some have codified the doctrine, other states have not. Since 1990, additional States have recognized the doctrine of *forum non conveniens*: see e.g. *West Texas Utilities Co* v. *Exxon Coal USA, Inc*, 807 P.2d 932, 935 (Wyo. 1991); CA. Code Ann. S8.01265 (Michie 1991).

[47] 202 Cal. Rptr. 773 (Cal. Ct. App. 1984).   [48] *Ibid*. 774.   [49] *Ibid*. 775.
[50] *Ibid*. 785.   [51] *Ibid*. 776–7.   [52] *Ibid*. 780.
[53] N. 23 above, at 255; see nn. 27–8 above and accompanying text.
[54] *Ibid*. 247–61; see n. 29 above.   [55] 819 P.2d 14 (Cal. 1991).
[56] *Ibid*. 18–19, 26–7; Cal. Civ. Proc. Code S410.30 (West, 1993).   [57] N. 55 above.

moved to dismiss or stay on *forum non conveniens* grounds, since virtually all the evidence relating to damages was in Scandinavia.[58] The Superior Court found that California was an inconvenient forum and stayed the actions, which was affirmed on appeal. The Supreme Court of California followed the federal standard developed in *Gulf Oil*[59] and *Piper*,[60] and held that a product liability action could be stayed on grounds of *forum non conveniens*, in order to permit actions to be tried in Sweden and Norway, even though the heart valves were designed, manufactured, tested, and packaged in California.[61] In *Stangvik*, the defendants stipulated that they would submit to jurisdiction in Sweden and Norway and to toll the statute of limitations.[62] The court also noted that there were already domestic actions pending in State courts which would provide an adequate deterrent to ensure quality production standards.[63]

2. Impact of Forum-selection Clause

(a) a party files a motion to dismiss on *forum non conveniens* grounds

If no forum-selection clause is in the agreement of the parties, then regardless of where the action is brought, the United States court of its own motion or on a party's motion can dismiss the case based on *forum non conveniens*.[64] However, when parties to an agreement use a forum-selection clause, *forum non conveniens* may be less readily applied because they consented to settle a dispute in a particular forum. The forum-selection clause is accordingly binding on the parties, unless the plaintiff who brings the action in another forum, or the defendant when the case is brought in the selected forum, can show that its enforcement would be unreasonable, unfair, or unjust.[65] Because the parties assume the risk that the selected forum may be inconvenient as part of the bargained-for exchange, this burden is higher than that applicable in *forum non conveniens* cases where the parties did not agree to a forum-selection clause.[66]

The Supreme Court in *Bremen* v. *Zapata Off-Shore Co*[67] held that if an action is brought in a forum other than the selected forum, the plaintiff has the burden of showing that the forum is gravely inconvenient or that the forum-selection clause is invalid.[68] In *Zapata*, the parties to an international towing contract had a forum-selection clause, naming London as

---

[58] *Ibid.* 16–17.   [59] N. 4 above.   [60] N. 23 above.
[61] N. 55 above, at 14.   [62] *Ibid.* 17, n. 2.   [63] *Ibid.*
[64] E.g. *Gulf Oil Corp*, v. *Gilbert*, n. 4 above; *Koster* v. *Lumbermans Mutual Casualty Co*, n. 16 above.
[65] *Bremen* v. *Zapata Off-Shore Co*, 407 US 1 (1972).   [66] *Ibid.* 16–18.   [67] *Ibid.* 1.
[68] *Ibid.* 15.

the appropriate forum to settle disputes.[69] A dispute arose, and Zapata brought its action in Florida, whereby the defendant, Unterweser, moved for dismissal for lack of jurisdiction or on *forum non conveniens* grounds.[70] The District Court treated the motion to dismiss under normal *forum non conveniens* doctrine, giving no weight to the forum-selection clause, and denied the motion.[71] The Supreme Court held that the choice of forum in London was made in an arm's-length negotiation by experienced and sophisticated businessmen and, absent some compelling reason, it should be honoured by the parties and enforced by the courts.[72] It ruled that it would be improper to place the burden on the defendant to establish that Florida was an inconvenient forum because the contract expressly resolved that issue.[73] The proper approach was to enforce the forum-selection clause, unless the plaintiff, Zapata, clearly showed that enforcement would be unreasonable and unjust, or that the clause was invalid due to fraud or overreaching.[74]

Similarly, if an action is brought in the appropriate forum, under the forum-selection clause, and the defendant brings a motion for dismissal based on *forum non conveniens*, the defendant has the burden of showing that the forum-selection clause is invalid, or that the chosen forum is so manifestly and gravely inconvenient that it would effectively deprive him of a meaningful day in court.[75] Otherwise, bringing the motion may constitute a breach of contract.

(b) DISMISSAL BY COURT INITIATIVE ON *FORUM NON CONVENIENS* GROUNDS

The Supreme Court in *Zapata* did not consider what would happen if the forum court of its own motion dismissed the case on *forum non conveniens* grounds. Its perspective was only from the parties' point of view.[76] Although the parties moving to dismiss based on *forum non conveniens* grounds have a higher burden of proof, the court does not have this inherent limitation when it brings its own motion for dismissal. Although the forum-selection clause is a relevant factor, in that it implies that the parties believe that the court is a convenient forum, it is but one factor to consider in the balance of public and private factors.[77] Inconvenience to witnesses, administrative difficulties from court congestion, lack of local interest in the controversy, and the avoidance of unnecessary conflicts of law, and the application of foreign law can all justify dismissal based on the *forum non conveniens* doctrine.[78]

---

[69] *Bremen* v. *Zapata Off-Shore Co*, *ibid*. 2.   [70] *Ibid*. 3, 4.   [71] *Ibid*. 6.
[72] *Ibid*. 12.   [73] *Ibid*. 15.   [74] *Ibid*.   [75] *Ibid*. 15.   [76] *Ibid*.
[77] See *Gulf Oil*, n. 4 above, at 508–9.   [78] *Ibid*.

3. INTERNATIONAL CONVENTIONS AND *FORUM NON CONVENIENS*

(a) CONVENTION ON THE INTERNATIONAL SALE OF GOODS

The Convention on the International Sale of Goods (CISG) has governed the formation of certain international contracts since 1 January 1988, twelve months after the date of deposit of the tenth instrument of ratification.[79] The CISG is applicable if: (a) the parties to the contract have their 'places of business in different Contracting States;'[80] or (b) if the 'rules of private international law' (i.e. conflict of laws) lead to the application of the law of a State which has ratified the Convention.[81] The Convention is applicable if either of the two applicability procedures is met, unless the parties opt out entirely or partially.[82] The automatic applicability of the Convention if either the 'place of business in different Contracting States,' or the 'rules of private international law' basis is met has been affirmed in recent litigation in the United States and other countries.[83] The Convention may also become applicable by way of a choice of law clause agreed to by the contracting parties even though neither the 'place of business in different Contracting States' nor the 'private international law rules' basis for applying the Convention is met.[84]

While the Convention has many similarities to the UCC, significant differences also exist. Careful reading of comparable Convention and UCC sections is, therefore, required to determine whether a client's interests are better served by one or the other regime. For example, one of the basic assumptions of the remedies provision of the Convention is that the contract of the parties should normally be specifically performed.[85] Partial opt-out under Article 6 with reference to this provision would appear to be one way to avoid application of the specific performance remedy. However, Article 28 also states that 'a court is not bound to enter a judgment for specific performance unless the court would do so *under its own law in respect of similar contracts of sale not governed by the Convention*'.[86]

[79] 15 USCA App. 55, Art. 99 (Supp. 1993).
[80] N. 79 above, Art. 1(1)(a). 'Contracting States' refers to States which have ratified the CISG.
[81] *Ibid.*, Art. (1)(b).   [82] *Ibid.*, Art. 6.
[83] *United States, Filanto, SpA* v. *Chilewich Intern. Corp*, 789 F.Supp. 1229, 1237 (SDNY 1992), appeal dismissed, 984 F.2d 58 (2nd Cir. 1993); Germany, OLG Frankfurt a.M.; 5 U 261/90; OLG Frankfurt a.M.; 5 U 164/90; LG Munich I; 17 HKO 3726/89; LG Stuttgart; 3 kfH 0 97/89.
[84] Louis F Del Duca and Patrick Del Duca [1991] *Comm. L Ann.* 553, 557.
[85] *Ibid.* 563, 576. As an alternative to avoidance of the contract, a buyer may require performance by the seller of its obligations and also require delivery of substitute goods if the lack of conformity constitutes a fundamental breach of contract: *ibid.* 576; n. 79 above, Art. 46. This approach differs from that of the US courts, which are authorized to grant specific performance in sale of goods transactions only in cases where the goods are 'unique or in other proper circumstances': UCC s. 2–716.
[86] N. 79 above, Art. 28, emphasis added.

The specific performance remedy can therefore also be bypassed if the parties provide for a forum-selection clause naming a United States court as the appropriate forum for dispute resolution.

However, this advantage of naming a United States court as the dispute forum must also be weighed against the potential disadvantages of use of contingent fees to facilitate litigation, expanded discovery, jury trial, increased damages including the possibility of punitive damages, and the possible removal under *forum non conveniens*.

The substantive applicability of the International Sales Convention on the 'place of business', 'conflict of law', or 'opt-in' basis previously discussed is one factor, but not necessarily controlling, in balancing both private and public factors to determine applicability of the *forum non conveniens* doctrine. Although no litigation has yet addressed the issues of the application of *forum non conveniens* in a Convention on International Sale of Goods case, experience under the Brussels Convention on Jurisdiction and the Enforcement of Judgments in Civil and Commercial Matters[87] and the Multilateral Convention for the Unification of Certain Rules Relating to International Transportation by Air (Warsaw Convention),[88] when dealing with *forum non conveniens*, is instructive.

(b) THE BRUSSELS CONVENTION

The Brussels Convention,[89] which deals with jurisdiction and the enforcement of judgments in civil and commercial matters, is considered in balancing public and private interest factors, but it is not given determinative weight in *forum non conveniens* litigation in the United States.[90] In *Carbotrade SPA* v. *Bureau Veritas*,[91] the plaintiff sued the defendant for negligently certifying the MV *Star of Alexandria* seaworthy, because the ship subsequently sank. The defendant moved to dismiss the action on grounds of *forum non conveniens*, arguing that the plaintiff's choice of forum violated the Brussels Convention since the action was brought in a forum not provided for under the Convention. The court held that, because the United States was not a party to the Brussels Convention, it would not give the Convention determinative weight in deciding a motion to dismiss based on *forum non conveniens* and denied the motion to dismiss.[92] The court so ruled because the defendant failed to show that the balance of public and private factors strongly favoured an alternative forum.[93]

---

[87] [1968] OJ L299, revised in English at [1989] OJ L285/1.
[88] 49 USCA. s. 1502 (1976).   [89] N. 87 above, revised [1982] OJ L388/30.
[90] *Carbotrade SPA* v. *Bureau Veritas*, No. 92 Civ. 1459, 1993 WL 60567 (SDNY 2 Mar. 1993).
[91] N. 90 above.   [92] *Ibid*. 9 n. 2.   [93] *Ibid*. 6.

(c) THE WARSAW CONVENTION

The Warsaw Convention[94] of 1929, a multilateral treaty that regulates claims for damages and other disputes which arise between passengers and international air carriers, also does not suspend a court's power to apply the doctrine of *forum non conveniens* in a case governed by the Convention.[95] This is so even though Article 28 of the Warsaw Convention reads:

An action for damages must be brought, at the option of the plaintiff, in the territory of one of the High Contracting Parties, either before the court of the domicile of the carrier or his principal place of business, or where he has a place of business through which the contract has been made, or before the court at the place of destination.[96]

In *Air Crash Disaster* v. *Pan America World Airways*,[97] Pan American Flight 759 crashed in Louisiana, the foreign plaintiffs brought an action in Louisiana, and Pan American moved for dismissal based on *forum non conveniens*. The court stated that such language did not preclude the court from dismissing the case on *forum non conveniens* grounds.[98] The court noted that there was no evidence that the drafters of the Warsaw Convention intended to alter the judicial system of any country.[99] Nevertheless, it denied the motion on the ground that *forum non conveniens* requirements had not been met.[100]

4. SECTION 1404(A) TRANSFER

Section 1404(a) of the United States Code states: 'For the convenience of parties and witnesses, in the interest of justice, a district court may transfer any civil action to any other district or division where it might have been brought.'[101] Congress enacted this section to permit a change in venue between federal courts. Although the statute was drafted in accordance with the doctrine of *forum non conveniens*,[102] it was intended to be a revision rather than a mere codification of the common law.[103] Section 1404(a) provides for transfer, not dismissal, of a case,[104] which prevents the inherent risk of the *forum non conveniens* doctrine resulting in the running

---

[94] N. 88 above.
[95] *In re Air Crash Disaster* v. *Pan America World Airways*, 821 F.2d 1147, 1160 (5th Cir. 1987), modified, 883 F.2d 17 (5th Cir. 1989).
[96] *Ibid.* 1161.   [97] *Ibid.* 1147.   [98] *Ibid.* 1162.
[99] *Ibid.* 1162; Robbins [1963] *McGill L J* 352, 355.   [100] N. 95 above.
[101] 28 USC s. 1404 (a).
[102] See Revisor's Note, HR, Rep. No. 308, 80th Cont., Ist Sess., A132 (1947); HR Rep. No. 2646, 79th Conc., 2nd Sess., A127 (1946).
[103] *Norwood* v. *Kirkpatrick*, 349 US 29, 31 (1955).   [104] *Ibid.*

of the statute of limitations prior to bringing an action in the appropriate forum.[105]

Although federal transfer entails balancing similar criteria,[106] section 1404(a) requires a lesser showing of inconvenience than does the *forum non conveniens* doctrine. Section 1404(a) broadens the district court's discretion in granting or denying transfer.[107]

(a) DEVELOPMENT

Van Dusen v. *Barrack*[108] and *Ferens* v. *John Doero Co*[109] are key cases that developed standards of federal transfers under section 1404(a). In *Van Dusen*,[110] the plaintiff filed in the District Court of Pennsylvania forty wrongful death actions, which arose from an aeroplane crash in Massachusetts. The defendant's motion under section 1404(a) for transfer to the Massachusetts District Court was granted, since over 100 other actions that arose out of the same disaster were pending in Massachusetts and most of the witnesses resided there.[111] The Court of Appeals vacated the transfer, and the Supreme Court reversed.

The Supreme Court held that, following a transfer under section 1404(a) initiated by a defendant, the transferee court must apply the State law of the transferor court. Section 1404(a) does not effect a change in the law; it merely authorizes a change in courts, because to hold otherwise would greatly prejudice the plaintiff.[112]

In *Ferens*,[113] the plaintiff lost his hand in Pennsylvania when it allegedly became caught in a harvester manufactured by the defendant.[114] The plaintiff brought an action three years later in the District Court of Pennsylvania under contract and warranty claims, and also in the District Court of Mississippi for negligence and product liability claims.[115] The plaintiff then moved under section 1404(a) to transfer the tort action to Pennsylvania on the ground that Pennsylvania was a more convenient forum.[116] The Mississippi court granted the plaintiff's motion, but the Pennsylvania court declined to honour Mississippi's tort statute of limitations, and dismissed the tort action under Pennsylvania's two-year tort limitation. The court reasoned that, since the plaintiff moved for the transfer, the *Van Dusen* rule that the transferee court must follow the choice-of-law rules prevailing in the transferor court, was not applicable.[117] The Court of Appeals affirmed and the Supreme Court reversed, holding that a transferee forum must apply the law of the transferor court,

---

[105] *Norwood* v. *Kirkpatrick*, 349 US 29, 31 (1955).
[106] E.g., *Parsons* v. *Chesapeake & O. Ry Co*, 375 US 71, 73 (1963).
[107] N. 103 above, at 32.   [108] 376 US 612 (1964).   [109] 494 US 516 (1990).
[110] N. 108 above.   [111] *Ibid*. 612.   [112] *Ibid*. 639.   [113] N. 109 above.
[114] *Ibid*. 519.   [115] *Ibid*.   [116] *Ibid*. 520.   [117] *Ibid*. 521.

regardless of who initiated the transfer.[118] The Court reasoned that the policies underlying *Van Dusen* required the same result,[119] since applying the transferor law does: (1) not deprive the plaintiffs of any State-law advantages; (2) not contravene *Van Dusen's* policy against forum-shopping, since a plaintiff already has the option of shopping for a forum with the most favourable law; (3) continue the focus on convenience rather than on the possibility of prejudice resulting from a change in the applicable law; and (4) promote judicial economy.[120]

(b) SECTION 1404(A) AND THE FORUM-SELECTION CLAUSE

Where the parties agree to settle a dispute in a particular forum under a forum-selection clause, the case still may be transferred under section 1404(a).[121] The forum-selection clause is not dispositive of venue, yet it is a significant factor to be considered under section 1404(a).[122] The convenience of the selected forum, the fairness of transferring in the light of the forum-selection clause, the parties' relative bargaining power, and public-interest factors of systemic integrity and fairness, must all be considered in the balance under section 1404(a).[123] Although a valid forum-selection clause may waive a party's right to assert his own inconvenience as a reason for transferring a case, the district court still must consider whether the interests of justice or the convenience of the witnesses requires transfer.[124]

5. ARBITRATION AGREEMENTS

(a) FEDERAL ARBITRATION ACT—CHAPTER 1 PROCEEDINGS

The Federal Arbitration Act generally covers all arbitration agreements in contracts involving 'maritime transactions'[125] or 'commerce'.[126] 'Commerce' is defined, *inter alia*, to mean 'commerce among the several States or with foreign nations'.[127] Chapter 1 of the Act covers arbitration agreements in contracts involving 'commerce' among the States or commerce with foreign nations who are not contracting parties to the Convention on Recognition and Enforcement of Foreign Arbitral Awards (hereafter 'the

---

[118] Ibid. 531.   [119] Ibid. 516, 521–32.   [120] Ibid. 516–7.

[121] *Stewart Organ, Inc* v. *Ricoh Corp*, 487 US 22, 32 (1988).   [122] *Ibid.* 29.

[123] *Ibid.* 29, 30.

[124] *Heller Financial, Inc* v. *Surety Federal Sav. & Loan Ass'n*, 630 F.Supp. 1004, 1008 (ND Ill. 1986).

[125] 'Maritime transactions' are defined in the Act as 'charterparties, bills of lading of water carriers, agreements relating to wharfage, supplies furnished, vessels or repairs to vessels, collisions, or any other matters in foreign commerce which, if the subject of controversy, would be embraced within admiralty jurisdiction': 9 USC s. 1.

[126] N. 125 above, s. 2.   [127] *Ibid.*, s. 1.

Convention'). Chapter 2 covers arbitration agreements in contracts involving 'commerce' with foreign nations who are contracting parties to the Convention.[128]

Chapter 1 provides that an arbitration agreement shall be 'valid, irrevocable, and enforceable, save upon such grounds as exist at law or in equity for the revocation of any contract'.[129] In an action to compel arbitration, the function of the United States District Court is limited to deciding whether there is an arbitration agreement in existence and whether it has been breached.[130] If the court determines that the dispute is subject to arbitration, it must, on the request of one of the parties, stay the trial until arbitration is complete.[131]

The United States District Court also has the power to opt not to decide the question whether the parties were involved in an arbitration agreement which has been breached, and instead use the doctrine of *forum non conveniens* to dismiss a petition to compel arbitration.[132] Although the specific language of section 4 of the Act[133] mandates arbitration, the court can only compel arbitration after determining that an agreement to arbitrate was made and breached. Thus, prior to any such determination, the Act does not limit the District Court's inherent power to dismiss a petition based on *forum non conveniens* grounds. The court or the defendant can bring the motion, subject to the same test of balancing private and public factors under the federal standard. However, once a determination is made, the court cannot invoke the *forum non conveniens* doctrine to alter the chosen arbitration forum, no matter how inconvenient.[134]

In *Spring Hope Rockwool* v. *Industrial Clean Air, Inc*[135] Chapter 1 of the Act was applicable because the conflict was between parties in different States of the United States. Their contract provided for arbitration in California, yet all the events occurred in North Carolina. The plaintiff sought to enjoin the arbitration proceedings, alleging California as an inconvenient forum. After finding that a valid arbitration agreement existed, the court further ruled that arbitration in California was required because use of the *forum non conveniens* doctrine at this stage of the proceedings was not authorized under the Federal Arbitration Act.[136] So ruling, the court noted

[128] 9 USC 5 201, art. I, III, declar. 43.   [129] *Ibid.*, s. 2.
[130] *Naviera* v. *Del Valle*, 759 F.2d 1027, 1031 (2nd Cir. 1985).
[131] 9 USC s. 3. It is disputed whether the Convention permits a stay of the proceedings as an appropriate remedy: see *Filanto, SpA* v. *Chilewich Intern. Corp*, 789 F.Supp. 1229, 1241–2 (SDNY 1992).
[132] *Naviera* v. *Del Valle*, n. 130 above; *Action Corp* v. *Borden Inc*, 670 F.2d 377 (1st Cir. 1982).
[133] 'The court shall hear the parties, and upon being satisfied that the making of the agreement for arbitration or the failure to comply therewith is not in issue, the court shall make an order directing the parties to proceed': 9 USC, s. 4.
[134] E.g. *Spring Hope Rockwool* v. *Industrial Clean Air, Inc*, 504 F.Supp. 1385, 1389 (1981) (the court found no cases which applied *forum non conveniens* doctrine to arbitration agreements).
[135] *Ibid.*   [136] *Ibid.* 1389.

that the Act exclusively governs the arbitration caluse[137] and provides that only 'fraud, coercion, or other grounds for revocation of contract' are defences to enforcement of the arbitration clause.[138] Since the court had heard the case on the issue of whether the parties had entered into a valid arbitration agreement, the *forum non conveniens* doctrine could not be invoked to alter the chosen arbitration forum.

Although in a Chapter 1 proceeding the court generally has the power to apply the *forum non conveniens* doctrine to dismiss the petition to compel arbitration, if the petition is brought in the same forum in which the parties have agreed to arbitrate, it is usually held to be against the 'interest of justice' to dismiss under either *forum non conveniens* or section 1404(a) since the parties agreed the site was convenient.[139]

(b) FEDERAL ARBITRATION ACT — CHAPTER 2 — PROCEEDINGS UNDER THE CONVENTION

Chapter 2 of the Federal Arbitration Act incorporates the Convention which, as ratified by the United States, mandates that each Contracting State (i.e., a country which has ratified it) recognize written arbitration agreements and enforce arbitral awards made in the territory of a Contracting State.[140] The Convention also requires a court of a Contracting State, at the request of one of the parties, to refer the parties to arbitration, unless the agreement is 'null and void, inoperative, or incapable of being performed'.[141]

Like Chapter 1 of the Act, Chapter 2 allows an aggrieved party to file a petition to compel arbitration.[142] Similar to the result reached in a Chapter 1 proceeding, the court has the power to dismiss the petition based on the doctrine of *forum non conveniens*.[143] Although the specific language of the Convention mandates arbitration,[144] the court can only compel arbitration after determining that an agreement to arbitrate was made and breached.[145] Thus, prior to such a determination, the Convention does not limit the District Court's inherent power to dismiss a petition on *forum non conveniens* grounds.

---

[137] *Ibid.*   [138] 9 USC, s. 2.

[139] See *Naviera* v. *Del Valle*, n. 130 above; *Aaacon Auto Transport, Inc* v. *Teafatiller*, 334 F.Supp. 1042, 1044 (SDNY 1971); *Lawn* v. *Franklin*, 328 F.Supp. 791, 793–4 (SDNY 1971); *Iberian Tankers Co* v. *Terminales Maracaibo, CA*, 322 F.Supp. 73 (SDNY 1971). Under ch. 2, in *Interpetrol Bermunda Ltd* v. *Petchem Co Ltd*, No. 82 Civ. 694 (SDNY 19 Nov. 1982). There was no discussion of any such limitation.

[140] 9 USC, s. 201 art. 1(3) (1993 Supp.). The US has exercised the option to limit application to arbitrate agreements from other Contracting States and Commercial Contracts: *ibid.*, declar. 43.

[141] 9 USC, s. 201, art. II (1993 Supp.).   [142] *Ibid.*

[143] *Interpetrol Bermuda Ltd* v. *Petchem Co. Ltd*, n. 139 above.

[144] 9 USC, s. 201, art. II (1993 Supp.).

[145] *Interpetrol Bermuda Ltd* v. *Petchem Co Ltd*, n. 139 above.

In *Interpetrol Bermuda Ltd* v. *Petchem Co Ltd*[146] Interpetrol petitioned the New York District Court to compel arbitration in New York in accordance with the agreement of the parties specifying New York as the arbitration forum.[147] The respondent moved to dismiss the petition on the ground of *forum non conveniens*.[148] Interpetrol contended that the court lacked the power to dismiss based on *forum non conveniens* grounds because the parties had agreed to an arbitration clause which established New York as the *situs* of arbitration of disputes, and under the Convention that must compel arbitration.[149] However, the court held that the Convention was inapplicable to compel arbitration until it initially determined that such an arbitration agreement was made.[150] This initial determination could be properly dismissed based on *forum non conveniens* grounds if, in the District Court's discretion, the public and private factors set forth in *Gulf Oil*[151] justified dismissal.[152] Ruling that the respondent had properly established the *forum non conveniens* grounds for dismissing the action to compel arbitration, the court noted that the balance of convenience weighed 'heavily in favour of trial of this issue in Asia, where the majority of the witnesses reside, the bulk of the documents are situated, and the underlying transaction took place'[153] even though the arbitration would ultimately be held in New York if such an arbitration agreement were ultimately found to have been agreed to by the parties.[154]

While the court may use the *forum non conveniens* doctrine to dismiss a petition to establish the existence of the arbitration agreement, once a court hears the case and finds that an arbitration agreement was entered into between the parties, it then can no longer invoke the *forum non conveniens* doctrine to alter the chosen arbitration forum.[155] Even an inconvenient forum for arbitration is binding on the parties, and the court has no power to designate a more convenient forum.[156] This is illustrated by *Intercontinental Packaging Co* v. *China National Cereals*,[157] where the parties agreed to arbitration in China applying New York law. Intercontinental Packaging sought a petition to compel arbitration in New York. The Supreme Court of New York held that, although New York was a more convenient forum, the arbitration clause would prevail. In ruling, the court cited numerous factors establishing New York as the more convenient forum including (a) New York law was to be applied; (b) the

---

[146] *Interpetrol Bermuda Ltd* v. *Petchem Co Ltd*, n. 139 above.
[147] *Ibid.*   [148] *Ibid.*   [149] *Ibid.*   [150] *Ibid.*   [151] N. 4 above.
[152] See nn. 13–15 above and accompanying text. *Interpetrol Bermuda Ltd* v. *Petchem Co Ltd*, n. 143 above.
[153] *Ibid.* 4.   [154] *Ibid.*
[155] *Intercontinental Packaging Co* v. *China National Cereals*, 159 A.2d 190 (NY 1990); *Oil Basins* v. *Broken Hill Proprietary Co*, 613 F.Supp. 483, 489 (SDNY 1985).
[156] *Intercontinental Packaging*, n. 155 above; *Oil Basins*, n. 155 above, at 489.
[157] *Intercontinental*, n. 155 above.

contract was executed in New York; (c) attempt at resolutions were made through the efforts of the parties' mutual agent in New York; (d) the allegedly defective beer was distributed in the United States and evidence of plaintiff's damages would likely be proven by witnesses in the United States. China was nevertheless the required forum for arbitration by reason of agreement of the parties. The court accordingly followed the Supreme Court guideline in *Scherk* v. *Alberto-Culver Co*,[158] stating that '[a] contractual provision specifying in advance the forum in which disputes shall be litigated and the law to be applied is . . . an almost indispensable precondition to achievement of the orderliness and predictability essential to any international business transaction'.[159]

In *Filanto, SpA* v. *Chilewich Intern. Corp*,[160] an Italian-based manufacturer of footwear (Filanto) brought an action in the New York District Court against a New York export/import company (Chilewich) for breach of a contract requiring Filanto to produce shoes which Chilewich had contracted to sell to a Russian buyer. Applying the Convention on International Sale of Goods, the New York District Court held that an agreement to arbitrate disputes in Moscow was part of the contract and compelled the parties to arbitrate in Moscow. Despite Filanto's contention that the court should take judicial notice of the unsettled conditions in 1992 in Moscow and order arbitration to proceed in New York, the court required compliance with the agreement.[161] It noted that the chosen forum had a reasonable relationship to the contract, and that, although the conditions in the Republic of Russia were unsettled, they continued to improve and there was no reason to believe that Moscow could not provide fair and impartial justice to the litigants. The court failed explicitly to address the applicability of *Zapata*,[162] which suggested that a forum-selection clause might be invalidated if the chosen forum had become seriously inconvenient or dangerous.[163] Other courts have distinguished *Zapata* in the arbitration context because the selected forum was for litigation not arbitration.[164]

Thus, under either Chapter 1 or Chapter 2 of the Act, dismissal based on *forum non conveniens* can be ordered by a federal court on the initial question whether the parties actually entered into an agreement to arbitrate. However, if the court accepts jurisdiction, the court is required to

---

[158] 417 US 506 (1974).   [159] *Ibid.* 516.
[160] 789 F.Supp. 1229 (SDNY 1992), appeal dismissed, 984 F.2d 58 (2d Cir. 1993).
[161] *Ibid.* 1242.   [162] *Bremen* v. *Zapata*, n. 65 above.
[163] Filanto, n. 160 above, at 1242: 'Whatever the applicability of [*Zapata*] . . . in the arbitration context': *ibid.*
[164] *Spring Hope Rockwool, Inc*, n. 134 above, at 1389; accord, *Sibley* v. *Tandy Corp*, 543 F.2d 540 (5th Cir. 1976). reh'g granted, 547 F.2d 286 (5th Cir. 1977), cert. denied, 434 US 824 (1977); *USM Corp* v. *GKN Fasteners, Ltd*, 574 F.2d 17 (1st Cir. 1978); *Matter of Ferrara, SPA*, 441 F.Supp. 778 (SDNY 1977), aff'd, 580 F.2d 1044 (2nd Cir. 1978), aff'd *sub nom. Fratelli Moretti Cereali, SPA* v. *United Grain Growers, Ltd*, 580 F.2d 1044 (2nd Cir. 1978).

order arbitration if it finds that the parties have entered into an agreement to arbitrate and it has been breached.[165]

III
LIS PENDENS

In this Part we shall deal with the handling of parallel proceedings. In Section 1 we shall only deal briefly with parallel proceedings in courts of sister States. Section 2 will deal with our main focus—parallel proceedings in a court in the United States and in a court in a foreign country. We shall discuss the factors which guide the judge in determining whether to grant or refuse a preliminary or final antisuit injunction.[166] Section 3 will examine suggested solutions for the avoidance of parallel proceedings.

1. PARALLEL PROCEEDINGS IN SISTER STATES

In common law countries, the resolution of a *lis pendens* situation is sought by the use of an antisuit injunction. Application for a preliminary, and eventually a final, injunction is made in one of the courts that has jurisdiction. The injunction is directed against the party who intends to initiate or, as the case may be, to continue a parallel proceeding. The object of the injunction is to restrain the party from beginning or from continuing the action in a second forum. Failure to comply with the injunction will expose the plaintiff to contempt-of-court proceedings before the issuing court. If the person is found to be in contempt, he may be fined. In more extreme cases, he may be incarcerated until he agrees to comply.[167] An injunction can only be enforced by contempt proceedings if the person against whom the injunction was issued is physically within the jurisdiction. Imposition of a fine against a person who is outside the jurisdiction will raise problems of enforcement, and imprisonment is, of course, impossible. Sequestration of the property of an absent individual or foreign corporation will often prove impractical for lack of due process.

Attempts to restrain proceedings, even in an inter-State context, are not only often futile but lead to delay, costs, and friction between the two parallel jurisdictions. This is illustrated by the classic case of *James* v. *Grand Trunk Western Railroad Company*.[168] The facts were simple: James

---

[165] See nn. 134, 155–6 above and accompanying text.

[166] See Bermann, (1990) 28 *Colum. J Transnat. L* 589; Hartley, (1987) 35 *Am. J Comp. L* 488; Comment, (1985) 71 *Va. L Rev.* 1039.

[167] See e.g. *Shillanti* v. *United States*, 384 US 364, 370–2 (1966). *Scott* v. *Hunter Oil Company*, 398 F.2d 810, 811 (5th Cir. 1968). According to the old judicial saying, he has the key of the jail in his pocket.

[168] 14 Ill. 2d 356, 152 NE 2d 858 (1958).

was killed by the railway in Michigan, his State of residence. His widow brought an action in Illinois under the Michigan wrongful death statute, which provided for exclusive venue in Michigan. Illinois had *in personam* jurisdiction against the railway company. An injunction obtained by the railway company in Michigan restrained Mrs James from continuing the action in Illinois. Mrs James then sought to defeat that injunction by requesting a counter-antisuit injunction from the Illinois court. The Supreme Court of Illinois overruled the trial court and the Court of Appeals, and held that granting a counter-injunction would not violate full faith and credit or comity. Shaefer J and two other justices dissented. Shaefer J, a distinguished jurist, agreed that a counter-antisuit injunction to restrain proceedings contrary to a sister State's statutory venue provision did not violate full faith and credit or comity. However, he wrote that an antisuit injunction and counter-injunction in this particular context gave rise to an 'unseemly kind of judicial disorder'.[169]

The above decision accurately represents the state of the law in cases of parallel proceedings within the United States. Injunctions and counter-injunctions are widely used in divorce cases, where one of the spouses seeks a quick divorce in a State which will assume jurisdiction after his or her brief presence. These injunctions, however, are of limited effectiveness.

Inter-State conflicts between parallel jurisdictions in cases of child custody have been alleviated by the enactment in all States of the Uniform Child Custody Jurisdiction Act.[170] The purpose of the Act is to determine a single 'court of custody'; where such court is in a particular State, a court seised of the matter in another State must dismiss the action. Mere presence of the child in the State is not enough to ground jurisdiction, unless the child has been abandoned or an emergency exists. Local jurisdiction may be preserved when it is in the best interest of the child.

2. Parallel Proceedings in the USA and Abroad

Parallel proceedings similar to those discussed in an inter-State setting may also arise in a transnational context. Although the worldwide liberalization of divorce has minimized parallel proceedings in divorce and nullity cases, parallel proceedings still arise frequently in child custody cases. The Uniform Child Custody Jurisdiction Act is applied by courts in the United States to foreign custody decrees.[171] In contrast, the Parental

---

[169] *Ibid.* 868 (Shaefer J dissenting).   [170] 9 ULA 115 (1979).
[171] Custody of a Minor (no. 3), 392 Mass. 728, 468 NE 2d 251 (1984), where a Massachusetts court decided not to modify an Australian custody decree because it substantially conformed to the UCCJ Act's requirements. See also *Tishendorf* v. *Tishendorf*, 321 NW 2d 405 (Minn. 1982), cert. denied, 460 US 1037 (1983).

Kidnapping Prevention Act of 1980[172] applies only to sister-State custody decrees. In transnational cases, the Hague Convention on the Civil Aspects of International Child Abduction[173] will affect the law of the countries that have ratified the Convention.

(a) PERSONAL INJURY CASES

In personal injury cases, whenever there is jurisdiction abroad and in the United States, plaintiffs generally prefer to bring the action in the United States where they may obtain four advantages: (1) extensive pre-trial discovery; (2) a jury; (3) higher damages including in many cases punitive damages; and (4) a contingent fee arrangement. Judges are divided as to whether seeking higher damages is an acceptable motivation for filing in a particular jurisdiction.

The United States Supreme Court in *Piper Aircraft Co* v. *Reyno*[174] rejected the attempt by Scottish personal representatives of Scottish passengers killed by an aircrash in Scotland to bring an action against the aeroplane's manufacturers in a Pennsylvania federal district court in the hopes of recovering higher damages. In contrast, Lord Scarman, in *Castanho* v. *Brown & Root (UK)*,[175] wrote that seeking higher damages by bringing an action in the United States was a legitimate objective.

In addition to personal injury cases,[176] in which the favourite forum is the United States,[177] there is another area in which parallel proceedings have led to antisuit and counter-antisuit injunctions: alleged extraterritorial jurisdiction by the United States in antitrust cases. This situation is dramatically illustrated by the *Laker Airways* litigation.

(b) THE *LAKER AIRWAYS* LITIGATION

Throughout the years, there has been friction between the United Kingdom and the United States over what has been described as the exercise of 'extraterritorial' jurisdiction by the United States.[178] The United States was criticized for applying to antitrust a doctrine of effects, by which United States authorities and courts have prescribed, adjudicated and enforced United States antitrust laws against foreign corporations for conduct out-

---

[172] Pub. L. 96–611, 94 Stat. 3569 (1980) (codified as amended at 28 USCA s. 1738A (1988)).
[173] S. Treaty Doc. 11, 99th Cong. 1st Sess. (1980), reprinted in (1981) 19 ILM 1501. This came into force for the US on 1 July 1988.
[174] N. 23 above.   [175] [1981] All ER 143.
[176] See as to personal injury cases: Robertson and Speck [1990] *Tex. L Rev.* 937.
[177] See the observation of Lord Denning MR in *Smith Kline French Laboratories* v. *Bloch* [1983] 1 WLR 730 at 733 (CA).
[178] *US* v. *Imperial Chemical Industries, Ltd*, 104 F.Supp. 215 (SDNY 1952); *British Nylon Spinners Ltd* v. *Imperial Chemical Industries Ltd* [1954] 3 All ER 88.

side the United States whenever there was any effect within the United States.[179] Difficulties in enforcement,[180] foreign blocking litigation.[181] and threats of retaliation have gradually led the United States authorities and courts, when it comes to extraterritorial application of United States laws, to balance the United States national interest against the national interest of the other country or countries involved.[182]

Extraterritorial application of national laws may trigger an antisuit injunction. This is what occurred in the *Laker Airways* litigation which erupted both in the United States and in the United Kingdom[183]

Laker Airways (Laker) was a small British-based airline, founded by Sir Freddie Laker. It was not a member of the International Air Transport Association (IATA) and it managed to challenge the IATA fare system by instituting a low-cost service between the United Kingdom and the United States. Laker initially charged fares that were about one-third of the price charged by IATA airlines. It was so successful that, by the time of its collapse in February 1982, Laker was carrying one-seventh of all air passengers between the United Kingdom and the United States. As a result of its overstretched finances, Laker ceased operations and went into liquidation at the beginning of 1982.

At the end of 1982, Laker, by its liquidator, filed an action in the United States District Court for the District of Columbia against a number of IATA airlines: two of them, Trans World Airways (TWA) and Pan-American Airways (Pan-Am), were United States-based airlines and two of them, British Airways (BA) and British Caledonian Airways (BCal.), were based in the United Kingdom. There were also two non-airline defendants: McDonnell Douglas Corporation (McDD) and an associated company of McDD which provided financing for the purchase of aircraft from McDD. The complaint alleged two causes of action: (1) violation of

---

[179] See e.g. *US* v. *Aluminum Company of America*, 148 F.2d 416 (2nd Cir. 1945).

[180] *US* v. *Watchmakers of Switzerland Information Center Inc*, 1963 CCH Trade Cases 70,600 (SDNY 1962) and 1965 CCH Trade Cases 71,352 (SDNY 1965).

[181] Several countries have adopted blocking statutes forbidding the production of documents located within their territories to foreign authorities or courts. The violators are usually subject to criminal sanctions: see n. 189 below and accompanying text.

[182] *Timberlane Lumber Co* v. *Bank of America National Trust & Savings Association*, 549 F.2d 597 (9th Cir. 1976); *Mannington Mills Inc* v. *Congoleum Corp*, 595 F.2d 1287 (3rd Cir. 1979); Restatement (Third) of Foreign Relations Law of the United States §§401–3, s. 415(3); Zaphiriou, (1988) 10 *Geo. Mason U L Rev.* 301 at 322. Ironically, the EC has also adopted a doctrine of effects in the regulation of competition. Bermann *et al.*, *European Community Law* (1993) 690; Cases 48, 49, 51–57/69 *Imperial Chemical Industries, Ltd* v. *Commission* [1972] ECR 619; Case 60/81 *IBM* v. *Commission* [1981] ECR 2639.

[183] American cases: *Laker Airways* v. *Sabena, Belgian World Airlines*, 731 F.2d 909 (DC Cir. 1984); *Laker Airways* v. *Pan American World Airways*, 604 F.Supp. 280 (DDC 1984); *Laker Airways* v. *Pan American World Airways*, 577 F.Supp. 348 (DDC 1983); *Laker Airways* v. *Pan American World Airways*, 559 F.Supp. 1124 (DDC 1983). English cases: *British Airways* v. *Laker Airways* [1985] AC 58 (HL); *Midland Bank* v. *Laker Airways Ltd* [1986] 1 All ER 526 (CA 1985); *British Airways* v. *Laker Airways* [1984] 1 QB 142 (CA).

section 4 of the Clayton Act for predatory pricing intended to drive Laker out of business and for pressure applied to McDD and Laker's Bank, the Midland Bank, to withdraw from Laker's rescue operations; and (2) intentional tort based upon the foregoing facts. The complaint further claimed treble damages for violations of sections 1 and 2 of the Sherman Act and punitive damages for the intentional tort.

Midland Bank, which was not yet a party to the action, obtained an antisuit injunction from the English High Court, which restrained Laker from joining it to the antitrust suit in the United States. The validity of this injunction was upheld by the Court of Appeal,[184] even after the House of Lords rescinded the injunction against Laker. BA and BCal. applied to the English High Court for a declaration that they had not engaged in any unlawful conspiracy and for an antisuit injunction to stop the American proceedings. They also sought a counter-antisuit injunction to prevent Laker from obtaining an antisuit injunction in the United States Federal District Court against their request for relief from the English High Court. Laker did obtain an antisuit injunction in the United States Federal District Court to restrain the English proceeding, which was later upheld on appeal.[185]

In the meanwhile, an application by BA in England to convert the temporary antisuit and counter-antisuit injunctions into permanent injunctions was dismissed by the High Court,[186] granted by the Court of Appeal,[187] and finally rescinded by the House of Lords.[188]

Sir John Donaldson, MR, who delivered the judgment of the Court of Appeal,[189] justified the granting of an English injunction on an Order of 1983 and directions of the British Secretary of Trade and Industry that were issued under the Protection of Trading Interests Act of 1980, and were addressed to BA and BCal. The Act is a blocking statute which enables the Secretary of State to prevent a person doing business in the United Kingdom from complying with requests of foreign authorities or courts that would damage the trading interests of the United Kingdom.

The granting of an injunction of BA and BCal. to restrain the proceedings in the United States would have created a situation unprecedented in the United Kingdom or in the United States. As far as is known, it would have been the first time that a party was enjoined from further prosecuting proceedings in a foreign forum where there was no alternative forum available either locally or in a third State.[190]

The Court of Appeal's decision was overruled by the House of Lords on the ground that the plaintiffs in the English action had failed to make out a case of unconscionable conduct by Laker.[191]

---

[184] *Midland Bank* v. *Laker Airways* [1986] QB 689 (CA).   [185] 559 F.Supp., n. 183 above.
[186] N. 183 above (QB).   [187] *Ibid*. 169.   [188] N. 183 above (AC).
[189] *Ibid*. 183 (QB).   [190] See the observations of Sir John Donaldson MR, *ibid*. 199.
[191] N. 183 above (AC).

Both Lord Diplock[192] and Lord Scarman,[193] who were the only Law Lords who gave reasoned opinions, relied heavily on the fact that, unlike *forum non conveniens* cases, there was here only one exclusive foreign forum that could try the case.

(c) FACTORS GUIDING JUDICIAL DISCRETION

A court in the United States, when faced with the commencement or continuance of parallel proceedings, has three options: (1) to let the parallel proceedings proceed; (2) to stay or dismiss its own proceedings; or (3) to issue an antisuit injunction.

The court will follow the first option if it is not satisfied that the issues in both proceedings are the same or that the parties, either at present or potentially, are not the same. The second option will be applied whenever the judge is satisfied that the court is a non-convenient forum as was discussed in Part II of this chapter. We are here concerned with the first and third options.

The grant or refusal of an injunction is discretionary. A court in the United States will grant a preliminary or final injunction if it is satisfied that a refusal to grant the injunction will cause irreparable harm to the person seeking the injunction and will not impose undue hardship on the person against whom the injunction is sought. The public interest must also be taken into consideration.[194] In the case of a preliminary injunction, the analysis is necessarily speculative. It depends on tentative projections, often in the light of inadequate evidence. Unless the trial court abuses that discretion, commits an obvious error in applying the law or makes a serious mistake in considering the evidence, the appellate court must take the judgment of the trial court as presumptively correct.[195]

There is wide consensus that, when it comes to granting an injunction to restrain proceedings in a foreign country, comity is an important consideration and that therefore an injunction should not be lightly granted.[196] On the other hand, it is equally clear that, conversely, comity does not compel the foreign court to comply with the injunction, just as full faith and credit does not compel a sister court to comply with the injunction of another sister-State court. In both situations, the injunction is directed against the party, not the court.

---

[192] *Ibid.* 80.   [193] *Ibid.* 95.   [194] 559 F.Supp., n. 183 above, at 1129.
[195] *A. O. Smith Corp* v. *FTC*, 530 F.2d 513 (3rd Cir. 1976); *Bentie* v. *Bentie*, 456 NYS 2d 25 (1982); *Owens-Illinois Inc* v. *Webb*, 809 S.W.2d 899 (CA Tex. 1991).
[196] *Seattle Totems Hockey Club* v. *National Hockey League*, 652 F.2d 852, 855 (9th Cir. 1981). cert. denied, 457 US 1105 (1982); *Philip* v. *Macri*, 261 F.2d 945, 947 (9th Cir. 1958); *Canadian Filters (Harwich) Ltd* v. *Lear-Siegler, Inc*, 412 F.2d 577 (1st Cir. 1969); *Laker Airways* v. *Sabena*, n. 183 above, at 928 n. 52.

Simple convenience is not a ground for granting an injunction. The parallel foreign-country suit must be frivolous or vexatious.[197] The litigant who seeks the stay of the foreign parallel proceedings must make out a clear case of hardship or inequity.[198]

In cases that can broadly be described as commercial, which encompass carriage of goods by sea, insurance, and patent infringement cases, the tendency is to deny the antisuit injunction and to let the parallel litigation proceed in the foreign country.[199] After all, a foreign-country judgment that is irreconcilable with a judgment in the United States will not be recognized or enforced.[200] In patent infringement cases there is an additional reason for refusing the antisuit injunction. Foreign proceedings usually relate to the infringement of a foreign patent and there is therefore no identity of cause.[201] In contrast, if the foreign-country action would seek to enjoin a manufacturer in the United States and his foreign subsidiaries from manufacturing or selling a particular product, because of an alleged infringement of a patent, a preliminary antisuit injunction may be granted in the United States.[202] The injunction will be granted if more hardship is imposed on the plaintiff by refusing the injunction than would be imposed on the defendant by granting the injunction. The public interest will also be taken into consideration.[203]

Generally, federal courts in the United States favour parallel proceedings in the United States and refuse to abstain in favour of foreign pending proceedings, even when a slight balance of convenience favours the foreign proceedings.[204]

(d) CHOICE OF FORUM CLAUSES

There is now a wide universal practice to insert into transnational commercial agreements a choice of forum clause. Choice of forum clauses

---

[197] *Bethell* v. *Peace*, 441 F.2d 495 (5th Cir. 1971); *Chase Manhattan Bank* v. *State of Iran*, 486 F.Supp. 832 (SDNY 1980).

[198] *Landis* v. *North American*, 299 US 248. The case dealt with parallel proceedings in the US. However, it is submitted, Cardozo J's opinion is also important in a transnational context and in two respects: (1) the parties to the two causes of action need not be the same and the issues need not be identical; and (2) there should be hardship and inequity to justify the granting of an injunction.

[199] *China Trade and Development Corporation* v. *m.v. Choong Yong*, 837 F.2d 33 (2nd Cir. 1987); *In re Maritima Aragua, SA* (SDNY 1990); *Brinco Mining Ltd* v. *Federal Insurance Co*, 552 F.Supp. 1233 (DDC 1982); *Black & Decker Corp* v. *Sanyei America Corporation* (ND Ill. 1986).

[200] *Ambatielos* v. *Foundation Co*, 203 Misc. 470, 116 NYS 2d 641 (1952).

[201] *Western Electric Co, Inc* v. *Milgo Electronic Corporation*, 450 F.Supp. 835 (SD Fl. 1978).

[202] *Metronic, Inc* v. *Catalyst Research Corp*, 518 F.Supp. 946 (CD Minn.), 664 F.Supp. 660 (8th Cir. 1981).

[203] *Ibid.*

[204] *Neuchatel Swiss General Insurance Co* v. *Lufthansa Airlines*, 925 F.2d 1193 (9th Cir. 1991); *American Home Insurance Co* v. *Insurance Corp of Ireland, Ltd*, 603 F.Supp 636 (SDNY 1984) (litigants enjoined from pursuing the foreign litigation).

submit disputes, arising between the parties to the agreement, to the exclusive jurisdiction of a particular court or to arbitration. Without going into much detail, as this would exceed the scope of this chapter, choice of forum clauses are generally upheld.[205]

It is submitted that filing an action in violation of a valid choice of forum clause tips the scale in favour of granting an antisuit injunction. The factors outlined in the previous section are of importance, but they are overshadowed by the blatant disregard of an agreed forum.

It is assumed that the agreement was reached without coercion, as interpreted by the applicable law, and that no new circumstances are frustrating the agreement or rendering the submission inequitable. It is further assumed that the choice of a foreign court is reasonable and that the submission to arbitration relates to an arbitrable dispute. Practical considerations, particularly in business contracts, outweigh judicial over-sensitivity. Commerce should not be burdened with costs and delays created by protracted transnational litigation. In the light of new develop-ments strongly supporting the choice by the parties to an agreement of an exclusive forum, the Hague Convention of 1965 on the Choice of Court[206] should be redrafted and the Model Choice of Forum Act of 1968,[207] which was withdrawn in 1975, should be reintroduced. They both should pro-vide that, subject to specified limited exceptions, fora other than the forum chosen by the parties should dismiss their proceedings in favour of the chosen forum, and that failure to do so would render their judgments unenforceable.[208] Choice-of-court clauses are of secondary importance compared to the overwhelming importance and wide enforceability of arbitration clauses and arbitration awards.

3. Solutions by Convention or Statute

The Hague Convention on the Recognition and Enforcement of Foreign

---

[205] See on choice of court clauses *Carnival Cruise Lines* v. *Shute*, 499 US 585 (1991); *Bremen* v. *Zapata Off-Shore Co*, n. 65 above. See on arbitration clauses: *Sherk* v. *Alberto Culver Co*, n. 158 above; *Mitsubishi Motors* v. *Soler Chrysler Plymouth*, 473 US 614 (1985); *Rodriguez* v. *Shearson/ American Express*, 490 US 477 (1989); New York Convention on the Recognition and Enforce-ment of Foreign Arbitral Awards, Art. II (1958); European Community: Brussels Convention 1968, Art. 27, reprinted in (1990) 29 ILM 1413; Lugano Convention 1988, reprinted in (1989) 28 ILM 620. See generally Borchers, (1992) 67 *Wash. L Rev.* 55; Gruson, [1982] *U Ill. L Rev.* 133; Zaphiriou, (1978) 3 *Intl. Trade LJ* 311.

[206] Hague Conference of Private International Law, Collection of Conventions (1951–80) xv, (1965) 3 ILM 348 (adopted only by Israel).

[207] Handbook of the National Conference of Commissioners on Uniform State Laws 219 (1968); Reese, (1969) 17 *Am. J Comp. L* 292.

[208] The Uniform Foreign Money-Judgments Recognition Act, 13 ULA 263, which has been adopted by 23 States of the USA provides in s. 4(b)(5) that a foreign judgment need not be recognized if 'the proceeding in the foreign court was contrary to an agreement between the parties under which the dispute in question was to be settled otherwise than by proceedings in that court'.

Judgments in Civil and Commercial Matters of 1971 and Protocol[209] provides in Article 5 that recognition or enforcement of a decision may be refused if 'proceedings between the same parties, based on the same facts and having the same purpose . . . are pending before a court of the State addressed and those proceedings, were the first to be addressed', the 'state addressed' being the country where recognition and enforcement of the foreign judgment is sought.

Article 20 of the same Convention provides that, where two countries which are parties to the Convention have concluded a Supplementary Agreement, provided for by Article 21, courts in either country may dismiss or stay an action when parallel proceedings are pending in a court of another country which may lead to a judgment recognizable or enforceable under the Convention.

The Hague Convention, by favouring the proceeding first introduced, encourages a race to court and therefore provides an incentive rather than a disincentive to the institution of parallel proceedings.

Some preference for the court 'first seised' is shown by the Brussels Convention on Jurisdiction and the Enforcement of Judgments in Civil an Commercial Matters of 1968[210] in Articles 21, 22, and 23, and the Lugano Convention of 1988[211] in identical Articles. These Conventions, like the Hague Convention on Recognition and Enforcement of Foreign Judgments, provide for dismissal or stay by fora other than the forum first seised. Dismissal is provided for where the proceedings involve the same cause of action between the same parties, unless the jurisdiction of the forum first seised is contested, in which case a stay may be ordered. If the actions are related rather than identical, there is a third alternative: consolidation of the actions on the motion of one of the parties.

It is submitted that the Conflict of Jurisdiction Model Act (the Model Act),[212] which was proposed in 1989 by a sub-committee of the American Bar Association Section on International Law and Practice, contains elements that could usefully be introduced into future conventions for the recognition and enforcement of judgments and into a possible revision of the relevant Hague Convention.

In the event of parallel proceedings, it is useful to have a provision, in a statute or in a convention, that notice of the parallel proceedings should

---

[209] Hague Conference of Private International Law, Collection of Conventions (1951–80), xvi, xvii.

[210] (1990) 29 ILM 1413.   [211] N. 205 above.

[212] The Conflict of Jurisdiction Model Act is appended to an art. by Tietz, [1992] *Int'l Lawyer* 21, 56. The Model Act was adopted by the State of Connecticut as part of the Act Governing International Obligations and Procedure, Public Act No. 324 (1991), Conn. Legis. Serv. PA 91–324 (HB 7364) (West). The 'Declaration of Public Policy' in s. 1 of the Model Act has not been included in the Connecticut Act.

be given to all known courts that are seised of the same or similar matter. Upon such notice, all parties having an interest should be heard and, if possible, one court should be designated to decide all related matters. In deciding which court should be designated, the factors determining which route is the most convenient should be taken into consideration. These factors, broadly speaking, give weight to judicial efficiency, effectiveness, and economy, the interests of the jurisdictions involved and of the parties.

In addition to the initiative of the parties which, in judicial systems similar to that of the United States, is of primary importance, one must emphasize the need for some judicial initiative and for wide judicial co-operation. Even in extreme adversarial systems, judicial initiative is on the increase in the form of pre-trial conferences. Particularly in transnational cases, there are preliminary hearings in arbitration proceedings. Similarly, judicial co-operation in transnational litigation is encouraged by letters rogatory or letters of request,[213] by which the judges of one country seek the assistance of judges of other countries.

Refusal of a particular forum to desist in favour of what appears to be, in the light of exchanged information and evidence, the most appropriate forum will deprive its judgment of recognition by other fora and will render it unenforceable. 'Appropriate forum' does not necessarily mean the most convenient forum. Convenience is one of the factors. Effectiveness in regulating a particular activity and efficiency so as to minimize delay and costs are other important factors. The interests of the jurisdictions involved and the interests of the parties are of vital importance even if difficult to evaluate objectively. The jurisdiction in which the judgment is sought to be recognized and/or enforced will have the last word. It is for that jurisdiction to evaluate conflicting views on the public and private interests involved. The concern that a judgment will not be recognized or enforced will compel the parties and the fora involved to choose the most appropriate forum.

POSTSCRIPT

Relevant conventions and implementing statutes should provide for and encourage transnational judicial co-operation for the resolution of problems created by parallel proceedings. This should be carried out within the bounds of due process with the participation of all parties concerned.

---

[213] See Convention on the Taking of Evidence Abroad in Civil and Commercial Matters of 1970, TIAS 7444, s. 1.

Experience under the Hague Service Convention[214] and the Hague Evidence Convention,[215] has shown that parties and courts found ways to circumvent them.[216] However, there is a difference between provisions ordering a course of action, as in the case of the Hague Service and Evidence Conventions, and a provision providing for co-operation in order to determine the appropriate course of action.

Judicial co-operation has been constructively used in transnational child custody cases, where the interest of the child is paramount. Even in the sensitive fields of antitrust and technology protection, that are often dominated by conflicting national interests, the prospects for judicial co-operation are improving. This is due to a number of factors: worldwide harmonization of the relevant rules, difficulties in extraterritorial enforcement, and increasing judicial concern about the interests of all countries involved and not only about the interest of the forum.

---

[214] Hague Convention on Service Abroad of Judicial and Extrajudicial Documents in Civil and Commercial Matters of 1965, 20 UST 361–73, TIAS No. 6638, 658 UNTS 163.

[215] Hague Convention on the Taking of Evidence Abroad in Civil and Commercial Matters of 1970, 20 UST 2555, TIAS No. 7444.

[216] *Volkswagenwerk* v. *Schlunk*, 486 US 694, 196 SCt. 2104 (1988); *Société National Industrielle Aérospatiale* v. *US District Court*, 482 US 552, 107 SCt. 2542 (1987).

Appendix
Questionnaire

RULES FOR DECLINING TO EXERCISE JURISDICTION
IN CIVIL AND COMMERCIAL MATTERS:
FORUM NON CONVENIENS, LIS PENDENS

Les régimes relatifs au refus d'exercer la competénce juridictionnelle en matière civile et commerciale.

QUESTIONNAIRE

The topic of rules for declining to exercise jurisdiction is of major practical importance and of considerable academic interest, involving, as it does, major differences between states following the common law tradition and those that follow the civil law tradition.

National reporters for the 1994 Athens/Delphi Congress of the International Academy for Comparative Law are, of course, free to cover the subject in whatever way they deem fit. However, it would be extremely helpful if they were to address the following points at some stage during the course of their Report. It is to be noted that in order to provide a complete picture, it is intended that, the General Report will discuss declining of jurisdiction in cases involving arbitration and choice of jurisdiction agreements as well as *forum non conveniens* and *lis alibi pendens*.

National reports should be submitted by the end of September 1993, and should not exceed 8,000 words. They may, of course, be shorter than this.

Forum Non Conveniens

1. Do you have in your state a doctrine of *forum non conveniens* (a general discretionary power to stay or dismiss actions on the basis of the appropriate forum)?

    If you have such a doctrine:

    (a) What is the origin of this doctrine?

    (b) What are the considerations when determining what the appropriate forum is?

    Do these include public interest factors as well as private?

    (c) Are these considerations contained within a framework of rules or is a more flexible position taken by the courts?

    (d) What role does your doctrine of *forum non conveniens* play? (e.g. is it used as an antidote to excessively wide bases of jurisdiction, to provide justice?).

2. If you have no doctrine of *forum non conveniens*:

    (a) Why is this?

    (b) Do you have in your state any power to stay or dismiss actions on some other basis, e.g. in cases of extreme injustice to the defendant? What are the considerations when exercising this power?

    (c) Is this power to stay or dismiss actions contained within a strict framework of rules or is a more flexible position taken by the courts?

    (d) What role does this power play? (e.g. is it used as an antidote to excessively wide bases of jurisdiction, to provide justice?)

3. Is forum-shopping a problem in your state?

    If it is, how is this problem tackled in your state (for example, by adopting narrow bases of jurisdiction, by using a doctrine of *forum non conveniens*, by using choice of law rules)?

4. How does your doctrine of *forum non conveniens* or your power to stay or dismiss actions on some other basis relate to your bases of jurisdiction (for example, is it only used in relation to certain bases of jurisdiction but not others)?

Lis Alibi Pendens

5. Do you have in your state a *discretionary* power to stay or dismiss proceedings [or declare that there is no jurisdiction] in cases of *lis alibi pendens* (i.e. two actions involving the same parties and the same cause of action taking place in two different states at the same time)?

    If so:

    (a) What are the considerations when determining whether to stay or dismiss an action in your state?

    (b) How are these considerations different from those employed under your doctrine of *forum non conveniens*?

6. Do you have in your state a mechanical rule that requires you to decline jurisdiction in cases of *lis alibi pendens*? (An example of such a mechanical rule is contained in Article 21 of the European Community Convention on Jurisdiction and the Enforcement of Judgments in Civil and Commercial Matters whereby the court seised second must decline jurisdiction in favour of the court seised first).

    If so:

    (a) What are the terms of this rule?

    (b) If your state is a European Community or EFTA state: when are your courts first seised of jurisdiction? Have you encountered or do you anticipate any particular problems in your state in relation to Article 21 of the Brussels/Lugano Convention?

7. Do you have in your state specific provisions on *lis alibi pendens* contained in bilateral treaties? What are the terms of these provisions?

8. Do you have in your state a separate rule to deal with cases involving actions which are related but do not fit within the above definition of *lis alibi pendens*?

Foreign Choice of Jurisdiction Clauses

9. Do you have in your state a *discretionary* power to stay or dismiss proceedings in cases involving a foreign choice of jurisdiction clause?

   If you have such a power:

   What are the considerations employed when exercising this discretionary power?

   How are these considerations different from those employed under your doctrine of *forum non conveniens*?

10. Do you have in your state a non-discretionary rule that requires you to decline jurisdiction in cases involving a foreign choice of jurisdiction clause? (an example of such a rule is contained in Article 17 of the European Community Convention on Jurisdiction and the Enforcement of Judgments in Civil and Commercial Matters according to which the EC State on which jurisdiction has been conferred by the parties is allocated exclusive jurisdiction and other EC States must decline jurisdiction.)

    If you have such a rule:

    (a) When does it operate?

    (b) If your state is a European Community or EFTA State have you encountered or do you anticipate any particular problems in relation to Article 17 of the Brussels/Lugano Convention?

Arbitration Agreements

11. Do you have in your state a power to stay court proceedings in cases where the parties have agreed to go to arbitration?

    If so:

    (a) Are there separate rules in respect of domestic and non-domestic arbitration agreements?

    (b) Do your rules involve a discretionary power or are they mandatory?

Restraining Foreign Proceedings

12. Do you have in your state a discretionary power to restrain foreign proceedings by means of an injunction?

    If you have such a power:

    (a) What are the criteria for the exercise of this power?

    (b) How are these criteria different from those employed under your doctrine of *forum non conveniens*?

13. At the stage of recognition and enforcement of a foreign judgment do your courts take into account the fact that there was forum-shopping abroad? How is this taken into account?

J. J. FAWCETT

Index

Index

Index